SECOND EDITION

MORAL COMPETENCE

An Integrated Approach to the Study of Ethics

James Jakób Liszka

University of Alaska Anchorage

Prentice
Hall

Upper Saddle River, New Jersey 07458

Library of Congress Cataloging-in-Publication Data

LISZKA, JAMES JAKÓB, [date].
   Moral competence: an integrated approach to the study of ethics / JAMES JAKÓB
LISZKA.—2nd ed.
      p. cm.
   Includes bibliographical references and index.
   ISBN 0-13-034154-1
   1. Ethics. I. Title.
BJ1012.L57   2002
   170—dc21   00-054712

VP, Editorial Director: *Charlyce Jones Owen*
Acquisitions Editor: *Ross Miller*
Assistant Editor: *Katie Janssen*
Editorial Assistant: *Carla Worner*
Editorial/Production Supervision: *Joanne Riker*
Prepress and Manufacturing Buyer: *Sherry Lewis*
Director of Marketing: *Beth Gillett Mejia*
Marketing Manager: *Chris Ruel*
Cover Art Director: *Jayne Conte*

This book was set in 10/11 New Baskerville by East End Publishing Services, Inc.
and was printed and bound by Hamilton Printing Company. The cover was
printed by Phoenix Color Corp.

Acknowledgments appear on pages xv and xvi, which constitute a continuation
of the copyright page.

 © 2002, 1999 by Pearson Education, Inc.
Upper Saddle River, New Jersey 07458

Printed in the United States of America

10 9 8 7 6 5 4 3 2 1

ISBN 0-13-034154-1

Prentice-Hall International (UK) Limited, *London*
Prentice-Hall of Australia Pty. Limited, *Sydney*
Prentice-Hall Canada Inc., *Toronto*
Prentice-Hall Hispanoamericana, S.A., *Mexico*
Prentice-Hall of India Private Limited, *New Delhi*
Prentice-Hall of Japan, Inc., *Tokyo*
Pearson Education Asia Pte. Ltd., *Singapore*
Editora Prentice-Hall do Brasil, Ltda., *Rio de Janeiro*

For my son, Zachary James Liszka

A child who suffers confounds all claims
For a caring cosmos.
But your gentle nature proves against cruelty;
Your tears a kind rain
That gathers in words, the verse of your life,
A poem stronger than order.

Contents

Preface, xi

Acknowledgments, xv

INTRODUCTION

Why Study Ethics?, 1

The Study of Ethics, 7

CHAPTER ONE

Moral Sentiment, 16

1.1 The Variety of Moral Emotions, 19
　1.1.1 Sympathy, 25

1.2 The Absence of Moral Emotions, 33
　1.2.1 Psychopathy, 33
　1.2.2 Sociopathy and Wickedness, 36

1.3 The Varieties of Moral Sentiment, 38
　1.3.1 Duty, 40
　1.3.2 Honor, 44
　1.3.3 Caring, 46
　1.3.4 Nobility, 48

1.4 The Development of Moral Sentiment, 52

    1.4.1 Rawls's Three Laws of Moral Psychology, 52

    1.4.2 The Development of Trust and Its Importance, 52

    1.4.3 The Importance of Parenting Style in Moral Development, 55

    1.4.4 Art, Literature, and Moral Education, 57

1.5 Feminist Ethics: Moral Sentiment Should Be the Basis of Morality, 63

1.6 Kant: Reason, Not Moral Sentiment, Should Serve as the Basis of Morality, 65

1.7 Emotivism: Morality Is Nothing But Moral Emotions, 69

    Review Questions, 71

    General Discussion Questions, 72

    Stories for Discussion, 72

    Suggested Readings, 76

CHAPTER TWO

Autonomy and Strength of Will, 80

2.1 The Issue of Free Will, 81

    2.1.1 Determinism, 84

    2.1.2 Libertarianism, 86

    2.1.3 Compatibilism, 88

2.2 Moral Luck, 90

2.3 Moral Strength and Weakness, 92

2.4 Responsibility, 97

    2.4.1 Causation, 99

    2.4.2 Accountability, 101

    2.4.3 Voluntariness, 102

    2.4.4 Voluntary Action, 104

    2.4.5 Acting out of Ignorance, 105

    2.4.6 Acting in Ignorance, 105

    2.4.7 Acting under Duress, 109

    2.4.8 Tort Liability, 112

2.5 The Concept of Autonomy, 120

2.6 Kant and the Notion of the Good Will, 123

2.7 Nietzsche: The Strong Will Is the Good Will, 125

2.8 Developing Autonomy, 127

    Review Questions, 130

    Questions for Discussion, 131

    Case Studies for Discussion, 132

    Suggested Readings, 133

CHAPTER THREE

Virtue and Vice, 137

3.1 Virtue as a Golden Mean, 140

3.2 Virtue and Character, 142

3.3 The Virtues of Self-Control, 145

    3.3.1 Temperance, 145

    3.3.2 The Relation between Virtue and Pleasure, 148

    3.3.3 Good-Temper, 154

    3.3.4 Ambition, 155

    3.3.5 Curiosity, 157

    3.3.6 The Work Ethic: Industry, Frugality, and Contentment, 160

    3.3.7 Issues in Sexual Continence, 162

3.4 The Virtues of Self-Efficacy, 163

    3.4.1 Courage, 164

    3.4.2 Patience , 168

    3.4.3 Perseverance , 170

3.5 The Virtues of Regard, 170

    3.5.1 Fair-mindedness, 170

    3.5.2 Tolerance, 180

    3.5.3 Truthfulness and Honesty, 182

3.6 The Virtues of Respect, 187

    3.6.1 The Polite Virtues, 191

3.7 The Virtues of Kindness, 194

    3.7.1 Forgiveness, 195

3.8 Is Being Virtuous Sufficient for Being Moral? 198

    Review Questions, 201

    Stories for Discussion, 203

    Suggested Readings, 210

CHAPTER FOUR

Wisdom, 212

4.1 The Relation between Wisdom and the Virtues, 213

4.2 The General Features of Wisdom, 214

4.3 How Wisdom Is Acquired, 215

4.4 Reasoning Wisely, 217

4.5 Moral Vision, 218

    4.5.1 Cosmic Vision, 221

    4.5.2 The Common Good, 229

    4.5.3 Happiness and the Vision of the Good Life, 234

    4.5.4 The Life of Pleasure, Adventure, and Entertainment, 241

    4.5.5 The Life of Security and Comfort, 244

    4.5.6 The Life of Wealth, 247

    4.5.7 The Life of Fame and Power, 250

    4.5.8 The Virtuous Life: Does Virtue Lead to Happiness? 252

4.6 Deliberation, 255

    4.6.1 Rational Calculation, 255

    4.6.2 Cunning, 257

    4.6.3 Aristotle's Account of Deliberation, 259

    4.6.4 Cicero's Model of Deliberation, 261

    4.6.5 Memory, 265

    4.6.6 Discernment, 272

    4.6.7 Foresight, 275

    4.6.8 Methods of Moral Deliberation: Casuistry and Narrative Ethics, 277

4.7 Judgment and Decision, 283

    4.7.1 Kidder's Paradigms of Moral Judgment, 284

    4.7.2 Bad Judgment, 288

    4.7.3 Decision, 289

4.8 Wisdom and the Question of Moral Knowledge, 297

    4.8.1 Aristotle's Dispute with Socrates and Plato, 297

    4.8.2 Kant's Notion of Practical Reason as Opposed to Aristotle's, 301

    4.8.3 The Unity of the Different Senses of Practical Reason, 302

    Review Questions, 305

    Questions for Discussion, 306

    Case Studies for Discussion, 307

    Suggested Readings, 309

CHAPTER FIVE

Moral Knowledge, 311

5.1 Moral Intuition, 312

    5.1.1 The Conflict between Moral Intuition
and Moral Knowledge, 313

5.2 Stages of Moral Knowledge , 315

    5.2.1 The Stage of Clarification, 316

    5.2.2 The Stage of Systematization, 317

    5.2.3 Integrity and Moral Codes, 320

    5.2.4 The Stage of Justification, 321

    5.2.5 Kohlberg's and Gilligan's Stages of Moral Reasoning, 321

    5.2.6 Subjectivism, Dichotomous Thinking, Relativism,
and Other Roadblocks to Inquiry, 326

    5.2.7 Ways of Justifying Ethical Principles and Their Problems , 330

    5.2.8 Feminist Criticisms of the Principle Approach, 336

5.3 Deontological Principles, 340

    5.3.1 The Principle of (Deontological) Egoism , 341

    5.3.2 The Principle of Nonmaleficence (the Libertarian
Principle), 343

    5.3.3 The Categorical Imperative, 345

    5.3.4 Contract Ethics and Discourse Ethics, 350

5.4 Teleological Principles, 358

    5.4.1 The Principle of (Consequentialist) Egoism , 358

    5.4.2 The Tit-for-Tat Principle, 360

    5.4.3 The Golden Rule, 363

    5.4.4 The Utilitarian Principle, 365

    5.4.5 Bentham's Account of Utilitarianism, 365

    5.4.6 John Stuart Mill's Version of Utilitarianism, 367

    5.4.7 The Preference versus Happiness Versions of Utilitarianism, 369

    5.4.8 Act- versus Rule-Utilitarianism, 369

    5.4.9 Justification and Criticism of the Utilitarian Principle, 370

5.5 The Natural Law Theory and Rights-Based Ethics, 374

    5.5.1 History of Natural Law Theory, 374

    5.5.2 The Natural Law Expressed as a Principle of Benevolence, 376

    5.5.3 The Beginnings of Natural Rights Theories , 378

    5.5.4 Rights-Based Ethics, 381

5.6 Using Principles in Moral Decision Making, 385

Review Questions, 393

Questions for Discussion, 394

Suggested Readings, 394

EPILOGUE

Moral Competence, 400

APPENDIX

Writing Ethics Term Papers, 403

The Purpose of Writing Philosophy Papers, 403

Choosing a Subject for the Paper, 403

    1. Choose a Subject of Interest to You, 404

    2. Choose a Controversial Subject, 404

    3. Choose a Manageable Subject, 404

    4. Make Sure the Subject Is Approved by the Instructor, 404

Finding Sources, 404

Doing the Research, 406

Constructing the paper, 406

Writing the Paper, 407

Ethical Use of Source Material, 407

Sources for Writing Philosophy Papers, 408

Reference and Bibliography Style, 408

Glossary, 409

References, 418

Index, 439

Preface

Don't be too hasty to trust or admire teachers of morality; they discourse like angels, but live like men.

—Samuel Johnson

Most people prefer theory to practice, under the impression that arguing about morals proves them to be philosophers, and that in this way they will turn out to be fine characters.

—Aristotle

Why does virtue consist in having read Chrysippus through? If so, progress is confessedly nothing else than understanding a great deal of Chrysippus.

—Epictetus

In this revision of the first edition of *Moral Competence*, I have tried to remain faithful to its original intent: to be a readable and relevant text for those interested in the traditional and enduring questions of ethics. I have made every effort here to introduce philosophers, ethical theories, concepts, and problems in a clear way—and for the benefit of those without much philosophy background—but in a manner that still preserves their depth and complexity. Thanks to a number of suggestions and criticisms from students and colleagues, the second edition has a number of improvements, including updated relevant research, more examples and cases studies, significant revisions, and the addition of new material in several places.

The basic theme of the text, however, remains the same. *Moral Competence* is an *integrated* approach to the study of ethics. By that I mean to show how the various concepts, issues, approaches, and theories which make up the panoply of ethical traditions play an important part in understanding the whole of moral life. The effort here is to weave these together into a coherent, contextual picture. Rather than a pastiche of topics and thinkers, students will see where each topic and concept fits into a larger scheme of things and how each important thinker contributes significantly to the matter of moral competence. In this regard, the book can be viewed not only as a tool of ethical reflection, but also a means of personal improvement.

Competence is a term that is used in a number of fields to convey the idea of a person's mastery and internalization of the rules, procedures, and use of a language, skill, a profession, or a body of knowledge. That is certainly the sense here. Moral competence is a mastery that permits general consistency in doing the right thing. It is defined by the interdependence of the elements that constitute good moral behavior. The ability to do the right thing consistently requires a coordination of a desire to do the right thing, the will to do it, a disposition to keep on doing it, knowing how to do it, and knowing what the right thing to do is. A little reflection shows their necessary interdependence. Surely there are many who desire the right thing yet can't seem to muster the will to do it. But even those with strong will may not have the virtuous character or disposition to will the right thing consistently; moreover, even those with virtuous character may not have the wisdom required to know how to do the right thing. Of course, all of these attributes are useless if one does not know what the right thing to do is.

To use more traditional language, what is needed to do the right thing consistently is an interconnection among moral sentiment, moral strength, virtue and vice, wisdom, and moral knowledge (see figure below). The text is designed so that one chapter is devoted to each of these aspects; its initial sense is then developed as

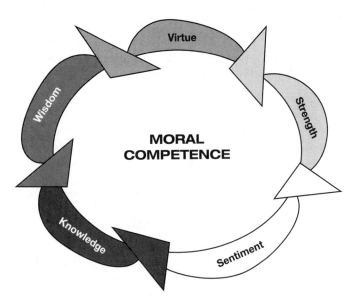

Moral competence is the integration of a number of important abilities: moral sentiment, the desire to do the right thing; moral strength, the power to do it; virtue, the disposition to keep on doing it; prudence, knowing how it's done; and knowledge, knowing what the right thing to do is.

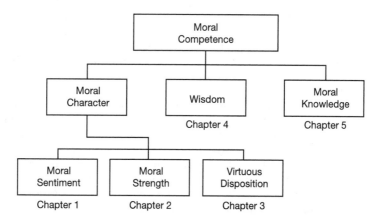

The Components of Moral Competence

it is related to the whole—much in the way in which the events in the first chapter of a novel acquire so much more significance as the story unfolds. The book is divided into three broad sections: Chapters One to Three on Moral Character, Chapter Four on Wisdom and Practical Reasoning, and Chapter Five on Moral Knowledge (see figure above). The first chapter begins with an examination of moral emotions and general characterizations of duty, honor, and the sense of caring. Theories concerning the acquisition of moral sentiment and pathologies of moral emotion are discussed, with the relevant psychological material included. Moral strength is the topic of the next chapter, starting with a discussion of free will and moving on to questions concerning moral weakness. Responsibility and blame are discussed in some detail. The nature of autonomy is analyzed, and various means of exercising moral strength are listed. In Chapter Three the virtues and vices are catalogued and described, and the issues pertaining to them are addressed. The character of wisdom, prudence, and practical reasoning is discussed in Chapter Four. Finally, questions of moral knowledge, principles, and justification are reviewed in Chapter Five. In the Epilogue several theses concerning the connection among these different aspects of moral competence are presented.

The reader will also notice a number of text boxes strategically placed throughout the book. These serve several purposes. Sometimes they are used to summarize the biography and thinking of an important ethical philosopher or thinker, or they may provide relevant information to a topic being discussed. They may also pose a query or problem related to the topic or present a case study for reflection.

The end matter of each chapter includes the usual review questions, questions for discussion, and additional bibliographic sources organized by topic. Some chapters include brief summaries of relevant stories and additional case studies.

The book is provided with a glossary and also a useful guide for writing ethics papers, complete with hints, general sources, and references to other writing guides and references. There is a complete bibliography of works cited. References in the body of the text are indicated by (author date: page), or where the author is mentioned in body, just (date: page) or (date) alone is indicated. If classical sources are used, an abbreviation of the work is indicated along with its scholarly indexing; for example, Aristotle's *Nicomachean Ethics* is referenced as (*Nic. Ethics* 1107a2). References in the bibliography employ a version of the American Psychological Association style, unless they refer to a classical source; the latter are indicated by author and title, with references to the appropriate translations and their dates. To insure proper gender representation in the text, "he" and "she" are randomly interspersed throughout the text.

Instructors and students are invited to visit my Website (http://cwolf.uaa.alaska.edu/~afjjl/JamesLiszka.htm). There are a number of PowerPoint presentations that have been especially prepared to accompany this text. These can be downloaded and modified by instructors for presentation in class or used by students as tutorials or for preparation for tests. Students can access study guides, chapter summaries, review presentations, practice quizzes, additional case studies, updates, and other useful information at the site. Please direct any questions or comments you have about the text to me at: afjjl@uaa.alaska.edu.

James Jakób Liszka

Acknowledgments

I owe a debt of gratitude to the hundreds of students who, over the years, have contributed their insights, criticisms, and helpful suggestions to the development of the first and second edition of this textbook. I hope it will continue to be a useful tool for other students as well. There are also a number of colleagues I wish to thank for their helpful remarks and suggestions, including Joseph Tarala, Krishna Mallick, Tom Morrow, Jon Stratton, Maurine Stein, and Geoffrey Frasz. For help with permissions, I would like to thank the following people: Marj Blixhavn of *The Anchorage Daily News*, who was especially helpful in this regard, Chuck Shepherd, Sharon Wenhil, L. Roche, Alec Wilkinson, Jill Frisch, and Naomi Warren Klouda.

Many thanks to the Prentice Hall editors for thoughtful suggestions for improvements in the material: Angela Stone, Karita France, and Ross Miller. I also wish to thank the Prentice Hall reviewers: Jeremiah Hackett, University of South Carolina and Mary Giegengack-Jureller, Le Moyne College for their helpful comments for this edition.

Most of my gratitude, however, is saved for my family, Genie Babb, with whom I spent countless hours discussing the material in this text and who was a constant source of encouragement and support; Zachary Liszka, to whom this book is dedicated; and Alexandra Liszka, whose cheerfulness, enthusiasm, and smile were always an encouragement.

Republication rights have been received from

Anchorage Daily News for the following: Susan Braund, "Story Medicine," Mike Doogan, "A Very Determined Woman Looks for Money for a Special Trip, Dr. Lael Conway, "Doctors without Borders," Craig Medred, "You Have to Learn to Deal With Fear," Bruce Melzer, "The Politics of Lies," Robert Meyerowitz, "Boarder Hurt on Denali," Liz Ruskin, "Memory of Killing Gone," "Doug Gustafson," "Adam Barger," Tracy Barbour, "Tearful Driver Gets Nine Months."

Nicholas Kristoff, "Japanese Serious about Fairy Tales," copyright © 1996 by The New York Times Co. Reprinted by Permission.

Alec Wilkinson, "Conversations with a Killer," quoted by permission of Alec Wilkinson, and first appeared in *The New Yorker*, April 18, 1994.

Deborah Blum, "Scientists Say Psychopaths Born–Not Made," Copyright, *The Sacramento Bee*, 1995.

"Arnold and Uma Relish Roles as Evil Mr. Freeze and Poison Ivy," Copyright 1997, *USA TODAY*. Reprinted with permission.

Into Thin Air by Jon Krakauer. Copyright © 1997 by Jon Krakauer. Adapted by permission of Villard Books, a division of Random House, Inc.

Living Faith by Jimmy Carter © 1996, by permission of Random House, Inc.

For Cause and Comrades by James McPherson © 1997, by permission of Oxford University Press.

Associated Press for the following: Claudia Coates, "Amish Torn Over Murderer"; Allesandra Galloni, "Nazi Ordered Retried"; Anne Gearan, "Silencing the Scream"; Niki Kapsambelis, "Big Jackpot Draws Misery"; Paula Story, "Zen and the Art of Survival on the Freeway"; "Robbers Test Walker's Faith"; "Mass Killings of the 20th Century"; "Following Orders Defense"; and "Vaccines Were Tested on Orphans."

INTRODUCTION

Why Study Ethics?

Isn't a moral philosopher … a thinker who considers morality question-able, as calling for question marks, in short, as a problem? Should moral-izing not be—immoral?

—Friedrich Nietzsche

In the spring of 1991 Fred Turner set out from Beaufort, South Carolina, with a plan to walk across America to prove that most people are good. He only got as far as the state line before he was robbed and pushed off a bridge. Two men in a faded red pickup truck pulled up next to him as he was walking across the Tuck-aseking Bridge at the Georgia–South Carolina line. "They asked me if I was the guy walking across America. I told them yes and they said, 'Good, give me your wallet'." He lost his balance and tumbled over the bridge railing when one of the men pushed him. With his backpack on, he drifted with the current until it took him to shore. He spent the night in a vacant cabin. He wanted to prove to himself that only one of every one hundred people is bad. "I found my one bad one," he said in an interview from a hospital bed where he was recovering from his injuries. Unde-terred Turner pledged to make another walk the next year. As far as it is known, he has not attempted that second walk (Associated Press, 1991).

This disheartening story feeds a prevalent feeling that most advanced industri-al cultures are undergoing a moral decline. University of Georgia professor Fred Schab found that in 1969 more than 80 percent of high schoolers agreed that "hon-esty is the best policy"; in 1989, that figure dropped to 60 percent (cf. Kidder 1995: 53). In the McFeely-Wackerle-Jett Survey on Ethics conducted in 1987, 56 percent of respondents felt that during the past 20 years people have become less ethical, while 36 percent felt that people were just as ethical now as then. A September 1992 Gallup survey showed that 63 percent felt that there is an overall moral decline in the United States, while 80 percent of a Shearson-Lehman Brothers survey felt that the United States was "pretty seriously on the wrong track" (cf. Kidder 1995: 48). Recent cheating scandals at West Point and other military training institutions, thought by many to be places where honesty, honor, and integrity are placed at a

After an opinion survey of 2000 people selected at random, which gave participants a guarantee of anonymity, James Patterson and Peter Kim, authors of *The Day America Told the Truth* (1991), came away with the following statistics:

- Only 13% of Americans believe in all Ten Commandments.
- 91% of Americans lie regularly at work and at home.
- 20% of women say they were raped by their dates.
- 33% of AIDS carriers have not told their spouses or lovers.
- 31% of married people are having or have had an affair.
- 7% of participants say that for $2 million they would commit murder.

premium, have also seemed to disillusion the optimistic and reinforce the more cynical. A *Newsweek* poll (June 2–3, 1994) seemed to confirm this general tenor. Of those interviewed, 76 percent felt that there was indeed moral decline in America.

Two recent, influential studies have tracked this perception of moral decline with more detail. In *Bowling Alone* (2000), Robert Putnam presents evidence for a steady drop in trust over the last part of the 20th century. Most Americans today believe that we live in a less trustworthy society than their parents did. In 1952, Americans were split about 50-50 as to whether society was as upright morally as it had been in the past. In 1998, however, people believed by a margin of three to one that American society is less honest and moral than it used to be (2000: 139). In general, Putnam's research showed that whereas early generations had a trust quotient of nearly 80 percent, Gen-X has a trust quotient of barely half that (2000: 141). Putnam traced a significant change in the amount of trust in the mid-1960s: 60 percent of the baby boomers born between 1946–1960 agreed that "most people are honest," and the percentages of people who held this view seemed unchanged even 30 years later; but of those born after 1960, roughly half have denied that "most people are honest" (2000: 141). In *The Great Disruption* (1999), Francis Fukuyama has detailed similar declines. In 1958, 73 percent of Americans surveyed said they trusted the federal government to do what is right "most of the time"; by 1994, only 15 percent did (1999: 49). Trust in corporations, organized labor, banks, the medical professions, organized religion, the military, education, and the press have all seen significant declines between the 1970s and 1990s (1999: 50).

Although there is a growing *perception* of moral decline, the question of whether there is an *actual* moral decline is much harder to determine. Perceptions can obviously vary from what is actually the case. A common hypothesis is that media coverage of events increases awareness of crime and often focuses on the underside of life (Fukuyama 1999: 86). Since the media in our "information age" are pervasive, and since they seem to focus on negative or sensational content, they promote negative perceptions of the condition of society. Since the media have become progressively pervasive over generations with the advent of radio, television, and the Internet, the people in previous generations had more positive perceptions of the moral quality of life simply because

How Do Adults Feel about the Moral Behavior of Adolescents?

A recent study was done by Public Agenda, a research organization based in New York City. The study, based on a poll of over 2000 adults, was entitled *Kids These Days: What Americans Really Think about the Next Generation*. According to the study, adults' negative views of the nation's teenagers and younger children are so widespread that only 37 percent believe that today's youngsters will eventually make this country a better place. Two-thirds of adults surveyed thought teenagers were rude, wild, and irresponsible. The study argues that the responses demonstrated a fundamental concern about youngsters' moral and ethical values: The adults stressed the need to teach kids integrity, ethical behavior, respect, civility, compassion, and responsibility. Americans are convinced, the report concluded, that today's adolescents face a crisis in their values and morals.

they were less exposed to the negative aspects of society. Robert Putnam argues that television may be one of the most important factors in promoting a decline in trust (1995; 2000: 216ff.), but he does not blame it on the news aspect of the media. Although readership in newspapers has declined steadily over the generations, it is not because it has been replaced by television news; interest in the news per se is declining generationally. If anything, the two types of news work as complements (2000: 219). Putnam points the finger to entertainment instead, especially television entertainment. Television has the effect of first isolating viewers from other viewers. It becomes a passive form of entertainment that can be easily accessed within the confines of one's home. Second, it controls the information presented to viewers. Third, it presents a great deal of content that could promote distrust in its viewers (2000: 224).

There is another aspect of such perceptions that also needs to be considered. The perception of others' perceptions can reinforce or change one's own perception. The data which Robert Putnam (2000) and Francis Fukuyama (1999) put forth show a generationally progressive decline of trust. When this is compared with the data which show that older generations view younger ones as having less moral quality, this may provide a partial explanation of generationally declining trust: General distrust of the younger generation by the older one may feed into the younger one's growing distrust of others. If we become aware that someone does not trust us, we may be less trusting in return; it could then be argued that it is the perceptions which cause the perceptions rather than any actual condition.

Fukuyama in general dismisses the claim that the perception of moral decline is due to nostalgia, poor memory, or ignorance of earlier generations (1999: 5). He also considers television and the media to be less important in the cause of these perceptions (1999: 85–86). He believes instead that the perceptions are accurate—that there is indeed actual moral decline. To determine that, of course, is much more difficult. It is relatively easier to portray perceptions accurately because how one perceives things is readily available to oneself just through simple reflection. Polling, if it is done right statistically and methodologically, can give a relatively accurate picture of these per-

---

Which Occupations Are Considered to Have People with Good Moral Standards?

In a Harris poll conducted in 1992

- 63% of those polled thought small business owners were honest;
- 39% thought journalists were honest;
- 31% believed business executives were;
- only 25% thought lawyers were honest;
- a mere 19% thought members of Congress were.

According to *The Sourcebook of Criminal Justice Statistics* (1998), issued by the Bureau of Justice Statistics, the highest rated occupations for honesty and ethical standards (in rank order) are

> pharmacists
> clergy
> medical doctors
> college teachers
> dentists
> police
> engineers
> funeral directors
> bankers
> journalists

Which Occupations Are Considered to Have People with Poor Moral Standards?

The following rank (starting with the worst) was made in *The Day America Told the Truth* (1991):

- street peddlers
- prostitutes
- TV evangelists
- organized crime bosses
- drug dealers
- local politicians
- members of Congress

Are Women More Ethical Than Men?

A 1997 nationwide survey conducted by Yankelovich Partners for the Lutheran Brotherhood yielded the following results:

- 51% of those surveyed believed women are more ethical than men.
- 26% of those surveyed believed men and women are equally ethical.
- 16% were undecided.

Louise Thoreson of the Lutheran Brotherhood claimed that the disparity between the estimation of men and women was due to the fact that women tend to be nurturers in our society and the role models and teachers of children. It is precisely these qualities in women that make them more trusted.

Question for Discussion

Do you agree with Thoreson's claim?

ceptions, but the perceptions may not be accurate about the way life is. Trying to show that there is actual moral decline requires some relatively objective standard of what is right and wrong and then a measure of conformity with or deviation from those standards over time. How we count something, objectively speaking, as moral or immoral is, in itself, a difficult matter and forms the subject of most of this book.

Fukuyama takes the following approach to this problem. He believes that actual moral decline can be measured by shifts in a small number of indices that would appear, by general consensus, to be morally undesirable. These include the crime rate for violent crimes and thefts, lower fertility and higher divorce rates, and increases in the rates of births to single mothers. Since these rates have seen dramatic shifts since the 1960s—a period which Fukuyama calls "the great disruption"—he concludes that moral decline has occurred over the last three decades. He also argues that this is a pattern—previous centuries have also witnessed such a periodic decline, followed by a moral renewal and regeneration.

Some of the indices which Fukuyama uses seem clear: Murder, assault and battery against the innocent, rape, and theft are counted as immoral in most people's books. However, it is not clear why lower fertility rates are inherently morally undesirable; curbing the population of an overly populated planet, especially among those societies with high per capita consumption rates, might actually be considered a good thing by many. Although divorces are undesirable because of their consequences to children and the stability of families, counting all divorces as morally problematic may be questionable. For example, there may be divorces that are the result of avoiding abusive relationships, which many people may view as perfectly justifiable. But one has to be careful here even in using the crime statistics as an absolute index of moral decline. First, there may be morally unrelated reasons for such increases. Low crime rates may also be the result of effective measures of crime prevention rather than an increase in moral health. That is to say, assuming a relatively constant segment of the population with criminal intent, they may be prevented from being successful, either because of efficient or oppressive measures. Thus, conversely, one could reasonably argue that an increase in crime rates is due to ineffective prevention or less oppression. Certainly Russia, since the fall of communism, is experiencing the latter. Sicily, for example, has experienced the former for years. Second, focus on a single index, or even a few indices, may ignore the moral ecology of a society. As Robert Putnam remarks,

> The fifties and sixties were hardly a "golden age," especially for those Americans who were marginalized because of their race or gender or social class or sexual orientation. Segregation, by race legally and by gender socially, was the norm, and intolerance, though declining, was still disturbingly high. Environmental degradation had only just been exposed by Rachel Carson, and Betty Friedan had not yet deconstructed the feminine mystique. Grinding rural poverty had still to be discovered by the national media.

Infant mortality, a standard measure of public health, stood at twenty-six per one thousand births—forty-four per one thousand for black infants—in 1960, nearly four times worse than those indexes would be at the end of the century (2000: 17).

Paradoxically speaking, the result of moral improvements in some areas may result in the increase in undesirable behaviors in others. The assessment of a society's moral health should then require a comparison of both positive and negative aspects of the society. It might be argued, for example, in the case of divorce, that the rise of divorce rates results from what many might consider positive changes in the ethos of marriage, women's social position, and their socialization. Career opportunity, civic equality, equity in the household, and less tolerance of abuse and male dominance may have questioned the older norms and created tension and some anomie in traditional marriages. But it may also be the case that marriages are being reconstituted at a higher moral plateau and that new, better patterns of intimacy are emerging.

As it turns out, Fukuyama seems to be laying claim to the same thing, more generally speaking. There have been recent positive declines in these same indices—including a recent report by the U.S. Justice Department, which shows that the rate of violent crimes fell by 10 percent in 1999. This suggests, in Fukuyama's view, that there is a turn toward some sense of moral renewal in America, and this is a repeating pattern found in previous centuries (1999: 7). In Gallup polls in the 1980s, the number of people insisting that a "strict moral code" is "very important" had risen steadily from 47 percent in 1981 to 60 percent in 1989 (Kidder 1995: 47). When the Center for Business Ethics at Bentley College in Massachusetts surveyed *Fortune 1000* corporations in 1992, one-third of the respondents said they had set up a formal ethics officer position in their corporation. The result of a survey of 4000 upper-level executives in 1987 by the consulting firm of McFeely-Wackerle-Jett showed that 90 percent felt that "good ethics is good business in the long run" (Kidder 1995: 47). The Marine Corps added a 12th week of basic training devoted to values discussion and training (AP July 6, 1996). *The New York Times* index from 1969 to 1989 shows that articles under the rubric of ethics have grown by 400 percent during that 20 year period (cf. Kidder 1995: 45–46). Interest in ethics is also indicated by the rise in the numbers of university affiliated ethics centers, so that presently all but seven states have one or more such centers. There is an increasing numbers of books and articles on morals education, a growth in the number of graduate degrees in applied ethics, and an interest among the professions in the use of specially trained ethicists to help with relevant moral problems. Private institutes, such as the Josephson Institute and Rushworth Kidder's Center for Global Ethics, along with movements such as the Commission on Civic Renewal have attempted to bring ethics education to the public consciousness.

But whether we are presently undergoing a moral renewal or whether we are still sliding into further decline or whether we have not really declined at all, the need to study ethics is clear. In the first case, we need it to give ourselves the vision necessary for change in the right direction. We need it in the second case to correct our deviation from the right path; and in the third case, we need to study ethics to maintain those things we do well and rightly. In general, it is clear that before we can determine whether there has been moral decline, we must inquire into what counts as morally right and wrong—and this is exactly what the study of ethics does.

But even if we can agree that there is a need to study ethics, there are often questions about its effectiveness and usefulness. Finding the proper moral vision and some relatively objective standards of moral conduct is considered by many to be very difficult if not impossible. *Relativism*—the view that morality differs in all societies and is nothing more than what is socially approved in a particular society—has many adherents. It seems to be an especially popular view in modern industrial cultures where diversity of religions and institutions makes it confusing for individuals to find a consistent moral compass to navigate the terrain of life. We are often given conflicting messages. Depending on the source, we can be told that, on the one hand, abortion is murder or, on the other hand, that it is morally permissible. We can be told that homosexuality is wrong, wrong but tolerable, or completely permissible. Islam says no more than four wives are permissible, whereas Christianity insists on monogamy; certain groups may insist on the immorality of premarital sex, yet the culture at large seems to endorse it. Moral competence is hard enough to achieve in a homogeneous culture, where norms, roles, and rules of conduct are relatively clear and straightforward, yet alone in one in which we are offered a cafeteria of values.

We will discuss the matter of relativism in Section 5.2.7, but still, despite the variety of values and norms in the moral marketplace, one might not be so surprised after all in finding a common ethical core in most cultures and groups. Many of the virtues, such as honesty, courage, fairness, as well as basic rules of cooperation, reciprocity, and nonaggression are honored in nearly every culture—and for good reason: Without them, a cooperative, mutually beneficial society would not be really possible. Robert Putnam argues that "the norm of generalized reciprocity is ... fundamental to civilized life. ... " (2000: 135). Reciprocity, trustworthiness, and its associated norms form the basis of what Putnam and others have called *social capital*, understood as a network among individuals and groups which helps to facilitate cooperation among them (Putnam 2000: 19). Those societies with large amounts of social capital generally flourish and prosper, whereas those with little live poorly in the many senses of the term. A society in which people wantonly steal, lie, cheat, and kill could not generate trust and could easily lead to what Thomas Hobbes described as a life "nasty, brutish and short."

In his book *The Sorcerers of Dobu* (1963), anthropologist Reo Fortune describes a society that is preoccupied by sorcery. Mistrust among even the closest relatives develops, and there is a plague of vindictive behavior. Just going to the bathroom was a problem since it involved going outside the village into the bush, where it was imagined one could be easily attacked by the magic of others. The result was a web of fear and lack of trust that pervaded everyday life. For a culture to thrive and for a people within it to flourish, a predominance of some virtue and moral order must be the case. The studies of the Sicilian Mafia by sociologist Diego Gambetta show a society impoverished in every way by its lack of trust and general norms of reciprocity—especially as compared to its more prosperous neighbors in Northern Italy, where a long democratic tradition has prevailed. "Societies which rely heavily on the use of force are likely to be less efficient, more costly, and more unpleasant than those where trust is maintained by other means" (1988: 221; cf. Putnam 2000: 136). But to maintain trust, the norms of honesty, keeping promises, and generalized reciprocity must predominate. Thus, it would not be surprising to find these very same norms present in cultures that have flourished and prospered over time simply because they are the very means to their longevity. Thus, despite Fred Turner's awful experience as related in the book's opening paragraph, we would expect to confirm his intuition that most people in societies are morally decent or at least trustworthy enough not to go out of their way to harm others.

THE STUDY OF ETHICS

Ethics is primarily concerned with addressing the questions of what should count as morally good behavior, what makes a person good, what is the good life, and what sort of rules and principles we should use in guiding our decision making; it provides evidence and justification for these matters and conveys wisdom and understanding about ethical life. All ethical studies are guided by some account or presumption of the human condition, and they are constrained by what Owen Flanagan calls the *principle of minimal psychological realism*: "make sure when constructing a moral theory or projecting a moral ideal that the character, decision processing, and behavior prescribed are possible ... for creatures like us" (1991: 32). Setting the standards of angels for humans is fruitless.

Ethics has two broad traditions: the classical and the modern. Generally speaking, the earlier and classical tradition was concerned with what it means to be a good person. As the great Greek philosopher Aristotle (384–322 B.C.E.) says, the goal of studying ethics is not to know the good, but "in order to become good, else there would be no advantage in studying it" (*Nic. Ethics* 1103b26–27). For this reason, the followers of this tradition have focused primarily on the question of character and the proper way of living. This tradition relies especially on wisdom, understood as a practical but inexact form of reasoning, as the means by which good character and good lives are achieved. This tradition is exemplified by Socrates (470–399 B.C.E.), Confucius (551–479 B.C.E.), Mencius (321–289 B.C.E.), Plato (428–348 B.C.E.), Aristotle (384–322 B.C.E.), Diogenes (412–323 B.C.E.), Epicurus (341–270 B.C.E.), Epictetus (c. 55–135 C.E.), and Cicero (106-43 B.C.E.). This sagacious tradition is also exemplified by many of the founders of the great religions, including Buddha, Moses, Jesus, and Muhammad. What we get from the moral sages is a plan for the *practice* of the good life and not simply answers to larger theoretical questions.

The modern period, for the most part, has forgone this sagacious tradition. Its emphasis, especially since the 18th century, has been on questions of what is the right thing to do, rather than what it means to be a good person. In doing so it has focused on questions of principles and rules for action, and it has believed that such principles could be determined systematically and justified by exact and rigorous means. By finding such a rigorous justification for a principle, then to the extent that such principles can help us decide what to do in any situation, we have a credible guide to action. This tradition is exemplified by the great German philosopher Immanuel Kant (1724–1804), who attempted such a systematic account of ethics. It is also the character of utilitarianism, developed in the 19th century, whose best known advocate is John Stuart Mill (1806–1873). Utilitarians especially believed that they had found a moral formula that made moral decision making clear and reliable. But despite the modernist trend, there are some current ethical thinkers who wish to return to the sagacious tradition and are doubtful of the ability of ethical theory to live up to its claims. The position of this text is that both traditions have something important to contribute to a more comprehensive picture of ethics. The systematic justification of ethics is a worthwhile project, but principles are insufficient for making good moral decisions. Attending to how we become good and how we do the right thing are complementary rather than contrary processes. An ethic that looks to both character and principle, wisdom and knowledge is a richer one for the effort.

The Ancient Moral Sages

Solomon (970–928 B.C.E.), son of David, was considered the wisest among the ancient Hebrew kings. Ecclesiastes, a writing attributed to him, stresses the vanity of a life seeking pleasure and happiness. Life is no more than a succession of unrelated and meaningless events, where death befalls wise and foolish, rich and poor alike. There is a season for everything in this endless cycle. The best one can hope for is wisdom, a faith in God, the enjoyment of whatever goods come one's way, and acceptance of life's sorrows.

Confucius (551–479 B.C.E.), an itinerant teacher and successful government minister, is considered the greatest and most revered of the Chinese philosophers. His focus was on humanistic rather than religious-based morality. He did not care to talk about spiritual beings or even about life after death. Instead, he believed that human beings "can make the Way [Tao] great," not that "the Way can make humans great." His philosophy argued for the harmony of the perfect individual with a well-ordered society. The perfect individual, the *chun-tzu*, was a morally superior person who retained a certain nobility. This was distinct from the traditional idea of nobility by status and inheritance. The characteristic of the *chun-tzu* was *jen*, understood by Confucius to be something like the golden rule: "Wishing to establish his own character, he also establishes the character of others, and wishing to be prominent himself, he also helps others be prominent." *Jen* is expressed in terms of conscientiousness and altruism.

The good society, on the other hand, was one based on the mutual moral obligations of the five human relations between ruler and subject, father and son, elder and younger brother, husband and wife, and one friend with another. In these cases, filial piety and brotherly respect were the primary virtues. Confucius's most important work is *The Analects*. (For more on Confucius, see Sections 1.3.4 and 4.6.5.)

Socrates (470–399 B.C.E.) was an ancient Greek philosopher living in Athens during its golden age. He was the teacher of Plato; later, despite his courageous military and civic service to Athens, he was charged with worshiping gods the city did not recognize and corrupting the youth. He was found guilty and put to death. Since the Athenians felt it was taboo to kill prisoners, the practice was for those condemned to death to die by their own hand; the usual practice was to drink hemlock. Plato suggests that Socrates had an opportunity to escape but refused to take it on the grounds that, as a citizen of Athens and a beneficiary of its practices, he had a

duty to obey its laws and an obligation to accept his sentence.

Socrates had the habit of discussing philosophical and ethical questions in the marketplace of Athens (the *agora*) with his young students and sometimes with prominent Athenian and foreign citizens. Socrates himself wrote nothing, but Plato immortalized Socrates in his various dialogues. The death of Socrates is captured in the dialogues *The Apology, The Crito,* and *The Phaedo.* The trial and character of Socrates is also portrayed by Xenophon in *Memorabilia.* A parody of Socrates is made by Aristophanes in his play *The Clouds.*

Because Socrates left no writings and Plato often uses Socrates's in his *Dialogues* as a voice for his own philosophical thought, it is hard to determine Socrates's views. Most scholars suggest that Socrates was one of the earliest Greek philosophers to be concerned with the ethics of human conduct. For him, wisdom (*sophia*) was not so much a matter of knowing the nature of the cosmos—as it was for the pre-Socratics—but concerned the right thing to do. Happiness did not depend on external or physical goods, but proper moral conduct. The way this was achieved was through genuine knowledge of self; hence, Socrates's motto—"know thyself." Socrates argued that wisdom lay in knowing the essence of the virtues and that, beyond social conventions or nominal definitions, the virtues could be captured in terms of their true nature.

Plato (428–348 B.C.E.) was the student of Socrates and the teacher of Aristotle, who later came to rival him for the status of the greatest classical philosopher. Plato wrote a number of philosophical pieces in dialogue form, among these *The Republic, The Meno, The Laws, The Apology, The Crito, The Phaedo,* and *The Symposium.* Plato developed a theory which argued that the Good was a transcendent Form that could be known through pure reason. The Form of the Good could not be ascertained through perception or observation of the world as it appears to us, but required special training and insight. Plato's "Allegory of the Cave" (*Rep.* 532b) illustrates this idea. Plato likens the condition of human beings to slaves who, confined inside a cave, are exposed only to shadows cast from afar by a fire. The slaves come to believe that these are the only things that are real. Once a slave is allowed to see the source of the shadows, he realizes that the projection of the fire is their reality, and he understands that what he once thought was real was only appearance. Yet, when he is dragged from the cave and exposed to the daylight, he understands that the sun is the paradigm of light, and fire is merely its example. This parallels the

The Ancient Moral Sages *(continued)*

process by which we come to understand the nature of the Good, and the distinction between appearance and reality. (For more on Plato, see Sections 2.2 and 4.8.1.)

Aristotle (384–322 B.C.E.) is thought to be one of the greatest Western philosophers. He was the student of Plato and the teacher of Alexander the Great. Aristotle was a prolific and systematic thinker, writing on logic, metaphysics, physics, biology, psychology, rhetoric, poetics, and politics. His principal work on ethics is the *Nicomachean Ethics*. In this study Aristotle makes a number of important claims that serve as the foundation for the study of ethics in generations that followed him. Aristotle argued that the end of all human activity was happiness (*eudaimonia*), better translated as flourishing. Flourishing consisted in the performance of human activity with excellence (or virtue). To flourish, then, one must be virtuous. Virtue, in turn, was constituted as a mean between extremes; for example, temperance was a mean between self-indulgence and insensitivity to pleasure; courage was a mean between cowardliness and rashness. Aristotle further argued that prudence was needed to attain this mean properly. Prudence was not a scientific form of reasoning, but a sort of practical wisdom that dealt with probabilities and the nuances of life. (For more on Aristotle, see Sections 2.2, 2.4, 3.1, 4.1, 4.4, 4.5.3, 4.5.8, 4.6.3, 4.8.1, and 4.8.2.)

Epictetus (c. 55–135 C.E.) was born a slave but gained his freedom sometime after the death of Nero in 68 C.E. He became lame because of maltreatment while in bondage. He studied with the powerful Stoic teacher C. Musonius Rufus. Later in life he was banished from Rome and died in Nicopolis in Greece, where he had established a school and had a large following. He married very late in life but only to bring up a child whose parents planned to expose it (a practice among Greeks and Romans for unwanted infants).

Epictetus lived a simple, austere life in a house with only a rush mat, a pallet (for his bed), and a small lamp. He was said to be a person of kind disposition—especially to children—and humble and charitable.

The Stoic ideal was tranquillity or peace of mind, which was not the absence of feeling but gave a certain tone or tenor (*tonos*) to one's life. This was accomplished by rigorous, continuing moral education, daily self-examination, and the practice of making clear and firm judgments. These practices were enabled by a certain submissiveness to the inexorable. Indeed, Epictetus's motto was "bear and forbear." As articulated in Epictetus's surviving work,

The Manual (probably compiled by Arrian, a student of Epictetus), the key to the tranquil life lies in determining what is truly in our power from what is not and to accept what is not in our power and to properly direct what is. What is in our power are our intellect, will, and judgment; what is not in our power are things, for example, pertaining to our body, wealth, and fame. If we can use what is in our power, judgment, to properly ascertain those events that happen to us, then genuine tranquillity is attainable. As Epictetus claims, "what disturbs men's minds is not events but their judgments on events." This ability leads to *autarkeia*, the independence of the virtuous person from external circumstances and the vagaries of life. (For more discussion of Epictetus, see Section 3.3.2.)

Epicurus (341–270 B.C.E.) studied philosophy at a very early age. He soon became a teacher himself and founded a school and community at Athens called The Garden. The Garden stressed the cultivation of friendship as the basis of community. Its members included women, courtesans, and slaves. He was so loved by his students that they celebrated his memory in a monthly feast after his death. His teachings became very popular and spread quickly through the Greek world.

According to Epicurus, the good life is only attainable by the philosopher, and it is marked by the enjoyment of the right sort of pleasure. Although pleasures have an intrinsic good to them, there is no guarantee of their permanence. To guarantee this, a person must choose pleasures wisely. This is accomplished by prudence or practical wisdom. It entails weighing pleasures against pains, enduring pains that lead to greater pleasures, and rejecting those pleasures that lead to greater pains. For Epicurus, the virtues are a means to attain the truly pleasurable life; consequently, virtue is practiced for the sake of the good life. (For more discussion of Epicurus, see Section 3.3.2.)

Diogenes of Sinope (fl. 4th c. B.C.E.) was considered the paradigm of the Cynic, a school of thought that disdained convention, wealth, and all external trappings. It is thought that Diogenes was a disillusioned teacher who protested against what he saw as a corrupt world of pleasure, desire, and luxury. He lived life as simply as possible with little or no possessions. Legend has it that his only possession was a cup—which he threw away when he noticed a child drinking water with cupped hands. Diogenes believed that happiness was constituted in self-realization and self-mastery, and he extolled drastic mental and physical training to achieve a state of self-sufficiency.

The Founders of the Great Religions

Buddha (fl. 5th c. B.C.E.) was the son of wealthy nobility in India. Legend has it that on his first excursion outside of a well-protected environment he encountered human suffering for the first time. This had such a profound effect on his life that at the age of 29 he abandoned his privileged life, his wife, and young son and set off to discover the cause of human suffering and its cure. After a legendary struggle with the forces of temptation and illusion, Buddha became enlightened in this regard. His teaching contains "four noble truths." First, all life is suffering; second, the cause of this suffering is ignorant desires; third, the suffering can be suppressed; fourth, the way of suppressing suffering is through the Eightfold Path. This includes the right view, right aspiration, right speech, right conduct, right means of livelihood, right endeavor, right mindfulness, and right contemplation.

Moses was a Hebrew foundling raised by the Pharaoh's daughter. At this time the Israelites were enslaved by the Egyptians, who issued an edict threatening the life of every first-born male child. Moses's mother hid him as long as possible until she was forced to abandon him in a cradle near the Nile River, where he was found by the Pharaoh's daughter's servants. After fleeing to Midian because he had killed an Egyptian slavemaster, Moses returned to Egypt with the aim of freeing his people from bondage. After a number of plagues and pestilences struck the Egyptian population, the Israelites were allowed to leave. Moses led his people through the Sinai wilderness for nearly 40 years, escaping the Egyptian army, but dying before seeing his people settle in Canaan.

Moses is responsible for bringing the Ten Commandments, the Decalogue, to the Western world. This list of prescriptions and proscriptions is recognized by all the major Western religions. Besides the first three commandments, which emphasize religious proscriptions, the remaining seven set certain definite moral commands:

4. you should honor your mother and father;
5. you shall not kill;
6. you shall not commit adultery;
7. you should not steal;
8. you should not bear false witness against your neighbor;
9. you should not covet any of your neighbor's possessions;
10. you should not covet your neighbor's wife.

Jesus (d. 33 C.E.) is the founder of Christianity. He began teaching at an early age and, because of his teachings, was arrested by the Romans with the collusion of some of the Jewish priestly hierarchy; he was tortured and crucified.

Jesus disdained earthly pleasures, wealth, and power. Instead, he emphasized a strongly altruistic way of life, saying that one should "love your neighbor as yourself." This was coupled with a strong pacifism: "If anyone hits you on the right cheek, offer him the other as well," and "offer the wicked man no resistance." Jesus also stressed forgiveness, urging people not only to love their neighbors, but also their enemies, and to pray for those who persecuted them. In the Sermon on the Mount, Jesus outlined whom he considered the most admirable: the poor, the gentle, those who strive for what is right, those who are persecuted, the merciful, the pure in heart, and above all, the peacemakers.

Muhammad (c. 570–632 C.E.) is the founder of Islam. He was born into a wealthy family near Mecca, and his parents died when he was very young. He married Khadija, 15 years his senior, to whom he was devoted, and he took no other wife while she lived. None of his children except his daughter, Fatima, outlived him.

Muhammad was troubled by the oppressiveness of the old Bedouin religion and the feuding tribal particularism of his people. He was motivated to find a principle of community that might transcend these problems. Although he initially relied on teaching to spread his ideas—which emphasized submission to the will of one God, Allah, and the modeling of all moral behavior on his—he eventually conquered his opponents through force of arms, the most important victory being the Battle of Badr, fought on March 15, 624. With this, Muhammad was able to replace the old feudal tribalism with a consistent doctrine that stressed compassion, protection of the weak, justice, and opposition to all forms of evil.

Ethics, in the modern tradition of a theoretical discipline, seeks to establish justifications for a certain way of life, preferred sorts of behaviors, and rules and principles for moral conduct. As such, it engages in both normative and empirical claims; it employs definitions and uses logical inferences to validate its positions. *Empirical claims* are assertions of truth about our physical and human world. They are exemplified by the sort of claims often made in the empirical sciences, including physics, biology and psychology. *Definitions* are descriptive propositions intended to convey an understanding of terms or concepts as they are employed in some discourse. There are various types, including lexical definitions, which track the ordinary usage of a term, precise definitions, which serve to reduce the vagueness of certain terms, and theoretical definitions, which draw on a number of theoretical or empirical claims to give what is intended as a true characterization of the term in question. *Logical inferences* are processes of reasoning which aim to show how a proposition follows from others treated as premises in an argument. For example, from the claim that "all human beings are mortal" and the claim that "Frederica is a human being," it follows that she is mortal. Finally, as opposed to empirical claims, which aim toward the truth about something, *normative claims* are assertions about what is *right, good,* or the *proper* thing to do. Whereas the use of empirical claims and definitions is common throughout every discipline, what makes ethics unique is its attempt to account for this notion of *normativity*.

To the extent that it draws on empirical evidence, ethical theories and arguments must do so with the usual scientific standards appropriate to the relevant discipline, whether it is psychology, biology, or physics. In this regard the findings of ethics are dependent on the reliability of empirical knowledge from these disciplines. For example, in understanding the character of moral emotions and motivations, ethicists may have to rely to some extent upon the findings of psychologists in this regard; or in a discussion of the issue of free will, reference to current theories in physics or neuroscience may be of some importance. We can disagree with this aspect of ethical theory by using contrary empirical evidence or by criticizing the methodology or findings of the evidence presented.

In defining basic terms and relevant concepts, the study of ethics must employ standard criteria for good definitions: a statement of the critical or essential attributes of the *definiendum,* avoidance of circularity, broadness, and ambiguity; the definition must be clear and also avoid indirect language.

Since a large part of ethics involves inference and logical reasoning, such argumentation must also meet standard logical criteria. Ethics is concerned to show that, given the initial claims certain thinkers make, certain other claims do or do not follow. As such, the reasoning that moral thinkers make must avoid both formal and informal fallacies, such as hasty generalization, abusive or emotional appeals, and circularity, among others.

As mentioned, what is unique to ethics as opposed to other disciplines is the establishment of normative claims and the very notion of normativity. Whereas the sciences seek to establish the credibility of empirical claims—that is, the claim either *is* or *is not* the case—moral thinkers in the modern tradition seek to establish, in part, that something *ought* or *ought not* to be done. This seems to require a different kind of justification involving some of the most difficult and complex thinking in ethical theory, and it has been a source of dispute among moral thinkers themselves. In a famous passage, 18th-century philosopher David Hume (1711–1776) was one of the first to note this particular problem:

> In every system of morality, which I have hitherto met with, I have always remark'd, that the author proceeds for some time in the ordinary way of reasoning, and establishes the being of a God, or makes observations concerning human affairs; when of a sudden I am surpriz'd to find, that instead of the usual copulations of propositions, is, and is not, I meet with no proposition that is not connected with an ought, or an ought not. This change is imperceptible; but is, however, of the last consequence. For as this ought, or ought not, expresses some new relation or affirmation, 'tis necessary that it shou'd be observ'd and explain'd; and at the same time that a reason should be given, for what seems altogether inconceivable, how this new relation can be a deduction from others, which are entirely different from it (1739: 469).

Why do we feel *obligated* to do something? What is the *binding* force of an action? Some have attempted to reduce this normative question to an empirical one: that the "ought" can be based on an "is." For example, 19th-century philosopher John Stuart Mill reasoned that since everyone *does* seek happiness, then they *ought* to abide by the utilitarian principle, which claims that the goodness of an action is measured by how much happiness it produces. In other words, abiding by the utilitarian principle is nothing more than maximizing a natural disposition in human beings to seek their own happiness. Thinkers such as turn-of-the century English philosopher G.E. Moore (1873–1958) have called this the *naturalistic fallacy* (1903: 13ff): The fact that beings are naturally disposed towards some kind of behavior is not necessarily a moral recommendation for it. If it turns out that human beings do have a disposition toward violence, that is not a reason to recommend it, morally speaking (see Section 5.49). One might say that the naturalistic fallacy attempts to reduce normativity to empirical fact.

Another attempt to settle the question of normative claims suggests that an "ought" can be derived logically from other oughts in combination with certain empirical claims. For example, consider an encapsulated version of the pro-life and pro-choice arguments in regard to abortion:

> One ought not to kill innocent human beings.
> A fetus is a human being.
> Consequently, one ought not to kill a fetus by abortion or any other means.

> One ought to have autonomous control over one's body.
> A fetus is part of a woman's body.
> Consequently, a woman ought to have autonomous control over her fetus, including the option of aborting it.

In both cases the conclusion is an "ought" derived from the fact that the second premise is an instance relevant to the general situation described in the first; a fetus is a human being, and it is wrong to kill human beings. Or a fetus is part of a woman's body, and a woman ought to have control over her body; consequently, in each case we are logically committed to the conclusion. Clearly, however, in this case we have just pushed the problem of justification one step backward, since we address the "ought" of the first premise in each argument: Although the "ought" in the conclusion is logically inferred, we still are not sure how the "ought" of the first premise is established. Moreover, some claim that logical inference is itself a species of normativity (Peirce 1965: CP 1.191). Thinking logically is thinking rationally, and thinking rationally is a normative way of being. There is no necessity that a person must infer from the claim that all human beings are mortal that he is mortal because he is a human being. That is a way of thinking that conforms to a logical standard; a person who does not conform to such a standard may be thought to be illogical and her way of thinking fallacious—but those are normative ascriptions.

Since normativity seems to be something different from the factual and not subsumed under the logical, then some thinkers argue for its uniqueness. Among this group the claim is that normativity is the result of *internalization* in some form or another, that is, the sense that there is something in the perception or conception of the rightness of an action which obligates us to it or in the fact that a person has freely and autonomously chosen something as a norm for herself. In an argument that goes back to the 18th century, this internalization is accounted for in two broad ways. Advocates of what is called *sentimentalism,* such as David Hume, Adam Smith, and Francis Hutcheson, argue that moral emotions and sentiments give us this perception of rightness and so establish internalization: The emotion of sympathy for the suffering of others, for example, generates the binding force to relieve them of their suffering or aid in their betterment. The *rationalists,* such as Samuel Clarke and Immanuel Kant, on the other hand, claimed that it is our cognitive judgment that something is right—understood as giving reasons for its rightness—which obligates us to it. When we have internalized a norm, we have justified it to ourselves, so that if we believe lying is wrong, we feel bound to tell the truth. It would be odd indeed if we did not feel obligated to do what we believed right. The disconnect between believing something right yet not feeling obligated about it would be a sure sign of lack of internalization. We will have an opportunity to discuss this very difficult and complex issue in Chapter Five.

Besides accounting for the sense of obligation we find in our moral lives, philosophers are also interested in accounting for what *motivates* us to do the right thing. Of course, this is a concern of other disciplines as well, such as psychology, sociology, and anthropology. Usually these disciplines are interested in answering the question of what causes people to conform with or deviate from cultural norms. Some of the more common answers include fear of punishment, peer pressure, conformity to law, socialization, conventionalization, and rewards in the form of honors and recognition. Although philosophers certainly recognize these as real motivators for moral action, they are concerned about this question from a somewhat different framework. They usually divide into three camps on this issue. Sentimentalists, such as David Hume, argue that it is our moral emotions and sentiments that primarily serve as motivators. Moral emotions are more indurate and infused in the human psychology than reason could possibly hope to be. The key, then, to motivating people to do the right thing is to create, encourage, and enhance the development of moral emotions in ourselves, in our children, and in others. Although cognitivists like Kant agree that moral emotions, such as sympathy, can be a motivation to do the right thing, they argue that such sentiments are not genuine *moral* motives, since they really help us do what we already feel like doing. The only genuine moral motive is the sense of obligation we get when we internalize something by means of having some reason to believe that something is the right thing to do. Understanding something as the right thing motivates us to do it. Consequentialists, on the other hand, argue that people are motivated to do the right thing because of the results it brings or because of the consequences it entails. Some ethical thinkers have argued, for example, that we should act virtuously or abide by certain principles since that will lead to peace of mind, happiness, or the good life. The question of moral motivation in this regard is the principal topic of Chapter One.

Another issue which distinguishes the concern of ethicists from psychology and the social sciences is the matter of determining which norms are right. It is not enough to discover why people conform to norms, whatever those norms may be. It is more important from the ethical point of view to determine which norms are the right ones to follow. This is usually expressed in modern ethics as a quest for an ethical principle, something which can serve as a sort of algorithm or formula for decision making. It is something that gives us a relative guarantee that our actions will be right to the extent that they conform to these principles. A detailed analysis of the classical ethical principles and some of the more prominent contemporary ones will be the subject of Chapter Five.

Questions of normativity, motivation, and principle are primary concerns of the modern theoretical tradition in ethics. The sagacious tradition, on the other hand, has different concerns. For its followers, the issue is not so much the right thing to do, but the question of the right way to be, not only in terms of the individual's character, but in the sense of what should count as the good life and the good community. In this view, especially as advocated by Aristotle, Cicero, and other Stoics, Confucius, Mencius, among others, good actions flow from good character as exercised in good communities. In this way character and community are interrelated. Good communities promote good character in their members, and the good and wise within the community promote its overall good. Consequently, most of these thinkers focused on virtue and character: What makes an individual a good person? Contemporary philosophies that continue and develop these traditions include what has come to be called *virtue ethics*. Virtue ethics, as advocated by such contemporary thinkers as Alasdair MacIntyre (1981) and Bernard Williams (1985), suggests that virtues are paramount in ethical life. Virtues are the means by which we can accumulate those goods that can be found inherently in the better practices that constitute our communities. It is the virtuous friend, spouse, parent, and citizen who can not only better these practices, but who can get the most benefit from them. The nature of virtue and its importance are the subject of Chapter Three. Communitarianism, as found in the work of Michael Sandel (1982) and Amitai Etzioni (1993), among others, is a contemporary doctrine which takes up the sagacious tradition's basic outlook on the relation between communities and their members. Its focus is on what constitutes good communities, and it argues for an integral connection between our sense of self and the communities in which we live: Who we are is bound up with others in a community that aims at certain common goods and values. Communitarianism moves against the grain of the sort of individualism that both liberal and libertarian traditions have advocated, but at the same time it upholds many of the basic democratic values which that tradition entails.

Another important feature that distinguishes the modern theoretical tradition in ethics from its older sagacious tradition is its account of moral reasoning. Theoretical ethics sees the job of moral reasoning as the discovery of rationally justified principles that can then be applied to particular cases, analogous to the way in which physical laws would be determinate for any single case to which they apply. For this reason the modern tradition has been focused on discovering these ethical principles. On the other hand, according to the sagacious tradition, moral reasoning is a form of practical reasoning. Its function is to persuade ourselves and others why we should do one thing rather than another in this particular situation; theoretical reasoning is concerned to show us why we should believe one thing rather than another (Aristotle, *De Motu* 701a8–12), that is, why we should believe in a particular law or principle. Moral reasoning results in decision and action rather than belief *(De Motu* 701a8–12). To be persuaded to act, a person must be convinced that this action is the right thing to do. The core of wisdom in the sagacious tradition is a kind of intelligence that involves making judgments about what the right thing to do is in a given situation. Both MacIntyre and Williams argue that moral decision making is far too complex and situated to imagine a moral principle that can transcend culture and place to evaluate moral action in any objective manner. Both argue that we think and decide within the moral tradition in which we live. Moral decision making works between our traditions and intuitions in response to novel moral situations which require new and challenging ways to address those traditions. Moral decision making always takes place within the context of a community that has some shared values, but it is often directed toward a resolution of conflicts in some manner. It is not something that can be handled by a principle, objectively administered by persons supposedly freed from the constraints of their tradition, and applied to a moral situation. What matters, as Williams suggests, is the dispositions, the character that people acquire by living in their societies. Good can only come from good ethical culture generated by means of the better character dispositions (1985: 201). The matter of moral wisdom and its relation to ethical principles and knowledge are the subject of Chapter Four.

This book attempts to integrate all of the various concerns raised by the two traditions of ethics into a coherent picture of moral life. In general, we are looking at the following sorts of questions:

1. What is the right thing to do?
2. What motivates us to do the right thing?
3. What give us the capability and power to do it?
4. How do I go about doing it?

It is only when these questions are answered satisfactorily—when persons are motivated to do what they have good reasons to believe is the right thing to do, and when they have acquired the will and power to do it—can we seriously begin to talk about their moral competence. It is clear that the wrong answer to any one of these questions or the absence of any one of these aspects of moral conduct can lead to wrong actions. Persons might perfectly well be motivated to do the right thing, yet they are wrong about what the right thing is; they might understand what the right thing is, yet have no motivation to do it or little moral strength to try. Their characters might be so corrupted that they do not have the fortitude it takes to accomplish it or the self-control to resist that which inhibits it. Their characters might be perfectly good, but they simply do not have the wisdom or savoir-faire to get it done in the right way.

Moral competence involves the whole person: the health of their moral emotions and motivations, their strength of will and autonomy, their virtuous habits, wisdom, and know-how, and their insight and knowledge about what is right and good. Each chapter of this book is dedicated to a detailed analysis of one of these vital aspects of moral life. Let's begin with a discussion of moral emotions and sentiments, and the basic motivations for doing the right thing.

CHAPTER ONE

Moral Sentiment

If it is reason that makes us, it is sentiment that leads us.

—Jean-Jacques Rousseau

Sentiment enters into all decisions of praise or censure.

Morality is ... more properly felt than judged.

Reason can never alone be a motive to any action of the will ... [and] it can never oppose passion in the direction of the will.

Extinguish all the warm feelings ... in favour of virtue, and all disgust or aversion to vice: render men totally indifferent towards these distinctions; and morality is no longer a practical study, nor has any tendency to regulate our lives and actions.

—David Hume

In the last week of October 1994, millions of Americans saw a mother plead on television for the safe return of her young children, Michael, 3, and Alex, only 14 months. Susan Smith told a story of a carjacking in the late evening in a small town in South Carolina. An armed man jumped into her car at a stoplight, ordered her to drive 7 miles, then forced her out and drove off with her two sons still strapped in their safety seats. The emotional outpouring from the American public was remarkable: There were yellow ribbons around trees, prayer vigils, letters of concern, and offers of help. The sympathy for the mother, her children, and their plight was palpable—and when she confessed a few days later to the killing of her own children, the emotional reaction of the public was just as manifest. When it was discovered that she drowned her own children, how she drove the car into the John D. Long Lake while the children were still strapped in their safety seats, and how it took several minutes before the car filled with water, the moral outrage was just as strong as the sympathy had been previously. When Sheriff Howard Wells

David Hume (1711–1776) is considered one of the most important philosophers of the 18th century. His books *A Treatise of Human Nature* and *An Enquiry Concerning the Principles of Morals* are among the most influential books of 18th-century philosophy. Hume argued that reason could not serve as basis for moral concepts, nor could it serve as motivation for doing the right thing. Such motivation came from moral sentiments and feelings, especially sympathy, which he thought to be relatively universal and natural; the limits on our feelings of benevolence, however, cause us to establish laws of justice to supplement this sentiment. Ultimately, social ethics and moral philosophy rest on tradition and convention. Generally speaking, Hume argued for a version of utilitarianism, that all our moral approvals are directed toward acts which serve the general good. (For more on Hume, see Sections 1.1.1, 1.5, and 1.7.)

made the 1-minute announcement of Smith's arrest, a collective gasp and spontaneous cries went up from the crowd. Fights nearly broke out among the crowd of spectators, and police had to close one block in front of the courthouse to control the crowd. The next day an angry group met Susan Smith at the Union Court House, calling her a "baby killer" and "murderer." All of her neighbors in the small town were disappointed and angry. Sympathy for the children intensified, as a spontaneous memorial with flowers, symbols, and other tokens sprang up near the spot where the children died. Television personality Willard Scott, who had been personally involved with finding the children, could barely hold back his tears as he announced the weather to millions of people across the country that day on *Today*. The sense of betrayal was great among those who had believed Susan Smith's original story: One neighbor had thought she was a wonderful person and proclaimed that, if anybody had told him that she had done such a thing, he would have called him a liar. But now, after realizing the truth, he was clearly shaken in the revelation.

The sympathy, outrage, and disgust expressed by the many people in this awful, tragic case are called *moral emotions*. Along with guilt, shame, resentment, remorse, and admiration, these form an integral part of most people's emotional life. Indeed, feelings and emotions are essential to any engagement with life, for any care about what happens to oneself and others. The philosopher, David Hume, said it plainly: "life, without passion, must be altogether insipid and tiresome" (1777: 121). Daniel Goleman, author of *Emotional Intelligence*, relates the case of a man who had to have his amygdala surgically removed in order to control severe seizures (the amygdala along with the prefrontal cortex is thought to constitute the fundamental emotional circuitry of the brain). The results were telling: The man was left with a fundamental indifference to his life and those he once loved. Without his center of emotion intact, "his life was stripped of personal meaning" (Goleman 1995: 15; cf. LeDoux 1992). Antonio Damasio, a neurologist at the University of Iowa, has also made several studies of patients who have had damage to the amygdala and the prefrontal lobe. He observed that decision making in patients with such impairments was terribly flawed, even though their IQ remained relatively intact. They made disastrous choices in business and in their personal lives, and often they labored over even the most trivial decisions (1994). This supports Ronald DeSousa's claim that emotions help us make judgments precisely because our cognitive processes alone leave us too indecisive (1980: 136). Without emotions, life would not matter, and without *moral emotions*, how one lived would be of little concern.

Emotions are thought to have certain general characteristics. First, they are *intentional states*, meaning that they are always "about" something (Kenny 1963; Solomon 1980: 252). A person is angry at Fred, or guilty about lying, afraid of the dark, disgusted with this person, happy about the new job, or regrets loaning a friend money. All emotions have an object toward which they are directed.

Second, each emotion is usually associated with certain distinguishable feelings and sensations, what psychologists call peripheral responses such as heart rate, blood flow, gestures, and facial expressions (Levenson, Ekman, and Friesen 1990, 1983; Ekman 1993; Levenson et al. 1992). In other words, emotions are very visceral. When a person is afraid of the bear he has encountered on the trail, his heart rate increases, he may feel that "sinking feeling" in the pit of his stomach, and his face may express all the recognizable signs of fear. When he becomes angry, there may be an increase of blood flow to his extremities, his fists may clench, and his face forms the expression typically associated with that emotion.

Third, although emotions can sometimes be generated without apparent cognitive input (LeDoux 1995; cf. Greenspan 1988), most emotions involve beliefs. A person must believe that the animal is a bear and that bears are dangerous before he can be said to be afraid of the bear. A person may be angry at her friend because she believes that he lied to her. Yet that emotion would change should she now believe that he did not lie; in that case her emotion may turn to guilt or shame for thinking such a thing of her friend. Just as people felt sympathy for Susan Smith when she was believed to have been a victim, they felt anger when they believed she had killed her own children.

Fourth, as David Hume suggests, emotions are usually involved with desire and aversion (1739: 574; cf. Solomon 1980: 274). It is one thing to believe that the bear is dangerous, but to be afraid, one also has to have a desire not to be in dangerous situations, and have a desire to stay alive. It is plausible, for example, that a person who thrives on danger may not be fearful of the bear.

Fifth, emotions involve judgments and evaluations (Solomon 1980: 258). As Hume also suggests, emotions are always accompanied by judgments of approbation and admiration (1739: 574). To be afraid of a bear is to make a judgment that because the bear is dangerous, this is a life-threatening situation, and such situations are not good. In being angry at a friend for lying, the anger is at the same time a judgment that lying is a wrong done to you. People were outraged at Susan Smith not only because they believed that Susan Smith killed her children, but also precisely because of their judgment that it was absolutely wrong for her to do so. If a person did not judge murder wrong, then the belief that someone murdered someone else would not be sufficient for her to feel moral outrage.

Emotions can be considered as quickly formed or spontaneous judgments about matters or events in one's life (Solomon 1980: 258, 262). Since moral emotions evaluate emotionally rather than intellectually, they affect us more deeply than mere formal rules, orders or commands, or other abstract criteria might. Many would argue that moral emotions are the heart of moral life; without moral emotion, there is little desire to do the right thing and little reaction to harm done by others. As Catherine Lutz, an anthropologist and psychologist, writes, "morality requires emotion because affect provides the motivation for taking particular moral positions towards events" (1988: 76). In sum, *emotions can be defined as visceral experiences, framed by our beliefs and desires, which function to make judgments about their intentional objects.*

Some Common Moral Emotions

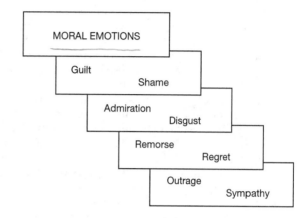

1.1 THE VARIETY OF MORAL EMOTIONS

> It is better to die in hunger, exempt from guilt and fear, than to live in affluence and with perturbation.

> —Epictetus, from *The Enchiridion*

There are over 500 names for the emotions in the English language (Averill 1980). Moral emotions form an important part of this set. Guilt is among the most familiar of these to people living in Western cultures. *Guilt* is a feeling of anxiety one has for deviating from an internalized moral standard. People don't feel guilty about something they do not acknowledge as wrong (Rawls 1971: 481). They feel guilty when they have acted contrary to their sense of right and justice (Rawls 1971: 445). For this reason guilt is more of a self-generated anxiety rather than created out of a fear or anxiety about the reactions of others to one's deeds, as is more typical of shame. The anxiety can become intense enough that a person becomes committed to confess to a crime or an immoral act. L.N., who worked as a bank teller in Juneau, Alaska, decided for a number of reasons that he would just walk out of the bank with $30,000 in November 1995. He didn't expect to succeed, but when he did, he went on a spending spree that lasted for 6 months. But he turned himself in afterward because, as he said, he didn't want to live with something that he did wrong. He felt he had a pretty good conscience. (Of course, he had already spent the money.) The psychological origins of guilt may be found in parental disapproval, withdrawal of affection, or punishment for anticipated actions (Walters et al. 1965). Guilt is most often felt in the context of some real or imagined injury

John Rawls (b. 1921) is one of the most important contemporary political and ethical thinkers. His most important work is *A Theory of Justice.* The argument in that book is that principles of justice should be based on the idea of fairness, where participants in a social and political arrangement ought to have equal power in making decisions about the rules that will govern them. (For more on Rawls, see Sections 1.4.1, 3.5.1, and 5.3.4.)

a person has done to others and so is more directed to the victim of the actions. *Guilt, then, can be defined as a self-generated feeling of anxiety resulting from the violation of an internalized norm that has caused harm to others.*

Guilt and shame can be closely associated (Rawls 1971: 482; Williams 1993: 92). The same act, for example, lying to a friend, can evoke both: guilt for having harmed a friend and shame for giving into the temptation of lying. Both reflect the concern with others and with one's performance "that must be present in all moral conduct" (Rawls 1971: 484). However, there are important differences between the two. *Shame* appears to be more directed to a deficiency in oneself than to the harm done another (Williams 1993: 222). The deficiency is usually expressed in light of the standards or expectations of the community or group in which one lives—but standards which the person has also internalized. It is not enough to feel shame simply on the basis of what others believe is wrong; a person must also have *internalized* this belief as well. A certain community may believe that it is shameful for unmarried couples to cohabit, but a couple in question may not feel ashamed, even if the group has admonished them, simply because they see nothing wrong with it. Philosopher Bernard Williams argues for this reason that shame involves an "internalized other" (1993: 98). As John Rawls notes, a person who feels shame believes that "he has fallen short of a standard of excellence, given in to weakness, and shown himself unworthy of association with others who share his ideals" (1971: 483–484).

Whereas guilt is often associated with the metaphor of hearing—that is, the sound in oneself of the voice of judgment, often called *conscience*—shame often involves vision metaphors. Because shame is connected, metaphorically speaking, with the "gaze of the other" and involves a sense of a "witness" or "watcher" (Williams 1993: 219), most often it becomes intensified when the act is publicly exposed, although it can still be generated simply through imagining such exposure. Guilt, on the other hand, is something that one lives with internally, is subvocalized, so to speak, "inside the head," even when no one else knows about the deeds that have been done. Guilt can be a powerful motivator since it can be a constant and nagging source of anxiety, but the avoidance of shame can also serve as a strong motivator because people often wish to avoid the ridicule or disdain of others if exposed (Williams 1993: 79). Indeed, there are many etymological and cultural associations between shame and nakedness, that is, being completely exposed without cover to the gaze of others (cf. Williams 1993: 78). As Takeo Doi, one of Japan's leading psychiatrists, says, "the sense of shame originates in awareness of the eyes of the outside world and is directed in toward the self" (1977: 53), and it is especially connected with the group (Doi 1977: 54). *Shame, then, may be defined as an other-generated feeling of anxiety directed toward one's own failings, as measured by an internalized, group-recognized norm or standard of behavior.*

There are some other important differences between guilt and shame. In general, in guilt we hear the judgment of our own voice, whereas in shame we hear the voices of others; shame is based on a sense of self-worth, while guilt comes from a sense of the worth of others. Guilt is more the result of the violation of those duties and expectations we have pertaining to our roles, for example, as a parent, a daughter, a friend, a spouse, a student, but shame is a lowering of our status relative to those very same roles and practices. In feeling guilt one is anxious about the resentment and indignation of those you have harmed; if your friend should learn of your lie, you worry about the hurt, anger, and loss of love that would result. Bernard Williams argues that guilt is based on a fear of anger as expressed by the victim or enforcer (1993: 219). In shame, on the other hand, the anxiety is about the derision, ridicule, and contempt others may show toward your flawed behavior and failings (Rawls 1971: 483; Williams 1993: 89–90). Thus, guilt and anger or moral outrage are correlative emotions, meaning that guilt is felt by the perpetrator and anger by the victim. Similarly, shame and disgust are often thought correlative, with shame being felt by the violator and disgust by the members of the group. Guilt is often relieved by repairing the harm and getting forgiveness from the victim, while shame is relieved by proving oneself worthy again to others; for example, a cowardly act can be rectified by proving one's courage or bravery (Rawls 1971: 484).

Some disputes have arisen about the differences between shame-based and guilt-based societies. Many Western societies are thought to be guilt-based, whereas many Eastern ones, such as Japan, are believed to be shamed-based (Benedict 1954). However, it is clear that some Western societies, such as ancient Greece, are also considered shame-based (Williams 1993) and that, even for those societies who predominate in one emotion or the other, the contrary emotion still operates at some level. As Takeo Doi points out, it is clear that Japanese certainly feel guilt, but its expression has less significance and is framed somewhat differently than in many Western cultures (1977: 48ff.), and shame is no stranger to most Western societies. Bernard Williams argues that although the ancient Greeks had no specific word for what we call "guilt," their understanding of shame was complex enough to incorporate some of the characteristics typically associated with it (1993: 90–91).

Well-known anthropologist Ruth Benedict argued that guilt is a superior moral emotion to shame because it lends itself more to moral autonomy than does shame (Benedict 1954). The reasoning is that since guilt is self-generated it relies more on individual conscience and internalization and so is not susceptible to group influence as is shame. Shame, on the other hand, is always related to community norms, involves less internalization, and seems to work on the basis of group-based standards. Shame, therefore, may push individuals toward conformity, convention, and acceptance of authority, while guilt seems to promote individually considered norms or standards. For example, consider the case of Paul Hill, prolife activist and former Presbyterian minister, who felt no guilt or remorse for shooting and killing Doctor John Britton, an active abortion advocate, and his security escort, James Barrett, in an ambush in 1994. Despite the fact that the act was condemned by most on both sides of the abortion issue, in court Hill reasoned that although what he did was not legal, it was moral because it appealed to the highest laws of God. He proclaimed that he felt no remorse for his actions and that he in fact felt better about himself and about his life than ever before. That sort of stand would seem more difficult for one primarily motivated by shame, since such feelings depend on a collective response to one's actions.

However, Benedict's argument is questionable. First, shame involves as much internalization as guilt (cf. Lynd 1973; Williams 1993: 94ff., 102). Whereas a person may avoid lying to another out of guilt for hurting that person, someone with a strong sense of shame would avoid lying for fear of being exposed for doing something as disgraceful as lying. This should be understood as different from someone who does not lie merely to avoid punishment, that is, someone who has not internalized the norm against lying; that sort of person would lie if she knew she wouldn't get caught. But a person with a strong feeling of shame is internally motivated not to lie whether or not she gets caught; such a person would experience a feeling of shame knowing she lied precisely because she shares the belief of the group, whereas the first sort of person would be delighted if she were able to get away with lying and so does not share the belief that it is wrong. Second, as Bernard Williams argues, the impression that the "inner voice" of guilt is autonomously structured may be misleading. Conscience may be as much the voice of the group as shame is. Just because it seems to be individualized and internally manifest does not necessarily mean that it is without influence from the group; it involves as much socialization as shame in this regard. In fact, Williams argues that in many respects shame is the superior moral emotion. Shame requires identification with the sort of community one can respect; shame makes one focus, then, on a person's character and roles in the context of living with others. Guilt, on the other hand, has a tendency to promote allegiance to a progressively abstracted moral rule or standard and to the sorts of roles and character that engenders. Guilt generally promotes a more individualized ethic, which also has its weaknesses.

Remorse is a feeling of sorrow or sadness occasioned by doing something morally imprudent that results in harm to others. It is often experienced when the consequences of an action are played out, and a person finally recognizes the full impact of what harm he or she has done to others. Eric Eckardt, the bodyguard of skater Tonya Harding, had arranged, on Harding's request, to have thugs attack Nancy Kerrigan, Harding's archrival for the 1994 women's Olympic figure skating team. The attack left Kerrigan with a battered knee, causing her to miss some of her critical training. Apparently when Eckardt saw the image of Kerrigan sobbing on television, he had a sudden rush of remorse and sought out a friend to bare his secret, leading to the disclosure and arrest of the attackers (cf. Goleman 1995: 106). Whereas he previously may not have fully realized the consequences of his actions, or may not have cared, in seeing the suffering and harm he caused, there was a clear reevaluation of his behavior. The key factor in remorse, then, is a feeling of repentance for what one has done. This is expressed well by the philosopher Philip Hallie, a veteran of World War II:

I do not repent the killing I did in combat. I can repent having done something only when I change my mind about having done it, only when I would not do it again under similar circumstances (1997: 57).

Remorse happens when there is a change of mind, a point at which you realize you would not do again what you did in those particular circumstances, a wish that you could somehow take the action back. This is different than guilt. One may feel guilt consequent to harming another because you immediately recognize that it is a violation of a norm you already believe to be valid, but remorse usually involves more of a process over time that results in the eventual realization of the validity of the violated

---

The Errant Missile Apology

In January 1999, during the continuing Iraqi–U.S. confrontations over the no-fly zones, an errant missile intended for a military target hit a residential neighborhood, killing an unconfirmed number of civilians. The United States claimed that it fired in self-defense when Iraqi radar sites locked on to the plane. A State Department official delivered the official reaction: "We deeply regret the loss of any civilian life in this unfortunate circumstance." Yet the spokesman went on to argue that it was within the act of self-defense and that, furthermore, Saddam was primarily to blame for this matter since he was provoking U.S. airplanes in firing on such targets.

Questions for Discussion

1. Would you say this is an expression of genuine regret?

Although the spokesman indicates regret for the consequences of the action, he doesn't seem to indicate regret for the action itself.

2. Would you say there is an expression of remorse here for the loss of civilian life?

One sign of remorse would be to accept full responsibility for the action, yet the spokesman seems to place most of the blame on Saddam. Also, remorse would be indicated by some attempt to change one's actions, but that is not mentioned here either.

3. What is your view on this?

norm, precisely because the harm to others is so palpable. Someone may have not taken that norm seriously, and perhaps that is why she did what she did; but now she recognizes why she should heed that norm. At this point she realizes that what she did was heartless, reckless, imprudent—or just plain wrong—and sees the error of her ways.

Remorse should also be distinguished from *regret, which is the feeling occasioned by doing something imprudent or inadvertent that results in harm to oneself* (Rawls 1971: 442). Thus, you may regret an action or a plan because it has failed to achieve your goal or has led to an undesirable consequence for yourself. Certain criminals may regret their actions because they got caught, yet feel no remorse for whatever suffering they may have caused their victims. For this reason judges, when deciding on sentences, look for signs of remorse as opposed to simple regret in the convicted defendant. This is an indication that the person recognizes that he has done a wrong and a harm to others, that he has violated some code which he now recognizes as valid precisely because of the harm its violation has caused, and as a result intends to change his behavior. In this case there is some chance of rehabilitation. A sign of genuine remorse is the case where the perpetrator not only feels saddened by the act, but wishes to right the wrong, as opposed to just expressing the wish that it had never happened.

For example, N.C., who had participated in an especially brutal robbery, in which one of the victims was clubbed into a coma, tearfully told the court how sorry she was for what she had done: "I'd like to do whatever I can do to make up for it—whatever I can do." The victim, who was not at first expected to live, was left partially paralyzed. After hearing the victim speak in a slurred voice about the crime, N.C. broke down: "I don't know what possessed me to do what I did. I allowed myself to be persuaded ... I feel awful about what happened. I know there's no way to make what happened up, but I'd like to do anything I can. And I'm sorry. I'm sorry" (Barbour 1995). J.T. was a very active member of the community, doing hours and hours of charitable work for local children's sports organizations. So when he admitted to forging checks, it was quite a shock to the people he had helped. It was clear, however, that he felt remorse for his actions. Just so there was no question of his motives, he sent a letter to the editor of the local newspaper after he had already been sentenced to jail time. In that letter he made "an acceptance of full responsibility" for his criminal action and felt that it was necessary to apologize publicly for his action and to apologize directly to those he defrauded. He recognized where he went wrong and pinpointed when he began to err. He referred to a code (in this case the Boy Scout code) which he had violated and decried his dishonesty. He gave no excuses for his action, claiming that even though some of his supporters saw good intentions involved, it did not cancel out the wrongdoing. He spelled out the harm that his actions have done to others, and he resolved to correct his ways with a specific plan.

Moral outrage is anger directed toward the perpetrator of a wrong, while sympathy is a feeling directed toward the victim of a wrong done by others. This is clearly illustrated in the public reaction to Susan Smith before and after her confession. Many people feel outrage toward Timothy McVeigh, who was convicted in the bombing of the Federal Center in Oklahoma City, while simultaneously feeling great sympathy for his victims. However, some persons are more directed by anger toward the perpetrator than sympathy for the victim. A study by California sociologists Samuel and Pearl Oliner (1988) on Christian rescuers of the Jews during the Holocaust showed that at least one-sixth of the rescuers acted out of sheer outrage toward the

Nazis rather than sympathy for the victims, whereas one-third of the rescuers acted more out of sympathy for the plight of the Jews, especially as they saw it in face-to-face encounters. In the last case certain neighbors, who might not otherwise be involved in defying the Nazis, did so when they saw the plight of their neighbors' children. Certainly, as depicted in the film *Schindler's List,* a direct encounter with the suffering was what motivated Oskar Schindler to do the right thing. Those motivated by outrage, on the other hand, did not even necessarily want to know the victims of Nazi atrocities they were helping—it was simply a matter of justice for them.

  Admiration is a positive feeling toward the behavior or character of another person (Oakley 1991: 176–177). Sometimes these feelings may evolve into ones of adulation or reverence. Often for this reason it becomes a motivation for imitating or modeling that behavior. Admiration of heroes is a typical paradigm. The behavior of the hero so exemplifies one's internalized standard of behavior that it serves as a model for one's own. Admiration, and especially reverence, facilitate taking direction from others. To the extent that one recognizes another as a paradigm of being—a way to behave, dress, talk, think, and so forth—then whatever codes or values that person represents are more easily conveyed to the admirer. Albert Bandura's work on what he calls observational learning is relevant here. To model another's behavior, four factors must be present: A person must be attentive to the model's behavior, must be able to retain what is essential about the behavior, must have the ability to produce the actions, and finally must be motivated to perform the actions (1986). Bandura demonstrated that the motivation to model can stem from external reward and punishment. Children who see aggression rewarded will often emulate it, while those who see it punished will avoid it (1965). But in the case of admiration, where one has internalized certain norms, the motivation to model is based on the fact that the person exemplifies those standards or norms. For example, it's quite possible to admire someone who is punished by the system; indeed, many heroes are those who fight the norms of a particular group. But for the same reason there is no guarantee that the one admired will be one the group considers morally admirable. Informal or popular polls asking for lists of most admired persons often place the president or the pope in the first two slots, but the remainder are often filled by movie stars, who obviously have more of a celluloid image than a real one. There is no guarantee that whoever is admired is worthy of that admiration.

  Disgust, according to William Miller,

> has ... powerful communicating capacities, and is especially useful and necessary as a builder of moral and social community. It performs this function obviously by helping define and locate the boundary separating our group from their group, purity from pollution, the violable from the inviolable (1992: 194).

"It is hard," he continues, "in normal conversation to give voice to moral judgments without having recourse to the idiom of disgust or reference to the concept of the disgusting" (1992: 180). *Disgust is the polar opposite of admiration. It is a feeling of revulsion toward the behavior or character of another* and is an effective way of cutting off sympathy to that agent (Miller 1992: 194). Just as we admire those whose lives or actions exemplify our moral standards, the objects of disgust are those who fall far short of those standards. This sort of feeling is experienced every day in reading the newspaper; in any one day you can read, for example, how a woman's two teenage granddaughters stole her life savings and went on a lavish trip to Disney World and, in the very next column, how a 5-year-old boy was dropped from the fourteenth floor of a building by 10- and 11-year-olds simply because he wouldn't steal candy for them. Or you will read how a 12-year-old was shot and killed because he wouldn't lend someone a quarter or the case of a man who robbed his neighbors' house just as they were trying to rescue his family from his own burning house. There is the case of an anesthesiologist who stole anesthesia from his patients to feed his own habit and the case of a mother who, ignoring her doctor's order to take her severely malnourished infant to the hospital, went instead to the beauty parlor to get her nails done—while her baby died lying nearby. Recently, the nation was shocked by the actions of a high-school senior who, unknown to anyone, allegedly delivered her baby in the bathroom while attending her senior prom. She allegedly left the infant, dead, in a trash can and returned to the dance, laughing and talking with her friends and date as if nothing had happened. There is no dearth of examples. The calendars of Jerry Springer, Ricki Lake, Geraldo, Sally Jessy Raphael, Jenny Jones, Maury Povich, and other such shows are filled with them, and much to our own shame and disgust, viewers crowd these programs to watch people who are willing to parade their often loathsome behavior for the sake of 15 minutes of fame.

1.1.1 Sympathy

Many moral thinkers and psychologists give sympathy special prominence among moral feelings. Some, such as Hume, thought it was the most basic moral emotion:

> We are certain, that sympathy is a very powerful principle in human nature. ... We find that it has force sufficient to give us the strongest sentiments of approbation, when it operates alone, without the concurrence of any other principle. ... We may observe, that all the circumstances requisite for its operation are found in most of the virtues. ... If we compare all these circumstances, we shall not doubt, that sympathy is the chief source of moral distinctions (1739: 618).

Words such as sympathy, empathy, compassion, and pity have a wide variety of meanings and are sometimes used interchangeably; it's nearly impossible to track any consistent usage (Duan and Hill, 1996; Verducci 2000). However, for purposes of explication, the following distinctions can be made. First, it seems important to distinguish the capability of reading or sensing the suffering of another from the feeling of distress over the suffering of another. *Empathy will be used here for the native ability to read the emotional state or feelings of others as based on past experience or the experience of one's own feelings, emotional states, and suffering.* Empathy allows one to understand, predict, and explain another's behavior (Gordon 1995: 730; Gladding, 1988: 194). In this case empathy involves the perception of what the other feels and may include attunement and sensitivity to their feelings. Such abilities are not only important for moral life and for our ordinary roles as parents, spouses, and friends, but are also vital for helping professionals, such as counselors, social workers, psychiatrists, and health professionals. On the other hand, *sympathy is the feeling of distress, sadness, or joy that may occur when we understand the emotional state of another.* It is literally a "feeling-with," a joy in others' joy, a sorrow in another's sadness. Given the distinction between empathy and sympathy, it is quite possible to understand that a person is distressed (empathy), yet not feel distressed over it ourselves (lack of sympathy), or it is quite possible to recognize great joy in another, yet not be glad about his or her joy. Sympathy has more of an *evaluative* character than empathy and involves judgments about whether the person is deserving of it.

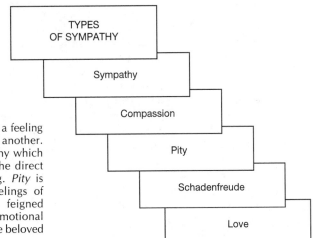

Types of Sympathy *Sympathy* is a feeling of distress over the suffering of another. *Compassion* is a type of sympathy which involves a change of heart in the direct presence of another's suffering. *Pity* is sympathy accompanied by feelings of superiority. *Schadenfreude* is feigned sympathy. *Love* is an intense emotional bond in which the suffering of the beloved becomes one's own suffering.

The difference between empathy and sympathy is brought out by some recent development studies, including research on autism (cf. Gordon and Baker 1995). Consider the following example: A boy puts his candy in location A, but while he is out of the room, someone else relocates it to B. Where will the boy go to get the candy when he returns—A or B? The obvious answer for adults is A, the place where he left it. However, children younger than 4 years typically respond by saying the boy will search the place where it has been moved. In other words, it is difficult for children this young to distinguish their belief-states from those of others. Given the information they have, they will also believe that others have it too. Younger children do not seem to have robust empathy at this stage; they cannot imaginatively project themselves into the situation of the other, but can only remain egocentrically situated.

Psychologist M.L. Hoffman (1984) has argued for four basic stages to empathy development. Infants are not able to separate self from others, but they do have proto-empathic responses, such as joint visual attention, emotional contagion, and the ability to read the mother's facial expressions. Joint visual attention is the propensity of infants to follow the gaze of another person; 6-month-old infants can be pretty accurate in locating the object referred to by the mother's change of gaze (cf. Butterworth 1991; Butterworth and Cochran 1980). This seems to be an early phenomenon of tracking or mimicking another's mental orientation (cf. Goldman 1993: 352). Babies as young as 1 day old engage in facial imitation of adults (Meltzoff and Moore 1977, 1983). Emotional contagion is the ability to respond reactively to another's emotional state with an identical state. At funerals one will cry as others cry; laughter is certainly contagious; often one yawns as others do. Neonates will cry in reaction to the cry of another (Stimmer 1971). The second level develops as the child is able to physically differentiate self from others. At 2 to 3 years of age the third level begins to develop. Children become aware that others might have feelings which are different from their own based on the other person's needs. Around the age of 2, the so-called "terrible twos," psychologist Judy Dunn (1987: 107) claims that young children learn how their action affects others. As a result, they learn how their actions can not only please but also bother or hurt people, and often they take as much delight in the latter as the former. As children develop a sense of another self, their ability to empathize becomes stronger. As language develops children begin to empathize with a wide range of emotions. In the primary education years children develop the ability to empathize with a person who is not present. At this point perspective taking is a part of the process. The fourth stage develops in late childhood when children become able to empathize not only with a person who is not present, but also with a group of people or society as a whole.

Although most children develop a capability for empathy after the age of 4, most autistic children do not. When versions of the experiment mentioned above are administered to autistic children of ages 6 to 16, almost all give the 3-year-old's answer. Studies also suggest that autistic children have difficulty reading basic emotions, even as compared to children with Down syndrome (Baron-Cohn et al. 1993; Maris et al. 1995). The incapability of empathy may explain the many reports which suggest that people with autism often view people and objects alike; they fail to treat others as subjects, as having points of view distinct from their own, and have difficulty feeling and expressing emotions toward others (cf. Gordon 1995: 737).

Temple Grandin, a well-known autistic who is profiled in Oliver Sacks's book, *An Anthropologist on Mars*, confirms many of these findings. Although she was able to recover somewhat from her milder form of autism and to become quite successful at her own business, she still has great difficulty understanding the emotional life of others. Indeed, her phrase, "I feel like an anthropologist on Mars," served as an inspiration for Sacks's title. In her autobiography, *Thinking in Pictures*, she talks about how she began to develop feelings of gentleness and sympathy for animals, although she could never quite progress toward humans:

> to have feelings of gentleness, one must experience gentle bodily comfort. As my nervous system learned to tolerate the soothing pressure from my squeeze machine [a machine she invented to comfort animals, but then used on herself], I discovered that the comforting feeling made me a kinder and gentler person. It was difficult for me to understand the idea of kindness. ... From the time I started using my squeeze machine I understood that the feeling it gave me was one that I needed to cultivate towards other people. ... I would've been as hard and as unfeeling as a rock if I had not built my squeeze machine (1996: 82).

The famous study on rhesus monkeys by psychologist Harry Harlow confirms this anecdote with broader experimental basis. Harlow and Zimmerman (1959) separated infant monkeys from their parents and peers and raised them for 6 months with two "surrogate mothers." The surrogates were wire monkeys with wooden heads. One surrogate was covered with terry cloth and the other was left bare. Harlow found that the monkeys preferred to cling to the cloth-covered surrogate, even though milk was available only from a bottle attached to the bare-wire surrogate. Harlow concluded that physical contact is a more important factor than nourishment in promoting infant attachment to the mother. Because autistics typically cannot tolerate the sort of hugging or holding children ordinarily get, this could explain the lack of attachment to parents characteristic of autistics. Because, as Harlow writes, "the development of attachment during the first year of infancy is important to a person's ... ability to interact successfully with others," this would also suggest why autistics such as Temple Grandin have not been very good at interpersonal relations.

As Temple Grandin notes, she just doesn't get Shakespeare's *Romeo and Juliet* or *Hamlet* (Sacks 1995: 259). She does not understand social relations (Sacks 1995:

260). When she was younger she was unable to read even the simplest expression of emotions in others (Sacks 1995: 269), and even now with much experience, she cannot read subtle emotional cues: "I have to learn by trial and error what certain gestures and facial expressions mean" (1996: 135). She has, over time, developed a catalogue of how people behave in certain situations, and she uses it to infer the intentions of others (Sacks 1995: 270). In other words she has merely a conventional, supernatant assessment of the emotional life of others, but no depth of understanding many of the more complex emotions, such as jealousy and love (1996: 89). As she describes it, she does have emotions, "but more like the emotions of a child than adult." Her anger is intense, but short-lived. Fear and anxiety are her dominant emotions, but she feels peacefulness now that she is on antidepressants. Her conversations with other autistics show similar patterns, some capable of feeling one or more of the basic emotions, but none of the more complex ones (1996: 89).

Alexithymia is another disorder which illustrates the same idea. In this case the inability to read another's emotions is due to the inability to understand one's own emotional life, although such a life is present. Alexithymics are confused about their own feelings and, as a result, are equally bewildered when other people express their feelings to them (cf. Goleman 1995: 96). They too, apparently, have difficulty in basic affect recognition (Mann et al. 1994).

The capability of not only being able to understand the suffering of another but also to feel distress about it is called *sympathy*. "As for 'sympathy'," Jonathan Bennett writes, "I use this term to cover every sort of fellow-feeling, as when one feels pity over someone's loneliness, or horrified compassion over his pain, or when one feels a shrinking reluctance to act in a way which will bring misfortune to someone else" (1974: 125). As opposed to empathy, sympathy adds an evaluative dimension to our reaction to another's suffering. Adam Smith (1723–1790) made the same point: In sympathy we don't simply respond to another's pleasure with pleasure and to another's suffering with suffering; rather we imagine ourselves being in the other's situation, ourselves faced with whatever is causing the other's emotion. Then, in imagination, we respond independently in our own way to the imagined cause. "We either approve or disapprove of the conduct of another man according as we feel that, when we bring his case home to ourselves, we either can or cannot entirely sympathize with the sentiments and motives which directed it" (1759: 109). Empathy allows one to predict and explain behavior; sympathy allows one to be distressed by it.

Adam Smith (1723–1790) was one of the most influential political economists in the West. In 1759 he wrote *The Theory of Moral Sentiments,* in which he argued that sympathy is the basis of all morality. In 1776 he published *The Wealth of Nations,* partly a history and description of the European economy, partly a theory of wealth and the notion of surplus value.

Psychological research shows, however, that this distress may be of two sorts: egocentric and altruistic. Some may react sympathetically toward another's suffering and act to relieve it primarily to relieve their own distress at seeing another suffer (Piliavin and Piliavin 1972; Cialdini, Darby, and Vincent 1973; Cialdini et al. 1987; Cialdini and Fultz 1990;

Was Adam Smith Right?

Self-described fishing fanatic, T.G., of East Moriches, Long Island, told a reporter the day after the crash of TWA Flight 800, a mysterious crash that killed some 200 people: "I felt bad when I heard about the wreck, real bad, but to be honest with you, the first thing I wondered was how it would affect the fishing."

This remark suggests that we can still feel sympathy for the suffering of others, yet not so much that it interferes with our own relatively trivial concerns.

Amato 1986). Others may act to relieve suffering primarily for the other's benefit (Batson et al. 1988; Eisenberg et al. 1989). The two sides of this issue have engaged in lengthy debates about this question (Cialdini and Brown 1997; Neuberg and Cialdini 1997; Batson and Sager 1997; Batson 1997), but some researchers (Davis 1983; Unger and Lakshmi 1997) argue that both types are part of a global concept of sympathy, are not necessarily mutually exclusive, and can be co-present in long-term behavior.

Many thinkers believe that sympathy works by means of analogy, an imaginative process of "putting oneself" in that situation and understanding what that would feel like (Smith 1759: 48; cf. Blum 1980: 510). Hume concurs: "The sentiments of others can never affect us, but by becoming, in some measure, our own; in which case they operate upon us, by opposing and encreasing our passions, in the very same manner, as if they had been originally deriv'd from our own temper and disposition" (1739: 593). Through this imaginative projection one realizes the horror of the situation which generates a fear in you. This analogizing may make us feel sympathetic toward the homeless, toward starving children, or toward the survivors of accidents, about whom we have little personal knowledge except what we read in the paper. Sympathy is the ability to reenact in those cases, for example, their suffering in us, causing us to feel distress and so be motivated to act on their behalf or at least to relieve our own distress. Sympathy also contains an element of fear that arises from seeing the horror of the situation the person undergoes. So it is an odd mixture of distress for another and fear for oneself. Consequently, it is said that to feel sympathy for someone we must also be able to fear what he or she is suffering or at least understand what the person is undergoing (Blum 1980: 507). Conversely, to share joy with others, we must be capable of enjoying such things ourselves. To feel sympathy for another's suffering, we must imagine that what is happening to another could (or has) happened to us or a loved one. But that is so horrifying that it shakes us with fear. However, the realization that it is not us in that situation also affords us a certain relief. That relief allows certain possibilities, either a selfish impulse simply to turn away from the other's suffering, glad that it is not us, or even a cruel impulse to pretend interest and sympathy but with a secret enjoyment of the other's suffering (*Schadenfreude*). Or it could have the more positive effect of genuine motivation to relieve another of his suffering. Similarly, we may take joy in another's joy and, as a result, join with them in an union of celebration or victory. Or we may refuse that for somewhat selfish reasons, precisely because we wish it were us in the victory seat instead. Because sympathy is often felt in the context for those with whom we have no special relationship, there is still some psychical distance between us and the persons who suffer. As Adam Smith (1759: 233–234) writes,

---

Jonathan Edwards (1703–1758), a Puritan theologian and philosopher, expresses the more negative elements of pity and Schadenfreude in the following passage:

> The seeing of the calamities of others tends to heighten the sense of our own enjoyments. When the saints in glory, therefore, shall see the doleful state of the damned, how will this heighten their sense of the blessedness of their own state. ... When they shall see how miserable others of their fellow-creatures are ... when they shall see the smoke of their torment ... and hear their dolorous shrieks and cries, and consider that they in the meantime are in the most blissful state, and shall surely be in it to all eternity; how they will rejoice!

(from "The End of the Wicked Contemplated by the Righteous," *The Works of President Edwards,* Vol. 4. London, 1817). (For a commentary on this passage, see Jonathan Bennett 1974.)

The most frivolous disaster which could befall himself would occasion a more real disturbance. If he was to lose his little finger tomorrow, he would not sleep to-night, but, provided he never saw them, he would snore with the most profound security over the ruin of a 100 million of his brethren.

"Nature, it seems," Smith continues, "when she loaded us with our own sorrows, thought they were enough, and therefore did not command us to take any further share in those of others than what was necessary to prompt us to relieve them" (1759: 108). In a marvelous interpretation of Pieter Bruegel's painting *Landscape with the Fall of Icarus* (1554–1555), poet W.H. Auden reinforces this idea. Icarus, of course, is the story of a boy who took his father's invention—a pair of waxed wings—too close to the sun, despite his father's warnings. The wings melted, and he plunged to his death. As opposed to what might be expected from Bruegel's title, however, the visual focus of the painting is a farmer plowing his fields and a shepherd tending his flock, with a vista of the sea in the background. In the periphery, if you look closely, you notice Icarus, having just plunged into the water from his fall, the lower parts of his legs now all that are visible. In the poem *Musée des Beaux Arts*, Auden interprets the visual arrangement of the painting as meaning something similar to Smith's account of sympathy. Despite the great tragedy of a father losing his son by means for which he is partially to blame, life goes on—the farmer's plow their fields, the shepherd tends his flock, and even a ship, close to the body of Icarus, sets sail and moves on to its destination.

Because sympathy is based on analogy, that is, your understanding of the sort of suffering a person is undergoing, it can be evoked even when you are not acquainted with the victim. For example, a story in the *Anchorage Daily News* (Doogan 1995) recounts the efforts of a woman, Teri, who wanted to help four little girls—none of whom she ever met—whose mother was dying from cancer. She wanted to arrange a trip to Disneyland for them to help assuage some of the grief she knew they would endure, even though there was no way she could afford the money for such a venture. "It just hurts my heart," she said. "It makes me cry every time I think about it." She learned of the family's plight through her husband's adopt-a-family program at work. She had never seen the girls, yet she understood their suffering: "because they're little children who are losing their mother. ... it's just not fair." She worked to arrange for donated tickets and rooms from Disneyland, hotels, and a local airline. She also related analogously to her own possible situation: "If I was dying before my time and there was something that might make my family happy, just think how that would make me feel."

Pity is a form of sympathy that involves a superior attitude on the part of the sympathizer (Blum 1980: 512). In pity we may still be motivated to relieve the suffering of another, but it also involves an impression that precisely because of a person's suffering, condition, or misfortune, he is in some sense inferior to us. It is because we have escaped the misfortune, and the other has not, that he is to be pitied.

Compassion is a term that is often used synonymously with sympathy, but *we may designate it here to mean a species of sympathy which, like pity, focuses on the suffering of another but, unlike pity, creates a feeling of mutuality, a recognition of the victim's common humanity or likeness with oneself.* An additional feature of compassion is that it is usually generated out of a direct witnessing of, or connection with, the suffering of a person. As a result it often takes the more altruistic forms of sympathy, as Batson argues (Batson et al. 1988; Eisenberg et al. 1988) and so is directed to the other as a person. Sometimes it may also involve a change from indifference to another's plight or create a sudden "softening of the heart" when confronted with another's suffering. The classic example is Achilles' decision in the *Iliad* to return the body of his bitter enemy, Hektor, to his father Priam after hearing the pleas of the old man. In that encounter Priam begins to remind Achilles of his own father, and as a result, he begins to understand Priam's great suffering. He sees Priam no longer as an enemy, but as a person like his father—like any father—whose son has met a tragic end. Compassion inhibits cruelty and encourages kindness precisely because a person—who may have been perceived previously as not worthy of sympathy—is now understood as a fellow human being. Robert Coles (1986: 27–28) relates a story about a 14-year-old white boy and racist—a popular athlete—who participated in harassing the African-American children who were trying to integrate his school; however, he slowly began to change his perception of one boy in particular:

> [I] began to see a kid. ... a guy who knew how to smile when it was rough going, and who walked straight and tall, and was polite. I told my parents, "It's a real shame that someone like him has to pay for the trouble caused by all those federal judges." Then it happened. I saw a few people cuss at him. "The dirty nigger," they kept on calling him and soon they were pushing him in a corner, and it looked like trouble, bad trouble. I went over and broke it up. ... They all looked at me as if I was crazy. ... Before [they] left I spoke to [him]. ... I didn't mean to. ... It just came out of my mouth. I was surprised to hear the words myself: "I'm sorry."

Unlike sympathy, which is motivated by the type of suffering a person undergoes and frames that suffering in terms of its possibility for the benefactor, compassion focuses on the fact that it is *this* person in this situation who is suffering; the direction is more toward the person's suffering, rather than the fact that the suffering could be one's own.

The sympathy one feels typically becomes more intense the more intimately you are connected with the person. Jean-Jacques Rousseau noted this: "The commiseration will be the more energetic, the more intimately the spectator identifies himself with the sufferer" (cf. Schopenhauer 1841: 185). This is echoed by David Hume: "We sympathize more with persons contiguous to us, than with persons remote from us: with our acquaintances, than with strangers: with our countryman than with foreigners" (1739: 581). In the case of love, of course, we have the most intimate sorts of relations with others, in which our emotional life and well-being are bound up with the beloved. Consequently, when there is a special relation involved, such as romantic love, parental love, or friendship, the distress over the other's suffering becomes much more emphatic. Love, unlike sympathy, affords no psychical distance and consequently no relief from the fact that the suffering is not ours; rather than being glad that the suffering is not ours, often we would gladly take on that suffering of our child, for example, if the child didn't have to undergo it. In love relations the beloved's suffering is yours precisely because he or she is that person and no other. Certainly if we saw a child suffering, a decent person would feel sympathy for that child and do whatever she could to help. But imagine it is your child who is suffering. In this case you do not, rightly speaking, pity your child (unless you are emotionally estranged from him or her), but you too suffer, as your child suffers—perhaps even more so. There is no distance between your suffering and this child's in the last case.

Besides understanding the various kinds of sympathy we experience, it is an interesting question as to why we do or do not feel sympathy for people and, when we do, what causes or inhibits us from acting to relieve their suffering. One possible answer is that sympathy may be a trait in some personalities, but weak or nonexistent in others (Rushton 1976). (A trait, as opposed to a disposition or a situational behavior, is thought to be a stable internal characteristic of a person displayed consistently over time and across situations (Carver and Sheier 1995). Consequently, it is the trait which causes altruistic behavior (Batson, Fultz, and Schoenrade 1987; Davis 1983; Eisenberg and Miller 1987; Barnett 1987; Batson et al. 1981, 1988; Eisenberg 1986; Eisenberg and Miller 1987; Piliavin and Chang 1990). In some ways, however, this is an unsatisfactory explanation—it suggests a person acts sympathetically because he has a tendency to do so. If this were the only reason, it would seem that a person would have a tendency to do so no matter what the situation or circumstance, but surely that is not the case, and there are several other conditions for acting sympathetically.

For example, although most people who feel distress over the suffering of another are more likely to help altruistically in that situation, they are even more likely to help when there is a personal encounter with the suffering of others (Oliner and Oliner 1988). There is something about the presence of the person suffering that is a powerful motivator. But there are inhibitors in personal encounters as well. Generally speaking, the motivation to help others when their suffering is distressful is inversely proportional to the risk incurred by or inconvenience to the benefactor and the unpleasantness of the suffering (Piliavin et al. 1990). This is so except in the case where the suffering is great or traumatic; in that case people motivated by sympathy are more likely to help (Piliavin et al. 1990), unless they are more motivated by great fears for their safety (Wilson and Petruska 1984). Other factors that might mediate this outcome include the bystander's belief in his or her competence to help (Clark and Word 1974).

Another motivator for acting sympathetically is identification with the victim. Familiarity, kinship, or similarity is likely to motivate others to help you. Kin are more likely to help and incur greater sacrifice on behalf of kin than nonkin, as suggested by Hamilton's (1964) theory of "inclusive fitness." Amato (1986) points out that much prosocial behavior occurs continuously between close friends and relatives: the self-sacrifices of parents for children, the care of aging parents, community voluntarism, neighborliness, and similar activities. He also indicates that such regular, planned altruism is much more common than emergency situations, real or simulated. Helping unrelated persons is more likely if the person is perceived as a benefactor in some respect (Feldman 1968; Hornstein, Fisch, and Holmes 1968; Piliavin, Rodin, and Piliavin 1969). The tighter the community, the less likely members of that community will help nonmembers (Wilson 1993). In general, the intensity of sympathy is inversely proportional to its extension; the more intensely it is expressed for some, the less its extension to others outside that circle. Identification with the victim is influenced by sociocultural characteristics such as race, gender, age, education, and economic status. For example, a study by Carl Enomoto (1999) showed that sympathy for O.J. Simpson during his highly publicized trial was significantly affected by these sociocultural categories. He found that blacks were more likely than whites to be sympathetic to Simpson and to believe he was innocent of the crimes he was charged with. Older individuals, males, those with higher incomes, and those with more education were less likely to be sympathetic to Simpson and more likely to think he was guilty. For blacks who were more likely than whites to perceive that the criminal justice system is biased against blacks, the implication was that Simpson was a victim of an unjust criminal system.

This suggests another important motivator for sympathy and sympathetic action. Sympathy will vary as the victim is perceived or not perceived as deserving of the suffering (Vitz 1990: 714; Hoffman 1984). In other words sympathy is evoked in the context of a story in which the person must be situated by the observer as an innocent victim of injustice, or undeserving of harm, and not responsible for his own situation (Schmidt and Weiner 1988). Clearly, someone suffering because of a brutal crime he's committed is less likely to receive sympathy than his victims.

In addition, helping others on the basis of sympathy is likely to be attenuated if a person is part of a larger group, so that responsibility gets diffused. This is exemplified by the Kitty Genovese case (Latane and Darley 1968). On March 13, 1964, the 28-year-old woman was returning home from her job as a bar manager in the early morning. As she walked to her apartment building in Queens, she was attacked by a mugger who repeatedly stabbed her. Thirty-eight of her neighbors reported that they had been awakened by her screams and had rushed to look out their windows, yet none did anything. The assailant left twice, returning each time to continue his attack. Psychologists Bibb Latane and John Darley (1968), among others, have studied this case and similar ones and came to the following conclusion: Among strangers, as the number of bystanders increases, the likelihood of a bystander's intervening decreases. This is probably the case because responsibility for helping becomes too diffused; roles and responsibilities become too confused with so many people present. Latane has come away with the outlines of a decision process that is involved in what's called "bystander intervention." First, the victim must be noticed. Second, the situation must be interpreted as an emergency. Third, a decision must be made whether to take responsibility for helping. Fourth, if such a decision is made, then a course of action is decided on.

1.2 THE ABSENCE OF MORAL EMOTIONS

The importance of moral emotions for right conduct can be shown indirectly by examining the results of their absence in people's lives. Many people are capable of occasional cold-hearted and cruel actions, where there is a loss of sympathy. Sometimes such people will feel remorse for their actions afterward, and when they are confronted with the consequences, they wake to their moral feelings as if they were emerging from some trance. Others may have had their moral sensibilities dulled through traumatic experience, such as war or exposure to other forms of brutality. In such cases it may take years for a person to recover full moral feeling. But in addition to these cases where there is a relatively temporary loss of moral emotions, there are the well-known maladies of psychopathy and sociopathy involving either a chronic loss of moral feeling or an inability to have moral emotions at all.

1.2.1 Psychopathy

In his book *The Mask of Sanity*, Hervey Cleckley (1982) describes psychopaths as people often from good families, intelligent and rational, sound of mind and body, who lie without compunction, cheat, steal, and casually violate any and all norms of social conduct whenever it suits their whim. Moreover, they seem surprisingly unaffected by the bad consequences of their actions, whether visited upon themselves or on their families and friends. *In general the psychopath is characterized by a lack of restraining effect of conscience, concern, and sympathy for other people* (1982). The classic definition includes persons who lack remorse or shame, have a total disregard of the feelings of others, and have an enormous ego. "Though psychopaths know, in some sense, what it means to wrong people, to act immorally, this kind of judgment has for them no motivational component at all. ... They feel no guilt, regret, shame, or remorse (though they may superficially fake these feelings) when they have engaged in harmful conduct" (Murphey 1972: 285–287). Pathological personalities do not seem to understand their behavior as vicious (cf. Hare 1970), except in a conventional sense, that is, when they do something that they know most people do not like to see in others, and they feel they should conceal it (Benn 1985: 798). They have knowledge of right and wrong—at least as conventionally understood—but are unmotivated by that knowledge (Deigh 1995: 746). For this reason they often treat clearly immoral behaviors as if they were ordinary sorts of behaviors. Often in talking with a truly pathological person, the vicious acts are related on a par with ordinary events, as if they had no special moral weight. They are persons who are adept at pretense, role playing, and imitation. They know what the proper roles are, but they can only imitate them superficially; they don't adopt them internally.

Adam B., 18, murdered his friend, P.M., 19, in a brutal and callous way. He had fallen in with Rick Johnson, a convicted thief, who wanted revenge on P.M. for turning him in for the theft of some restaurant equipment. On the pretense of stealing car stereos, they lured P.M. to his death. The murder was particularly gruesome. After two different guns misfired, Adam B. finally pulled out a gun that did work and shot his friend twice in the head. Johnson finished him off with a shotgun blast to the face after he lay on the ground pleading for help. Adam B. was someone who could easily imitate a certain code—at first, the code of his parents, their church, and even the Boy Scouts. In fact, he had been hoping to become a state trooper (and strangely enough at the trial he framed his actions in the language of the state troopers). But as the judge in this case noted, "none of the rules took root inside him" (*Anchorage Daily News*, April 5, 1995). Thus, it was just as easy for him to adopt the criminal code of Rick Johnson, which required revenge on informers. When Adam B. gave a videotaped confession of the killing, he spoke in a casual monotone about the most gruesome aspects of the murder. As the evaluating psychologist noted, "Adam has the ability to say 'I love you,' 'I hate you,' and 'Let's order pizza' in the same tone of voice" (*Anchorage Daily News*, April 5, 1995).

Psychopaths are capable of reasoning, weighing evidence, estimating future consequences, understanding the norms of their society, anticipating the blame and condemnation that result from the violation of those norms, and are quite capable of using cognitive skills to make and carry out their plans (Deigh 1995: 743). They are not maniacs; they can be persistent wrongdoers, but they are not driven to commit misdeeds; they are smooth and bloodless operators, a trait well depicted by Richard Hickock in Truman Capote's *In Cold Blood*. This coldness is confirmed by recent studies of wife abusers by Larry Jacobsen and John Gottman at the University of Washington (1994). The most aggressive wife beaters, nearly a third of whom may be formally classified as psychopaths, don't become angered or enraged when they strike, but in fact become calmer in the face of hot arguments. This is probably due in part to their high threshold of fear. Hare and Schalling (1978) found that psychopaths are hard to condition because they are less apprehensive than others about situations that would make most people very anxious. They do not readily develop a fearful response to an event; they do not seem capable of internalizing fear, and hence, they have difficulty internalizing anxieties. They are often thrill seekers simply because they are underaroused.

Psychopaths in general seem to have the inability to enter into genuine friendships or form attachments of loyalty and love. Often they are bothered by petty emotions; they are shallow, always scheming, and incapable of deeper feelings either for themselves or others. They feel no compunction about their actions, however wrong or injurious they may be (Deigh 1995: 743–744). Alec Wilkinson, in his many interviews with John Wayne Gacy—who brutally murdered thirty-three boys between 1972 and 1978—had this to say about the man:

> Visiting Gacy is like spending time with a person who is pretending to like you in order to separate you, violently, if necessary, from something you possess. ... he [is] ... capable of charm in the service of deception. ... He appears to have no inner being. I often had the feeling that he was like an actor who had created a role and polished it so carefully that he had become the role and the role had become him. What personality he may once have had collapsed long ago and has been replaced by a catalogue of gestures and attitudes and portrayals of sanity (1994: 59).

Wilkinson noted that Gacy "conducts his life as if he possessed a complete and sensitive emotional capacity, which he has not" (1994: 10). Indeed, Wilkinson observed that Gacy had no capacity to listen to the other person in the conversation, that he had no friends, and that he appeared to have no capability for intimacy (1994: 10).

Not only do psychopaths seem incapable of deep personal relations, but generally they seem incapable of sympathy; even if they have some ability to read the suffering of others, they don't have the capability of feeling for their suffering (cf. Blair et al. 1995). Some argue that because there is a shallow interior to psychopaths, a sort of interior death as one psychiatrist put it, and they cannot feel something in themselves, they cannot be sympathetic with others. In fact, it is argued that some psychopaths get relief from this condition precisely by causing and observing suffering in others. It is almost as if the psychopath needs a surrogate in order to feel some suffering or feel anything at all. It is as if by cruelly killing someone, they might feel something themselves.

Because psychopaths have a shallow emotional interior, a lack of sympathy, and difficulty forming attachments to others, they seem incapable of the internalization necessary for proper socialization and for developing moral emotions and a sense of right and wrong. Internalization occurs when persons feel that a set of beliefs, norms, or codes is their own, so to speak. At the point of internalization, they are willing to correct their own behavior without external prompts, and when they violate those norms, there is some anxious emotional response to it—that is, one of the more negative moral feelings normally associated with conscience. In other words, a person's feelings and emotions become integrated with these beliefs or norms.

It is not entirely clear whether these inabilities in the psychopath are congenital or environmentally based (for a review of some of the more recent literature, cf. Martens 2000; Mitchell and Blair 2000). Allinsmith (1968) claims that internalization is unrelated to matters of care, feeding, weaning, or toilet training; rather it is related to the sort of nurturing children receive in their early years. Without attachment to an adult in these early years, internalization is unlikely. This is supported by Magid and McKelvey, who claim that "conscienceless" children were typically destructive and violent and most had severe attachment problems (1989). Indeed, McCord and McCord (1956) argued that psychopaths often have a history of parental neglect and abuse, although Magid emphasizes that not all attachment-deprived children necessarily become psychopaths, nor do all children successfully attach to their parents even when optimal conditions are present; some children simply resist attachment. Recent studies by Robert Hare (1999), a psychologist at the University of British Columbia, seem to back up the latter claim. He argues that he can pick up signs of psychopathy in children as young as 6 and that there are certainly remorseless killers who come out of loving homes (cf. Blum 1995; Hare 1970, 1978, 1999). Indeed, there is a continuing debate between a nurture and a nature view of psychopathy. Bruce Perry, a neurobiologist working at the Baylor School of Medicine, takes a position somewhat opposed to Hare. Perry's work suggests that a wretched childhood may alter the critical balance between neurotransmitters such as serotonin, which has a calming and controlling effect on people, and noradrenaline, which has the opposite effect. A hostile environment might act like an acid on the brain, Perry speculates, making permanent changes in the way in which the brain responds to fear and chaos, allowing children to develop a cold and calm attitude toward violence and aggression. David Lykken attempts to settle this dispute by making a distinction between psychopathy and sociopathy (1996: 29; 1995). The psychopath resists socialization because of a congenital inability, whereas the sociopath's antisocial behavior is a direct result of failed socialization. "The primary psychopath has failed to develop conscience and empathic feelings not because of the lack of socializing experience but, rather, because of some inherent psychological peculiarity that makes him equally difficult to socialize" (1996: 30; 1995). Psychopaths cannot internalize, and so lack many of the ordinary moral emotions. Not only are most psychopaths incapable of acquiring emotions such as guilt, recent studies seem to indicate that psychopaths have difficulty even recognizing guilt displayed by others (Blair et al. 1995).

In successful internalization or socialization, the desire to do the right thing comes organically from within the person and does not require constant external rewards and punishments alone, although certainly rewards and punishments are necessary to reinforce the internalization. A life without some reward for doing the right thing, or confirmation from others, would make the desire to do the right thing fade in most people. But generally speaking, the existence of moral emotion is confirmation that such persons have internalized certain norms and are willing to correct and control their behavior toward those norms. Persons primarily motivated by external punishment or reward will behave accordingly in the presence of that authority; in its absence they will do what they will. Those who have moral emotions are internally motivated to do the right thing whether some authority is present or absent, and they may exhibit the tendency to do the right thing even where punishment for doing it is threatened. Those who have not achieved a point of internalization do not typically engage in self-control but are out of control, as we say. Consequently, they must be directed by others, specifically by fear of punishment or hope of reward from others. Or as in the case of many psychopaths who seem incapable of internalization, they transfer the control of self to control of others in their environment; that is, instead of controlling oneself to better satisfy one's desires, the psychopath will attempt to control others and their environment to achieve the same goal. Certainly, people at different times and at different stages of their lives act morally out of fear of punishment and other similar motivations, while still, during the same period, acting out of moral feeling. But generally speaking, the internalized acquisition of moral emotion is the point at which moral competence is possible for a person.

1.2.2 Sociopathy and Wickedness

If we can accept David Lykken's distinction between psychopathy and sociopathy, the causes and characteristics of the latter differ somewhat from those of the former. Whereas the psychopath appears to have a congenital condition which frustrates any socialization, the sociopath is often the result of failed socialization (1996: 29). To put it differently, the psychopath is incapable of moral emotion, but the sociopath has lost moral feeling.

Sociopathy may be another label for what has been traditionally called "wickedness." Wicked persons have some understanding of right and wrong; they understand that their actions create a significant harm for others—that is, they have the capability of seeing the suffering from another's perspective, yet still choose destructive or harmful behaviors precisely for those consequences, and with little remorse. Wicked people may very well have the capacity for empathy, yet no sympathy, at least for their victims. Wicked persons are those who exhibit a relatively constant tendency to harm others and engage in these destructive behaviors for deliberate reasons. These reasons may be political or personal. Often they find gratification in harming and humiliating others. The philosopher Arthur Schopenhauer (1818) had an insightful characterization of such a person. Wickedness is motivated not by a desire to do oneself good, but by a privation of good for others. The suffering of others is an enjoyment not because it creates a good for oneself, but because it reduces the other to the state which is the ordinary state for the wicked person. The philosopher Georg Hegel (1770–1831) writes that wickedness "is despicable, for it is a quality which arises from the envy and hatred of all that is noble, and does not shrink from distorting—even a power that is essentially based upon the good—into a means ... for its own perverse and shameless passion." John Rawls (1971: 439) notes that the evil man "delights in the ... humiliation of those subject to him and he relishes being recognized by them as the willful author of their degradation." Leon Bing, who spent a great deal of time with Los Angeles gangs, writes about one member in particular, Faro, who paralyzed a mother and her child in a drive-by shooting. While driving, Faro tells Bing that he's "gonna look crazy" at the people in the next car. The driver sees Faro, his eyes connect with Faro's, then he breaks the contact and looks down and away (cf. Goleman 1995: 108). Vicious people do not find pleasure in the good, even the good for themselves, which they believe themselves to be either unworthy or incapable of receiving. Rather they find gratification in the suffering of others. As Bing says of Faro: "His look tells you that he doesn't care about anything, not your life and not his" (1991).

Doug Gustafson was convicted for shooting and killing a young driver who had cut in front of him. While in prison, he plotted along with his sister and brother to send a mail bomb to G.K., a former friend, who was in the car with him that night and had gone to police with his firsthand information. It was on the basis of G.K.'s testimony that Gustafson was convicted. During a phone conversation with his sister, after they had worked out the details of the bomb, Gustafson said that when everything was over, "I'm gonna sit back. I'm gonna have a nice big juicy cigar.

The Banality of Evil?

In her famous book *Eichmann in Jerusalem*, philosopher Hannah Arendt promotes the thesis of "the banality of evil." Eichmann was the driving force behind the concentration camp system and ultimately responsible for the murder of millions of Jewish men, women, and children. But rather than seeing Eichmann as the incarnation of evil and wickedness, Arendt characterized him as simply an unimaginative bureaucrat who was interested in career advancement and who had no particular awareness or concern with the broader consequences of his actions. Eichmann was characterized as someone not particularly ideologically motivated, nor as someone who might take particular pleasure in seeing others suffer.

Question for Discussion

Do you agree with Arendt that much evil in the world occurs because of these sorts of people?

Mass Killings of the 20th Century

1904–1907: Colonizers of Namibia kill 100,000 Hereros.

1905–1907: Colonizers of Tanzania kill 120,000 Africans.

1915–1918: 1.5 million Armenians killed in Iraq.

1932–1935: 4–7 million peasants starved in Soviet Union.

1937–1953: 4–5 million people killed in Soviet Union.

1939–1945: Nazis kill approximately 11 million people in Europe.

1944–1945: 1 million Nazi collaborators killed in Europe.

1962–1963: 14,000 Tutsi killed in Rwanda.

1965–1966: 1 million people killed in Indonesia.

1966–1976: 1.5 million people killed in China's cultural revolution.

1971–1972: 1.5–3 million Bengali Hindus and Muslims killed in Pakistan.

1971–1979: 100,000–500,000 killed in Uganda.

1972: 80,000–150,000 Hutus killed in Burundi.

1975–1985: Indonesia invaded East Timor killing 60,000–200,000 people.

1975–1979: 1.7 million killed by Khmer Rouge in Cambodia.

1976–1983: 10,000–20,000 "disappeared" in Argentina.

1979–1987: 255,000 killed in Uganda.

1980–1984: 100,000 killed in Guatemala.

1980–1992: 45,000–75,000 murdered in El Salvador.

1983–1984: 1 million killed in Ethiopia.

1983–1993: 1.3 million killed in the Sudan.

1987–1988: 100,000 Kurds gassed by Iraqi forces.

1992: 1 million Muslims killed by Serbs in Bosnia.

1994: 500,000 killed in Rwanda.

Source: Associated Press

Or I'm gonna buy some expensive ones from the commissary. A nice big cigar … and um, I want to sit back and just enjoy it and then I'm gonna go off in the room, cover up the little phone vent … and I'm gonna laugh so hard" (*Anchorage Daily News* Feb. 17, 1995). It is understanding the actual or potential suffering of another that gives the vicious person satisfaction. (As it turned out, the bomb killed G.K.'s father and seriously injured his mother-in-law. G.K. was not home at the time.)

One of the clearest literary examples of such a person is found in the character of Claggert in Herman Melville's *Billy Budd.* Claggert hates the handsome young sailor, a sweet, innocent, and pleasant young fellow; in attempting to destroy the young man, Claggert is not acting for his own good or anybody else's, but rather he is motivated by his hatred and spite (cf. Benn 1985: 386). One might think of it as a jealousy and resentment of the good. Because vicious people think they are incapable of good, their goal is to destroy it. Instead of seeing the good as a worthy goal, their character is such that they would rather see the world reduced to their level than strive to

Arthur Schopenhauer (1788–1860) was a German philosopher of pessimism; he developed a metaphysics in which "The Will" in all its variations formed a crucial part of his thinking. His most relevant ethical work was *The Basis of Morality*. In that text he argued that the ethical person is someone who rises above egoism and comprehends himself and his relations with others from a higher standpoint, a view which addresses the unitary nature of all things.

ascend to its level. "Precisely because the good that he sees cannot motivate him, he hates it for its very inaccessibility" (Benn 1985: 798).

1.3 THE VARIETIES OF MORAL SENTIMENT

The examples of psychopathy and wickedness emphasize how important it is to have moral emotions. Moral emotions, however, are usually experienced as reactions to single events; it is also important that a person develop a more generalized

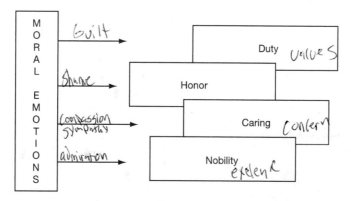

The diagram shows "MORAL EMOTIONS" on the left connected by arrows to a series of overlapping boxes. Handwritten annotations appear alongside: "Guilt" → Duty *values*; "Shame" → Honor; "Compassion sympathy" → Caring *concern*; "admiration" → Nobility *extent*.

Over time moral emotions configure into various types of sentiment. *Duty* is a sense of obligation relative to certain roles; *honor* is based on the status one has as a good moral agent; *caring* is feeling of concern for the suffering of others and their well-being; *nobility* is based on a sense of personal excellence.

feeling for the good over time. This higher-order moral feeling is called *moral sentiment,* and it establishes emotional dispositions which *incline* a person toward the good (Rawls 1971: 479). John Rawls defines moral sentiments as "governing dispositions such as the sense of justice and the love of mankind" (1971: 479). It can be thought of as driving a desire for the good, however vaguely we may understand that sense of the term.

Those who have acquired a moral sentiment have successfully internalized some moral norms. They have a different motivation to act morally than those who are primarily motivated by punishment and reward. In the last case, one does the good to avoid displeasure or to gain reward; a moral sentiment prods us to do the right thing because that's what we *feel* we *should* do—in other words, it creates a sense of *obligation* in us. Depending on what sort of moral sentiment guides us, if we don't do what we feel we should, often we are visited with the pangs of what is popularly called *conscience,* a feeling which Immanuel Kant calls an "instinct of self-judgement" (1775–1780: 129), or some other form of anxiety about our behavior. When moral sentiment is fully developed in a person, the pleasure of doing what the person believes to be the right thing is *internally* generated rather than *externally* imposed.

The Ring of Gyges

In *The Republic* (2.359d) Plato has Glaucon advocate the position that people are motivated not to do wrong only out of fear of punishment. To illustrate his point, he tells Socrates about the story of Gyges, a Lydian shepherd who acquired a magical ring which could make him invisible. Realizing this, he first committed adultery with the king's wife, attacked the king with her help, killed him, and took over the kingdom. Glaucon argues: If there were two such rings, one worn by the just and good man, the other by the unjust, both would end up doing immorality because there would be no external constraint.

Questions for Discussion

1. Is Glaucon correct? If the concept of internalization is accurate, then even in the absence of external punishment or some authority, some people may be willing to correct or control their own behavior. Do you believe this happens?
2. If internalization is a genuine process, what is its relation to externalization, to reward and punishment? Is the latter necessary to reinforce the former? Is it possible for people to persist in doing the right thing despite the lack of reward or punishment?

Moral sentiment can be expressed in various ways depending on the predominance of moral emotions in the agent. Although people can experience a wide range of moral emotions, some are more prone to guilt, others are more readily shamed, or someone may respond strongly to another's suffering more than any other moral feeling. If guilt is the primary motivator, then moral sentiment may be expressed as a sense of *duty*, that one is to do certain things or to refrain from doing certain things as a matter of obligation to others. Duty is felt most strongly by most people within the practice of certain roles: parents, professionals, or citizens. This is a sentiment especially emphasized by Immanuel Kant, Cicero, and other ancient Stoic thinkers. Shame and *honor* are often thought to be correlative. A sense of honor is the emphatic feeling that a moral person does or does not engage in certain types of acts, that an individual's identity is bound up with this conduct, which is becoming of certain roles and status, and that it is beneath one to engage in anything less or contrary to it. This is a sentiment also found in Plato, Aristotle, Cicero, and Confucius. If sympathy is the primary motivator, then moral sentiment is expressed as a sense of *caring*, which is a general regard for the welfare of others, distress over their suffering, and good fellow-feeling. This is a view primarily associated with 18th-century philosopher David Hume. If moral sentiment is bound up with admiration, then it is expressed as a sense of *nobility* in human conduct. Nobility is an aspiration toward excellence and a connection with morally worthy goals, causes, and visions larger than oneself. This is a sentiment especially associated with 19th-century philosopher Friedrich Nietzsche, but it is also found in many classical thinkers.

Each sentiment may complement another, although one may predominate in a person. Some persons may have a strong sense of honor or duty, and some are motivated by their general sympathy and compassion for the suffering of others; similarly, some may simply find themselves bound up with a great and admirable cause. Perhaps the most balanced person, morally speaking, is one who exhibits all of these various sentiments in a complementary way. For example, good parents are those who have a strong sense of sympathy and love toward their children, but also a strong sense of duty, given their role as parent, to tend to the children's needs and wants. They feel a certain sense of honor, in which they pride themselves for being the sort of parents they are, and all the while they hold up as ideal a certain model of a parent, to which they aspire, and a belief that parenting is a noble and important thing to do.

1.3.1 Duty

In 1947 Chuck Yeager was the first man to break the sound barrier in an experimental jet aircraft. Many test pilots before him had died trying. A civilian pilot was willing to do it for $150,000, but in a recent interview, Yeager said he was willing to do it for one reason—"duty," his duty as an Air Force officer (*ABC Evening News*, October 14, 1997). James Wilson defines the sense of duty as "the disposition to honor obligations even without hope of reward or fear of punishment" (1993: 100). More specifically, *duty may be defined as a sentiment that certain obligations to others are required to be performed because they are commanded by one's roles or by the moral norms and rules one has internalized.* Cicero thought so much of duty that be believed "the inquiry into duty is common to all philosophers: is there anyone who would dare to call himself a philosopher without having handed on instructions about

Do You Agree with Cicero's Ranking of Duties?

In *On Duties* Cicero argues that "if there should arise any need to estimate or choose by comparison those who are entitled to receive your highest duty, the fatherland and the parents should come first: our debt to their kindness is the largest. The children and the household in general come next: they depend on us alone and cannot look to any other refuge. The last place goes to the deserving friends: your destiny is often intertwined with theirs" (44 B.C.: 29). Cicero's criteria seem to be that our first duties should be to those we owe the most, our second to those who depend on us the most, and the third to those who are peers and friends. (For more on Cicero, see Section 4.6.4.)

duty?" (*De officiis* 5). Immanuel Kant thought that duty exemplified the very nature of morality (1797).

Duty is closely associated with guilt, although certainly one can feel shame for failing in one's duties. Since guilt is directed toward what we are obligated to do or not to do to others, and what we owe others is considered the essential aspect of duty, then its developmental tie with guilt makes sense (cf. Williams 1993: 219–220). Although duty can be driven by what is expected of us given our specific roles as parents or citizens, Bernard Williams argues that the inner voice of guilt can develop into a more abstract and generalized sense of obligation so that the focus of duty becomes thought of as adherence to a set of moral rules and principles (1993: 219–220). This is certainly what Kant believed. For him duty is bound to a respect or reverence for the moral law (1785: 16). Kant selected duty as exemplary of morality precisely because it seems to pro-

Many philosophers and psychologists believe that the sense of duty has an emotional and sentimental basis. The 18th-century philosopher Immanuel Kant thought otherwise. For Kant duty is the result of a purely rational understanding of obligation, of what must and should be done, and so the result of a cognitive process. One discerns what is right through reason; understanding that something is right is also an understanding that it must be done—and it is this that generates the sense of duty. Consciousness of duty generates the feeling of "conscience" so "moral feeling, is identical with the consciousness of one's duty" (1797: 58ff.; cf. Beck 1960: 222). For Kant then, an understanding of duty precedes any feeling or emotion associated with duty. The 19th-century philosopher Arthur Schopenhauer argued that reason alone would not be sufficient to generate a feeling of duty toward a moral law, but a person would already have to be emotionally motivated to do so; reason by itself would make us indifferent (1841: 74). *With whom do you agree?* (See Section 1.5.)

mote this more abstract sense of obligation, that is, doing what is right because it is the right thing to do. In this way duty can command us to act morally or fairly to others even if we don't like them personally or have much sympathy for their circumstances. Those who act from duty to relieve the suffering of others may not necessarily do so out of any feeling of sympathy for them, but out of a general sense of what is owed others in time of need. As Adam Smith suggests, acts of altruism may be more motivated by devotion to moral principles, concepts of honor and nobility, rather than by love for one's neighbor (1759: 235). Duty can also urge us to do something when we have little time or inclination to perform it. For this reason, duty is often felt by people as something imposed upon them, as something that they "must" do. Often we hear of people who have persisted in doing their duty despite suffering greatly or enduring terrible harm.

Duties are more ordinarily associated with the specific roles we play within certain practices and are directed to certain types of people. As a teacher you may have duties to your students, to your employer, to your community, and to your peers. Usually, then, our sense of duty becomes more specific as we mature into certain roles within a community, so that we come to learn what is expected of us in that regard. The culture at large, or the particular subcultures to which we belong, will often give us an idea of these expectations, although there may be individual variation and some ambiguity about less essential duties. For example, the culture

Duties of the Corporation

Here is a list of duties thought to apply to the corporation, relative to its various constituencies.

Duties to Customers

1. to ensure product safety.
2. to use truth in selling and advertising.

Duties to Local Community

1. to contribute to the economic stability of the community.
2. to engage in philanthropic acts beneficial to the community.

Duties to Environment

1. to avoid pollution.
2. to dispose of waste safely.

Duties to Employees

1. to practice nondiscrimination in hiring.
2. to reward for performance.
3. to preserve privacy and confidentiality.
4. to show concern for safety, health, and economic security.

Duty to Shareholders

1. to maximize profits

Question for Discussion

How many of these duties do you agree are core to corporate responsibility?

at large makes it fairly clear what duties we have as parents: We need to feed and clothe our children, make sure they get a proper education and training, give them guidance, and most important, tend to their emotional and moral life. Paying for their college education, giving them music lessons, or providing their own car may be duties subject to debate even among parents who can afford such things. Moreover, duties may often be negotiated where they are not entirely clear; for example, within a household a question of household chores and cleaning may be debated until some clarity is reached. We have duties to our friends, our family, our employer, our community, our country, and so on; there are the duties of the teacher, duties of the student, and many others.

In addition to these role-specific duties, some philosophers argue about more general duties. The 20th-century philosopher W.D. Ross called these *prima facie* duties (1930). These duties should be done regardless of the role or practice, such as keeping a promise. In other words, a prima facie duty is one that is incumbent on persons no matter who they are or what they do. There must be extenuating or stronger conflicting duties present for them to say that it is not an actual duty in some particular case. But if a person has to make an exception, it must result in a decision that "would discharge in the

W.D. Ross (1877–1971) was a Scottish philosopher and educator at Edinburgh and Oxford University. He was known for his work on Aristotle and for his two books, *The Right and the Good* and *Foundations of Ethics*.

fullest possible measure the various … *prima facie* duties in that situation" (1939: 190). That is to say, every qualification of a prima facie duty must be for the sake of maximizing the prima facie duties relevant to the situation. For example, the duty to tell the truth may be qualified if it violates a number of other such duties, such as the duty not to harm or the duty to help. Prima facie duties include fidelity (i.e., keeping promises and truth telling), reparation (i.e., duties resting on the righting of a wrong), gratitude (i.e., obligations to those who have benefited you), duties of justice, which require us to give others what is owed them, duties not to harm, duties of benevolence, and duties of self-improvement.

Generally speaking, the desire to take on role-specific duties as well as the more prima facie ones is the core of this moral sentiment. Certainly, one advantage of the sense of duty over some of the other sentiments is that it prompts us to do what we know we should do, even if we don't feel like doing it. Paradoxically, it is a feeling to do something in the absence of a feeling to do it.

Case Study: Just Doing One's Duty?

On March 24, 1944, two German SS officers, Erich Priebke and Karl Hass, ordered their soldiers to take 335 Italian men and boys to the Ardeatine Caves, outside of Rome, and shoot them in retaliation for an Italian resistance action that killed 33 German soldiers the day before. It wasn't until 1996 that the two soldiers were extradited from Argentina to Italy and stood trial for the massacre. Priebke had been living a quiet life as an innkeeper in an Andean mountain resort. He claimed that, although he gave the orders, he personally killed only two of the civilians.

Priebke had two defenses for his actions. First, it was an order that was his duty as a soldier to obey. Second, if he did not obey the order, he would be shot. It was the general policy of the Nazis to kill ten times as many civilians as Nazi soldiers killed in any irregular or resistance action (Source: Galloni 1997).

Questions for Discussion

1. The Priebke case brings up the issue of whether a soldier always has the duty to obey an order. Is that your opinion?
2. Assuming that Priebke was right in saying that he would be shot for disobeying the order, what should he have done? Some argue that, as in the case of self-defense or combat, one is sometimes forced to kill since one's own life is threatened, and these actions are justifiable since they were done under duress. Do you agree with this assessment of the situation? Others might argue that even though people are sometimes forced to act under duress, still they can be responsible to a large degree for placing themselves in such situations; for example, consenting to participate in an unjust war with corrupt commanders may place you in situations in which you are under duress to commit atrocities. What do you think of this assessment of Priebke's situation?

In Priebke's first trial, the Italian judge was sympathetic to Priebke's situation and found him not guilty of premeditation and cruelty (although guilty of slaying the 335 civilians). This, in effect, allowed Priebke to evoke the 30-year statute of limitations on murder in Italy and so to be free of any charges. (If someone was found to be guilty of cruelty in murder, the 30-year statute of limitations could be waived.)

Question for Discussion

3. Do you think this was a judicious and reasonable judgment for Priebke?

The decision was met by outrage from Jewish groups, former Italian partisans, and families of the victims. The judge in this case, Agostino Quistelli, was found to be biased, and Priebke was ordered to be retried. On Wednesday, July 23, 1997, Priebke was found guilty and given a 15-year sentence, which was reduced to 5 years because of mitigating circumstances, including the fact that he was acting under orders. Many of the victims' families were satisfied with the verdict. Priebke's commander, Herbert Koppler, the Gestapo chief in Rome—who was responsible for giving the original order for the executions—was tried, convicted, and sentenced to life imprisonment, but he escaped Italy shortly before his death, having been smuggled out of a military hospital in a suitcase by his wife.

Question for Discussion

4. Which judgment do you think was more judicious for Priebke—the first or the second?

Consider the related case of Otto Ohlendorff, head of Action Group (*Einsatzgruppen*), who was given direct orders to exterminate Jews in Eastern Europe. At his trial and inquiry after the war, he discussed his role in the killing of hundreds of Jewish women and children. His particular method was to gather the victims into vans under the pretense that they were being transported somewhere (in this way he said they would cooperate better); however, the vans were rigged with gas, which would then kill them as they desperately tried to get out. The Tribunal asked, "but did you have no scruples in regard to the execution of these orders?" Ohlendorff replied, "Yes, of course." Tribunal: "And how is it that they were carried out regardless of these scruples?" Ohlendorff: "Because to me it is inconceivable that a subordinate leader should not carry out orders given by the leaders of the State" (cited in Hallie 1997: 101).

Question for Discussion

5. Tobin Siebers (1992: 115) notes that some people view duty "as an opiate, a blindness, a rationalization, capable of condoning tyranny and conformity to violence. It is not a concept of respect for society but its nemesis. Rigid laws, totalizing views of conduct—these are the tools of fascism and the enemies of the modern ethical project." In light of the Priebke case, do you agree with this view?

1.3.2 Honor

As mentioned earlier, a sense of *honor is the emphatic sense that a moral person is one who does or does not engage in certain types of acts; that an individual's identity is bound up with this conduct, which is becoming of certain roles and status, and that it is beneath one to engage in anything less or contrary to it.* As Cicero says, "Is there anything of such great value or any advantage so much worth winning that you are willing to lose the glory and reputation of being a 'good man'? What can your so-called advantageousness bring you of value equal to what it can remove if it whisks away your reputation as an 'honest man' and takes away your trustworthiness and justice?" (*De officiis* 158). Honor plays to a strong sense of dignity and worth, based on who people are and what they do. A strong sense of honor stresses not only how people feel about themselves, but about how they want others to perceive them and the sorts of behavioral expectations they would demand from others in that regard. For example, they may feel they have a duty to be honest with others, and so they refrain generally from lying. On the other hand, they pride themselves on being honest, and they certainly do not want others to perceive them as liars. That is why generally they tell the truth, but also because they are the sort of people who do not lie, and questioning a person's honesty is an insult to his sense of honor and dignity. To be treated badly by others, despite who people are and what they have done, is great disrespect; to fail at one's duties with respect to that role is to bring dishonor. Whereas duties specify what people are to do for others, given their role, an honor code has to do more with status within their position and role and how others should treat them in that regard. In other words, they act honorably because they have a certain sense of self which others should also have.

Whereas duty is probably more connected to guilt, honor is more closely associated with the feeling of shame. Indeed, Aristotle defines shame precisely as the "fear of dishonor" (*Nic. Ethics* 1128b10). James Wilson, author of *The Moral Sense*, claims that when the family is the primary source of social approval and ridicule is used to control misconduct, the fear of being shamed leads to a strong sense of honor (1993: 154). Honor, then, is more associated with a sense of group or community, an attempt to achieve a certain recognition from others. For this reason, honor codes are very effective in keeping individual behavior in conformity with a group's standards. Honor codes are often developed with the context of a sense of solidarity with the group, for example, honor codes among military units. As a result, it is expressed more in those cultures which value community over the individual (Doi 1977: 58). Honor

---

Death before Dishonor?

In May 1996, Admiral Jeremy Boorda, Chief of Naval Operations, committed suicide. The act occurred after he was told that there were press inquiries concerning his decorations. The accusation was that Boorda wore combat ribbons which were not earned on the battlefield. The claim was made by Colonel David Hackworth, a *Newsweek* columnist and himself a highly decorated and well-respected combat veteran. Hackworth argued that the very bedrock of any military organization was honor. Combat ribbons are the ultimate status symbol to soldiers. They bring a special recognition and respect. Consequently, it would be disgraceful to wear unearned valor awards—especially by a high-ranking officer. Some argued that Admiral Boorda had committed suicide precisely to avoid such disgrace, to avoid inquiries by the press that would not only bring shame to his office, but—as Chief of Naval Operations—to the Navy itself, especially after the Tailhook scandal and other incidents had tarnished its reputation.

Questions for Discussion

1. Do you think Colonel Hackworth had a duty to investigate Admiral Boorda?
2. Is there a point at which doing one's duty can cause greater harm than it's worth? Or do you think that one should do one's duty regardless of the consequences to oneself or others?
3. Is one's honor worth one's life? Certainly, many have felt so strongly that they chose to die rather than to be dishonored. What do you think? Do you agree with the motto, "death before dishonor"?

Bushido, or the Way of the Samurai

Bushido is the honor code by which the samurai lived. The samurai flourished for nearly 800 years in Japan from the late 10th century to the middle of the 19th century. In *Hagakure: The Book of the Samurai* Tsuentomo Yamamoto explains that the Way of the Samurai is found in death. If by setting one's heart right every morning and evening one is able to live as though his body were already dead, he gains freedom in the Way. His whole life will be without blame, and he will succeed in his calling. To continue to live without success in this calling is to live a cowardly life; to die without success in the calling is to die the death of a dog. The samurai is guided, above all, by loyalty to his master. He perfects three virtues: wisdom, courage, and humanity.

codes are an important part of most military units because using an individual's sense of honor and the desired recognition from her comrades is a means of ensuring the individual's conformity to certain kinds of conduct. Often, then, duty and honor become correlative and complementary in certain groups. Creating a strong sense of honor among individual members of a group is a way of ensuring they do their duties in regard to their roles or positions in the group. James Wilson gives an excellent example of how these two sentiments can work in conjunction (1993: 110ff.).

In *A Vietnam Experience* Admiral James Stockdale relates his 8 years of suffering as a prisoner of war in North Vietnam (1984). Stockdale and his fellow prisoners were routinely tortured for military information and political concessions. The method used was called "the ropes," a process in which a prisoner's arms were pulled up behind his back while his head was forced down toward the floor. The pain is excruciating, a compound of slow suffocation because the lungs are no longer able to expand, dislocation of the shoulder joints as the arms were pulled in an unnatural direction, and constriction of the blood supply to the extremities. Stockdale endured the ropes fourteen times and signed many documents, as did other prisoners, but only after enduring unbearable torture. Several prisoners died as a result of the torture.

What made these soldiers endure, even if they knew they would eventually give in? In analyzing Stockdale's reflections, Wilson argues that it was a strong sense of duty and honor among the prisoners which kept them from easy capitulation. Through secret communication (the captors kept each prisoner isolated from the others), a well-defined sense of one's duty as a soldier in this situation was clearly circulated: One should not capitulate without first enduring significant torture. In other words, one's duty to one's country dictated this sort of behavior. This duty was reinforced by a strong honor code, which was upheld strictly by peer observation and communication: do not bow to your captors in public; make no broadcasts on behalf of the enemy; admit no crimes in your confessions; if you are ever rescued, don't kiss the captors good-bye. This code pertains to the dignity and worth of the prisoners as soldiers, rather than their particular duties as prisoners of war. Soldiers with a certain amount of dignity simply do not do these kinds of things, even given their extreme circumstances. By group reinforcement of

Family Honor?

UNICEF and Amnesty International report the practice among some conservative Muslims of "honor killings" in Pakistan (approx. 1000 in 1999), Yemen (approx. 400 in 1997), Egypt (52 in 1997), Lebanon (36 between 1995–1998), Jordan (approx. 25/year), West Bank and Gaza Strip (two-thirds of all homicides in 1999). These are killings of family members (mostly women) by family members (mostly men), when the female family member is thought to have violated strict Muslim laws concerning contact with other men. The honor of the family is thought to be preserved by killing the alleged violator.

Questions for Discussion

1. How are appeals to honor always appeals to what is right?
2. How is sexism revealed in these honor killings? Why is the woman's sexual activity such a focus of honor?

this dignity, the duty to resist torture is reinforced, so the sense of duty and honor complement each other in this case. Wilson concludes, "a tiny and remote chance that one would be honored intangibly by one's comrades was more valuable than a high and immediate chance that one would be rewarded materially by one's enemies" (Wilson 1993: 113). Fear of punishment can be overcome more easily if guilt and shame are assuaged; if doing your duty means endangerment, the sense of duty and honor can motivate you to fulfill it. Having a sense of honor means that you value highly a certain public or outward image of yourself that is genuinely deserved (as opposed to hypocritical behaviors). Such an image motivates you to continue to do those things that will accord with it, and a fear of losing that image (of "losing face") motivates you to avoid doing those things that would diminish or destroy it. For this reason, those with a strong sense of honor have a keen sensitivity to insults or slights by others (De Vos 1973).

1.3.3 Caring

Moral sentiment can also be expressed primarily in terms of compassion and sympathy. Philosopher Richard Taylor defines it as "goodness of heart, tenderness towards things that can suffer, and loving kindness. ..." (1970: 26). David Hume (1739), Jean-Jacques Rousseau (1755), Adam Smith (1759), and Arthur Schopenhauer (1841: 170) are among some of the classical thinkers who believe that the development of sympathy is the primary means by which we acquire moral sentiment. Schopenhauer was so confident of this claim that he believed "boundless compassion for all living beings is the firmest and surest guarantee of pure moral conduct" (1841: 172). This view is currently championed and eloquently interpreted by feminist thinkers, including Carol Gilligan (1982), Nel Noddings (1984), Annette Baier (1985), and Rita Manning (1992).

Raoul Wallenberg (1912–?) was a Christian Swedish diplomat who risked his life to help thousands of Jews escape from Hungary and thus avoid being murdered by the Nazis. After the war he was captured by the Soviets and is presumed to have died in their custody.

According to feminist theory, a caring life is not preoccupied with rights, duties, obligations, and honor, but with a strong sense of attachment to others and the world in the broadest sense of the term. As Carol Gilligan puts it, the problem is "not how to exercise one's rights without interfering with the rights of others," but how to lead a moral life of commitment and concern for others (1982: 21). Commitment, obligation, and responsibility to others are defined in terms of an understanding of the needs of others, a responsiveness to those needs, and preventing harm from happening to others. In caring there is an emphasis on loving attachments, on preserving and strengthening existing relationships while extending others, and within the context of those relationships, there is a deep concern to reduce

Mother Teresa, who died in 1997, is viewed by many as a contemporary exemplar of the caring person. An Indian Catholic nun, she founded The Missionaries of Charity in 1948, an order devoted specifically to the care of the poor and sick, and she devoted her life to tending to their needs. She received a Nobel Peace prize in 1979 for her contributions to the welfare of others. John Sannes of the Nobel committee said, "The loneliest and the most wretched, the dying destitute, the abandoned lepers have been received by her and her sisters with warm compassion devoid of condescension." In her acceptance speech she dedicated the prize to the poor and infirm she served.

She purposefully worked in Calcutta among the "poorest of the poor." Over the years she founded more than 500 charities in 120 countries, including AIDS hospices, soup kitchens, homes for unwed teen mothers, and orphanages. Despite the fame and honors, she managed to avoid their trappings, and she remained devoted to the goals of her work until her death.

Doctors Without Borders is an organization devoted to helping the sick and injured regardless of political affiliation or consideration. Dr. Lael Conway knew ever since she attended medical school that she wanted to volunteer for the organization. Her tenure was in Sri Lanka, which is presently in the midst of a civil war between Tamil rebels and the government. Her day typically consisted in first finding out from the army whether travel to a certain region was safe; next setting up a makeshift medical camp by a tree or building; then treating as many as 125 patients in a day for a variety of ailments; and finally, spending the night close to a bunker in case of rebel attack (*Anchorage Daily News*, May 12, 1997).

the suffering of others, to want them to do well. In caring one is more open to emotions and feelings, especially the feeling of sympathy; indeed, as Annette Baier emphasizes, sympathy is one of the primary moral guides and the source of moral responsiveness (1985: 210ff.). In general, caring can be defined as *a moral sentiment that derives commitments and a sense of obligation through emotional, sympathetic, and relational connection with others.* Nel Noddings argues that "there can be no ethical sentiment without [this] initial, enabling sentiment" (1984: 79) and goes so far as to claim that "the caring attitude that lies at the heart of all ethical behavior is universal" (1984: 92).

According to Noddings, a sense of obligation arises in the caring attitude not from a sense of duty, but from the overall effects of caring and being cared for (1984: 79). The "I must" in obligation is not created *de novo* or out of respect for some inchoate moral law—as in Kant—but simply by the results of being cared for. In caring we accept the impulse to act on behalf of another, even if we may not be particularly inclined, and partly because we cherish our connectedness to others. "The source of obligation [to others]," Nodding says, "is the value I place on the relations of caring" (1984: 84).

Can Ordinary People Lose Their Sense of Sympathy and Compassion?

In his recent, controversial book, *Hitler's Willing Executioners: Ordinary Germans and the Holocaust* (1996), Daniel Goldhagen claimed that, as opposed to a view which suggested the Holocaust was perpetrated without the cooperation or even knowledge of ordinary German citizens, in fact many ordinary citizens were willing participants in such efforts. For every stormtrooper bounded by a personal oath of loyalty to Adolf Hitler, there was, he claims, a squad of common soldiers and policemen doing the everyday work of the Holocaust. Goldhagen focuses on Police Battalion 101, a group of men drawn from ordinary German citizens who had no special status within the Nazi party and who were given special assignments in regard to the massacre or imprisonment of Jews. These men "failed to avail themselves of opportunities to avoid the killing" and in fact "incessantly volunteered" for such duties. Goldhagen, whose parents survived the concentration camps, describes one particularly brutal scene that took place in Meidzyczec, Poland, on May 26, 1943: Jewish men, women, and children, forced to squat for hours, were kicked and mocked; a game was played in which "whoever was hit by a bottle in the head would be dragged out and beaten amid roaring laughter." The book has created great controversy in Germany and elsewhere; for a critical review of the book, which disputes much of Goldhagen's evidence and claims, see Norman Finkelstein and Ruth Birn, *A Nation on Trial* (1998).

The caring attitude is expressed well by one of the many women Carol Gilligan interviewed in *In a Different Voice*. Diane, a woman in her late twenties, defines her sense of morality in the following way:

Some sense of trying to uncover a right path in which to live. ... It is part of a self-critical view, part of saying, "How am I spending my time and in what sense am I working?" I think I have a real drive, a real maternal drive, to take care of someone—to take care of my mother, to take care of children, to take care of other people's children, to take care of my own children, to take care of the world. When I am dealing with moral issues, I am sort of saying to myself constantly, "Are you taking care of all the things that you think are important, and in what ways are you wasting yourself and wasting those issues?" (1982: 99).

(For more on feminist ethics, See Sections 1.4.1, 1.4.2, 1.6, 5.2.5, and 5.2.6.)

1.3.4 Nobility

In the famous last scene of *Casablanca* (1942), the American expatriot Rick, played by Humphrey Bogart, has a tough decision to make. He has in his possession two transport papers, which would allow two people to exit Nazi-controlled Casablanca, Morocco, and escape to freedom. He could give these to Victor Laszlo, who is an important figure in the French resistance, and his wife, Ilse. The difficulty is that he is in love with Victor Laszlo's wife, with whom he had a deep romantic involvement while it was thought that Victor had died in a Nazi concentration camp. Rick and Ilse planned to escape France together as it was being occupied by the Nazis at that time, but when Ilse discovered that Victor was still alive, she returned to him immediately. But now they all find themselves together in Casablanca. What makes Rick's decision more complicated is that Ilse had just expressed her love for Rick the night before, and she is torn between her husband and her former lover. So Rick could also keep the letters of transport for himself and Ilse, and the two could escape out of the clutches of the Nazis, leaving Victor behind. He could also simply send Victor out alone and persuade Ilse to stay behind with him. In coming to his decision, he tells Ilse in a now famous line, "I'm not good at being noble, but in this crazy world, the lives of three people don't amount to a hill of beans." His decision is to give the letters of transport to Ilse and Victor, to convince Victor that Ilse no longer loves him (Rick), and to persuade Ilse that Victor needs her to continue his struggle against the Nazis. So perhaps Rick is good at being noble after all.

The sentiment of *nobility can be defined as a desire for moral excellence that often lets one set aside personal interests in favor of some purpose or cause larger than self.* Nobility involves admiration of what is fine and excellent in others and a desire to strive for what is best in us. The noble person is one who admires goodness and greatness and has a loathing for injustice and immorality. Aristotle writes that in progress toward the genuine good life, "there must first be a character that somehow has an affinity for excellence or virtue, a character that loves what is noble and feels disgust at what is base" (*Nic. Ethics* 1179b29–30). Cicero describes the noble person in the following way:

> a genuine, wise nobility of character decides that the moral excellence that nature requires above all consists of accomplishments, not of reputation; a man of such character prefers to be a true leader, not an apparent one. ... One trait is contempt for external circumstances, when one is convinced that men ought to respect, to desire, and to pursue only what is moral and right; that men should be subject to nothing, not to another man, not to some disturbing passion, not to Fortune. The second trait ... is to perform the kind of services that are significant and most beneficial (*De officiis*, 32).

Cicero argues here that the noble person is someone who is singular in her pursuit of the what is right and not discouraged by what is in the way of that goal, but also—and importantly—is devoted to something significant and beneficial and more vital than self-interest. The Chinese philosopher Mencius (321–289 B.C.E.) makes a similar claim. The noble person (*junzi*) is someone who pursues that which is right (*yi*), in contrast to ordinary persons, who are small-minded and pursue profit and self-interest (*li*) (cf. Goldman 1995: 331). Confucius argues that the noble person "takes as much trouble to discover what is right as lesser men take to discover what will pay" (*Analects* IV.16). The noble act, like Rick's, is something that allies itself with something greater or grander than the person's individual interests. Often those whom we historically consider noble, for example, recent figures such as Martin Luther King and Nelson Mandela, are bound up with

Confucius (551-479 B.C.E.). Considered to be the greatest of the Chinese philosophers, his most important work is *The Analects*.

Presidential Medal of Freedom Recipients

Often we look for heroes in our lives, people whose actions and character we can admire. In 1996 The Presidential Medal of Freedom went to the following people:

- Cardinal Joseph Bernadin of Chicago for fighting against social injustice and poverty.
- James Brady for his leadership in the fight for gun control.
- Rosa Parks for work on human-rights issues.
- Morris Udall for leading the way on landmark environmental legislation.
- Millard Fuller, who founded Habitat for Humanity, which has built more than 50,000 homes for poor families.
- David Alan Hamburg, president of the Carnegie Foundation, who has lobbied for family legislation.
- John Johnson, who founded *Ebony* and *Jet* magazines, for building self-respect among African-Americans.
- Eugene Lang, who adopted a sixth-grade class and paid the tuition of anyone who went to college and created the I Have a Dream Foundation.
- Jan Nowak-Jezioranski, who risked his life as a member of the Polish underground during World War II.
- Antonia Pantoja, who has devoted her life to promoting community development.
- Ginetta Sagan, a member of the World War II Italian resistance, who has fought rights abuses worldwide.

---

important causes and have overcome tremendous odds or obstacles to see them prevail. They are willing to endure personal costs for what they believe right—for Mandela it was years of imprisonment and for King it was his life.

One significant feature of noble persons, according to Confucius and Mencius, is a desire to perfect themselves morally (cf. Goldman 1995) and, as a result, a desire to emulate what is best in others and promote what is excellent in oneself. As Confucius said: "When you see the wise, think of equaling him: when you see the unwise, examine yourself" (*Analects* 4.17). And also: "When on my way I meet three men, there must be at least one from whom I can learn something: he who is a good example I shall follow; the bad example will make me rectify myself" (*Analects* 7.22). *The Great Learning* (Confucius, 6-7) regards the cultivation of the personal life extremely important. Mencius uses an analogy with the body to describe the noble person's process in this regard—we can determine whether a person is nourishing their body properly by seeing "the choice he makes for himself. Now, some parts of the body are noble and some are ignoble; some great and some small. We must not allow the ignoble to injure the noble, or the smaller to injure the greater. Those who nourish the smaller parts will become small men. Those who nourish the greater parts will become great men" (*Book of Mencius* 6A.14).

A second feature of noble persons is that, precisely because they have a strong desire for moral perfection, they often serve as models or exemplars. Confucius seemed to think that only a few could achieve this moral perfection (*Analects* 8.9), but those few would naturally prove to be worthy of emulation and leadership (*Analects* 4.25). Confucius also points out that the noble have an effect on others that emanates out in wider and wider circles, first fostering a good family life, and then social harmony, good government, and peace in the largest circle. The noble person is immanently admirable and so obviously imitable. Thus, just as guilt is associated with duty, shame with honor, and sympathy with caring, admiration is tied to the notion of nobility.

Friedrich Nietzsche, the 19th-century German thinker, is also a philosopher deeply concerned with the notion of nobility. Although his concepts are similar to those of Cicero, Mencius, and Confucius in some respects, there are important differences and a different tenor to his analyses. Like Confucius, he does believe that the noble are few, and precisely because of their nobility they become natural leaders. But the relation between the noble and the less noble is differently articulated in Nietzsche. The noble people for Confucius and Mencius are those who aim at a good that is somehow not only greater than themselves, but exists in some objective form to be grasped and understood. Ordinary people can share in this good to the degree possible for them, but importantly, it is the noble person who shows them the way. The noble person brings good to the common person and to the human condition precisely by being noble. For Nietzsche, on the other hand, what is good is determined by the noble person: "the noble type of man feels *himself* to be the determiner of values ... he creates values" (1886: Sect. 260). "The noble soul has reverence for itself" (1886: Sect. 287). To this extent, the noble one despises the cowardly, the timid, the petty, and those who think narrowly in terms of utility: "the dog-like type of man who lets himself be mistreated, the fawning flatterer, above all the liar. ... " (1886: Sect. 260). But second, the relation between the noble person and the common one is not—as in Confucius and Mencius—between benefactor and beneficiary but, for Nietzsche it is one of means and end, master and slave. The purpose of the common man is to serve the noble ones precisely because the noble ones retain the highest values; it is the highest values that are served in serving noble persons. The noble ones feel they are the meaning and "supreme justification" for others. Therefore, they accept "with a good conscience the sacrifice of innumerable men who *for its sake* are to be suppressed and reduced to imperfect men, to slaves and instruments" (1886: Sect. 258) (For more on Nietzsche, see Sections 2.7 and 5.3.1.)

Thus, although both concepts of nobility involve ranking and a claim of superiority, Nietzsche infers a master–slave dynamic from this account, which allows him to view the noble person as the embodiment of the highest values and the less noble as instruments to the realization of those values. On the other hand, Confucius and Mencius—perhaps paradoxically—imply a servant dynamic for noble persons. Even though they should be considered superior to others in the aspect of morality, they are first servants to some good greater than themselves which they should serve; second, they are the instruments by which the good is realized for others and for the community of which they are a part.

Those motivated by this sentiment are often driven by a desire toward excellence, an inclination to perfect themselves in the performance of whatever role is required of them and to actualize what they can be. Unlike a sense of duty, in which one performs those duties out of a desire to benefit or avoid harm to others, this sentiment stresses the excellence of the performance, which then ideally benefits others. Unlike a sense of honor, which stresses recognition and dignity, this sentiment internally drives one outward toward actions, causes, or purposes that the person believes are larger or more significant than personal honor and recognition. As a result, persons with a sense of nobility may be egoless or selfless precisely because they are more interested in the cause than the honor. Unlike the sentiment of caring, a sense of nobility is not always motivated by a caring relation with the beneficiaries, but it is bound up with a more objective sense of the good that the actions or visions achieve.

An Illustration of the Four Sentiments:
Why Did Men Fight in the Civil War?

General John Wickham commanded the 101st Airborne Division in the 1970s and subsequently became chief of staff. On one occasion he visited the Antietam Civil War battlefield in Maryland. He gazed out at Bloody Lane, the scene of one of the worst parts of the day-long battle—a battle that cost more American lives than any other day in the entire Civil War. He looked in amazement as he recounted the several assaults that federal troops had to make over relatively open ground before they were successful in dislodging Confederate forces from their position. Incredulous as to what those soldiers did, he said, "You couldn't get American soldiers today to make an attack like that" (McPherson 1997: 5).

In his book on the Civil War, *For Cause and Comrades: Why Men Fought in the Civil War*, James McPherson (1997) tries to address Wickham's puzzle and answer why so many men voluntarily fought in a war that was so brutal and required so many sacrifices. "What possessed these men? How could they sacrifice themselves in that way?"(1997: 4). He found a number of letters sent by soldiers from both sides of the conflict to their family and friends, explaining their motives for participating in that awful, bloody war. What he discovered was a number of motives, some of which were based on a sense of duty, others on honor, the occasional call for glory, and some who did it and continued to fight out of a love and care for their comrades.

A common motivation was duty. McPherson claims that the phrase, "I went from a sense of duty," was frequently used in the letters (1997: 22). One young soldier from Massachusetts writes, "I am going ... [as a] duty which everyone ought to perform—love of country" (1997: 17); another echoes the same sentiment, "It is every one's duty to enlist, if he possibly can" (1997: 22). An 11th Michigan recruit writes to his fiancée: "No Jenny ... while your happiness is as dear to me as life, duty prompts me to go" (1997: 22).

Honor was also often cited as a reason for enlisting or fighting and went hand-in-hand with duty. John DeForest, a veteran and novelist, wrote: "The man who does not dread to die or to be mutilated is a lunatic. The man who, dreading these things, still faces them for the sake of duty and honor is a hero" (McPherson 1997: 5). A 42-year-old Confederate planter writes, "No man now has a right to stay at home, duty, patriotism and aye, honor, calls him to the field" (1997: 24). A sergeant in the 24th Mississippi writes to his wife: "Life is sweet but I always prefer an honorable death to a disgraceful and shameful life" (1997: 23). McPherson says that many

soldiers lacked confidence in their courage, but most of them wanted to avoid the shame of being known as a coward—and that is what gave them courage (1997: 77). One soldier writes that "I'd rather be shot by a comrade than have any disgrace attach to my family" (1997: 78); another says, "I would sooner lose my life than have my children ashamed of their Father" (1997: 24). In a letter to his father in 1864, a Union soldier writes: "A soldier has but one thing in view, and that is two [sic] fight the Battles of his country with oner [honor]. ... " (1997: 6).

But besides duty and honor, others looked to the supposed glory of war and nobility of the cause, as a motive for enlisting and fighting. According to Bell Wily, "the dominant urge of many volunteers was the desire for adventure ... the glory and excitement of battle" (1997: 26). A Pennsylvania cavalry recruit writes, "How often in boyhood's young days when reading the accounts of soldiers' loves have I longed to be a man, and now the opportunity has offered" (1997: 27). A South Carolina planter writes, "I am blessing old Sir Walter Scott [author of *Ivanhoe* and other romances] daily for teaching me when young how to rate knightly honor and our noble ancestry for giving me such a State to fight for" (1997: 27).

Another common motivation for fighting was care and love for one's comrades. Joshua Chamberlain, hero of Gettysburg and Medal of Honor winner, argued that love or camaraderie was a common motive in this regard: "Here is Bill, I will go or stay when he does" (1997: 6). In general, McPherson says, "Men are fighting for each other" (1997: 86). "We feel like the kindest of brothers together," a 10th Virginia cavalry soldier writes. "We love each other like a band of brothers," another writes. We all "seem almost like brothers. We have suffered hardship and dangers together and are bound together by more than ordinary ties" (1997: 86). "A soldier is always nearly crazy to get away from the army on furloughs," another soldier writes, "but as a general thing they are more anxious to get back. There is a feeling of love—a strong attachment for those with whom one has shared common dangers, that is never felt for anyone else, or under any other circumstances" (1997: 87).

Questions for Discussion

1. Do you identify with any of these motivations? Which one of these motivations, if any, is most likely to cause great self-sacrifice in you?
2. Do you see any danger in moral sentiment? Could moral sentiment cause people to do great harm or to incur unnecessary sacrifice?

1.4 THE DEVELOPMENT OF MORAL SENTIMENT

Moral sentiment is critical to the development of moral competence. Vicious and pathological persons clearly live without it, and although moral sentiment alone is not a guarantee of moral competence by any means, without it moral competence is impossible. Clearly, the best opportunity to acquire moral sentiment is in the ordinary process of childhood. Since a child develops within the family, among other institutions, this makes the family the center of the development of moral sentiment in the child.

Perhaps it is safe to say that a more robust moral life begins with an opportunity to develop a variety of moral sentiments. Since many of the moral sentiments complement one another, providing a child with the means of developing all of them would be most helpful.

1.4.1 Rawls's Three Laws of Moral Psychology

David Hume believed that sympathy develops out of the experience of being loved and cared for primarily in the context of the family. This seems to be borne out by psychological studies (Stroufe 1983: 63) and is echoed by other philosophers such as John Rawls (1971: 490ff). Being loved creates in us a desire to love which, in the arena of public life, gets attenuated into the form of general desire to act benevolently toward others. Because one is genuinely distressed by the suffering of others, there is a motivation to act in such a way toward others that not only prevents harm, but often seeks to remove and remedy harm done to others. John Rawls articulates this process in terms of three "laws" of moral psychology (1971: 490–491):

> *First law:* given that family institutions are just, and that the parents love the child and manifestly express their love by caring for his good, then the child, recognizing their evident love of him, comes to love them.
>
> *Second law:* given that a person's capacity for fellow feeling has been realized by acquiring attachments in accordance with the first law, and given that a social arrangement is just and publicly known by all to be just, then this person develops ties of friendly feeling and trust toward others in the association as they with evident intention comply with their duties and obligations, and live up to the ideals of their station.
>
> *Third law:* given that a person's capacity for fellow feeling has been realized by his forming attachments in accordance with the first two laws, and given that a society's institutions are just and are publicly known by all to be just, then this person acquires the corresponding sense of justice as he recognizes that he and those for whom he cares are the beneficiaries of these arrangements.

1.4.2 The Development of Trust and Its Importance

Feminist philosophers also stress the importance of trust in moral development. Annette Baier argues that sympathy, care, and love within the family generate a certain level of "appropriate trust" (1985: 56), a feeling that is absolutely crucial to cooperative and communal practices. Baier claims, indeed, that morality can only thrive with some form of trust. The work of psychologist Erik Erikson (1991) confirms these claims as well; constant, reliable care promotes the baby's sense of trust, which is one of the first stages of psychosocial development in the child. The work of Robert Putnam (2000) has also clearly shown the importance of trust for the health and well-being of communities.

Trust is confidence in the good will of others (Baier 1986: 235); it is a willingness to place what one values in the possession or power of another (Baier 1986: 235), and may be generally defined in those terms: *an implicit or explicit confidence that others intend no harm and can be counted on to work toward the good of those things held in common.* Trust is necessary for any cooperative arrangement and the generalized reciprocity needed to make societies work well (Putnam 2000: 135). "It seems fairly obvious that any form of cooperative activity, including the division of labor, requires the cooperators to trust one another to do their bit. ..." (Baier 1986: 235). Societies that rely heavily on the use of force are likely to be less efficient, more costly, and more unpleasant than those where trust is maintained by other means (Gambetta 1988: 221; cf. Putnam 2000: 136). Several economists have argued that trusting communities, other things being equal, have a significant economic advantage (Fukuyama 1995; La Porta et al. 1997; Knack and Keefer 1997; cf. Putnam 2000: 135). Life expectancy appears to be enhanced in more trustful communities (Kawachi et al. 1997). Low levels of trust and cohesion in neighborhoods feed into the crime rate in those areas; neighborhoods with relatively high levels of trust are more successful at programs that aim to reduce the crime rate (Putnam 2000: 317). Trust is necessary for developing friendships and other intimate relationships, and it marks the special relationship between parent and child. Trust is the basis of nearly all professional relationships: between doctor and patient, teacher and student, customer and proprietor.

Annette Baier is a contemporary feminist philosopher. Her most important ethical works are *Postures of the Mind* and *The Progress of Sentiment*. She argues in these books that what feminist theory in ethics has shown is a wider appreciation of the role of moral sentiments and feelings in ethical actions and judgments. On the other hand, those theories which promote reason, rules, and principles as the basis of moral judgment and decision making force decision makers into a certain framework that disallows compromise and a genuine connection with others. (See also Sections 1.6 and 5.8.)

Most people operate at two levels of trust—what Robert Putnam calls *thick* and *thin* trust (2000: 136). Thin trust has a long radius and involves those who are at a greater social distance from the truster; thick trust has a short radius, encompassing those who are socially close to the truster (Putnam 2000: 466 n. 12). Thin trust can be viewed as one which gives most people the benefit of the doubt—even those whom one does not know directly (Rahn and Transue 1998: 545). Those who engage in a certain level of thin trust are more likely to participate in politics and community organizations, contribute more to charity, serve more willingly on juries, give blood, comply with their tax obligations, be more tolerant of minority views, and display many other forms of civic virtue (Putnam 2000: 137). Those who view others as honest and trustworthy are also more likely to be honest and trustworthy so that one mutually reinforces the other (Brehm and Rahn 1997). Conversely, those who are not civically engaged believe they are surrounded by dishonesty and feel less reason to be honest themselves (Putnam 2000: 137). Those who are at the lower end of the socioeconomic scale of a society trust less than those in the middle and upper end. Those who suffer racism trust less than whites, people in urban centers trust less than small-town populations, and those who are victims of crimes feel less trusting (Putnam 2000: 138). Political and social trust also ought to be distinguished. It is quite possible for people to trust other people, yet not to trust institutions or political authorities (Putnam 2000: 137). It is also quite possible for people to have very little thin trust, yet substantial thick trust, so that they form strong bonds with family and friends but otherwise remain civically disengaged. Yet, although thick and thin trust are essential for both collective cooperation and intimate relations, it is a fragile relation: It is much easier to maintain than it is to get started, and it is never hard to destroy (Baier 1986: 241).

As Annette Baier claims, we count on all sorts of people for all sorts of things without contract or promises. "Trust in people to do their job conscientiously and not to take the opportunity to do us harm once we put things we value into their hands are different from trust in people to keep their promises, [this is] in part because of the very indefiniteness of what we are counting on them to do or not to do" (Baier 1986: 249). Trust involves the trust in a person's judgment, a person's intentions and good will, and serves as a background to specific contracts, promises, and obligations. For example, in promise keeping, trust allows not only a judgment about when promises should be kept, but also allows the possibility that one would forgo the promise should great harm befall those involved in the contract. I might promise to drive you to the store, but because my car has suddenly become unsafe, I can be trusted to inform you of that and suggest that you find someone else to give you a ride. Without this background of trust, promises and contracts become merely mechanical rule following. Promise making involves trust, as Hume suggests: "To perform promises is requisite to beget trust and confidence in the common offices of life" (1978: 544). Promises employ both honesty and trust in a complementary way. On the one hand, the making of a promise requires that one intends to keep to the bargain; on the other, we must trust that they will do as they say. A promise makes explicit just what we count on another person to do and so defines the parameters of the trust involved (Baier 1986: 249).

Certainly, there are people who are not worthy of trust, but distrustful people are those who fear, excessively, that others may not keep their end of the bargain or intend to harm them in some way. Often such a belief leads to self-fulfilling sabotage of cooperative arrangements simply because other people easily sense such a feeling. On the other hand, naively trusting in others allows one to often be taken advantage of. As Robert Putnam writes, "generalized reciprocity is a community asset, but generalized gullibility is not. Trustworthiness, not simply trust, is the key ingredient" (2000: 136). Trusting is rational when there is no reason to suspect the trusted person's motives or when there is a strong belief that the trusted and trusting person share a caring value for the same thing (Baier 1986: 253). Baier, in fact, proposes a test for the moral decency of a trust relationship. If the continuation of the trust relies on successful threats held over the trusted or on successful cover-up of breaches of trust, then the trust relationship is morally bad. Put differently, if the psychological means by which trust is established between parties, when made explicit, causes distrust, then the trust relationship is immoral. Thus, if it becomes clear to me that you trust me because you are relying on my fear of whatever revenge you will impose on me by breaking that trust, then that may be enough for me to distrust you. However, if it becomes clear to me that you trust me because you believe that I share with you the same goals and values concerning the thing entrusted, then that would be sufficient to reinforce the trust. We can certainly distrust our known enemies, but it is those who engage in deceit, dishonesty, and cunning who are problematic. As Kant notes, we can have either an honest or a treacherous enemy. "We can defend ourselves against the former, but not against the latter. Deceit and cunning destroy all confidence, but open hostility does not. He who openly declares himself an enemy can be relied upon, but the treachery of secret malice, would mean the end of all confidence" (1775–1780: 215). Treachery employs the semblance of trust to destroy or harm another. What makes Iago so despicable is that he uses the implicit trust of his (feigned) friendship with Othello to ruin Othello's and Desdemona's lives. (See also Section 3.5.3.)

1.4.3 The Importance of Parenting Style in Moral Development

Parenting is important to moral development not only because parents may convey a certain moral code to their children but also because of the emotional attune-ment that proper parent–child relations establish. As Daniel Goleman notes, this emotional attunement between parent and child lets the child feel a sense that other people care and share in his feelings. "Prolonged absence of attunement between parent and child takes a tremendous emotional toll on the child. When a parent consistently fails to show empathy with a child—the child avoids expressing, and perhaps feeling the emotion" (1995: 101). Without this opportunity for emo-tional connection, a person can acquire a strong propensity for cruel and violent behavior toward others (cf. Goleman 1995: 102 n 10). Those children who develop a strong capacity for empathy and sympathy are more emotionally adjusted, more popular, more outgoing, and more sensitive than those with a weak capacity (cf. Rosenthal et al. 1977; Bowlby 1988). These traits, of course, contribute to success in life (Park and Waters 1989).

Besides building a capacity for empathy and sympathy, strong attachments between parent and child also help a child develop a sense of duty according to James Wilson (cf. 1993: 103ff.). Boys are more likely to acquire strong moral stan-dards when they have a loving and nurturing, rather than a threatening or fear-inspiring, father (Ainslie 1992: 214–215; Aronfreed 1968: 308–309). The Oliner's study of Christian rescuers of Jews during the Nazi period showed that many of the rescuers, as opposed to bystanders, were very close to their parents. One rescuer, Suzanne, described her family as emotionally "very close," as did another rescuer, Louisa. Both women recalled growing up in families that combined love with an emphasis on accepting personal responsibility and taking one's obligations serious-ly. This was not a case of simply pleasing the parent; both women had so internal-ized their sense of duty that neither told their parents what they intended to do until they had begun, and in fact they ignored their mothers' urging not to take such risks (Oliner and Oliner 1988: 214, 217, 219–220). Studies have shown that many campus radicals and civil rights leaders during the 1960s were not so much rebelling against their parents, but were taking parental values seriously, behaving in a way that was consistent, although somewhat more extreme than their parents (Flack 1967; Braungart 1972). This was confirmed by a study of university students in 1970 in which Otto Klineberg noted that "many students express a feeling of closeness to their parents rather than conflict" (1979: 276).

If attachment, attunement, and closeness are essential for internalization of norms, the acquisition of moral sentiment naturally leads to the question of the best parenting style in this regard. Psychologists have identified three basic types of parenting style: permissive, authoritative, and authoritarian (Baumrind 1980; 1991). *Permissive* parents set few rules and rarely punish misbehavior. The obvious defect in this style of parenting is that without standards, norms, or guidelines, there is nothing for the child to internalize. In addition, a child must not only be shown what are the best rules to follow, but the parent must show enough interest and passion about these rules that their violation causes distress in the parent (cf. Zahn-Waxler et al. 1979). A parent must show the child that the violation of the rules has consequences and that the parent is willing to take the time to carry out discipline for their violation. If a parent is lax about the violation of rules or does not even convey that there are rules to follow, this sends a clear message to the child that basic moral rules have little value, and so their violation is inconsequential.

Authoritarian parenting is the other extreme. In this case the parents set strict rules and rely on physical punishment especially for disciplining. Most justifications for rule following are based on simple command authority, rather than on reasoning or inferences from consequences. Instead of love and attachment as the motivation for rule following, fear and threat of punishment predominate. Such strategies are not very successful at internalization. Children disciplined by severe and unexplained punishment rarely develop an effective sense of guilt or self-regulation; instead, they learn to behave so they will not get caught. Psychologists Bacon, Child, and Barry (1963) did cross-cultural studies which showed a high incidence of theft and lack of guilt among children in societies that use *severe* socialization. Windmiller et al. (1980: 146) suggest that severe discipline doesn't promote internalization because children are conditioned by fear of the parent to behave the way they do; so when the parent is absent, there is no control. When it is out of attachment to the parent, the desire of the child to please the parent becomes generalized, and so the absence of the parent doesn't matter as much.

Another danger in this approach is that severe physical punishment can escalate to child abuse. Not only is there the potential for injury to the child in this case, but child abuse is associated with lasting emotional effects: Abused children have poorer self-esteem and are more socially withdrawn (Kaufman and Cicchetti 1989); they tend to be more aggressive and less empathic toward children in distress (Main and George 1985; Klimes-Dougan and Kistner 1990); and they are more likely to become juvenile delinquents (Bowers 1990). As Daniel Goleman writes:

> These children, of course, treat others as they themselves have been treated. And the callousness of these abused children is simply a more extreme version of that seen in children whose parents are critical, threatening, and harsh in their punishments. Such children also tend to lack concern when playmates get hurt or cry; they seem to represent one end of a continuum of coldness that peaks with the brutality of the abused children. As they go on through life, they are, as a group, more likely to have cognitive difficulties in learning, more likely to be aggressive and unpopular with their peers ... more prone to depression, and, as adults, more likely to get into trouble with the law and commit more crimes of violence (1995: 198).

As opposed to these two extremes of parenting style, *authoritative* parenting seems the most successful in helping children, other things being equal, to flourish both psychologically and morally (cf. Burton et al. 1963; Baumrind 1983). Authoritative parents tend to be warm and loving, yet insist that their children behave appropriately. Some studies show that mild punishment, coupled with a temporary withdrawal of affection, appears to establish guilt and self-regulation much more efficiently than severe physical punishment does (Hoffman 1977). They encourage independence within well-defined limits, show a willingness to explain the reasons for their rules, and permit their children to express verbal disagreement with them. Berkowitz (1998) argues that the single most powerful parental influence on children's moral development is explaining parental behavior and its implications for the child and others; it is linked to greater empathy, more highly developed conscience, higher levels of moral reasoning, and altruism. Studies by Hoffman and Saltzstein (1967) and Aronfreed (1969) suggest that reasoning with children and pointing out the effects of their wrongdoing are just as effective as the temporary withdrawal of love. Verbal explanations and reasoning encourage children to take the role of others, and they help them internalize moral standards by providing thoughts they can associate with their feelings and with any rewards or punishment they receive (Hoffman 1980). The discussion of acceptable behaviors helps children understand and internalize particular standards for behavior (Schulman and Mekler 1985). More democratic approaches to family problems and issues seem to promote moral development in children (Berkowitz 1998). If all stakeholders are given equal power to enter into the discussion and participate in decision making, this leads to morality in two ways: First, decisions and rules are more likely to be just; second, the participation in the process is more likely to stimulate the moral development of the participants (Berkowitz 1998). This has been demonstrated empirically in Kohlberg's *Just Community* school approach (Powers 1982) and seems to work in the family as well. By maintaining a delicate balance between freedom and control, authoritative parents help their children internalize standards of behavior. Generally speaking, children of authoritative parents are less likely to use drugs (Baumrind 1991), are more likely to perform better in school (Steinberg et al. 1992), and show better social adjustment (Durbin et al. 1993).

1.4.4 Art, Literature, and Moral Education

Providing good moral models is thought to be another relatively effective way of establishing moral sentiment in children. However, modeling alone is not sufficient to produce moral sentiment, since the model chosen may not be a moral exemplar. Psychological studies suggest that if a model goes unpunished for transgressions, then children are likely to follow suit; furthermore, if they see a model go unrewarded for moral behavior, they also fail to copy him or her (Staub 1975). If children are exposed mostly to a certain class of models, they may adopt that model, even if most of the population find those models bad examples. Children may form an attachment to models who appear exciting, powerful, and interesting rather than morally good. For example, when asked to name their heroes, most young people will list sports figures or entertainment personalities rather than genuine heroes (Keyes 1995). As Bruno Bettelheim observed, for a child the question "Who do I want to be like?" is more important than "Do I want to be good?" (1977: 10). Children may then be attracted to drug dealers if that is the predominant model in their environment. As the narrator in the film *Goodfellows* says, when he went to see the Cagney gangster films, he always rooted for the bad guy. Indeed, in most of those films, it is the villain who is the most interesting and more daring character, even if his life ends badly.

Plato recognized the power of models, especially the power of literary models, for the young, but he also recognized how easily they can sway people away from an attachment to the good. Plato's particular nemesis was Homer, whose epic poems, *The Iliad* and *The Odyssey*, he believed gave the young the wrong impression about the gods and about the best moral life in general (*Rep.* X 606ff.). Story and poem can serve to set attachments in a certain direction, especially if these are part of the cultural canon. (Of course, in our current culture, children are exposed to more than just stories and poems; there is film, video, TV, advertisements, comic books, and so on to contend with.) In any case, for this reason Plato advocated a highly controlled censorship of what citizens of his ideal state might see, read, or listen to. The goal was to create a literature that reflected only certain sorts of values and promoted certain sorts of character traits (*Rep.* X 605ff.). In other words children and the young must be cultivated and value educated. The desire for the good is generated through the exposure to nobility, goodness, and all things beautiful.

The general Platonic view is championed by a number of contemporary moral educators (Bloom 1987; Bennett 1993; Kilpatrick 1994; Kilpatrick, Wolf, and Wolf 1994; Lickona 1991; Sommers 1993). The argument is that the right sort of literature, the right type of story, can promote not only moral sentiment but also good character, and it can serve as a laboratory for prudence. "Stories can create an emotional attachment to goodness, a desire to do the right thing" (Kilpatrick et al. 1994: 18). "The dramatic nature of stories enables us to 'rehearse' moral decisions, strengthening our solidarity with the good" (Kilpatrick et al. 1994: 24). Stories often provide codes of conduct and good paradigms of people attempting to live by those standards (Kilpatrick et al. 1994: 28).

How do stories generate moral sentiment and promote virtuous character? Moral emotions themselves are evoked in the context of stories. For example, to experience moral outrage, one must witness a drama of opponents in which an undeserving victim and an unjust perpetrator must be identified. In that context sympathy for the victim may also be evoked. Similarly with other moral emotions. To admire someone we must be able to see them do something that we believe, however we believe it, to be excellent, noble, or exceptional. To do that also requires a narrative context. Aristotle was one of the first thinkers to recognize the correlation between stories and moral emotions. The success of a tragedy rested on its ability to evoke sympathy and terror in the audience, which in turn depended primarily on the organization of character and events through a specific form of plot. The character had to be one of high station and neither an exceptionally good person nor a particularly vicious one; the plot had to move from one of complication to reversal of fortune, ending with the suffering of the tragic character (*Poetics* 1452b 30ff.; 1453a; 1453a10). This can be applied to other types of literary genre as well. In a melodrama or romance, as it is traditionally called, the hero stands in conflict with a villainous opponent. Despite setbacks, twists and turns, and a great struggle or combat, the hero usually prevails, the villain is defeated, and justice is restored. In these kinds of stories, our admiration is usually directed toward the hero, and we feel disgust or moral outrage for the villain. A sense of righteousness is ordinarily felt when the villain is defeated and the victim is saved. In this way stories are structured to evoke certain moral emotions in the audience precisely because moral emotions are themselves "little stories." All emotions have a storied character, and all stories have an emotional response. Emotions become the means by which we are drawn into the stories. The ability of make-believe or fiction to create an intense reaction in the audience is well known. It's not unusual to see people cry in the theater, even while they know full well that the story is not real. Stories and emotions are matched closely enough that even the simulation of life can evoke them.

If emotions serve as a means of pulling us into a story, still the emotional effect of a story depends on our ability to identify with its characters. If a person is viewing a melodrama, yet fails to identify with or admire the hero in some fashion, the emotional effect of the story will be lost or changed. If a tragedy does not evoke pity or sympathy in the spectator, then it will not work as a tragedy for that audience. Stories make identification easy because there is a parallel between the way narratives organize events and the way we organize our lives (Scheibe 1986; Sarbin 1986; Robinson and Hawpe 1986; Vitz 1990). In other words, since our lives are narratively organized, it is much easier to place ourselves in a story than

The Censorship of Art, Music, and Stories

The appraisal of the moral fitness of music or stories immediately raises the issue of censorship. When, if ever, should art be censored? Here's a list of some of authors who have been censored at one time or another by some official state or organization: Homer, Confucius, Aristophanes, Ovid, Dante, Erasmus, Machiavelli, Michelangelo, Martin Luther, John Calvin, Galileo, Shakespeare, René Descartes, John Milton, Molière, Blaise Pascal, John Locke, Daniel Defoe, Jonathan Swift, Miguel Cervantes, Voltaire, Jean-Jacques Rousseau, Denis Diderot, Immanuel Kant, Thomas Paine, Thomas Jefferson, Goethe, Friedrich Schiller, Shelley, Victor Hugo, Nathaniel Hawthorne, Hans Christian Andersen, Elizabeth Browning, John Stuart Mill, Charles Darwin, Harriet Beecher Stowe, Karl Marx, George Eliot, Walt Whitman, Charles Baudelaire, Gustave Flaubert, Oscar Wilde, Arthur Conan Doyle, Rudyard Kipling, H.G. Wells, Bertrand Russell, Jack London, Alexandre Dumas, Henrik Ibsen, Mark Twain, Thomas Hardy, Emile Zola, George Bernard Shaw, Upton Sinclair, James Joyce, Sinclair Lewis, Eugene O'Neill, Boris Pasternak, Henry Miller, Aldous Huxley, William Faulkner, Ernest Hemingway, Allen Ginsberg, Phillip Roth, Eldridge Cleaver, Walt Disney, John Steinbeck, Jean-Paul Sartre, William Burroughs, Tennessee Williams, Arthur Miller, J.D. Salinger, Kurt Vonnegut, Joseph Heller, Norman Mailer, James Baldwin. Here are some books that have been censored by some state or official organization at some time in their history: *The Bible, The Talmud, The Koran, The Adventures of Sherlock Holmes, The Wizard of Oz, Jaws, Father Christmas, The Adventures of Robinson Crusoe, Les Miserables, Mary Poppins, Charlotte's Web, Where the Wild Things Are, Alice's Adventures in Wonderland.* Mickey Mouse has also been the subject of censorship.

Questions for Discussion

1. Have you found some of your favorites among these?
2. Which ones seem the most surprising to you and why?
3. Why do you think they might have been censored by some group?

Censorship usually has three purposes: (1) it may be used politically as an attempt to silence opposition and to secure power; (2) it may be employed to avoid offense to someone or some group; (3) and it may be used to protect someone from harm, such as children. On the other hand, censorship is condemned mostly on the grounds of the violation of rights of liberty and free speech. Rights are usually characterized as entitlements that should not be interfered with even if their restriction would lead to some good, in some sense of the word. Thus, much of the debate about censorship focuses on the tension between the purposes of censorship and liberty rights. Many fears of censorship stem from their possible political motives. Protection of basic liberties of expression are vital for good forms of government. Censorship of "hate speech" is usually justified on the basis of offense and harm to others. Yet some claim that some forms of free political expression could be labeled as hate speech. Feminists, such as Catherine MacKinnon and Andrea Dworkin, want to censor all forms of pornography and erotica because it is both offensive and harmful to women. The opposing side argues that it is an unjustified infringement of liberties of individuals to view it. Recent attempts to ban pornography on the Internet had the purpose of preventing harm to children. Opposition to the ban again argued that such attempts are an infringement on the liberties of individuals.

Questions for Discussion

1. Which of the three purposes of censorship seems most justifiable? Which is the least desirable?
2. Which of these two rights seems more important?
3. Is there a way to balance the better purposes with the more important rights of individuals?
4. Sometimes attempts to censor art backfire so that the material in question becomes even more in demand (examples are the film *I Am Curious Yellow* and attempts by certain groups to censor Fox's *Married with Children*). Why do you think that is so?
5. Do you know of any parents who do not engage in some form of censorship for the benefit of their children? Why do you think parents are especially worried about their children? Why has there been so much concern lately about Hollywood and the prevalence of violence in film?

it is to identify with a logically arranged system of beliefs. If a story is set up in such a way as to admire the hero, then to the extent that we wish to be admired, we may identify with that hero (cf. Kilpatrick et al. 1994: 29). But the hero must have some characteristics that the audience can share. It would be difficult to create such identification with a completely alien character, no matter how admirable. Conversely, villains must be characterized negatively and in such a way that identification is unlikely. Still, many villains are attractive because of their power and lack of constraint. No less an authority than Arnold Schwarzenegger confirms this. In commenting on his role as Mr. Freeze in the third *Batman* movie, he said, "As a villain you can do much more than you can as a hero. You can be nice, sweet, emotional, warm and charming, but you can also at the same time be evil, cold, chilling, intimidating and as threatening as possible." Jeff Parson, a Batman enthusiast, said, "Quite frankly, you could stick Pavarotti in a Batsuit and I wouldn't care. I think George Clooney is going to make the best Batman so far, but I'm here to see the bad guys." "Without villains, Batman and Robin would just be two guys running around in costumes," said Harold Vogel, an entertainment industry analyst with Cowen and Co. (*USA Today,* June 20, 1997). As Alfred Hitchcock argued, "The more successful the villain, the more powerful the story" (Truffaut 1967: 141).

    The drama of the story helps incorporate us into the narrative and into an imaginative process of participation and identification. Once we have identified and associate positive moral emotions with the character, then that character can become model for us to emulate. Of course, it is difficult to say how strong or long-lasting that particular effect will be. But generally speaking, stories are appealing ways to offer models for behavior. They engage the imagistic and imaginative parts of our brain (Vitz 1990). This approach is more delightful, typically and especially for children, than a reasoned approach (Kilpatrick et al. 1994: 21; Vitz 1990). Telling stories is a form of enchantment that draws our attention (Bettelheim 1977). In this manner stories concretize moral norms in terms of images and particularities through a narrative process that has a tendency to incorporate us into the moral vision of the story. By asking the question "What sort of story am I in?" stories enable us to give moral meaning to our lives through comparison with the story, and stories provide models and practical examples, visions, and outlooks. As Robert Penn Warren says, "We turn to fiction for some slight hint about the story in life we live." Human beings require stories to give meaning to the facts of their existence. Stories, in short, help to make sense of our lives. However, as we'll discuss in Chapter 4, there are several different types of stories, which create different senses of heroism, and some of which many people feel do not promote the right sort of moral outlook.

    This raises the interesting issue of how to evaluate the moral quality of a story. It also brings up the issue of censorship of stories at the same time. One of the most common ways of evaluating the moral fitness of a story is in terms of its content (cf. Booth 1988: 5–6). Currently, for example, some parents and religious groups wish to censor the *Harry Potter* series by J.K. Rowling because of its "content"—in this case the fact that witchcraft is among its events and happenings. Often the ordinary objections to stories such as *Catcher in the Rye*, which is everyone's favorite book to censor, are in reference to the language used or certain scenes that involve sexual

---

Japanese Versions of Little Red Riding Hood

In several Japanese versions of the famous Western fairy tale, instead of the hunter killing the wolf, he cuts open his stomach while he's sleeping, releasing both Little Red Riding Hood and her grandma. The hunter replaces them with rocks and sews the stomach back up. The wolf later complains of a stomachache, saying perhaps he ate too much. In some versions the wolf apologizes to Little Red Riding Hood and promises to be good from now on. The Japanese believe that the young can be taught values in school, and they use these stories to emphasize that children "ought to be harmonious citizens, thoughtful of each other, and even of wolves" (Kristof 1996).

explicitness. When assessed in terms of content, nearly everything ends up on someone's censored list as immoral, including every sacred text and a surprising number of children's books.

In this manner stories or films may be evaluated in terms of offensive content: the graphic quality and amount of violent scenes, sexual explicitness, or vulgar language. Films may be evaluated morally on the basis of their racial, gender, or ethnic stereotypes; condemnations may also extend to character depiction, whereby a character may be considered so loathsome (as in Bret Easton Ellis's *American Psycho*—but compare this to the film version) that the story should not be read simply on that basis. This may also hold for the depiction of religious or historic figures, for example, the representation of Jesus in Martin Scorsese's *The Last Temptation of Christ*.

Indeed, the current American movie rating system is based on content (i.e., whether the film contains vulgar language, explicit sex, or too much violence), and it certainly reflects the behavior of other national media regulatory organizations that assess potential harm to viewers (cf. Federman, 1996; BBFC, 1995). What is underlying content censorship is the assumption that reading or watching such events and happenings—regardless of whatever else happens in the story—will offer undesirable models for the audience, especially for an immature or unsophisticated one. These are usually expressed as: (1) increased aggression or sexual activity after watching graphic violence or sex, (2) desensitization toward real-life acts of violence or sexual aggression or assault, (3) increased levels of anxiety, fear, depression, or phobias from viewing graphic or sexual violence. In other words, to the extent that it is undesirable to have vulgar, violent-prone, and sexually aggressive or intemperate persons, so it is wrong to have such stories for general public consumption. What we need to do, under this view, is to create stories that express more positive models.

In many respects the validity of this position rests on empirical studies which can establish points (1)–(3). Indeed, there is strong evidence that media violence can have a profound effect on levels of anxiety both in children (Berry and Gray 1999; Cantor and Reilley 1982; Palmer, Hockett, and Dean 1983; Sparks 1986; Wilson, Hoffner, and Cantor 1987) and in adults (Buzzuto 1975; Heisler 1975; Johnson 1980; Mathai 1983). The causes of this may be viewer specific; several studies show that differences in sex (Gunter and Fumham 1983; Tamborini, Stiff, and Zillmann 1987), personality (e.g., Edwards 1984; Gunter 1983; Tamborini, Stiff, and Heidel 1990), social viewing conditions (e.g., Mundorf, Weaver, and Zillmann 1989; Sparks 1989), socioeconomic status (e.g., Greenberg and Gordon 1971), and occupational status (Payne 1993) may be predictive of how enjoyable individuals find media violence or graphic horror.

But several studies have show that it is the contextual organization of the violence that may increase the anxiety, specifically what might be recognized as the narrative organization of those violent events. For example, studies show that the graphic violence may elevate state anxiety among viewers because they may experience strong empathic reactions to the suffering of victims, especially sympathetic or attractive victims (Zillmann 1980; Zillmann and Cantor 1977). Some studies have shown how the reward or punishment meted out to the perpetrators of violent behavior (Bandura 1971) or the justification for the violence (Berkowitz and Rawlings 1963) plays a role in this regard. The most widespread study of violence on American television to date, the recent report of the National Television Violence Study (Wilson et al. 1997), seems to focus on the specific context in which violence was presented, and there seems to be an increasing consensus among researchers that presentations of violence may have differential effects on individuals and that some of the contextual factors just mentioned may mediate between viewing media violence and subsequent aggression (Comstock and Paik 1991; Comstock and Strasberger 1990; Donnerstein, Slaby, and Eron 1994; Gunter 1994).

Thus, although concern for the content of stories is an important factor in assessing their moral fitness, focus on the content alone may ultimately be an incomplete approach. Examining the organization of this content within the narrative may be a fairer or more sophisticated means of appraisal. What matters—contra Plato—is not so much that villainy is represented but that, given the sense of the story, when villainy is defeated, it creates a moral worth to the story that exceeds the plain presence of a villainous figure. In a certain sense, this suggests that the risk of introducing immoral agents or offensive scenes is lessened by the fact that such a character or the events surrounding it may serve a moral purpose. Moreover, raising anxiety in the viewer may in fact be good from a moral point of view, if its purpose is to unsettle the audience away from complacency. Violence against victims may be used by a story to rightly raise sympathy in an audience for a good cause; rather than being a paean to violence, the use of violence in a film may serve the purpose of decrying it.

But besides stories, Plato argued for a general role of the aesthetic, the beautiful, in cultivating moral sentiment, an approach that was to include the exposure of the young to certain kinds of music. Plato believed that certain kinds of rhythms and melodies promoted self-control and attenuation of the passions (*Rep.* 398ff.). For example, he believed that continual exposure to melodies composed from certain scales, such as the Ionian (equivalent to our major diatonic scale) would make people conducive to drunkenness, whereas exposure to Lydian scales would make people too soft. He favored both Dorian and Phrygian scales for their "solemnness" (*Rep.* 398b). Of course, Plato can't be right about the Ionian scale, since almost every modern church hymn is based on it, but his general concern about the power of music to influence the emotions of children and young people is nothing new. Our century has seen plenty of attempts to censor or restrict the sort of music the young hear—whether it was swing, jazz, or rock-'n'-roll. Plato's larger point is expressed by the statement that "education in music is most sovereign, because more than anything else rhythm and harmony find their way to the inmost soul and take strongest hold upon it, bringing with them and imparting grace, if one is rightly trained, and otherwise the contrary ... " (*Rep.* 401e).

Music is a way of training the emotions, and if they are refined in the right way, they become more moral-ready, so to speak. Establishing this connection between the aesthetic and the good is what 19th-century poet and philosopher Friedrich Schiller (1759–1805) called *aesthetic education.* He argued that it is the experience of the beautiful in fine art which creates in the individual a certain harmony, a harmony that confers a certain social character on the individual (1795). The experience of beauty in the fine arts cultivates taste, which should not be understood in the elitist, aristocratic sense, but simply as the desire for the truly fine and excellent. Taste, then, becomes the basis for the desire for the good and the avoidance of vulgar and base desires or feelings. Those who express their moral sentiment in this fashion are motivated out of sense of what is highest, best, and noble in themselves and others. In this way the aesthetic training of the emotions through beauty creates a love of the noble and the good. (For more on stories and morality, see Sections 4.5.1, 4.5.2, 4.6.5, and 4.6.7.)

1.5 FEMINIST ETHICS: MORAL SENTIMENT SHOULD BE THE BASIS OF MORALITY

In an *Enquiry Concerning the Principles of Morals*, David Hume reviews a controversy

> started of late ... concerning the general foundation of Morals; whether they be
> derived from Reason, or from Sentiment; whether we attain the knowledge of them by
> a chain of argument and induction, or by an immediate feeling and finer internal
> sense. ... (1777: 2).

Reason is concerned solely with matters of fact—truth and falsity. Reason, as it is
exemplified in science or logic, is an instrument used to determine those sorts of
questions. The ends of human action, on the other hand, are matters different
from questions of truth and falsity. The ends of human action are those things
which precisely guide instruments, such as reason. Thus, rather than reason guiding our ends, it is our ends which guide reason and determine for what purposes it
should be used. Where, then, does the source and impetus for these ends originate? Hume concludes that "the ultimate ends of human actions can never, in any
case, be accounted for by reason, but recommend themselves entirely to the sentiments and affections of mankind, without any dependence upon intellectual facul-
ties" (1777: 225). It is in the passions and sentiments that we find the drive toward
human ends, such as happiness and the desire for pleasure. Second, moral decision
making is a matter of value rather than truth. In determining what to do in a situation, we are not considering what is true, but what is good, beneficial, useful, pleasurable, and admirable. Consequently, because of its narrow concern with truth,
reason cannot be the source of these values. These values are clearly the domain of
the emotions. Hume concludes that sentiment can be the only foundation of ethics
(1777: 135).

Feminist thinkers concur with Hume on the importance of sentiment in
moral matters and the displacement of reason as its foundation. But feminist ethics
also attempts to show how women's experience of morality is important in the
transformation and understanding of moral theory generally. Many feminist
thinkers see reason and rationality in the Western traditions as something associated with the transcendence and control of the feminine. The paradigm of that tradition has been the control of reason by the unruly passions, which can be seen as
beginning with Socrates and Plato, and is used as a metaphor of the control of the
masculine over the feminine (cf. Lloyd 1984: 104). Traditionally, women have been
seen as emotional rather than as rational beings and so somehow as lesser moral
agents (Held 1990: 325). The dominance of reason in ethical theory has led to a
view of ethics as controlled by abstract, impartial rules and principles, which then
serve as guidelines for decision making in particular situations. This has altogether
ignored the sphere of the emotions and sentiments which serve us in a down-to-
earth manner and in our daily, ordinary moral deliberations and encounters with
people to whom we are connected in some manner. Hume's philosophy is one of
the few that affirms the importance of sentiments in moral life. "Hume," according
to Annette Baier, "gave authority to feeling, custom and tradition" rather than giving authority to sovereign reason (1985: xii). For Baier, Immanuel Kant represents
the extreme in rationalist moral philosophy, based as it is on obedience to universal
ethical law. Such an approach is both wrong and wrongheaded. It is wrong because
most so-called universal moral rules turn out to be cultural conventions, subject to

historical variations and change (1987). It is wrongheaded because, in reality, morality develops from intimate caring relations and is directed toward particular persons in specific contexts, rather than in terms of abstract universal principles of justice. Moral theory, as dominated by the rationalist approach, needs to reassess the role emotions and sentiment play in moral life and understand how they engender relations with others and focus on particular situations and contexts. "Feminist theorists begin ethical theorizing with embodied, gendered subjects who have particular histories, particular communities, particular allegiances, and particular visions of human flourishing" (Morgan 1990: 2; cf. Held 1990: 319).

These views are supported by the research of Carol Gilligan. In *In a Different Voice* (1982), she claims that women's moral development is distinct from men's, and this has generally been disregarded. She found through her research that women and girls don't focus on abstract questions of right and justice so much, but more on responsibilities of *care* deriving from attachments to others. The woman's paradigm is the family, which involves caring relations among unequals who take responsibility for each other.

According to Baier, care offers a model for dealing with moral concerns that may not be found in larger-scale public institutions. In the context of the caring family, partiality and emotional attachment are crucial for solving conflicts. This concept of morality is different from one based on rationally justified principles. The principle-based approach frames moral questions in terms of conflicts that must be resolved one way or another and on the basis of "objective" principles that say one side is right and the other is wrong. If caring serves as the paradigm, the framework is different. The goal is not to resolve moral conflict by means of determining which side is right but by promoting a sympathetic connection or relationship among the disputants that aims at a compromise which will ensure that all concerned are not harmed (cf. Baier 1985: 53, 56). To take a case in point, consider the decision whether to remove a loved one who is terminally ill from a ventilator. The caring approach argues that such a decision should be made by those who are connected to the person through bonds of sympathy and love, not in terms of some abstract rule following. This approach is partial and takes into consideration the feelings, emotions, and connectedness of all those affected by the decision. A rule-based approach, on the other hand, is impartial and indifferent to the personal relations that exist in this situation. The goal, in general, of the care approach is to build a certain level of "appropriate trust" among those participants in cooperative and communal practices (Baier 1985: 56).

One criticism of feminist ethics is that it seems to apply only to family, private life, but cannot be appropriately applied to public life which, as in the legal system, works on the very idea of impartiality and emotional detachment. One vice of judicial decisions is partiality: Justice should be blind; when it comes to matters of distributive justice, again impartiality is an admirable virtue of such practices. Feminists respond by arguing that the distinction between the private and public is itself a continuing masculine tradition (Held 1990: 330ff.). Such a tradition sees the family and mothering as "natural" and inappropriate for the public sphere, which is concerned with the law, politics, and the economy. The public is the sphere of the contract; the family is the place of caring relations constituted by emotions and sentiments. Feminists argue that not only is it wrong to think that the public sphere is somehow detached from personal connection and sentiment, but by ignoring that, the public sphere can lose a model for improvement, as found in the paradigms of mothering and care relations (cf. Friedman 1989; Ruddick 1989;

Held 1990: 333). Still, critics argue that using caring family relations as a paradigm for the public sphere may be misplaced, if not appropriate. If the paradigm of special partial relationships is enlarged to the public arena, this could result in some form of tribalism. Nepotism and the like are all based on certain forms of partiality. Also, since we can't have a connection to everyone, what are we to do in those cases in which particular feelings of sympathy or compassion are absent? Something must fill in the gap. Although the family may serve as an appropriate paradigm for many sorts of social practices, it may not be appropriate for all. Although we may wish to recognize the importance of moral sentiments for character and moral life, it may not be the most appropriate basis for a morality.

John Rawls gives an interesting account of this difficulty, which may prove to mediate between rationalist approaches, such as Kant, and feminist thinking. Rawls recognizes, as feminist theorists do, that sympathetic and caring connections—especially as they are experienced in the family—are vital for the development of a sense of trust concerning the practices and institutions of the society in which we live. As we have seen, he summarizes this process in terms of three "laws" or "tendencies" of moral psychology (1971: 490–491). Although this is vital in that it accounts for the motivation to support just institutions and serves as the glue which bonds members of a community to such institutions and practices, still the question of the morality or the justice of those institutions may be addressed within the framework of rational discourse. In other words, Rawls seems to agree with feminist thinkers that sympathy, love, and caring relations are the heart of moral development and generate the desire to see just institutions and practices flourish; but he would disagree with their view that, consequently, rational assessment or the systematic development of moral principle is not viable. Without the sort of moral psychology that caring relations bring, institutions and practices, no matter what their moral status, could not be held together. Still, the question of their moral status can be satisfactorily determined through reasoned discourses. Conversely, then, he agrees with thinkers such as Kant that moral principle must be founded on reasoned discourse, but he disagrees with Kant that moral principle alone is sufficient for moral motivation. (For more on feminist ethics, see Sections 5.2.5 and 5.2.6.)

1.6 KANT: REASON, NOT MORAL SENTIMENT, SHOULD SERVE AS THE BASIS OF MORALITY

As we have just seen, David Hume, Virginia Held, Carol Gilligan, Annette Baier, and other feminist thinkers argue that moral sentiment forms the basis of morality. In so doing they argue against advocates of a cognitive or rationalist basis. There is no stronger proponent of this rationalist position than the 18th-century philosopher Immanuel Kant. He held the strong opinion that reason alone served as the foundation of morality (1788: 123). Kant not only felt that sentiment was an unsure and unstable foundation for ethical conduct (1780: 13, 37) but that acting from motives such as sympathy was morally inferior to acting from a rational understanding of one's obligations. Kant explains his thinking in a well-known passage:

> For inclinations vary; they grow with the indulgence we allow them, and they leave behind a greater void than the one we intended to fill. They are consequently always burdensome to a rational being, and, though he cannot put them aside, they nevertheless elicit from him the wish to be free of them. Even an inclination to do that which accords with duty ... can at most facilitate the effectiveness of moral maxims but not produce any such maxims ... Inclination, be it good-natured or otherwise, is blind and

slavish; reason, when it is a question of morality, must not play part of mere guardian of the inclinations, but, without regard to them … must care for its own interest. … Even the feeling of sympathy and warm-hearted fellow-feeling, when preceding the consideration of what is duty and serving as a determining ground, is burdensome even to right-thinking persons, confusing their considered maxims and creating the wish to be free from them and subject only to law-giving reason (1788: 122–123).

In arguing that moral sentiment should not serve as the *basis* or *ground* of morality, he is addressing two questions. Looking for the basis of an action is searching for *justifications* for why it is right. Once we understand that something is right to do, we can also address issues of how we might be *motivated* to do the right thing. As far as Kant is concerned, moral emotions such as sympathy only address the second question; they are not really factors in addressing what is right. We first have to determine that helping someone is the right thing to do, in which case sympathy may serve as a motive to do it. However, sympathy alone does not serve to justify an action. It is quite possible, under this view, that acting out of sympathy could lead us to do the wrong thing. It may be difficult for us to discipline our children when they deserve it because their tears play on our heartstrings, but it may be the right thing to do and, in the long run, benefit both child and parent. Thus, sympathy only incidentally leads to the right thing. "It stands on the same footing as other inclinations—for example, the inclination for honor, which if fortunate enough to hit on something beneficial and right and consequently honorable, deserves praise and encouragement, but not esteem … " (1785: 14). Barbara Herman, a philosopher who advocates Kant's position, takes this one step further:

> **Immanuel Kant (1724–1804)**
>
> A German philosopher of great importance, Kant contributed significantly to the theory of knowledge, ethics, and aesthetics. His major works on ethics include *Foundations of the Metaphysics of Morals* (1785) and *The Critique of Practical Reason* (1788). In his first major writing, *The Critique of Pure Reason,* Kant argued that there could be no proofs by use of reason for such notions as God, immortality, and human freedom. However, these ideas could serve as practical postulates for human existence and moral agency. Such notions must be practically postulated to make sense out of our lives and to give any meaning to moral agency as such. *The Critique of Practical Reason* takes up this issue in detail. Kant makes it clear that without freedom the concept of moral agency is impossible. Without freedom how would it be possible to blame or praise since no one would be responsible for his or her actions? Kant consequently explicates the notion of moral agency as autonomy, or freedom to be responsible for one's choices and the moral rules which will govern one's actions. Kant argues further that if autonomy is understood in terms of moral laws, freely chosen, then the true and genuine notion of law—understood as having a universality and compellingness—argues that we should always choose those actions which, when generalized, could be reasonably implemented as laws. This forms the basis of what Kant calls a categorical imperative. (For more on Kant, see Sections 2.5–2.6, 3.3.2, 4.5.8, 4.8.2–4.8.3, and 5.3.3.)

> The man of sympathetic temper, while concerned with others, is indifferent to morality. … If we suppose that the only motive the agent has is the desire to help others, then we are imagining someone who would not be deterred by the fact that his action is morally wrong. And, correspondingly, the moral rightness of an action is no part of what brings him to act. … [W]hile sympathy can give an interest in an action that is (as it happens) right, it cannot give an interest in its being right (1993: 5).

However, what makes Kant's position especially controversial is his view that acting from sympathy has little moral worth. He writes:

> there are many spirits of so sympathetic a temper that, without any further motive of vanity or self-interest, they find an inner pleasure in spreading happiness around them

and can take delight in the contentment of others as their own work. Yet I maintain that in such a case an action of this kind, however right and amiable it may be, has still no genuinely moral worth (1785: 14).

There should not be as much praise for the action if it is something someone is already inclined to do. For Kant, acting from duty has much more moral worth since, at least as he understands duty (see Section 1.3.1), it does not involve inclination but a firm commitment to do the right thing despite consequence or disinclination. This is the same sort of reasoning Kant invokes to dismiss ethical theories, such as those espoused by Epicurus, which use pleasure as the basis of moral action (1788: 115). If one does the right thing because it leads to pleasure, in some sense of the term, then one's motives are corrupt: Moral actions are done solely for the pleasure they afford rather than for the fact that they ought to be done for their own sake. Consequently, should it turn out that the right thing to do affords no pleasure, then all incentive for doing it would vanish under Epicurus's account of things (see Section 3.42). Kant believes firmly enough in the unworthiness of sympathy as a motive that he argues that in moral education it is better to weaken inclinations such as sympathy than to ally them with consciousness of duty (1788: 88). In other words, we should try to destroy the sentiment of sympathy for others so that their motive for moral action is more purely identified with duty. For many parents and educators, this may have a tinge of perversion to it.

Is Duty Morally Superior to Sympathy?

In a wonderfully developed argument, Jonathan Bennett (1974) makes the claim that sympathy is a superior guide to moral behavior than duty and that in fact the absence of sympathy in a person is a sign of the greatest evil. Bennett articulates three scenarios to illustrate his point. The first scenario describes the conflict Huck Finn faces when he must decide whether to turn in his friend, Jim, a slave. Huck feels that it is his duty to turn in runaway slaves because that is the law; he even believes that he will be condemned to hell for not doing it. Yet he cannot do such a thing precisely because of a sympathetic bond with his friend. In the end it is Huck's sympathy that wins out. The second scenario involves Heinrich Himmler, the notorious Nazi responsible for the deaths of millions of Jews. Analyzing his historical speeches, Bennett argues that Himmler was also a man constituted by a conflict between duty and sympathy. He was not unsympathetic to the suffering of the millions of Jews he ordered to death. But he insisted that it was his duty "to cleanse" the race, and despite his sentiments, he thought it a noble thing to carry out his duty. The third case is that of Jonathan Edwards, the 18th-century American philosopher and Puritan, best known for his sermon, "Sinners in the Hands of an Angry God." Bennett argues that Edwards's Calvinist theology leads him to a complete loss of sympathy for human beings, because he believes that all human beings are worthless enough in the eyes of God to condemn to eternal damnation. Such a loss of sympathy makes Edwards an even more despicable person than Himmler. For Bennett, sympathy always serves as a check on our duties, understood as the embodiment of moral principles.

Thus, Kant makes four points for the dismissal of moral sentiment and emotion as the basis of morality. First, emotion and sentiments are neither secure, stable, nor consistent in people, so the ground for doing the right thing vanishes when the emotion is not present or inhibited. Should a person suddenly lose heart, become involved in her own troubles, or lose the general sense of sympathy for others, then the inclination to be moral is also lost. Second, because sympathy is an emotion and an affective rather than cognitive process, it cannot help us to determine our obligations or the rightness of our actions. Moral feeling does not precede and serve as the basis of moral principle, but rather should be understood as the effect on the person of his consciousness of moral law or principle. Third, because it cannot help determine the right thing to do, actions based on it are good only incidentally, and acting from sympathy is not necessarily acting for what is morally right. Fourth, because acting out of sympathy is acting from inclination, it is not a morally worthy motive; those acts which are done despite or against inclination are more morally worthy.

Let's look at some of the arguments against these four points. First, Kant's claim that sympathy cannot help us determine the right thing to do because it is a purely affective process may be questionable. Although sympathy is certainly an affective process, it is also involves a judgment and so a cognitive process as well. Kant does not seem to fully appreciate the characteristics of sympathy or emotions in that regard. As we argued earlier, emotions are evoked through certain kinds of stories or scenarios; for a person to feel sympathy for another, she must see the person as an innocent or undeserving victim, which is a judgment that is made. Emotions *are* judgments and evaluations. For that reason, sympathy does not direct us to do the right thing incidentally, but intentionally—although perhaps mistakenly. Still, there is no guarantee that just because we reason things out, we are infallible in our deliberation. Reasoning also leads to mistakes, and history is replete with horrors and immoralities committed out of duty (Sverdlik 1999; Bennett 1974). Conversely, it may be argued that there can be no purely rational decisions, that is, decisions made on the basis of reason alone. In *Descartes' Error* (1994), Antonio Damasio argues case studies of brain lesions show that emotion is crucial for rational decision making; intelligence alone is not enough to decide between one course of action and another: "We can't decide whom we're going to marry, what savings strategy to adopt, where to live, on the basis of reason alone."

It may be true that emotions are not consistent or may be inhibited, but there is no guarantee that reason is any more consistent and stable; reason may fail us, and our thinking may prove as inconsistent or unstable as any emotion; there is also no reason to think that a sense of duty will be any more available than the feeling of sympathy (cf. Blum 1980a: 30). Moreover, it may be the case that not only is Kant wrong about the purely affective nature of sympathy, but also wrong about the purely cognitive character of duty. There is sufficient argument, as we have seen (Section 1.3.1), to warrant the claim that duty is a moral sentiment like any other and so also contains an affective component. The claim that sympathy is a less morally worthy motive for action than duty because duty is done without the push of inclination may also be suspect. As Lawrence Blum points out, acting from compassion does not typically involve doing what one is in the mood to do or feels like doing; in that regard it is as worthy as duty, as Kant understands it.

An additional point can be made against Kant's position. As mentioned, Kant suggests that it is consciousness of our duty, understood as a generalized sense of obligation, a moral law, which generates our feelings of conscience (1788: 79). But there seems to be a certain circularity in Kant's account. If the moral feeling is generated through our apprehension of the moral law, what motivates us to apprehend the moral law? Why shouldn't we be indifferent or even adverse to the moral law, unless we are already inclined toward the good, that is, already have acquired some moral sentiment? Schopenhauer picks up exactly on this point: "[Kant] presupposes that it would occur to man quite automatically to look around for and inquire about a *law* for his will, to which his will would have to be liable and would have to submit. This, however, cannot possibly of itself occur to him, but at best only after the first impetus and occasion for it had already been given by another, positively effective, real moral motive. ... " (1841:74).

Kant's ultrarationalism leaves a bad taste in many people's mouths. They argue that it makes morality a passionless science and moral agents bloodless followers of principle or slaves to duty. The German poet Friedrich Schiller ridiculed Kant in this regard: "In the Kantian moral philosophy the idea of duty is presented with a hardness which frightens away all the graces and which could mislead an obtuse mind to seek moral perfection on the path of a dour and monkish asceticism" (Schiller, *Über Anmut und Würde*, quoted in Beck 1960: 231). Indeed, Schopenhauer remarks that Kant's moral agent must be characterized as a "loveless doer of good, who is indifferent to the sufferings of others" (1841: 66; cf. Schopenhauer 1841: 66). As 19th-century philosopher Henry Sidgwick noted, those benefits which are done from affection and lovingly bestowed are often more welcome than those given simply out of duty (1981: 223), and as Michael Stocker points out, surely a person would be disappointed if he found out that a friend who he thought visited him in the hospital out of sympathy really did so out of duty (1976: 462). (For more on Kant, see Sections 2.6, 3.32, 4.59, 4.82–4.83, and 5.33.)

1.7 EMOTIVISM: MORALITY IS NOTHING BUT MORAL EMOTIONS

Beginning in the early 1930s, the philosophers Alfred Ayer (1952) and Charles Stevenson (1946) developed what is called the emotive theory of ethics. Like feminist theory, this particular account was inspired by certain claims made by David Hume, especially the claim that "when you pronounce an act vicious you only mean that you have a feeling or sentiment of blame from the contemplation of it" (1739: 469). In general, the emotive theory espouses the view that all moral claims and judgments are nothing more than expressions of ethical feelings or sentiment and/or attempts to get others to feel similarly. "[Ethical terms] are used to express feeling about certain objects, but not to make any assertion about them. ... They are calculated also to arouse feeling and so to stimulate action" (Ayer 1952: 108). Ayer continues,

> **A.J. Ayer** (1910–1989) was one of the principal proponents of logical positivism, a 20th-century movement which advocated the paradigm of science and logic as a model for evidence and proof. Since ethical behavior was not amenable to adjudication by such criteria, emotivism was a consequence of his ethical theory. His most important book is *Language, Truth and Logic*.

> Thus if I say to someone, "You acted wrongly in stealing that money," I am not stating anything more than if I had simply said, "You stole that money." In adding that this action is wrong I am not making any further statement about it. I am simply evincing my moral disapproval of it. It is as if I had said "You stole that money," in a peculiar tone of horror, or written it with the addition of some special exclamation marks. The tone, or the exclamation marks, adds nothing to the literal meaning of the sentence. It merely serves to show that the expression of it is attended by certain feelings in the speaker (1952: 107).

Ayer's characterization of ethical judgments as expressions of feeling stem from his theory of *positivism.* Positivism argues that there are only two kinds of truth: that which can be determined factually, in the manner in which the sciences proceed, and that which can be determined tautologically, that is, the manner in which mathematics proceeds. All other claims of judgments must be capable of being reduced to one or the other or otherwise be designated as meaningless—that is, incapable of making any meaningful judgment. As we saw in the Introduction, ethical judgments are *normative* claims and suggest a category distinct either from empirical fact or logical reasoning. Ayer argues that the normative cannot be

reduced to either the empirical or the logical and so is meaningless: "the fundamental ethical concepts are unanalysable, inasmuch as there is no criterion by
which one can test the validity of the judgment in which they occur … the reason …
they are unanalysable is that they are mere pseudo-concepts. … " (1952: 107). In
other words, Ayer denies the distinctness of normativity and its justification. He
characterizes normative judgments as expressive statements of wish or command,
but in themselves they form no meaningful judgment.

C.L. Stevenson agreed with Ayer's account of the status of morally normative
claims, but he stressed their particular function as a means of getting others to
share a person's feelings:

> The emotive meaning of a word is the power that the word acquires, on account of its
> history in emotive situations, to evoke or directly express attitudes, as distinct from
> describing or designating them. … ethical judgments alter attitudes, not by appeal to
> self-conscious efforts … but by the more flexible mechanism of suggestion. Emotive
> terms present the subject of which they are predicated in a bright or dim light … and
> thereby lead people, rather than command them, to alter their attitudes (1946: 33).

To say that "murder is wrong" is to express disgust or disapproval; but in saying it to another, it has the function of trying to create the same attitude in that
person. It is precisely the emotive power of the term that causes it to be suggestive
or persuasive. In saying that a particular action is wrong, one is really saying that it
is morally disgusting and that a person ought to be shamed by it or at least show
some signs of remorse. What one is conveying in such moral ascriptions is a certain
feeling about actions that ought to be shared by others such as yourself. One cannot really say anything in terms of the rightness or wrongness about moral action.
One can only express how he or she feels about it in such a way as to exhort others
to share that same sort of feeling. Moral judgments and claims are just disputes
concerning moral tastes and preferences, based as they are on moral emotions.

There have been several criticisms of emotive theory over the years, and it is
certainly less of a force than it once was in the middle of the 20th century. We may
employ both a Kantian criticism and a Humean–feminist one. From a Kantian
point of view, one problem with the theory is that the reduction of normativity to
feeling doesn't seem to capture some of the experience of normativity. If people
feel that murder is wrong, in some sense they must also believe that it is wrong, and
we assume, believe it for some reason—even if they are unable to articulate it consciously. Their feeling that murder is wrong is based on their reasons for believing
so. The fact that a person feels a certain way would not seem to be sufficient for
wanting to persuade or influence others to it. It would simply warrant expressive
attitudes. It would be equivalent to saying that because a person is in a terrible
mood, she wants to persuade others to be in such a mood. In fact, such a person
may want others' help to get out of that mood. Just because a person feels that
murder is wrong doesn't, in itself, say why that person would want to persuade
another. Normativity means that a person believes another should believe as he
does. Simply feeling something does not alone convey that characteristic.

The Humean–feminist criticism would suggest that the reduction of moral
emotions to mere feelings is an impoverished analysis of these emotions which casts
aside the fact that they are already judgments. Someone who feels sympathy has
already made a judgment as to the moral worthiness of the victim and the villainous
character of the perpetrator. Moral emotions are inherently normative, and it is
through them that we establish our commitments and obligations.

If emotivism is taken seriously, the consequences are quite clear. Since disputes about moral feeling are not resolvable, then one can only express what one feels about them. In other words, the only purpose of moral discussion is to achieve a certain solidarity with others who feel as you do (or incidentally, to ensure that those who do feel as you do understand that this particular case is one in which they should feel that way). Although many moral disputes may seem to be simply an expression or ventilation of feeling that gets nowhere, the question is whether this is the only possibility in regard to moral dispute. If all moral disputation is of this sort, then it acts in a way similar to propaganda. It attempts to bypass critical thinking, reflection, and reasoned judgment in favor of directly causing us to feel a certain way. Although this clearly happens in regard to certain moral issues, the fact of the matter is that many people come to change their beliefs about the rightness of certain normative claims and so come to feel differently about a particular moral matter. Indeed, this requires precisely a certain emotional detachment from moral or other feelings one may have. Giving reasons why certain norms should hold or not provides a course which allows the possibility of rational resolution between conflicting groups, but emotivism eliminates in principle such a possibility.

REVIEW QUESTIONS

1. What are some general characteristics of emotions? What is a moral emotion? How important are emotions, and what sort of role do they play in our lives? How do emotional pathologies illustrate this?
2. What is guilt? What is shame? How do they differ?
3. What are the differences among empathy, sympathy, compassion, pity, and love?
4. What are, generally speaking, the circumstances which will motivate or prevent people from acting on their sense of sympathy?
5. What is the difference between regret and remorse?
6. What is admiration?
7. What are some general characteristics of psychopathy?
8. What is meant by internalization? How is it different from motivation by punishment and reward? How does psychopathy help us understand it?
9. What is the difference between psychopathy and sociopathy (wickedness) according to David Lykken's theory?
10. What is the difference between moral emotion and moral sentiment?
11. What are some characteristics of the sense of duty?
12. What are the essential characteristics of the sentiment of honor? How does a sense of honor differ from a sense of duty? How do they work together?
13. What is the nature of care?
14. What are the characteristics of nobility as a moral sentiment?
15. What are John Rawls's three laws of moral psychology?
16. What are the differences among authoritarian, authoritative, and permissive parenting styles? Which one seems most conducive for acquiring moral sentiment and why?
17. How do stories serve as moral models for us?
18. What is Kant's argument concerning the sense of duty? Why does he distrust moral sentiment as a basis for morality?
19. Why is moral sentiment so important according to feminist theory? Why is something like trust so essential to moral and social life?
20. What is the emotive theory of ethics?

GENERAL DISCUSSION QUESTIONS

1. Granted that feelings of guilt help motivate us to do the right thing, can they also become harmful?
2. How can shame be used to exert peer pressure and conformity on others?
3. Is the better way to motivate people morally through shame or through guilt? Or are both good to have? What are the differences between the two, and what sort of society is required for each one to work well as a motivator?
4. Do you think that empathy is necessary for any moral emotion? Do you agree with Kant that one really shouldn't rely on sympathy to do the right thing? Can sympathy make you do the wrong thing?
5. Knowing what we know about psychopaths, how should their actions be punished? Can they be held responsible for their actions if they have no moral sense? Can they be blamed for their behavior?
6. What would be more effective for public life, a strong sense of caring or a strong sense of duty? What would be more effective for family life, a strong sense of caring or a strong sense of duty? Could the two senses be complementary? Are both necessary for these sorts of practices?
7. Is fulfilling obligations always the right thing to do? Could it be that some obligations are dictated by roles that are inherently unjust or unfair? For example, does a wife have an obligation to obey her husband, as some religions argue? What about the obligations that Himmler felt that led him to create the Holocaust?
8. Is an honor code always a guarantee of moral behavior? For example, the Mafia has an honor code and so do many gangs. What about the claim that there can be "honor among thieves"? In the past duels were often fought over breaches of honor, one example being the famous duel between Alexander Hamilton and Aaron Burr. Can a strong sense of honor lead to the wrong thing?
9. Reflect on any historical or current actions by well-known people which you consider noble and admirable. Why do you consider them so?
10. Do you agree with Kant that moral emotions and sentiments are a shaky foundation for moral behavior? Do you agree with feminist theory in this respect that moral sentiment, especially the sense of caring, is essential for moral life? How important is moral sentiment and feeling for moral life? Can one be moral without having a sense of caring?
11. Are the moral claims we make nothing more than expressions of our feelings about the act? When we make such claims are we simply exhorting people to feel as we do?

STORIES FOR DISCUSSION

On the Theme of Duty and Honor

High Noon. 1952. Directed by Fred Zinnemann. Will Kane has just been married and has resigned as marshal of Hadleyville, but a killer he helped put in jail and his gang are now looking for him. Kane tries to get the townspeople to stand by him, but they turn their backs. Even his friend Herb backs out on him, as does his deputy marshal. Everyone seems to want him to go, especially his wife, who wants to start a new life with him. Will Kane is now faced with a choice to stand and fight the gang, with no support from the town, or to leave town with the blessing of the townsfolk and the desire of his wife and ideally escape harm from the gang. Will Kane chooses to stay in town and fight the gang.

Questions for Discussion

1. Why do you think Will Kane felt he must stay and fight? Was it out of a sense of duty and obligation or a sense of honor? Could other motives be present?

2. Do you think Kane owed the townspeople any obligation to stay and fight? Do you think the townspeople had an obligation to support him?
3. What about the obligations Will Kane had to his new wife? Should they have overridden his reasons for staying to fight? Was his wife right in asking him to leave the town with her, or should she have supported his plan to stay and fight?

Casablanca. 1943. Directed by Michael Curtiz. Rick, an American who has fled Paris in advance of the Nazi invasion, owns a café in Casablanca, Morocco. One day he is visited by his former lover, Ilse Laszlo, a woman he still strongly loves. They planned to leave Paris together, but she never showed at the train station. As it turns out her husband, Victor, whom she thought had died in a Nazi concentration camp, managed to escape and return to Paris just at that time. Both of them are now in Casablanca. Victor is a dedicated resistance fighter, and the Nazis are anxious to detain him in Casablanca. Rick has come upon two specially authorized transport papers, which would allow their bearers safe passage out of Casablanca and out of the hands of the Nazis. In the meantime feelings of love are rekindled between Rick and Ilse, and Ilse, having trouble deciding between lover and husband, wants Rick to decide for her. Rick now faces the following choice: He can do what is best to defeat the Nazis or do what would be personally satisfying and continue his love relation with Ilse. In the end he helps Victor escape and encourages Ilse to go with him so that she may help support the cause and he may join the local resistance.

Questions for Discussion

1. Rick convinces Ilse to leave with her husband, in part, with the following remark: "In this crazy world, the lives of these people don't amount to a hill of beans." How do you think this remark characterizes a sense of nobility?
2. Why do you think Rick sacrifices his own personal happiness for the sake of contributing to the defeat of the Nazis?

The Seven Samurai. 1954. Directed by Akira Kurosawa. The setting is a period of chaotic civil war in Japan, just at the decline of the power of the samurai. Seven samurai are recruited by poor farmers to defend their village against a group of bandits who exact tribute from them. Despite the fact that they are offered only food for payment, the samurai agree to defend the village, and almost every one of them dies in the process. Americans are probably more familiar with its American version, *The Magnificent Seven.*

Question for Discussion

1. What do you think motivates the samurai or the gunslingers to risk their lives for villagers they do not know and for no external reward?

On the Theme of Moral Emotions

Crime and Punishment. 1866. Fyodor Dostoyevsky. Raskolnikov, a young student down on his luck, becomes obsessed with killing an especially despicable, old pawnbroker. He is motivated by a certain Nietzschean-like philosophy which suggests that the great man has a right to transgress morals and the law precisely because of his greatness. The ordinary person, on the other hand, must remain conventional and follow the morals and laws of his culture. To prove himself in regard to these beliefs, he decides to kill the old woman. Yet he has a great deal of conflict about the matter. After an especially terrible nightmare, he expresses his doubts about the act. Will it be possible for him to strike her with the ax, to split her skull open, to be covered in her blood? Despite these qualms he does kill her. In the process he must also kill an innocent girl he likes because she witnesses the crime. Under the pressure of a relentless inquiry by a detective and the influence of his association with a kindly prostitute, his own psychological defenses unravel, and he confesses to the crime and seeks redemption for the act.

Questions for Discussion

1. Is Raskolnikov a wicked person in the classic sense? If not, what do you think caused him to kill the old woman?
2. Why do you think Raskolnikov could not overcome his sense of guilt for committing the crime? What does that say about moral emotions and sentiments? Can they be denied or overcome once they are established in a person?
3. Could Kant's account of duty explain Raskolnikov's confession? Why are moral emotions so powerful an influence on our behavior? Can we be moral without some moral feeling?

The Scarlet Letter. 1850. Nathaniel Hawthorne. An older English scholar sends his young wife, Hester Prynne, to Boston to set up their home. When he arrives a few years later, he finds that Hester has an illegitimate child and has been publicly humiliated in the pillory and made to wear a scarlet A, signifying Adulteress. She refuses to name her lover. Her husband conceals his identity and changes his name to Roger Chillingworth in order to find out who is her secret lover. He discovers that it is the Rev. Dimmesdale, a well-respected and seemingly saintly young minister. Dimmesdale has struggled for years with his burden of hidden guilt, and even though he does secret penance for it, pride prevents him from confessing publicly, and he remains tortured by this guilt. Chillingworth, on the other hand, has become ruined by his obsessive and cruel search. Hester, who in the meantime has won back much of the respect and forgiveness of the community through her good works helping the unfortunate, tries to convince Dimmesdale to flee with her to Europe. Instead he makes a public confession on the pillory in which Hester had once been placed. He dies there in her arms, broken by his concealed guilt. Hester goes on, free of her shame, to devote herself to helping her daughter and others in misfortune.

Questions for Discussion

1. How could public confession and shaming be beneficial for a person? How could it be harmful?
2. Why is internalized and secretive guilt so harmful for a person to bear?
3. Should Hester have made public her lover?
4. Would this sort of incident be as shameful today?
5. Why does revenge often lead to self-destruction?

Schindler's List. 1994. Directed by Stephen Spielberg. Novel by Thomas Keneally. Oskar Schindler is an unscrupulous businessman, womanizer, adulterer, and charming rogue living in Nazi Germany. He is a war profiteer, who bribes officials to get business deals. As the Jews are systematically rounded up and placed in ghettos and concentration camps, he exploits the Jewish businessmen to financially back his scheme to set up factories to produce war materiel. However, one day as he is riding his horse, he comes across a scene in which Nazi soldiers are brutally routing Jews out of the ghetto for transportation to the death camps. The event completely turns him around. He now becomes devoted to saving as many Jewish lives as he can. In the process he places himself at grave risk and loses his fortune, but manages to succeed in saving a number of lives.

Questions for Discussion

1. Would you call Schindler a good man?
2. Do good and noble acts make a person good and noble?
3. Why is compassion often a stronger and more intense feeling than sympathy? How can compassion be transformative in a way that sympathy cannot be?
4. Do you think Schindler felt pity or genuine compassion for those he rescued?

On the Theme of Guilt

Sophie's Choice. 1979. William Styron. A Southern writer, Stingo, moves to New York City and meets an unbalanced but brilliant man, Nathan, and his Polish girlfriend, Sophie, a woman who survived the Nazi concentration camps. In the course of their relation, the writer discovers a horrifying decision that Sophie made in the concentration camp.

The Tell-Tale Heart. 1843. Edgar Allan Poe. The murderer of an old man buries the dismembered body beneath the floor in his room. While the police are investigating, he begins to hear the heartbeats of his victim. He confesses in a frenzy. When the body is recovered, the murdered man's watch is found to be ticking.

On the Theme of Wickedness

Billy Budd. Published 1924. Herman Melville. Billy Budd is a handsome and innocent sailor with a fine singing voice. He is well-liked among his shipmates. One day while sailing, his ship is boarded by the crew of a British frigate, whose officers impress Billy into the Royal Navy. Among the petty officers is Claggart, who fixes on the innocence of Billy Budd and plots to bring him down. Claggart uses every opportunity to treat Billy cruelly. In his simplicity Billy cannot understand why Claggart hates him so and why evil should desire to destroy good. Claggart concocts a fantastic story of mutiny, supposedly plotted by Billy, whom he accuses to the captain. Billy, unable to speak, in his only act of rebellion strikes Claggart with a fatal blow. Claggart smiles as he dies, knowing that he has condemned Billy to death. Captain Vere, who sympathizes with Billy and recognizes his innocence, is nevertheless forced to hang him.

Questions for Discussion

1. Can you answer Billy's question: Why would Claggart be so determined to destroy the good in Billy?
2. Why was Claggart pleased with Billy's demise, even though it meant his own death?
3. Would it have been reasonable for the captain to override his duty and not hang Billy? Was there an alternative, keeping in mind the strictness of discipline aboard British ships in the 19th century?
4. Is Billy's innocence a fault? If he had been more worldly and prudent, would that have benefited him?

Other Familiar Stories on Wickedness for Discussion

Lord of the Flies. 1955. William Golding. A group of boys become stranded on an island after a plane crash. In spite of the efforts of a few boys to form an organized society, the group reverts to primitive rites and ritual murder.

A Clockwork Orange. 1962. Anthony Burgess. Film version directed by Stanley Kubrick, 1971. Alex is a sinister delinquent living in a future society. When he commits an especially brutal crime and rape, he is imprisoned and made to undergo brutal behavioral modification. Now conditioned to respond negatively to violence, he is released into a society in which he falls prey to the violence he cannot respond to.

Blue Velvet. 1986. Directed by David Lynch. All seems well in a small, ordinary town. But beneath the surfaces lies brutality and the sinister operation of underground figures.

East of Eden. 1952. John Steinbeck. Adam Trask marries Cathy, a vicious prostitute. She gives birth to twin boys, Caleb and Aron. Hating her situation, she shoots her husband after he attempts to stop her from leaving and takes up in a brothel. She slowly poisons the madam and takes over the establishment. After years of lethargy and denial, Adam finally confronts Cathy's wickedness and no longer loves her. In the meantime Aron grows up innocent, open-hearted, and religious, while Caleb has a stormy adolescence, torn between his desires for innocence and his proclivity toward viciousness. To hurt Adam, who dotes on his brother Aron, Caleb takes him to see his wicked mother. Aron is so shocked by the experience that he gives up his girlfriend and enlists in the army during World War I, where he is killed. Adam suffers a stroke with the news. But on his deathbed Adam forgives Caleb, which gives Caleb a chance to rethink his life.

In Cold Blood. 1966. Truman Capote. The story of the murder of a well-to-do farmer, his wife, and two children in Kansas by two ex-convicts. The story follows their escape, capture, trial, judicial appeals, and hanging.

SUGGESTED READINGS

On Moral Emotions and Sentiment

Aronfreed, Justin. 1968. *Conscience and Conduct.* New York: Academic Press.
———. 1969. The Concept of Internalization. *Handbook of Socialization Theory and Research.* Edited by D.A. Goslin. Chicago: Rand McNally, pp. 263–323.
Baier, Annette. 1985. *Postures of the Mind.* Minneapolis: University of Minnesota Press.
———. 1991. *The Progress of Sentiment.* Cambridge, MA: Harvard University Press.
Blum, 1980. *Friendship, Altruism and Morality.* London: Routledge and Kegan Paul.
Damasio, Antonio. 1994. *Descartes' Error: Emotion, Reason and the Human Brain.* New York: Grosset/Putnam.
De Sousa, Ronald. 1987. *The Rationality of Emotions.* Cambridge, MA: MIT Press.
Eisenberg, Nancy. 1986. *The Altruistic Emotion, Cognition and Behavior.* Mahwah, NJ: Erlbaum.
Goleman, Daniel. 1995. *Emotional Intelligence.* New York: Bantam.
Gordon, Robert. 1987. *The Structure of Emotions.* New York: Cambridge University Press.
Green, O.H. 1992. *The Emotions: A Philosophical Theory.* Dordrecht, the Netherlands: Kluwer.
Greenspan, Patricia. 1995. *Practical Guilt: Moral Dilemmas, Emotions, and Social Norms.* Oxford, England: Oxford University Press.
Hume, David. 1739. *An Enquiry Concerning the Principles of Morals.* 3rd edition. Edited by L.A. Selby-Rigge. Oxford, England: Oxford University Press, 1975.
———. *Treatise of Human Nature.* Edited by L.A. Selby-Rigge and P.H. Nidditch. Oxford, England: Clarendon Press, 1978.
Lynd, Helen. 1973. *On Shame and the Search for Identity.* Cambridge, MA: Harvard University Press.
Lyons, William. 1980. *Emotion.* New York: Cambridge University Press.

Margolis, Diane. 1998. *The Fabric of Self: A Theory of Ethics and Emotions.* New Haven, CT: Yale University Press.

Oakley, Justin. 1991. *Morality and the Emotions.* London: Routledge.

Oliner, Samuel, and Oliner, Pearl. 1988. *The Altruistic Personality.* New York: Free Press.

Piliavin, J., and Chang, H. 1990. Altruism: A Review of Recent Theory and Research. *Annual Review of Sociology* 16: 27-65.

Planalp, Sally. 1999. *Communicating Emotion: Social, Moral, and Cultural Processes.* Cambridge, England: Cambridge University Press.

Rorty, Amelie, editor. 1980. *Explaining Emotions.* Berkeley: University of California Press.

Schopenhauer, Arthur. 1841. *On the Basis of Morality.* Translated by E. Payne. New York: Bobbs-Merrill, 1965.

Smith, Adam. 1759. *The Theory of Moral Sentiments.* Edited by D. Raphael and A. Macfie. Oxford, England: Clarendon Press, 1976.

Soble, Alan. 1990. *The Structure of Love.* New Haven, CT: Yale University Press.

Solomon, Robert. 1976. *The Passions.* New York: Doubleday.

Sternberg, R. 1985. *Beyond IQ.* New York: Cambridge University Press.

Taylor, Gabriel. 1985. *Pride, Shame and Guilt: Emotions of Self-Assessment.* Oxford, England: Oxford University Press.

Williams, Bernard. 1993. *Shame and Necessity.* Berkeley: University of California Press.

Wilson, James. 1993. *The Moral Sense.* New York: Free Press.

On Psychopathy and Wickedness

Benn, S. 1985. Wickedness. *Ethics* 95: 795–810.

Cleckley, Hervey. 1982. *The Masks of Sanity.* St. Louis, MO: Mosby.

Hare, Robert. 1999. *Without Conscience: The Disturbing World of the Psychopaths Among Us.* New York: Guilford Press.

Hare, Robert, and Schalling, D. 1978. *Psychopathic Behavior.* New York: Wiley.

Heginbotham, Christopher, editor. 2000. *Philosophy, Psychiatry and Psychopathy.* New York: Ashgate.

Lykken, David. 1995. *The Antisocial Personality.* Mahwah, NJ: Erlbaum.

Martens, Willem. 2000. Antisocial and Psychopathic Personality Disorders: Causes, Course, and Remission—A Review Article. *International Journal of Offender Therapy and Comparative Criminology* 44(4): 406–430.

Millon, Theodore, Simonsen, E., Birket-Smith, M., and Davis, R., editors. 2000. *Psychopathy: Antisocial, Criminal and Violent Behavior.* New York: Guilford Press.

Mitchell, Derek, and Blair, James. 2000. State of the Art: Psychopathy. *Psychologist* 13(7): 356–364.

Murphey, Jeffrey. 1972. Moral Death: A Kantian Essay on Psychopathy. *Ethics* 82: 284–298.

Rieber, Robert, and Bakan, David. 1997. *Manufacturing Social Distress: Psychopathy in Everyday Life.* New York: Plenum.

On Moral Development in Children

Coles, Robert. 1986. *The Moral Life of Children.* New York: Atlantic Monthly Press.

———. 1997. *The Moral Intelligence of Children.* New York: Random House.

Damon, W. 1988. *The Moral Child.* New York: Free Press.

Erikson, Erik. 1991. *Childhood and Society.* New York: W.W. Norton.

Gerwirtz, J., and Kartines, W., editors. 1983. Morality: Moral Development and Moral Behavior. New York: Wiley.

Gesell, Arnold. 1948. *Studies in Childhood Development.* New York: Harper.

Gilligan, Carol. 1982. *In a Different Voice.* Cambridge, MA: Harvard University Press.

Kagan, Jerome, and Lamb, S. 1987. *The Emergence of Morality in Young Children.* Chicago: University of Chicago Press.

Kohlberg, Lawrence. 1981–1984. *Essays on Moral Development. The Psychology of Moral Development.* 2 vols. New York: Harper and Row.

Lapsley, Daniel. 1996. *Moral Psychology.* Boulder, CO: Westview Press.

Pritchard, Michael. 1991. *On Becoming Responsible.* Lawrence: University of Kansas Press.

———. 1996. *Reasonable Children.* Lawrence: University of Kansas Press.

Reimer, Joseph et al. 1983. *Promoting Moral Growth.* New York: Longman.

Rest, James. 1979. *Development in Judging Moral Issues.* Minneapolis: University of Minnesota Press.

Rick, John, and De Vitis, J. 1994. *Theories of Moral Development.* Springfield, IL: Charles C Thomas.

Rosen, Hugh. 1980. *The Development of Sociomoral Knowledge.* New York: Columbia University Press.

Siegal, M. 1982. *Fairness in Children.* London: Academic Press.

Verducci, Susan. 2000. A Conceptual History of Empathy and a Question It Raises for Moral Education. *Education* 50(1): 63–81.

Windmiller, M., Lambert, N., and Turiel, E., editors. 1980. *Moral Development and Socialization.* Boston: Allyn and Bacon.

Wren, Thomas. 1991. *Caring About Morality: Philosophical Perspectives in Moral Psychology.* Cambridge, MA: MIT Press.

Zahn-Waxler, C., Cummings, E., and Iannotti, R., editors. 1991. *Altruism and Aggression: Biological and Social Origins.* Cambridge, England: Cambridge University Press.

On Stories and Moral Education

Bennett, William. 1993. *The Book of Virtues.* New York: Simon and Schuster.

Bettelheim, Bruno. 1977. *The Uses of Enchantment.* New York: Vintage.

Booth, Wayne. 1988. *The Company We Keep.* Berkeley: University of California Press.

Coles, Robert. 1989. *The Call of Stories.* Boston: Houghton-Mifflin.

Kilpatrick, William. 1992. *Why Johnny Can't Tell Right from Wrong.* New York: Touchstone.

Kilpatrick, W. Gregory, and Wolf, Suzanne. 1994. *Books That Build Character.* New York: Touchstone.

Lickona, Thomas. 1991. *Educating for Character.* New York: Bantam Books.

Newton, Adam. 1995. *Narrative Ethics.* Cambridge, MA: Harvard University Press.

Nussbaum, Martha. 1990. *Love's Knowledge.* Oxford, England: Oxford University Press.

Palmer, Frank. 1992. *Literature and Moral Understanding.* Oxford, England: Oxford University Press.

Plato. *The Republic. Collected Dialogues.* Edited by Edith Hamilton and H. Cairns. Princeton, NJ: Princeton University Press, 1973.

Rosenstand, Nina. 1994. *The Moral of the Story.* London: Mayfield.

Sarbin, T., editor. 1986. *Narrative Psychology: The Storied Nature of Human Conduct.* New York: Praeger.

Sieber, Tobin. 1992. *Morals and Stories.* New York: Columbia University Press.

Sommers, Christina. 1993. Teaching the Virtues. *The Public Interest.* Spring: 3–11.

Vitz, Paul. 1990. The Uses of Stories in Moral Development. *American Psychologist.* 45(6): 709–720.

On Feminist Ethics

Andolsen, Barbara et al., editors. 1985. *Women's Consciousness, Women's Conscience: A Reader in Feminist Ethics.* New York: Winston Press.

Baier, Annette. 1985. *Postures of the Mind.* Minneapolis: University of Minnesota Press.

———. 1991. *The Progress of Sentiment.* Cambridge, MA: Harvard University Press.

Bat-Ami, Bar on, and Ferguson, Ann, editors. 1998. *Daring to Be Good: Essays in Feminist Ethico-Politics.* New York: Routledge.

Bowden, Peta. 1997. *Caring: Gender-Sensitive Ethics.* New York: Routledge.

Brabeck, Mary, editor. 1989. *Who Cares? Theory, Research and Educational Implications of the Ethics of Care.* New York: Praeger.

Cannon, Katie. 1988. *Black Womanist Ethics.* Atlanta, GA: Scholars Press.

Card, Claudia, editor. 1991. *Feminist Ethics*. Lawrence: University of Kansas Press.

Clement, Grace. 1999. *Care, Autonomy, and Justice: Feminism and the Ethic of Care*. Boulder, CO: Westview Press.

Elshtain. 1981. *Public Man, Private Woman*. Princeton, NJ: Princeton University Press.

Frazer, Elizabeth, Hornsby, J., and Lovibund, S., editors. 1992. *Ethics: A Feminist Reader*. Oxford, England: Blackwell.

Gilligan, Carol. *In a Different Voice: Psychological Theory and Women's Development*. Cambridge, MA: Harvard University Press.

Held, Virginia. 1989. *Rights and Goods: Justifying Social Action*. Chicago: University of Chicago Press.

———. 1993. *Feminist Morality*. Chicago: University of Chicago Press.

———, editor. 1995. *Justice and Care: Essential Readings in Feminist Ethics*. Boulder, CO: Westview Press.

Hoagland, Sarah. 1988. *Lesbian Ethics: Toward New Value*. Palo Alto, CA: Institute of Lesbian Studies.

Jaggar, Alison. 1983. *Feminist Politics and Human Nature*. Totowa, NJ: Rowman and Allanheld.

Kittay, Eva, and Meyers, D., editors. 1987. *Women and Moral Theory*. Totowa, NJ: Rowman and Littlefield.

Noddings, Nel. 1989. *Care: A Feminist Approach to Morals and Education*. Berkeley: University of California Press.

Okin, Susan. 1979. *Women in Western Political Thought*. Princeton, NJ: Princeton University Press.

Pateman, Carol. 1988. *The Sexual Contract*. Stanford, CA: Stanford University Press.

Ruddick, Sarah. 1989. *Maternal Thinking: Towards a Politics of Peace*. Boston: Beacon Press.

Tong, Rosemarie. 1993. *Feminine and Feminist Ethics*. New York: Wadsworth.

On the Relation between Reason and Moral Feeling in Kant

Aune, Bruce. 1979. *Kant's Theory of Morals*. Princeton, NJ: Princeton University Press.

Kant, Immanuel. 1788. *Critique of Practical Reason*. Translated by L.W. Beck. New York: Bobbs-Merrill, 1956.

Korsgaard, Christine. 1996. *Creating the Kingdom of Ends*. Cambridge: Cambridge University Press.

Nell, Onora. 1975. *Acting on Principle: An Essay in Kantian Ethics*. New York: Columbia University Press.

On the Emotive Theory of Ethics

Ayer, A.J. 1952. *Language, Truth and Logic*. New York: Dover.

Hare, R.M. 1952. *The Language of Morals*. Oxford, England: Oxford University Press.

Stevenson, C.L. 1946. *Ethics and Language*. New Haven, CT: Yale University Press.

Urmson, J.O. 1968. *The Emotive Theory of Ethics*. London: Hutcheson.

On David Hume's Ethical Theory

Baier, Annette. 1985. *Postures of the Mind*. Minneapolis: University of Minnesota Press.

———. 1991. *The Progress of Sentiment*. Cambridge, MA: Harvard University Press.

Bricke, John. 1996. *Mind and Morality: An Examination of Hume's Moral Psychology*. Oxford, England: Clarendon Press.

Harrison, Jonathan. 1981. *Hume's Theory of Justice*. Oxford, England: Clarendon Press.

Hope, Vincent. 1989. *Virtue by Consensus*. Oxford, England: Clarendon Press.

Jaap, Anne, editor. 2000. *Feminist Interpretations of David Hume*. State Park: Pennsylvania State University Press.

Mackie, John. 1980. *Hume's Moral Theory*. London: Routledge and Kegan Paul.

Norton, David. 1982. *David Hume: Common Sense Moralist, Sceptical Metaphysician*. Princeton, NJ: Princeton University Press.

CHAPTER TWO

Autonomy and Strength of Will

A man without force is without the essential dignity of humanity. Human nature is so constituted that it cannot honor a helpless man, though it can pity him, and even then it cannot do that for long if signs of power do not arise.

—Frederick Douglass

Freedom is nothing more than an opportunity to discipline ourselves, rather than to be disciplined by others.

—Thomas Murphy

I wish my life and decisions to depend on myself, not on external forces of whatever kind. I wish to be an instrument of my own, not of other men's acts of will. I wish to be ... moved by reasons, by conscious purposes, which are my own, not by causes which affect me, as it were, from outside. I wish to be a doer ... deciding not being decided for, self-directed and not acted upon by external nature.

—Isaiah Berlin

The importance of moral emotions is clear. The analysis of psychopathy and wickedness shows that without moral feeling, a person can become cold-hearted and cruel. Those who lose the capacity to feel sympathy or remorse, guilt or shame, increase their capacity for atrocity and viciousness. Moral emotion and sentiment create a desire to do the right thing—manifest as a certain style of internalization: a sense of duty or honor, caring, or a striving for nobility. In general, throughout all these various sentiments, there is a willingness to correct behavior toward what is thought to be good without the constant prod of some external constraint.

But although it is impossible to be morally competent without moral sentiment, moral sentiment alone is not enough to guarantee it. It is one thing to desire the good, to be motivated toward self-correction, but it is another to have the strength of will to do the right thing. Kant defines strength of will simply as "not mere wish but as the summoning of all the means in our power" (1785: 10). Most parents know what strength of will it takes to act on their desire to see their children happy. Good parents must spend countless hours attending to their children's physical needs and wants, forgoing most of their own comforts. First, there is the loss of sleep, the rituals of feeding, the effort it takes simply to drive an infant safely to the store, and nursing them through illnesses and injuries, accompanied by the anxiety not only over ordinary childhood sickness but very serious ones as well. There is the matter of their upbringing: helping them to walk, to talk, to acquire innumerable skills; to set the rules of etiquette, to enforce moral rules; to tend to their education, helping them learn addition and multiplication tables, preparing for spelling tests, helping with science projects, helping with homework, and the infinite number of hours of correction and monitoring required for all these matters. Add to this the endurance of adolescence and the constant worry about whether they will turn out right. Throw in the economic sacrifice involved in it all, and one can easily calculate what great strength of will it takes to do the ordinary task of raising kids. There is a scene in *The Magnificent Seven,* a story of seven gunslingers who decide to defend a poor village against marauding bandits. Some of the village children begin to admire one of the gunslingers. "You are a brave man. Our parents are not like you," one little boy protests, "they are cowards." At which point the gunslinger grabs the little boy angrily, saying, "It takes more courage and strength to be a parent than a gunslinger like me. I don't ever want to hear you say that again!" He may have a point.

To accomplish any significant task requires the strength of will to do what it takes. If moral sentiment involves an internalization, a willingness to correct behavior toward the good, then strength of will involves a power to do it. As the list of parenting tasks illustrates, this power is expressed as the ability to endure, to refrain, to stay the course, to direct, to avoid, to forgo, to wait, to sacrifice, to retain, to resist, to overcome. Doubtless the person who has these powers also has autonomy, which is the power to control and direct oneself, a sort of self-mastery.

Autonomy and strength of will assume that people have a power either to change the events in their environment to suit their goals or to change their own behavior to conform to the constraints of that environment. Autonomy assumes that the world is somewhat changeable and not absolutely determined; it also assumes that one's behavior is not so determined that a person cannot change. In ordinary parlance, autonomy assumes free will—that issue, then, is the first order of business.

2.1 THE ISSUE OF FREE WILL

In Slawomir Mrozek's play *Striptease,* two identically dressed commuters on their way to work suddenly find themselves transported to a room of unknown location. The room has two stools and two doors, one on the left and one on the right. As the two discuss what they should do, a large hand comes through one of the doors, and as it reaches the two commuters, it silently points alternately to the two suit jackets they are wearing. After gesturing in such a manner for a while, the commuters realize that the Hand wants the articles of clothing; they take them off and hand them to the Hand, which promptly exits the room with the goods in tow. The two commuters start bickering about the event. Commuter A believes that it was

The Peter Paradox

In Luke 22:31–35, Jesus, anticipating his arrest, torture, and death, tells Peter that he will deny that he knows him (Jesus) three times and predicts precisely that this will occur before the "cock crows." Peter insists that he could never do such a thing and that he "was ready to go to prison" with him "and to death." Of course, Peter does deny him three times and exactly at the time foretold.

If Jesus could foretell what Peter would do, that is, if it was fated for Peter to deny knowing his master, could Peter have done otherwise? Could Peter be blamed for his actions then?

The Omniscience Paradox

There is a theological paradox related to the Peter Paradox that has plagued thinkers for centuries. If God is an omniscient, omnibenevolent, omnipotent being, then because of his omniscience, he can foretell what human beings will do; if we do something other than what is foretold, God cannot be omniscient. Consequently, if God is omniscient, then we have no choice in what we do.

Question for Discussion

Do you agree with this claim?

A parallel but more secular argument can be made. A scientist can predict the behavior of the planets precisely because she knows the laws pertaining to them. The ability to predict accurately is an indication of existing laws; laws in the strict sense are deterministic. Consequently, the successful ability to predict, or to predict comprehensively (as in omniscience), would be proof of determinism.

because they were discussing how to escape the room that the Hand came in and demanded the suit jacket; Commuter B argues instead that they must do something to find a way out of their circumstances. Acting upon their respective beliefs, Commuter B pounds on one of the doors to see if it will open, while Commuter A sits passively waiting on the stool. Suddenly, the Hand appears through the other door, walks to Commuter B and demands another article of clothing—this time his pants. As Commuter B obliges the Hand, Commuter A proclaims that he was right all along—the thing to do was to do nothing under these circumstances so as not to provoke the Hand. But just then, the Hand turns to Commuter A and points to his pants, which he apologetically removes, behaving obsequiously. Commuter A and Commuter B dispute again, A insisting on passiveness and B on activism. In the meantime the Hand comes into the room periodically to demand various articles of clothing. B begins to realize that no matter what he does, the Hand will appear; to prove his point he stands on one of the stools and sings Schubert's "The Trout." The Hand appears again. Eventually, the two are handcuffed together by the Hand and made to wear duncelike hats that obscure their vision. In the end they wander around the room blindly, with no pants.

One plausible interpretation of this play relevant to the theme here is that the appearance of the Hand seems regular and planned and irrelevant to the actions or inaction of the agents in the room. In other words, the outcome was fixed by the Hand, and the agents' actions had no bearing on it. To put it differently: In a system that is fixed, determined, or fated, what will happen to you will happen regardless of what you do. *Determinism is the view that all events happen within a closed, causally connected system that dictates the necessary occurrence of those events. Fatalism* usually has a somewhat different connotation. *It suggests that one's life and events are guided by some superior force and cannot be altered; it often involves the sense of destiny.*

Fatalism is one of the principal themes of the more famous and familiar story of Oedipus. The Oracle (a priestess connected with Apollo, the god who knows the future) tells Laius, king of Thebes, that his son will commit patricide and will marry his wife. Fearing his fate, Laius vows not to have sexual intercourse with his wife, Jocasta; he fails in his resoluteness, and a male child is born. Out of fear, Laius binds the feet of the infant and abandons him on a hillside. He is found by a shepherd who returns him to his home in the city of Corinth. The king and queen of Corinth, who are childless, adopt the foundling but try to conceal his orphan status

Can the Most Powerful of the Gods Overcome Fate?

In the Iliad, Homer depicts a scene in which Zeus, the mightiest of all the Greek gods, and Hera, his wife and queen, are observing the 10-year battle between the Achaians and the Trojans for the prize of the city of Troy and the release of Helen. This is war that the gods themselves have created by manipulating and interfering with human plans. At one point in the battle, Zeus sees one of his (many) mortal sons in the heat of a fight; he knows that his son is fated to die, but moved by love and compassion for his son, he thinks about rescuing him from his fate. Hera admonishes him, arguing that if Zeus were to do this, then the other gods would attempt to meddle in the matters of destiny. Zeus realizes the wisdom of this argument and allows his son to die in battle.

This scene seems to suggest that Zeus could change fate if he chose to do so. But does that really make sense? If fate can be changed, then by definition it wouldn't be fate, but something that could be altered by the intervention of gods and mortals.

There is a similar paradox found in Christian theology. God is thought to be omniscient (all-knowing), omnipotent (all-powerful), and omnibenevolent (all-good), among other characteristics. If God is all-good, could he do something evil? Certainly, if he is omnipotent, he could, but if he is all-good, he can't.

from him. Nonetheless, as the child grows into a young man, he is plagued by rumors of his foundling status. Seeking the truth, he goes to the Oracle, who promptly tells him that he will kill his father and marry his mother. Horrified by this prophecy, Oedipus flees Corinth, hoping thereby to avoid committing acts of murder and incest against the people he believes to be his parents. On the way to the neighboring city of Thebes, he is accosted by a chariot driver and his passenger who run him off the road and try to kill him; he kills both the driver and the passenger.

When Oedipus arrives at Thebes, it is besieged by the Sphinx. The monster demands that the city solve a riddle it poses. Each week an answer must be given, brought by a young man; if the answer is wrong, the young man is killed by the Sphinx. After months, no one has solved the riddle ("What walks in the morning on four legs, in the afternoon on two, and in the evening on three?"). Oedipus reflects on the riddle and volunteers to present a solution (the answer is "man," who crawls on all fours as an infant, walks on two legs as an adult, and uses a cane as an old man). With the right answer in hand, the Sphinx is forced to destroy itself, and the city of Thebes is saved. As a reward for his rescue, Oedipus is made king, since the previous king had recently been killed, and is given the king's wife as bride. As Oedipus discovers later, one of the men he had killed on the road to Thebes was indeed the former king who abandoned an infant with bound ankles on a hillside. Well aware of the scars that mark his ankles, Oedipus doesn't take long to realize that, as the prophecy had foretold, he killed his father and is presently married to his mother.

Although both *Oedipus* and *Striptease* show that, if outcomes are determined, it matters not what one does or does not do. Still it can be argued that, even if this is the case, morality still matters. There is a moral difference between how Commuter A and Commuter B deal with their fates, and certainly, the Oedipus who abhors his fate and strives to avoid it, simply because he does not want to do such horrible things, would be morally superior to the one who embraces such actions and decides to kill his father and get it over with. But if a stronger form of determinism is supposed so that how one reacts to the fatalism of a system is itself fated, then it seems that morality is a meaningless consideration. In other words, if who you are is also determined, then what you do in a system which is determined is also fixed. This is the strongest possible version of fatalism.

Many people find fatalism comforting. The idea that the path of your life is chosen for you—either by fate, by God, by the stars, or by one's genes—relieves you of the responsibility of making choices, on the one hand, and of taking blame for your actions, on the other. Choosing, especially depending on the sort of choice involved, is stressful for many, and accepting the blame when some choice has gone awry is painful for most. People appeal to determinism for all sorts of justifications for their actions: a husband, married 20 years, who has an affair, claims that his new relationship was "fated to be." This attitude toward the situation allows him to do two things. First, it exonerates his infidelity. Since it was meant to be, then he had no choice in the matter and cannot be blamed. It also releases him from the responsibility of making a painful choice between his wife of 20 years and his questionable new love. By proclaiming it a matter of fate, there is no choice. When people look to the stars or to psychics, not only are they searching for their futures, but they are also searching for comfort in knowing that their future is out of their hands. If someone is not fatalistic, they show signs of strength of will; conversely, those who are fatalistic are anxious to give up choice in their lives in favor of someone or something taking control.

As mentioned, fatalism shows that if there is no possibility of directing our own behavior, and we are powerless to change ourselves or the world, then the study of ethics makes no sense. If there can be no self-correction of behavior, there is no reason to persuade ourselves to do the right thing. Obviously, the very reason for practicing ethics hinges on a positive answer to the existence of what is traditionally called "free will."

There are three basic positions in regard to the issue of free will: determinism (sometimes called hard determinism—and of which fatalism is a species), compatibilism (sometimes called soft determinism), and libertarianism (not to be confused with the political and ethical theory).

2.1.1 DETERMINISM

Determinism argues that there is no free will in the ordinary sense of the term. Human behavior is determined through the interrelation of a number of physical, biological, and social laws and the conditions surrounding them. This can be defined more strictly in the following way: (1) every event is caused and (2) given all previous relevant causes of an event, that event and only that event could have been the result. Therefore, any action a human being performs is the unique result of a previous set of causes, and given those causes, only that action could have happened. If we add to this conclusion the *principle of alternative possibilities*, that is, people are morally responsible for what they have done only if they could have done otherwise (Frankfurt 1969: 829), it follows that human beings are not responsible for their actions. Given what has preceded an action, human beings have no choice but to act in the way they are about to. "The sum total of a person's experiences, desires and knowledge, his hereditary constitution, the social circumstances and the nature of the choice facing him, together with other factors that we may not know about, all combine to make a particular action in the circumstances inevitable" (Nagel 1987: 51). It is specifically the second thesis of determinism which gives it its

---

Query: Would the Ability to Control Human Behavior Actually Prove the Existence of Free Will?

In 1971 Kenneth Clark, in a presidential address to the American Psychological Association, proposed that all political leaders should be given biochemical treatments which would block the possibility of using power destructively. Imagine that, either through biochemistry or genetics, it was possible to design personalities and behaviors.

Question for Discussion

Wouldn't the choice to do that itself become an ethical question and, therefore, a matter of ethical choice?

fatalistic edge: Given all that has preceded, nothing else could have occurred. A wider view of hard determinism was advocated by the 18th-century philosopher-mathematician, Pierre Laplace (1749–1827). Laplace imagined that if one knew the present state of the universe and the laws that pertain to it, then one could predict the next state of the universe: "Nothing would be uncertain and the future, as the past, would be present to our eyes" (1814).

There are several difficulties with determinism. First, some scientific theories infer some kind of indeterminism. Both quantum theory and the theory of chaos suggest that certain systems found in nature are inherently indeterminate. For example, we have all the laws necessary to explain the weather (namely, the laws of fluid mechanics). Yet we cannot predict the weather with a great deal of accuracy. Weather is an inherently chaotic system, meaning that conditions can appear nearly instantaneously in a way that affects the character and direction of the entire system, and small changes in the system can lead to large, unpredictable results (cf. Gleich 1987: 11–15). Quantum theory also seems to serve as a counterexample to the deterministic thesis. Under the older Newtonian view of subatomic physics, every atom moves along a trajectory that is uniquely determined by the forces which act on it, thus upholding the two theses of determinism. Quantum theory contradicts this view by suggesting that subatomic particles of light behave in such a way that, depending on initial conditions, the photon may subsist in several states. This is evidence against the second thesis of hard determinism (cf. Davies 1983: 100–119).

The ability to predict human behavior would be an indication of the credibility of determinism. This is possible in some cases, marginal in others, and nonexistent in some. Of course, this could be a problem with our state of knowledge. Human behavior could still be determined, yet we do not have the science to explain it. The closest hard science we have to predicting human behavior is genetics. Yet genetics shows that genetic determination is not hard determined in the way in which the motion of the planets is. Genes and genetically based behaviors are not fatalistic, but subject to permutation and variability over time; that is, there is a great deal of plasticity in this sort of behavior. If there were not, the entire theory of evolution would make no sense; adaptability, permutation, and variation are the very core of evolutionary growth. Genetically determined behavior is more of a disposition that often requires certain environmental conditions to trigger, and it can be culturally directed or controlled. After all, some of the more hardwired behaviors, such as sexual behaviors, are often tightly controlled by cultures: A culture may insist on virginity prior to marriage and even lifelong celibacy for certain members of its subgroups. This is despite the fact that sexual proclivity seems to be a genetically based behavior. Conversely, despite the fact that incest-avoidance behavior is apparently hardwired, incest of course does occur (cf. Shepher 1980).

In addition to these considerations, human systems and human thinking form a self-reflexive system, meaning that knowledge about how the system works affects the system. That is different from most physical systems. The fact is that no amount of knowledge of how the planets orbit the sun will change their orbit. Astrophysicist Stephen Hawking describes this characteristic of human behavior neatly:

> The concept of free will belongs to a different arena from that of fundamental laws of science. If one tries to deduce human behavior from the laws of science, one gets caught in the logical paradox of self-referencing systems. If what one does could be

predicted from the fundamental laws, then the fact of making that prediction could change what happens. It is like the problems one would get into if time travel were possible. ... If you could see what is going to happen in the future, you could change it. If you knew which horse was going to win the Grand National, you could make a fortune by betting on it. But that action would change the odds (1994: 135).

But self-reflexivity does not necessarily disprove determinism; it may simply indicate a more complex determinism. It is quite possible that a self-reflexive system is a system that causes other systems to cause other events within the total system. Both chaos and quantum theory lend credence to the possibility of a certain indeterminacy in the basic structure of things, yet it is never clear in these accounts whether the indeterminacy is an actual condition of these systems or whether it is a perception due to the inadequacy of our state of knowledge. Chaotic systems may still be determinate ones, though the character of their determinacy is different than the classic Newtonian model.

The strategies for proving the existence of "free will" in some sense of the term are clear. One way is to show—as paradoxical as it may sound—that free will and determinism are somehow compatible. *Compatibilism*, as the name implies, accepts this assumption. The challenge for compatibilists is to show how such a claim makes sense since, offhand, the two seem inconsistent. *Incompatibilism*, on the other hand, argues that a determined system is incompatible with any ordinary sense of free will (cf. Van Inwagen 1983). Free will is possible only if there is indeterminacy. But even if some systems are indeterminate, they would not necessarily prove the existence of free will. If our actions are random or a matter of luck, then we cannot really be praised or blamed for them. Thus, it would seem that, in order to hold someone responsible for an action, she would require some latitude of control over alternative possibilities (Fischer 1999: 99). This is the position known as *libertarianism* (not to be confused with libertarian political thought). The challenge for libertarians is to show how it makes sense to say that human agents can have control over indeterminate events, without resorting to some causal-deterministic model.

2.1.2 Libertarianism

As we have seen, *libertarianism is the view that free will and determinism are incompatible.* To count a choice as a "free" choice, there had to be some alternative to the one made; that is, there must be the assumption of a principle of alternative possibilities. For it to have been otherwise, there must be some indeterminacy in the process. Thus, the principle of alternative possibilities presupposes indeterminacy. Yet for a choice to be free, it cannot be a completely random, indeterminate process either. It's certainly an ordinary experience to feel that the outcomes of our choices are beyond our control and may have consequences we did not anticipate. But it would be strange to say that we have free will if our decision processes are also random and, hence, beyond our self-control. If a person had no idea what they were going to choose or why, their situation would have the same effect as a completely determined outcome. Whether it is random or determinate—in both cases—a person has no control over these events. The challenge for libertarianism is to show how self-control and indeterminacy are possible, without inferring some form of determinacy.

One strategy libertarians take is to argue that brain processes are indeterminate, chaotic systems, which often result in conflicts but are resolved determinately by a decision we make. Our decisions take control of indeterminate processes and move them in a certain direction (cf. Kane 1996; Van Inwagen 1983; Ginet 1990). Our beliefs, desires, and emotions merge in an indeterminate way, often resulting in a common experience of inner conflict. But in making a decision, we bring the force of will to bear upon that chaos. Thus, the decision process is one that forcefully directs the indeterminate process in a certain way. Because the process it directs is indeterminate, it does not causally determine the process, and so a person could have chosen otherwise.

It is not clear why this solves the problem. The claim that some brain processes are under self-control and others are not seems like an arbitrary claim. Second, as the decision process is described by these philosophers, it seems like an arbitrary force of will. Yet we would expect that for our decisions not to be arbitrary, we should have reasons, desires, and beliefs for choosing the way we do. Consequently, those beliefs, desires, values, and plans must have some influence on our decision making. In that case we're back to square one: Either our beliefs and desires do seem to causally influence our decisions, in which case they may be determined, or they randomly influence our decisions, in which case we also have no self-control.

Some libertarians take a different strategy. They argue that decision processes are indeterminate not in the sense of chaotic, but in the sense of having a different kind of relation than cause and effect. Thinkers associated with this position include A.I. Melden (1961), Roderick Chisholm (1964), Richard Taylor (1992), Timothy O'Connor (1996), and Randolph Clarke (1996). For them, intentional action is a prime example of noncausal relations. Intentional behavior is determinate in the sense that it directs actions toward a certain end, but it is not determinate in the sense in which cause determines an effect. The relation among choice, intention, and action is fundamentally different from the causal relation between two events, and doing something intentionally is different than having something happen to something else. For example, in viewing someone raising her arm, one could say that the brain has caused the musculature in the left arm to raise itself. However, if the context is a classroom and the person is a student, then a more accurate description would be to say that the student is raising her left arm in order to get the teacher's attention. More accurately, she is making something happen in order to make something else happen. Whereas cause and effect are blind and mechanical, in the sense that A causes B without regard to what B causes, it is clear that, at least in the case of intelligent agency, the latter causes A specifically for the purpose of causing B. To put it differently, an agent causes A because he believes that A is likely to cause B, which is the result that the agent intends. Consequently, the actions of intelligent agents, such as human beings, cannot be entirely framed within a causal framework. The end, so to speak, predates the means by which it is achieved and so violates the normal asymmetry found in cause and effect.

But does this explanation really avoid causal language? There are a few things to consider. Although it is true that the goal of the action guides the means by which it is accomplished, it does not necessarily predate the means because it exists, at least in cognitive form, in the agent's ideas or plans. Second, intentional behavior may be considered similar to steering behaviors or cybernetic processes, which can be viewed as complex causal processes. Consider an example that may be too simplistic to apply analogously to a complex system such as the brain, but still might be illustrative. A thermostat controls the behavior of the furnace through a negative feedback loop that can be explained purely in terms of cause and effect. As the temperature in the room cools, the metal conductor inside the thermostat contracts, reconnecting a circuit that turns on the furnace. As the furnace works to heat up the room, the metal conductor expands and breaks the circuit, thus turning off the furnace. The behavior involves self-guidance, but it does not involve anything other than cause and effect relations, although at a more complex level than things simply bumping into one another. Although the brain could not be explained so simply, there is evidence to suggest that self-reflexive and self-directed behaviors may still be complex causal ones. Self-directed behaviors are present in many biological forms where such behaviors are required for adaptability and survival. Such beings form complex systems that are difficult to understand. However, using the criterion of simplest explanations (called "Occam's razor"), there is no need to invoke the existence of new relations when old ones might do in their explanation.

But whether or not we accept intentional relations or causal relations, the important point is that there is still a determinate process involved. A person who is not able to direct his behavior intentionally so that when he wants to raise his arm, his arm does not rise, or he cannot say what he intends to say, or his body acts randomly despite his wishes are all circumstances that suggest he has no "free will." Thus, it seems inconsistent to say that a person has control over events, yet these events are indeterminate. This leads exactly to the position of compatibilism. Compatibilists argue that there is no inconsistency between "free will" understood as self-control and determinacy.

2.1.3 Compatibilism

Compatibilism agrees with the two principal theses of determinism, namely, that (1) every event is caused and (2) given all previous relevant causes to an event, only that event and no other could have occurred. However, compatibilists, such as philosopher Harry Frankfurt, disagree with the claims of the principle of alternative possibilities, which would then infer the impossibility of responsibility for human behavior. *The claim by compatibilists is that even though no alternative possibility exists, there can still be cases where we are held responsible for our action* (Frankfurt 1969: 829). This requires some clarification.

There is no doubt that all human actions are caused. In fact, as mentioned earlier, if it is the case that behavior, or some behavior, is not caused, that it just "happens," then that does not make a person "free" either. If behavior just happens for no reason, then it is just as difficult to say that persons are responsible for their behavior as it is in the case in which all behavior is determined. Thomas Nagel says this nicely: "This raises the alarming possibility that we're not responsible for our actions whether determinism is true or whether it's false. If determinism is true, antecedent circumstances are responsible. If determinism is false, nothing is responsible" (1987: 56–57). What we want to say instead is that *we* cause our behavior rather than something or someone else. If this is the case, then the principle of alternative possibilities may be false. It is quite possible that, given the critical set of causes, no alternative result to the action exists, yet we can still be held responsible for our actions as long as the significant causal determinants are made by a certain aspect of the self (Frankfurt 1969: 829; 1994).

Contemporary philosopher Harry Frankfurt illustrates this point through an interesting thought experiment. Imagine you're going to vote for a certain candidate. You stand at the booth, look at the names, and a number of thought processes and emotions transpire as you pose to make a choice. However, unbeknown to you, an evil genius bent on seeing his candidate win has rigged your brain so that at the precise moment you make your choice, should you not choose his candidate, a brain scan will occur so that you do choose his candidate. Thus, there is no alternative but to choose his candidate. But let's suppose, however, you *do* choose his candidate. In that case his brain scan does not kick in, and even though there was no alternative, it could be argued that you "freely" chose that candidate.

Even though this thought experiment is a bit odd, it illustrates a very common and ordinary thing. In practice we are held responsible for our actions when we control the beliefs, values, desires, intentions, and emotions that cause the action and its outcomes, not because an alternative was possible. Conversely, we are excused from responsibility for our actions and their outcomes when either we have done nothing wrong in what we have caused or when we are not in control of those mental states. As R. Jay Wallace (1994) points out, excuse from responsibility for our actions is not due to the fact that there was no alternative possibility, but rather that the person in question was not under self-control in some sense of the term. For example, if a person is seriously ill mentally, or mentally disabled, or mentally immature as a child is, we excuse them from responsibility for certain actions. We don't excuse them because they had no other choice. To put the same point a bit differently, if the self, in some sense of that term, is the predominant part of the proximate causes of an action, then to that extent the action is free; otherwise it is not. "The claim is that for an action to be something you have done, it has to be produced by certain kinds of causes in you" (Nagel 1987: 57). "According to this position, causal determination by itself does not threaten freedom—only a certain kind of cause does that" (Nagel 1987: 57), namely those causes that are not associated with "self." Freedom in this sense is *self-determination,* or what is sometimes called *autonomy.* Coercion and force, either by others or by nature, are the contrary of this freedom.

The immediate difficulty is to define what we mean by the "self" in this case. If we include everything that belongs to our body, then that seems to contradict the fact that many of our bodily functions, desires, wants, feelings, and so forth do not seem to be under our control. For instance, if someone has an uncontrollable urge to steal, to drink, or even just to scratch an itch, our experience suggests that although he cannot control the urge, he can control how he acts upon that urge to some degree. It is that part of the self that we want to delimit in that regard. It is that which involves consciousness and awareness to some extent, attention, centers of recall, centers of decision making, and that which is capable of directing voluntary movement in a very generous sense of the term. In this regard Frankfurt draws a distinction between first-order and second-order volitions. First-order volitions are the ordinary kinds of wants and desires that seem to well up in us from time to time with little conscious control; second-order volitions are those which we consciously formulate and develop. Thus, there can be basically three situations that arise in relation to first and second-order volitions: (1) they can be discordant in the sense that the second-order volitions are contrary to the first-order ones; (2) they can be concordant in the sense that the first-order volitions are caused by the second-order ones; or (3) they can be concordant in the sense that the second-order volitions do not conflict with the first-order ones even though they are not their cause.

To put the distinction between first- and second-order volitions differently, we can identify the moral self and its second-order volitions with the higher cortical functions of the brain. Therefore, even though the hypothalamus and limbic system are parts of the person, they are not parts of the moral self so understood, since they involve for the most part subconscious processes or first-order volitions that seem to be out of our control. Put simply, free will is the ability of one part of the brain (the higher cortex) to control or direct other parts of the brain. For example, in the case of the control of many primary emotions, it is the ability of the pre-frontal cortex to control the amygdala (cf. Goleman 1995: 13–29). Free will is nothing mysterious in that regard. Compatibilism allows the reasonable assumption that all our actions sit in a nexus of causes in the ordinary sense of the term but still allow us to describe some of them as free. By defining freedom as self-determination, self-direction, self-control, or autonomy, this fits well with the sense of ourselves as agents capable of directing our own behavior within a certain latitude of direction and to various degrees of strength. Psychologist David Shapiro expresses this idea exactly:

> We have no reason to find human self-directedness intrinsically puzzling or philosophically doubtful. We recognize self-regulation of various sorts not only in other living organisms and in biological processes but also in certain kinds of machines, organizations, and even political entities. The functions of the organism … are regulated by processes internal to it. These processes confer a certain degree of autonomy, of independence of circumstance and surroundings, and endow the organism with a range of adaptability. In none of these cases do we regard self-regulation or autonomy as tainted with vitalism, or requiring any notion of free will, or implying any exception to natural law or predictability (1981: 14).

2.2 MORAL LUCK

Even if we assume that the compatibilists or the libertarians are right—that we are free, in some sense of the term—still there is a question of the latitude of that freedom. How much self-determination do we really have? Thomas Nagel argues that when one really thinks about it, most of our behavior seems to be out of our control and simply a matter of "moral luck" (1976: 573). There are roughly four ways in which this is so: (1) in terms of the kind of person we are, that is, our personality and temperament; (2) our circumstances, the kind of problems and situations we face; (3) the chain of antecedent conditions to our choices; and (4) the chain of consequences to our choices and actions (1976: 575).

We might grant that, if the self is the proximate cause of our behavior, still, what has constituted the self may not be under the self's control, and the way in which you are as a person will constrain latitude of self-determination. Similarly, some persons are faced with more tragic, tempting, or critical situations than others, situations that are not under their control; thus, they are tested more often and more intensely than others. You may be a decent person and live enough of a fortunate life that

---

Run Lola Run

The fascinating film *Run Lola Run* (1999, directed by Tom Tykwer) explores some themes of moral luck. Lola has 20 minutes to save her boyfriend from death. He has botched a drug deal and needs to deliver $100,000 to a drug boss. He accidentally lost the money on a subway, and it was picked up by a homeless man. The film shows how a shift in a few seconds changes circumstances, allowing for three different scenarios with three completely different results. In the first scenario, Lola runs to her father's bank, which refuses to loan her the money, and the chain of events leads to her inability to prevent her boyfriend's desperate act of robbing a store. In the second scenario, a 1-second delay causes her to take a completely different direction, robbing her own father's bank and, in the end, being shot and killed by police. In the third scenario, she is delayed another second, which sets off a set of circumstances allowing her boyfriend to run into the homeless man who took the money, ending with the safe return of the funds to the drug dealer.

your courage or perseverance or mettle is not tested to the extreme. On the other hand, you may find yourself in circumstances where even apparently decent persons end up doing terrible things. In Nazi Germany many ordinarily decent folks ended up supporting atrociously immoral actions. Should we fall into that situation, how would we act? (cf. Nagel 1976: 579)

In addition, the consequences of our choices and actions may, to a large degree, be out of our control, yet the moral success or failure of these determines our moral culpability. Consider a firefighter who rescues someone from a burning building. Whether the victim lives or dies depends on medical causes that are out of the firefighter's control; still, if the victim lives, the rescuer may receive more praise for the rescue than if the victim dies. Consider the difference between a trucker who runs a red light with no consequence and another who, unaware of a pedestrian crossing the street at exactly that time, hits and kills the person. More blame is placed on the second situation even though the trucker was not in control of the person crossing the street. Another example is the tragic death of Jessica Dubroff, the 7-year-old pilot who, along with her father and flight instructor, was attempting to break a record by flying across the United States. Had she been successful, many people might have praised her father and mother for allowing her to undertake this adventure. But because it ended in her death, more are willing to blame them for being foolish in letting her take such a risky journey. The same could be said for the antecedents of your choices. The context in which one must make choices or act upon them is one that highly constrains those choices, yet it is not under your control.

In all these cases, there is a paradoxical result: Although we are not in control of our personality and temperament—or in terms of the situations we find ourselves in or in terms of the consequences of our choices—still we use these things to assign blame and praise. One is morally lucky if she has a sanguine temperament and personality, does not encounter many great temptations, and is not thrown into situations that require important moral decisions, or she is lucky in terms of the consequences of her actions. But since most of this is a matter of moral luck, praise and blame are really undeserved, and responsibility for actions is a matter of things that are not in her (or our) control.

The reasonable response to the paradoxes of moral luck is the following. Obviously, certain sorts of pathologies or pathological personalities are in many cases beyond self-help; nevertheless, many defects in your personality seem to be subject to self-correction. A person aware of a short temper may compensate accordingly, just as someone may attempt to improve his physical stamina. Second-order volitions may cause first-order volitions to attenuate. Granted that those who do not anger easily have an easier time controlling their anger than those who are short-tempered, still such limited control is possible. It is true that your moral situations or temptations are often not a matter of choice, but certainly you can do things that make them more likely to happen than not. Someone who drinks and drives is more likely to be involved in an accident than is someone who does not; even if the choice to drink is not under one's control, the choice to drink and drive is still, for the most part, in a person's power. The consequences of the actions are also under a person's control to a certain extent. A pilot who safety checks the plane, does a careful flight plan, and reviews weather conditions and possible problems is more likely than not to return safely; the pilot who takes no precautions is simply an accident waiting to happen. It is possible for the first case to end in disaster, but at least the pilot can be praised for taking proper precautions; the second can be blamed for being careless. If the truck driver in the previous example ran the red light, that action in and of itself places the trucker in greater likelihood of doing someone harm. Similarly, if someone allows a young, immature child to pilot a plane across the country, that is more likely to lead to disaster than not flying. A person can be part of the chain of causes that will likely lead to certain outcomes. Part of what people are responsible for is the calculation of the likely consequences of their actions. Part of good judgment is determining the risk in a certain plan or action. By choosing certain things to do, people also increase the likelihood of certain consequences; there is still a difference between those who attempt some good and fail and those who attempt some good and succeed. But in certain cases, like those who died at the Alamo, they may be even more praised, despite the inevitability of failure.

2.3 MORAL STRENGTH AND WEAKNESS

In compatibilism free will is understood simply as varying degrees of self-control and self-direction. Although some psychologists employ the common-sense term "self-control," others call this characteristic of persons *ego-strength* (Rothman 1971; Grim, Kohlberg, and White 1968; Krebs 1967; Rest 1979). This is generally thought of as the ability to control impulses and delay gratification. It is also, in its active form, a characteristic clearly necessary for the accomplishment of any type of task, including moral ones. Consequently, self-control is not alone sufficient for producing morally good behavior, since it would also support immoral behaviors requiring impulse control and delay of gratification; it is a necessary feature of executing plans, whatever the plan may be and whether the plan is a morally good or bad one (Rest 1979: 177). Clearly, strong will alone is not sufficient to generate moral behavior. In the 1995 film *The Usual Suspects*, there is a certain underground character by the name of Keyser Soze. Much of what is known about him is only through reputation; only a few are able to identify him. One story that is passed around has Soze living in Turkey working the drug trade. A group of Bulgarians want to muscle in on his business. They want to show him the strength of their will in this regard, so they break into his home, hold his wife and two children, a boy and a girl, hostage, and wait for his return. When he enters the house, the Bulgarians show him their hostages, and just to prove to Soze that they will do anything to meet their goals, they kill his boy in front of him. Soze reacts in an unbelievable way—he shoots his surviving daughter and wife, then several of the Bulgarians; he allows one to escape only so he can tell others that Soze's will is stronger than theirs.

History has many illustrations of great strength of will: some who act for negative visions or dreams of conquest, such as Alexander, Caesar, Attila, Ghengis Khan, Napoleon, Hitler, Stalin, and those who have more positive visions, such as Confucius, Buddha, Abraham, Jesus, Paul, Mohammad, Gandhi, Susan B. Anthony, Martin Luther King. These are people willing to undergo great personal risk, to overcome great obstacles, to endure great suffering and doubt, to enlist large numbers of people in their cause, to put their welfare at risk, to risk a change in the world. But strength of will needs to be combined with other factors of moral competence before it can consistently generate moral outcomes. Moral strength is strength of will directed toward the attainment of some morally satisfactory goal.

Aristotle makes a number of interesting classifications in this regard. He calls a person *self-controlled* (*sōphōn*) if she is well-balanced and gives the impression of being in control of pleasures and passions without effort or strain (*Nic. Ethics*

Query: What Causes Moral Weakness?
Plato's and Aristotle's Answers

What causes moral weakness? Plato offered the view that moral weakness (*akrasia*) was not a question of character flaw so much as a question of ignorance. That is to say, a person would not act contrary to what he knows or believes is good (Protag. 352–353), but often acts immorally because he is mistaken about what is good for him. To put it differently, moral struggle would vanish in a state of complete knowledge. If moral weakness can be characterized as being overpowered or overcome by immediate pleasures, then such a situation is due to the fact that the person does not understand fully the measure of that immediate pleasure compared to its painful, long-run consequences (Protag. 356–357). One might get immediate pleasure out of drinking and partying all night, but assuming that such practices continue, inevitably your health declines. As a result, the harm to yourself in the long run outweighs the immediate pleasure. Those who continue such actions simply don't understand these consequences fully, so they are acting in ignorance.

Aristotle's response to this position is somewhat complex. On the one hand, he wanted to recognize the apparently common experience of persons acting contrary to what they know they should do, yet on the other hand, he wanted to uphold Plato's view that knowledge and wisdom are principles of strength (cf. *De Anima* 434a10–15). Aristotle tried to accommodate the contrary views by making a number of plausible distinctions. According to Aristotle, moral weakness can be due either to acting out of ignorance or acting in ignorance. Acting out of ignorance happens for two reasons: ignorance of general moral principles or ignorance of particulars (cf. *Prior Analytics* 67b1–5; *Nic. Ethics* 1147a25–30). To take a simple, practical example, I may be ignorant of the general principle that saturated fats are unhealthy to eat, and I can also be ignorant of the fact that granola contains many saturated fats. In either case I would be inclined to do something that is unhealthy. Moral weakness in this case is due to the fact that although I may know the general principle, I am ignorant of the particular (cf. *Nic. Ethics* 1147a25–30) or conversely. You might want to avoid saturated fats but eat granola because you enjoy it and are unaware that it is harmful to you in that respect.

On the other hand, moral weakness may be due to acting in ignorance (*Nic. Ethics* 1113b25). This is the case where the process of apprehending generals and particulars is affected, resulting in acting differently than you otherwise would. For example, drunkenness affects our ability to process information and be attuned to our surroundings. Being overwhelmed by anger may make us fail to see something important in a certain situation. Pleasures or passions may reduce people to a state of ignorance and render them incapable of actually knowing or realizing what they are doing.

There are some questions that can be raised about Plato's and Aristotle's accounts. Acting out of ignorance—specifically, ignorance about particulars—seems to be a question of perception and information. Knowing that granola is unhealthy is a fact one acquires or does not; understanding that a life of partying is costly or harmful may be a result of experience and understanding, characteristic of wisdom. But the fact of the matter is that people eat granola despite that information, smoke cigarettes despite the high probability that it will cause cancer, and party despite enduring its consequences. This may be due in part to people's willingness to take risks: I might not get caught if I steal this item. If that is the motivation, then Plato and Aristotle may be right in part. If the person were to know for certain he would be caught, then it is unlikely that he would do it; persons may start to smoke because they think that, although smoking leads to lung cancer, they may not contract cancer. But if they knew they were going to die from cancer, if they could see it in a clear vision, then they would not smoke. It is precisely because it is not entirely certain that some people are prompted to act contrary to their general knowledge. As Aristotle suggests, they are acting out of ignorance because they are ignorant of the particulars. They know that smoking has a high probability of causing cancer, but do not think that they will be one of the cases—and they may be right. Such risk calculations may be mistaken in a sense closer to Plato's view. Smokers may even believe they will die from cancer but believe that it will be later in life, and the pleasure that has been gained from smoking in the meantime would outweigh that outcome. People might also start to smoke because they lack moral imagination: They do not have the ability to see anything but the present; because the future is not immediately experienced, it has no urgency or no effect on their thinking. This might also be in line with Plato's and Aristotle's thinking. Setting aside the risk takers, there are motivations that would seem contrary to this sort of thinking. Some people know full well the consequences of their actions, but may act nonetheless; some simply do not care about the future, either because of depression, pessimism, or some other ideology or attitude. Or it may be the case that they are destructive or self-destructive types of persons; revengeful persons, for example, may not care about the consequences of their actions as long as the object of their revenge is harmed. These cases seem

Continued

Query: What Causes Moral Weakness?
Plato's and Aristotle's Answers, *Continued*

to weigh against the view that moral weakness is simply a question of knowledge.

On the other hand, acting in ignorance does not seem to be a question of knowledge but rather a psychological state. In that state you lose self-control. That is something much different than not being informed or not having wisdom about certain matters. The distinction between acting out of ignorance and acting in ignorance, then, is an important one; the first is a question of information or wisdom acquired from experience, while the second is really a psychological state or condition that prevents the ability to understand a situation or apply that knowledge. That suggests that acting in ignorance has little to do with knowledge, or at least knowledge in the

first sense. It is quite possible that your passions, desires, or urges could easily corrupt your deliberation and distort any understanding you might have of certain information. Leon Festinger's classical studies on cognitive dissonance illustrate the point. Festinger (1957) showed that heavy smokers have less of a tendency to believe in a link between smoking and lung cancer than do lighter smokers. Because heavy smokers are more addicted to nicotine and have more investment in that habit, their understanding of the harm and benefit is more likely to weigh in favor of their habit. In the case of cognitive dissonance, the problem is not that of knowledge, but the fact that such processes have been altered by the very things such information hopes to control.

1146a10ff.). Such a person has neither excessive nor base appetites. *Morally strong* persons (*enkratēs*), on the other hand, are those who have a general sense of what is right, have strong moral sentiment, but still may feel a struggle between their desires and the right thing to do; but precisely because of their strength of will, they are able to prevail and do the right thing (*Nic. Ethics* 1146a15). People with moral strength have an intense and passionate character, but are able to control it—though with some struggle. Self-controlled persons have no such struggle to overcome. As William James (1842–1910) notes, unlike *weak-willed* persons who must call upon all sorts of external and internal aids to stay the course of their will, and who must always be engaged in inner dialogue of pros and cons,

> The strong-willed man, however, is the man who hears the still small voice unflinchingly, and who, when the death-bringing consideration comes, looks at its face, consents to its presence, clings to it, affirms it, and holds it fast, in spite of the host of exciting mental images which rise in revolt against it and would expel it from the mind (1890: 563–564).

Often morally strong persons do not require drastic measures in a struggle between what they consider right or wrong but can address it directly through "force of will." They are less subject to moral blindness, or what Daniel Goleman calls "emotional hijacking" (1995: 14). For example, often in Christian hagiography, the saints are depicted as undergoing great struggles with vices and temptations before they find the right path. This was certainly the characterization of Augustine's life as portrayed in *The Confessions* (397–400). Consider Gregory the Great's description of how St. Benedict overcame a certain temptation (593–594: 6–7):

> The Devil came to tempt Benedict and made him bring to mind a certain woman whom he had once seen. So intensely did the devil inflame him that he could hardly control his passion. He was overcome by sensuality, and almost considered abandoning his solitary retreat. Then suddenly God graciously looked upon him and he returned to himself ... he stripped off his garments and flung himself naked upon ... stinging thorns and burning nettles. ... So through the wounds of the skin he drew out from his body the wound of the mind by changing his lust to pain. ... He conquered

Current Debates about Weakness of Will

Some contemporary thinkers, such as Donald Davidson (1980), take up Plato's and Aristotle's theses and try to articulate them in somewhat different terms. Davidson argues that one's reason for an action must also be a cause of that action. Therefore, one's best judgment for doing something should be a sufficient cause of doing it, provided there is no other interfering, nonreason cause. In other words, one would always act on what one believes is the best thing to do unless something other than that rational belief interferes with it. To act otherwise is irrational. For example, smokers who believe that smoking is bad for them, yet continue to smoke, are acting irrationally. All forms of weakness of will, then, are cases of irrationality. As a consequence of his claims, Davidson supposes that the mind has at least two relatively autonomous structures, one rational and the other nonrational, such that in some cases a thought or impulse can cause another to happen which bears no rational relation with it (1982). Some have criticized this two-system view of the mind as unnecessarily complex and subtly circular (Mele 1987; Heil 1989). John Heil's argument, for example, is that the mind is not divided between a rational and an irrational system, but is a set of subsystems, all of which are rational and have various degrees of motivational clout. The subsystem that urges the smoker to smoke is just as rational as the belief system that urges the smoker not to smoke, but the smoker who judges that it is best not to smoke simply misjudges the motivational intensity of the subsystem. The limbic system, let's say, is just as rationally going about its business of satisfying its needs and goals, as the higher cortex is trying to achieve its particular goals. The reason why the smoker continues to smoke despite his belief that it is a bad thing to do is that the limbic system, let's say, has more motivational strength than the person's belief system in this case. Thus, the brain is not divided between a rational and an irrational system, but is composed of rational systems which may have different degrees of motivational strength, the greater of which will prevail.

Yujian Zheng (1998) believes that Heil's argument can be supported by an application of George Ainslie's picoeconomic model of the brain (1992), specifically in terms of the "matching law." Such a law is based on a number of empirical studies of animal behavior which suggest that there is a general tendency to devalue or discount future events. This leads to two consequences of the law: There is a temporary high preference for imminent reward, and preference reversals will occur when lesser but more imminent rewards compete with bigger but more distal ones. In the last case, even though one may set oneself to accomplish a long-term goal that has a big reward, if an imminent but lesser reward—which conflicts with the long-term one—presents itself, then a preference reversal for the imminent one might occur unless the person is successful in employing self-control. These combine and lead to two results: The value of an imminent reward rises very sharply when it is proximate, being able to exceed values of other rewards previously preferred but more delayed in time; at the same time, when both rewards are somewhat delayed, the larger reward will always have a higher value than the smaller one. Thus, the smoker is constantly confronted by the imminent rewards which a dose of nicotine will yield, and even though the benefits of quitting smoking are greater, they are more distal and somewhat nebulous. Consequently, there is ample opportunity for preference switching in the smoker unless the smoker is able to exercise the necessary self-control. This theory allows for the general rationality of actions, but also accounts for why we exhibit moral weakness and often choose something despite our better judgment. (See also Section 4.7.2 on bad judgment.)

---

sin, then, by transforming the fire. From that time on, as he later used to tell his disciples, he had such control over temptation of the flesh that he never again experienced a sensation like that.

People with true moral strength would not require such extreme measures to control their desires, and self-controlled persons are those with so much self-control that they can face whatever temptation comes their way directly and still move in the direction they have willed to do. The poet Milton has a good description of the self-controlled person:

He that can apprehend and consider vice with all her baits and seeming pleasures, and yet abstain, and yet distinguish, and yet prefer that which is truly better. ... I cannot praise a fugitive and cloister'd vertue, unexercis'd and unbreath'd, that never sallies out and sees her adversary, but slinks out of the race, where the immortall garland is to be run for, not without dust and heat. ... [T]rue temperance [is that which can] see and know, and yet abstain (1644: 2: 514–516).

Morally weak persons (*akrasia*), on the other hand, can be characterized in the following way: They know, generally, that acting in a certain way is wrong, but they often fail to resist those passions or appetites which urge them to do what is contrary to their knowledge (*Nic. Ethics* 1145b10). They are persons who feel this moral struggle between desire and moral goals more strongly than others; they also may be more attracted to base pleasures than others. Put more precisely, with the morally weak person, whenever there is discordance between first- and second-order volitions, often the first-order volitions will be the proximate determinant of behavior. For the morally strong person, whenever there is discordance between first- and second-order volitions, the second-order volitions are more likely to be the proximate cause of behavior. Weak-willed persons are often susceptible to what is called moral blindness or emotional hijacking. This occurs when passions or appetites overwhelm individuals, thus making them impervious to the consequences or understanding of their actions; or it might be the case that those overwhelming passions or appetites place them in a state or condition which has the same effect. According to Goleman, emotional hijacking occurs when the amygdala, which according to the work of LeDoux (1992) processes information before the prefrontal lobe does, recruits the rest of the brain in its urgent agenda. Wired as it is on the basis of the fight or flight response, the amygdala, which acts like a sentinel, can spring into action while the slightly slower but more fully informed neocortex unfolds its more refined plan for action (cf. Goleman 1995: 18). Then the result is often a person who flies into a rage or is overwhelmed by sexual desire to the point where he may not even remember what took place.

In general, once the passion or appetite has waned, morally weak persons show regret and strive to control or correct their future actions. A person may be morally weak, generally speaking, but also may be so in regard to one particular appetite or passion; for some it is sex and for others it is money or power. As a result, this sort of person will have a tendency toward the corresponding vice and otherwise may be virtuous. In those cases it is said that such people have a certain character flaw. Otherwise upstanding persons may be led to ruin or misfortune because of this "fatal" flaw. The great tragedies often depict this sort of ruin: For Oedipus it is arrogance and curiosity; for Prometheus, disobedience; for Hamlet, vacillation; for Macbeth, ambition; for Othello, jealousy.

A *self-indulgent* (*akolasia*) person, according to Aristotle, is someone who has an appetite "for everything pleasant ... and ... is driven by his appetite to choose pleasant things at the cost of everything else. As a result, he feels pain both when he fails to get what he wants and when he has an appetite for it" (*Nic. Ethics* 1119a1–4). This sort of person thrives on immediate gratification and may often set aside moral values and principles for the sake of those pleasures.

Pathologically weak persons are those who have a general sense of what is right and have moral sentiment, but are incapable of resisting or find it extremely difficult to resist a certain appetite, urge, passion, or desire. One way to define the difference between the morally weak and the pathologically weak is to stress the difference between one who, as David Shapiro suggests, cannot control an undesirable behavior as much as he wants versus someone who cannot stop wanting the undesirable behavior (1981: 7). In other words, the person's second-order volitions are helpless in determining the first-order ones. The pathologically weak typically have a weakness in regard to a particular sort of urge; otherwise they exhibit various degrees of moral strength in regard to desires. Various sorts of manias, for example, kleptomania, or phobias are examples of this. Addictions, whether to drugs or alcohol, are also clear illustrations. In some cases addictions can lead to extreme loss of control. William James relates an incredible example of this, related by a Dr. Mussey of Cincinnati in the year 1874. An alcoholic (then called dipsomania) was put into a poorhouse in Ohio.

> Within a few days he had devised various expedients to procure rum but failed. At length, however, he hit upon one which was successful. He went into the wood-yard of the establishment, placed one hand upon the block, and with an axe in the other, struck it off at a single blow. With the stump raised and screaming he ran into the house and cried "Get some rum! get some rum! my hand is off!" In the confusion and bustle of the occasion a bowl of rum was brought, into which he plunged the bleeding member of his body, then raising the bowl to his mouth, drank freely, and exultingly exclaimed, "Now I am satisfied" (1890: 543).

David Ohlms's work on alcoholism seems to confirm the possibility of this extreme behavior. Rats, who normally avoid drinking alcohol, will become severely addicted once the rat's brain is bathed with a chemical called tetrahydroisoquinolin:

> One wretched rodent in particular caught my eye. The animal was so intoxicated that he literally had to squirm and crawl across his cage to reach a saucer containing alcohol and water. Once there, he dropped his snout into the solution up to his eyeballs and drowned. My gosh, I thought, the poor creature reminds me of some of my patients (Ohlms 1988: 56).

Ohlms's conclusion is that the alcoholic's brain as opposed to a normal brain produces this tetrahydroisoquinolin, a neurochemical much more addicting than morphine, every time it takes a drink to feel better. This sort of loss of control due to addiction also explains the willingness of crack-addicted mothers to forgo the physiological well-being of their fetuses or for pregnant alcoholic women to continue to drink despite their full knowledge of the effects of fetal alcohol syndrome. It was crack addiction that led a mother to allow a crack dealer to have sex with her 8-year-old daughter in exchange for a supply of the drug (Associated Press, January 16, 1996). It takes an extreme effort to overcome urges or impulses that incline the addict toward the activity, and generally, it requires professional help to reach a point of self-control. Pathological weakness implies a loss of the controlling centers in the brain.

2.4 RESPONSIBILITY

Our discussion of free will, moral luck, and moral strength raise interesting questions about responsibility, accountability, fault, blame, and praise for behavior. If, as compatibilism suggests, our actions are free to the extent that the self is a cause of those actions, then how is responsibility for actions and their consequences to be determined on that basis? Intentional behaviors would seem to make a person more responsible for the action and its consequences than unintentional ones, since the beliefs and desires of the person involved are formative causes. But what of reckless behavior? Even if it is unintentional, shouldn't a person be held responsible for such carelessness? If the consequences of much of what we do are out of our control, as proponents of moral luck suggest, how much should we be held responsible for them? To what degree is a person responsible for accidental results or negligent behaviors? If some persons are pathologically weak, should they be blamed for their actions? To what degree should we hold an alcoholic or drug addict responsible for her behavior? How should we treat the mentally ill when they commit a crime?

Responsibility is used in a variety of senses (see Hart 1968: 210–237), and it is often used synonymously with such words as "blame," "fault," "liability," or "accountability." Sometimes it implies a simple causal relation between an event and its source, as when we say that "the hurricane was responsible for loss of life," or that Fred is responsible for the spilled milk. We also often use it to designate duties relative to a role, for example, John is responsible for doing the dishes and Mary is responsible for cleaning the floor. We also use it as a character description. Someone is a responsible person if she has a habit of fulfilling her obligations and duties. We also say that someone is responsible when we mean that she is mentally or developmentally competent. If a person is clearly mentally ill, we will say that "he is not responsible for himself." However, the term "responsibility" is principally used in ethics and the law to determine who can be morally censured for an action, or who should be punished for the violation of a law, or who is liable for harm done to others. In this sense ethics and the law are looking for who can be "held responsible" for the action and its outcomes. As we will see, "being held responsible" for an action involves some of these other senses of responsibility but is something generally more complex and comprehensive than any one of the senses mentioned here. In this section we will try to sort out these differences and give an account of the basic conditions for holding someone responsible for an action.

Determining responsibility for an action is a critical matter in ethics and the law. Our judicial system can serve as a good model for identifying the conditions for determining responsibility. Usually the law separates between criminal and civil (tort) matters, although some cases are subject to both. The first is concerned with establishing guilt or innocence of violating the criminal code and punishments for crimes committed, usually in the form of fines, imprisonment, or, in some cases, execution. Criminal law looks to the public good, to see that justice is done, and to remove a dangerous person from society. Criminal law is a grave matter since it affects the life and liberty of those involved. Civil or tort law is interested in determining fault in order to find a remedy for harm done to a victim, usually in the form of restitution or compensation. Its focus is on individuals rather than a public good. Civil or tort law affects a person's property or economic interest primarily, since it results in damages paid to the harmed party. As we will see, these two areas of law can have different criteria for liability or responsibility.

In criminal law, determining the responsibility for an action or its outcomes requires that a prosecuting attorney first show that the accused performed a certain set of actions, for example, that the accused shot the victim on a certain date, at a certain time, and in a certain location. Second, it must be shown that those actions caused the outcome, namely, the death of the person (*actus reus*). An autopsy can reveal that the person died of a gunshot wound rather than a heart attack. Third, it must be shown that those actions violated a norm, duty, or law that exists between the accused and the alleged victim. In the case of the accusation of murder, for example, there are both moral norms and legal laws against it. Fourth, the *mens rea*, or mental state of the person, must be established. Were the actions intentional and premeditated, impulsive, unintentional, negligent, and so on? To what degree were those actions and circumstances under the control of the accused? Once all four conditions have been established, the responsibility of the accused can be determined.

Desperate Efforts to Excuse Responsibility

No one usually enjoys taking responsibility for blameworthy actions or consequences that lead to harm to oneself or others. But here are some examples of extreme attempts at exoneration:

- J.D. and his parents filed a lawsuit in January 1997 against some county officials in California for at least $700,000. The lawsuit was for J.D.'s total disability that resulted from a car crash. J.D. and some friends had been out drinking. J.D. was in the back seat of a car and had stuck his head out the window to vomit just as the driver veered off the road, ramming J.D.'s head into a tree. The lawsuit claims that it was the county's fault that the tree was so close to the road.
- In New Mexico a high-school football player, G.J., 18, was arrested after he reacted to his ejection from a game (for two unsportsmanlike conduct penalties) by tackling a referee, causing the man to flip over and land on his head, knocking him unconscious. G. J.'s mother later blamed the referees and coaches, saying that her son was simply tired and frustrated.
- In September 1997 Patrick Bark, 59, pleaded guilty in Kansas City, Missouri, to selling more than 1300 guns illegally over a 2-year period—including many to juveniles and felons. Bark said at his sentencing that he blamed half of it on the government for letting him go as long as he did. He also claimed that he had no idea that the guns would be used in crimes.
- Burglary suspect, W.S., 57, said in November that he was temporarily insane when he allegedly robbed a home in West Palm Beach, Florida, because he had just eaten too much cotton candy. In Montgomery County, Maryland, C.S., who originally plead guilty to an accusation of hiring a hit man, said that tranquilizers, plus the ingestion of an entire bottle of an extra-strength antacid before he made his plea, caused impaired judgment, and consequently, he should be allowed to withdraw that guilty plea.
- In Santa Fe, New Mexico, a former teacher, Roger Katz, says his relationship with a 14-year-old female student was justified because it dated back to their past lives in Tibet more than 1000 years ago, when she saved his life by taking an arrow meant for him; consequently, he had to repay the debt of love. The judge didn't buy the story and sentenced Katz to 18 months in prison.
- Here's one from Ann Landers (October 5, 1997): A woman in Memphis has filed suit against a small mom-and-pop pharmacy because she purchased a tube of contraceptive jelly, spread it on a piece of toast and ate it. She then had unprotected sex, believing she was safe, and became pregnant. Despite the fact that the contraceptive came with instructions, the woman says the pharmacist should have put a specific warning on the box not to eat it. "Who has time to sit around reading directions these days, especially when you're sexually aroused?" She's suing for one-half million dollars.

Generalizing this framework, it can be reasonably argued that *responsibility is determined by a configuration of three important factors:* (1) *causation:* establishing that the person's actions or omissions were the proximate cause of the event, (2) *accountability or blame:* determining that the actions or omissions caused a harm which violated a norm, duty, or law that existed between the agents in question and which the agent was under obligation to do or not to do, and (3) *voluntariness:* establishing the degree of both inner and external control of the actions and the circumstances surrounding it. Let's look at each of these factors in some detail.

2.4.1 Causation

Establishing causation is considered an essential step in determining the responsibility of an agent for an action and its outcomes. Generally speaking, a person is usually held responsible for a result caused by her own conduct. However, as we'll see, there are certain types of tort liability and kinds of criminal acts that are exceptions to that rule.

Causation is established by showing factually that the agent did a certain set of actions, and those actions caused the outcome in question. Legally, this is called the *cause in fact*

(Black et al. 1980: 221). More specifically, a person's actions must be shown to be the *proximate* cause of an outcome or event, understood as that which is nearest to the effect in the order of causation. Thus, a proximate cause may not necessarily be the one closest in time or space to the event in question, but only to its happening or not (Black et al. 1980: 1225). It is the one most significant and nearest in the causal sequence related to the outcome. A proximate cause is further refined as being both *relevant* and *salient*. Two events, or two facts, are said to be relevant to each other when they are so related that according to the common course of events, one either taken by itself, or in connection with other events, causes or makes probable the past, present, or future existence or nonexistence of the other (cf. Black et al. 1980: 1290). The fact that the defendant went to get some cigarettes just before going to the victim's house is not relevant to the victim's death, although it is certainly near in time to the event. A proximate cause should also be salient, the most significant in accounting for the event in question. Legally, it is often referred to as the *producing cause* (cf. Black et al. 1980: 1209); the term sufficient cause is also appropriate. A *sufficient cause* is one which, in conjunction with neces- sary causes, produces the event. A necessary cause is something without which another event could not occur. For example, oxygen is necessary for combustion, but alone it is not sufficient to produce it. One also needs a number of sufficient causes, such as combustible materials, a source of high heat, and the means of applying one to the other. Thus, it might be true that the fact that a person was born is a cause of that person murdering the victim, but it is hardly salient and so not proximate. Birth is a necessary condition for anybody murdering someone—in fact, it is a necessary condition for anybody doing anything—but it is not a suffi- cient condition.

   Claiming that a person's conduct is the cause of a result may be qualified in a number of ways. For example, although the person's conduct may be the proxi- mate cause of an event, it may be *concurrent* with other proximate causes (cf. Black et al. 1980: 221). For example, if a group of people assault another person, it may be hard to determine which blow was the death blow, and it may be the case that the defendant struck the victim only once, while the others did so several times or with more deadly instruments. The defendant's actions may also have been a *con- tributing* cause; for example, he may have driven the car to the location where his passengers then assaulted the victim.

   A classic 1928 legal case gave some sense of what could be counted as a proxi- mate cause (*Palsgraf v. Long Island R. Co.*, 248 N.Y. 339, 162 N.E.99, Sup. Ct. N.Y. 1928). A man was late attempting to catch a train. Railroad employees tried to assist him. One employee took a package from him which, unbeknown to him, contained a quantity of fireworks. But as he handled it, it dropped on the rails, causing an explosion, which started a chain of events that led to the tipping of a set of scales on the platform, which then fell on Mrs. Palsgraf, causing her injury. Although the lower courts had initially ruled that the railroad could be held liable for the injuries, the higher courts overturned that decision, claiming that because the porter could not reasonably foresee the consequences of dropping the package, and since there would be, in any case, an unusual causal chain of events that could lead to the outcome, he and the railroad that employed him could not be held responsible for the injury.

   Although causation is an important factor in determining responsibility, there are clear cases where even if a person's action can be counted as a proximate cause, he may not be held responsible for the result. Homicide is a good example; not every person who is the proximate cause of a homicide is held responsible for the death of that person. Situations of self-defense are a clear example. If it can be shown that the defendant killed a person because her life was placed in imminent danger by the person in question, then that is counted as an *excusable homicide* (cf. Black et al. 1980: 734). *Justifiable homicide* is another example (cf. Black et al. 1980: 734). The police may be justified in an act of homicide if the person in question poses a clear and present danger to the public and refuses to surrender a weapon. In these situations people are excused from responsibility because they are placed into circumstances beyond their control.

Conversely, it is also quite possible that a person can be held responsible for a harm, even if her conduct is not the proximate cause of that harm. For example, if someone hires another person to murder a business partner, as an accomplice she can be held as responsible for the murder as the hired hit man. Tort liability offers a number of examples in this regard. In a classic case (*Summers v. Tice*, Cal. 2d 80, 199 P.2d 1 1948), Summers had gone quail hunting with the two defendants, Tice and Simonson. A quail was flushed, and the two men fired negligently in Summers's direction. One shot struck Summers in the eye. Because both were equally distant from Summers, both had an unobstructed view, and both were using the same kind of gun with the same kind of birdshot, it was not possible to determine which man's gun fired the injuring shot. The trial court found both men jointly liable. The California State Supreme Court upheld the ruling, arguing that "they [were] ... both negligent towards plaintiff. They brought about a situation where the negligence of one of them injured the plaintiff. ... " Thus, in this case, even though neither of the defendant's actions were established as the proximate cause of the outcome, they were both held liable. As another example and as we'll see below (Section 2.4.8), an employer can be held liable for the actions of his employees when their conduct falls within the scope of their employment.

2.4.2 Accountability

Accountability is a second factor for determining responsibility. It is a normative process in the sense that *to claim someone is accountable for an action and its outcomes, it has to be shown that the person in question had some obligation or duty toward those affected by the actions, that there was a certain set of conventional expectations on their part, or that the accountable party was bound by existing law or moral norms.* The purported violation of those duties or expectations requires that the person be answerable in some venue. Depending on the kind of obligations involved, an employee may be accountable to his employer, a husband to his wife, a friend to a friend, or a citizen to a court of law.

As we discussed earlier (Section 1.3.1), duties or obligations may be relative to a role so that professionals have obligations of confidentiality and informed consent, for example, to their patients or clients. Employers have obligations to employees to provide a safe work environment and to be treated fairly; conversely, employees have duties to employers to obey directives and do an honest day's work. Parents have duties to their children, and conversely—and citizens have a number of duties to one other. In addition to role-specific duties, there are also *prima facie* ones to consider—those that transcend any one particular role; duties not to harm, to tell the truth, to keep promises, for restitution, and so on.

Accountability becomes complicated when a chain of command is involved. An employee, for example, may be accountable to her supervisor for her actions relative to duties and job expectations for that position. This would be true up the chain of command. However, the employee is also accountable to those customers, clients, coworkers, or fellow citizens who may be harmed by her actions when obligations not to harm them exist. Although she has obligations to obey the directives of her employer, she has stronger obligations not to harm others. If the employee acted under the implicit or explicit command or direction of the supervisor in causing harm to others, the supervisor can also be held accountable for the employee's actions, even though it was the employee's actions that served as the proximate cause of the harm. This is justified by two factors: (1) control, the fact that supervisors have more power, authority, or control over the actions of subordinates, and as such their commands or directives serve as salient causes of their subordinate's actions; correspondingly, such power and authority involves inherent duress for the subordinate; (2) relative to the chain of command, the higher one goes in the chain of command, the wider the range of obligations and so the more accountability. In some cases, the duress that results from an employer's directive to do something that resulted in harm to others may be sufficient to exonerate or excuse the employee's actions. In some cases the employer may be held fully responsible for the harm the employee has caused and receive the brunt of any consequences from that action. Within that context, the employer may in turn hold the employee accountable within the purview of the powers of the employer to demote, punish, or dismiss the employee. The recent Firestone case is a good example where the corporation and its executives are being held accountable to Congress (as a public forum)—and most likely to the courts—for the tire failures that are alleged to be the cause of a number of vehicular fatalities. If, as some have hypothesized, the fault lies in the design of the tire, there may be legitimate consequences for those design engineers and supervisors within the purview of the corporations involved. But—unless there was some criminal intent involved—it's unlikely those employees will be held publicly accountable other than in terms of public testimony.

2.4.3 Voluntariness

A third factor for determining responsibility is the degree and kind of voluntariness found in the acts performed. *Voluntariness is based on the degree and kind of inner and external control a person has over actions and their outcomes.* Control involves the power to originate, direct, prevent, or enact something; indirectly expressed, it involves the absence of coercion, understood both psychologically and physically. Inner control is the power to generate or restrain desires and emotions, set intentions and purposes, design plans and the means for their realization, and make decisions accordingly. External control is the power to perform certain actions and execute plans in the context of a variety of anticipated and contingent circumstances.

One of the earliest thinkers to address the notion of voluntariness was Aristotle. He argued that human actions could be classified in terms of their degree of voluntariness (*Nic. Ethics* 1110a15–18). In this regard he endeavored to chart the kinds and degrees of voluntariness that have since influenced legal traditions (*Nic. Ethics* 1110–1115, 1134–1137) (see Figure). In general, Aristotle divides human action between the voluntary and the involuntary. When a person has a reasonable amount of inner and external control, then that action is *voluntary*, and the person is fully responsible for her actions. Voluntary actions may be subdivided between the deliberate and the impulsive, that is, the kinds of inner causes. Deliberate

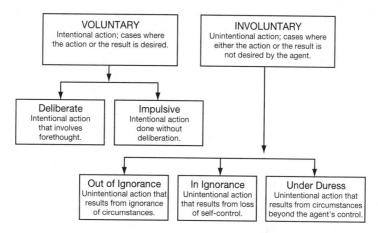

Aristotle's Classification of Human Action

actions involve planning and forethought, whereas *impulsive* ones have little deliberation and are usually the result of quick reactions to passions or desires.

Involuntary actions, on the other hand, are cases where there is a significant attenuation of either or both inner and external control of actions and their circumstances. To the degree that such controls are attenuated, the person has proportionately less responsibility for those actions, and usually the forms of punishment that follow in courts of law are attenuated accordingly. These may come under different headings, using Aristotle's terminology: When there is a lack of inner control, the person can be said to be *acting in ignorance*. A person's inner control is diminished when there is, for example, an internal compulsion of some sort or another, such as kleptomania, loss of control of the passions (e.g., phobias), and other forms of pathological weakness. A person's inner and external control are diminished when there is a lack of knowledge or awareness of the sufficient conditions of the outcome of an action. Aristotle calls this *acting out of ignorance*. A driver may be unaware of a rock in the road, which then causes her to swerve into oncoming traffic. When the psychological or physical force of those sufficient conditions for the actions is external to the person, and is greater than what is considered a reasonable amount of inner or external control, then the person is *acting under duress*. For example, sailors may find themselves in a middle of a storm and be forced to dump their cargo into the sea to save their lives and ship.

To illustrate Aristotle's distinctions, consider the following various legal descriptions of a homicide:

1. *First degree murder* is the case where persons are found to have committed homicide "with malice aforethought." In Aristotle's terms these acts are voluntary, the persons are held completely responsible, and as a result, are given the severest punishments. The desire to kill the person originated with them, they intended his demise, deliberated about the plans to do it, and executed the plan with whatever effort or difficulty that took.

2. *Voluntary manslaughter* is the case where persons are found to have committed homicides without deliberation or premeditation but in the "heat of passion." This corresponds to what Aristotle calls impulsive behavior. The desire to kill was present and the intent was present, but there were no plans or deliberations made ahead of time. The

person is still considered fully responsible for the action, since the ordinary presumption is that competent persons have inner control over their passions and emotions.

3. *Involuntary manslaughter* is homicide that results from reckless actions which grossly deviate from proper standards of caution. Persons in this case do not deliberate about the outcome, but in acting with such reckless disregard for human life, where it is clear that such actions will most likely result in death to another, they are considered to act intentionally. In Aristotle's language this corresponds to acting out of ignorance, or what he specifically calls *nonvoluntary actions*, where the person acts recklessly in a manner that indicates lack of regret for the actions (cf. *Nic. Ethics* 1110b22). Another type of involuntary manslaughter is cases of homicide committed under extreme mental or emotional disturbance. These correspond in Aristotle's language to cases of acting in ignorance.

4. *Negligent homicide* is the case where a person's negligent behavior is the cause of death. Negligence is usually defined as the failure to use such care as a reasonably prudent and careful person would use under similar circumstances. In these cases there is neither deliberation nor intent, nor is the behavior considered reckless. This corresponds to Aristotle's notion of acting out of ignorance.

5. *Justifiable or excusable homicide* is exemplified by self-defense, where a person's life has been threatened or placed in imminent danger by another, and under great duress she causes the death of the person. This corresponds to Aristotle's notion of acting under duress.

2.4.4 Voluntary Action

For an action to be counted as voluntary, there must be a reasonable amount of both inner and external control of the actions. In regard to inner control, the desire for the outcome must have its origin in the agent; second, the intention to attain the object of desire must be formed, deliberation about the means to attain that goal must be formulated, and a decision to act on the plan must have been made. Successful efforts must also have been made to arrange or account for events and circumstances that would lead to the intended outcome. Actions which meet these conditions can be said to be genuinely voluntary, and agents who act voluntarily in this matter can be held fully responsible for the actions and their outcomes.

Although actions which stem from passion and appetite, for example, anger or lust, are more impulsive and less deliberative, still a person, Aristotle argues, should be held fully responsible for actions and outcomes based on them:

> what is the difference in respect ... between errors committed upon calculation and those committed in anger? Both are to be avoided, but the irrational passions are thought not less human than reason is, and therefore also the actions which proceed from anger or appetite are man's actions. It would be odd, then, to treat them as involuntary (*Nic. Ethics* 1111b 1–5).

The assumption here is that a person ordinarily has control over passions and desires, and the expectation then is that a competent person should be held responsible for losing that control. Although a person who murders from rage as opposed to one who murders intentionally and with forethought is just as responsible, still intuitively many people want to characterize the actions differently in some respect. There is something thought to be more repulsive and vicious about a cold-blooded killer than the one who strikes out in anger. What makes him more vicious is that he is in control of the entire process, whereas the enraged killer has lost self-control of his anger. The enraged killer is morally weak, but the deliberate killer calculates the crime.

2.4.5 Acting out of Ignorance

By acting out of ignorance, as we saw earlier, Aristotle meant that *a person is unaware of the general rules that apply to a certain situation or the particulars of a situation* (*Nic. Ethics* 1111a5ff.). For instance, someone may drive around a sharp curve in the road unaware that a car is making a left turn, and a crash results. In this case, although the person voluntarily and intentionally drove around the curve, he did not voluntarily intend to hit the other car, say, as opposed to someone who intentionally wants to hit a car to commit suicide or collect insurance. In these sorts of cases, and following Aristotle's ideas, we can hold the person responsible for the action and its outcome in a qualified sense; we can hold the person responsible for driving in a way that voluntarily deviates from a rule that says "drive cautiously around blind curves." Although the person is not in control of the fact that a car is waiting to turn or that his car actually hits another, he is in control of how he performs the activity that leads to the crash. Simple negligence can be defined as a deviation from common or prescribed rules for the safe performance of a certain activity; sometimes it may imply neglect or failure to perform something. Criminal negligence might be defined as involving reckless behavior, that is, gross deviation from such standards of caution.

A reckless person is thought to be more responsible for the outcome of an action than a negligent person, and one whose actions lead to harm of another despite all reasonable cautions is thought to be even less responsible for the outcome (although as we'll see later questions of tort liability are more complex). Criminal penalties follow this logic, often reserving the harsher ones for those who act recklessly (i.e., are criminally negligent). As H.L.A. Hart suggests, "There seems a world of difference between punishing people for the harm they unintentionally but carelessly cause, and punishing them for the harm which no exercise of reasonable care on their part could have avoided" (1968). In general, responsibility can be assigned to actions done out of ignorance to the extent that the person was either negligent, reckless, or both.

In January 1987 a single-engine Cessna 207, piloted by F.S. of an Alaskan air service, crashed in Lake Clark Pass, an especially hazardous route through the Aleutian range on the Alaska peninsula. A 13-month-old boy was killed and six others were injured, including the pilot. It was alleged that F.S. decided to fly the pass despite the fact that he had been advised by flight controllers that visibility along his route was too poor for flying, and there was no radar or control tower in the area of Lake Clark Pass. Besides this, F.S. allegedly had not filed a flight plan; it was also alleged that the airplane was not properly stocked with emergency equipment as required by state law, and the emergency beacon, which helps rescuers locate downed planes, was not working. If all of this is true, although certainly the pilot cannot be held responsible for the weather, which was beyond his control, and did not intend the accident, he can be held responsible for those negligent actions which left the plane unprepared for an emergency and those agents which went against the grain of prudence and common sense in flying into bad weather without a flight plan.

2.4.6 Acting in Ignorance

By acting in ignorance, Aristotle meant the case where *one acts without being in control of one's centers of control.* Examples include intoxication and mental illness or impairment. In general, acting in ignorance is a case of being incompetent.

Case Study: Who's to Blame for Princess Diana's Death?

Princess Diana was killed in an auto accident in Paris on August 30, 1997, along with her boyfriend, Dodi Fayed, and the driver of the vehicle; her bodyguard was the only survivor. Apparently, the driver was attempting to elude a number of paparazzi who were relentless in their pursuit of Diana (and there is some evidence to suggest that the driver may have swerved to avoid a car that was in its path and then lost control). Pictures of Diana could fetch quite a lot of money, and the public's curiosity about Diana and her life fed the quest for this material. The driver was alleged to have been driving at a high rate of speed, but evidence from an autopsy also suggested that he may have had four times the legal level of alcohol for intoxication. There was also the accusation that he had taunted the paparazzi, claiming that they would not catch them that night. The driver was an employee of Fayed's father. There was also evidence that some of the paparazzi had driven ahead of Diana's limousine to slow it down. It was also alleged that when Diana's car crashed, some paparazzi had run to the vehicle to take pictures of Diana while she lay dying in the car. Who is to blame for her death? Assuming hypothetically that all of the allegations are true, consider the following claims:

1. If the paparazzi were not intent on photographing Diana, the driver would not have had to speed to elude them, and there may not have been an accident.
2. If the driver was not speeding, there may not have been an accident.
3. If the driver was not intoxicated, there may not have been an accident.
4. If the driver had not taunted the photographers, they may not have pursued them, and there may not have been an accident.
5. If the driver had not been called by Fayed or employed by his father or better supervised by his boss, he may not have been driving that night, and there may not have been an accident.
6. If the passengers prevented the driver from driving, there may not have been an accident.
7. If the passengers ordered him to slow down, there may not have been an accident.
8. If the passengers had worn seat belts, they may have survived the accident.

Question for Discussion

1. How would you assign responsibility for the death of Diana in this case?

Incompetence can be defined in at least three different senses. Incompetence might be due to the inability to exercise judgment, for example, if the person is persistently or temporarily unconscious. A second type of incompetence is the inability to form judgments either due to immaturity, as in the case of young children, or because of mental disability. Third, mental incompetence may be due to the inability to make sound judgments and in three different senses: (1) self-imposed, as in the case of drug or alcohol intoxication, (2) accidental, as in the case of mental impairment due to trauma or disease, and (3) inherent, as in the case of mental illness or pathology.

Certainly, the first sort of incompetence is irrelevant here. The second sort of incompetence is an important point of discussion for responsibility. In a way some children's actions are like acting in ignorance in that they simply do not understand or are not aware of what they are doing. Because of inexperience, children may not be aware of the consequences of certain actions. They may not know, for example, that taking certain medicines may harm them, or they may not realize that playing with pointed sticks could lead to serious injury. Children may also not fully understand their own powers, as when they kick or punch someone smaller than them. In addition, their centers of self-control may not be fully formed. Because they lack judgment, children are more easily influenced by social and cultural influences. Finally, young children may not even be capable of forming the necessary intent to commit a crime or serious harm.

Certainly, children can be blamed for their actions, and parents constantly do what they can to correct such behaviors. But responsibility is usually qualified due to the tenderness of age and the immaturity of judgment. Also, because of their lack of experience and their innocence, children are more susceptible to influence; poverty, parental abuse, and social environment are stronger mitigating factors in assigning responsibility than in the case of adults who, because of their maturity and strength of will, are thought to be capable of rising above many of these circumstances. When Leo Pritchard, 33, stabbed his wife brutally in a drunken rage, part of his defense was his unhappy childhood, replete with alcoholism and violence. But as M.W., a friend of the victim remarked, "Once you become an adult, you have choices. You have the power to change your life. You can't blame your childhood for your problems. It doesn't work" (Ruskin 1996).

This distinction between adult and child competence is also reflected in the legal system, which has a tendency to reduce responsibility and punishment for young offenders. We give them special consideration: more leniency, protection from public notice, separate judicial and punitive systems. Two widely publicized cases illustrate this point. In March 1998 two boys, 11 and 13 years of age, allegedly ambushed their seventh and eighth grade classmates in Jonesboro, Arkansas. It was claimed by authorities that the two—dressed in camouflage—lay in wait while their classmates filed out of the school after a false fire alarm. They were charged with killing four children and one teacher and wounding ten others using high-powered rifles. Despite the charge of murder, because they were under the age of 14, Arkansas law prevented them from being tried as adults, and should they be found guilty, they could only be imprisoned until they were legally considered adults, that is, until they are 18 years of age (as of this writing federal law and prosecution may be used to extend their prison time). A second case occurred in February 1993 in Liverpool, England. Two boys, just over 11 years old, abducted a 2-year-old boy from a shopping mall, beat him, and then killed him. Despite the awful brutality and viciousness of the crime, the judge allowed a number of considerations in his decision to sentence them so that they would be considered for release after 8 years.

For many people, the notion of diminished responsibility becomes more difficult to accept, given the severity and cruelty that crimes such as these illustrate. For this reason, legal systems are changing. In many states juveniles committing murder are often treated as adult offenders. In 1997 Michigan passed a law that allows children of any age to be prosecuted as adults for serious offenses. Nathaniel Abraham was the youngest person to be tried under such a law. He was convicted of murder for a killing he committed when he was 11. He shot a stranger outside a Pontiac convenience store in 1997 with a stolen rifle. He bragged about the shooting to friends afterward. The defense argued that the boy was firing at trees and a bullet ricocheted off a tree. The defense argued that the boy had the mind of a 6–8 year old and could not form the intent to commit murder. Although the judge had options ranging from life imprisonment to a sentence of time already served, he opted for imprisonment in juvenile facilities until the age of 21, citing the Michigan law as flawed.

Intoxication belongs to the third category of incompetence. It can be reasonably argued that in these cases individuals choose to lose control over their centers of control, although they may not desire or intend any results that occur while in that state. Suppose a person strikes someone while drunk and seriously injures or kills him. Even though that person may not have intended the action and consequence (or was not even aware that he struck the person), and the act is not strictly speaking voluntary, it is thought that person can still be held responsible for putting himself into a state of loss of self-control, since that part of the activity was voluntary. Leo Pritchard, whose case was mentioned earlier, would beat his wife nearly every

The Neuromechanisms of Addiction

In the spring 1997 issue of *Nature Medicine,* J.K. Zubieta et al. suggested that the fierce craving for cocaine is caused by the same molecular mechanism as heroin addiction and is linked to the brain's own natural opiate system, which is thought to function as a congenital mechanism for coping with stress. The research showed that cocaine, like heroin, interrupts the natural relationship between a neurochemical called enkephalin and receptors on the surface of brain cells that are specialized to trap it. Cocaine causes the brain to manufacture less enkephalin; in response, brain cells produce more enkephalin receptors on their surface to capture as much of it as possible. The increase in the number of unoccupied enkephalin receptors may produce the cravings experienced by cocaine addicts. The researchers also found that increased binding to enkephalin receptors in the brains of cocaine abusers lasted up to a month after withdrawal from the drug. That provides a strong clue as to why cocaine addicts relapse so readily.

time he drank. Despite a restraining order and the presence of some friends, he broke into his wife's trailer, flew into a rage, and in a struggle stabbed her several times, once through the heart, the knife going completely through her torso. Yet on the witness stand, Pritchard claimed he could not remember any of the struggle, that he loved his wife and did not intend to kill her, at which point he dissolved into sobs (Ruskin 1996). Clearly, his defense was trying to use this as a way to exclude the action as a case of first degree murder, since he could not have formed the intent while drunk and was unaware of the stabbing at the time. But even if this strategy were to succeed, which it did not in this case, many would argue that he must be held responsible for the decision to drink, knowing full well the disposition toward violence it creates in him.

Drunk driving that leads to death is an especially problematic circumstance within this category and the subject of national debate and action. In 1998 the national average of fatal car accidents involving either drunk drivers or pedestrians was 30 percent of all such fatalities. Often such incidents occur after several arrests of the driver for DWI. These are people who have had jail time, have undergone court-mandated therapy, have had their licenses revoked, yet still manage to find some way to get behind the wheel of a car drunk. Handling such cases is difficult since, prior to fatal results, the person has not committed a crime that warrants years of imprisonment, yet their behavior is so persistent and dangerous that they have to be taken off the roads for reasons of public safety. Often extreme measures are proposed to deal with them. Addiction to alcohol complicates these cases further, since from one point of view, addiction is loss of inner control, and so the person's responsibility for her behavior is highly attenuated. In this sense a person doesn't really "choose" to drink but does so compulsively and so is pathologically weak. An alcoholic can certainly be held responsible for initiating the determinants that led to the addiction, and the status of the decision to continue to drink becomes more problematic if the control centers have already been corrupted by the addiction. Sorting out that problem both ethically and legally is difficult, although from the legal side, pressure from public opinion has made the courts treat these cases as voluntary actions and as serious crimes. In February 2000 a man in Waco, Texas, was given a 60-year sentence after his ninth drunk-driving conviction. Prosecutors charged him as a habitual criminal, which allowed the judge to impose the harsher sentence.

Certain kinds of mental illness are also cases of the third sort of incompetence. However, unlike alcoholism or drug addiction, these are usually not self-imposed, and consequently, the agents are usually assigned less responsibility for actions that are caused by them, although that view is changing in the legal system. The courts in principle traditionally recognized certain kinds of mental illness as

Case Study: Can Someone Be Found Guilty Yet Mentally Ill?

In January 1996 multimillionaire John DuPont shot and killed Olympic world-class wrestler, David Schultz, in front of the guest house DuPont provided for him and his family on his estate in Philadelphia. DuPont had been a longtime supporter of the Olympics, especially Olympic wrestling. DuPont's lawyers pleaded an insanity defense on the basis of a clear diagnosis of paranoid schizophrenia. The prosecution argued that his illness stopped short of legal insanity and that DuPont killed Schultz out of jealousy for the respect Schultz commanded in the wrestling world. In Pennsylvania jurors had a choice of convicting him on first degree murder, finding him not guilty due to insanity, or guilty on a charge of second or third degree murder (i.e., cases where there is no premeditation to kill).

Questions for Discussion

1. Assuming that John DuPont had in fact killed Schultz and in fact was a paranoid schizophrenic, how would you have deliberated as a juror?

   On February 26, 1997, the jury found DuPont guilty of third degree murder, recognizing that he was mentally ill, yet rejecting the insanity defense.

2. Is someone who is mentally ill capable of being held responsible for his or her actions? If not, can there be degrees of culpability nonetheless? In other words, does it make sense to say that someone is mentally ill yet guilty for his or her actions?

an excuse for an action; in lieu of punishment, enforced treatment was prescribed. In other words, because they are incompetent, they cannot be held responsible for their behavior, but because they have harmed, their behavior must be stopped and changed. However, this trend has changed. The cases of Colin Ferguson, the man who in 1994 shot and killed a number of Long Island commuters, and Jeffrey Dahmer, the man who killed and cannibalized a number of young men and boys, illustrate this. Colin Ferguson was clearly suffering from classical paranoia and delusionary behavior; still he was deemed competent to stand trial in the sense of being aware of himself and his surroundings and of being able to form plans and intentions. Although that was true, it still could be argued that his paranoia caused him to view the world in a fundamentally flawed way. Even though he could form plans, his plans were dictated by the strange imagined conspiracies and delusions he had. Despite Dahmer's obviously deep mental problems, the same sort of conditions were laid out in his trial, namely, that he stalked his victims and so showed deliberation. Yet the compulsiveness of his desires demonstrated a pathological weakness. If these men have lost the power of self-control in a way that was not self-imposed, can they, strictly speaking, be held responsible for their actions? No doubt their behavior should be prevented or stopped, but can they be held responsible for it? This can be illustrated by problems often encountered in the treatment of those affected by bipolar (manic–depressive) illnesses. While the patients are taking their medication, they are cooperative, competent, and understand the benefits of the treatment. But because of the side-effects, they often stop taking the medication; soon they start to decline downward in a cycle in which their judgment becomes impaired. Getting consent to force them into treatment becomes problematic because they are really no longer competent, although medically they must be treated as such.

2.4.7 Acting under Duress

In the film *Air Force One*, the president's plane is captured midflight by a group of terrorists, who are not only holding the president, but also his wife, daughter, and a number of other hostages. The Chechnyan terrorists want their leader freed from a Russian prison. Unless he is freed, the hostages—including the president's family—

will be killed one by one. This creates a crisis in leadership among the remaining officials at the White House. Who's in charge? They ask the attorney general for a constitutional opinion. He replies that since the president is under duress (both his life and the lives of his family depend on his decision), then even though he is alive and in contact, his decisions can be overridden by a majority of the cabinet.

Acting under duress is the case where some external force, some force majeur, *compels a person to do something she would not ordinarily choose to do;* the circumstances are so overpowering or life threatening that one is compelled to act in a certain way. Aristotle gives the examples of sailors throwing goods overboard in a storm or a ruthless man holding your loved ones hostage to force you to do something base for him (*Nic. Ethics* 1110a5–15). We can add ordinary cases of being robbed at gunpoint or cases of self-defense to the list of examples. Usually in these situations you are not held responsible for whatever force impinges upon you (you did not ask for the storm to rise or for someone to rob you), although you might be held responsible to some degree if the duress is brought on through recklessness or negligence. You might know, for example, that a storm is present but choose to sail anyway; you might walk carelessly, flashing money, through a known crime-ridden neighborhood. Still, even if you are not responsible for the compelling force, you still act voluntarily to throw the goods overboard or to hand over your wallet. In this case you are still acting either appropriately or inappropriately, given the circumstances. Sailors could be blamed, for example, for not throwing the goods overboard, thus leading to the sinking of their ship and loss of life. Many would think you foolish, being unarmed and untrained, if you did not give your wallet up to the mugger. Killing in self-defense, under the right conditions, is treated as an excusable, justifiable action, since the other person threatens your own life.

More ordinary cases of acting under duress occur as an employee, where a person is given certain duties to fulfill, or given general directions, yet these may place that person in a situation in which they cause harm to others. An accountant may be told to "cook the books." The implicit threat is that unless the employee acts as directed, he will lose his job, not get the promotion, or otherwise be disadvantaged. The issue here is how much of this duress exonerates the employee's responsibility for an action. Whether the threat is real, whether the employee was personally advantaged, and whether there were opportunities for reporting the wrongdoing are all factors in determining the responsibility of the employee. Employers or supervisors act *vicariously* through their employees, and in many cases they are held responsible for the actions of their employees, and their employees are not responsible precisely because they are thought to be acting under the command and authority of the employer.

Even more familiar cases are situations in which a soldier is given a command to do something that is clearly immoral. Although it is clear in the U.S. military codes that soldiers are not under obligations to obey immoral orders, still the element of coercion is present in doing so. The infamous My Lai massacre which occurred during the Vietnam War illustrates some of the difficulties surrounding this issue. On the tip that there might be Vietcong hidden in the village of My Lai, a platoon of American soldiers entered the village. The action soon turned from reconnaissance to a killing that resulted in the deaths of innocent civilians. The platoon leader, Lt. Calley, was found guilty, yet none of his platoon members nor his supervising officers were found so. It was determined that the command to perform such actions were Calley's alone (although that was disputed). In that case his soldiers were considered to be acting under the duress of that command and were not held responsible for their actions.

Case Study: Acting under Duress?
The Case of Patty Hearst

On February 3, 1974, Patty Hearst, daughter of the heir to the Hearst newspaper dynasty, was kidnapped from her Berkeley, California apartment by the Symbionese Liberation Army (SLA), a small, radical revolutionary group. Hearst's fiancée, Steven Weed, was beaten severely in the armed kidnapping. The SLA, a leftist group, advocated armed and violent overthrow of the government. They had issued a "warrant" for Patty Hearst's arrest as a member of "the oppressive capitalist organization."

Over the course of the kidnapping, the SLA issued a number of communiqués concerning their ideology, justification for the kidnapping, and general demands. Their first demand was the distribution of food to needy people in the San Francisco area; they wanted Patty Hearst's father, William, to bring in about $1 million worth of food. Hearst complied, but the distribution of the food was so mishandled that riots broke out, ending with a number of injuries and arrests. There was also some question about the quality of the food distributed, which William Hearst wrote off as a tax deduction for that year. Another food distribution was attempted with more success. Later, William Hearst offered $1 million for the release of his daughter.

As the kidnapping dragged on and the SLA eluded police and FBI efforts to find them, a turn of events occurred. Communiqués from the SLA started to include messages from Patty Hearst which made it clear that she had chosen to join the revolutionary efforts of her former kidnappers. After identifying with the revolutionary ideology of the SLA, she adopted the name Tania, after a comrade who fought alongside Che Guevara. "I embrace the name with the determination to continue fighting in her spirit." From all appearances the quiet, shy, and reserved Patty Hearst had been transformed into a radical. The apparent proof of this transformation occurred when Patty Hearst was captured on videotape robbing the Hibernia Bank on April 15, 1974. She was seen on tape dressed in a leather coat, with a brown wig, holding an assault rifle. The guard at the bank, Edward Shea, said later, "She looked as though she knew what she was doing. She had a gun and she looked ready to use it." Two bystanders were shot and wounded in the robbery. Apparently, she had participated in the robbery of a sporting goods store earlier as well. Patty Hearst now moved from a kidnap victim to an armed and dangerous fugitive.

On May 17, 1994, there was a fiery shootout between police SWAT teams and the SLA at an SLA safe house. Six members of the SLA were either shot or burned to death as the house burned down. At first Patty Hearst was thought to be among the members killed, but as it turned out she had escaped out of the city earlier with two other members. In her communiqué after the battle, she eulogized her dead comrades.

Eventually, she and her two comrades were captured; she was charged with armed robbery and the use of a firearm to commit a felony. She was brought to trial in February and March of 1976 (her lawyer was F. Lee Bailey). Her defense at this time was based mostly on the argument that she had been acting under duress and had been completely brainwashed by the SLA (some of this had been supported by the testimony of various psychologists, with a well-known phenomenon in which kidnap victims sometimes begin to identify with their kidnappers and torturers). However, at the time Judge Oliver Carter emphasized to the jury that "the fact of a prior kidnapping would not of itself be sufficient to absolve her of responsibility for criminal acts committed afterwards." After some deliberation the jury found her guilty on both counts. She was sentenced on September 24, 1976. Judge William Orrich replaced Judge Carter, who had died that June. He sentenced her to 7 years in prison, with no chance of parole, despite the fact that the district attorney thought she might be eligible for a lesser sentence under the young offender's provisions. However, when a second set of charges were brought against her on the basis of the sporting goods robbery—charges that could net her 15 years to life—Judge E. Talbot Callister gave her 5 years probation, arguing that in his opinion Patty had never willingly joined the SLA and that "she had undergone 57 days of horrible torture as a kidnap victim."

On November 19 she was released on bail, pending appeal. About a year later, after the verdict, one of the jurors, Bruce Braunstein, said, "On the strength of our own experiences over the past year, of now realizing the drastic effects of changes from one's normal environment, we could never convict Patty again." On November 7, 1978, Judge Orrich set aside all petitions to reduce her sentence. Her lawyers at this point sought a presidential pardon, and on February 1, 1979, Patty Hearst's sentence was commuted by President Jimmy Carter.

Question for Discussion

1. Whom do you agree with here, Judge Carter or Judge Callister? Should Patty Hearst's act of robbing the bank be excused because she was the victim of kidnapping and torture, or is that irrelevant to the responsibility for her actions?

Sources: Shana 1979; Jimenez 1977; Weed 1976

2.4.8 Tort Liability

Tort liability is a legal determination of responsibility in cases of civil law that allows a plaintiff the right to compensation for damages or harm caused by another's action. However, it is a complex and evolving body of law. Some argue that its development is more guided by relief of the harm and suffering of innocent victims than to the assignment of blame and responsibility. The object of liability is to relieve the victim of harm of a burden as far as possible and to shift it to the persons or agencies closest to responsibility for it. For these reasons, it often uses a looser sense of responsibility. In many cases persons have been held liable even though they acted in a reasonably cautious manner. There are also well-established cases where the person's conduct need not even be the proximate cause of the results (see *Summers v. Tice* Cal. 2d 80, 199 P.2d 1 1948 above).

Tort liability is generally determined by two standards: the negligent or fault standard and strict liability. The negligent standard looks to the voluntariness of the agents involved. Did they intend the action? Were they acting in a state of ignorance? Did they behave in a reasonably cautious manner? Even the most careful behavior, of course, can result in harm to others, so under this view the plaintiff must show that the person acted negligently or recklessly to cause the harm. Otherwise, the defendant is not held responsible for the harm, even if they were the proximate cause. Strict liability, on the other hand, looks simply at the consequences of an action without regard for the state of the defendant's mind, or in some cases, even if his actions are the proximate cause. This account relies primarily on accountability, next on fault, and least on voluntariness. Strict liability was originally used in the area of consumer protection, where faulty manufacturers' goods could cause great public harm, even if usual precautions were taken. Holding manufacturers under strict liability had the effect of ensuring stronger and more stringent measures of consumer protection and safety. However, strict liability is now also used in other areas. Recent Supreme Court rulings have extended the use of strict liability to cases of sexual harassment (*Faragher v. City of Boca Raton*, 118 S.Ct. 2275 1998; *Burlington Industries Inc. v. Ellerth*, 118 S.Ct. 2257 1998). (See case study below.)

Liability often involves issues of what is called *vicarious responsibility*. Generally, it refers to the imposition on one person for the actionable conduct of another based solely on a relationship between the two persons (Black 1980: 1566). It is often used in the context of employers or corporations for the conduct of their supervisors, managers, or employees. Much of the legal determination of vicarious responsibility of corporations rests on the 1958 *Restatement of Agency* (Sect. 219). This sets the generally accepted legal principles governing the employee–employer relationship. Under these guidelines, Section 219(1) states that "a master is subject to liability for the torts of his servants committed while acting in the scope of their employment." Of course here, master represents employer, and servant, employee. According to Section 228, conduct of a servant is within the scope of employment if:

a. it is the kind he is employed to perform;
b. it occurs substantially within the authorized time and space limits;
c. it is actuated, at least in part, by a purpose to serve the master;
d. if force is intentionally used by the servant against another, the use of force is not unexpectable by the master.

However, Section 219(2) declares that a master is not subject to liability for the torts of his servants acting outside the scope of their employment unless:

a. the master intended the conduct or the consequences, or

b. the master was negligent or reckless, or

c. the conduct violated a nondelegable duty of the master, or

d. the servant purported to act or to speak on behalf of the principal and there was reliance upon apparent authority, or he was aided in accomplishing the tort by the existence of the agency relation.

The use of agency principles helps explain why corporations or institutions can be held liable for the acts of their employees even if they did not intend such actions to occur. So long as the actions were performed within the context of the scope of employment, the corporation can be counted as negligent if it did not properly supervise or create measures that would prevent the harm resulting from the employees' actions. In most cases the individual persons who are members of the corporation are facilitated in their action by the power which the corporation has delegated to them. When they use that power to create harm to others, the corporation can be held liable under certain circumstances. Larry May (1983) has cited two conditions for defining these circumstances:

a. causal factor—the member of the corporation was enabled or facilitated in his harmful conduct by the general grant of authority given to him by corporate decision; and

b. fault factor—appropriate members of the corporation failed to take preventative measures to thwart the potential harm by those who could harm due to the above general grant of authority even though:

1. The appropriate members could have taken such precautions, and

2. These appropriate members could reasonably have predicted that the harm would occur.

This suggests that it is not enough that a corporation does not intend nor desire the harm which its employees have created; it must also be vigilant in setting up measures and procedures which would prevent such harm from happening. Two case studies discussed below, the *Exxon Valdez* oil spill and *Faragher v. City of Boca Raton*, illustrate some of the complexities involved in determining vicarious responsibility.

Case Study: Responsibility for the *Exxon Valdez* Spill

The Accident

The story of the largest oil spill in North American waters is familiar to most people. On March 24, 1989, the *Exxon Valdez*, while traveling outside of normal traffic lanes, ran aground on Bligh Reef in Prince William Sound, spilling 11.2 million gallons (257,000 barrels) of North Slope crude.[1] The details of the events leading up to the spill are also well known. The master of the ship, Joseph Hazelwood, was drinking prior to the departure of the *Exxon Valdez*. The ship left the dock at 9:12 P.M., piloted by the harbor pilot Edward Murphy and accompanied by a single tug.[2] Hazelwood left the bridge at 9:35, while Chief Mate James Kunkel stayed on. This was in clear violation of the Exxon manual, which required two officers on the bridge while the ship

was under condition C—defined as a measure of navigational hazard that indicated closely bounded waters or limited visibility (Keeble 1991: 38). At 9:50 Third Mate Gregory Cousins came to the bridge to relieve Kunkel. At 10:49 Murphy reported to the Valdez Marine Vessel Traffic Center that it passed out of the narrows without event. At 11:05 Hazelwood called the bridge to intercept Murphy's departure and returned there at 11:10 P.M. Murphy was off the ship by 11:24, at which time the ship was up to a speed of 11 knots, good maneuvering speed.

Shortly after Murphy's departure Hazelwood radioed the Valdez Marine Vessel Traffic Center notifying them that they planned to divert from the usual shipping lanes to avoid ice. Traffic Valdez confirmed the plan.[3] Hazelwood informed Cousins that they would divert around the ice that had been calv-

Continued

ing off the Columbia Glacier nearby. Hazelwood also ordered helmsman Claar to put the ship on autopilot without informing Cousins. Shortly after this Robert Kagan, the helmsman, came to relieve Claar, and Maureen Jones relieved Radtke on watch. Claar testified that he told Kagan, "I'm steering one-eight-zero and I'm on the iron mike (the autopilot)" (Keeble 1991: 39). Hazelwood told Cousins that he wanted to "bring it down to abeam of Busby, and then cut back to the lanes." Cousins testified that Hazelwood went through the course change with him three times and was asked twice if he felt comfortable with the procedure, enough so that Hazelwood could go below and finish some paperwork. Cousins said that he understood the orders, was capable of the maneuver, and felt comfortable with everything. However, Cousins did not have an endorsement for Prince William Sound required for all watch commanders.

At 11:52 Hazelwood ordered that the engines be placed on "load program up," which would put the engine under the control of a computer program that would increase the engine speed to about 14 knots in about 45 minutes. After conferring with Cousins about where and how to return the ship to its designated traffic lane, Hazelwood left the bridge about a minute later. Leaving one officer on the bridge again violated Coast Guard regulations and Exxon company policy.

At 11:55 the lookout, Jones, reported seeing the flashing red light for Bligh Reef on the starboard side instead of the port side where it should have been sighted had they been traveling in the outbound shipping lanes. At this point Cousins ordered the 10-degree turn and then notified Hazelwood. The captain said he would return to the bridge in a few minutes. During this time Cousins had his back to Robert Kagan, the helmsman. When he went to check on the rudder indicator, he saw that it read around 6 degrees rather than the ordered 10 degrees. He immediately ordered the 10-degree right, but instead of watching Kagan carefully, he stepped out to get a reading on the Bligh Reef light. When Cousins returned he ordered a 20-degree right rudder because the ship still had not turned. Cousins knew the ship was in serious trouble now and would end up on the reef. He ordered a hard-right command somewhere around midnight. He called Hazelwood to tell him that he thought "we were getting into trouble." Just after that the first shock was felt, and within seconds the ship came hard aground on Bligh Reef. It was 12:04 A.M. Before Hazelwood arrived on the bridge, Cousins ordered a hard left to avoid having the engine room hulled. Kagan hesitated and Cousins grabbed the wheel and turned it himself. When he switched on the exterior floodlights, he could see oil bubbling up from beneath the surface. In the meantime Chief Mate Kunkel, who was awakened by the grounding, had gone to the engine control room and determined that eight cargo tanks and two ballast tanks had been ruptured and that there was loss of oil. When Hazelwood arrived he ordered a fix on their position and had the engines placed on idle. He called Valdez Traffic and reported his predicament: "We should be on your radar there. We've fetched up, run aground north of Goose Island around Bligh Reef. And evidently we're leaking some oil. And we're going to be here awhile. And if you want to say you're notified."[4]

At 12:30 Kunkel ran a computer program twice that determined that the ship had unacceptable stress levels and that it would have unacceptable stability without being supported by the reef. This was conveyed to Hazelwood; yet despite this he continued with a number of maneuvers to try to get the ship off the reef and notified Valdez Traffic accordingly (Davidson 1990: 19–20). He finally abandoned his efforts at 1:41 A.M.

The Response

Under the Prince William Sound Contingency Plan approved by the Alaska Department of Environmental Conservation (DEC), the Alyeska Pipeline Co. was responsible for developing and maintaining a response to any oil spill in Prince William Sound (Piper 1993: 14). Their claim made to the state of Alaska was that they could respond to such a spill in about 5 $\frac{1}{2}$ hours (Davidson 1990: 21). Even though Alyeska was notified almost immediately by the Coast Guard after the spill, the Alyeska barge didn't arrive at Bligh Reef until 14 hours later. By then nearly 240,000 barrels of oil had already escaped into Prince William Sound.

The reasons for such a late response are now well known. Despite promises to the state of Alaska and the Department of Environmental Conservation, Alyeska had cut back its response team. Their response to the Coast Guard's notification of the spill was languid (Davidson 1990: 22). Larry Shier, the person placed in immediate charge of the spill, failed miserably in organizing the response (Davidson 1990: 22). By 5:00 A.M., about the time Alyeska should have arrived with the equipment, the thirty-nine workers assigned to this task were just arriving at the Alyeska terminal. But the needed equipment was not organized. The barge was in dry dock, and the large skimmers and boom, which were supposed to be in the barge, lay somewhere in a warehouse buried under tons of unrelated equipment. A forklift and a crane were deployed to begin sorting skimmers and sections of boom and loading them onto the barge. However, there was only one person who could operate both pieces of the equipment. But finally, as soon as all the equipment was loaded on the barge, the workers were told that the barge was needed for a more urgent task of lightering the ship to prevent the tanker from capsizing. However, no one knew where that equipment was.

After an hour's search, someone noticed them buried under a snowdrift. At 6:30 A.M. Dan Lawn called Larry Shier again noting the urgency of oil already forming a slick about 3 miles long. By 10:00 A.M. the *Exxon Baton Rouge* was diverted to Bligh Reef to take on oil from the *Exxon Valdez*. By 11:00 A.M. the barge with the necessary skimming equipment left the Alyeska terminal.

In the meantime officials from Exxon arrived, including Frank Iarossi, president of Exxon shipping. In the afternoon and evening, Alyeska mishandled an experiment with the effectiveness of oil dispersants, which convinced most state officials that the dispersant would not be effective. At this point Iarossi took over the lightering and dispersants operation from Alyeska. Now there was confusion among the DEC officials about who should be in charge. Although Dennis Kelso, head of the Alaska DEC, believed Alyeska was responsible according to the state-approved contingency plan, he seemed unaware of the agreements made between Alyeska and Exxon on this matter. But now with Exxon in charge, things were no better off because they also were starting from ground zero. Iarossi scrambled to mobilize equipment while Alyeska began to pull back from its participation.

Twenty-four hours after the spill, dispersants and planes arrived. But the controversy and conflicts around the dispersants would delay action. Tests of the dispersants were inconclusive as far as the Coast Guard was concerned, and a controlled burn was also challenged. After 48 hours of extraordinarily calm conditions, little ground had been made with the cleanup—a total of 3000 barrels had been recovered.

On the third day dissension among the principal decision makers—Iarossi from Exxon, Kelso from the DEC, and McCall from the Coast Guard—on the effectiveness and environmental safety of dispersants and controlled burns further delayed action. By the fourth day, when a storm came up, it was too late to act on the spill by means of those methods. The wind had driven the oil slick 40 miles overnight, and by the next morning it was showing up on the shores of Knight Island.

The Harm

The oil spread for 56 days, reaching as far as 470 miles southwest of the original spill site. The oil soiled beaches in the Prince William Sound, along the eastern edge of the Kenai Peninsula, and as far as the Alaska Peninsula through the Shelikof Strait across from Kodiak Island. Altogether it affected 1300 miles of shoreline, roughly the length of shoreline from New Jersey to South Carolina, and spread over an area of 900 square miles, approximately the size of Luxembourg. Of the 257,000 barrels spilled, 32,500 were recovered by cleanup efforts and 77,100 evaporated, leaving 147,400 barrels in the environment.

The toll on the biota of the sound was remarkable.[5] Among birds in the region, it was estimated that 250 bald eagles had died, with anywhere from 50–500 black oystercatchers killed. The common murres took the brunt of the spill, and nearly 22,000 carcasses were found; it was estimated that between 12,000–14,000 marbled murrelets were killed. The carcasses of 838 cormorants were found, 200 harlequin ducks were counted, 300 pigeon guillemots were found, and it was estimated that half of their population died as a result of the spill. About 400 loon carcasses were retrieved.

Among fish populations nearly half of the pacific herring eggs laid in 1989 in the area of the spill were exposed to oil during early development; the population collapsed in 1993 and 1994 with an 85 percent decline. Oil reached one-third of the pink salmon's spawning streams in the southwestern part of Prince William Sound. Exposure to oil may account for decline in runs after 1990.

Among sea mammals probably around 2800 sea otters died; a few river otter carcasses were also found. An estimated 300 harbor seals died directly from oil exposure, and their population declined by 43 percent in the oiled areas. Disruptions in the killer whale populations were found. Of the thirty-six known to inhabit this region, seven were missed when observed 6 days after the spill; a year later six more were missing.

The effect on intertidal and subtidal communities was enormous, given that 1300 miles of beach were soiled by the spill. Mussels, clams and bivalves, snails, sea stars, and crabs were severely affected, and countless invertebrates and vegetation such as fucus seaweed, kelp, and eelgrass were destroyed in these oiled areas.

Besides devastating harm to the sound's ecology, there was also, of course, the human cost. The way of life for a number of villagers and fishers was gravely disrupted. People in Tatitlek, Chenega, Nanwalek, Eyak, Cordova, Port Graham, and Kodiak were all seriously affected by the environmental disaster. Subsistence hunting was greatly curtailed in the years immediately following the spill (Philips 1999: A-6). Even though subsistence has returned to its ordinary levels, the spill "damaged people's confidence in the resources" (Philips 1999: A-6).

There were a number of economic consequences to the spill for the fishing industry. In April 1989 the Alaska Department of Fish and Game was forced to

Continued

close the herring fishery. Closures for shrimp and crab were made shortly after this. The most devastating closing, however, was for pink salmon. Since the ocean fisheries were closed, there were so many fish at the spawn sites that they were in danger of being smothered by an oxygen-burning carpet of pink salmon detritus (Piper 1993: 101).

The disruption in the supply of pink salmon to the usual markets probably triggered changes in the canned salmon market, as buyers turned more to fish farmers from Canada, Chile, and Norway (Piper 1993: 101). The closing of the fisheries also caused local processing plants to close for all or part of the season (Piper 1993: 102). Many of the plants did not reopen, and this has caused problems for local workers and affected city tax revenues. The closing of the Port Graham plant was especially devastating for the village (Piper 1993: 103). The gillnet fleet in the upper Cook Inlet was also badly affected. This area is the second most important sockeye salmon fishery in Alaska, and it was already poorly positioned because of the effects of the 1987 Glacier Bay spill. The Kodiak fisheries were also shut down at this time.

Some of the economic downturn was countered by the revenue brought in by the cost of cleaning the spill. Many, although not the majority, of the fishers affected by the spill made a substantial amount of money from Exxon in assisting with the spill (Piper 1993: 105). However, the jobs were not plentiful nor were they equitably given. Even though some fishers made money from the cleanup, and profited from a few years of good pink salmon runs consequent to the spill, the decline of pink salmon runs after that, the devaluing of their permits, overinvestments in equipment, and the current failure of Exxon to pay its civil penalties have caused many fishers in Cordova to sell their businesses at a considerable loss and have left many with little resources for retirement.

Service companies that provided catering and other support to the offshore cleanup forces had a prosperous season. Retail sales in all towns in the area were generally high. The state's unemployment rate dropped (Piper 1993: 115). But given the short- and long-term economic problems, it was clear that boosting an economy on the basis of an environmental disaster was not a good strategy (Piper 1993: 115).

The social and psychological consequences of the spill should also be noted. The effects of the spill and its cleanup greatly disrupted the lives of the villages and people in the areas of the oil contamination (Piper 1993: 106). The problem for the villages was not just a lost harvest of food, but the loss of a way of life. For the Alutiq, subsistence was integrated into the social fabric of the communities in a way in which occupations or economies may not be for the non-Native and larger communities (Piper 1993: 107).

The invasion of spill cleanup workers, Exxon, state and federal officials, reporters, and transients seeking employment disrupted the community life and taxed the town's resources. Fights, thefts, domestic violence, and drunkenness all rose substantially in all the towns of the spill area. In Seward crime went up 100 percent (Piper 1993: 116). Mental health suffered, and so did the service providers (Picou and Arata 1997). In Kodiak mental health admissions were up 72 percent; in Homer it was 177 percent, and mental health workers in Cordova saw a 28 percent increase in drug and alcohol abuse referrals. Whereas prior to the spill Ahkiok on the Kenai Peninsula had managed to curb an alarming trend in alcohol abuse among its population, during 1989 the sobriety rated dropped some 30 percent. The local women's shelters in the Kenai-Soldotna-Homer area were full. In general, "the stress levels, the sudden flow of money, the influx of transients with no obligations or connections to the communities, all helped make day-to-day life in the spill town a bizarre, unsettling, and occasionally dangerous experience" (Piper 1993: 117).

The Trial

Both Hazelwood and Exxon were brought to trial in 1990, and the trial lasted more than 4 months. At Hazelwood's trial he was accused of the negligent discharge of oil in the spill. Evidence for negligence was based on four factors. (1) Since it was discovered that Hazelwood had several drinks before his departure from Valdez (his blood-alcohol level 9 hours after the grounding was 0.06, slightly above the Coast Guard level of 0.04), he acted negligently by violating the Coast Guard rule prohibiting drinking within 4 hours of active duty. (2) He acted negligently by leaving the bridge, against Exxon's rules. (3) He acted negligently by leaving an unqualified man in charge. (4) He acted negligently by giving the "load up program" command too early and without further supervision. The jury found Hazelwood guilty of negligent discharge of oil, a misdemeanor. He was made to do 1000 hours of community service and pay a fine of $5000 (the conviction was thrown out on appeal but reinstated by the Alaska Supreme Court; Hazelwood appealed that decision, but it was also upheld).

The jury also argued that Exxon acted negligently by not properly supervising Hazelwood and making decisions which contributed to the accident. The attorneys for the plaintiffs in this case argued that Exxon tried to save money by reducing crew levels and that they gave little concern to the level of competence of the crew. Gregory Cousins had little competence to navigate the ship, and Robert Kagan, the helmsman, also had little competence. Exxon also gave little concern to the training of the crew; Exxon did not concern itself with the fatigue levels of the crew. It was claimed that Exxon was aware of the risks involved with these policies. First, the attorneys argued that Exxon failed to supervise Hazelwood properly. Despite the fact that Hazelwood had been hospitalized for depression and alcoholism, Exxon continued to employ him to captain their ships; Exxon knew that he was a risk to himself and to others long before the vessel ran aground. Second, it was argued that there was enough scientific data to prove that the oil spill had caused long-term ecological damage to Prince William Sound, disrupted the fishing industry, and upset the lives of the coastal village inhabitants. Third, because of the failure to supervise Hazelwood, Exxon acted negligently and deserved punitive damages. The attorneys argued that in 1993 Exxon had revenues of $111 billion, assets of $84 billion, a cash flow of $12 billion, and after taxes, a profit of $5.3 billion. The jury concurred, and Exxon was charged with $5.5 billion in civil and criminal penalties (the award is still under appeal).

Notes

[1] Ricki Ott, Cordova biologist, fisherman, and environmental activist, claims there were more than 11 million gallons spilled.

[2] The ship was piloted at that time 7 miles to Rocky Point. Formerly, the pilot was required to take the ship through the sound to Hinchinbrook Island—a cost-saving practice implemented by Alyeska.

[3] U.S. Coast Guard, Valdez Station recordings, March 24, 1989.

[4] U.S. Coast Guard, Valdez Station recordings, March 24, 1989. Notifying the Coast Guard of an oil spill would, under regulations at that time, exonerate a captain from certain kinds of criminal prosecution from an oil spill. Later, Hazelwood's lawyers used this to defend their client from prosecution. Judge Johnstone in that case denied the defense this strategy since a spill of this magnitude, he argued, would have been discovered soon enough.

[5] A research industry has grown up around the *Exxon Valdez* oil spill. Funded partly by the federal government, by the *Exxon Valdez* Oil Spill settlement, by Exxon corporation, and partly by universities, there are thousands of published articles related to the research on recovery of Prince William Sound. The *Exxon Valdez* Oil Spill Trustee Council offers a bibliography of the published research on recovery of the sound that it has sponsored (http://www.oilspill.state.ak.us/tcbib.html), and it recently organized a conference, "Legacy of an Oil Spill: 10 Years after the *Exxon Valdez*," in Anchorage, Alaska, on March 23–26, 1999 (cf. http://www.oilspill.state.ak.us/posters.htm). On the basis of this research, the Trustee Council has divided injured resources into the following categories: recovered, recovering, not recovering, recovery unknown, and not affected. Sea lions, brown bears, Sitka black-tailed deer, crabs, shrimp, among other species were considered not to be notably damaged by the spill. The bald eagle is the only species cited that has recovered. Common murres, mussels, pink salmon, sockeye salmon, and the intertidal and subtidal communities are thought to be recovering. The species not recovering include cormorants, harbor seals, harlequin ducks, killer whales, marbled murrelets, pacific herring, pigeon guillemot, and sea otters. The recovery status of black oystercatchers, clams, common loons, cutthroat trout, dolly varden, Kittlitz's murrelets, river otter, and rockfish is unknown (cf. http://www.oilspill.state.ak.us/injuredresource.html). The Exxon corporation-sponsored research disputes many of these findings (cf. http://www.valdezresearch.com/abstract/pp-894.htm for abstracts of some of the more critical research). Exxon's vice president, Frank Sprow, has been quoted as saying that "Prince William Sound is a robust, healthy, thriving place today" ("The *Exxon Valdez* Oil Spill," KTUU, Anchorage, Alaska, aired March 24, 1999). According to the Auke Bay Research facility, part of the Alaska Fisheries Science Center, "although it is 10 years past the spill, oil still remains in the impacted area; intertidal and shallow subtidal habitats are still contaminated; some species have not recovered; and the production of the ecosystem appears 'out of sync' as major salmon and herring fisheries have not returned to stability" (cf. http://www.afsc.noaa.gov/abl/evos/index.htm).

Questions for Discussion

1. Who caused the spill? Were there contributing or concurrent causes? Who caused the failure to recover the oil?
2. What were the duties and obligations of Kagan? Of Cousins? Of Hazelwood? Of Exxon? How can they each be held accountable? What were the duties of Alyeska and Exxon in the oil spill recovery? How can they be held accountable? Do you think the Coast Guard should be held accountable? What about the Alaska Department of Environmental Conservation, which was supposed to oversee Alyeska's operation? Should they have been held accountable?
3. Who was most responsible for the spill? Who was most responsible for the failure to recover the oil?
4. Do you think responsibility for the spill was properly assigned?
5. Do you think the punishments were fair, given the various assignments of fault?
6. Should a company that makes a large profit from its activities be given large penalties if one of its employees does something in the line of work that does great public harm? How accountable are oil companies in the transport of oil?

Case Study: Vicarious Responsibility for Sexual Harassment

Two recent Supreme Court cases, *Faragher v. City of Boca Raton* (118 S.Ct. 2275 1998) and *Burlington Industries Inc. v. Ellerth* (118 S.Ct. 2257 1998), illustrate the complex reasoning involved in the notion of vicarious responsibility.

In *Burlington*, Kimberly Ellerth brought action against Burlington Industries for sexual harassment from her supervisor, Theodore Slowik, who was the vice president of sales and marketing. She claimed that Burlington had violated Title VII of the Civil Rights Act of 1964. She was hired as a merchandising assistant, and she alleged sexual harassment from Slowik in the form of personal remarks of a sexual nature and sexually oriented remarks and jokes on several occasions; he also rubbed her knees several times. Although Ellerth was aware of Burlington's sexual harassment policy, she failed to tell anyone in authority about the harassing behavior. In her resignation letter, she also failed to mention the harassment. It was 3 weeks later that she sent a letter stating her reasons for the resignation. The District Court of Illinois concluded that Burlington was not liable. Ellerth appealed to the United States Court of Appeals for the Seventh Circuit, which reversed part of the lower courts decision—although the decision produced eight different opinions. The Seventh Circuit Court allowed that Burlington was liable. Burlington appealed to the U.S. Supreme Court, which upheld the Seventh Circuit's decision, but on grounds different than the majority decision in the lower court. However, it also gave Burlington Industries the opportunity to establish a defense against such liability and articulated the conditions of that defense.

In *Faragher*, Beth Ann Faragher and Nancy Ewanchew brought suit against the city of Boca Raton for sexual harassment by their immediate supervisors, claiming the city violated Title VII of the Civil Rights Act. Bill Terry often touched the bodies of the female lifeguards, including waist, neck, buttocks, and breasts, and simulated sexual activity, inviting them to have intercourse with the male guards. In 1990, some months after her employment ended, Ewanchew wrote a letter to the director of personnel for the city complaining of Terry and another supervisor, David Silverman. As a result, the city initiated an investigation that led to the reprimand of the two and a forfeiture of their annual leave. A few months later Faragher resigned from her job. It was afterward that they brought suit against the city. The District Court for the Southern District of Florida found the city strictly liable for the sexual harassment. On appeal the Eleventh Circuit reversed the lower court's decision. On appeal the U.S. Supreme Court reversed the judgment of the Eleventh Circuit finding the city of Boca Raton liable in this case.

On face value it would appear that both Burlington Industries and the city of Boca Raton are not responsible, and therefore not liable, for the actions of their employees, not only because they did not know of these actions during the time they took place, but because the actions of their employees were not sanctioned by them relative to their sexual harassment policies and so seemed out of the scope of their employment. How could they be held responsible for another person's action when they did not authorize such behavior? Moreover, when the city of Boca Raton did find out, it took punitive action against the offending supervisors. The U.S. Supreme Court's reasoning on this matter is both fascinating and complex and does require some background.

Both of these cases refer to the Civil Rights Act of 1964, section 2000e-2, subsection 2a, commonly known as Title VII. It declares that

> It shall be an unlawful employment practice for an employer (1) to fail or refuse to hire or to discharge any individual, or otherwise to discriminate against any individual with respect to his compensation, terms, conditions, or privileges of employment, because of such individual's race, color, religion, sex, or national origin; or (2) to limit, segregate, or classify his employees or applicants for employment in any way which would deprive or tend to deprive any individual of employment opportunities or otherwise adversely affect his status as an employee, because of such individual's race, color, religion, sex or national origin (42 U.S.C. section 2000e-2a).

Before an individual can bring a sexual harassment claim under Title VII, a complaint must be filed with the Equal Employment Opportunity office in the individual's state within 300 days of the date the actionable conduct occurred. The EEOC reviews the circumstances surrounding the alleged harassment on a case-by-case basis. To do that job the EEOC passed the Title VII interpretive guidelines, which became effective November 10, 1980 (29 C.F.R. sect. 1604, 1997). The guidelines define sexual harassment as unwelcome verbal or physical conduct of a sexual nature, including sexual advances or sexual favor requests, that occur when: (1) submission is explicitly or implicitly made a condition or term of employment; (2) compliance with such demand affects the individual's employment; or (3) the pur-

Case Study: Vicarious Responsibility for Sexual Harassment, *Continued*

pose or effect of such conduct unreasonably interferes with work performance or creates an intimidating, hostile, or offensive working environment. Conditions (1) and (2) make up what is often called the *quid pro quo* (this for that) clause; condition (3) is often referred to as the hostile work environment clause and was established by the U.S. Supreme Court in *Meritor Savings Bank v. Vinson* (477 U.S. 57, 1986). There Judge William Rehnquist, writing for the majority, argued that "sexual harassment which creates a hostile or offensive environment for members of one sex is every bit the arbitrary barrier to sexual equality at the workplace that racial harassment is to racial equality" (477 U.S. 57, 1986, 66–67).

Part of the argument in both *Burlington* and *Faragher* also rests on some concept of the scope of employment, understood as what actions of an employee fall within the performance, function, or duties of the job. As discussed earlier in Section 2.4.8, the 1958 *Restatement of Agency* (sect. 219) sets the generally accepted principles governing the employee–employer relationship and, according to *Meritor*, is to be the guideline for liability under Title VII (cf. Gill 1999). To repeat these guidelines, Section 219(1) states that "a master is subject to liability for the torts of his servants committed while acting in the scope of their employment." Of course, here, master represents employer and servant represents employee. According to Section 228, conduct of a servant is within the scope of employment if

a. it is the kind he is employed to perform;
b. it occurs substantially within the authorized time and space limits;
c. it is actuated, at least in part, by a purpose to serve the master;
d. force is intentionally used by the servant against another, the use of force is not unexpectable by the master.

However, Section 219(2) declares that a master is not subject to liability for the torts of his servants acting outside the scope of their employment unless

a. the master intended the conduct or the consequences, or
b. the master was negligent or reckless, or
c. the conduct violated a non delegable duty of the master, or
d. the servant purported to act or to speak on behalf of the principal and there was reliance upon apparent authority, or he was aided in accomplishing the tort by the existence of the agency relation.

The Supreme Court argued in both *Burlington* and *Faragher* that employers should be held strictly liable for hostile work environment sexual harassment created by supervisory personnel (*Burlington* 118 S.Ct.: 2270; *Faragher* 118 S.Ct.: 2292–3). In the *Burlington* case it argued that Burlington Industries should have the opportunity of defense against the charge of liability, but it found the city of Boca Raton strictly liable in this case. The Court reasoned in the following way. Although sexual harassment by supervisory personnel is not within the scope of employment, nonetheless strict liability should be imposed under a theory of apparent authority found in Section 219(2d) of the *Restatement of Agency* (*Faragher* 118 S.Ct.: 2287, 2290; *Faragher* 118 S.Ct.: 2267). The Court held that vicarious liability for supervisor misconduct centers around Section 219(2d) above, because the very nature of the supervisor relationship creates an atmosphere less likely to be questioned by the employee than, for example, co-worker harassment (*Faragher* 118 S.Ct.: 2290-91). Further, the Court reasoned that the employer is most capable to guard against supervisory misconduct than it can against the conduct of ordinary employees; the employer can more easily screen, train, and monitor supervisors' performance (*Faragher* 118 S.Ct.: 2291). Because only supervisory personnel can make tangible employment actions, such as hiring, firing, and promotion, the supervisor retains a special threatening character. The Court also laid down the conditions for defense against such liability: Assuming that there has been no tangible employment action such as firing, then the employer may raise a defense on the following grounds: (1) that the employer exercised reasonable care to prevent and correct promptly any sexually harassing behavior and (b) that the plaintiff employee unreasonably failed to take advantage of any preventive or corrective opportunities provided by the employer or to avoid harm otherwise (*Burlington* 118 S.Ct.: 2270). Thus, since Burlington Industries did have a widely distributed sexual harassment policy and a process in place for complaints of sexual harassment, which the plaintiff in this case did not take advantage of, it had a reasonable defense it could use against the charge of liability. On the other hand, because the city of Boca Raton did not distribute information about its sexual harassment policy to the department in question and did not take reasonable care to monitor its supervisors in this area, it should be held vicariously liable for the actions of its supervisors, even though they did not fall within the scope of their employment.

Case Studies for Assigning Responsibility and Blame

A. Should subsequent generations be held accountable for the harms done to others by preceding generations? This is sometimes a claim that is made to support practices such as affirmative action, although, of course, many proponents of affirmative action argue that the program is not established to punish white Americans but to ensure equal treatment for minorities in the process of hiring. In any case some argue that if preceding generations received unfair economic, social, and political benefits from exploitation and discrimination of other groups, and because these benefits were, generally speaking, something that enriched the generations which came directly from that group, then why shouldn't the present generation repair that original harm in some way if it hasn't already been redressed. If generations of African Americans were enslaved and then systematically discriminated against so that economic, social, and political advances were denied to them, then once this harm has been recognized and admitted, why shouldn't the present generation make appropriate reparations? What do you think of this argument? For example, the U.S. government has tried to make amends for the internment of thousands of Japanese Americans during World War II, even though, as far as we know, the present U.S. officials had nothing to do with that original decision.

B. How responsible should we be held for the consequences of our actions? In *Watkins v. U.S.* (589 F. 2d 214 5th Cir. 1979), a man was injured when his car collided with a serviceman's car. He sued the United States, charging that a government doctor had improperly given the serviceman an excessive supply of Valium and that this negligence caused the accident. The court concluded that the physician's negligence in prescribing the tranquilizer without checking the serviceman's known psychiatric history and condition was a proximate cause of the victim's injuries. A foreseeable consequence of prescribing Valium under such circumstances is that a patient with psychiatric problems will drink and that such a patient, after ingesting Valium and alcohol, may injure others, as happened here. Comments?

C. A 4-year-old boy was tragically killed when his head became stuck in an electric window of a GM truck. The child was alone in the truck while his stepfather was inside the house, and the keys were in the ignition. The father sued GM for faulty design and the stepfather for negligence. Comments?

D. A Louisiana State University student who nearly died after a night of drinking that killed a fellow fraternity pledge filed a negligence suit in September of 1997 against the school, the fraternity, and the bar where they drank. The student alleges that he and other pledges were forced by members of the fraternity to consume pitchers of drinks and that the fraternity did not do enough to help nearly two dozen drunken pledges. When paramedics were called, the student was not breathing and near death, with a blood-alcohol level at 0.588 percent—nearly six times the legal level for intoxication. The student was also one year under the legal drinking age. The suit claims that the bar owner—who happened to be the fraternity's president—should have stopped the drinking at the private party, and the university should have regulated or discouraged fraternity bid night. The university's spokesperson argued that while they regret any misfortune suffered by the students, they have no legal liability. Comments?

E. In *Penn Tanker Co. v. U.S.* (310 F. Supp. 613 1970), a 27-year-old seaman injured his eye while using a welding torch aboard a ship. The company that owned the ship was negligent in supervising the procedure. The seaman was hospitalized for eye surgery. Although the seaman's eye had not been properly prepared for surgery, the ophthalmologist proceeded to operate, tearing the patient's iris, puncturing his lens, and then failing to control postoperative bleeding. Each defendant, the company and the physician, paid the portion of damages caused by his own negligent conduct. Comments?

2.5 THE CONCEPT OF AUTONOMY

Notions such as free will, responsibility, and moral strength are thought by many philosophers to be best explicated by the notion of autonomy ("autonomy" etymologically means "self-governance," from the Greek *auto* meaning "self" and *nomos* meaning "law"). *Autonomy should be understood as a mastery of self that also involves self-direction. True freedom under this view is the employment of strength of will for the purposes of self-determination or self-governance.* This definition may contradict the popular understanding of freedom. For example, William Williams, a self-styled lifestyle guru and author of *Future Perfect* (1995), writes,

> I eat when I want to eat, sleep when I want to sleep; go wherever I want, and whenever
> I want. There is no place I ever have to be, and no time I ever have to be anywhere. In
> short, I am free.

What Williams means here by freedom is a life without constraints. But in looking
at this passage carefully, it is clear that Williams is constrained by basic desires such
as eating and sleeping. Under the view of compatibilism, all actions are caused, i.e.,
constrained. There is no escape from some kind of constraint. What makes one
free is when one's actions are under self-imposed constraint, that is, self-control.
Under the notion of autonomy, Williams's behavior is far from free; rather it is simply a life in which you are controlled and constrained by your desires and wants,
your first-order volitions, rather than by your second-order ones—to use Frankfurt's terminology presented earlier. In fact, those who would eat whenever or
whatever they want and sleep whenever they want would soon find themselves both
in ill health and poor to boot. Rather than doing anything you like, genuine freedom is paradoxically understood as self-mastery. Indeed, autonomy as self-mastery
and self-determination is echoed in the very idea of internalization, the means by
which we acquire norms or standards for behavior: It is only when we have adopted
standards as our own that we can really be considered to have internalized such
norms. As psychologist David Shapiro argues, internalization is crucial for the development of autonomy (1981: 33, 45, 46).

Autonomy appears to have two aspects. On the one hand, it involves *self-mastery*, the ability to exert control over your inner life (*self-control*) as well as your outer
life (*self-efficacy*), and *self-direction*, the ability to set rules and limits for yourself. This
distinction is confirmed by psychological studies on autonomy (cf. Shapiro 1981).

Self-mastery is reactive, whereas self-direction is proactive (Shapiro 1981:15). In self-mastery or self-reg-ulation, one responds to an impulse, feeling, or desire and reg-ulates it accordingly; in this sense the source of the motivation to act comes from outside the control of

---

"the conception of autonomy is connected with each indi-vidual's capacity to form projects, plans, and goals. An autonomous person is able to form such projects and execute them."

—Jules Coleman, Professor of Jurisprudence
and Philosophy, Yale University

---

the agent, and the agent controls the motivation. In self-direction, on the other
hand, the motivation to act comes from a conscious or internally represented goal,
or what Frankfurt calls second-order volitions. This seems to be confirmed by a classical study made by Kurt Goldstein and M. Scheerer in 1941. Lesions to the brain
which affected abstract thinking processes also had the effect of diminishing self-
direction in the patient. The typical symptom was the inability of the patient to initiate tasks. Goldstein and Scheerer characterized these patients as "will-less"—they
were unable to draw a map of their own ward but could complete one if it was started for them. One patient was unable to set the hands of a clock at a given hour but
could recognize the time when the clock was presented. These patients had lost the
ability of self-direction because they had lost the power of internally representing a
goal for themselves; they were stimulus bound, confined to what was immediately
before them. They were, therefore, unable to plan, to guide, or to initiate an action
toward an end that had to be imagined (Goldstein and Scheerer 1941)

The notion of *self-direction* is illustrated by what David Shapiro calls pathologies of autonomy (1981: 18). Hysterical personalities (as opposed to conversion disorders) are people who are often passive, nearly paralyzed in terms of
decision-making capacity. They feel they have no aim of their own, and their actions

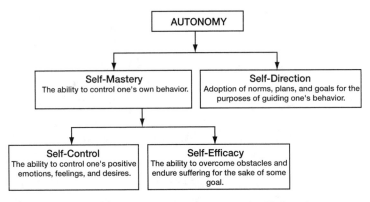

Autonomy Involves Both Self-mastery and Self-direction

are entirely determined by force of circumstance and by the expectations of others. "I didn't mean to, I just did" or "I didn't want to, but he asked me to" are typical responses to misbehaviors. Obviously, these sorts of people are easily susceptible to the influence and direction of others. In the hysterical personality, consciousness of intention, deliberateness, and planning have all been diminished; at the same time there is a tendency to quick and relatively spur-of-the moment action (1981: 18). Rigid character, on the other hand, is the polar opposite of the hysterical one. This is marked by an extraordinary degree of articulation, self-consciousness of aim and purpose, and often excruciating consciousness of choice and decision (Shapiro 1981: 69–77).

Granting this distinction between self-mastery and self-direction, the former can be subdivided into self-control and self-efficacy. *Self-control* is control over your inner life in terms of emotions, feelings, passions, wants, needs, dispositions, flaws, drives, and so forth. *Self-efficacy* is a general mastery over the events of your life and the ability to meet challenges as they come up (cf. Goleman 1995: 89–90) (see figure). Without self-control you are simply a set of raging hormones or a bundle of needs and wants; without self-efficacy you are helpless and passive. The virtues, such as temperance (control of pleasure), courage (control of fear), and fairness (the limitation of self-interest), are examples of self-control and self-efficacy in this regard.

Self-direction, on the other hand, involves giving oneself certain standards, rules, and principles of conduct. Philosopher John Kekes (1992: 16) defines it as a process of self-transformation, involving the gradual change of our present self

"Making decisions about the quality of life you want for yourself and affirming these choices is partly what autonomy is about.

"Autonomous individuals have a desire to become both free and responsible and to do for themselves what they are capable of doing.

"People moving in the direction of autonomy have a sense of identity and uniqueness. Rather than only looking outside of themselves, they also find answers within. Instead of looking primarily to what others expect of them and seeking their approval, they ask: 'Who is it that I want to become? What seems like the right thing to do? What do I expect of myself?'

"People moving in the direction of autonomy have a sense of commitment and responsibility. They are committed to some ideals and personal goals that make sense to them. Their sense of commitment includes a willingness to accept responsibility for their actions rather than blaming circumstances or other people for the way their lives are going."
—from Gerald and Marianne Corey (1997)

into a future self that approximates more closely the ideals we aim at. Typically, these standards, rules, and principles are initially selected from an array of those available in your immediate culture, although over time they may be exchanged for others modified or others developed. The idea in genuine autonomy is that these are not selected simply by osmosis or by association but through a sorting process that involves reflection, information, and honesty. Whereas the virtues are the means by which self-mastery is achieved, self-direction is fulfilled through wisdom and moral knowledge.

Autonomy is contrasted with *heteronomy*, which can be understood as being controlled by something other than self-control. Being controlled by your passions rather than controlling your passions is one example, and having moral standards or rules imposed upon you without reflection or deliberation is another. Psychologist Jean Piaget stresses this contrast between heteronomy and autonomy in his studies on moral development in children (1932: 65). By the age of 10

> the consciousness of rules undergoes a complete transformation. Autonomy follows upon heteronomy; the rule of a game appears to the child no longer as an external law, sacred in so far as it has been laid down by adults; but, as the outcome of a free decision and worthy of respect in the measure that it has enlisted mutual consent.

A fully autonomous person is one who has not only self-mastery but has also deliberately chosen the moral rules and principles for self-direction (whether or not these conform to the conventional moral standards of his or her community). One can also be partially autonomous in the sense that one is heteronomously directed although self-mastered and, conversely, self-directed but failing in self-mastery.

Perhaps an ancient metaphor would be of help in explaining the two aspects of autonomy: self-mastery and self-direction. Imagine that your passions, emotions, feelings, and so on are the horses that drive the chariot. Before you can go anywhere you, as the driver, must control the horses—your strength of will must be stronger than theirs. Yet to go somewhere, you need a compass, map, and guide, and for this purpose you must have knowledge and information about the right way to the desired destination, and to get there at all, you must be able to overcome obstacles and endure the long journey. The most striking thing about autonomy is that it is something that only you can give yourself. Although people can certainly help you, as long as you are guided in your behavior purely by external reward or punishment, you are truly not autonomous. Only by self-mastery and adopting some standard of conduct for yourself is that possible.

2.6 KANT AND THE NOTION OF THE GOOD WILL

There is an important difference between moral sentiment, the desire or the wish to do the good, and the will to do the good, or the good will. A person with good will (not to be confused with someone who has goodwill toward others, which is simply a form of moral sentiment) is someone who brings all of her power and self-control for the good. Immanuel Kant believed that good will was the most important aspect of moral life, even more important than virtuous character and prudent deliberation:

> Moderation in emotions and passions, self-control and calm deliberation not only are good in many respects but even seem to constitute a part of the inner worth of the person. But however unconditionally they were esteemed by the ancients, they are far from being good without qualification. For without the principle of a good will they

can become extremely bad, and the coolness of a villain makes them not only more dangerous but also more directly abominable in our eyes than he would have seemed without it. The good will is not good because of what it effects or accomplishes ... it is good only because of its willing, that is, it is good of itself (1785: 10).

The good will, according to Kant, is manifest in a person's sense of duty, that is, given our earlier language, the fact that someone has internalized a certain code of obligations toward others. The person with a good will, then, is different than someone who will act according to this sense of duty, but only because of the rewards and benefits it brings to their lives. A shopkeeper may be honest with his customers only because he believes that it is good for business. A shopkeeper with good will is honest to customers without that consideration: A person should be honest with others, and that is that. Often people will act according to duty only to avoid trouble or to get ahead or to please someone. In this case one does one's duty for what it brings rather than for the fact that it is one's duty. On the other hand, when one acts from duty, according to Kant, that is the purest expression of the good will (1785: 14ff.). In acting from duty one is not interested in the consequences, good or bad, but simply in the fact that it is one's duty. It is for these reasons that Kant makes his famous pronouncement: "Nothing in the world—indeed nothing even beyond the world—can possibly be conceived which could be called good without qualification except a good will" (1785: 9). Although many talents, abilities, virtues, and excellences are desirable and can achieve marvelous things, still they are not good without qualification because intelligence, courage, and the like can always be used for some malicious or self-fulfilling purpose. Because the good will acts without regard to consequence, benefit, or harm, it must be considered the purest expression of goodness; even if one acts virtuously for the sake of happiness, still in that case one's motives for acting good are subordinated to the goal of happiness, and one has tainted the motives for acting morally. It would seem, then, that Kant would count as better those who will the good although they fail to attain it over those who attain the good, but for ulterior reasons (1785: 10).

Kant also draws a distinction between the holy or saintly will and the good will. In the last case an ordinary person with good will brings all of his power and self-control to bear for the sake of the good, yet there is often a conflict between this duty and other alternatives. In the holy will, such as God's will, there is no such conflict. In fact, in the holy will duty makes no sense since there is only one thing to do, namely, the good. In other words, there is no inclination contrary to the good to sway the holy will from its course. The holy will is constituted with the good (1788: 84ff.).

The good will, understood as the commitment to duty for the sake of duty, translates into the notion of autonomy for Kant. In acting from duty one is literally giving oneself a code or law by which to live, which as far as Kant is concerned is the essence of freedom. Often freedom is imagined as the ability of a person to do whatever she wants. But in Kant's view this is an example of servility to the whims of passion, desires, and wants. It is only when one has mastery over one's desires, wants, passions, and needs that one can call oneself truly free. Paradoxically, then, in doing one's duty despite an inclination against it, one is exhibiting the greatest form of freedom. Thus, autonomy and freedom are synonymous in Kant's view.

There are several criticisms of Kant's position, however. In emphasizing the good will, Kant seems to belittle the role of moral sentiment. He seems to be opposed to the idea that if we are inclined to the good, that somehow that does not count, since it is only through the power of the force of will over our inclinations that we have the true sense of goodness. But surely the inclination toward the good, combined with a strong good will, serves the matter of moral competence much better than the force of will against any contrary inclination and in spite of positive ones. It seems that there are two strategies toward doing the good in this regard: the use of will to constrain negative inclinations and the use of moral sentiment to build positive ones. Moral sentiment requires internalization, which seems to be at the basis of the very concept of duty. Consequently, the notion of the good will seems to rely on this moral sentiment to some degree. Although it is clear that duty is not the sole moral sentiment, Kant narrowly viewed it this way. It is as wrong to think, as Hume did, that sympathy is at the basis of all our moral actions as it is wrong for Kant to think that duty is the primary form of expression. In this matter the narrowness of these views prevents the thinkers from seeing a broader basis for moral competence.

2.7 NIETZSCHE: THE STRONG WILL IS THE GOOD WILL

Nietzsche argues "life itself is the instinct for growth, for an accumulation of forces, for power" (*The Antichr.* 6). Since all life exhibits this will to power, then the "good" will is the will which expresses it well. To say, as Kant does, that the good will is simply that will which does its duty is simply to say that it conforms to custom, and specifically the custom of the herd disguised as the mores of the community. Nietzsche makes a distinction between two fundamental kinds of morality: slave (or herd) and master morality. Those who live a master morality express the will to power well: It is the self-affirmation, self-consciousness of the noble, powerful, high-

Friedrich Nietzsche (1844–1900) was a German philologist and philosopher. His most important notion was the concept of the "will to power," explained in this section. He developed a number of interesting ideas in the areas of aesthetics, ethics, and cultural criticism. His most famous works are *Beyond Good and Evil, The Birth of Tragedy,* and *Thus Spake Zarathustra.* (For more on Nietzsche, see Sections 1.3.4 and 5.3.1.)

stationed, and high-minded individuals, who established themselves and their actions as good, especially in contrast to the low-minded, common, and plebeian (*Gen. Morals* I: 2). On the other hand, the herd morality—the exemplars for Nietzsche being common Christian morality, utilitarianism, socialism, or any other morality that values the lowly or the common good—is a reaction of the weak; it is a morality based on what they feel is threatening, on resentment against those who threaten them. It is a nay-saying to the power of life and to those who are exceptional and powerful (*Gen. Morals* I: 10). In fact, slave morality is hostile to life, so understood as the will to power; human life diminishes in vigor and quality by domination of the herd morality. Herd morality aims at the removal of everything dangerous to life as it seeks the common security, whereas master morality aims at the bold. It transgresses and seeks to establish something new despite the risk (*Dawn* 174). The herd morality reinterprets as vice the natural drives of the strong; not only is it directed to the preservation of the mediocre, but it is against the strong: "the more dangerous a quality seems to the herd, the more thoroughly it is proscribed" (*Will to Power* 276). To make a person noble requires pressing "the mightiest powers," while the herd morality strives to restrict strength and passion (*Will to Power* 383).

However, the strong will is not simply an arbitrary will, or despotic will; it is a will that exhibits self-mastery to the highest degree—a self-mastery that is necessary to create new value and order (*Gay Sci.* 335). It has achieved for this reason the highest degree of autonomy, or the power necessary to direct oneself toward higher forms of life (*Will to Power* 403). In Nietzsche's words such autonomy means, "a yes, a no, a straight line, a goal" (*Antichr.* 1). In this sense master morality is not simply self-indulgence, of which everyone is capable, even those bound by slave morality. And it is not self-centeredness because it involves an indifference for oneself in favor of higher forms of life (*Dawn* 146). In the end the strong will is "beyond good and evil," as it creates the very sense of that distinction:

> Self-interest is worth as much as the person who has it: it can be worth a great deal, and it can be unworthy and contemptible. Every individual may be scrutinized to see whether he represents the ascending or the descending line of life. ... If he represents the ascending line, then his worth is indeed extraordinary—and for the sake of life as a whole. ... (*Twilight Idols* IX: 33).

What is necessary for the strong will is the establishment of autonomy or self-mastery; only then can it go on to enhance life, to create new order, and generally to affirm higher forms of life.

There are, of course, numerous complaints against Nietzsche's position; many find it shocking and distasteful since it does, indeed, seem to go against the grain of those moralities which serve to protect the weak against the strong. In addition, its formulation is unclear enough that it could simply serve as an ideology for any individual who has power. The 20th century after Nietzsche has seen the effects of this, especially in light of Hitler and Stalin. The mastery by the few over the many and the ruthlessness of the powerful have created suffering for millions; this, of course, is a lesson learned throughout history, although the power of

---

Does Nietzsche's View Suggest Hitler's?

In *Mein Kampf* Hitler argued the following: "The strength which each people possesses decides the day. Always before God and the world the stronger has the right to carry through what he wills. ... The whole world of Nature is a mighty struggle between strength and weakness—an eternal victory of the strong over the weak. There would be nothing but decay in the whole of Nature if this were not so."

technology in the 20th century has made it all the more clear. There is a problem with Nietzsche's theory in addition to these considerations. His account of morality relies on a sort of naturalism that is dependent, interestingly enough, on a certain biological interpretation of the world and a certain anthropological understanding of culture, neither one of which might entirely support his theory of the will to power. The idea that nature is permeated with power and its expression may itself be a value prejudice, a sort of projection onto nature of certain aspects of human life.

2.8 DEVELOPING AUTONOMY

Given the character of autonomy, becoming autonomous requires self-mastery and self-direction. Self-direction is a matter of wisdom and moral knowledge, and so its acquisition will be dealt with in the following chapters. Self-mastery, as mentioned, involves self-control, which is control over your inner life, and self-efficacy, which is adeptness in your social and cultural environment. Psychologist Samuel Klausner (1965: 14) noted that when it comes to self-control there are essentially four objects of control: (1) actual physical movements, such as restraining yourself from striking another or motivating yourself toward movement, for example, straining to win a race; (2) inhibiting drives, such as sexual impulses, or enhancing drives, such as building up a desire to work; (3) cognitive functions, such as inhibiting vicious thoughts or using thoughts to distract from anxieties and worries; and (4) controlling affects or emotions, for example, combating sadness or restraining anger.

Self-control involves both a restraining and a restorative aspect. It acts to restrain when something overpowers the person, when the person is on the edge of loss of control. Controlling one's temper requires restraint prior to a critical point, when the feeling of anger floods the brain. But it can also involve an attempt to restore a lack or loss, for example, to promote positive feelings in a difficult situation and to go on despite tiredness or obstacles.

There are several methods of self-control pointed out by Klausner (1965: 20ff.). Most are complementary, but some are effective enough when used exclusively. The paragraphs that follow summarize Klausner's version.

First, control can sometimes be established rationally in terms of ordinary deliberation about cost–benefit ratios or employing more elaborate principles. The belief that there is great loss in acting in a certain way may inhibit a person from such behavior, a traditional form of advice stemming from Plato, as we saw (cf. Bain 1859). For this reason, it might be convenient to call it the *Platonic method*. The idea is that the greater we understand the benefit of a certain course of action, the more likely we will seek it. The will to achieve some goal, then, is proportionate to the knowledge of its benefit plus the degree of the benefit. The disadvantage of such means is that calculations may have to occur each time in order to be convincing, and objective calculations may be overwhelmed by the very emotions, impulses, and feelings you hope to control. Rational calculations can be easily corrupted so that they become rationalizations. As mentioned earlier, Leon Festinger's classical studies on cognitive dissonance illustrate the point (1957). Plato may have been convinced that you needed only a rational understanding of what is good to do the good, but there are some doubts about that claim.

A second means of self-control is *affective*. This would employ those moral sentiments, such as guilt, shame, dishonor, and so on, in an effort to inhibit more negative feelings, emotions, or desires. In other words, you fight emotion with emotion. Guilt may serve as a deterrent to harshly punishing your children out of anger, since you are aware of how guilty you would feel if such a thing should happen. This can be very effective and suggests how moral sentiment contributes to self-control. Strong moral sentiment can often outweigh negative desires or emotions.

A third means of self-control is *habituation*. This is the idea of training yourself in regard to certain kinds of control. Desired control may result simply by practicing it. For example, if you enjoy coffee, but desire to control the amount, establishing the habit of drinking coffee only in the morning and denying it the rest of the day creates a pattern of behavior that automatically controls the desire. Habituation was a favorite means of self-control for Benjamin Franklin (1706–1790):

> It was about this time I conceived the bold and arduous project of arriving at moral perfection. ... But I soon found I had undertaken a task of more difficulty than I had imagined. ... I concluded at length that the mere speculative conviction that it was our interest to be completely virtuous was not sufficient to prevent our slipping, and that the contrary habits must be broken and good ones acquired and established before we can have any dependence on a steady, uniform rectitude of conduct (1771–1790: 94).

Franklin's typical day looked something like this (1771–1790: 100):

5 A.M.–8:00 A.M.	Rise, wash and address Powerful Goodness;
	contrive day's business and take the resolution of the day;
	prosecute the present study;
	and breakfast.
8 A.M.–12 noon	Work
12–2:00 P.M.	Read or overlook my accounts; and dine
2:00–6:00	Work
6:00–10:00 P.M.	Put things in their places;
	supper;
	music, diversion or conversation;
	examination of the day
10:00 P.M.–5:00 A.M.	Sleep

Indeed, we can see the source of Franklin's dictum: "Early to bed, early to rise, makes a man healthy, wealthy, and wise," the idea being that a regular habitual order to one's life brings about an inner order, which in turn can lead to success in life.

The 19th-century philosopher and psychologist Alexander Bain said this of moral habits:

> The peculiarity of the moral habits ... is the presence of two hostile powers, one to be gradually raised into the ascendant over the other. It is necessary, above all things, in such a situation, never to lose a battle. Every gain on the wrong side undoes the effect of many conquests on the right. The essential precaution, therefore, is to so regulate the two opposing powers that the one may have a series of uninterrupted successes, until repetition has fortified it to such a degree as to enable it to cope with the opposition, under any circumstances. This is the theoretically best career of mental progress (quoted in James 1890: 123).

This is followed by three maxims of advice: (1) launch a habit with all possible determination, (2) never suffer an exception to occur until the new habit is securely rooted in your life, and (3) seize every opportunity to act on one's resolution so that "the actual presence of the practical opportunity alone furnishes the fulcrum upon which the lever can rest, by means of which the moral will may multiply its strength, and raise itself aloft" (quoted in James 1890: 124).

William James, a 19th-century American philosopher and psychologist, thought habits to be the great "fly-wheel" of society (1890: 121), and in that sense habitual behavior was for both good and bad, since it could keep the most awful arrangements indurate but at the same time preserve the best of human actions. His view was that the plasticity of the brain allowed humans to solidify their patterns of behavior into various habits, good or bad. "Could the young but realize how soon they will become mere walking bundles of habits," he urges, "they would give more heed to their conduct while in the plastic state. We are spinning our own fates, good or evil, and never to be undone" (1890: 127).

William James (1842–1910) was an American psychologist and philosopher. Along with Charles Peirce, he developed the philosophy of pragmatism. His most important books include *The Principles of Psychology* and *The Will to Believe*. Pragmatism, as James interpreted it, was the view that the meaning of a concept was found in the practical effects which the employment of the concept would entail.

A fourth means of self-control is by *externalization*. Instead of achieving self-control through internal manipulation (through cognition or affect), you address the external variables of your social environment in a way that facilitates self-control. To use the language of behaviorism, you control your behavior by manipulation of appropriate environmental variables. To use a simple illustration, if you find that you eat too much, then you avoid fattening temptations and make available only nonfattening foods.

Popular literature on sexual continence, especially in the 1940s and 1950s, was replete with this sort of advice: Don't become involved in conversations which stimulate your imagination about sex; avoid pornography and erotica; avoid petting; dress modestly; use diversions when aroused (Buschke and Jacobsohn 1948; Davis 1958; Derstine 1943, 1944). This method includes group participation when it aims to enhance self-control. For example, joining a sports team may help teach self-discipline; joining the Girl Scouts or the army may accomplish the same thing. Affiliation with strongly directed groups, such as Alcoholics Anonymous, or self-help groups may do the same. It is well known that a good, strong leader can provide disciplinary inputs that help an individual with her own task of self-control, even in extremely stressful situations (Strauss 1944; Shaffer 1947). This sort of self-control is established through voluntary abdication of power over self to another (or a group), whose recognized authority will be used to impose a regimen of discipline. For obvious reasons this is the least satisfactory expression of self-control because it does not rely on self but on others for the wherewithal of autonomy; since self-control is directed by others, the person is at least partially heteronomous. At the same time, it is often the last hope of those who are morally or pathologically weak.

A fifth means of self-control is simply *the direct exercise of those centers of control*. It is one thing to employ reason, moral sentiment, habituation, and external controls to gain self-control, but exercising self-control through pure "force of will," so to speak, is likely the most difficult means, yet the most striking expression of autonomy. We know, as mentioned earlier, that the prefrontal lobe is one such center in relation to the amygdala. A person who has mastered such centers of self-control is able to face whatever may prove tempting or violative directly, without the mediation or direction of the other means. In his autobiography, *The Ragman's Son*, Kirk Douglas tells an amusing story about his father, a poor immigrant. At some point in

The Purposes of Tae Kwon Do

Tae kwon do trains both mind and body through strict discipline and places a great emphasis on the development of moral character. Thus, control of the mind over body, patience, kindness, self-restraint, and humility must accompany physical grace. (from *Tae Kwon Do* by Richard Chun. Santa Clarita: Ohara Publications, 1975)

his life he had made a decision to quit smoking. To stick to his goal, he always carried a cigarette in his shirt pocket. Whenever the urge to smoke struck, he pulled out the cigarette, looked at it intently, and said, "Who is stronger, you or me?" The method worked and illustrates exactly the method of conquest. As Klausner points out, this method promotes a polar view of the self, that you have bad tendencies as well as good ones, and self-control is a matter of encouraging the good ones to conquer the bad. The method involves strengthening the desired pole until it overcomes the resisting force or, conversely, to weaken the negative pole until it cannot resist effectively. Each of the objects of control can be brought to bear on the matter.

Whereas self-control is control over your inner life, self-efficacy is control of yourself in the context of external constraints or obstacles to your goals. In other words, whereas self-control serves as the basis for controlling our anger or desire for pleasure, self-efficacy sets the intensity of effort, our persistence in the face of obstacles and unpleasant experiences, and helps us reduce our anxiety about the performance of certain tasks (cf. Bandura, Reese, and Adams 1982). Self-efficacy works together with self-control to allow you to accomplish your goals. Getting a college degree takes a great deal of self-control; you have to forgo many immediate pleasures for long-term ones, give up leisure in favor of study time, apply yourself to difficult materials, and perform countless other tasks requiring self-discipline. Self-efficacy provides the drive to succeed, the persistence to overcome obstacles, and a sort of confidence in the ability to do the necessary tasks to accomplish the goals.

According to the work of psychologist Albert Bandura (1986), there are four determinants to self-efficacy. First is previous success. You will have a greater feeling of self-efficacy in a college course if you have done well in previous courses. The second determinant is vicarious experience. You will also have a greater feeling of self-efficacy if you know others who have succeeded at the task you are about to undertake. This is why, for example, children will often be more adventurous in their play with others than when alone; if they see their friends succeed at some task (e.g., climbing a tree), then they will feel more confident and less anxious about their own success. The third determinant is verbal persuasion, which is the ability to make rationally persuasive arguments for your plausible success at a task. Finally, there is physiological arousal. You will have a greater feeling of self-efficacy if you are at an optimal level of physiological arousal; high anxiety in the performance of tasks will affect the quality of that performance.

REVIEW QUESTIONS

1. What is meant by fatalism? Why can fatalism be comforting?
2. What is meant by determinism? What are the two theses of determinism? How does quantum theory and chaos theory discredit determinism?
3. What is meant by libertarianism? What are some of its versions?
4. What are some criticisms of libertarianism?
5. What is meant by compatibilism? What are some of its difficulties?
6. What is moral luck? How does moral luck address the issue of free will?

7. What is meant by moral strength? moral weakness? pathological weakness? What's the difference between the self-controlled person and one with moral strength according to Aristotle? What is the difference between the morally weak person and the self-indulgent one?

8. What is Plato's account of moral weakness? What are some of its difficulties?

9. What is Aristotle's account of moral weakness? What is the difference between acting out of ignorance and acting in ignorance? How does Aristotle's account differ from Plato's? What are some of its difficulties?

10. What are the three basic factors for determining responsibility? When is an action a proximate cause? What is meant by salience and relevance?

11. What is meant by accountability and blame?

12. What is the difference between acting voluntarily and involuntarily? between acting with deliberation and spontaneously? What is the difference between acting with ignorance and acting under duress? What is the difference between recklessness and negligence?

13. What is meant by mental competence? What are the types of mental incompetence?

14. What are the conditions under which a person might be held fully responsible for an action? What are the conditions under which a person might be held partially responsible for an action?

15. What is meant by tort liability? What is meant by vicarious responsibility?

16. What is meant by autonomy? What is Kant's definition? What is heteronomy? What are self-mastery, self-control, self-efficacy, and self-direction?

17. What does Kant mean by the good will? Why is it good without qualification according to him?

18. Why is the strong will the good will according to Nietzsche?

19. What are the various ways in which one can gain self-control? What are the limitations of each method? How can self-efficacy be strengthened?

QUESTIONS FOR DISCUSSION

1. Ironically, some people construe chance events as if they were fated to be. In other words, precisely because events were such seeming improbabilities, they somehow were meant to be. For example, lovers who met by accident or circumstance often feel this way. What do you think of this account?

2. Suppose we are, as the hard determinists argue, so determined that even each one of our individual actions has to have happened exactly the way it did. Second, suppose that we are able to determine all the laws that pertain to those actions so, in effect, we could predict behavior. Assuming an adequate technology, would we then be able to change it? If we are determined to act, can we change that behavior if we know the laws that determine that behavior? Is there a difference between saying that something is fated to be and something will act in such and such a way, given its conditions and the laws that pertain to it?

3. Can persons make their own moral luck? Do you think that moral luck is all a matter of chance and circumstance, or is it possible to make yourself luckier in that regard?

4. Talmudic law forbids women to sing in public places in which men are present, since the woman's voice is thought to be very seductive. Islamic law requires women to dress especially modestly, covering the face and nearly all other parts of the body; Victorian culture also insisted on very modest attire for women. Is it better, in your opinion, to suppress the temptation or to strengthen the tempted? Is it right to restrict the conduct of some people because they serve as a temptation to others? Why should women in particular bear the brunt of restrictions on their behavior for the sake of men's

morality? Does that not imply that men are the weaker sex? Why is it assumed that women are not seduced by men's voices or dress?

5. Autonomy in part is defined as self-direction, that is, giving oneself a moral guide; heteronomy is defined as simply the implicit acceptance or compliance with rules and directions set by others. Is it possible to be truly autonomous in this sense? The very act of living in a certain culture which promotes certain values, rules of conduct, and notions of the good life makes it seem impossible to escape these strictures or to strike out a course different than what one's culture dictates. Consider, for example, how the advertising and the entertainment industries influence our lives in this regard.

CASE STUDIES FOR DISCUSSION

1. An obese hospital patient in severe pain was placed in a hospital bed that was on rollers and had no side rails. The patient was sedated, foggy, drowsy, and disoriented. While under the effects of this sedation, she fell from her bed and was injured. The nurses had neither set up side rails nor removed the wheels from the bed. *A Nurses' Procedures Manual* for the hospital was introduced into court. It provided that side rails should always be applied to the bed of a patient who is restless, very obese, under deep sedation, or in any other case in which side rails would be an added protection. Any omissions of the rails had to be on written order of the physician. The manual also provided that, if the patient was permitted to get up alone, the rollers must be removed. Evidence indicated that the patient was permitted to be out of bed. Therefore, the rollers should have been removed. *Who was at fault here? Why could the nurses be held accountable? What were the* mens rea *of the nurses, using one or more of Aristotle's classifications? Should the hospital be held liable for the actions of the nurses? Why or why not?* (*Burks v. The Christ Hospital,* 249 N.E. 2d 829 Ohio 1969).

2. Christian Scientists do not believe in the physical reality of diseases; instead they see everything as mental and spiritual. Consequently, diseases can be cured by prayer. Gerry and June were practicing Christian Scientists. In 1990 their 2-year-old son developed a fever and began to vomit. They called their prayer counselor, and after a few sessions, the fever seemed to diminish. However, the next day the fever rose again to higher levels, and the vomiting was more severe. The prayer counselor was called again, but it did not help this time. They rushed the boy to the hospital, but it was too late, and their son died. The child had an intestinal blockage that could have been easily corrected if given prompt treatment. The parents were charged with involuntary manslaughter. *Do you think the charge was justified? What should be done if the parents' beliefs, no matter how sincere, could reasonably harm the child? How responsible was the prayer counselor in this matter?* Some Christian Scientists believe that if you seek any assistance other than a prayer counselor for medical conditions, then the effects of the prayers will not work. *Is that a form of coercion?*

3. In *Sindell v. Abbott Laboratories,* the plaintiff Sindell had brought an action against eleven drug companies that had manufactured, promoted, and marketed diethylstilbestrol (DES) between 1941 and 1971. The plaintiff's mother took DES to prevent miscarriage. The plaintiff alleged that the defendants knew or should have known that DES was ineffective as a miscarriage preventive, that it would cause cancer in the daughters of the mothers who took it, and that they nevertheless continued to market the drug as a miscarriage preventive. The plaintiff also alleged that she developed cancer as a result of the drug taken by her mother. Due to the passage of time and to the fact that the drug was often sold under its generic name, the plaintiff was unable to identify the particular company which had manufactured the DES taken by her mother, and the trial court therefore dismissed the case. The California Supreme Court reversed. It held that the plaintiff did not have to carry the burden of showing which manufacturer made the quantity of DES that her mother took; rather the burden shifts to them to show they have not manufactured it. If damages are awarded to her, they

should be apportioned among the defendants who cannot make such a showing. *Do you think this is fair? Doesn't this seem to violate one of the basic tenets of responsibility, namely, that you can be shown to be the cause of the outcome in question? How do you think the reasoning of the court would go to support its finding?*

4. One of the most infamous cases of self-defense was the trial of Bernhard Goetz, a white man who, on December 22, 1984, shot four boisterous black youths in a subway car after being approached by one or two of them. There were four teenage boys in the car—Barry Allen, Troy Canty, James Ramseur, and Darrell Cabey. They were sprawling across the seats and generally behaving in a rowdy manner. They were later found to be carrying screwdrivers. Goetz may not have noticed as he entered, but the other passengers had moved to the far end of the car. One of the boys, lying stretched out on the bench opposite, asked casually, "How are ya?" Then either one or two of the boys approached Goetz and asked for $5. Goetz, interpreting this behavior as the prelude to a mugging, took a gun from his pocket and fired five bullets. He may have fired all five in rapid succession or he may have paused after the fourth and said, "You seem to be all right; here's another." One of the youths was left paralyzed. Goetz then went to the platform between the subway cars, unfastened the safety chain, and escaped into the tunnel. On December 31 he surrendered to the police in Concord, New Hampshire. In the year and a half that followed, Goetz faced two grand juries, a criminal trial, and a civil one. The first grand jury refused to indict him on grounds of self-defense; a second allowed his case to come to trial. At the first criminal trial, he was acquitted of murder out of self-defense. At a civil trial in 1996, the jury awarded the paralyzed plaintiff he shot $18 million for past and future suffering and $25 million in punitive damages. Goetz declared bankruptcy and legal moves were made to garnish 10 percent of his wages for the rest of his life. According to the New York penal law in effect at the time, there were four requirements for a reasonable claim of self-defense: (1) imminence, that the time for defense is now, so that the defender cannot wait any longer; (2) necessity, that there are no other less deadly means of defense; (3) proportionality, the probable harm intended by the attacker should be proportionate to the harm dealt by the defender; (4) intentionality, the defender must believe there will be an attack and act with the intention of repelling it. *Do you think Goetz's actions satisfied these four conditions? Is there a contradiction between the criminal and the civil trials?*

SUGGESTED READINGS

On Free Will

Augustine. 388. *On Free Choice of the Will.* Translated by A. Benjamin and L. Hackstaff. New York: Bobbs-Merrill, 1964.

Bennett, Jonathan. 1980. Accountability. *Philosophical Subjects: Essays Presented to P.F. Strawson.* Edited by Zak van Straaten. Oxford, England: Clarendon Press, 14–47.

Bernstein, Mark. 1992. *Fatalism.* Lincoln: University of Nebraska Press.

Berofsky, Bernard, editor. 1966. *Free Will and Determinism.* New York: Harper and Row.

_____. 1995. *Liberation from Self: A Theory of Personal Autonomy.* Cambridge, England: Cambridge University Press.

Bratman, Michael. 1987. *Intention, Plans, and Practical Reason.* Cambridge, MA: Harvard University Press.

Campbell, C.A. 1957. *On Selfhood and Godhood.* New York: Macmillan.

Chisholm, R.M. 1964. *Human Freedom and the Self.* Lawrence: University of Kansas Press.

Dilman, Ilham. 1999. *Free Will: An Historical and Philosophical Introduction.* London: Routledge.

Duff, R.A. 1990. *Intention, Agency, and Criminal Liability.* Cambridge, England: Blackwell.

Ekstrom, Laura. 2000. *Free Will: A Philosophical Study.* Boulder, CO: Westview Press.

Feinberg, Joel. 1992. *Freedom and Fulfillment: Philosophical Essays.* Princeton, NJ: Princeton University Press.

Fischer, John. 1999. Recent Work on Moral Responsibility. *Ethics* 110: 93–139.

Frankfurt, Harry. 1971. Freedom of the Will and the Concept of a Person. *Philosophical Review.* 68(1).

Ginet, Carl. 1990. *On Action.* Cambridge, England: Cambridge University Press.

Honderich, Ted. 1990. *Consequences of Determinism : A Theory of Determinism.* Oxford, England: Clarendon.

_____, editor. 1973. *Essays on Freedom of Action.* London: Routledge and Kegan Paul.

Hook, Sidney, editor. 1958. *Determinism and Freedom in the Age of Modern Science.* New York: Collier.

Kane, R. 1985. *Free Will and Values.* Albany: State University of New York Press.

_____. 1996. *The Significance of Free Will.* New York: Oxford University Press.

Klein, Martha. 1990. *Determinism, Blameworthiness, and Deprivation.* New York: Oxford University Press.

Lehrer, Keith, editor. 1966. *Freedom and Determinism.* New York: Random House.

Libet, Benjamin, Freeman, Anthony, and Sutherland, Keith, editors. 2000. *The Volitional Brain.* Bowling Green, KY: Philosophy Documentation Center.

Melden, A.I. 1961. *Free Action.* New York: Routledge and Kegan Paul.

Midgley, Mary. 1994. *The Ethical Primate: Humans, Freedom and Morality.* London: Routledge.

O'Connor, Timothy, editor. 1995. *Agents, Causes, and Events: Essays on Indeterminism and Free Will.* Oxford, England: Oxford University Press.

Swanton, Christine. 1992. *Freedom: A Coherence Theory.* Indianapolis, IN: Hackett Publishing.

Thorp, John. 1980. *Free Will: A Defense of Neurophysiological Determinism.* London: Routledge and Kegan Paul.

Van Inwagen, Peter. 1983. *An Essay on Free Will.* Oxford, England: Clarendon Press.

Watson, Gary. 1983. *Free Will.* Oxford, England: Oxford University Press.

On Moral Luck

Nagel, Thomas. 1976. Moral Luck. *Proceedings of the Aristotelian Society* Supp. 50.

Nussbaum, Martha. 1986. *The Fragility of Goodness: Luck and Ethics in Greek Tragedy and Philosophy.* Cambridge, England: Cambridge University Press.

Williams, Bernard. 1981. *Moral Luck.* Cambridge, England: Cambridge University Press.

On Moral Weakness

Aristotle. *Nicomachean Ethics. The Basic Works of Aristotle.* Book VIII. Edited by R. McKeon. New York: Random House, 1941.

Milo, Ronald. 1966. *Aristotle on Practical Knowledge and Weakness of Will.* The Hague, the Netherlands: Mouton.

On Responsibility and Blame

Aristotle. *Nicomachean Ethics.* Books III, V. *The Basic Works of Aristotle.* Book VIII. Edited by R. McKeon. New York: Random House, 1941.

Baier, Kurt. 1972. Types and Principles of Responsibility. In *Individual and Collective Responsibility.* Edited by Peter French. New York: St. Martin's Press.

Bradley, F.H. 1962. *Ethical Studies.* Oxford, England: Oxford University Press.

Burke, John. 1988. *Bureaucratic Responsibility.* Baltimore, MD: Johns Hopkins University Press.

Dworkin, Gerald. 1988. *The Theory and Practice of Autonomy.* Cambridge, England: Cambridge University Press.

Feinberg, Joel. 1970. *Doing and Deserving: Essays in the Theory of Responsibility.* Princeton, NJ: Princeton University Press.

Fingarette, Herbert. 1972. *The Meaning of Criminal Insanity.* Berkeley: University of California Press.

Fischer, John, and Ravizza, Mark. 1991. *Perspectives on Moral Responsibility.* Ithaca, NY: Cornell University Press.

French, Peter, editor. 1991. *The Spectrum of Responsibility*. New York: St. Martin's Press.
_____. 1984. *Collective and Corporate Responsibility*. New York: Columbia University Press.
_____. 1995. *Responsibility Matters*. Lawrence: University of Kansas Press.
Glover, Jonathan. 1970. *Responsibility*. London: Routledge and Kegan Paul.
Gorlin, Rena, editor. 1999. *Codes of Professional Responsibility: Ethics Standards in Business, Health, and Law*. New York: BNA.
Hart, H.L.A. 1968. *Punishment and Responsibility*. Oxford, England: Oxford University Press.
Leoni, Bruno, editor. 1991. *Freedom and the Law*. Indianapolis, IN: Liberty Fund.
May, Larry. 1992. *Sharing Responsibility*. Chicago: University of Chicago Press.
May, Larry, and Hoffman, Stacey, editors. 1991. *Collective Responsibility: Five Decades of Debate in Theoretical and Applied Ethics*. New York: Rowman and Littlefield.
Meyer, Susan. 1993. *Aristotle on Moral Responsibility: Character and Cause*. Oxford, England: Blackwell.
Pritchard, Michael. 1991. *On Becoming Responsible*. Lawrence: University of Kansas Press.
Russell, Paul. 1995. *Freedom and Moral Sentiment: Hume's Way of Naturalizing Responsibility*. Oxford, England: Oxford University Press.
Schlossberger, Eugene. 1992. *Moral Responsibility and Persons*. Philadelphia, PA: Temple University Press.
Schoeman, Ferdinand, editor. 1987. *Responsibility, Character, and the Emotions: New Essays in Moral Psychology*. Cambridge: Cambridge University Press.
Trusted, Jennifer. 1984. *Free Will and Responsibility*. Oxford, England: Oxford University Press.
Wallace, R. Jay. 1994. *Responsibility and the Moral Sentiments*. Cambridge, MA: Harvard University Press.
Zimmerman, Michael. 1988. *An Essay on Moral Responsibility*. Totowa, NJ: Rowman and Littlefield.

On the Notion of Autonomy

Bain, Alexander. 1859. *The Emotions and the Will*. London: John Parker and Son.
Bandura, Albert. 1965. Influence of Model's Reinforcement Contingencies on the Acquisition of Imitative Responses. *Journal of Personality and Social Psychology* 1: 589–595.
———. 1986. *Social Foundations of Thought and Action: A Social-Cognitive Theory*. Upper Saddle River, NJ: Prentice Hall.
———, Reese, L., and Adams, N. 1982. Microanalysis of Action and Fear Arousal as a Function of Differential Levels of Perceived Self-Efficacy. *Personality and Social Theory* 13: 173–199.
Benn, Stanley. 1988. *A Theory of Freedom*. Cambridge, England: Cambridge University Press.
Christman, John, editor. 1989. *The Inner Citadel: Essays on Individual Autonomy*. New York: Oxford University Press.
Clement, Grace. 1999. *Care, Autonomy, and Justice: Feminism and the Ethic of Care*. Boulder, CO: Westview Press.
Dworkin, Gerald. 1988. *The Theory and Practice of Autonomy*. Cambridge, England: Cambridge University Press.
Goleman, Daniel. 1995. *Emotional Intelligence*. New York: Bantam.
Hill, Thomas. 1991. *Autonomy and Self Respect*. Cambridge, England: Cambridge University Press.
Holt, Robert. 1967. On Freedom, Autonomy and the Redirection of Psychoanalytic Theory: A Rejoinder. *International Journal of Psychiatry* 3: 524–536.
Johnson, Oliver. 1977. Heteronomy and Autonomy: Rawls and Kant. *Midwest Studies in Philosophy* 3: 277–279.
Klausner, Samuel, editor. 1965. *The Quest for Self-Control*. New York: Free Press.
LeDoux, Joseph. 1992. Emotion and the Limbic System Concept. *Concepts in Neuroscience* 2(1).
Mele, Alfred. 1995. *Autonomous Agents: From Self-Control to Autonomy*. New York: Oxford University Press.

Shapiro, David. 1981. *Autonomy and Rigid Character*. New York: Basic.

Turner, Dean. 1996. *The Autonomous Man: An Essay in Personal Identity and Integrity*. Bethany Press.

Wegner, D., and Pennebaker, J. 1993. *Handbook of Mental Control*. Upper Saddle River, NJ: Prentice Hall.

Young, Robert. 1986. *Personal Autonomy: Beyond Negative and Positive Liberty*. New York: St. Martin's Press.

On Kant's Notion of Autonomy

Baron, M. 1984. The Alleged Moral Repugnance of Acting from Duty. *Journal of Philosophy*. April 197–220.

Beck, L.W. 1960. *A Commentary on Kant's Critique of Practical Reason*. Chicago: University of Chicago Press.

Kant, Immanuel. 1785. *Foundations of the Metaphysics of Morals*. Translated by L. W. Beck. New York: Bobbs-Merrill, 1959.

———. 1788. *Critique of Practical Reason*. Translated by L. Beck. New York: Bobbs- Merrill, 1956.

———. 1775–1780. *Lectures on Ethics*. Translated by L. Infield. New York: Harper and Row, 1963.

———. 1797. *The Metaphysical Principles of the Virtues*. Translated by J. Ellington. New York: Bobbs-Merrill. 1964.

Kneller, Jane, and Axinn, Sidney, editors. 1998. *Autonomy and Community: Readings in Contemporary Kantian Social Philosophy*. Albany: State University of New York Press.

Korsgaard, Christine. 1999. *Creating the Kingdom of Ends*. Cambridge, England: Cambridge University Press.

Ross, W.D. 1954. *Kant's Ethical Theory*. Oxford, England: Oxford University Press.

On Nietzsche and the Will

Nietzsche, Friedrich. 1881. *Dawn. Complete Works*. Edited by O. Levy. 18 vols. New York: Russell and Russell, 1964.

———. 1882. *The Gay Science*. Translated by W. Kaufmann. New York: Vintage, 1964.

———. 1886. *Beyond Good and Evil*. Translated by W. Kaufmann. New York: Vintage, 1966.

———. 1887. *The Genealogy of Morals*. Translated by W. Kaufmann. New York: Vintage, 1968.

———. 1883–1888. *The Will to Power*. Translated by W. Kaufmann. New York: Vintage, 1968.

———. 1888. *The Antichrist*. The Portable Nietzsche. Translated by W. Kaufmann. New York: Viking, 1954.

CHAPTER THREE

Virtue and Vice

Nothing too much.

—Solon

Moderation is the greatest virtue.

—Heraclitus

Virtue is the link of all perfections, the center of all felicities ... Virtue is the sun of our world. ... Nothing is lovable but virtue, nothing detestable but vice. A person's capacity and greatness are to be measured by his virtue and not by his fortune. She alone is all-sufficient. She makes people lovable in life, memorable after death.

—Balthasar Gracian

In his book *Living Faith* (1996), Jimmy Carter relates the following story about his early years in Plains, Georgia. In 1953 Carter left the navy and, with his wife Rosalyn and their three little boys, came home to the small Georgia town. They lived in a tiny apartment in a public housing project while their oldest child attended first grade. Carter struggled alone with a farm supply business, while Rosalyn struggled with home life. After investing all their savings and borrowing a substantial amount of money, they only managed an income of $300 the first year—plus a heavy debt. An application for a $10,000 loan at a local bank was rejected, but Carter managed to get some credit from the company he did business with. The next year was better, and their income was almost $3000. But then a problem arose. Carter's business was threatened with a boycott by the farm warehouse customers because he was seen as too liberal on the issue of racial desegregation. All the white men of Plains belonged to the White Citizen's Council, and some were suspected of belonging to the Ku Klux Klan.

The White Citizen's Council was an organization publicly sponsored by most of Georgia's political leaders, including the incumbent U.S. senators and the governor of the state. When Carter was asked to join by the local marshal, he told him he wasn't prepared at that time to join; he discussed the matter with Rosalyn. Both agreed that they could not yield to the community pressure, even if the decision might severely reduce their marginal income. When the marshal (who was one of the officials of the council) returned, Carter refused to join. The marshal told him he was making a serious mistake.

Some time later twenty of his best customers came to see him. The spokesman for the group, Paul, tried to convince Carter that he ought to join the group, and he articulated the segregationist principles of the organization. They emphasized that this was not a militant, violent organization, not associated with the Ku Klux Klan, and that it was sponsored by prominent politicians. Paul also reminded Carter that they had traded with his father; they had affection for his family, and they knew he was struggling with the business. For that reason, they were willing to pay his dues for the year, and all he needed to do was sign the membership card.

In a somewhat shaky voice, Carter told them that he appreciated their helpfulness and loyalty but that he had resolved not to join the council. It was not a matter of money—he said he would be willing to take a $5 bill and flush it down the toilet rather than contribute it to an organization in which he did not believe.

After that group meeting, Carter visited each of the men individually. One-on-one they seemed less concerned about the issue, and many in fact expressed resentment at being pressured to join. Although some of the customers went to the competition, many stayed with Carter. As race relations in his town began to improve in the 1960s, Carter's business was able to survive, and he eventually became a successful peanut farmer.

However, a few years later, after Carter had already served as state senator, his business was threatened with another crisis. This time the group in question was the John Birch Society. While vacationing in Mexico, two prominent members of the John Birch Society had gone to the county courthouse and examined the public agricultural records, obtaining a list of everyone who had ever sold peanuts to Carter. They visited everyone on the list and urged them not to do business with Carter because they claimed he had secretly gone to a communist training camp in northern Alabama to help expedite segregation. As a result business dropped off greatly after Carter's return from Mexico.

Upon learning what had happened, Carter confronted the two men—one was president of the largest insurance agency in the state, and the other had served in the state legislature for 8 years. They grudgingly admitted the truth. Carter diffused the crisis by visiting each of his customers, showing them the receipts from his Mexican trip.

Jimmy Carter, of course, went on to become governor of Georgia and president of the United States and after his term served as an important negotiator in a number of international crises and promoted Habitat for Humanity. In this story of his early life, Carter exhibits a number of important virtues. He showed courage by his willingness to put himself (and his family) at risk for the sake of some principle or cause he felt important. He was steadfast in his beliefs and did not cave-in to the enormous amount of peer and community pressure put against him. He treated everyone with respect and civility, even those who viciously conspired against him, and he did not seek revenge or retribution against them. He was honest and forthright about all the matters that concerned him in this respect.

The virtues, as the important medieval philosopher and theologian Thomas Aquinas (1225–1274) suggested, are "the perfection of power" (*Summa*, Pt. II, Q. 55). This is a felicitous definition. *If strength of will or autonomy is the power to endure, to refrain, to stay the course, to avoid, to forgo, to sacrifice, to retain, or to resist, then the virtues are the perfection of these various powers.* For example, temperance is usually viewed as the power to resist the wrong sorts of pleasures, patience and persever-ance are the power to endure for the sake of something worthwhile, persistence is the power to stick to a task, and so forth. Virtue can be seen in this regard as the completion or specification of autonomy. If autonomy is understood as self-mas-tery—that is, self-control in regard to passions, feelings, emotions, and self-efficacy, the determination and drive to succeed in our goals—then success at self-mastery is virtue, whereas its failure is called vice.

The list of virtues is well-known: courage, temperance, generosity, fairness, friendliness, ambition, honesty, wit, modesty, and the like. The vices are just as well-known: greed, envy, lust, sloth, anger. The virtues primarily involve the proper response to feelings, emotions, desires, needs, wants, and wishes. All emotions are in essence impulses to act; they are instant plans for handling life that evolution has instilled in us (Goleman 1995: 6). Virtues in turn are the manner in which we han-dle those emotions in the service of some sense of the good. Virtues give us the abil-ity to motivate ourselves and persist in the face of frustrations, to control impulse and delay gratification, to help regulate our moods, and to keep distress from swamping our ability to think (cf. Goleman 1995: 34).

The virtues can be divided into three basic categories: virtues of self-control, virtues of self-efficacy (these two form the basis for the third), and the virtues of regard (see figure). The virtues of self-control involve the ability to moderate our desire for pleasure, to restrain our emotions, desires, wants, and wishes, or in gen-eral, the ability to modulate selfish impulses and direct self-fulfillment. Temper-ance is considered the cardinal virtue in this respect (cf. Pieper 1975). The virtues of self-efficacy, on the other hand, concern our ability to persist in our goals despite pain, suffering, hardship, discouragement, obstacles, and personal risk. Courage is thought to be the cardinal virtue of this category (cf. Pieper 1975). The virtues of regard generally involve the ability to look to the interests of others or to show

Temperance, courage, and fairmindedness are tradition-ally thought to be the cardinal virtues. Prudence is often included in the list. Temperance is self-control of pleas-ure; courage the ability to endure for something greater than oneself. Both are essential for developing a sense of justice or fairmindedness.

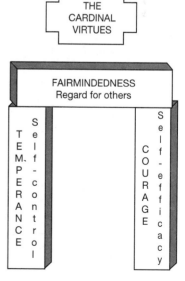

respect and concern for another; its cardinal virtue is fair-mindedness, the mark of a just person (cf. Pieper 1975). Temperance and courage serve as the basis for fair-mindedness. Temperance gives us the ability to control ourselves in terms of what we want and desire; before one can learn to regard the interest of others or share goods with others, one must be capable of modulating self-interest. Thus, the vices of intemperance—greed, ill-temper, arrogance, ruthlessness, envy, contempt, covetousness, miserliness—are not constitutive of fair-minded persons. Courage opens us up to the possibility of the sacrifice of our interests or even ourselves for some greater goal. By being able to control what we want and to allow ourselves to work for goals larger than ourselves, we become primed for cooperation with others; fair-mindedness, a regard for the interests of others, is the cardinal virtue of cooperative practices. Those who are not capable of casting off self-interest in favor of what is right are also probably not capable of genuine fairness.

Becoming virtuous, then, is a matter first of learning self-control, especially in regard to the variety of pleasures and emotions; second, it is practicing self-efficacy, the ability to endure pain, fear, hardship, and obstacles; and finally, it is learning regard for others. The promise is that a person with these combined qualities not only exhibits graceful character but is someone who would be sought after as a companion, trusted as a colleague and citizen, and a rich contributor to the public good.

3.1 VIRTUE AS A GOLDEN MEAN

"Whoever cultivates the golden mean (*aurea mediocritas*)," the Latin poet Horace says, "avoids both the poverty of the hovel and the envy of a palace." The concept of the golden mean is expressed in a number of cultures and time periods. Confucius claims that "the superior man exemplifies the mean." He argues that:

> Before the feelings of pleasure, anger, sorrow, and joy are aroused it is called equilibrium (*chung*). When these feelings are aroused and each and all attain due measure and degree, it is called harmony. Equilibrium is the great foundation of the world, and harmony its universal path. When equilibrium and harmony are realized to the highest degree, heaven and earth will attain their proper order and all things will flourish (*The Doctrine of the Mean* I.1).

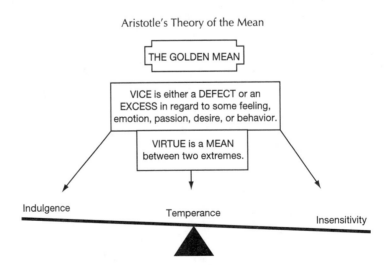

Aristotle's Theory of the Mean

THE GOLDEN MEAN

VICE is either a DEFECT or an EXCESS in regard to some feeling, emotion, passion, desire, or behavior.

VIRTUE is a MEAN between two extremes.

Indulgence   Temperance   Insensitivity

Aristotle also believed that the *virtues could be seen as a balance between two extremes, that is, an excess or defect in regard to the "matter" with which the virtue is concerned* (*Nic. Ethics* ii.6) (see figure). As Horace writes, "There is a measure in things, there are definite limits this side of which, or beyond which, the good cannot lie" (*Sermones* I.l. 106). "The vices," according to Aristotle, "fall short of or exceed what is right in both passions and actions, while the virtue finds and chooses that which is at the mean" (*Nic. Ethics* 1107a4–7). Thus, temperance is the proper control of pleasure, indulgence the enjoyment of too much pleasure or the wrong sorts of pleasures, while insensitivity, the excessive control of pleasures, is the inability to enjoy proper ones. By the mean, Aristotle does not refer to the average. He uses a wonderful analogy to illustrate the beauty of the virtues. He imagines that virtue is something like an artistic masterpiece, so that for "good works of art ... it is not possible either to take away or to add anything, implying that excess and defect destroy the goodness of works of art, while the mean preserves it" (*Nic. Ethics* 1106b10–12). Consequently, the mean should be thought of as the perfection rather than the average of behavior in regard to a certain emotion, feeling, or desire. Just as the great work of art is the accomplishment of training, talent, and experience, so it is with moral behavior. The ability to achieve the mean—to enjoy the right sort of pleasures at the right times, with the right people, with the right motive, and in the right way—is "no doubt difficult," as Aristotle says with understatement. It is for this reason that the prudent person is looked up to as the paradigm for such competence (*Nic. Ethics* 1107a2). Understood in Aristotle's sense, the virtues and vices could be organized triadically so that the vices form a pair demarcated by excess and defect, while virtue is bound by the mean between these extremes. For example, courage is the mean between cowardliness and rashness or good temper between apathy and bad temper, whereas frugality is the mean between extravagance and miserliness (see figure).

A Classification of the Virtues Considered in this Chapter

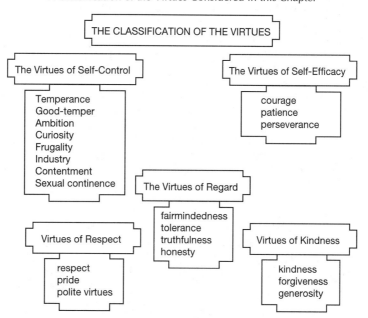

3.2 VIRTUE AND CHARACTER

When we think of "Honest Abe," we have a tendency to think of him as exhibiting this virtue as a trait, consistently expressed through many different contexts and situations. However, it is important to keep in mind the difference between virtuous acts, dispositions or habits, and traits. A *virtuous act* is a one-time event that exhibits the characteristics of a certain virtue but may be performed by someone who does not exhibit that character trait or disposition. A person may act courageously in a certain situation, or a certain type of situation, but may often act cowardly otherwise. *Dispositions* are habits people have acquired over time in responding to certain situations in certain ways.

"A man's character is his destiny."
—The Instruction of Ankshesbonq

"Character is destiny."
—Heraclitus

"Character is destiny."
—Novalis

Question for Discussion

1. As these quotes from different cultures and different periods suggest, what happens to your life depends on your character. Do you agree?

Traits are thought to be inherent characteristics of a person, which move them toward a certain type of action such as honesty or trustworthiness (cf. Flanagan 1991: 277).

There is a debate in the psychological literature precisely about whether virtues can be considered character traits of persons (the debate also extends more generally to personality traits) or whether they are simply dispositions of persons present in certain contexts (Flanagan 1991). We do like to think that if someone is honest, they are so in a global sense. But there is evidence to suggest that a person may be honest in one context but not in another. This would account for the shock or surprise of the neighbors when a person who is considered by them to be an upright, honest citizen is found to be dishonest at work or, conversely, when a person thought to be honest at work is found to be deceiving in his personal life. A classic study by H. Hartshorne and M. May (1928) suggested exactly this sort of thing. Their study of hundreds of children's moral behavior in a variety of settings showed inconsistency in regard to characteristics such as honesty and the like. The findings seem to suggest that virtues are not unified character traits, but specific behaviors that conform to certain situations in life. If the situations are similar, then similar behavior may result. Persons may be cautious when it comes to money matters but rash or impulsive when it comes to ideas or innovations. However, this study has been reviewed and reevaluated by a number of other psychologists. Burton (1963) found some methodological flaws in the study which led him to suggest that there is more generality underlying, for example, honesty than the original study suggested. Burton also claimed that consistency in honesty seems to increase with age, which suggests that had Hartshorne and May studied adults, character dispositions may have been more transparent.

But even if certain virtues are globally expressed in some characters, it is fairly clear that under certain situations, an honest person may turn dishonest, or a kind person cruel. For example, many people might feel distressed over inflicting severe electrical shocks to innocent people as a form of punishment. Yet Stanley Milgram's (1974) classic experiments on authority showed that a vast majority of people will do so if directed by some authority figure. As discussed earlier in a different context, in these experiments, which occurred during the period 1960–1963, the subjects were initially told that the experiment had to do with the effects of punishment on learning. The subject would act as a teacher, a learner was placed in a booth, and the experimenter would supervise the procedures. The subject's job was first to read word pairs to the learner and, second, to read only the first member of each pair with four possible associations. If the learner did not choose the correct pairing, the subject was to administer an electric shock for each error. The shock generator consisted of a panel with thirty levers, each with a voltage rating of 15 to 450 volts. The subjects were instructed to move up the voltage ladder after each error. Engraved on the panel at various intervals were labels indicating slight shock, moderate, strong, very strong, intense, extreme intensity, danger, and severe shock. The last two levers were simply marked XXX. What the subjects were not told, however, was that there was a collusion between the learner and the experiment, nor were they told that the voltage was not real, and the learner would simply act out pain and distress over receiving the shock. Nevertheless, what is interesting is that 65 percent of the subjects went all the way to 450 volts, even though the learner was pounding the walls at 300 volts. Even where administration of the shock required the experimenter to forcibly place the learner's hand on the shock plate, the subjects still gave the shock in 60 percent of the cases. A later study (Elms and Milgram 1966) showed that there were no significant differences on standard personality measures between the maximally obedient subjects and the maximally rebellious ones.

There is the additional question of whether certain moral traits are associated with certain personality characteristics or with other sorts of moral traits. In a classic study by Asch (1946), given a list of traits—intelligent, skillful, industrious, warm, determined, practical, cautious—the majority of persons inferred that the persons were also honest (98 percent), good-looking (77 percent), altruistic (69 percent), happy (98 percent), and generous (91 percent). Varying "warm" with "cold" in the description produced huge changes in whether certain traits—generous, humorous, sociable, popular, humane, happy, and altruistic—were inferred.

This view is also given some support in the psychological literature; indeed, the psychologist G. Allport thought that moral character "is personality evaluated" (cf. Coles 1986: 137–138). There seems to be a compatibility between characteristics such as being carefree, lively, easygoing, responsive, talkative, outgoing, and sociable and having the virtue of friendliness, and someone without the first group of traits would have difficulty developing the latter trait. According to Eyesenck's (1960) two-dimensional type theory of personality, there are four underlying poles to any personality: introversion, stability, extroversion, and instability. Jerome Kagan (1994) developed an updated version of this based on a biological model—timid, bold, upbeat, melancholy. Eyesenck's poles combine to form four permutations: stable-extrovert, unstable-extrovert, stable-introvert, and unstable-introvert. Each of these generates a quadrant of personality types. A stable extrovert is likely to have a set of personality characteristics including carefree, lively, easygoing, and so on, listed earlier, whereas an unstable extrovert might exhibit the following: touchy, restless, aggressive, excitable, changeable, impulsive, optimistic, active. Intuitively, one would say that such characteristics would have a tendency to promote many of the polite vices; such characteristics probably suggest a tendency toward arrogance, unkindness, and so forth. Cattel's early theory of personality (1946) argued for a number of characteristics that seem to cluster with one another. Honesty, loyalty, and fair-mindedness seemed to do so. These seem to have their source in affectothymia, that is, an even-tempered person who is considerate and trusting of others. The work by Theodore Adorno (1950), later confirmed by

Query: Can We Be Saints?

If Flanagan's thesis is correct, it is unlikely that anyone can be a saint in the sense of consistently holding a predominance of the virtues mentioned in the text discussion: "The idea of moral excellence as consisting of a life instantiating the full complement of the entire set, even if the idea of the entire set could be rendered coherent, is a nonstarter" (Flanagan 1991: 10). Instead, Flanagan suggests that there might be several different types of virtuous persons, depending on the type of virtue competence or dispositional module they fit. In fact, a recall of examples of saints or moral exemplars demonstrates that such models really are usually thought to be proficient in a few of the virtues or exemplify one the most: "Indeed, no saint in any tradition of which I am aware displays all the excellences that are recognized as such, even within the tradition of which he or she is part" (1991: 4). John Coleman (1987) writes that within the hagiographic tradition of Catholicism it is impossible to find a single list of virtues exemplified by all the canonized saints. Mother Teresa, for example, was especially known for her kindness and compassion to the poor—"the saint of the gutters." As Flanagan points out, most of the Buddhist *avadanas* are stories of Buddhist disciples who display particular virtues rather than practicing the full complement. The *tzaddik* in Judaism is someone who is better than most, and he tries always, as best he can, to do what is right, but typically embodies a single virtue, for example, great compassion, humility, trust, and so forth.

In addition to the questions of what is a saint and whether we can be saintly, there is an interesting question of how much we truly admire the saintly. Some have argued that because the saintly are so removed from ordinary human beings, it is very difficult to identify with saints and, consequently, to use them as a model of behavior. Consider in this regard the amount of media coverage, honor, and recognition accorded Princess Diana compared to Mother Teresa, when they died around the same time in September 1997. Many people complained that the media devoted too much coverage to Princess Diana and too little to Mother Teresa. Relative to their accomplishments—Mother Teresa was a winner of the Nobel Peace Prize who sacrificed herself for the poor, sick, and needy, while Princess Diana was a jet-setting aristocrat who promoted occasional charitable causes—the coverage seemed unfair.

Question for Discussion

Why do you think there was so much attention paid to Diana and so little to Mother Teresa?

R. Brown (1965), suggests that there are ten sorts of attitudes that cluster with the authoritarian personality: conventionalism; a submissive, uncritical attitude toward in-group ideals; punitive and aggressive attitudes toward violation of conventional norms; opposition to the imaginative, subjective, and tender-minded; a tendency to think in rigid and stereotyped ways and to believe that things are fated; preoccupation with power, hierarchy, strength, and toughness; generalized disdain for human nature; projection of unconscious impulses and terrors onto the world, for example, believing that the world is evil and dangerous; an exaggerated concern with sex and a rigid conception of sex roles; and idealization of one's parents and oneself (cf. Flanagan 1991: 289).

Because some findings suggest that certain moral traits will cluster with certain personality characteristics and attitudes, some persons will have more of a talent for certain virtues than others. Also, the Hartshorne and May studies suggest that virtues, such as honesty, do not seem to be as consistently exercised by a person as thought. Finally, the Milgram studies warn us of how even the most virtuously disposed are subject to situational deviancies. This all argues for a more cautious understanding of moral traits according to the philosopher Owen Flanagan (1991). He bases his view on Howard Gardner's (1983) theory of multiple intelligences. According to Gardner, there is evidence that there are several relatively autonomous human intellectual competencies: linguistic, musical, logical-mathematical, spatial, bodily-kinesthetic, intrapersonal, and interpersonal (1983: 8). Each of these intelligences is fitted with a unique process in the brain that facilitates and expresses it (1983: 278). In general, these intellectual competencies can vary to different degrees within the same person (1983: 278). The idea is that the mind in this case is a sort of "modularized economy." Similarly, Flanagan imagines that there are several sorts of virtue competencies. Consequently, it is misleading to think of a virtuous person as someone who exhibits most if not all of the major virtues in a consistent pattern through various situations. Instead, a virtue trait should be understood as a dispositional module (1991: 277).

3.3 THE VIRTUES OF SELF-CONTROL

Recall that autonomy is divided into self-mastery and self-direction; self-mastery in turn is divided into self-control, the ability to constrain one's more positive emotions, feelings, and desires, and self-efficacy is the ability to endure obstacles and suffering to accomplish some goal. The virtues of self-control are concerned, then, with mastery of those more positive passions; they are thought of as inwardly directed discipline and are often considered the fundamental and essential virtues for moral character. As Kant said, "virtue requires, first of all, control over oneself" (1797: 67).

3.3.1 Temperance

Temperance can be defined as self-control in regard to pleasure. As the ancient Greek philosopher Epimarchus said, "Pleasures for mortals are like impious pirates: for the man who is caught by pleasures is straightaway drowned in a sea of them" (485 B.C.E: 23.44a). Obviously, then, without temperance pleasure can be overwhelming and oftentimes destructive as Aristotle suggests (*Nic. Ethics* 1119a 1). This is why Daniel Goleman stresses its importance: "There is perhaps no psychological skill more fundamental than resisting impulse. It is the root of all emotional self-control, since all emotions, by their very nature, lead to one or another impulse to act" (1995: 81). Goleman recounts Walter Mischel's famous "marshmallow test" in this regard. Mischel, Shoda, and Peake (1990) present an offer to 4-year-olds: They can have a marshmallow now, or they can wait for a period of time and have twice as many. Those who resisted the immediate gratification of grabbing the marshmallow at 4 were now, according to Mischel's long-term study, more socially competent as adolescents; they were personally effective, self-assertive, and better able to cope with the frustrations of life. They were less likely to go to pieces, regress under stress, or become rattled and disorganized when pressured. They were self-reliant and confident, trustworthy and dependable; they took initiative and plunged into projects (cf. Goleman 1995: 81).

Temperance and the Seven Deadly Sins

"I can resist everything but temptation."
—Oscar Wilde

Among the most frequently given versions of the seven deadly sins are:

> anger
> avarice
> envy
> gluttony
> lust
> pride
> sloth

At least five of these fall under the category of intemperance and are due to lack of self-control. Anger is lack of good-temper; lust is lack of sexual continence; sloth, lack of industry; gluttony, inability to control appetite; avarice, lack of control over what one wants or possesses; envy, the inability to curtail a desire for what others possess.

Temperance includes the ability to forestall lesser pleasure for greater pleasures or to forgo immediate pleasures for long-term ones but also, conversely, to feel good in the enjoyment of appropriate pleasures, an enjoyment that gives one drive, ambition, and enthusiasm for certain goals. Pleasure is essential to most social activity. As Peter Kramer notes, it influences attachment and learning, the willingness to participate in groups and obey rules. It regulates appetite for food and other substances. It reaches broadly into every aspect of personality, through enthusiasm, passion, aesthetic sensibility, and self-satisfaction (Kramer 1993: 227).

Some psychologists (cf. Klein 1987) divide pleasures into two types: *consummatory* and *appetitive.* Consummatory pleasures are those that are created when, for example, the pang of hunger is satisfied by a good meal; it is the pleasure derived from relieving an undesirable or uncomfortable state. Appetitive pleasure is more excitatory. This is pleasure derived from anticipation rather than satiation and so serves more as a drive mechanism. Sexual flirting, pursuit, and foreplay may yield appetitive pleasures for a person, while orgasm yields consummatory ones. More generally, we might say that appetitive pleasures are involved in the drive for the goal, whereas consummatory pleasures are experienced in the achievement of a goal. To justify this distinction, Klein showed that anhedonic patients (people with chronic insensitivity to pleasure and enjoyment) would respond to the drug imipramine at only one level; that is, the drug would restore sleep normality and appetite for food, but not drive or interest in their work. On the other hand, if he added an amphetamine to the imipramine, then the person's drive and interest in work would also return.

In addition to this distinction between appetitive and consummatory pleasures, psychologist Mihaly Csikczentmihali argues for a difference between pleasure and *enjoyment.* Pleasures are certainly important components for the quality of life, but the pleasures of sleep, rest, food, and sex provide merely restorative, homeostatic experiences that return the body to a certain order or thermostatic level. Pleasure occurs when, after the neurochemical thermostat, so to speak, falls below where it should be, it is returned to its proper level (1990: 46). Pleasure does not lead to growth or complexity of life—it simply helps to maintain a steady state (1990: 46). Enjoyment, on the other hand, occurs when needs are not only satisfied, but also where the event or activity leads to something novel or unexpected, something more than what was anticipated (1990: 46). For example, everybody takes pleasure in eating. To enjoy food, however, is more difficult. A gourmet enjoys eating. The unexpectedly delightful taste of a well-prepared meal goes beyond the mere satisfaction of hunger.

But besides the self-control of pleasure and enjoyment, temperance also involves the ability to control emotions and desires that may cloud judgment, although Aristotle argues that it has only to do with bodily pleasures (*Nic. Ethics* 1118a1). Temperance allows a steady and calm emotional state, a state necessary for sound judgment (cf. Kant 1797: 68). Aristotle seems to think that lack of temperance also leads to the development of improper tastes, that is, a taste for base pleasures (*Nic. Ethics* 1118b20ff.).

In regard to the vices associated with temperance, *self-indulgence* is thought to be one that leads toward personal decline, especially if many pleasurable temptations are possible. Those who acquire sudden wealth and fame are often led this way simply because so many opportunities for enjoyment are now possible. Sybaritic lifestyles often lead to addiction, disease, death, or at least ill health; more serious or noble goals and pursuits are cast aside in favor of more immediate rewards, and talents and abilities are ruined. Certainly, the lives of Elvis Presley, Jim Morrison, Keith Moon, and a number of other popular entertainers are illustrative of this result. Morrison was known for his liberal use of drugs, drink, sex, food, and various other entertainments, the results being a wasting of his talent and an early death. In the movie *Tender Mercies*, Robert Duvall plays a country singer who has ruined his native talent and an outstanding career through excessive drinking. He has lost his wife's love and become estranged from his daughter. The beginning of the movie finds him at the bottom of his luck, abandoned by his last friend after a night of drinking. Broke, he has nowhere to turn; it is only through the kindness of the motel owner, who requires that he give up drinking, that he manages to find his way back toward a simple, decent life. Still he is racked with regret, remorse, guilt, and a sense of loss of what he had and what could have been. In one of the most dramatic scenes of the story, his (adult) daughter comes to visit him in his new home. It is clear that she loves her father but resents the fact that he was not around enough or that he was always too drunk to be a good father to her. She tries to make him recall a song he used to sing to her when she was young, at a time when they were more of a loving family. He claims he doesn't recall the tune, but as soon as she leaves he picks up his guitar and sings the tender ballad. The memory of such a time was just too painful for him to bear in front of her.

On the other hand, those who are *insensitive* are led into dull, monotonous lives, devoid of the enjoyment of basic human pleasures; such persons deny themselves even those aspects of life which often make it worth living. Aristotle suggests that "people who fall short with regard to pleasures and delight in them less than they should are hardly found; for such insensibility is not human" (*Nic. Ethics* 119a7). However, psychologists seem to suggest, on the contrary, that it is a malady not too uncommon among humans, which they call *anhedonia* (cf. Kramer 1993: 223–249; cf. also Clark and Fawcett 1987; Bloomfield and Kory 1980). Peter Kramer describes one of his more seriously anhedonic patients in the following way: "She had no passion, no enthusiasm, no drive, no initiative, just a sort of lazy passivity grounded in her indifference to the pleasures of life. ... [she] had few close friends and no boyfriends; men invariably developed the impression that she was bored with them. ... [She] complained that she was bored, lonely, and under-scheduled. She never had the willpower to bring order to her life. Nothing touched her or meant much to her ... without enthusiasm it was hard for her to sustain projects" (1993: 224). This description shows how necessary the proper enjoyment of pleasure is for many of the other virtues in life, especially ambition, friendliness, industriousness, and other sorts of goal-driven virtues: "The inability to experience pleasure as others do not only interferes with the motivation necessary to ambition or affiliation, it also leaves a person subtly uncomprehending of social behavior, and therefore utterly isolated" (Kramer 1993: 227). Anhedonia prevents goal-directness since success is no longer rewarding (Kramer 1993: 229). Sometimes hypohedonia can lead to a false drive or overambition. Because anhedonics have such a high threshold for enjoyment, they must perform especially exciting or thrilling acts just to come away with the sort of pleasure another person experiences in ordinary events (Kramer 1993:231). They may live in hyper-drive but derive little reward or pleasure from such great efforts; accomplishments are not rewarding, and there is no pleasure derived from recognition of those accomplishments.

3.3.2 The Relation between Virtue and Pleasure

Moral philosophers have been interested in the role pleasure and enjoyment should play in our lives. How temperance ought to be exercised hinges on one's outlook. But also, as will become clear, the answer to this question has profound consequences for moral theory.

There have been, generally speaking, three broad estimations of the relationship between pleasure and virtue. *Hedonism* (from the Greek *hedon* for "pleasure") *is the view that pleasure does or ought to constitute the good life.* Eudaimonism (from the Greek *eudaimonia* for "happiness" or "flourishing"), especially as promoted by Aristotle, *argues that the good life is not constituted by pleasure but by virtuous activities, which result in a certain kind and level of happiness.* Stoicism, which is opposed to both hedonism and eudaimonism, *argues that a life of virtue should constitute our end in life, and in fact, an indifference to pleasure (and pain) must be cultivated to achieve such an end.* There are a range of positions within each of these major divisions of thought.

Within hedonism, *sybaritism advocates the unbridled and intensive pursuit of all pleasures.* Sybaritism is reflected by the dictum "if it feels good do it." This position certainly has its critics. For one thing, such conduct could lead to obvious immoralities. It might feel very good for someone to kill somebody he hates immensely. If pleasure is paramount, the right thing to do may often become subordinate. In addition to this serious complaint, maintaining a life which feels pleasurable, even the majority of the time, is difficult if not impossible. First, one requires a great deal of resources to accomplish such a thing; unless you're heir to Bill Gates's fortune, you must work in order to get such resources. Work can be painful, tedious, and boring, and it may consume the majority of your day and your life. This is why the sybaritic life is often more available to those who make quick fortunes while young, especially in the entertainment industry. Usually people who struggle to earn their wealth over a long period of time already have acquired habits which, precisely because they are needed to endure over the long run, dictate against sybaritic behavior. Second, the psychological features of pleasure may make sybaritism impractical. Pleasure has various thresholds which are determined by repetition and acclimation. Because repetitive pleasures become less pleasurable, you need to vary pleasures. You may like steak, but steak every day soon becomes barely palatable. The variation of pleasures, especially over a lifetime, requires hefty means and opportunity. In addition to the problem with repetitiveness, human bodies become acclimated to certain pleasures—some pleasures require more of the same to achieve the same effect. Addictive practices have this characteristic. The irony of addiction is that one needs more to be satisfied at the same level as previously; yet the more one requires, the more difficult it becomes to maintain that same level of satisfaction. You may remember how it felt to have your first car, the old junky Chevy, but now you're lusting for a BMW. Because desire is infinite, pleasure is asymptotic.

Epicureanism (a view associated with the philosopher Epicurus) *argues that although pleasure is the end of life, one must choose only those pleasures in life that provide the most of the highest pleasures.* Choose the wrong pleasures or the right pleasures without the right constraints and one's life becomes a miserable morass of pain, worry, and trouble. For Epicurus, pleasures of the mind are paramount *(Letter to Menoeceus).* Ataraxia, or peace of mind, is the highest of the mind's pleasures. It is achieved through the coordination of several aspects of one's life, all of which must achieve a state of repose, or more technically speaking, a catastematic state. According to Epicurus, there are two sorts of pleasures (somewhat similar to the distinction just made): *kinetic* pleasures are those associated with the activity, and they cease when the activity ceases. For instance, the pleasure in eating fine food ceases when one is done eating. These are momentary pleasures that come and go with the activity. *Catastematic* pleasures result from not being hungry and so are associated with a stable or prolonged condition. To achieve ataraxia, the body must first be put into a state of repose. Temperance, then, is a crucial factor in this regard, and its goal would be to ensure catastematic pleasures for the body: "And since pleasure is the first good and natural to us, for this very reason we do not choose every pleasure, but sometimes we pass over many pleasures, when greater discomfort accrues to us as the result of them: and similarly to us when we have endured pains for a long time. Every pleasure then because of its natural kinship to us is good, yet not every pleasure is to be chosen" *(Letter to Menoeceus)*. Contrary to the image of Epicureanism that grew up around it, for example, as the connotation of "epicure" might imply, Epicurus advocated a very simple life that involves modest meals and accommodations and the loosening of desires as a way of procuring repose of the body:

> And again independence of desire we think a great good—not that we may at all times enjoy but a few things, but that, if we do not possess many, we may enjoy the few. ... To grow accustomed therefore to simple and not luxurious diet gives us health to the full, and makes a man alert for the needful employments of life, and when after long intervals we approach luxuries disposes us better towards them, and fits us to be fearless of fortune (*Letter to Menoeceus*).

Thus, the motto "eat, drink, and be merry," sometimes associated with Epicurus, is really more appropriate for sybaritism or some of Epicurus's unorthodox adherents.

Second, one's way of life must avoid heavy responsibilities and serious involvements. Epicurus himself seemed to avoid any political life. In general, it is better to lead a life that avoids fame and the notice of others. A life that is quiet and reserved is most conducive to ataraxia.

Third, the mind must also be put into a state of repose by freeing it of its basic fears and psychological discomforts. Among the most important fears to eliminate are fear of the gods and fear of death. This can come about only by the right understanding of the nature of things. A clever argument against the fear of death, repeated by the Epicurean philosopher Lucretius (94–55 B.C.E.), claims that since we are not dead yet, there is no need to fear from death; and once we are dead, then it does not matter (*On the Nature of the Universe*, Bk. III, 1.830ff.). Lucretius blames religion for instilling in people all sorts of superstitions and accounts of the gods which make them cower with a heavy burden on this earth and make them feel guilty about even the simplest of pleasures.

Epicurus makes a nice summary of his brand of hedonism:

> When, therefore, we maintain that pleasure is the end, we do not mean the pleasures of profligates and those that consist in sensuality, as is supposed by some who are either ignorant or disagree with us or do not understand, but freedom from pain in the body and from trouble in the mind. For it is not continuous drinking and revelling, nor the satisfaction of lusts, nor the enjoyment of fish and other luxuries of the wealthy table, which produce a pleasant life, but sober reasoning, searching out the motives for all choice and avoidance, and banishing mere opinions, to which are due the greatest disturbance of the spirit (*Letter to Menoeceus*).

Several criticisms are often made of Epicureanism. First, it leans toward an egocentric outlook on life. It focuses mostly on the inner sense of happiness, a withdrawal into the center of one's own life. Even though Epicurus especially counts friendship as among the important pleasures of life, he disdains civil and political involvement. According to Epictetus (*Moral Discourses*, XXIII), Epicurus even recommends not raising children since parents may "fall into anxieties about them." But it is precisely in relationships, friendships, and civil and political activity that many of the virtues are exercised.

Second, Epicureanism clearly subordinates virtue to pleasure; in other words, virtue becomes a means of attaining pleasure. Consequently, if it turns out that being virtuous prevents us from leading a pleasant life, we should then act viciously. Thus, Epicurus would have to prove that being virtuous does lead to a pleasant life (this issue is raised again in Section 4.5.8). This leads to the third basic criticism that Epicurus's philosophy really rests on an empirical account of the psychology of pleasure; that is, to ensure that his ethical doctrines are correct, he must first assure us that his psychology is credible. This in turn leads to a fourth criticism which is called the "naturalistic fallacy" (discussed in the Introduction). This is a criticism that is also appropriate for a hedonistic theory called utilitarianism (discussed in Section 5.4.7). Utilitarianism argues that an action is good in proportion to the amount of happiness it promotes, where happiness is defined in terms of pleasure. John Mill, one of the advocates of this principle, argues that such a principle is justified precisely because people find pleasure intrinsically good and naturally pursue it; consequently, the right thing to do is to maximize it. Epicurus, too, claims that pleasure is something that is intrinsically good to us. But there is a fallacy here in thinking that because something is natural to us, it might be good. Biologist Konrad Lorenz (1997) thought that aggression was natural to human beings—but that is certainly not always a good. If pleasure is inherently good, then the pleasure that someone might get from killing or raping should be counted as a good, and if an ethic allows that, then it's in big theoretical trouble.

The eudaimonism of Aristotle is certainly more complex than the bald pursuit of pleasure found in sybaritism, but it is also subtly different from Epicureanism. Under this view it is not merely feeling good that matters but living the happy life, which Aristotle calls flourishing (*eudaimonia*). As it turns out, flourishing is living one's life with excellence or virtue; thus, although the end of one's life is happiness, virtue constitutes happiness, and it is not simply a means to it. In this case temperance, as the moderation of pleasurable feelings, is one aspect of living the good life. Flourishing is not identified with the pleasantness of life, but happens in the living of a virtuous life. The subtle relation between pleasure and flourishing is articulated by Aristotle in the following passage toward the end of *The Nicomachean Ethics:*

> Pleasure completes the activity not as a characteristic completes an activity by being already inherent in it, but as a completeness that superimposes itself upon it, like the bloom of youth in those who are in their prime (1174b32).

To explain this, he likens it by analogy to perception:

> All sense perception is actively exercised in relation to its object, and is completely exercised when it is in good condition and its object is the best of those that can be perceived by the senses. ... From this it follows that in any sense perception that activity is best whose organ is in the best condition and whose object is the best of all the

> objects that fall within its range, and this activity will be the most complete and the most pleasant (*Nic. Ethics* 1174b15–22).

Put more simply, when the eye is functioning well, viewing a beautiful object results in a certain pleasure; pleasure accrues within the activity performed well. By analogy, then, if we live our lives with excellence, with virtue, then a certain pleasure will accrue. This may sound like nitpicking, but it makes an important difference. Those forms of hedonism which see pleasure or the pleasant life as the end of human activity suggest that activities are not sought for their own sake but for the pleasure they might bring. But many think that the pursuit of pleasure in and of itself is seldom rewarding. This is because—if Aristotle is right—pleasure is, first of all, something that accompanies certain activities. Consequently, if you seek the activity because it is worthy, then the pleasure is something that crowns or "completes" the activity. But if the goal is pleasure, then the activity becomes simply a means to pleasure, and the worth of the activity is less important to you. As a result, you may be more willing to participate in less worthy activities as long as they produce the desired pleasure. Engaging in unworthy activities for the sake of whatever pleasure they may bring can lead to trouble. If one lives life well, with excellence, then pleasure results; if one lives for pleasure, then the activities that generate it can become corrupted. Proper pleasures are those that accompany the virtuous exercise of worthy practices.

This difference between Aristotle's eudaimonism and Epicureanism can be expressed, for example, in a certain estimation of acts of generosity and kindness. There is a certain worth in helping people through generosity and kindness that has its own sort of pleasure. But if you are helping people in need by being generous and kind because that makes you feel good, then the purpose in doing it is to feel good, not to be generous and kind. If that is the basis of your behavior, then there's no particular reason to be kind and generous if some other sort of behavior makes you feel as pleasurable.

Consider a variation of a thought experiment presented by philosopher Robert Nozick (also discussed in Section 5.4.7). Imagine a machine capable of creating the exact feeling of pleasure one would get from being kind and generous; the hedonist would be committed to the plausibility of the claim that this would be just as good as actually being kind and generous, since the purpose of being kind and generous is the pleasure it affords; if you can get the pleasure without the activity, then that seems even more pleasurable. In the film *Strange Days* (1996), the principal character is addicted to a machine that allows one to experience the experience of others. The machine is worn like a skullcap which somehow connects to the brain's neural network. A tape, which has recorded someone else's real experience (e.g., of robbing a bank, walking in the woods, having sex), is inserted into the machine, and the person experiences all the feelings, sensations, and emotions of the other person, while seeing everything they do. Since pleasure is the goal of activities, then the hedonist would have to say that living vicariously like this would be just as good as actually living.

Eudaimonism is critical of hedonism because it subordinates virtue to pleasure; for hedonists, virtue is a means to an end, pleasure, or at least a certain kind of qualitatively enduring pleasure. Consequently, if there is no such connection between virtue and pleasure, there is no reason for being virtuous. But the same logic would seem to apply to eudaimonism. Eudaimonism would also have to show that there is an inherent connection between the virtuous life and flourishing, and

The Matrix

The film *The Matrix* (1999, directed by Larry and Andy Wachowski) presents a thought experiment similar to Nozick's "experience machine." In the future human life has been taken over by a vast computer called "The Matrix." Human beings are reproduced by The Matrix essentially for their electrical power—as batteries to run The Matrix. Human beings therefore must be kept alive, but to keep everything in order, they must be made complacent. The Matrix devises machinery that allows human beings to live virtual lives so realistic that they believe their lives are actual. A few individuals have discovered the truth and have extricated themselves from this virtual world. A small band of these individuals strives to free others from this virtual imprisonment. However, "real" life is gray, dull, harsh, and brutal. One of the members of this band, Cypher, secretly makes a deal with the agents of The Matrix to be restored to a virtual life of his choosing in exchange for betraying his comrades. He tells the agents exactly what sort of virtual life he wants—rich, famous, handsome, and powerful.

Questions for Discussion

1. If you had the power to choose a virtual life, would you choose it over an actual life?
2. If you knew your life was virtual rather than actual, what would be your attitude toward your virtual friends, lovers, family, children, spouses? The film *The Truman Show* (1999, directed by Peter Weir) covers some of the same themes. What would you rather have, a perfect virtual lover or an actual lover?
3. Cypher adds that he doesn't want to remember that the world he chose is virtual. Would that make a difference to your choice if you could build in that possibility?

if there is no such connection, then the basis for acting virtuously seems to drop away.

The Stoics appreciate this point and take the criticism to heart perhaps more than any other thinkers. Even if there is no connection between virtue and pleasure or virtue and flourishing, one must still be virtuous according to the Stoics. What is the incentive, then, for acting virtuously? Simply for its own sake. To put it a bit differently, hedonism and eudaimonism both suggest that acting morally is in one's self-interest. In other words, to lead a pleasant life and to flourish, you need to be virtuous. But in the Stoic account, you need to forgo this self-interest in favor of a generalizable interest in what the right thing to do is regardless of how it affects you personally. The motives for doing the right thing should not be from any prospective reward, benefit, or pleasure, but simply because it ought to be done, that is, by the fact that it has moral worth. As Cicero, the great Roman orator and confirmed Stoic, put it, "By moral worth, then, we understand that which is of such a nature that, though devoid of all utility, it can justly be commended in and for itself, apart from any profit or reward" (*De finibus*, Bk. II, 45–46). This eventually becomes the basis of a theoretical position in ethics called deontology (from the Greek *deon* meaning "duty" or "obligation"). Deontological ethics is contrasted with what is called consequentialist ethics, which, as the name implies, argues that one should do the right thing precisely because of what the consequences of doing it entail (this matter is discussed in Section 4.8.3).

For the Stoics the best way to illustrate the deontological basis of virtuous behavior is indeed by means of the notion of duty. Duty is acting regardless of whatever pleasure or pain it brings and whatever consequences that action may incur. Kant (as discussed in Sections 1.5 and 2.6), who was heavily influenced by Stoic thinking, sees duties in this manner and is careful to make a distinction between acting from duty and according to duty. The shopkeeper who is honest because it is good for business acts according to duty, whereas the one who is honest for the sake of honesty acts from duty. Thus, the person who acts from duty becomes an exemplar of the person who acts on the basis of the moral worth of the action rather than of self-interest.

If the good life is constituted by virtue and not by pleasure, then we ought to act virtuously for its own sake, indifferent to either the pleasure or pain it brings. In fact, because the pursuit of pleasure can be a corrupter of virtuous activity, its pursuit ought to be expunged from the sense of the good life. Temperance, as seen by Aristotle and the hedonists, is a way of moderating pleasure and choosing the right sort of pleasures so that flourishing or ataraxia can be attained. But pleasure and the emotions definitely play a central role in any sense of the complete and good life. For the Stoics pleasure, as well as the other emotions, take away from the life of virtue. It is in a growing indifference to the pleasures and sufferings of life and the emotional attachments to this world that one will find tranquillity or *euthymia,* as Seneca calls it (*On Tranquility,* 58). This indifference is achieved through the perfect employment of reason in understanding the nature of things; once this understanding is achieved—by which one understands one's part in the whole and the character of that whole—pain, suffering, and loss become accepted and tolerated. In learning about the true nature of things, one learns what is in his power to do or not to do and to accept what he cannot change (Epictetus, *The Manual,* 1): "If you attempt to avoid disease or death or poverty, you will be unhappy" (*The Manual,* 2).

> The opinion that death is terrible is the terrible thing. When then we are impeded or disturbed or grieved, let us never blame others, but ourselves, that is, our opinions (*The Manual,* 5).

It is precisely this indifference to suffering (and its consequent diminishing of pleasure) that many argue generates certain paradoxes within Stoicism and makes it untenable. Epictetus argues,

> In everything which pleases the soul, or supplies a want, or is loved, remember to add this: "What is its nature?" If you love an earthen vessel, say it is an earthen vessel which you love; when it has been broken, you will not be disturbed. If you are kissing your child or wife, say that it is a human being whom you are kissing; if the wife or child dies, you will not be disturbed.

But this account seems to undermine the purpose of living. The distrust of emotions and passion, indifference to genuine human suffering, and the avoidance of emotional bonds are contrary goals to precisely those things that engage us as human beings, that are the center of our lives and the source of our compassion. If you must treat your child not as this child with whom you have a deep love and emotional connection but as a generalized human being that has a certain nature, then you can, we suppose, be removed from the suffering the loss of that child might involve. But that also causes us to remove ourselves from the emotional connection we have with that child that causes us great joy. The price of indifference to suffering is the loss of connection to this life. Pleasure of all sorts is what engages us in life, but it is precisely because we take pleasure in these things that their loss or lack can lead to suffering and pain. The price of engagement in life is the possibility of suffering because we care about what happens to ourselves and others.

Indeed, what we find within the philosophy of Stoicism is the seed of asceticism, which is the polar opposite of sybaritism. *Asceticism is generally understood as the attempt to withdraw from the pleasures of life; in fact, it stresses the purposeful denial of bodily pleasures to achieve a higher spiritual or mental plane of existence.* The complaint against asceticism is that it is not a philosophy that tells us so much how to live in this world as it tells us how to escape it. Ascetics, who disengage themselves from sexuality, property, and strong human bonds, loosen those connections thought to be essential to human life in all its forms. What should we demand of an ethic, then:

an understanding of how to lead our human lives well or of how to lead extra-human lives in this world?

Second, there is a suspicion of another inconsistency in Stoicism. Stoicism criticizes both hedonism and eudaimonism for apparent subordination of virtue to pleasure; yet Stoicism could be similarly accused. Peace of mind, tranquillity, or euthymia seems to be the reward for the virtuous life and the sort of indifference to suffering that is promoted by Stoic thinkers. Epictetus says, "Seek not that the thing which happens should happen as you wish; but wish the things which happen to be as they are, and you will have a tranquil flow of life" (*The Manual*, 8). It would seem then that this tranquillity is the reward of acting virtuously so that there is still a certain subordination between virtue and something else; since euthymia is a certain kind of pleasure, virtue is also subordinate to pleasure. Under this reading both Epicureanism and Stoicism agree that virtue is subordinate to pleasure; they simply disagree on how best to attain and maintain a certain pleasurable state.

3.3.3 Good-Temper

In April 1997 two drivers on the George Washington Memorial Parkway in McLean, Virginia, started chasing each other after the first driver cut off the second. They reached speeds of 80 mph while screaming profanities at each other. The two drivers lost control of their vehicles, crossed a median, and slammed into two oncoming vehicles, killing three people. The wreckage was unbelievable—the tops of the cars were sheared off, with the twisted and broken wreckage of a van scattered all over the highway. Narkey Terry, the only survivor of the deadly altercation, was sentenced to more than 10 years in prison for his role in the 7-mile chase (Story, 1997).

Control of anger is called good-temper, which is temperance in regard to the emotion of anger. Feeling angry or indulging in your anger is a pleasurable thing—it is a pleasurable feeling of release that is painful or stressful to control. Daniel Goleman relates a very common cab ride routine that illustrates exactly this point (1995: 64):

> As I settle into a New York City cab, a young man crossing the street stops in front of the cab to wait for traffic to clear. The driver, impatient to start, honks, motioning for the young man to move out of the way. The reply is a scowl and an obscene gesture. … The driver yells, making threatening lunges with the cab by hitting the accelerator and brake at the same time. At this lethal threat, the young man sullenly moves aside, barely, and smacks his fist against the cab as it inches by into traffic. At this, the driver shouts a foul litany of expletives at the man. As we move along the driver, still visibly agitated, tells me, "You can't take any shit from anyone. You gotta yell back—at least it makes you feel better."

Because it is a form of pleasure, anger properly fits in the category of temperance. It may be the most difficult of the passions to control (Zillmann 1993; Goleman 1995: 59). Anger may be prompted by some perception of endangerment—not just physical threat but also a threat to self-esteem or dignity; it may be a reaction to being treated unfairly, rudely, or it may be a reaction to a frustrated goal.

Good-temper is a necessity for any social interaction. Those who cannot control their temper are often avoided by others, and should they gain a position of power or authority, subordinates suffer greatly because of the instability of their decision making. The subordinate is never sure of what sort of mood they will be in or what sort of event will trigger their anger. An ill-tempered superior may, in this

Aristotle seemed especially aware of the various ways in which people express their anger. Accordingly, he made the following distinctions. *Hot-tempered* persons get angry quickly, with the wrong persons, at the wrong things, and more than is right, but their anger ceases quickly, which is the best point about them. This happens to them, according to Aristotle, because they do not restrain their anger but retaliate openly owing to their quickness of temper, and then their anger ceases (*Nic. Ethics* 1126a12–15). *Choleric* persons are quick-tempered and ready to be angry with everything and on every occasion (*Nic. Ethics* 1126a17–19). *Sulky* people are hard to appease, and they retain their anger long because they repress it. It ceases when they retaliate, according to Aristotle, for revenge relieves them of their anger. If this does not happen, they retain their burden. "Such people are most troublesome to themselves and to their dearest friends" (*Nic. Ethics* 1126a25–26). *Bad-tempered* people are those who combine the worst of the other types: they are angry at the wrong things, more than is right and longer, and cannot be appeased until they inflict vengeance or punishment (*Nic. Ethics* 1126a27–29).

regard, secure her position or get her way through fear and intimidation, that is, by threat of outbursts and tirades. Being ill-tempered in this sense is not necessarily an advantage toward security, for those with undisciplined temper often have their visions and judgments clouded. They can often be taken advantage of by a more even-tempered, rational, and calculating person; and subordinates may be motivated to do so precisely because of the dislike brought on by the superior's ill-temperedness. As the Swahili say, "The anger of the cuttlefish is the joy of the fisherman" (Scheven 1981). As Aristotle notes, the ill-tempered person is prone toward revenge (so a person needs to be more cautious in any partnership with them), while the even-tempered one is capable of making allowances (*Nic. Ethics* 1126a2).

As opposed to most popular beliefs, some studies of anger management show that ventilation of anger is the worst thing you can do to control it (Zillmann 1993). Rather than providing catharsis, outbursts of anger typically pump up the emotional brain's arousal, leaving people feeling angrier, not less angry. When people told of taking their rage out on the person who provoked it, the net effect was to prolong the mood rather than end it. It was far more effective for people to cool down first and then confront the person in a more constructive or assertive manner (cf. Tice and Baumeister 1993; Tavris 1989).

On the other hand, those who are *apathetic* are most likely to be taken advantage of by others. If you are not angered by unfair actions against you or others and if there is no resistance or emotional display of anger for transgressions committed against you, then persons who are so inclined will be more likely to take advantage of you. Apathy leads to self-inflicted injustice. Anger is a way of letting others know that they have harmed or offended you, and when that offense is unfair, then you are justified in expressing the anger. This is why Aristotle says, "The man who is angry at the right things and with the right people, and, further, as he ought, when he ought, and as long as he ought, is praised" (*Nic. Ethics* 1125b32). In articulating it in this manner, Aristotle also shows that the virtue of good-temper is a matter of not only controlling inappropriate anger, but allowing anger to be expressed when it should. Knowing when, against whom, and how much anger to express is an essential aspect of this virtue.

3.3.4 Ambition

Ambition is concerned with a desire to achieve a certain status or position or to attain some sought-after goal. However, there is some ambiguity as to the virtuous status of ambition. The word itself often connotes a vice. In Shakespeare's *Julius Caesar*, Brutus defends his assassination of Caesar precisely in those terms:

As Caesar loved me, I weep for him; as he was fortunate, I rejoice at it; as he was valiant, I honour him; but, as he was ambitious, I slew him (Act III, Scene ii).

It was because Caesar had personal ambitions to become emperor of Rome and to destroy the republic that Brutus felt the assassination was justified. Perhaps the ambiguity of the word can be clarified by making a distinction between ruthlessness and ambition and contrasting ambition with directionlessness. In that context the willingness to abandon morality for success is the characteristic of *ruthless* people, while *directionlessness* is a kind of apathy: Such persons are not sure of what they want to do in life, or if they do act, they're not entirely sure they want to do it.

Ruthless people will do nearly anything to attain something they truly desire. The ruthless, like Shakespeare's Macbeth, become blinded by their passion for a certain goal, as John Dean's book *Blind Ambition* suggests. Blind ambition involves keeping eyes on the prize without eyes on the road. It is a kind of lust for success. That's why it properly belongs to the category of temperance. Ruthless persons may forsake all virtue for achievement so that it will not be beneath them to lie, deceive, cheat, coerce, or worse to attain their goal.

Query: Does the End Justify the Means?

Should it be the case that certain goals are so noble and worthy that they justify any means to attain them? The paradox can be expressed in the following thought experiment: Suppose you could guarantee the happiness of some thousands of your family, friends, and compatriots; all you had to do was administer various forms of torture to an innocent child over an extended period of time. Would you be justified in doing it? Does its justification compare to the thinking of Hitler, Stalin, or Pol Pot, all of whom tortured and killed millions in the name of a better society? Or is the comparison inaccurate?

Some, such as Leon Trotsky, who rivaled Stalin for power after Lenin (and who was assassinated by agents of Stalin in Mexico in 1940), had a more subtle answer to the question of whether the ends justified the means. He wrote:

A means can be justified only by its end. But the end in its turn needs to be justified. From the Marxist point of view, which expresses the historical interests of the proletariat, the end is justified if it leads to increasing the power of humanity over nature and to the abolition of the power of one person over another. ... That is permissible ... which really leads to the liberation of humanity (1969: 48).

Trotsky's theses, then, are the following: (1) an end must be justified and (2) any means to achieve the end that has been justified is itself justified only if it really achieves that end. *Do you agree?*

Trotsky argued that the only way to eliminate oppression in society was to oppress the oppressors. Therefore, the only difference between the right thing to do and the wrong thing to do lay in the end to be achieved. The oppressors had only their interests in mind, while those who sought to overthrow the oppressors had the interests of the oppressed in mind. Since the acts of oppression were vicious, then vicious means were justified in overthrowing them, which would be the only effective way of eliminating the oppression.

Some argue that the end does not justify the means and that how we achieve our goals is just as important as the goals. It is argued that if means are employed which contradict the ethical ideal implicit in the end, then that will corrupt those goals. A society which uses torture and genocide to achieve its goals will become an oppressive society, even if its goal is to eliminate oppression. Contrast the philosophy of Trotsky with that of Gandhi and Martin Luther King. In employing nonviolent civil disobedience, the goal was not to overthrow the oppressors by oppression but to appeal to certain ethical ideals which would eventually hold sway over the opponents. Since no violence was perpetrated by the protesters, yet such protest persisted, those in authority would have to act in an especially oppressive way to squash such resistance. Many have argued that both Gandhi and Martin Luther King were successful in large part in achieving their goals. *Do you agree? Which strategy do you think is ultimately more effective, Trotsky's or Gandhi's?*

Properly ambitious people have a sense of what they want; they have definite goals in life. However, they are not so desirous of those goals that they are willing to forgo all integrity to achieve them. While the ambitious may have goals such as a good job, a family, and a home, a *high-minded* person is an ambitious person with more noble goals in mind. The high-minded person is keen on accomplishing a collective good or doing some public service—a better community, the improvement of others, a safer neighborhood—and not just a good

Wanda Webb Holloway wanted her teenage daughter to succeed at cheerleading so badly that she offered her diamond earrings in a murder-for-hire plot aimed at eliminating her daughter's chief competitor's mother. It was Holloway's hope that the death of the mother would so upset the competitor that she would withdraw from the competition. Holloway was caught and sentenced to 10 years in prison.

for herself. The *directionless* are those who drift from goal to goal but fail to accomplish much. As Montaigne says, "The soul that has no fixed goal loses itself; for as they say, to be everywhere is to be nowhere" (1572–1588: 7).

3.3.5 Curiosity

Curiosity is the desire to seek information and discover the means necessary to accomplish goals or ends. This can be of two sorts: intellectual curiosity, which deals primarily with knowledge and knowledge seeking, and curiosity understood as an attempt to understand the affairs, motivations, and plans of others. Those who are too curious intellectually are often distracted from their goals; as Solomon says, "He that considers the wind shall not sow, and he that looks to the clouds shall not reap" (Ecclesiastes 11:4). If we take the Adam and Eve myth in Genesis as representative of the Biblical attitude, then curiosity (in the context of disobedience) is the root of our miserable condition; curiosity associated with knowledge (the tree of the knowledge of good and evil) led to the expulsion from paradise. Similarly with the ancient Greek myth of Pandora's box. Pandora was a beguiling woman fashioned by Zeus. She had gathered in her box all forms of evil and disease. Zeus sent Pandora to Prometheus's brother, Epimetheus, as revenge for theft of fire by Prometheus (Prometheus in turn had given it to humankind against Zeus's wishes). Epimetheus, being the weaker of the brothers, was seduced by the

Will the Truth Set You Free?

In Plato's dialogue *The Republic,* Socrates tells a story, which has come to be known as the "Allegory of the Cave." Men have been raised inside a cave since childhood, fettered in such a way that all they can see are shadows flitting about on the walls. Since this is all they've known their entire lives, they take these as the only real things in the world. Yet when one is freed from his bonds and forced to turn around, he sees a fire and the shadows it casts as the true source of the shadows. And when he is made to exit the cave through a rough and painful road, he witnesses the sun for the first time. The brilliance of the sun causes him great pain, yet he soon realizes that the sun is the paradigm of fire. Now whereas he once believed shadows to be the only real things, he recognizes their position on a true hierarchy of reality. Yet when he tries to convince his compatriots of his new found knowledge when he returns to the cave, they threaten him with death.

Questions for Discussion

1. Why do you think the other men rejected this knowledge?
2. Why was it so painful for the freed man to experience these new levels of reality?
3. What is better, to live in comfortable beliefs—some of which, if not all are illusions—or to know what is real and true even if it is disconcerting?

charm of Pandora and his own curiosity about Pandora's box. When it was opened all forms of evils, plagues, and diseases visited humankind. Curiosity can not only be downright deadly ("curiosity killed the cat"), but generations may suffer as a result of it.

Many admire curiosity, but others see it as a fault; hence, Sophocles portrays Oedipus's downfall in part as overzealous curiosity. Many folktales and myths begin with curiosity as the motivation for transgression or disobedience that consequently leads to some dangerous adventure or misfortune (cf. C.S. Lewis 1955). Some suggest that there are simply things that one should not inquire about at all, and curious people only destroy themselves when they seek such knowledge. For example, in the popular films *Raiders of the Lost Ark* and *Indiana Jones and the Last Crusade,* the villains also seek, respectively, the ark of the covenant and the holy grail and are destroyed by their efforts to unlock their mysteries. Augustine (*Confessions,* Bk. X, Chap. 35) calls curiosity the "lust of the eyes," a sort of greed to know (cf. Meilaender 1984: 138ff.), and that is probably why it belongs to the category of temperance. It may drive us to see what is not pleasurable at all; we may suffer greatly "simply because of the lust to find out and know" (Meilaender 1984: 135). Whereas Aristotle delights in curiosity and wonder, claiming it to be the motivation for all science and philosophy (*Meta.* 982b11), Augustine sees a certain uselessness in the scientific pursuit of nature: "From the same motive [of curiosity] men proceed to investigate the workings of nature which is beyond our ken—things which it does no good to know and which men only want to know for the sake of knowing" (*Confessions,* Bk. X, Chap. 35). Indeed, curiosity is dangerous since it seeks answers to questions and puzzles, and these answers often upset the status quo or worldview concerning the matter. Curiosity is a means of going beyond what is already known and believed, and thus, it transgresses boundaries. Curiosity can be disrespectful and disobedient of authority, especially those considered authority in regard to knowledge. Many cultures, such as the early Christian culture, see such potential for transgression as a vice; they look more favorably upon what Aquinas calls *docilitas* or "teachableness" (*Summa* IIa.IIae. q. 166), that is, the passive receptiveness of knowledge or information rather than the active pursuit of it. It is often dangerous to the knower, too, since knowledge may often bear information that is unbearable or revelatory; curiosity about dangerous or powerful things also has the potential of harming or destroying the knower.

Augustine (354–430) was a philosopher and theologian, considered to be one of the early Church fathers. His best known work is *The Confessions.*

Aquinas seems to support Augustine's view to some extent; yet at the same time he wants to pay homage to his master, Aristotle. To this end he makes a distinction between *studiositas,* a disposition to be diligent in the pursuit of knowledge, and *curiositas,* which he considers a vice (*Summa* IIa.IIae, q. 166). Curiosity as opposed to studiousness is a sort of unfettered ruthlessness in the pursuit of knowledge—a willingness to do what is necessary in order to know. The Gothic image of the mad scientist is an example of this sense of curiosity. As portrayed in Mary Shelley's *Frankenstein* or Robert Louis Stevenson's *Dr. Jekyll and Mr. Hyde,* the scientists delve into matters that fallible humans should not investigate, and they use means that are morally and prudently questionable, with the result that the knowledge attained leads to their own destruction and harm to others.

Those who are too curious about others' affairs are called *meddling,* and this is often a sign of *envy.* The purpose of such meddling is primarily to learn enough about someone to harm them. Francis Bacon believed that the meddling or strongly inquisitive person was commonly envious of the persons inquired about. This is probably the sense of Plautus's statement that "all inquisitive persons are malevolent" (*Stichus* I.iii.55). A specific kind of meddling concerned with spying on the morals of others, which Kant calls *allotrioepiscopia*, is, he claims, "an inquisitiveness offensive to the proper knowledge about mankind, and everyone may rightfully oppose it as a violation of the respect owed him" (1797: 132). Often relations with others rest on appearance, beyond which one does not wish to penetrate simply because the relation works well in that context. One is comfortable with a certain understanding or image of the other. Investigating too deeply into the past or into the character of another with whom one is especially connected may lead to unpleasant results. Kant seemed to think that the more one knew of another, the more one was likely to dislike that person; consequently, intimate relations were to be capped at a certain level, below which fondness or love would be lost.

Are We a Society Afflicted with Allotrioepiscopia?

We seem to be a society extremely curious about the moral affairs of others, if sales of tabloid newspapers are any index. Tabloid TV shows hosted by Jerry Springer, Jenny Jones, Maury Povich, Ricki Lake, Leeza, Sally Jesse Raphael, and others are very popular. Often they deal with the seamier side of life. Many have noted that mainstream news has also shifted some of its emphasis to tabloidlike material. The fascination with every detail of the lives of the "rich and famous" has made for a very profitable business. Although many blame the death of Princess Diana on the paparazzi, some argue that the people who make such accusations should look to themselves, since they're the ones who had an interest in the affairs of Diana and who, consequently, bought the tabloids that bought the photos from the paparazzi and so made it profitable for them to pursue her aggressively.

This curiosity has extended to every detail of public figures' lives, of religious, civic, and political leaders, so that the newspapers are rife with accounts of real or supposed sex and corruption scandals. The personal history of nearly every candidate for major political office is scrutinized by the press, which seems to see its task as not articulating what the candidate stands for, but what sort of dirt can be dug up in his or her past. *What effect do you think this might have on the society as a whole? Does it serve a good purpose or an unworthy one?*

In a 1997 article in *The Atlantic Monthly*, "In Praise of Hypocrisy," Henry Louis Gates, Jr., called for a lessening of this sort of prurient interest in the intimate details of our public figures' lives. In a way Gates makes a point similar to Kant's condemnation of allotrioepiscopia—it diminishes the dignity of humanity by demonstrating to everyone that even the best of us has some indignity. Do we want saints in public office or relatively decent people with good intentions who have the skills and abilities to get the public good accomplished? Finding a saint—like Diogenes's search for the honest man—may be an impossible mission; shouldn't we tolerate a lower standard? For example, how does the adultery of a public officeholder bear on his or her public duties?

Contrary to this position, some would argue that such immoralities as adultery and cheating in business or on one's taxes are a reflection on character, and character is important in building trust in a person in public office—that such a person will perform the duties of public office with the public interest in mind. Consequently, we need to know about any scandals such a figure may have engaged in. Epictetus argued,

> if, laying aside ... fidelity, we form designs against the wife of our neighbor, what do we [do] ... but destroy and ruin ... fidelity, honor and sanctity of manners. ... And do not we ruin neighborhood? Friendship? Our country? In what rank do we then place ourselves? How am I to consider you, sir? As a neighbor? A Friend? What sort of one? As a citizen? How shall I trust you? (*The Manual*, Bk. II, Chap. IV).

Questions for Discussion

1. Do you agree with Epictetus?
2. Should a middle ground between these two positions be adopted? Certainly, those who are accused of corruption, sexual harassment, or even more serious acts should be investigated, and we should be made aware of their actions, but should there be some reasonable limit to this? Should a public figure be afforded the same amount of privacy as an ordinary citizen?
3. How do the charges against former President Clinton in the Monica Lewinsky case illustrate these various issues?

Those who are *incurious* are often docile and passive in regard to information or knowledge. They accept what they are told and are not curious enough to question the basis or evidence for such knowledge. As a result, they are likely gullible. They show little initiative in pursuing information and require simply enough to satisfy whatever is necessary to get by. They are good at regurgitating what others have told them and so often do not have the independence to adopt their own beliefs. Consequently, they may be easily swayed by others and adopt whatever is conventional or appropriate. Since they recite the beliefs of others, they really don't understand the basis of their own beliefs and are often incapable of justifying them. They are subject, then, to easy loss of conviction in the face of challenges to their beliefs.

3.3.6 The Work Ethic: Industry, Frugality, and Contentment

The work ethic—sometimes called the Protestant ethic—is thought to be at the heart of the American character and at the center of the American dream. It is believed by many that, if you work hard and save money, you will have a successful and comfortable life. At the core of this ethic, then, are the virtues of industry, frugality, and contentment.

Frugality is temperance in regard to spending one's money, that is, temperance in regard to material lifestyle. Frugal persons meet debts, save money, and live within their means. Frugality is necessary for attaining long-range goals; it allows one to forgo immediate gain for long-term rewards. Thus, saving money for a house may require one to give up certain vacations or other material pleasures, but owning a comfortable home may turn out to be a lifelong pleasure. *Extravagance* is the tendency to spend more on oneself than is appropriate for one's income. *Miserly* persons, on the other hand, are insensitive to material comforts; they do not save money for long-range goals but simply save obsessively.

One of the most frugal families in America is undoubtedly Amy and Jim Dacyczyn and their six children. Amy Dacyczyn received national attention through her magazine, *Tightwad Gazette*, a very successful monthly newsletter. In the publication she offers advice to consumers on how to stretch every dollar and save money on everyday items by using and reusing everything around the house to its limit. Using the techniques she expounds in her newsletter, Amy Dacyczyn claims she was able to cut her annual expenses to about half of what an average family of eight spends per year. Although this required a great deal of sacrifice of the ordinary pleasures of middle-class life—as far as she was concerned—it yielded a greater reward of a nice house in the country and the ability to be a stay-at-home mother.

The case of the Dacyczyns raises questions most central to frugality as well as the other virtues of temperance: the cost versus the benefit of attaining certain goals relative to the worthiness of the goals pursued. Clearly, the Dacyczyns had to make such a choice. They made the decision that it was worthwhile scrimping and saving in order to reach the quality of life they wanted. The payoff was that they could attain this life much sooner than most folks could. The cost was in terms of the denial of many things that most middle-class or upper-middle-class Americans would have while working toward their higher goals: new clothes, vacations, fancy TVs, and other electronics. Are these benefits worthwhile and, if so, are they worth the sacrifices they entail?

This issue of cost versus benefit in the context of lifestyle is addressed in a book entitled *Your Money or Your Life* by Joe Dominguez and Vicki Robin (1992). In it they argue that America's current rabid consumerism has led to lives that are busier, more stressful, and less connected to community and family than ever before. Although people have more things, they must spend more time earning enough money to get them; this takes away not only from the enjoyment they might get from using them, but it also forces them to neglect other aspects of their lives, such as relations with their loved ones, that are by and large more important. Frugality is therefore linked to the virtue of *contentment*—of how much to be satisfied with. The lack of willingness to forgo immediate pleasures for long-term ones, combined with easy access to credit, has led many down the road to bankruptcy. A general complaint of modern American culture is that it is so consumer oriented and people are so directed toward possessions that many have lost connection with community as a result. Would frugality correct that?

Industriousness is the ability to temper the desire for play, entertainment, recreation, or relaxation in order to do what is necessary to get something done: "Only he who goes into the forest comes back with firewood," as the Swahili say. Industrious persons are directed and focused on a goal and the steps necessary to achieve it. "A beginning is a beginning, there is no beginning which is bad," the Swahili add. Industrious persons are able to forgo immediate pleasures and desires to that end. When most everything else in one's life is forsaken for such goals, then for lack of a better word, such persons are often classified as workaholics. *Workaholics* do not know how to relax or enjoy the pleasures of doing nothing, or if they do find the time to recreate, they make work out of it as well. On the other hand, *lazy* or *slothful* persons do not have the discipline to forgo the distractions of body and mind that prevent people from accomplishing their goals. *Idleness* is an amalgam of directionlessness and lack of industry.

Contentment is temperance in regard to desire for what others possess and, conversely, satisfaction with what one has. It is the virtue that is concerned with setting the proper limit to acquisition. *Covetous* or *envious* persons try to "keep up with the Joneses" and so may exhibit a tendency toward extravagance. Contentment is being grateful for what one has and being able to enjoy it for what it offers. The content person sets a limit to goals; one accomplishes the goal set and remains satisfied with its accomplishment. If ambition drives one to succeed, contentment tells one when to stop. *Covetousness* generates a desire for more than what one has by wanting what others possess. One may not be content with this house, but want a larger house, a fancier car, a better job, or a prettier partner. Covetousness is considered such a powerful vice that there are two separate commandments against it in the Decalogue (Exodus 20:17): "You shall not covet your neighbor's house. You shall not covet your neighbor's wife, or his servant, man or woman, or his ox, or his donkey, or anything that is his." Covetousness may often lead to ruthlessness,

---

Jealousy

Jealousy is an exaggerated desire to keep exclusively as one's own what one already has, whether it is property, possessions, friends, lovers, or a spouse. Jealousy directed toward persons is especially offensive since it treats them as property rather than as autonomous agents. *Security* is confidence in one's importance to others with whom they have special relations. Security in regard to possessions is the ability to emotionally disengage from possessions; secure persons do not see themselves defined in terms of what they own, but who they are.

forgoing friendships and principles for the sake of personal gain. In a certain way the desires of covetous persons are dictated by others; it is the desire for what others have that directs their own desire. Envious persons may also have a tendency toward unfairness because they may want more than they probably deserve. On the other hand, *undesirous* persons are not motivated by material gain or what others possess; they may have a tendency toward directionless for this reason. It may not really be the case that undesirous persons are content with the little they have; it may be the case that they do not have the desire, ambition, or industriousness needed to get what they could in a fair and reasonable way. (For more on the importance of these virtues, see Section 4.5.6.)

3.3.7 Issues in Sexual Continence

Confucius said that "I have never yet seen anyone whose desire to build up his moral power was as strong as sexual desire" (*Analects* IX.17). We must presume that would hold for Confucius as well. But Confucius's point is clear: Sexual desires are among the strongest we have, and sexual continence for most is among the most difficult of the virtues of temperance.

Sexual continence, more than any other species of temperance, shows more clearly what has been progressively hinted at in the various accounts of virtues so far—namely, that often the question of what is temperate hinges on what kind of pleasure, how much, when and with whom, and for what reason.

To illustrate this point—and as an exercise—consider the following claims within each of the categories listed. Try to identify where your initial preferences lie. How would you cut the line between lasciviousness and prudishness?

With Whom

1. A consenting adult who is one's spouse is the only person you should ever have sex with (thus, sex prior to marriage or outside of marriage would be immoral).
2. Sex should be exclusive to a partner who is a consenting adult in a committed relationship.
   a. sex before marriage would be permitted as long as it was exclusively in the context of a seriously committed relationship.
   b. this would hold especially for marriage, which is the ultimate committed relationship.
3. Sex can be with any number of consenting adults in any combination or sequence.
4. Sex can be with anyone.

What Kind

1. Sex should be exclusively heterosexual and restricted to vaginal intercourse.
2. Sex should be exclusively heterosexual but involve whatever sexual practices bring mutual pleasure.
3. Sex can involve any sexual practices that bring mutual pleasure.
4. Sex can involve any sexual practices that bring pleasure of any sort.

When

1. When there is a desire on the part of at least one partner.
2. When there is mutual desire.

For What Reason

1. Exclusively for the purposes of procreation.

2. For any purposes mutually desired such as procreation, affection, communication, or mutual pleasure.
3. For pleasure only.

This exercise illustrates how problematic the doctrine of the mean is for making decisions about what counts as virtue. The golden mean suggests that we should avoid the extremes, that is, a life of sybaritic sex, on the one hand, and a celibate life, on the other. But many possibilities lie in between that are left unaddressed. Beyond the recommendation of avoiding extremes, it doesn't help us locate the mean in any practical way and so address the more germane issues of sexual continence. The doctrine by itself does not tell us with whom we should have sex or what sort of sex is morally appropriate. Thus, it creates a great degree of latitude in our decision making. The doctrine of the mean may be a good analytic tool for categorizing virtues and vices, but it doesn't help much with the nitty gritty of choosing right conduct. For this task, as we'll see later, we need to appeal to wisdom and moral knowledge.

This exercise also illustrates how defining sexual continence hinges on the relation between virtue and pleasure discussed in Section 3.3.2. Generally speaking, hedonists would see the purpose of sexual practices as primarily a means of getting pleasure of some sort. More specifically, sybarites would permit themselves to engage in any sexual practice with anybody as long as there was some degree of pleasure involved. Epicures, on the other hand, would be more temperate in regard to sexual practices, engaging in those in which they could be reassured of qualitative and not just quantitative sorts of pleasures. The Epicure would be interested primarily in those sorts of relations, partners, and practices that would lead to repose of body and mind. It is easy to imagine the Epicure seeking exclusive and special relations with persons of worth, modeled on friendship, which the Epicureans hold as the highest sort of relationship. As opposed to the hedonist, the eudaimonist is concerned primarily with goodness of the practices; the pleasures resulting from good practices are the most appropriate ones. The goodness of the practices are measured by how well participants flourish within them, that is, how well they succeed at perfecting their character within that context. The worst sorts of relations are those that destroy or foul the character of a person. The Stoic, on the other hand, is not concerned with the pleasure that might result from such practices. Pleasure is subordinate to the proper role and duties performed within a relationship. For the Stoic there is more of an emphasis on the importance of the function and purpose of the activity than the personal benefits or pleasures it might bring. For the Stoic there is a stronger sensibility of what is owed another in a relation and a stress on duty and loyalty to the standards of the relationship. The ascetic, of course, would be the least interested in sexual practices. True ascetics often forgo sexual practices altogether, since it is these that are the most exemplary of bodily pleasures.

3.4 THE VIRTUES OF SELF-EFFICACY

Whereas the virtues of self-control deal with constraining our more pleasurable feelings, desires, and emotions so that we may accomplish our goals in the morally right way, the virtues of self-efficacy are concerned with overcoming the obstacles, pain, and suffering that we may encounter in the pursuit of those goals. To the extent that pleasure and pain dominate a person's behavior, then courage and temperance work to control the one and endure the other for the sake of the right thing.

3.4.1 Courage

Early on a Monday morning Air Force Sgt. Daniel Lake was hanging on a rope beneath a helicopter at 15,500 feet on the side of Mt. McKinley. Below him he could see a ledge where a tent was pitched. Inside rested a battered mountain climber. To the side of the ledge there was a sheer 1500-foot drop that had killed an Air Force climber 2 years earlier. The 100-foot rope beneath the helicopter swung in an arc back and forth over the sweep of the ledge. "We all have fear of heights. What you have to do is learn to deal with that fear." When Lake's feet touched ground, he was 5 feet from the precipice. The artificial wind from the giant Chinook helicopter could have easily blown him off the edge. It was difficult just to unhook the harness from the safety of the hoisting line. Lake curled up in a ball and waited for the helicopter to leave. He found the injured climber, 45-year-old Stanley Darke, who had fallen 800 feet. He was unconscious and his breathing was raspy. Lake had to take every precaution, so he fitted Darke with a neck collar and a back board after he had been stabilized. By then Lake was feeling both the effects of the altitude and the cold. But despite his own difficulties, he managed to get the injured climber back into the helicopter and to safety (cf. Medred 1994).

Consider the following queries:

1. Who is more courageous, the climber who scales a difficult peak or the rescuer who rescues him?
2. Who is more courageous, the well-equipped, experienced, and trained firefighter who enters a burning building to rescue a child or the ordinary citizen who does the same thing?
3. Does a bank robber act courageously?

Plato poses the second question in the *Laches* (cf. 193aff. for what follows). Socrates, who is discussing the question of courage with two Athenian generals, poses the following problem: Who is braver, the skilled person who engages in a dangerous task or the less-skilled person who accomplishes a similar task? The skilled person may not fear as much because with his experience and understanding of the situation, he does not have to overcome so much fear to accomplish the task. The unskilled or inexperienced person has more to fear and so must strive harder to perform the task. Thus, Socrates seems to think the unskilled person is the more courageous because courage has more to do with the mastery of fear than just with the mastery of the particular circumstances of the situation, which could lead to a reduction of fear.

However, this solution—that courage is simply mastery of fear—would seem to lead to a strange paradox articulated by the first example just listed. Assuming the same level of fear in both climber and rescuer (let's say both are equally skilled), this solution would suggest that they are both equally courageous. Yet many would argue, intuitively speaking, that somehow the rescuer is more courageous because he is risking his safety and life to save another's life, while the climber is risking his life for a less clear or noble purpose. In other words, it is not facing fear alone that makes an act courageous but the purpose of the act as well. If we accept Plato's solution, then an amateur bank robber would have to be called courageous, since he must work harder than a professional bank robber to master his fear.

To solve this problem, Douglas Walton suggests a distinction between courage and bravery. *Bravery can be defined as the ability to accomplish something despite fear, with-*

out consideration of the nobility of the purpose (Walton 1986: 98). In some sense it is a more difficult virtue than temperance: "It is harder to face what is painful than to abstain from what is pleasant" (*Nic. Ethics* 1117a34), most likely because "pain upsets and destroys the nature of the person who feels it, while pleasure does nothing of the sort" (*Nic. Ethics* 1119a23). On the other hand, Walton defines courage more specifically as the case where "an agent contributes to some highly worthwhile outcome by bringing about something very difficult or dangerous" (1986: 133). *Courage is the willingness to do the right thing despite serious pain, significant harm, or risk to one's well-being or even to one's life.*

Applying these distinctions to the climber–rescuer story, it could be argued that Sgt. Lake exhibited both courage and bravery: He not only had to control his fear to accomplish his mission, but since his mission was saving the life of another, that gives it a noble purpose. Darke, on the other hand, at best demonstrated bravery, since climbing North America's tallest peak also requires control of fear, but it may not be considered an act of courage, as climbing the mountain serves no noble purpose and is only a sort of vain adventure. At its worst, then, it could also have been considered foolhardy, since the risks to life were not worth the goal. In regard to Plato's question, again the distinction between courage and bravery becomes useful. We can say that depending on the end or goal of the action, both sorts of persons (the trained soldier and the citizen-soldier) are acting courageously; however, the unskilled one may be exhibiting more bravery due to the greater fear to control than the more experienced person has to master. In the context of the third query listed, it is also clear that, although it may take some bravery to rob a bank, it's certainly not a courageous act, since it has an ignoble purpose.

Given this distinction between bravery and courage, it would appear, then, by this definition, there are two essential features of courage: the presence of fear or at least the presence of a risky or dangerous task and the fact that the action is performed for some noble, collective, or suprapersonal reason. Most commentators believe that the experience of fear is an essential feature of courageous acts (cf. Aristotle, *Nic. Ethics* 1107a33; Aquinas, *Summa* II.IIQ123; Von Wright 1963: 147; Wallace 1978). Others dispute this (Foot 1978: 12; Walton 1986: 80ff.). Walton (1986: 82) argues that it doesn't matter so much whether the person experiences fear as whether the situation is truly dangerous or risky. Thus, persons who have enough confidence, gained from experience, to act in a dangerous situation, may not feel fear, although they still recognize the situation as risky. Such acts would still be called courageous, but the feeling of fear may not be present. Walton uses a study of astronauts by Ruff and Korchin (1964) to support his claim. The study argued that although the astronauts admitted to fear, their anxiety levels were not high because of their confidence in their training and technical readiness. Also, observations of parachute jumpers have indicated that successful execution of jumps tended to lead to a reduction of fear.

But besides the fact that the situation must be perceived as dangerous or risky, another essential feature of courage is that the end or the goal of the action must be for a noble cause or for another's

---

Linda Seals, 45, lost her life in the surf off Santa Catalina Island after rescuing a group of children being swept to sea by riptides. Exhausted after rescuing the children, barely making it ashore, she was on the beach when she saw her husband, Randy—still in the surf from the rescue attempt—being pulled to the sea. Without hesitation, she dove in after him, but the tide was too strong and her strength was gone. Randy Seals was swept to safety on rocks that line the shore, but Linda died in the surf.

good, that is, for other than selfish or self-interested reasons (cf. Walton: 97ff.). Courage is the cardinal virtue of abnegation since it demands self-denial in favor of something larger than the person, such as a cause, principle, or sacrifice for the sake of others. As Aristotle argues, courage concerns overcoming fear in the face of the noblest circumstances (*Nic. Ethics* 1115a30): "It is for a noble end that the brave man endures and acts as courage directs" (*Nic. Ethics* 1115b22). For this reason, courage is the primary virtue of heroes, and heroes are specifically those who sacrifice or who incur great risk for the sake of a collective good or another's welfare. War heroes are often the paradigm of heroism, and so courage in battle is thought to be the paradigm of courageous action (cf. *Nic. Ethics* 1115a30). For one thing, it involves the very real possibility of loss of life, the supreme sacrifice one can make; second, it can involve a noble end, that is, at least a cause which is greater than the person. The courageous person, according to Aristotle, sees the matter as a point of honor; some soldiers may engage in battle simply out of a fear of the punishment from commanders, but that is not genuine courage. An honorable soldier does not fight out of compulsion (*Nic. Ethics* 116b22ff.). Also, a courageous soldier is one who fears dishonor over death; professional mercenaries may appear courageous simply because of experience and an assumption that their force is greater than the enemies', but these will often flee in the face of superior force, whereas the truly courageous soldier would be willing to stand up to it (*Nic. Ethics* 1116b22ff.). Furthermore, although truly courageous soldiers exhibit passion and anger, they are not primarily motivated by them but by the sense of honor or the cause for which they fight.

This second criterion for courage also helps distinguish the genuine hero from someone who may simply serve as a role model. Heroes should not be confused with role models such as sports figures, movie stars, or popular figures from entertainment; such persons are simply models of success rather than genuine heroes, especially since they receive a large benefit for their efforts. Such role models may exhibit skill, physical virtues, plus character virtues such as ambition, industriousness, and so on, but they do not typically exhibit genuine courage. Of course, there are exceptions to this, as in the case of Jackie Robinson, who incurred many hardships when he broke the color line in baseball; it was clear that much of his purpose in doing so was to advance the cause of African Americans—and indeed, his success led to further integration of the major leagues. Every year the Carnegie Institute puts out a list of the ten top heroes it wishes to recognize. Many are persons who have sacrificed their lives to save others or who have forgone their own personal benefit for the sake of others. There is no comparison between these sorts of heroic acts and those who make millions of dollars because of physical ability or acting talent. But this doesn't stop people from confusing the two. According to Dick Keyes, author of *True Heroism* (1995), when young people are asked for their heroes, most respond with the names of well-known sports or entertainment figures. "Celebrity and ability seem to have replaced courage and character as most qualifications for respect."

What Is Your Reaction When People Say Pro Athletes Should Set an Example for Youngsters?

Some people have argued that athletes are not really heroes and shouldn't necessarily serve as models for children. With lucrative contracts, endorsements, and the publicity of frequently reported bad behavior, many argue that athletes are, at best, models for how to make money or paradigms of success while, at worst, they are exemplars of greed and excess. Some athletes themselves have argued that they shouldn't be held up as role models. *What do you think?*

Types of Bravery

Those who strike out of anger or fear are not genuinely brave, so Aristotle claims, "for even asses would be brave when they are hungry" *(Nic. Ethics* 1116b30). He calls this type of bravery *faux bravery.* In these cases the passion overwhelms prudence, and a person appears brave only because he is blinded to the consequences or perils of his action. Fearlessness, as discussed earlier, is more of a psychological state or part of a person's constitution. *Daring* is the willingness to take a new or novel course of action, and it might be thought of as bravery in regard to ambition; *valor* is strength of mind and body required to act courageously. *Intrepidity* is courage in the context of a specific goal or mission. The lesser passive virtues of courage include *dauntlessness,* which might be defined as the determination, despite hardship and risk, to stick with something, and is related to perseverance, and *mettle,* which is a resilience or ability to endure. It is quite possible for people to exhibit mettle, valor, and bravery, for example, yet not genuine courage simply because the actions are not in the context of some larger, suprapersonal context. Mountain climbers, for example, might be brave, daring, and intrepid, yet because the purpose of climbing mountains does not generally serve any higher noble purpose, they may not be courageous. Those who fight out of anger or for revenge are more *pugnacious* than courageous: "for they do not act for honor's sake nor as the rule directs, but from strength of feeling" *(Nic. Ethics* 1117a9). Being *stalwart* means that one has the bravery to stand up for herself; such a person has enough valor and self-reliance to defend herself against attack, either verbal or physical. *Conciliatory* persons give up on a struggle too easily, or they waiver as soon as they are attacked. Persons with *conviction* have the courage to defend their beliefs, especially when they put themselves at risk for those beliefs. This should not be confused with dogmatism; *dogmatic* persons do not have the bravery to admit the falsehood of their beliefs. *Vacillating* persons do not have the courage of their convictions.

Besides bravery, genuine courage should also be distinguished from a number of other related virtues. For example, *fearlessness* should not be confused with courage. Glenn Gray (1967: 109), a philosopher who had much combat experience, characterized the fearless soldiers as having indomitable strength of will. They have an extraordinary will to victory and an iron nerve. They are war lovers and seem to find their element in battle. He observes, however, that they are contemptuous of other men who are not like themselves. Such men are motivated primarily by a kind of sense of themselves, a sort of will to power and egoism rather than a sense of higher purpose.

In the summer of 1995, Y.T., 24, attempted to snowboard down one of the most dangerous parts of Mt. McKinley, the Messner Couloir, a steep, funnel-shaped slope that descends from about 19,000 to 14,000 feet. A few years earlier four Canadians plunged to their deaths in the same spot. As Ken Kehrer, the chief ranger at Denali National Park put it, "It's an incredibly dangerous place." Yet Y.T. and a companion were intent on snowboarding the couloir. The inevitable resulted; they set off an avalanche and Y.T. fell, resulting in injuries that left him partially paralyzed (Meyerowitz 1995). As easily suggested, this is an example of foolhardiness. Bravery is one thing, but *foolhardiness* is facing dangers that lead to nearly inevitable, negative results for no particularly good purpose. Such dangers may be endured if the cause is great, in which case we talk about heroic self-sacrifice. But if the dangers are great yet the cause is small, then the act is plain foolishness. However, a foolish act can also be one in which the person may not be aware that a situation is dangerous and act despite that danger without fear, but still, we would not want to call that action

Bravery or Foolhardiness?

In March 1996 a motorcycle stunt rider, Butch Laswell, crashed to his death while trying to break a record by jumping over a bridge. Although he cleared the 38-foot bridge, he landed off to the left of the landing ramp and hit the concrete pavement. He was pronounced dead at the scene.

brave. In that sense foolhardiness might be defined as accidental bravery; the person is simply ignorant of the danger or does not perceive the situation as dangerous when she should. Those who act in ignorance or out of ignorance should not be counted as truly courageous according to Aristotle. For example, the intoxicated person may have false confidence, "liquid courage" as it is often called, while those who do not understand the dangers consequent upon their actions may simply be fortunate in not being harmed or in succeeding in their goals. It is only when people are fully aware of the dangers involved in the enterprise, and face them nonetheless, that they can be truly called courageous (*Nic. Ethics* 1117a 10–27).

Cowardliness is thought to have two sources. On the one hand, it may result from a distorted perception of the risks or dangers involved; on the other, it may be due to the inability to control one's fear, even if the fear is rightly perceived. "The cowardly person fears both what he ought not and as he ought not," as Aristotle says (*Nic. Ethics* 1116a2). This idea is reinforced by Gray in his observations of men in battle (1967: 112ff.). The constitutional coward tends to be constantly troubled by his own imagination; he seems to perceive danger everywhere, and so the cowardliness is due to misperception of risk or danger. What Gray calls the occasional coward may be due mostly to a sudden loss of self-control in regard to fear and so exemplifies the second source of cowardliness. As Gray notes, on occasion even the bravest veterans might flee in terror. Gray characterizes this as a group phenomenon and a highly contagious failure to cope with sudden emotions. Gray also points out another interesting feature of cowardliness. The constitutional coward seems to have the inability to see himself as part of the group and is not committed to any altruism; that is, he has difficulty seeing how the group outweighs the value of his own life. This would suggest that cowardliness stems from the person's inability to take on suprapersonal goals; such a person is simply more egoistic than others in this regard. This observation seems to confirm the view that courage involves, as one of its essential conditions, a supraindividual goal and that courageous persons are capable of adopting such goals. In addition to these considerations, Aristotle argues that the cowardly person is someone who displays a tendency toward despair and lacks confidence (*Nic. Ethics* 1116a3–4).

3.4.2 Patience

> Patience and the mulberry leaf become a silk gown.
>
> —Chinese proverb

Patience is the ability to delay or wait for what is desired; as the Swahili say, "What is in the sea, go and wait for it on the beach" (Scheven 1981). But it also often involves suffering or enduring pain, trouble, or evil for the sake of some greater good, as Lactantius defines it: "The bearing with equanimity of the evils which are either inflicted or happen to fall on us"(1867–1872: 347). Precisely for this reason, Cyprian of Antioch felt that all other virtues rely on it (357: 12). Prudentius (1949: ll 109–177) and Miles Coverdale (1550: 169; cf. Schiffhorst, 1978: 6) seem to concur. Augustine emphasizes the self-efficacy involved in patience: "The patience of a man ... is that by which we tolerate evil things with an even mind, that we may not with a mind uneven desert good things" (1888: III, 527). Because it involves enduring pain, in some sense of the term, it is often associated with courage or fortitude. As Henry Hawkins writes in *Parthenia Sacra* (1633: 155), "The Vertues of Fortitude and Patience may seeme as two but are easily reduced to one, that is, to a stout Patience, or patient Fortitude" (cf. Gerald Schiffhorst 1978: 25 n.2ff.). For example, patience and fortitude are often placed together in iconography (see, e.g., *Patientia and Fortitude* by Hendrik Golzius 1584). But more strictly speaking, stout patience might be called perseverance (discussed later).

Patience allows one often to accomplish the goal in a manner that has better results than if one rushes to its pursuit. Waiting for something to grow or improve within its own time, of course, is the virtue of the parent or teacher. As Chaucer writes in *Canterbury Tales* (l. 773–778), patience can bring about what action and exigence are powerless to effect.

The paradigm of patience is Job according to most Judeo-Christian commentators. Job demonstrates a willingness to endure suffering, hardship, and trouble simply for the sake of God, without question and with a quiet faith and trust that such suffering will be justified. Patience is what is denoted when one submits oneself to God's will amid the fortunes and the misfortunes of life; it is the will holding on through faith to a belief that life has meaning in spite of appearances (cf. Schiffhorst 1978: 6). This is a view promoted by Isaac Barrow in his writing of 1685, *Of Patience:* "[patience] is the disposition to bear anger and injuries with charitable meekness, and second, the pious sustaining of the adversities dispensed to us by Providence" (quoted in Schiffhorst 1978: 7). It involves the hope that such suffering will pass eventually into a happier state and so allows one to bear the suffering joyfully. In this context patience is often contrasted with *tristitia,* or *melancholia*—a sadness in the face of diversity.

The Impatient Culture?

Richard Carlson, author of the best-selling book *Don't Sweat the Small Stuff ... and It's All Small Stuff* (1997), argues that people in modern life lack the virtue of patience. The hurriedness of modern life has caused people to expect more things immediately. Computers, faxes, e-mail, and car phones have led much of the American public to believe they have a right never to wait for anything. "We have developed this belief in the age of technology that we shouldn't have to ever wait at the post office or sit in traffic," Carlson says. "We're all going somewhere very quickly, but where? ... As a culture, we've lost perspective." The rewards of patience are great, Carlson says. "When a person becomes more patient, his or her life is so much calmer."

Do you agree with Carlson?

This Christian account of patience contrasts somewhat with the Stoic sense, which involves more of an indifference to hardship or suffering than a hope that in the end all will be well (cf. Schiffhorst 1978: 7). In general, the distinction between the Stoic and Christian sense of patience is the difference between a cold, proud, defiant character and a humble, ardent, submissive one. Stoic patience is born of hardened indifference to suffering; Christian patience is born of humble submission to the will of God.

But being too forbearing leads to *passivity,* that is, waiting for something to happen to you without actively attempting to attain it. So the Swahili have a twin proverb that goes with the one above: "Today is yours, tomorrow is not." As with most of the virtues discussed so far, the proper use of patience requires an assessment of the goal of patience: Is the thing waited for worthy of our time and effort? How long should we wait for something?

Impatience is often thought to be akin to a kind of anger. For example, in Christian iconography patience is often opposed to *ira,* rash, impatient anger (cf. Cyprian of Antioch 357: 12; cf. Schiffhorst, 1978: 3). Losing one's patience has a marked similarity to anger, but it is really an amalgam of anger and frustration. Like anger, it is a sudden loss of control: "Whosoever is out of patience is out of possession of his soul" (Bacon 1625: 188). It is partly frustration of not seeing the result of one's efforts. In this regard patience is seen as necessary for a peaceful, happy, and serene disposition, as the 15th-century author of *Patience* suggests: "For anyone who knows how to endure misfortune, happiness would follow, and whoever cannot endure because of his anger, the more he suffers" (Unknown 1918).

3.4.3 Perseverance

Perseverance is courageous patience. It is the wherewithal to endure a series of tests or trials that put one at risk, an ability to overcome difficult obstacles, or simply the ability to suffer through a long and agonizing ordeal without falling into despair or, in fact, by maintaining a cheerful hopefulness. Perseverance involves a certain ability to go on despite setbacks, defeats, and difficulties. Often, as a study by Seligman (1991) showed, success is not only a function of talent and intelligence but your capacity to stand defeat. Perseverance is allied with hope and optimism. *Hope*, as Snyder defines it, is believing you have both the will and the way to accomplish your goals, whatever they may be (1991); *optimism* is the manner in which people explain their successes and failures to themselves. Optimists see failure as due to something that can be changed so that they can succeed the next time around, while *pessimists* take the blame for failure, ascribing it to some lasting characteristic they are helpless to change (cf. Seligman 1991). This is supported by the new psychological literature on resilience (cf. Higgins 1994). Higgins studied 40 young people who had gone through significant traumas and difficulties in their lives, yet managed to succeed in life to various degrees. They seemed to have the following in common: a higher than average intelligence, an optimistic and flexible temperament, an ability to distance themselves from abuse, a refusal to see themselves as victims, and above all, the presence of caring adults or parental surrogates.

Often those with terrible diseases or severe disabilities, such as illustrated by the case of Christopher Reeves, show perseverance and bravery. There are thousands of such examples. In addition, when the disabled, in the context of their disability, work toward some collective good, then perseverance is also courageous, as Walton suggests (1986: 93ff.).

Persistence is a close relative of perseverance. This involves the willingness to endure years of training or effort for some goal. Studies of Olympic athletes, chess masters, concert violinists, and so forth show the ability of people to train for years and to endure routines that most others would find numbing. *Resignation* is spiritless endeavor, a feeling that one is bound to fail even before an effort is made. *Doggedness* is foolish perseverance, a waste of effort on attempts that are fruitless or without hope of success.

3.5 THE VIRTUES OF REGARD

Temperance and its related virtues involve self-control of the positive pleasures and emotions, courage with self-efficacy, and endurance. Consequently, these are virtues that deal primarily with the self. The virtues of regard, on the other hand, are primarily concerned with one's proper relation to others. In the virtues of regard, self-control and self-efficacy are applied to the interests of others.

3.5.1 Fair-mindedness

Justice, along with temperance and courage, has been traditionally thought of as a cardinal virtue. However, it is important to make a distinction between the just or fair-minded person and justice as a system of principles. *Principles of justice address questions of rights, citizen duties and responsibilities, the distribution of goods, and the right sort of punishments for wrongs.* When we talk about the just person, we're referring to the moral character of someone. Perhaps to avoid confusion, it is better to talk about *fair-mindedness* as the virtue character and *justice* as a question of the proper arrangement of rights, punishments, and so on. It is clear that without fair-minded persons, the best forms of justice could not operate. As John Rawls argues, it must be presupposed that citizens of any well-ordered society, that is, a society founded on some principles of justice, will have the capacity for a sense of justice (i.e., fairness; cf. Rawls 1971: 505, 132).

In regard to what we are calling fair-mindedness, Aristotle suggests, "this form of virtue" is in "relation to our neighbor" (*Nic. Ethics* 1129b25), and he approves of Plato's characterization of it as "another's good" (*Nic. Ethics* 1130a4; Plato *Rep.* 343c). Fair-mindedness is the primary virtue of cooperative arrangements. Every cooperative arrangement involves rights and duties, costs and benefits, punishments and rewards; justice and fairness involve precisely the proper adjudication of those matters. Fair-mindedness draws on the other cardinal virtues. Temperance teaches us self-control, which involves not being greedy, covetous, and indulgent. Courage teaches us to think of people other than ourselves. *Fair-mindedness is concerned with giving others their due in cooperative arrangements that benefit a collective good.* Thus, we can see the elements of both temperance and courage in fair-mindedness. Although one may justly expect benefit from cooperative arrangements, fair-minded people are interested in getting only what is their due. But they are interested that others get their due as well. If they were intemperate, they may want what is the others' due. Justice also concerns collective goods, and to that extent, it requires self-abnegation. For this reason, fair-mindedness is considered by many to be the supreme virtue since it incorporates the other cardinal virtues. As Aristotle puts it, it is virtue in the "fullest and complete sense, ... because he who possesses it can exercise his virtue not only in himself but towards his neighbor also" (*Nic. Ethics* 1129b30–35).

Generally, we want to have fair-minded people in our societies since they are thought to have certain valuable characteristics. First, they are generally willing to participate in fair or just cooperative arrangements—they're willing to "do their part." Second, they don't seek more than what is their due in cooperative arrangements or practices—they seek only their "fair share." Third, they abide by the rules that are either implicitly or explicitly set by that practice—they "play fair" and don't cheat. Fourth, they are impartial in the sense that they treat others equitably without bias or regardless of likes or dislikes. Fifth, they want to "see justice done" in the sense that they are willing to correct a practice or arrangement so that it is fairer—even if it is not particularly to their advantage. Each of these characteristics needs elaboration.

Fair-minded persons are willing to participate in fair cooperative arrangements for the following reasons. Cooperative arrangements are necessary for any society. When members of a group cooperate to achieve common goals, they usually stand much more of chance of accomplishing the goals than if individuals pursue them singularly. A road is necessary to get from home to work, but if a person tried to build it single-handedly, it would occupy his lifetime and a lifetime of resources. A large community—either through cooperative labor or pooling of funds (i.e., taxes)—can easily accomplish the task, and it is something that can benefit a large number of people. If these cooperative arrangements are fair, they will lead to mutual benefit in the sense that each participant gets more advantage from their existence than from their nonexistence. Thus, commuters in the vicinity of the road are more advantaged by its existence than its nonexistence. Moreover, they are also likely to advance the good of the group as a whole. Having this road will allow people from outside of that vicinity to access it. Perhaps people who want to live in that area now can do it, the road may increase commerce to the area, and so forth.

Fair-minded persons are thus willing to participate (by means of some contribution) in these cooperative practices not only because they benefit themselves individually, but because they also benefit others and contribute to the overall good of the group of which the person is a member. Persons act unfairly when they refuse to participate in a cooperative arrangement yet still take advantage of the benefits that such arrangements entail. Such people are often called free-riders. Of course, not everybody can physically participate in all arrangements that benefit them, although certain arrangements—such as tax practices—are efficient ways to guarantee that it happens to some extent. Thus, a person who fails to pay a fair share of taxes yet uses the benefits which those taxes bring for the community could be called a free-rider. As a society becomes more complex, divisions of labor occur which allow for a wide reciprocity of benefits and services. Some people may participate exclusively in the military, which serves to protect the community as a whole, while others may work exclusively in providing weapons that make the military more likely to succeed in defending the community. However, there are certain practices, such as voting, jury duty, and participation in local government, that are expected of each community member.

Besides being willing to participate in fair arrangements, fair-minded persons do not seek unfair advantage for themselves under such arrangements. This could be understood in at least four ways: (1) fair-minded persons do not seek more than what they are due from the arrangement; (2) they do not seek to deprive others of their due; (3) they do not seek something from the arrangement without proper contribution to the arrangement; or (4) they do not require others to contribute more than they should to the arrangement. Put simply, fair persons do not take advantage of possibilities for unfair gain. Fair persons are not greedy and do not act ruthlessly. Fair persons generally act virtuously. This is why Aristotle says that fairness ("justice") is not part of virtue but "virtue entire" *(Nic. Ethics* 1130a10) since to be fair a person must also employ the other virtues. It is hard to imagine that someone who is greedy, dishonest, cowardly, and intemperate will also be fair-minded.

Third, fair-minded persons are willing to "play fair." This means they are willing to abide by the rules of the practice even when the rules may not particularly advantage them.

Fourth, they are also willing to grant that other players deserve something even if they don't particularly like that person or even if they are disadvantaged by it. In other words, fair-minded people are impartial and unbiased in whatever practice they are engaged in. Fair-minded persons have a talent for looking at both sides of an issue or conflict regardless of who the participants are. Impartiality is the virtue of those who serve in disputes, such as judges, referees, and arbitrators. A referee who enforces infractions and penalties more strictly for one team than for another is called unfair. A judge who applies the law differently to two persons similarly situated is considered biased and partial. An arbitrator who hamstrings one side in negotiations cannot be trusted to be fair.

Fifth, fair-minded persons are also willing to correct a cooperative arrangement toward a more just or fairer outcome should it prove to be lacking or wanting in that regard, even if they are personally advantaged by the present arrangement. Fair-minded persons are not just concerned with self-interest; they are also concerned with the interests of others in the sense that they have an interest in seeing that cooperative arrangements are genuinely fair. Fair-minded persons acknowledge and respect the interests of others. They recognize that each person who participates in a cooperative practice has as much right as they themselves do in getting some benefit from it. Fair persons are rightly outraged at the exploitation and abuse of others.

It is often not enough that people be fair-minded; we must also have fair cooperative practices to ensure a cooperative, mutually beneficial society. The capacity to be fair-minded will always be constrained by the fairness of the practices we participate in. It is quite possible that fair-minded people may find themselves participating in unfair practices and so can still be said to be acting unfairly. Thus, to be completely fair it is important to understand what constitutes a fair practice. A fair practice is one with rules and procedures that are mutually advantageous, equitable, have some element of mutual consent, and for that reason can serve as a final court of appeal. Consider the condition of mutual consent. For something to be counted as fair, the rules which constitute the practice must be reasonably understood by the participants and agreed to in principle (cf. Rawls 1971: 133). To have some participate in a practice where the rules are not made explicit to them is blatantly unfair. The ordinary example is the contract with "fine print." When an attempt is made by the negotiator to hide or obscure certain conditions in the contract that may be unfavorable to the signees and lead them with the favorable explicit conditions into signing the contract, most would think this an unfair practice.

Second, to count something as fair, it must be of mutual advantage. Hardly anyone who is rational is willing to participate in a practice designed to disadvantage them or in a game they are destined to lose, unless for reasons of self-sacrifice. If a person joins a political organization that seeks to oppress people just like them, one would want to say that either the person has been duped or forced by that organization into participation or "their elevator just doesn't stop at certain floors." Disadvantages inherently assigned to certain participants must be only for the sake of "leveling the playing field." For example, if you're playing a game with someone who is light years ahead of you in terms of experience, knowledge, and ability, then a handicap might be a fair arrangement to make the game enjoyable and allow a partner some possibility of winning.

Third, the rules of the practice should be equitable; that is, the rules should be designed so that what happens to one happens to the other. Similar cases should be treated similarly (Rawls 1971: 237). If two people are working at the same job for the same employer, yet one is paid more than the other, this is clearly an inequity that makes the practice unfair. In ancient Roman law, a husband could have his wife put to death for adultery, but the wife could not do the same for an errant husband (cf. Boren 1992: 80). In some Islamic practices, there is a provision that allows a husband to divorce a wife by simply pronouncing "mutallaqa" ("divorced") three times; such an opportunity is not afforded the woman, though (cf. Bahadur 1898: 47). The ancient code of Hammurabi made clear distinctions between social classes and appropriate punishments. For example, if a lord destroyed the eye of another lord or a member of the aristocracy, then his eye was also destroyed. But if he destroyed the eye of a commoner, then he had to pay the commoner one mina of silver, and if he destroyed the eye of another's slave, then he had to pay half of the slave's price to the owner (Hammurabi 1792–1750 B.C.E.: 175). In this sense there is no special treatment or special rules that apply to subcategories of participants. Recent laws prescribing penalties for the use or distribution of crack cocaine are much more severe than for other forms of cocaine. Some critics of these laws argue that they are inherently unfair because they are biased toward upper- and middle-class white people, who are the predominant users of ordinary cocaine, and against African Americans, who are the predominant users of crack cocaine. Inequitable laws promote partiality (Rawls 1971: 187). Jim Crow laws were inherently unfair because they targeted the African-American population and imposed restrictions not made for other citizens.

Fourth, the rules should serve as a final court of appeal. There should be no secret rules or rules that can be dismissed as soon as they disadvantage someone (cf. Rawls 1971: 131–132). It is often the practice of tyrants to dismiss the results of an election if it should not go their way. It is clear, then, that their intent all along was simply to remain in power. If the election allowed that, then fine; if not, then they change the rules.

To illustrate these four conditions for fairness, one might take the simple example of playing a game. First, the game is mutually enjoyable, that is, not performed at the cost or expense of another; if the game was one in which one person was designated to be the object of harm, ridicule, or abuse, while all other players enjoyed exception from that, then the game wouldn't be considered fair, and the unlucky participant would undoubtedly have to be coerced into playing. The same could be said if the game was so designed that one of the participants couldn't possibly win. Second, the rules are general enough so that they do not distinguish among persons or types of persons; most board games, for example, generalize the rules so that they refer to a "player" as such, although they specify roles such as "opponent" but without reference to any particular person or class of person. Third, for the game to be considered fair, the rules must be universal in the sense that they apply to all players alike. Fourth, the rules are publicly displayed and acknowledged. Fifth, competing claims are resolved by an appeal to the rules, without any element of coercion. Sixth, the rules publicly acknowledged are the ultimate appeal in adjudication of claims or the ordering of the game.

Having made the distinction between fair-minded persons and fair practices, an account of justice is still needed. As mentioned earlier, justice is concerned with providing the underlying rules or precepts for practices that determine rights, obligations, rewards, and punishments for cooperative arrangements. Put simply, it should ensure that people get what they deserve and meet their obligations to others.

To illustrate the differences among justice, fairness, and fair-mindedness, consider a practice very familiar to most students—grading. The grade a student receives for a course is obviously very important to the student and to the teacher as well. Generally speaking, grading is a practice which involves some set of tests and assignment of the grade on the basis of the performance on those tests. In general, grading is a system of reward or benefit for doing well in the course, and consequently, it is a question of justice.

Starting with the basic conditions for fairness, a fair grading system would be one in which there is, first, advantage to the participants. A good grade, for example, contributes to the student's ability to meet requirements for a degree, which has all sorts of personal benefits, from economic to psychological. Conversely, grades assure standards of performance in a particular profession, which in turn assures us, for example, that when she builds a bridge, an engineer knows what she is doing or, when his patient is on the operating table, a doctor will not kill him. Second, to be fair the rules for the grading practice must be publicly explicit and accessible; the students must be made aware of them and implicitly or explicitly consent to the procedures and standards (usually this is acknowledged by the students willing participation in the course). Third, the rules for the practice must be equitable so that whatever standards apply, they apply to all, and there are no inherent biases or favoritism built in.

Assuming the fairness of the practice, it is quite possible for students or teachers to act unfairly in their respective roles in that practice. For example, students can cheat. In other words, rather than getting the benefit of the practice (the grade) by performing well on the tests (i.e., working hard to know the material), they find a way to copy another's work. In this way they also act like free-riders, since they get the benefit of the practice by hanging onto the backs of those who work hard at it. Teachers can also act unfairly by assigning undeserved grades to people they like, while not giving a break to people just shy of a higher grade because they dislike them. They can show more partiality to men rather than women, or vice versa, in the classroom.

The justice of the grading practice, on the other hand, concerns the underlying precepts or principles of the practice. Since grading is a reward or benefit for good performance, how should that benefit be assigned? For example, consider the following three precepts of grading:

1. Grades should be assigned on the basis of individual merit. A person should be assigned a grade on the basis of his or her performance on specified tests in comparison to an independent standard. For example, if a student answers 90 percent or more of the questions on an exam correctly, then he should be assigned an A.

2. Grades should be assigned to an individual on the basis of the performance of the group to which that individual belongs. A person should be assigned a grade on the basis of how the group as a whole performs on a test. For example, if the class average for a particular exam is 90 percent or more, then each student in the class will be assigned an A.

3. Grades should be assigned in rank order on the basis of a finite set of slots for each grade level. For example, only 10 percent of the grades in a class of thirty will be As. Thus, the top three students will receive an A, the next six a B, the next twelve a C, the next six a D, and the last three an F.

Most students might find the second and third set of rules alien and blatantly unjust, but perhaps mostly because they're used to the first rule. But think of the differences between these three precepts and how they will affect the tenor of the class and what sorts of behaviors they might promote among students who have a certain level of self-interest and regard for others.

In the first case each student, independently of another and under ideal conditions, will strive for the best grade she can get. All the student has to do is meet the objective criteria set by the teacher, achieve a certain point score, and she will be assigned the grade she deserves accordingly. In this case the student does not compete with other students directly and, for that reason, has no incentive not to cooperate with other students in the class in getting a good grade. On the other hand, because each student can achieve a grade independently of other students, there is no incentive to cooperate with other students. In other words, if a student is especially good in a class, he will have no motive to share that expertise or skill with others, unless he is willing to do this for altruistic reasons. In that case the expert student is being asked to devote more time and energy to a subject he's mastered, which could take away from study time for subjects he hasn't quite mastered. Students who are not as competent in the subject matter might pool their resources, study together, and thereby improve their grades more so than if they tackled the subject independently. They would also benefit from participation in the study group by expert students—but as already mentioned, this would be an altruistic act. Students who are doing poorly, on the other hand, would certainly benefit from participating in the study groups of more competent students; they might also benefit greatly by help from the expert students. However, because they are having a more difficult time understanding the material, there may be less motivation for these groups or individuals to help them since the time and energy it would take to bring them up to par might be too much of a sacrifice, given their own time and needs. Thus, students doing poorly in the class would have to appeal to the instructor for extra help, hire a tutor, or simply rely on the altruism of other students. In general, then, this arrangement would benefit the most talented in the class and would not especially advantage or disadvantage the less talented, but it could be seen as having the least benefit for the least talented in the group. But to the extent that the purpose of the practice is an evaluative one—to sort out the more qualified from the less qualified—this might be seen as a perfectly just arrangement. In that framework the practice might want to reward the most talented since one of the purposes of education at the university level is to generate competent and skilled people in their particular field of study.

In the second precept the grade each student receives depends on the performance of the group as a whole. In this case the most talented in the classroom would still be motivated to do their best and also be more motivated to help the less talented in the classroom. There would also be more pressure on the least talented to do their best, and there would most likely be a spontaneous policing of slackers and so forth. The least talented in the group might even be pressured by other students to drop the class. In general, in this arrangement the people who benefit the most would be the less talented. For example, if by means of studying on their own. they would receive a D or F for the class, then since C is the average grade, let's say, their grade will be better under this arrangement than the first one. The least advantaged in this group, then, would be the most talented since their grades are more likely to be lower than in the first arrangement—this despite the fact that they performed better on the exam than most others in the class. In addition, precisely because of their talent, there would be more demand on their time and energy to help improve the overall average of the class.

From this perspective, these sets of rules may be considered unjust precisely because they do not give people in this context what they are due. Still it could be argued that, depending on the purposes of the practices being graded, this might be a perfectly just arrangement. For example, if the goal of the practice is to promote team effort, such a grading system might be perfectly appropriate and just. In a team there will be different levels of talent and ability, yet only a team can do the job. Consequently, what an instructor or coach would want to strive for is maximizing the collective or cooperative talent of the group rather than looking for the most talented within that group. Military instructors, for example, stress this sort of evaluation; what they want is for the unit to perform well, not for individual members to excel. Similarly with sports teams, although some members may be more talented than others, the team cooperates as a whole, drawing on various talents to create the greatest score for the team as a unit. The purpose is not to maximize the scoring of individual members of the team, but to maximize the score for the team (which may involve giving the better scorer more opportunity to score). In this case the most talented member works for the team rather than just herself.

In the third precept students would not be motivated to cooperate with other students, since they are competing for a few slots within a certain category. Each person you help to improve his grade means less chance for you to get the same grade. The exceptional students would prevail in this arrangement. The least talented students would not be either especially advantaged or disadvantaged since the percentage of grades they would make in the first arrangement, for example, would be roughly the same as this one. In other words, the real competition is for the As and Bs. The least advantaged in this group, then, would be students of moderate and strong talent. In the first arrangement, for example, for students to get an A they would only need to get 90 percent of the answers correct. But in this arrangement one might need to know 98 percent or 99 percent of the answers to receive the A. These are percentages usually reserved for exceptional students. Again, some may consider this to be blatantly unjust, yet it might be considered perfectly just for certain sorts of practices. For example, in the case of sports, tryouts for the Olympics are based on this model. There are a few slots, let's say, for the marathon, and the purpose of the evaluation is to find the three most talented athletes for the purposes of competing with the best of the best from other groups. Because the practice demands the best, then a grading system which favors the best would seem appropriately just.

Given this example of justice, it would be convenient to look at some of its more general parameters. As mentioned, the justice of cooperative arrangements is typically concerned with three areas: (1) people's rights and duties, (2) the benefits and recognition they are due, and (3) the punishment people can expect if there is violation of the conditions of the arrangement.

Rights can be thought of as the most fundamental guarantees of regard from others in the community. (For more on the notion of rights, see Sections 5.5.3 and 5.5.4.) They are entitlements to protection from others and participation in the cooperative arrangement. For example, the most fundamental rights guaranteed by the American Constitution are the right to life, that is, a guarantee that another person or the state cannot take someone's life, unless she violates the right of another in that regard; liberty, or the right of self-determination and consent to laws which would restrict that self-determination; and the pursuit of happiness, that is, the right to set a course of life that will attain what people believe to be of greatest benefit to them. Duties are those fundamental activities which are expected of a person as a contributor to this collective arrangement. As an American citizen, there is a duty to vote, to contribute to the defense of the country, to pay taxes, to sit on juries, and so on.

Second, principles of justice are concerned with the fair distribution of goods and benefits in the collective arrangement. This is traditionally called distributive justice. Distributive justice can range over a number of different goods, both economic and social. The example of grading just discussed is an illustration of distributive justice. There are different common-sense precepts which attempt to satisfy these questions (cf. Rawls 1971: 303–310). Aristotle argued that these questions should be articulated in terms of equality, balance, and proportion, but although

Aristotle is perhaps correct in identifying questions of justice in those terms, the issue of what is to be balanced or proportioned varies greatly. Proportion, as understood by Aristotle, is a proportion between merit and benefit, although what counts as meritorious will vary (*Nic. Ethics* 1131a25ff.). Under a democracy it would be simply the status of a "freeman"; under an oligarchy, wealth or noble birth; under an aristocracy, excellence (*Nic. Ethics* 1131a28). As articulated by Aristotle, distributive justice supposes an inequality between persons based on differences in merit, and the proportion is a geometric ratio between merit and benefit; that is, P_1 is to B_1 as P_2 is to B_2, where P is a person and B is the particular benefit or reward (*Nic. Ethics* 1131bff.). Thus, if oligarchy is the measure of merit, then the wealthy in a particular cooperative arrangement should expect the greatest benefit from that arrangement, and the poor should expect the least. If it is in terms of birth classes, then the higher-status classes (e.g., Brahmins) should receive more benefit from the social arrangement than the lower-birth classes (e.g., the untouchables). If it is in terms of an aristocracy (in Aristotle's sense of "the most excellent"), then those of moral or other forms of excellence should receive the greatest benefit from the social arrangement. If it is in terms of democracy, then simply the status as a person (or freeman in Aristotle's sense) merits benefit. Clearly, then, what is needed in this case is an account of which concept of merit is justified.

But besides the precept "each according to merit," other precepts are offered as the best account of distributive justice; for example, "each according to contribution." However, contribution can be understood in different ways, such as the amount of effort or the actual contribution. The distinction means a difference in benefit for those who have worked hard to contribute but have not succeeded in contributing much as opposed to those who have actually contributed much regardless of the effort involved.

For example, consider the issue of fair wages. Assuming a market system something like the capitalist one (and setting aside issues of justice in political economy), many precepts are involved in determining fair wage: "each according to skill," "each according to training," "each according to experience," "each according to education," and so on. The difference between a physician's wages and a janitor's wages might be justified as, first, a difference in the amount of talent and ability involved; second, a difference in the amount of training and education required to perform the job; third, a difference in terms of the particular good the occupation contributes to the collective good or the good of others; fourth, a difference in the amount of effort (i.e., time and energy devoted to the occupation). Since the physician is required to have many years of training, education, and a certain talent and ability, fewer people could meet the requirements for being a physician, and more could qualify for the position of janitor; and since health is considered an important good, and the amount of time and energy devoted to the occupation is considerable, then the difference in wages could reasonably be considered justifiable. On the other hand, if one assumes that talent and ability are not deserved, in the sense that they are simply accidents of birth, and if it is assumed that training and education are themselves opportunities provided by a collective effort, including janitors' efforts, then one could reasonably argue that the significant difference between the salary of the physician and that of the janitor is unwarranted. Under this framework all occupations contribute to a collective good achieved by the harmonious productivity of its members, and therefore, the collective pie need not be sliced up in terms of individual contribution. An arrangement guided by the Marxist precept, "from each according to ability, to each according to need," could justify that account.

Consider the issue of fair taxation as another example. Should citizens be taxed at a flat rate, that is, a certain percentage of one's income no matter what the income? This might be justified by the precept each according to his or her ability. Or should the wealthy be taxed at a higher rate than the middle class or lower-income groups based on the precept that those who benefit the most from a collective arrangement ought to contribute the most to it?

The third concern of principles of justice is in the area of rectification of wrongs, or what might be called *corrective* or *retributive* justice (cf. *Nic. Ethics* 1121b25ff.). Corrective justice is traditionally subdivided into criminal and civil concerns. Criminal justice is concerned with establishing principles and rules for just punishments if the rules of the collective arrangement are transgressed while civil punishment is concerned with rectification and compensation to the victim of a wrong. For example, O.J. Simpson had both sorts of trials; he was first tried for criminal behavior and then for civil wrongs. Assuming an element of fairness to the arrangement (in terms of equity and impartiality), then the classical precept concerning criminal justice is "the punishment should be in proportion to the crime." More traditional precepts, expressed by the *lex talionis*, prescribe a stronger, more literal sense of equality: A tooth for a tooth suggests that the punishment of the transgressor ought to be the same as the crime perpetrated against the victim. Thus, if one per-

> The Federal Sentencing Guidelines were the result of the Sentencing Reform Act passed in 1984 by Congress. It accords punishment to a defendant found guilty of a crime on the basis of the following criteria: the seriousness of the offense, to what degree the guilty party was a participant in the offense, whether the victim was especially vulnerable, whether the offender obstructed justice, how many offenses were committed, whether the offender accepted responsibility, and the offender's criminal history.

son has killed another, then that person in turn ought to be killed; if one has beaten another, then he too should be beaten and so forth. In the case of compensation to the victim, the sense of it, especially as expressed by Aristotle, is that the perpetrator should be made to restore to the victim that which was unfairly taken, leading to the restoration of balance between the two. In general, the sense of corrective justice is that if one has unjustly gained at another's expense, then the balance ought to be restored. In the case of corrective justice, the same sort of simplified scheme is expressed by the idea that the punishment received for a transgression should be in proportion to the seriousness of the transgression. As Aristotle suggests, in corrective justice everyone is treated equally no matter what status they have or what contribution they make to the group, whereas in distributive justice persons are unequal due to the quality and degree of their contribution, but equality is expressed in terms of the proportion between contribution and benefit.

But of course, these simplified schemata encounter all sorts of complications in context. For example, in family life it seems that the rule "to each according to need, from each according to ability" is more appropriate, so that young children, who contribute little to the economic means of the family, nonetheless receive a disproportionate benefit. There are some goods in a cooperative arrangement that are shared equally despite differences in contributions; for example, persons pay differing amounts of taxes, but all receive the same general quantum of military protection, or use of the highways, etc. Justice, for these reasons, is a very complicated matter. A fair-minded person is concerned with these particular questions in the context of a certain cooperative arrangement: What sort of rights do participants have? What sort of duties are they expected to perform? What are the principles for the distribution of rewards and benefits? What are the principles and rules for the rectification of wrongs?

3.5.2 Tolerance

An artist who called himself Dred Scott (after the famous legal decision) created a piece of work that was very simple in design. A podium was placed against a wall and on top of the podium there was a book in which viewers were instructed to write their comments about the piece. However, to get to the podium they had to walk across an American flag that was strategically placed on the floor in front of the podium. In several places where the work was exhibited, there were vocal protests from citizens and veterans' groups. In some cases local veterans would walk into the exhibition and take the flag for the purpose of treating it reverently. Should Scott's work be tolerated and allowed to be displayed unhampered?

Ku Klux Klan officials apply for a parade permit to demonstrate in your town. Jews and African Americans protest the demonstration vigorously. Should the KKK be allowed to demonstrate?

Students in a local high school form a Gay Students' Club promoting acceptance and tolerance of gay lifestyles. Many parents and religious groups protest the existence of the club; they threaten to recall the school board members unless the club is banned. Should the club be allowed to operate?

Peter Melzer openly admits to the fact that he is sexually attracted to boys under 16 and is a longtime member and leader of the North American Man/Boy Love Association. He has worked to raise money, has written articles, and worked for the repeal of laws that forbid sexual relationships between men and boys. Melzer is also a physics teacher at the Bronx High School of Science. The New York City board of education has said that Melzer, because of his beliefs, is disruptive, dangerous, and immoral, and they want to fire him. In his defense Melzer has argued that all his activities have been solely intellectual, and he has never had sexual relations with any of his students, nor has he ever been accused of it. Should his views be tolerated and should he be allowed to keep his job?

Tolerance is the willingness to allow others to lead a life based on a certain set of beliefs contrary to one's own. This is based on the view that there is a wide range of beliefs which, although contrary to one another, either complement or at least do not cause significant harm to others. Peter Nicholson (1985: 235) defines it in the following way: "toleration is the virtue of refraining from exercising one's power with regard to others' opinion or action although that deviates from one's own over something important, and although one morally disapproves of it."

The central issue in tolerance is its limits. What sort of things should one tolerate? One of the simplest criteria for tolerance was devised by 19th-century philosopher John Stuart Mill in his book *On Liberty:* tolerate any behavior so long as it does not cause harm to people other than those who practice it (1859: I, 9, IV, V). One difficulty with this criterion is determining whether a practice is harmful, what sort of harm it creates, and how much harm should be permitted. For example, an argument could be made for the toleration of homosexuality by heterosexuals and, in the case given earlier, for the toleration of the Gay Students' Club because the harm, if any, of its practice is incurred mostly by the participants, assuming that their homosexual acts are consensual. However, many of those opposed to homosexuality on religious grounds argue, first, that since it is "abomination against God" (Leviticus 18:22; 20:13), it should be morally condemned regardless of who is or is not harmed, but second, in fact, society as a collective whole is affected by homosexuality in terms of its alleged harm to the institution of marriage and the family.

Indeed, this sort of debate concerning homosexuality was made by Lord Patrick Devlin (1965) and H.L.A. Hart (1959) in England in the 1960s (cf. Warnock 1987: 127ff.). Devlin argued that since there was a consensus of hostile feeling toward homosexual practices, the law must therefore enforce such feelings and both morally and legally condemn the practice. In general, certain practices should not be tolerated by the state if they are intolerable to the majority or to the common morality. Otherwise, state tolerance of morally intolerable acts would threaten the moral fiber that holds a society together. Hart responded in a number of ways, but the crux of the argument is as follows: If the harm that is incurred by forcefully forbidding that which is intolerable by the majority outweighs the harm of tolerating the practice, then the practice should be tolerated. In the case of legally repressing homosexuality, the prosecution would require, for example, the violation of privacy and other related individual rights since homosexuality includes, after all, sexual acts between consenting adults; sanctioning such actions by the state would create greater harm to the collectivity than acts of homosexuality which mainly affect the individuals involved. Allowing no limit to the power of the majority also involves a further degradation of state power, and legal persecution of homosexuality could easily engender that step. If translated to the question of religious tolerance, the history of persecution and pogrom speaks volumes about the ill effects of socially sanctioned intolerance.

The distinction between tolerance of practices and tolerance of beliefs complicates this issue. Karl Popper suggests a rather broad criterion in this matter: All beliefs should be tolerated including those which do not tolerate beliefs other than their own, unless those beliefs or acting on those beliefs lead to violence. "As long as these intolerant minorities discuss and publish their theories as rational proposals, we should let them do so freely. But we should draw their attention

---

Karl Popper (b. 1902) is an Austrian-American philosopher best known for his work on the philosophy of science. His most important political work is *The Open Society and Its Enemies.*

---

to the fact that toleration can only exist on a basis of mutuality, and that our duty to tolerate a minority ends when the minority begins to act violently" (1987: 19). In other words, we should tolerate much more intellectually than we should concerning actual practices. The justification for this position rests on the idea that rational discourse is not inherently violent, and it can lead to consensus and resolve questions of truth in a manner much better than action might achieve. Whereas discourse may persuade rationally, actions may involve force and coercion. Furthermore, not to tolerate a wide diversity of beliefs threatens the fabric of a democratic culture and so would do more harm than good (1987: 18–19).

The case of Peter Melzer cited earlier tests the limit of this criterion expressed by Popper. Applying Popper's criterion to this case, as long as Melzer has not acted on his beliefs, especially in the context of his own students—that being an act of violence perpetrated against an underage boy—then his beliefs should be tolerated and allowed to enter into the intellectual marketplace. There is more difficulty in addressing the issue of whether his peaceful attempts to change legislation should be tolerated. To the extent that he is employing means available to anyone interested in affecting legislation, then another argument could be made for tolerating that activity. But the real issue is whether he should be tolerated in the classroom. Assuming that he has not sexually abused his children (and there was no evidence that he had), then the argument could be made that, given his inclination, he is a threat to the security of the children in the school.

Another issue is tolerance of the intolerant. Should we tolerate the KKK, which is intolerant of African Americans, Jews, and other ethnic minorities? John Rawls makes it clear that the intolerant have no title to complain if they are not tolerated, since people's rights to complain are limited to violations of principles they themselves acknowledge (Rawls 1971: 217). Still that does not infer that the liberty of the intolerant person or sect should necessarily be suppressed. For example, one might grow intolerant of persons or sects if they pose a genuine threat to one's security. Intolerance out of self-defense is not grounds for the restriction of one's own liberty (1971: 218). It can be inferred, then, that the restriction of the liberty of the intolerant should happen only in the case where the tolerant sincerely and with reason believe that their own security is in danger (1971: 220). Under this argument only those activities of the KKK which threaten the security or involve intimidation or coercion of the persons or groups who are the target of their particular ideologies should be suppressed. Without the possibility of threat, coercion, and intimidation, the beliefs of the intolerant groups simply become one set among others in the marketplace of ideas; their appeal will stand or fall on their intellectual, moral, or political merit alone. The merit of this arrangement is that it allows intolerant groups the possibility of seeing a reasoned and public reaction to the quality of their beliefs and, ideally, why they have no merit. Second, the experience by the intolerant of being tolerated may allow them to recognize the value of those arrangements that do tolerate them; consequently, there is the good possibility that the intolerant may accept the necessity of tolerance (1971: 219). Thus, we might justify allowing the KKK to demonstrate peacefully or otherwise exercise freedom of speech, if only because it would subject their views to public ridicule and criticism. Should their activities in this regard be suppressed, then there is little opportunity that they should be persuaded differently toward their views. The suppression or coercion of their views would not in and of itself be persuasive but might, in fact, harden them to their defense.

3.5.3 Truthfulness and Honesty

In the film *Shiloh* (1997), a young boy is faced with a moral dilemma. A puppy that has befriended him is seriously abused by a neighbor in this rural community that values privacy and property. The puppy's owner is a hunter who makes his living by trading game meat to a local butcher and processor. The boy's father, Ray, who is an honest and forthright man—and strongly patriarchal—demands the same sort of character traits in his family, and especially in his son. When the puppy is first found, his father insists on returning it to its rightful owner despite obvious signs of abuse. When the owner threatens to shoot the dog should he run off again, the boy decides to hide the puppy when it returns to him once more. He hides the puppy in a shed near his house. To continue this, he must engage in a certain amount of deception: He doesn't tell his father or his family that he has the puppy. To feed the puppy, he must pretend that he's not hungry at the table and later take the food to the dog. He tells his mother that he's going for a walk when in fact he's going to play with the dog. And when the owner comes to his house asking if anybody has seen the dog or knows of its whereabouts, he lies directly to the man. For the sake of protecting the puppy, the young boy engages in lying, deception, nondisclosure, dishonesty, and pretense.

Truthfulness is telling someone what you believe to be true in the context of a direct query; lying is a denial of what one believes to be true in response to a direct query. As Sallust said, lying is "when what the tongue utters is different from what is in the heart" (*War with Cataline* 10.5). *Nondisclosure* is when one chooses not to inform someone of information that could have a significant harm or benefit for her. *Deception* is planned lying and so has a more strategic character to it; it is a deliberate plan to fool someone into thinking one way rather than another. As Bok suggests, deceit is like force in that it can coerce people into acting against their will, but deceit controls more subtly than force, and those who cannot be subdued by force can often be overcome by deceit (1979: 19). *Dishonesty* involves a secret violation of the rules of a practice which a person participates in and agrees to.

Truthfulness can be thought of as fairness in regard to information: It is giving others what is their due, specifically in regard to information that can help or harm them. Lying, nondisclosure, and misleading people about information that could help them, or whose absence harms them, are forms of injustice, as Dante suggests (*Div. Com.: Inferno:* Canto 11). This is repeated by Montaigne: "Since mutual understanding is brought about solely by way of words, he who breaks his word betrays human society" (1572–1588: 287). This sense of it is expressed nicely by Sissela Bok: "To the extent that knowledge gives power, to that extent lies affect the distribution of power" (1979: 20). "All our choices," as Sissela Bok notes, "depend on our estimates of what is the case; these estimates must in turn often rely on information from others. Lies distort this information and therefore our situation as we perceive it, as well as our choices" (1979: 20). Nicholai Hartmann puts it more simply: A lie "injures the deceived person in his life; it leads him astray" (cf. Bok 1979: 20).

"You may [see] exaggeration [in advertising]. The law says that legitimate puffery is an acceptable characteristic of advertising. But there's a big gap between legitimate puffery and false claims."

"People think you can't lie in political advertising. And you can. You can lie with impunity. ... [Political advertising] is not limited in the way in which product advertising is ... yet they use the format and trappings of product advertising to make people think this is subject to the same restrictions that product advertising is."

—John O'Toole, President of the American Association of Advertising Agencies (quoted in Melzer 1992)

People usually want nothing to do with known or habitual liars. When lies and dishonesty are exposed, the liar becomes an object of distrust and scorn: "The deceit is regarded as treason, and the deceiver as a traitor, which is even worse," so Gracian argues. The deceived definitely feel wronged; they feel resentful, disappointed, and suspicious, especially if the liar stands in a special relation. Once a person has lied, then there is an uncertainty about whether they can be trusted to speak the truth again (Bok 1979: 24). It is much easier to maintain one's reputation for honesty than it is to regain it once it has been lost; as Gracian suggests, "A single lie destroys a whole reputation for integrity" (1637: par. 181). Liars are in a sense "free-riders": They do not

---

Balthasar Gracian was a 17th-century Spanish monk. His most famous book is *The Art of Worldly Wisdom.*

---

desire to be deceived, yet they feel they may do so. Deception works only in the background of mostly honest and trusting people. Once you are interacting with a group of dishonest persons, then deception is much more difficult; it is much

Is It Better to Lie or to Be Blunt?

To get around this dilemma, Robert Thornton, a Professor of Economics at Lehigh University in Pennsylvania, created a number of ambiguous phrases that could be used to convey double meanings in letters of recommendation. He calls his collection "The Lexicon of Inconspicuously Ambiguous Recommendations," or LIAR for short. Thornton pointed out that LIAR is not only useful in preserving friendships, but it can also help avoid serious legal trouble in a time when laws have eroded the confidentiality of letters of recommendation. Here are some of his examples:

1. To describe a person who is totally inept: I most enthusiastically recommend this candidate with no qualifications whatsoever.

2. To describe an ex-employee who had problems getting along with fellow workers: I am pleased to say that this candidate is a former colleague of mine.

3. To describe a candidate who is so unproductive that the job would be better left unfilled: I can assure you that no person would be better for the job.

4. To describe a job applicant who is not worth further consideration: I would urge you to waste no time in making this candidate an offer of employment.

5. To describe a person with lackluster credentials: All in all, I cannot say enough good things about this candidate or recommend him too highly.

---

easier to deceive unsuspecting people. Given that background, one can "get ahead" by lying and deceiving others simply because one can withhold information vital to another's interests and plans and still be relatively assured that others will be fair and supply you with the information necessary for your own goals and interests. Honesty relies heavily on a sense of fairness and the belief that others are due correct information so that they can fulfill their plans and interests. Honesty is not entirely in regard to others but of mutual benefit: An honest society benefits all its members.

Lies certainly harm the deceived, but many argue that dishonesty also harms the liar. Lies affect integrity, and so knowing that one is a liar reduces self-respect and, if exposed, loses the trust of others. "Lying," as Kant says, "is the ... obliteration of one's dignity as a human being." Kant suggests that lying makes one even less than a mere thing, since at least a thing can be useful to someone (1797: 91). Another consequence of lying is that often other lies must be told to support the first lie; lying leads to a web of lies and a pretense that may have to be supported for years. The problem is that it is often difficult to maintain this web of lies. It takes a great deal of caution about what one says; it is easy to remember the truth, but difficult to recall a lie. Eventually, lies are exposed, and if they are maintained for a long time, then the harm is greater than if they had been admitted to earlier on, and the way in which others regard you changes drastically. The danger of lying is that, as one begins to lie, lying becomes more habitual so that liars become more prone to create situations in which much of their life is tangled in such webs (cf. Bok 1979: 27). Another danger is that

Gerald Plecki was a teacher at a Chicago area high school that desperately wanted his team of students to win the school district's academic decathlon. The school was an underdog in the area and from a more economically disadvantaged and academically disreputable part of the district. Whitley High, an upper-class public school in the "good" part of town, was the 10-year reigning champs. Copies of the exam had been stolen by one of the students on the decathlon team. When Plecki found out, rather than returning the exam, he encouraged students to study it. He believed strongly that they deserved to win. He rationalized the cheating by believing that beating the ten-year reigning champions would give more fairness to the competition. However, when the underdogs won big—suspiciously big—there was an investigation, and the cheating was discovered.

Questions for Discussion

1. Even if the cheating had not been discovered, how do you think the team would have eventually felt about itself?
2. How does it feel to win when you don't deserve to win?

Case Study: Should She Tell the Guy She's Dating That She Has an STD?

Suppose a friend of yours comes to you for advice. She's seeing a man that she really likes; she thinks that they could go on to have a serious relationship. But she's afraid to tell him that she has herpes (genital herpes is presently an incurable STD that causes periodic sores in the genital region; a person is thought to be infectious only when the sores are present). You know that she got herpes from a former fiancé who didn't tell her about his disease.

After that she lost her feelings for him and couldn't trust him anymore. When she started dating again, she told her boyfriend about her herpes. He broke up with her almost immediately. She's afraid that the same thing will happen this time with a man she considers wonderful. She tells you that if she acts carefully, she thinks the guy doesn't have to know about the problem.

What's your advice?

---

liars who exhibit patterns of lying may often be self-deceived as well, literally beginning to believe their own lies.

Honesty is deliberate adherence to the rules of procedure of a practice or contract, and so it is strongly allied with fair-mindedness. *Cheating* is pretense of abiding by a set of rules which a person has implicitly or explicitly agreed to follow, but who in fact secretly violates those rules to gain some personal advantage. A cheater seeks the benefits a practice affords without using the same procedural rules that most others are using, and so it is inherently unfair. Cheaters have an advantage that others do not have to get those same benefits, and those who aid cheaters—even when they are friends—are foolish because they are promoting their own disadvantage. For example, most students will spend time and energy preparing for an exam. Usually they will get a grade that corresponds to that time, effort, and whatever talents they may have. Students who cheat get a grade based on their ability to bypass normal rules for taking a test. They're getting a grade on the basis of a different procedure than the one publicly announced and implicitly agreed to by the students.

Stealing is also a blatant form of unfairness since it involves the violation of the normal or implicit rules pertaining to property relations. The thief must gain possession or access to the property without the owner's knowledge or consent. The thief is in possession of property that was purchased by the owner, and so the owner is in effect involuntarily paying for something that benefits another in addition to whatever insult and invasion have occurred from the theft.

Rutgers professor, Donald McCabe, surveying more than 6000 students in thirty-one colleges and universities around the nation during 1990–1991, found the following percentage of confessed cheaters (on exams or other major assignments) by intended specialties:

law schools: 63%
arts programs: 64%
public service: 66%
medical schools: 68%
engineering programs: 71%
graduate schools of business: 76%
(cf. Kidder 1995: 49–50)

In another piece of news, the Educational Testing Service, in Princeton, N.J.—a service that administers SATs and various standardized tests for teachers—revealed a major cheating scandal in Louisiana, a state which is near the bottom of almost every educational ranking. Apparently, copies of a test for teachers who want to be school principals was circulated among test-takers—perhaps for years.

Poor but Honest?

Among the college students surveyed by Donald McCabe of Rutgers, he found that 50 percent more were likely to be regular cheaters if they came from families who made more than $150,000, than if they came from families whose parents earned less than $25,000 (cf. Kidder 1995: 54).

Promise making is a combination of truthfulness and honesty. In making a promise, people first claim that they will do something they say they will do. Second, they must be sincere in the sense that they intend to do what they say they will do. Third, they must be honest in the sense that they will abide by the rules of promise making without secretly violating them for personal gain.

Is It Okay to Steal from Large Businesses and Corporations?

The Rev. John Papworth, an Anglican priest, suggested on a London BBC radio program in 1997 that it was no sin to shoplift as long as the victim is a big supermarket. Papworth drew a distinction between stealing from individuals or small merchants and stealing from giant retailing corporations. Those, he says, have run little stores out of business and harmed local communities: "With these institutions, all you are confronted with are these boardroom barons sitting round the boardroom plotting how to take the maximum amount of money out of people's pockets for the minimum in return" (Anchorage Daily News Wire Services, March 15, 1997).

Assuming that an institution is exploitative, does that justify stealing from it?

Is Some Kind of Lying Acceptable?

Leonard Saxe, PhD, a polygraph expert and professor of psychology at Brandeis University claims that "lying has long been a part of everyday life. We couldn't get through the day without being deceptive" (Kornet 1997). Bella De Paulo of the University of Virginia claims that "everyday lies are really part of the fabric of social life" (Kornet 1997). While some lies damage relationships and destroy trust, she found that most lies are meant to help the liar protect someone else's feelings, preserve one's own self-esteem, or maintain one's privacy. People lie an average of twice a day. She also found that 10 percent of lies are usually exaggerations, whereas 60 percent are outright lies. More than 70 percent of liars would tell their lies again. *Do you agree with these researchers who claim that lying can have positive social functions?*

Honesty, or at least a preponderance of honesty, is essential to any cooperative arrangement. Any society can scarcely do without honesty (Bok 1979: 19). As Samuel Johnson said, even the devils do not lie to one another, since the society of hell could not subsist without truth any more than others (cf. Bok 1979: 19). We could also quote Montaigne on this matter: "If [dishonesty] deceives us, it breaks up all our relations and dissolves all the bonds of our society" (1670–1688: 287). A complete lack of honesty among a group of people would lead to a complete breakdown of trust and with it any cooperative effort; honesty is therefore essential for trust. One would not know whether any information offered was true or false; relying on one's own discernment would be tedious and in some cases impossible. Since most of our knowledge, information, and beliefs are based on information supplied by others, honesty is the paramount virtue of all research, scholarship, and any practice involved in the public conveyance of information.

Other Types of Lying

Duplicity is when you must appear one way to a certain person but a different way to another person.

Insincerity is the false or pretended advocacy of a political, religious, or other wide-ranging belief.

Libel is defamation by writing, the telling of lies meant specifically to harm the reputation of a person; this should be distinguished from *slander*, which is defamation by saying.

Hypocrisy is an amalgam of insincerity and duplicity. Hypocrites must subscribe publicly to one view but must admit to themselves that they do not really advocate such a view. In public life they must speak and act in one way, yet in private life another way. Montaigne says of it that "of all vices, I know none that testifies to so much cowardice and baseness of heart. It is a craven and servile idea to disguise ourselves and hide under a mask, and not to dare to show ourselves as we are" (1670–1688: 269).

Dupery is tricking someone or being deceptive with someone who is especially gullible, vulnerable, or innocent, and so it is even more cowardly than duplicity. These are people who take advantage of the very young, the very old, or those new to a practice or organization.

Other Types of Lying, *Continued*

Exaggeration is enhancement or distortion of information for effect. If the intention is primarily to entertain, then many find little harm in such exaggeration; however, if exaggeration is in the context of boastfulness, then certainly it can be counted as a lie, although it still retains an element of truth.

Pretense should be distinguished from lying and deception; pretense is offering information which one really doesn't have or one is not certain of. Often those engaged in pretense offer advice and information for the sake of appearances, of seeming more knowledgeable, wise, skilled, or informed than they really are. It is not, strictly speaking, lying, since lying requires that one believes or knows the information to be true, but pretense is when the person does not know if the information is true or not.

Is There a Vice of Being Too Truthful?

Bluntness is the tendency to tell the truth even when it is harmful or hurtful, and it could be argued that it is done precisely for that reason; if that is so, bluntness can be considered an act of cruelty and disrespect for the feelings of others. As Gracian says, "nothing demands more caution than the truth—it is the lancet of the heart" (1637: par. 181). Great skill is needed in telling the truth; often, as Gracian suggests, "the most expert doctors of the soul pay great attention to the means of sweetening the pill of truth. For when it deals with the destroying of illusion it is the quintessence of bitterness" (1637: par. 210). Being truthful without being blunt is *tact*.

The Many Ways of Self-Deception

Self-deception is a form of dishonesty with yourself. Joan Didion suggests that it remains the most difficult of deceptions because the tricks that work on others count for nothing "in that very well-lit back alley where one keeps assignations with oneself: no winning smiles will do here, no prettily drawn lists of good intentions" (1968). Self-deception is a significant failing since it violates the dictum "know thyself" (cf. Butler 1726), a prerequisite for prudent deliberation. If you deceive yourself about your character or other matters, it is likely to lead to imprudent action. Being brutally honest with yourself saves you from foolish actions or endeavors, but also protects you from those who might prey on the vanity or arrogance that might follow from self-deceit. As Bishop Butler notes, self-deception may lead to self-partiality, that is, "they think, and reason, and judge quite differently upon any matter relating to themselves, from what they do in cases of others where they are not interested" (Butler 1726). As a result, self-deception can be a source of unfairness in this regard, since it leads to a feeling that certain rules or cases do not apply to oneself.

Self-deception takes either the form of magnification, aggrandizement, or its contrary, diminution. *Magnification* allows one to inflate the importance of one's actions; *diminution* deflates their importance. Magnification often leads to vanity and arrogance because it has a tendency to make more out of our actions or accomplishments than is warranted, whereas diminution has a tendency to make less out of our failings. Both evaluations lead to unfairness. The first suggests that one is owed more than what is proper and is a violation of distributive justice. The second suggests that one should be blamed less or punished less than what is warranted, is a violation of retributive justice, and also reduces accountability. Diminution is accomplished by *rationalization*, which takes on many forms. *Inversion* allows one to rationalize actions as good when they are really bad ("I did him a service by hitting him; now he's more aware of his failings"). *Projection* occurs when the fault is cast on the victim ("He deserved to be hit"). *Blaming* is an attempt to shift responsibility for the action to another ("It wasn't really my fault; the crowd prodded me on"). *Excuse* attempts to justify the action by showing how one could not help it ("I was in a terrible mood to begin with, and he said something that sent me into a fury"). *Comparison* is a means of justifying the behavior by showing that it is not as bad as other similar sorts of actions ("At least I didn't beat him to a bloody pulp like that guy in the fight last week"). *Conventionalization* allows one to rationalize the behavior by showing how it is standard or usual behavior ("Everybody gets into a fight at least once in their lives").

3.6 THE VIRTUES OF RESPECT

On a Friday night in September 1996, Roberto Alomar, all-star second baseman of the Baltimore Orioles, had a confrontation with umpire John Hirschbeck. That in itself is not unusual—in fact, such confrontations are quite common in baseball. But then Alomar went beyond the usual yelling and cursing and, in front of thousands of spectators, spit in Hirschbeck's face. Many commentators saw the act as the ultimate disrespect for not only the umpire but for the game and the institution. When Alomar received only a five-game suspension, the umpires were especially upset and voted to boycott the baseball playoffs until Alomar's suspension went into effect.

Respect is the tendency to regard another as having some worth and, consequently, the desire to treat them with civility. It is a form of fairness because in recognizing someone's worth you give them what is their due. Although each person deserves some level of respect, often it is allotted in proportion to worth; you should respect even a child, but not as much as a person of great accomplishment. As Kant claims, every person has a "rightful claim" of respect from others simply on the basis of their humanity, which is itself a dignity (1797: 127); however, it is clear that some are deserving of more respect than others. To respect persons more than what they deserve is to encourage arrogance in them and also to incur a charge of flattering obsequiousness upon yourself. Disrespect can take on many forms, and some forms of it under certain circumstances can be argued as justifiable. *Contempt* may be seen as lack of respect for authority. Contempt of court is a common charge brought against defendants, lawyers, or courtroom spectators who defy the authority of the judge. Kant thinks that contempt is any form of undeserving disrespect (1797: 128). He argues that cruel and unusual forms of punishment ought to be disallowed because even the vilest of criminals is owed the respect of their humanity and such punishments, for example, drawing and quartering, are contemptuous of any person (1797: 128).

Pride is proper self-respect and is based on an honest self-evaluation. Pride is the good feeling about who you are and what you have done. Pride, as Aristotle says, "is the crown of the virtues" (*Nic. Ethics* 1124a1). It is the afterglow of a virtuous character. Pride enhances motivation, reinforces the sense of justice, and encourages courage; for this reason, it serves to solidify virtuous behavior. Proper pride allows you to feel justified in getting what you deserve. Proud persons think themselves capable of good and noble things; consequently, it is often those sorts of things that motivate them. As Aristotle suggests, the proud person is someone concerned with honor (*Nic. Ethics* 1123b17). As a result, pride is essential for proper motivation and proper direction in terms of goals and plans.

Because pride requires self-honesty, it goes hand-in-hand with *humility, understood as the willingness to recognize and admit to your faults or limitations*: "Humility, on the one hand, and true, noble pride on the other, are elements of proper self-respect," Kant says (1963: 126). "People with self respect," as Joan Didion suggests, "have the courage of their mistakes" (1968: 53). They know the price of things, and as a result, they show "the willingness to accept responsibility for [their] own life" (1968: 53). Many people mistake pride and humility as contraries. Having self-respect and a good self-image makes persons less resistant to admitting faults and limitations simply because they are confident enough in their worth that even with these admissions they still feel valuable. The benefit of humility is that it allows you to grow or improve. Humility is necessary for any education. Someone who believes they know it all will end up knowing little.

Sometimes pride and *modesty* are confused (as in Kant 1797: 127), but a distinction could be justified, with the first pertaining to self-image and the other to special talents or abilities. People cannot really be modest about themselves, although they can be modest about their talents or their physical attributes, but they may have a healthy self-image because of what they have accomplished or what they're capable of. But as opposed to the Greek tradition, Christian thinkers have condemned pride and listed it as one of the seven deadly sins. Kant believes that pride is a kind of ambition, a desire to swim to the top which may really be a characteristic of ruthlessness more than pride (1797: 130).

Arrogance is the result of a self-image grander than what it should be. As Montaigne defines it, "It is an unreasoning affection, by which we cherish ourselves, which represents us to ourselves as other than we are" (1572–1588: 255). Or as Aristotle suggests, arrogance is when a person "thinks himself worthy of great things, being unworthy of them" (*Nic. Ethics* 1123b7–8). Arrogance is based on a form of self-deception and violates one of the more fundamental maxims necessary for proper moral judgment: "Know thyself." Misperceiving yourself is fatal for prudent action; consequently, the arrogant person is bound toward imprudence and self-deceit. This self-deception may take various forms, but the one that is most pertinent to arrogance might be called magnification or aggrandizement. Arrogant persons may feel that what they have done is greater than it actually is. As Samuel Johnson said, a person may deceive himself by thinking that one act of liberality or tenderness makes him liberal or tender.

Because arrogant people overvalue themselves, arrogance may also result in a certain patronizing attitude toward others. Arrogant persons are more likely to be less receptive to correction or instruction by others, since they often feel they are beyond that. Arrogant persons harm themselves in that regard because they fail to take advantage of opportunities to improve themselves. Also, because arrogant persons are likely to feel that they deserve more recognition, respect, or consideration from others, they may have a tendency toward unfairness.

Hubris is a special form of arrogance. *The term is applied especially to those persons who feel they are worthy enough to meddle in matters that they are actually unworthy of.* It was a term used by the Greeks to characterize any mortal who dared interfere with the business of the gods. In general, it carries the sense of a transgression into affairs of people who are more worthy, knowledgeable, or qualified than the transgressor.

Vanity should be distinguished from arrogance. *Vanity is excessive attention to one's appearance,* as opposed to an inflated regard of oneself. As John Woodforde notes, "It seems that self-respect ends and vanity begins where there is an element of narcissism, where a person keeps checking with pleasure on his appearance" (1992: 15). Beau Brummel, for example, made the ritual of his morning toilet legendary (Woodforde 1992: 39). But vanity is not restricted to physical appearance; for example, many strive to promote a certain image of themselves as a connoisseur or an intellectual or a pious person or a tough guy. The Roman emperor Commodus liked to portray himself as Hercules. Statuary depicted him

---

The Price of Vanity?

Cosmetic surgery can be very costly and risky. For women, some of the more popular procedures are facelifts, breast enlargements, tummy tucks, and liposuction. These procedures can cost anywhere from $3000 to $12,000. Facelifts, for example, can result in nerve injury or scarring, and breast enlargement—especially with the use of silicon implants—is alleged to have caused a wide variety of ailments in women.

For men, the most popular cosmetic surgeries are hair transplants, pectoral implants, and penis enlargements. These can cost anywhere from $2000 to $8000. Pectoral implants can shift or limit motion, and penis enlargements don't enlarge the erection, just the unerect appearance.

---

as draped in a lion skin and carrying a hero's club (Woodforde 1992: xiv). The point is, however, that vanity involves appearance rather than substance. The vain person acts on the surface, a sort of shell which is empty inside. As Candida McWilliam wrote, "vanity has its roots in insecurity and its crown in greedy dreams

... " (1990; cf. Woodforde 1992: xvi). It is a fragile shell which must be constantly bolstered and attended to; conversely, it allows others who recognize the superficiality of it to take advantage of vain persons and prey on their vanity. For example, Baldassar Castiglione wrote a book in 1529, *The Book of the Courtier,* precisely to develop this sort of art (cf. Woodforde 1992: xx). The vain person is more vulnerable to deception and flattery. In fact, in soliciting compliments the vain person may defeat his or her purpose: "Tell your lover with sobs that you look horrible and he may believe you. ... " (McWilliam 1990).

Proud persons, on the other hand, have a more representative sense of their accomplishments and so are not as vulnerable to flattery and the deceits of vanity; they are more aware of the possibility that praise is sometimes meant to harm them, even in some cases with purposes of generating envy in others; as Tacitus suggests, "the worst kind of enemies are they that praise" (*Agricola and Germany,* 41). The vain person gladly accepts praise from those who do not have the talent, ability, or taste to serve as good judges of these things, whereas the proud person, although they show gratitude toward such praise, realize that its value is not as significant as when it comes from equals or superiors. Vain persons seek fame as a means of acquiring false adulation and so will feign a persona that matches the sort of fame they are seeking. Such persons affect reputation, and as Bacon claims, these are the "sort of men commonly much talked of, but inwardly little admired" (1625: 182). Excessively vain persons may also pursue attempts at appearance that are in fact dangerous to their health or person, as recent problems with breast implants or attempts at maintaining a year-round tan illustrate. But not everyone thinks vanity is necessarily a vice. Lord Chesterton argued the following: "If a man has a mind to be thought wiser, or a woman handsomer, than they really are, their error is a comfortable one to themselves, and an innocent one with regard to other people; and I would rather make them my friends by indulging them in it, than my enemies by endeavoring (and that to no purpose) to undeceive them" (cf. Woodforde 1992: xx). Dressing well and having a clean appearance should not be confused with vanity. This is an indication of self-respect, as Woodforde suggests (1992: xx), and respect for others.

Self-debasing persons are those who are apt to be treated unfairly simply because they feel they deserve less than what they should get. Self-debasing persons (who have a poor self-images and little self-respect) may also have a tendency to place themselves in inferior positions unjustly and denigrate their genuine talents and abilities. "To do without self-respect," Joan Didion writes, "is to be an unwilling audience of one to an interminable documentary that details one's failings, both real and imagined, with fresh footage spliced in for every screening" (1968: 54). If we do not have self-respect, as Didion reflects, we are forced to despise those who have so few resources or qualities that they would look up to us. On the other hand, we are determined to live out their false notions of us. We flatter ourselves by thinking these compulsions to please others are attractive. We play roles for those we hold in contempt—roles that are doomed to failure. "A low opinion of oneself in relation to others," Kant says, "is no humility; it is a sign of a little spirit and of a servile character. To flatter oneself that this is virtue is to mistake an imitation for the genuine article" (1775–1780: 126–127).

Modesty is a virtue in the context of demonstrating accomplishments, ability, skill, talent, physical features, or other characteristics to others. *Modesty is also for this reason a recognition of the limit of our talents and abilities.* We must know not only what we are capable of but also what we are not capable of. This clearly makes modesty a vital virtue for any plan or endeavor. Modest persons are those who are not ashamed, that is, persons who are proud to demonstrate their talents at appropriate times and places, but who hesitate from doing this inappropriately or showing-off at any time. On the other hand, they do not hesitate to make it clear what they are not capable of doing. A modest person might be justifiably proud of being fluent in a foreign language and willing to use that talent to benefit others; yet, the same person would be the first to admit that they are weak in another language. Modest persons are interested more in sharing their talents so that others will receive enjoyment or benefit from them, than using them as means of self-aggrandizement. In a way modesty encourages cooperative behavior, since the talent is seen as having a collective benefit rather than a private reward. Modest persons may recognize that they have not earned the talent they are naturally inclined to; they did nothing to deserve the great voice they have or the raw intelligence or poetic ability they may exhibit, although they do feel justly proud of the manner in which they have developed and exercised that talent. This particular sort of attitude reinforces the idea that whatever talent they have is meant for the collective good rather than personal aggrandizement.

Shameless persons take every opportunity to show-off what they have, usually to impress others. *Boastfulness* is a combination of lying (often in the form of exaggeration), arrogance (an impression that one is worth more than what one really is), and shamelessness. Boastfulness is an exaggerated claim of what one is capable of doing or, on the other hand, an exaggeration of what one has done, an exaggeration of the contribution one is making toward something, as when one claims more responsibility for a good than one has really contributed. The latter is illustrated in Aesop's fable, "The fly sat upon the axle-tree of the chariot wheel, and said, 'What a dust do I raise!'" In the first case, as Francis Bacon notes, "when they have promised great matters and failed most shamefully, … they will but slight it over, and make a turn, and no more ado" (1625: 75), or as the French proverb suggests, "beaucoup de bruit, peu de fruit" [the more the boast, the less the result]. But boastfulness, as Aristotle suggests, can include downright lies: "the boastful man … is thought to be apt to claim the things that bring glory, and when he has not got them, or to claim more of them than he has" (*Nic. Ethics* 1127a20).

3.6.1 The Polite Virtues

Politeness is a form of respect. To speak to others when spoken to, to initiate social contact and not always wait for others, to carry on a conversation rather than fall back on "yes" or "no," to express gratitude toward others, to let another pass, to wait until another is served—all of these are examples of respectful politeness toward others.

Charm is an example of a polite virtue; it is a term we use for people whom we like to be with because their emotional skills make us feel good (Goleman 1995: 115). Charm is an attempt to please others with your personality and in doing so to win their favor and good will; in a sense it is an effort to establish a cooperative relation with another by getting that person to like you, and so it is allied with friendliness. It is, on the one hand, a consideration of another, since you are trying to please that person, but it is also a means of creating an image of yourself for others. Charm, therefore, is an implicit recognition of the need of approval from others and the desire to please them. The *vulgar* person offends others by the intemperate use of actions or words and thereby disrespects them; if it is done on purpose, it has the aim of dissociating the offended person from your company. Vulgar persons seek to exclude rather than include others. *Mannered* persons are artificial and thus transparent in their motives; many persons also take offense to such disingenuous attempts at winning favor.

Wittiness is a form of charm, specifically, *charming conversation.* Witty persons attempt to win favor in others by entertaining them with interesting stories, funny jokes, or clever remarks. The witty person, like the modest person, does not aim to dominate the conversation or use the wittiness to show-off, but delights in the fact that others are delighted by it. Typically, these conversations do not aim to debase but to entertain. As Aristotle suggests, wittiness involves tact and for this reason: "There are jokes he will not make; for the jest is a sort of abuse. ... " (*Nic. Ethics* 1128a29). Wittiness is a display of intellectual excellence and so reflects on the qualities of the person. *Buffoons* do anything to get attention or to make people laugh, usually by debasing themselves, as suggested by Aristotle: "The buffoon ... is the slave of his sense of humor, and spares neither himself nor others if he can raise a laugh, and says things none of which a man of refinement would say" (*Nic. Ethics* 1128a34). Buffoons have a tendency to act lowly and vulgar. *Boorish* persons are those who make conversation unfriendly, spoil jokes, and aim to insult others; they often act crudely and speak in a vulgar way. They demonstrate an inherent unkindness, disrespect, and inconsiderateness of other's feelings.

Unpretentiousness is also an expression of respect. *Unpretentious persons are those who, despite deserved reputation, position, or status, do not use these to intimidate others.* They are willing to act cooperatively with people less capable or deserving. Unpretentious persons are modest and do not attempt to show-off their abilities at every opportunity; rather they encourage others to test and experiment with their own talents while still offering a model to admire; they are patient and solicitous of others in this regard; they are encouraging and helpful to novices and the inexperienced. *Pretentious* persons are those who exhibit strong arrogance and an exaggerated air of superiority to their inferiors; they have a tendency toward unkindness in that regard, and they delight in making the inferior feel uncomfortable, lowly, and worthless. *Lowly* persons are those who pretend to be equals to their inferiors by mimicking or trying to fit in with them; as the result, they often appear buffoonish or foolish.

Friendliness is a form of respect that assumes a person is trustworthy and worthy of consideration. Being friendly toward strangers or co-workers helps create a certain atmosphere of cooperation and consideration. Aristotle notes that the friendly person is not necessarily interested in giving pleasure or avoiding pain to the stranger but in doing what is honorable and expedient. They will not acquiesce in another's action if it is not honorable. *Obsequious* persons go overboard in their friendliness or agreeableness; that is, they aim more to please another at whatever cost. They "praise everything and never oppose," as Aristotle says (*Nic. Ethics* 1126b14). For this reason, one begins to suspect their motives and sees through their artificiality. Obsequious persons lower themselves more than they should toward others. *Unfriendly* persons, on the other hand, set a tone of combat and distrust. As Aristotle suggests, "They oppose everything and care not a whit about giving pain" (*Nic. Ethics* 1126b16).

Commendation is proper praise for another, in a sense it is fairness in regard to praise or a proper form of respect for another who deserves it. As Pliny says, "In commending another you do yourself right; for he that you commend is either superior to you in that you commend, or inferior. If he be inferior, to commend him is to commend yourself more; if he is superior, then not to commend him, is to commend oneself less." Commending persons speak well of those who have done well and have a tendency to speak little of those who do not. It is a sort of graciousness, a charity of spirit toward others, that allows one to praise another. This often requires a secure person who is not envious of others.

Flatterers are those who try to win favor by exaggerating the accomplishments of another and pretending to debase their own; Kant suggests it may also be considered a form of hypocrisy (1797: 98). The flattering person is also likely to be fawning, mannered, and overly pleasing toward those persons. But typically, a modest person can see through the flattery as a calculated means of getting favor or special consideration. However, flattery can be used for contrary purposes; rather than seeking favor, the flatterer may intend to harm another by means of excessive praise, that is, by stirring envy and scorn in others (cf. Bacon 1625: 179–180).

Slanderous persons are usually envious of those whom they slander and wish to act unkindly toward them; they do not speak well of those who deserve it but attempt to find something that may be true about those persons but will debase them, thus offsetting any good said in their favor; or they may simply promote lies and so are often dishonest and libelous. Slanderous persons have a tendency toward deception and duplicity; they will say one thing to the person's face but another behind his back. Kant argues that slander or calumny creates a certain attitude toward others, "It casts the shadow of worthlessness upon our species." Put less grandly, slander creates an atmosphere of disrespect and enmity toward others (1797: 132). In fact, Kant suggests that we should act positively against slander, silencing it when it happens and softening the faults of others.

Sportsmanship is friendly and fair competition. Sporting persons have respect for competitors and play fair, but they have the ambition to win. They are commending when they lose, modest when they win, and deservedly proud of their victories. The consequences of poor sportsmanship on boys and girls are listed by Linda Lews (1997):

1. Poor sports feel lots of stress. Boys and girls unable to control their hostility and anger during athletic events often experience more anxiety than their better-mannered teammates.
2. Poor sports fail to learn proper standards of etiquette.
3. Poor sports have less fun; their continual whining, arguing, and complaining take the joy out of the game, and fellow teammates, competitors, and spectators usually don't like to be around them.

Competitive persons are keen on winning and so have a tendency toward ruthlessness; they cannot be relied upon to follow the rules fairly. They often feel that if they do not win, then somehow they will lose the respect and admiration of others; this shows a certain insecurity in their own self-image. They may act in an unsportsmanlike manner when they lose, debasing the winner and placing the blame for the loss on others. *Spiritless* persons have no ambition to win and no spirit to compete in challenging games or competitive events; they show little confidence or pride in themselves or their abilities.

Cleanliness shows respect for others by avoiding offenses in appearance; it is also an attempt to make oneself pleasing to another. This is true not only of cleanliness of body but also cleanliness in your home and environment. Inviting persons to a dirty house is often considered a sign of disrespect or disregard. On the other hand, *fastidious* persons are mannered cleaners; this is often a source of annoyance to others since it shows a standard of cleanliness that is too excessive; an excessively clean house does not feel comfortable, friendly, or welcome, and a person obsessed with clean appearance does not seem approachable, touchable, or warm.

Punctuality is a form of respect for another person, since it demonstrates a recognition that the other person's time is valuable and should not be wasted. Indeed, it is often the case that the more prestige or worth a person has, the more time we spend in waiting for a transaction with that person. At the same time, the more prestige or worth a person has, the more punctual we are apt to be. Inconsiderate persons are unlikely to notify someone that they will be late. *Meticulous* persons are annoying because of their preciseness and unforgiving character.

3.7 THE VIRTUES OF KINDNESS

Kindness is regard for those who are in our power to harm or help. People can only be kind to those who are in need of their help, and for this reason, it is concerned with the good of another primarily and not one's own good. Kindness raises one from mere reciprocity to benevolence, since like many of the other virtues of regard, it is not dominated by self-interest. In reciprocity you recognize that someone might receive benefit from an action you perform incidentally to your own purposes. Being punctual is a consideration of another, but not a kindness. Kindness is a special concern with those who are vulnerable, in need, or who lack something. The benefactor may be willing to alleviate the need even at some cost. As Francis Bacon says so eloquently, "If he be compassionate towards the afflictions of others, it shows that his heart is like the noble tree [frankincense] that is wounded itself when it gives the balm" (1625: 77). Kindness is distinct from sympathy, although the latter seems to be a motivation for the former. I may exhibit sympathy for someone yet not act kindly toward them; that is, I might flee rather than help.

Cruelty is pleasure in exploiting the vulnerability of others (Taylor 1970: 209). "Nothing shocks our moral feelings so deeply as cruelty does. We can forgive every other crime, but not cruelty" (Schopenhauer 1818: 169). Cruel persons are cowardly because it is easy to take advantage of the weak and vulnerable. Cruel persons have a tendency toward vengefulness should a person in a superior position now hold an inferior one. "Seek the good of other men," Francis Bacon says, "but be not in bondage to their faces or fancies, for that is but facility or softness, which taketh an honest mind prisoner" (1625: 76). *Softness* is unfairness toward oneself and others. Since soft persons more easily give in to the whims or wants of others, many of which may inconvenience or even harm the good-hearted benefactor; it is unjust to others because it allows them to get more than they deserve.

Generosity is the willingness to give money, time, service, or possessions to others who are genuinely in need of help. Aristotle said that generosity has to do with giving and taking things whose value is measured in money (*Nic. Ethics* 1119b21–27). Wallace qualifies this by giving genuine generosity three essential features (1978: 342):

1. the benefactor, because of his direct concern for the good of the beneficiary, gives something with the intention of benefiting him;
2. the benefactor gives up something of his that has a market value and he has some reason to value, and, therefore to keep;
3. the benefactor gives more than what is generally expected in such circumstances.

The generous person must be motivated by genuine kindness rather than self-aggrandizement. If your gift of money is motivated by public recognition or some other suspect motive, then it cannot be generosity in a genuine sense. That is why anonymous gifts are the most generous of all, since the motivation is beyond suspicion. Also, the thing or service given must be of some value to the benefactor, so that she would have good reason to hold on to it herself (1978: 341). If instead of throwing something away you give it to a neighbor or friend, that would not count as generosity although it would be inconsiderate simply to throw it away without inviting the neighbor to take it. That is to say, generosity must be more than simple consideration; it must be a form of kindness. Finally, the giver must give in excess of what he is required to give. Giving a person a birthday gift is in and of itself not a generous act, although it might be generous should its cost far exceed what is expected, and assuming that the intention is not one of self-aggrandizement. Generosity, like many virtues of this type, is not simply concerned with one's interests in the context of others' interests but is genuinely concerned with the good of another (cf. Wallace 1978).

Prodigality is the tendency to spend lavishly on others or to give of your own material goods in such a way as to harm yourself or those who are dependent on you. *Greedy* persons are those who try to get more than they need and hold on to what they have even if giving it to others would not significantly harm them. Greediness, therefore, is a species of unfairness.

3.7.1 Forgiveness

If there is one image that sticks in the mind of those living in the Vietnam War era, it is Nick Ut's Pulitzer Prize winning photo of a 9-year-old girl running down a road, screaming and crying from the pain of her napalm-inflicted burns. Her clothes have been incinerated by the napalm. She is desperately trying to flee her village as it burns in the background. Although the girl, Pham Thi Kim Phuc, survived the war, the napalm left thick white scars where it splashed on her arm, neck, and back. She had seventeen operations and still lives with the pain. She eventually married and moved to Toronto in 1991.

John Plummer had ordered the napalm attack on Kim's village of Trang Bang in June 1972. He was 24 and a gung-ho helicopter pilot and operations officer. When Plummer saw the Nick Ut photograph on the front cover of *Stars and Stripes,* "It just knocked me to my knees." He had been twice told that there were no civilians in the village, only soldiers. But although his comrades-in-arms accepted the incident, when Plummer went home, the images and consequences of his decision began to trouble him. Even though he had a successful career as a military and civilian flight instructor, he went through three marriages and two divorces. He began to drink too much. He eventually turned to religion and became a minister. He became a better husband to his third wife, a good father to his children, but still he could not forget about the little girl in the photo. Every time he saw the photo, he said to himself, "Look what I did. I did that to her. I'm responsible. ... It just hurt every time, it became very difficult to deal with."

That is why when John Plummer learned that Pham Thi Kim Phuc was alive, he knew he had to find her and seek her forgiveness. On November 11, 1996, Kim planned a rare appearance at the *Vietnam Veterans Memorial* in Washington, DC. He managed to get a note to her. After her speech Plummer approached Kim. When she was told who he was, "I couldn't move anymore, I stop and I turn, and he looked at me," she said. Suddenly, they embraced. "She just opened her arms to me. I fell into her arms sobbing," Plummer said. "All I could say is, I'm sorry I'm

Should He Be Forgiven?

In *The Railway Man* Eric Lomax relates the story of his forgiveness of a Japanese man, Nagase Takashi, who during World War II was a principal interpreter and investigator in his brutal torture. Lomax was a British soldier who was captured in Burma and forced to work on the infamous Burma-Siam Railroad, where over 250,000 men died. Believed to have information concerning underground resistance in Thailand, Lomax was tortured to the point of death. Among some of the awful torture that Lomax endured was a form of water torture in which water was forced down his nostrils to the point of drowning.

The torture was so brutal that, in fact, Takashi believed that Lomax had died some time later after his involvement. Some years after the war, Lomax became intent on finding his torturers, motivated by a strong sense of revenge by means of public exposure. However, when he discovered an article in a Japanese paper about the sorrow and remorse that Takashi had for his actions and how this had affected his life, Lomax set up a meeting with the man. After a year's worth of meetings, Lomax was convinced of the genuineness of Takashi's remorse, and accepted some of the reasons he gave for his actions.

just so sorry." She patted Plummer's back. "It's alright," she told him, "I forgive, I forgive" (Gearan 1996).

Forgiveness is a virtue of kindness because the transgressor who feels guilt and remorse for his or her actions must seek the forgiveness of the person who has been harmed. That power of forgiveness now lies in the hands of the victim, and only that person. *Forgiveness is the willingness to overlook transgressions made against you by repentant persons.* "A man's self-respect shows," as Solomon says, "when they overlook an offense" (Proverbs 19:11); that is, it is a willingness to forgive those who have acted unfairly toward you. "If he easily pardons and remits offenses," Francis Bacon says, "it shows that his mind is planted above injuries, so that he cannot be shot" (1625: 77). Those who forgive even if the person is not repentant or if the act was a great wrong are *soft-hearted*, which Kant calls the "weak toleration of wrongs" (*ignava injuriarum patientia*) (1797: 126). As Jeffrie Murphy suggests, "A too ready tendency to forgive may be a sign that one lacks self-respect" (1982: 505). Not to react strongly to the violation of our rights or to harm done to us by others is to convey emotionally that either we don't think we have rights or that we do not take our own rights very seriously. Forgiveness may restore the status of a relationship, but to seek restoration at all costs—even at the cost of your self-respect—can hardly be a virtue. This is even truer of personal relationships. Being a doormat for friends or lovers is a strong sign of codependence. Mur-

A new field of "forgiveness studies" is emerging in psychology, sociology, and social work. Among the more prominent researchers is Robert Enright who, along with Joanna North, has recently edited a book entitled *Exploring Forgiveness* (University of Wisconsin Press, 1998). Most of the research in this area concludes that forgiveness is a moral choice, but when it is done, it has significant health, emotional, and psychological benefits for those persons, as opposed to people who continue to hold a grudge or seek revenge.

phy also points out how in an indirect way, forgiveness is also an indication of respect for others (1982: 505). Nietzsche argued that truly strong people exhibit no resentment toward others who seek to harm them simply because they do not matter enough (*Genealogy of Morals*, I, 10). As Murphy suggests, forgiveness is distinct from mercy (1982: 392). *Mercy* is the granting of a plea from someone who is under your power to help or harm to be treated less harshly than is warranted. Forgiveness has more to do with how one feels toward the other, but mercy is an action that revolves about just punishment. Also, in forgiveness the forgiver is the victim, while a person may show mercy to someone who has not personally harmed them. Thus, a judge may show mercy, but the victim shows forgiveness.

Margaret Holmgren (1993) argues that forgiveness is morally proper under the following conditions: (parallel to Liska's list)

Liskus list.

1. The wrongdoer recognizes and acknowledges to herself that her act was wrong;

2. The wrongdoer recognizes the victim's status as a person due a certain amount of respect. The offender must start to see the victim as a person like herself, with his own needs and feelings;

3. The wrongdoer must allow herself to experience the feelings that arise from the injuries and harm she has done another;

4. The wrongdoer must also address the attitudes and behavior patterns that have led her to commit the wrong, with an eye towards their elimination;

5. The offender must make amends for the wrong.

Forgiveness can proceed under these conditions since it allows the forgiver to recognize that the harm done is also recognized as such by the offender; that the offender has in an implicit sense made a pledge to avoid such actions in the future; that the offender has worked to make amends for the harm; that the offender, in recognizing the wrong of the action and seeking forgiveness for it, intends no malice toward the victim. In addition, it does not suggest that the offender is a vicious person.

The *vengeful* person is someone who cannot forgive another for what he or she has done. As Alexander Theroux (1982) suggests, it is a feral branch of hatred. Vengeful persons seek to punish those who have transgressed against them in a way that makes them suffer more than they did, even if the persons are repentant; for this reason, it is a species of unfairness. It is not simply an eye for an eye, but the jaw, tongue, and ears must also be taken. It is unfairness in another sense. Typically, vengeful persons seek to punish the transgressor outside of the collective and sanctioned forms of punishment and simply to satisfy that feeling for revenge (Bacon 1625: 55); it is more important that punishment be collectively sanctioned than individually enacted. Kant explains the difference between just punishment and revenge in the following way: "Every deed which violates a man's rights deserves punishment, whereby the offense is avenged on the doer of the deed (and the wrong not merely redressed). Punishment, however, is not an act stemming from the private authority of the person wronged, but is an act of a court of justice dis-

Case Study: The Thief

While visiting the estate of a cousin, 17th-century essayist and philosopher Michel Montaigne encountered a man whom the villagers called "the thief." The man, as he says, was born a beggar, and finding that by earning his living by labor he would never protect himself against poverty, he decided to become a thief. He spent all his youth at this trade. He took from other people's lands, but due to his extraordinary strength, he was able to take more at one attempt than would be expected. He also stole from a variety of lands and with a schedule that prevented him from being caught. He was now, in his old age, rich for a person in his station. But to make his peace with God and those he robbed, he spent his days compensating, by good deeds, the successors of the people he robbed, and according to the amount he robbed from them. Montaigne comments: "Judging by this description, whether it is true or false, this man regards theft as a dishonorable action and hates it, but hates it less than poverty; he indeed repents of it in itself, but in so far as it was thus counterbalanced and compensated, he does not repent of it." Thus, the man is not repentant because he feels that he has compensated the harm by good. But is that fair? He has acquired a status through theft which affords him the opportunity to act generously toward others. He has not been harmed by such action and in fact has benefited, and although others were harmed, he has compensated for that harm by helping their successors.

With which position do you agree? Should the man be forgiven?

tinct from him, which gives effect to the laws of a sovereign to whom all are subject" (1797: 125).

Vengefulness is distinct from viciousness. In the latter case there is a desire to harm another without just cause, while in the former there is a justifiable reason for making the other suffer, although it is typically unfair, since the retribution is not balanced. Vengeful persons have a tendency toward cruelty. Vengeful persons are set on seeing someone pay for their offense in a way that demeans or humiliates them; they would prefer that things are so arranged that the transgressor must beg for mercy or forgiveness. The goal is to humiliate. But revenge also causes harm to the vengeful person; the desire to seek revenge often becomes obsessive, eating away at the soul of the person. As Francis Bacon says, "This is certain, that a man that studieth revenge keeps his own wounds green, which otherwise would heal and do well" (1625: 56); or as the old Chinese proverb says, "If you seek revenge, carry two shovels." The revenger, ironically, becomes like the thing hated; those who fight with monsters become one.

3.8 IS BEING VIRTUOUS SUFFICIENT FOR BEING MORAL?

Having finished an account of the most significant virtues, a question needs to be asked. Granted that it is hard to imagine that we would count someone morally competent who was not virtuous, might it be the case that a virtuous person could still do immoral acts? Consider the following paradox.

The Battle of Gettysburg was one of the most significant and bloodiest battles of the Civil War. There were many acts of bravery recorded at the Devil's Den, Little Round Top, and Pickett's Charge. It is clear that at least some soldiers from both armies acted courageously in the sense we have articulated it, as the willingness to undergo risk and danger for the sake of something greater than oneself, that is, for a cause that had collective significance (cf. McPherson 1997). Yet at least under one motivation of the Confederate army (the defense of slavery as a practice), we would have to say intuitively that fighting for such a cause is immoral. Thus, it is quite possible that people will exhibit virtuous behavior, yet not moral behavior. We can admire the Confederate soldiers who braved the withering fire to cross miles of open fields in Pickett's charge, yet we should not admire the purpose of that charge.

P.T. Geach (1977) presents a similar dilemma: Suppose there is a devoted and intelligent Nazi who also possessed the virtue of courage. We ought to say, according to Geach, that either it was not courage that he possessed or that in such a case courage of this sort is not a virtue. In clarifying the paradox here, Alasdair MacIntyre makes the following points (1981: 167). Let's suppose we had to morally reeducate such a Nazi. There would be many vices he would have to unlearn and many virtues about which he would have to learn. Humility and charity would be relatively new to him. But he would not

---

Alasdair MacIntyre is a contemporary philosopher who is instrumental in generating a new interest in the study of the virtues. His most important books on ethics are *After Virtue* and *Whose Justice? Whose Rationality?*

---

have to unlearn or relearn what he knew about avoiding cowardice and rashness in the face of harm and danger. As MacIntyre emphasizes, "it was precisely because such a Nazi was not devoid of the virtues that there was a point of moral contact between him and those who had the task of reeducating him, that there was something on which to build. To deny that the Nazi was courageous or that his courage was a virtue obliterates the distinction between what required moral reeducation in such a person and what did not" (1981: 167–168).

This paradox seems to promote what might be called an *instrumental view of virtue*. Under this claim, behavior can be characterized as virtuous but not necessarily morally good. This is a position which seems to be supported by Confucius: "A good man will certainly also possess courage; but a brave man is not necessarily good" (*Analects* XIV.5); "If a noble man has courage but neglects right, he becomes quarrelsome; if a small-minded man has courage but neglects right, he becomes a thief" (*Analects* XVII.23). Kant suggests the same sort of thing: "courage, resolution, and constancy of purpose, as qualities of temperament, are without doubt good and desirable in many respects; but they can also be extremely bad and hurtful when the will is not good. ... " (1785: 61). In the instrumental view, virtuous character is certainly of higher value than a vicious character and so is not value neutral (i.e., a means toward any end, both good and bad); but neither is it sufficient for moral behavior. Thus, the instrumental theory must make a distinction between merely virtuous behavior and moral behavior. The former exhibits the moral quality of one's character; the latter exhibits the moral quality of the action. Under the instrumental view, the vicious person is incapable of moral action (except by accident), but the virtuous person is capable of both moral and immoral actions, although the latter are caused primarily by a lack of understanding of when and for what reason it is proper to apply these virtues toward some goal. In other words, for virtuous behavior to tend toward moral behavior, it must be supplemented by something which can determine what is good; traditionally, this is understood as the province of prudence, wisdom, and moral knowledge, all of which supply us with suggestions as to what is the right thing to do or not to do. Virtue can supply us with the wherewithal to do the good, but wisdom and knowledge can supply us with the content of the good.

A second way to answer the paradox is given by Aristotle and Aquinas and, more recently, by Phillipa Foot. These philosophers would argue for what might be called an *integral theory*. Under this view, the practice of the virtues collectively is sufficient enough to lead to consistently moral behavior. Aquinas argues for a "connection" among the virtues based on a view advocated by Gregory: "A virtue cannot be perfect as a virtue, if isolated from the others: for there can be no true prudence without temperance, justice and fortitude," and so true for the other virtues (*Summa* Pt. I–II Q65 Art. 1; cf. Augustine, *De Trinitate* vi. 4). If fortitude is strength of mind, it is not commended as virtuous unless it is also accompanied by temperance and prudence (*Summa* Pt. I–II Q. 65 Art. 1). As MacIntyre comments, for Aristotle "One cannot possess any of the virtues of character in a developed form without possessing all the others" (*Nic. Ethics* 1145a; cf. 1981: 145). Under both Aristotle's and Aquinas's view, there is one particular virtue, however, which must be integrated into every virtue to ensure the moral quality of action: prudence or wisdom. For Aristotle, the exercise of prudence raises a certain virtuous disposition to one of true virtue (cf. MacIntyre 1981: 145). As Aquinas argues, "No moral virtue can be without prudence" (*Summa* Pt. I–II Q. 65 Art. 1).

Under the first thesis of the integral theory, moral action results from the integrated practice of the virtues. The discussion in Section 3.2 about character and the virtues would argue against such a claim. Although all the cardinal virtues must be exercised to some degree to have a decent moral character, not all the virtues are compatible with one another. Moreover, persons may have different virtue emphases in their character—some may be especially honest or especially kind or

Query: Are the Virtues Necessary to Maintain Good Institutions and Practices?

In an address to a Hillsdale College seminar in Oklahoma City, Jeb Bush—son of former President George Bush and recently governor of Florida—related the following story, which is summarized here:

> In his later years, an old man who was a great admirer of democracy and public education tried to bring them together in one great experiment. It was his intention to establish a public college where students would practice self-governance. There would be no regulations but only individual student judgment.
>
> But only in a few months after the opening of the school, many students became unruly. They would skip classes and drink excessively. One night, fourteen students disguised themselves with masks and got involved in a drunken rampage that ended with a brawl. Two professors were beaten, one with a brick, the other with a cane.
>
> After the brawl the college's trustees convened in a special meeting. The old man—now 82-years-old—addressed the student body. He reminded the students of the lofty ideals of the college and said he had expected more from the students. He said, finally, that it was the most painful event in his life. After that, he could no longer speak as he became emotionally distraught. The audience was so moved by the speech that the fourteen offenders admitted their guilt afterward. However, the trustees decided to set up a strictly enforced code of conduct.
>
> Not too long afterward, the old man died on the fourth of July. Engraved on his tombstone were the successes and failures of his most important experiments: "Thomas Jefferson, author of the Declaration of Independence, and father of the University of Virginia."

Jeb Bush claims that the reason why Jefferson's experiment failed was because he "took for granted the one essential ingredient necessary for success: virtue. Only a virtuous people can secure and maintain their freedom." According to Bush, the success or failure of self-governance "will ultimately be determined by our virtue" (from *Imprimis*, 1992).

Clearly, Bush agrees with James Madison, the American Constitution's chief architect, along with Alexander Hamilton and John Jay, author of the Federalist Papers. Madison wrote the following: "Is there no virtue among us? If there be not, no form of government can render us secure. To suppose that any form of government will secure liberty or happiness without any virtue in the people is a chimerical idea."

Questions for Discussion

Do you agree? Could good institutions and practices survive without a predominance of virtuous participants? Conversely, could virtuous people also support bad practices or institutions?

Ironically, Hillsdale College, which prides itself on its ethical education, was recently rocked by a scandal when it was alleged that its president for the last 28 years, George Roche, was having an affair with his son's wife. Matters came to a head when she was found to have committed suicide. Roche resigned. *What happens when institutions are faced with such behavior?* In an open letter to the student body, Donald Mossey, chairman of the board of trustees of Hillsdale College, used a naval metaphor to express his views about the scandal and resignation: "the ship awaits a new captain. But the vessel itself, its purpose and its resources remain intact and focused" (*Imprimis*, January 2000).

Question for Discussion

Do you agree with Mossey that institutions have a character or constitution over and above the individuals who compose it, which allows it to survive their misbehavior?

---

incredibly courageous—all of which are admirable, but some of which are more suitable for different moral purposes. As MacIntyre writes: "If any version of moral Aristotelianism were necessarily committed to a strong thesis concerning the unity of the virtues (as not only Aquinas, but Aristotle himself were) there would be a serious defect in that position" (1981: 168).

Where the instrumental and integral theories seem to hold common ground is in their estimation of prudence or practical wisdom as necessary to guide or correct the character virtues toward the good. The difference between the two theories hinges on the question of whether prudence or wisdom is to count as a virtue in the way in which temperance or courage or fairness does or whether it is something different from these virtues, properly speaking. Both Aristotle and Aquinas agree that prudence, even if it is to be counted as a virtue, is a virtue unlike the other virtues; more specifically, it is an intellectual rather than a character virtue. Certainly, if we take the very broad definition of virtue suggested by Aquinas, as the "perfection of a power," then any ability perfected in a human being could count as a virtue. But such a broad definition may be unhelpful. The important point to note is how different abilities contribute differently to moral competence; if there is a significant difference between temperance as a virtue and practical wisdom as a virtue in terms of how they perfect a power and what powers they perfect, then this is not just cause for lumping them together. There is no dispute between the two positions in saying that practical wisdom directs moral character to the good, only whether wisdom acts like a character virtue. To use an analogy, if one says that experience is necessary to perfect a skill but training is also necessary, one will want to say that both are necessary for the perfection of a skill; yet one can clearly recognize a significant difference in the way in which training and experience each contribute to that perfection. So it is with moral character and wisdom. Moral character contributes to moral competence, and so does practical wisdom, but in a way differently than character.

How does prudence or wisdom direct virtue to the good? Although this is a question addressed in the next chapter, there is a short answer. As noted in several places in this chapter, an answer to the question of what is virtuous hinges on answers to the following questions: How much? What kind? With whom? When? For what reason? For example, temperance is knowing what sorts of pleasures are worthy, how much of a pleasure is appropriate, when is it appropriate to enjoy certain pleasures, and with whom should they be shared. Sexual continence is sex with the right person, at the right time, for the right reasons. In short, wisdom is concerned with answering these sorts of questions, not only in a particular situation, but in a larger framework as well. Virtuous people may still act immorally, primarily by a lack of understanding of when and for what reason it is proper to apply these virtues toward some goal. In other words, for virtuous behavior to tend toward moral behavior, it must be guided by something which can determine what the good might be and how it is to be accomplished, given a certain situation. This is the province of wisdom.

REVIEW QUESTIONS

1. How is virtue related to strength of will?
2. Why is temperance considered the cardinal virtue of self-control?
3. Why can courage be considered the cardinal virtue of self-efficacy?
4. How do temperance and courage contribute to regard for others?
5. What is meant by Aristotle's claim that virtue is a "golden mean"? Give examples of how various virtues and vices from each of the three major categories of virtues follow this pattern.
6. What are some of the issues concerning the relation between virtue and character? Do you think honesty is a character trait or a situational disposition? Discuss Owen Flanagan's thesis. What is the general sense of saintliness? Might there be a difference between saintly and holy?
7. What is meant by temperance? What is meant by indulgence? What is meant by insensitivity? What is anhedonia? What are the two general categories of pleasure? What is the difference between pleasure and enjoyment?

8. Define generally the differences among sybaritism, hedonism, eudaimonism, Epicureanism, Stoicism, and asceticism.

9. What is good-temper? What are the varieties of bad-temper?

10. What is ambition? What is highmindedness? How is ambition distinguished from ruthlessness? What is a directionless person?

11. What are the differences among curiosity, docility, and studiousness? Do you agree with many who suggest curiosity is a vice? What is allotrioepiscopia? Do you agree with Kant's estimation of it?

12. What is your model of sexual continence? What value does sexual continence have? How might it lead to respect for the other gender? Why might prudishness be a vice? Is virginity being sexually continent or prudish?

13. Why do you think vices such as jealousy and envy might be so destructive?

14. What are the differences among courage, bravery, and fearlessness? Clarify the differences among daring, valor, intrepidity, dauntlessness, mettle, and pugnaciousness. What does it mean to be stalwart? To have conviction? Are mountain climbers in your opinion courageous, brave, or foolhardy? What are some of the sources of cowardliness?

15. Why is patience so valued by many? What does patience allow you to do? Give some models of perseverance. What is the difference between persistence and doggedness?

16. What is the difference among fair-mindedness, fairness, and justice?

17. What are some characteristics of fair-minded persons?

18. What are some essential conditions for a fair practice?

19. What is the difference between distributive and retributive justice?

20. What is tolerance? Why is it important to a community? What is Mill's criterion? What is Popper's criterion? What is your estimation of those criteria?

21. Characterize the differences among the following kinds of untruthfulness: lying, deception, duplicity, insincerity, libel, hypocrisy, dupery, exaggeration, pretense, and self-deception. What are the various ways in which we engage in self-deception? Define the various rationalization strategies: inversion, projection, blaming, excuse, comparison, conventionalization.

22. How is cheating different from stealing?

23. What are some of the effects and consequences of lying and dishonesty?

24. What is promise making?

25. What are pride and self-respect? Why are they important?

26. What are the differences among pride, arrogance, vanity, and hubris?

27. What is modesty?

28. Discuss the familiar polite virtues.

29. When can a person be genuinely considered generous?

30. What are some of the conditions under which a person might be deserving of forgiveness? What are some of the dangers in revenge?

31. What is meant by the integral theory of the virtues? What is meant by the instrumental theory of the virtues? Which, in your opinion, is the most plausible account?

STORIES FOR DISCUSSION

On Courage and Bravery

The Red Badge of Courage. 1895. Stephen Crane. Henry Fleming is a young, inexperienced Union soldier who has visions of glory as he faces his first battle. He's anxious to prove himself a hero, yet when he is suddenly placed in the midst of battle, he is overcome by fear and runs from the field. Falling behind his lines, he joins the wounded, but as he comes into contact with the "real" wounded, he grows ashamed because he has not earned their "red badge of courage." Among the wounded he meets with his mortally wounded friend, Jim Conklin. He becomes angry as he witnesses the horrid death of his friend. The next day he's accidentally struck on the head by a retreating Union soldier. Wrapping his head in a scarf, he pretends that he was wounded by enemy fire, and he makes his way back to his own lines. When his pretense is accepted by his comrades, he suddenly begins to fight frantically; in the battle he seizes the regiment's colors in a charge, reestablishing its reputation. Fleming emerges with a steady sense of his own courage.

Question for Discussion

1. In your opinion did Henry Fleming finally redeem himself? Should he be honest and tell his compatriots about his act of cowardliness?

Lord Jim. 1900. Joseph Conrad. Jim is chief mate on the *Patna*, a ship carrying a party of pilgrims in Eastern waters. He is young and often dreams of heroic deeds. When the ship is threatening to sink, the cowardly officers flee the ship in the few lifeboats, leaving the pilgrims to their fate. Despite the fact that Jim despises their actions, in the confusion and horror of the moment, he jumps into the lifeboat with the escaping officers at the last minute. But the *Patna* does not sink and the pilgrims are rescued. Jim, alone among the crew, remains to face the court of inquiry. Disturbed by the violation of his own code of honor and stripped of his papers by the courts, he moves from place to place whenever his past threatens to catch up with him. He searches for anonymity and the chance to redeem himself. Eventually, he moves to a remote trading station in Patusan, where he creates order and well-being in a formerly chaotic community. Because of his efforts he wins the respect and affection of the community, who call him "Lord Jim." When a gang of thieves arrives to plunder the village, Jim begs the chiefs of the community not to kill them, pledging his own life if they do not leave. But the thieves act treacherously and there is a massacre. Rather than flee, Jim delivers himself up to one of the chiefs whose son was killed in the massacre. Jim willingly accepts this honorable death, and the chief shoots him.

Questions for Discussion

1. Could Jim be forgiven for his last-minute act of cowardliness aboard the *Patna*?
2. If Jim had not felt such guilt and remorse over his act of cowardliness, do you think he would have found a more reasonable solution to his dilemma in Patusan?

Pentimento. 1973. Lilian Hellman. Film version, *Julia,* 1977. Directed by Fred Zinnemann. Author Lilian Hellman recalls her childhood friend's brave fight against the Nazis during World War II.

The Alamo. 1960. Directed by John Wayne. John Wayne tells the story of the battle of the Alamo in March of 1836, during Texas's fight for independence from Mexico. One hundred and fifty Texans fought against Santa Anna's army of four thousand.

Gettysburg. 1993. Directed by Ronald Maxwell. The film recounts the major events of the 3-day battle, including Col. Joshua Chambers's defense of Little Round Top and Pickett's Charge.

Bataan. 1943. Directed by Tay Garnett. After the invasion of the Philippines catches the Americans by surprise, a small group of soldiers fight off the Japanese to the last man.

Norma Rae. 1979. Directed by Martin Ritt. Norma Rae is a working-class woman in a small Southern town who has more than her share of trouble. When a union organizer comes to town, she struggles to help unionize her co-workers despite threats and sanctions.

Braveheart. 1995. Directed by Mel Gibson. The tale of the legendary William Wallace, who fought to rid English control of Scotland in the 13th century and the complacency of the Scottish nobles.

Glory. 1989. Directed by Edward Zwick. The story of the first all African-American regiment during the Civil War.

The Four Feathers. 1902. A.E.W. Mason. Film version 1939. Directed by Zoltan Korda. On the day before his wedding, and a few days before his enlistment is up, a British officer delays reading a telegram calling him to report for duty in the Sudan. His fiancée and his friends label him a coward. To win back their respect, he rescues each of his four friends from danger in the Sudan.

On Patience and Perseverance

The Odyssey. c. 9th cent. B.C.E. Homer. Having devised a clever ruse to enter the walled city of Troy after 10 years of struggle to conquer the city, Odysseus arrogantly brags to the gods that he did this on his own. Poseidon takes special offense at the boast, since he assisted the Achaians in their defeat of Troy. As punishment Poseidon makes Odysseus wander the seas for 20 years. During this time Odysseus undergoes many trials and tribulations but persists in his effort to return to his homeland and to his beloved wife, Penelope, and his son, Telemachus, who he has not seen since birth. In the meantime, despite the insistence of a number of suitors and rumors of his death, loyal Penelope waits patiently for her husband to return. Eventually, Odysseus returns to his home, kills the suitors with the help of his son, and reunites with Penelope.

Questions for Discussion
1. Would Penelope have been justified in giving up her wait and marrying one of the suitors? Are there limits to promises, vows, and patience?
2. Who do you think suffered more, Penelope, in waiting all those years, or Odysseus, in trying to get home?

El Norte. 1983. Directed by Gregory Nava. El Salvadorans struggle through a number of trials and tragedies to reach America to escape persecution in their native land.

Fitzcarraldo. 1982. Directed by Werner Herzog. Fitzcarraldo devises a scheme to transport rubber along the Amazon that requires moving a huge steamer overland.

My Left Foot. 1989. Directed by Jim Sheridan. A portrait of Irish poet Christie Brown, who was afflicted with severe cerebral palsy.

On Curiosity

Dr. Jekyll and Mr. Hyde. 1886. Robert Louis Stevenson. A generous and philanthropic man, Dr. Jekyll is preoccupied with the problems of good and evil and the possibility of separating them into distinct personalities. He develops a drug that transforms him into the demonic Mr. Hyde; he also creates an antidote that will restore him back to Dr. Jekyll. Gradually, however, the darker side begins to predominate, and he commits murder. As he struggles to regain control of his darker side, he realizes he is slipping more and more into the world of evil. Unable to get the necessary chemicals for his transformation and with the police closing in, he commits suicide.

Questions for Discussion

1. Do you agree with Stevenson's supposition that human beings have both a good and a bad side?
2. How would such a supposition affect an account of virtue? Is virtue necessary to hold back the darker side of human beings?

Frankenstein. 1818. Mary Shelley. Frankenstein, a young student, animates a being out of corpses from graveyards and dissecting rooms by means of electricity. The monster is shunned by everyone, but longs for human company. The creature ultimately turns to evil and destroys Frankenstein and everything he loves.

On Jealousy

Othello. 1602–1604. William Shakespeare. Desdemona, the daughter of a Venetian senator, has secretly married Othello, a Moor who is a well-respected general. Sent on a mission by the senate to prevent the Turks from attacking Cyprus, when the enemy fleet is dispersed by a storm, Othello, his wife, and his entourage land in Cyprus. Among his group is Cassio, who helped him woo Desdemona, and Iago, an old soldier and friend in the service of Othello. Othello has made Cassio his lieutenant, passing over Iago for promotion. Iago becomes bitterly resentful and plans his revenge. Iago uses Roderigo, a gentleman in love with Desdemona, to fight with Cassio after he gets him drunk. Othello deprives Cassio of his new rank. He then persuades Cassio to ask Desdemona to plead in his favor with Othello, which she gladly does. Iago suggests to Othello that Cassio is, and has been, Desdemona's lover. In the meantime he arranges for his wife, Emilia, who is Desdemona's lady-in-waiting, to get Desdemona's handkerchief and put it in possession of Cassio. As proof of Desdemona's infidelity, he tells Othello of the handkerchief. Othello is taken in by Iago's deception and in a jealous rage smothers Desdemona in her bed. Iago convinces Roderigo to murder Cassio, but when he fails, Iago kills him. He also kills his wife, Emilia, after he discovers that she has disclosed Desdemona's innocence to Othello. Iago and Othello are arrested. Othello, racked with remorse, kills himself.

Questions for Discussion

1. Why can people prey on your jealousy and use it to their advantage? Why would a jealous person be more prone to buy into a claim of infidelity? Why is it a flaw?
2. Who is more loathsome, Iago, who deceived his friend and committed the foulest crimes to satisfy his thirst for revenge, or Othello, who was willing to believe that his beloved was unfaithful, that his good friend was deceiving him, and who showed no pity for his wife?

On Anger

The Iliad. 8th cent. B.C.E. Homer. During the 10-year struggle of the Achaians to conquer Troy, a dispute arises between Agamemnon, leader of the Greeks, and Achilles, their greatest warrior. Since Agamemnon is forced to give back a female captive, he decides to take one of Achilles's. Achilles becomes extremely angry over this insult and refuses to fight for Agamemnon. Without their greatest warrior, the Greeks are eventually pushed into near defeat by the Trojans. Not wishing to see his own people defeated, Achilles's most beloved friend, Patroclos, dons Achilles's armor and pretends to be the mighty warrior. But in the fray that follows, Patroclos is killed. Mourning the death of his great friend, Achilles takes to the field and slaughters the Trojans. Eventually, he kills the Trojan hero, Hektor. Seeking revenge, Achilles is in turn killed by Paris, the brother of Hektor and the man originally responsible for the 10-year war.

Questions for Discussion
1. How can anger blind us to what is in our own interest?
2. How can an angry person be taken advantage of?

On Ambition

All the King's Men. 1946. Robert Penn Warren. Willie Stark is a self-educated rural Southerner who dreams of great power and public service. He becomes an unscrupulous and demagogic politician and is eventually elected governor of his state. He rises as an extremely powerful figure in the politics of his state and is known as "the Boss." He attracts Jack Burden, a journalist, into his employ. He wants Jack to return to Burden's Landing, his childhood home, to find some way to blackmail Judge Irwin—a dignified, old family friend and former attorney general—because the judge had reneged on a promise he made to the Boss. In the process Jack renews friendships with Adam Stanton, an idealistic surgeon, and his sister, Anne, who was Jack's first love. Jack gets them involved with Willie Stark. Stark makes Adam director of the hospital that he had built and soon starts an affair with Anne, scorning his old mistress, Sadie Burke. In the meantime Jack finds out that Judge Irwin once took a bribe, but rather than submit to Stark's blackmail, the judge commits suicide. Jack finds out from his grieving mother that Judge Irwin was her lover, and the he, Jack, is his son. At the same time Sadie anonymously tells Adam of the affair his sister is having with Willie Stark. Adam goes to the capitol and shoots Willie, getting killed himself. Jack returns to Burden's Landing, marries Anne, and settles into the realization of Stark's fundamental corruptness, despite his desire for great public service.

Questions for Discussion
1. How can even the finest goals become corrupted if the means are not salutary?
2. How much is Jack to blame for the consequences of his action? Why is naiveté dangerous? How difficult is it to walk the line between skepticism and loyalty?

Aguirre, The Wrath of God. 1972. Directed by Werner Herzog. Aguirre is one of Pizarro's lieutenants. Pizarro is in search of the lost city of gold, El Dorado, in South America. Pizarro sends a party down one of the tributaries of the Amazon to search for the city. He places a nobleman in charge, but Aguirre is sent along. Aguirre kills the nobleman and sets out to search for the gold for himself. Soon he and his party descend into madness and desperation as they are killed one-by-one.

Citizen Kane. 1941. Directed by Orson Welles. The rise and fall of a newspaper magnate. One of the great films of all time.

On Covetousness

Jean de Florette. 1966. Directed by Claude Berri. Two villagers attempt to grow flowers commercially in rural France. They hope to use a spring on the next property but are dismayed when it is bought by an outsider. Before he moves in, they conspire to hide the spring, hoping that the man will be discouraged and abandon the property. The stranger hopes to raise rabbits commercially but dies in an accident trying to dig for water. A startling revelation about the stranger causes a great tragedy for the villagers.

On Greed

The Treasure of the Sierra Madre. 1948. Directed by John Huston. Two men, Dobbs and his young companion, are down on their luck in Mexico. They meet up with an old prospector who befriends them. He tells them of the likelihood of gold in the Sierra Madre. They put a grubstake together and explore the region, soon discovering a profitable stream. They work the claim several months, when another adventurer comes into their camp. The new man wants to get in on the venture, but the others are wary of his intentions. Suddenly, the group is attacked by Mexican bandits, and the stranger is killed in the fray. A photograph of the dead man's wife is discovered among his possessions. The prospectors gather their gold and return home to cash it in. But on the way back, Dobbs begins to act strangely paranoid. He becomes overwhelmed by greed and attempts to keep all the gold for himself. Having left his partners, he's attacked by Mexican bandits and killed. Thinking the saddlebags full of sand rather than gold dust, the bandits scatter it to the winds. When his partners find him, and the gold gone, the old prospector laughs it off, and the young man vows to visit the woman in the photo.

Questions for Discussion

1. How does a disposition toward greed affect the trust that might exist in a cooperative arrangement?
2. After all their travail, why do you think the old prospector could laugh off the loss of his gold?

On Obedience

Gallipoli. 1981. Directed by Peter Weir. A colonel must make a choice of whether or not to obey orders to make a charge that will lead to the slaughter of his men.

On Calumny

Absence of Malice. 1981. Directed by Sydney Pollack. The son of a mobster is falsely accused of wrongdoing by a reporter.

On Loyalty

Antigone. Sophocles. After the defeat of the expedition against Thebes led by Polynices, Creon, now king, decrees that his body shall lie unburied in defiance of the rites due the dead. Antigone, Oedipus's daughter, gives her brother a token burial and though she is affianced to his son Haemon, Creon condemns her to burial alive. Warned by Tiresias, he regrets his act too late; Antigone and Haemon kill themselves and Creon's wife, Eurydice, does the same on hearing the news.

The Adventures of Huckleberry Finn. 1884. Mark Twain. Huckleberry Finn must make a choice between remaining loyal to his friend Jim, a runaway slave, or obeying the law.

Beau Geste. 1924. P.C. Wren. Film version 1939. Directed by William Wellman. A man assumes a new identity in the Foreign Legion to escape the accusation of stealing a valuable diamond from his adopted mother. His brothers follow him to the Foreign Legion with tragic consequences. As it turns out Beau Geste feigned the theft to hide the fact that his mother had sold the diamond without the owner's permission years before in order to pay off some debts.

On Honesty

All My Sons. 1947. Arthur Miller. A son discovers that his father—whose partner took the blame for manufacturing defective airplane parts that led to the deaths of American fliers during World War II—was actually in on the plan.

Quiz Show. 1995. Directed by Robert Redford. A Columbia professor, overshadowed by his famous poet father, agrees to participate in a dishonest scheme set up by producers of a popular game show. The professor is seduced by the instant celebrity and wealth his winnings bring.

House of Games. 1987. Directed by David Mamet. A psychiatrist and a con man try to outwit each other in a game of deception.

On Temperance

Babette's Feast. 1953. Karen Blixen. Film version 1988. Directed by Gabriel Axel. Two unmarried sisters belong to a fundamentalist Christian sect, founded by their father who has recently died in a remote Norwegian community in the 18th century. In their youth each gave up the love of their lives for their faith and the direction of their father. One had a beautiful voice and fell in love with her instructor, a great opera singer. The other sister fell in love with a young lieutenant, who later became a great general. One day a French expatriate, Babette, appears at their door. She is fleeing the French Revolution and is seeking refuge with them on the recommendation of the sister's former lover, the opera star. As an act of charity, they take in the mysterious Babette, who offers to serve as their cook. Although she is an excellent cook, on their insistence she learns to prepare the rather bland Norwegian food. Over time she becomes a pleasant companion and friend to the sisters. The sisters are troubled by the constant bickering and infighting of their religious community. When Babette learns that she has inherited a small fortune, she devises a plan. She asks the sister for a favor—that she be allowed to cook them a feast to celebrate their dead father's birthday. The sisters and the leaders of the religious community agree to the feast, but only out of politeness. In the course of the sumptuous meal, the leaders of the community renew their friendship and camaraderie. It is revealed that Babette was a famous French chef and now, because she has spent all of her fortune on the grand meal, she cannot return to France.

Questions for Discussion

1. How does shared pleasure and enjoyment bind people together?
2. Discuss some of the ironies of the story in this contrast between the ascetic and the gourmand.

The Doors. 1991. Directed by Oliver Stone. The story follows the rise and fall of a popular rock singer as his life spirals downward in a haze of drugs and sex.

On Revenge

Hamlet. 1601. William Shakespeare. The ghost of his father appears to Hamlet, informing him that his brother, Claudius, had killed him by poison, and Hamlet is commanded to avenge his death. Hamlet's mother, Gertrude, is now married to his uncle. He feigns madness in order to better carry out the revenge. In the process he rejects his love, Ophelia. Claudius conspires to kill Hamlet but fails. In the meantime Ophelia is destroyed by Hamlet's rejection and is found drown. Claudius sets up a duel between Hamlet and Laertes which ends with the death of Claudius, Hamlet, and Laertes. Gertrude commits suicide.

Questions for Discussion

1. Does Hamlet have an obligation to avenge his father? Does his father have a right to demand such a thing?
2. Why is revenge often destructive? Why is revenge so attractive?

Moby Dick. 1851. Herman Melville. Moby Dick, the great white whale, is pursued by Captain Ahab, who lost his leg in their last encounter. In his singular pursuit of the whale, he sacrifices his own dignity, his life, and the lives of all his crew, except Ishmael, who survives to tell the story.

The Virgin Spring. 1959. Directed by Ingmar Bergman. Transients rape and accidentally kill a nobleman's beloved young daughter. He discovers who they are and succeeds in taking his revenge.

The Searchers. 1956. Directed by John Ford. Returning from the Civil War, Nathan moves in with his brother and his family. While away, Indians kill the family and abduct the daughter. Full of racial hatred for the Indians, Nathan is bent on recapturing his niece and killing her, since he perceives her as being defiled. But when he finally finds her after years of searching, his anger fades and he brings his niece home.

The Count of Monte Cristo. 1844. Alexandre Dumas. Edmond Dantes is about to begin a blissful existence as captain of his vessel and husband of his longtime love when a false political charge condemns him to life imprisonment. He escapes and flees to the island of Monte Cristo, where he discovers a treasure revealed to him by one of his fellow prisoners. With the aid of the money, he becomes a powerful and mysterious figure who slowly wreaks his revenge on those who wronged him.

The Cask of Amontillado. 1846. Edgar Allan Poe. A tale of revenge against a man too prone to ridicule. His desire to taste a fine amontillado proves to be his downfall.

The Crossing Guard. 1996. Directed by Sean Penn. A man seeks revenge against the drunk driver who killed his child.

SUGGESTED READINGS

On Virtue

Aquinas, Thomas. *Summa Theologica.* New York: Benzinger Brothers, 1947.

Aristotle. *Nicomachean Ethics. The Basic Works of Aristotle.* Edited by R. McKeon. New York: Random House, 1941.

Bennett, William. 1993. *The Book of Virtues.* New York: Simon and Schuster.

Bloomfield, Morton. 1967. *The Seven Deadly Sins.* East Lansing: Michigan State University Press.

Cooper, John M. 1975. *Reason and the Human Good in Aristotle.* Cambridge, MA: Harvard University Press.

Crisp, Roger, and Slote, Michael, editors. 1997. *Virtue Ethics.* Oxford, England: Oxford University Press.

Darling-Smith, Barbara. 1994. *Can Virtue Be Taught?* Notre Dame, IN: Notre Dame University Press.

Foot, Phillipa. 1978. *Virtues and Vices.* Berkeley: University of California Press.

Fortenbaugh, William. 1969. Aristotle: Emotion and Virtue. *Arethusa* 2: 163–185.

Geach, Peter. 1977. *The Virtues.* Cambridge, England: Cambridge University Press.

Gray, Glenn. 1967. *The Warriors: Reflections on Men in Battle.* New York: Harper and Row

Gyekye, Kwame. 1987. *An Essay on African Philosophical Thought: The Akan Conceptual Scheme.* Cambridge, England: Cambridge University Press.

Heyd, David, editor. 1996. *Toleration.* Princeton, NJ: Princeton University Press.

Holmgren, Margaret. 1993. Forgiveness and the Intrinsic Value of Persons. *American Philosophical Quarterly* 30(4): 341–353.

Horton, J., and Mendis, S., editors. 1985. *Aspects of Toleration.* Oxford, England: Oxford University Press.

Hume, David. 1739. *An Enquiry Concerning the Principles of Morals.* Edited by L.A. Selby-Rigge. 3rd ed. Oxford, England: Oxford University Press, 1975.

_____. *Treatise of Human Nature.* Edited by L.A. Selby-Rigge and P.H. Nidditch. Oxford, England: Clarendon Press, 1978.

Hursthouse, Rosalind. 2000. *On Virtue Ethics.* Oxford, England: Oxford University Press.

Hutchinson. 1725. *An Inquiry Concerning Moral Good and Evil.* New York: Touchstone.

Jacoby, Susan. 1983. *Wild Justice: The Evolution of Revenge.* New York: Harper and Row.

Kant, Immanuel. 1797. *The Metaphysical Principles of the Virtues.* Translated by J. Ellington. New York: Bobbs-Merrill, 1964.

Martin, Mike. 1995. *Self-Deception and Morality.* Lawrence: University of Kansas Press.

MacIntyre, Alasdair. 1981. *After Virtue.* Notre Dame, IN: University of Notre Dame Press.

Meilaender, Gilbert. 1984. *The Theory and Practice of Virtue.* Notre Dame, IN: University of Notre Dame Press.

Mendus, S., and Edwards, D., editors. 1987. *On Tolerance.* Oxford, England: Clarendon Press.

Murphy, Jeffrie. 1982. Forgiveness and Resentment. *Midwest Studies in Philosophy* 7: 503–516.

Oakley, Justin. 1991. *Morality and the Emotions.* London: Routledge.

Paul, Ellen, Miller, Fred, and Paul, Jeffrey, editors. 1998. *Virtue and Vice.* Cambridge, England: Cambridge University Press.

Pieper, Josef. 1966. *The Four Cardinal Virtues.* Notre Dame, IN: University of Notre Dame Press.

Plato. *The Republic. Collected Dialogues.* Edited by Edith Hamilton and H. Cairns. Princeton, NJ: Princeton University Press, 1973.

_____. *Laches. Collected Dialogues.* Edited by Edith Hamilton and H. Cairns. Princeton, NJ: Princeton University Press, 1973.

_____. *The Symposium. Collected Dialogues.* Edited by Edith Hamilton and H. Cairns. Princeton, NJ: Princeton University Press, 1973.

_____. *Euthyphro. Collected Dialogues.* Edited by Edith Hamilton and H. Cairns. Princeton, NJ: Princeton University Press, 1973.

_____. *Meno. Collected Dialogues.* Edited by Edith Hamilton and H. Cairns. Princeton, NJ: Princeton University Press, 1973.

_____. *Protagoras. Collected Dialogues.* Edited by Edith Hamilton and H. Cairns. Princeton, NJ: Princeton University Press, 1973.

Rawls, John. 1971. *A Theory of Justice.* Cambridge, MA: Harvard University Press.

Sherman, Nancy. 1991. *The Fabric of Character: Aristotle's Theory of Virtue.* Oxford, England: Oxford University Press.

Scheven, Albert. 1981. *Swahili Proverbs.* Washington, DC: University Press of America.

Schiffhorst, Gerald. 1978. *Some Prolegomena to the Study of Patience. The Triumph of Patience.* Edited by G. Schiffhorst. Orlando: University of Florida Press.

Sherman, Nancy. 1997. *Making a Necessity of Virtue: Aristotle and Kant on Virtue.* Cambridge, England: Cambridge University Press.

Slote, Michael. 1983. *Goods and Virtues.* Oxford, England: Oxford University Press.

_____. 1995. *From Morality to Virtue.* Oxford, England: Oxford University Press.

Statman, Daniel. 1997. *Virtue Ethics.* Washington, DC: Georgetown University Press.

Uehling, T., French, P., and Wettstein, H., editors. 1988. *Midwest Studies in Philosophy: Ethical Theory: Character and Virtue.* Notre Dame, IN: University of Notre Dame Press.

Von Wright, Georg. 1963. *The Varieties of Goodness.* London: Routledge and Kegan Paul.

Wallace, James. 1978. *Virtues and Vices.* Ithaca, NY: Cornell University Press.

Walton, Douglas. 1986. *Courage.* Berkeley: University of California Press.

Wegner, D., and Pennebaker, K., editors. 1983. *Handbook of Mental Control.* Upper Saddle River, NJ: Prentice Hall.

On Moral Character and Personality

Adorno, T.W. et al. 1950. *The Authoritarian Personality.* New York: Harper.

Brown, Roger. 1965. *Social Psychology.* New York: Free Press.

Burton, R. 1963. The Generality of Honesty Reconsidered. *Psychological Bulletin* 70: 481–499.

Clark, David, and Fawcett, J., editors. 1987. *Anhedonia and Affect Deficit States.* New York: PMA Publishing Co.

Coles, Robert. 1986. *The Moral Life of Children.* New York: The Atlantic Monthly Press.

Damasio, Antonio. 1994. *Descartes' Error: Emotion, Reason and the Human Brain.* New York: Grosset/Putnam.

Flanagan, Owen. 1991. *Varieties of Moral Personality: Ethics and Psychological Realism.* Cambridge, MA: Harvard University Press.

Goleman, Daniel. 1995. *Emotional Intelligence.* New York: Bantam.

Hartshorne, H., and May, M. 1928–1930. *Studies in the Nature of Character.* 3 vols. New York: Macmillan.

Kupperman, Joel. 1991. *Character.* Oxford, England: Oxford University Press.

CHAPTER FOUR

Wisdom

Wisdom is the principal thing; therefore get wisdom; and with all thy getting get understanding.

—Proverbs 4:18

Wisdom denotes the pursuing of the best ends by the best means.

—Francis Hutcheson

Happy the man who discovers wisdom, the man who gains discernment;
gaining her is more rewarding than silver, more profitable than gold.
In her right hand is length of days; in her left hand, riches and honour.
Her ways are delightful ways, her paths all lead to contentment.
She is a tree of life for those who hold her fast, those who cling to her
live happy lives.

—Proverbs 3: 13-18

Simply put, wisdom attempts to answer Socrates's famous question: How should we live? (*Rep.* 352d). Wisdom is concerned with both the ends and means of the good life. It enables good judgment and decision making and facilitates the fine art of deliberation. The wise person is someone who has a sophisticated understanding of the world and is adept at taking that understanding and applying it to the nuances of life's situations in such a way that the result is morally satisfying. Whereas moral sentiment creates a desire for the good and moral strength the power to do it, and whereas the virtues infuse our character with habits which enable us to continue to do the right thing, wisdom is concerned with envisioning the good life and how best to achieve it. As we have seen, the virtues are successes at self-mastery, that is, self-control and self-efficacy. Temperance, patience, industry, courage, and fair-mindedness keep us on whatever path we set, but it is wisdom that sets the path, and the success of wisdom is success in self-direction. The 15th-century Italian artist Caesare Ripa, portrayed "Wise Counsel" (*Consiglio*) by a dignified old man, standing on a bear's head and a dolphin, and wearing on his neck a heart suspended on a chain. In his right hand he holds a book on which an owl is perched, and in his left what is known as the *tricipitum*, a three-headed beast representing prudence. Wise Counsel conquers haste (the dolphin) and anger (the bear); its decision must be approved by the heart as well as by the mind (the heart suspended from a chain); it must be founded on industrious nocturnal study (the book and the owl); and it must be directed by prudence.

　　Wisdom, prudence, and practical reasoning are sometimes used interchangeably in the literature; other times they are made distinct. Aristotle is especially keen on distinguishing a number of types of intelligence. Scientific knowledge (*epistēmē*)—to put it in relatively modern terms—is talent in deductive or inductive reasoning (*Nic. Ethics* 1139b25–30). Intellectual intuition (*nous*) is the ability to discern the first principles of scientific knowing, for instance, the axioms of mathematics or basic definitions (*Nic. Ethics* 1141a5). Artistic excellence (*aristē technes*) is the sort of genius great artists and musicians display (*Nic. Ethics* 1141a9–11). Political wisdom (*praktikē*) is talent at governing others and running affairs of state, of generally organizing practical affairs (*Nic. Ethics* 1141b: 23–25). Wisdom (*sophia*) is considered by Aristotle to be highest cognitive talent. It is concerned with the proper understanding of the ultimate order of things (*Nic. Ethics* 1141a10ff.). Prudence or "practical wisdom" (*phronesis*), on the other hand, is concerned with human affairs and what sorts of things are conducive to the good life in general (1140a 27). Thus, for Aristotle, one important difference between prudence or practical wisdom and wisdom in general is their scope, the former being restricted to human affairs. For our purposes here the term *wisdom* will refer to "practical wisdom." Often the connotation of "prudence" today suggests individuals who are shrewd in the management of their affairs, but this is certainly not the way Aristotle meant it nor was it the sense in the classical tradition.

4.1 THE RELATION BETWEEN WISDOM AND THE VIRTUES

Plato (*Laws* 631b–c) and Cicero (*De inventione* 159) thought prudence or practical wisdom was a cardinal virtue along with justice, temperance, and courage, a view continued by Christian thinkers (Pieper 1975). Plato ranks it the highest among the four cardinal virtues (*Laws* 631c). However, some—such as Aristotle—distinguish prudence or wisdom from the other virtues by emphasizing that it is an intellectual talent rather than a character virtue (*Nic. Ethics* 1103a14–25; 1103a1–3). This is not to deny that character plays no role in the development of wisdom, only that it operates differently than a character virtue such as courage. Aristotle argues, moreover, that as an intellectual virtue, wisdom is acquired differently from the character virtues. Wisdom is acquired through teaching since it requires experience and time, while moral or character virtues come about as a result of habit and training (1103a14–16). Modern psychological research seems to confirm this view to some extent. Although it is not identical to pure intelligence (Sternberg 1991), wisdom is primarily a cognitive process nonetheless (Csikszentmihalyi and Rathune 1991; Baltes and Smith 1991).

A second feature which distinguishes practical wisdom from the character virtues is that wisdom directs the character virtues and so plays a special role in each of the virtues. For example, given Aristotle's argument that virtue is a mean between two extremes, the mean is still defined in accordance with practical wisdom (*Nic. Ethics* 1103b31–34; 1144b21–28). If practical wisdom is a virtue, then it's a virtue like no other because it is necessary and integral to every virtue. Certainly, some virtues are dependent upon one another in the way in which fair-mindedness is dependent upon temperance; some virtues also cluster with one another in the sense that a temperate person will generally have more luck with frugality, industriousness, and other virtues that deal with various types of pleasures. We can also say that some virtues comprehend others in the sense that a fair-minded person, to assure fair treatment of others, must incorporate many of the other virtues, such as honesty, respect, consideration, and the like. But prudence or wisdom is integral to each virtue, and that is a different sort of relation.

Indeed, as it has been noted in the detailed analysis of the virtues, the question of what is temperate, good-tempered, industrious, frugal, courageous, and the like has centered on questions of how, how much, when, with whom, and so forth. These are all pertinent concerns of practical wisdom. This suggests that it is not a virtue among virtues but something at the basis of virtue: "The other virtues," as Gregory says, "unless we do prudently what we desire to do, cannot be real virtues" (*Moral.* xxii). Aristotle suggests the same thing when he talks about the distinction between "natural" virtue and "virtue proper" (*Nic. Ethics* 1144b1–5). Natural virtues are the result of untrained character disposition. Some people may have more of a tendency toward self-control, for example, or bravery than others. But practical wisdom perfects natural virtue into virtue proper.

4.2 THE GENERAL FEATURES OF WISDOM

Several psychologists have attempted to identify the more central features of wisdom by looking at its common understanding among a wide range of people. A study by Holliday and Chandler (1986) came away with the following *principal components of moral wisdom: exceptional understanding, meaning that a wise person has learned from experience and sees things in a larger context; judgment and communication skills, that is, the ability to understand and judge correctly in matters of daily living; general competence in the sense of a strong ability to manage affairs, broadly understood; interpersonal skills, that is, someone who was sociable and sensitive; and social unobtrusiveness, meaning that such a person was discreet and nonjudgmental.* Based on their studies, psychologists Paul Baltes and Jacqui Smith define it as an expert knowledge

> about important matters of life, their interpretation and management. Included is knowledge about the variations, conditions, and historicity of life span development, human nature and conduct, life tasks and goals, social and intergenerational relationships, and life's uncertainties. Knowledge about one's self and one's own life biography and goals is also part of the domain (1991: 96).

Probably one of the best studies of the popular understanding of wisdom was done by Robert Sternberg (1991) and includes the following features:

1. *Reasoning ability.* Wise persons have the unique ability to look at a problem or situation and solve it; they have a clear, logical mind; they can draw on a huge store of knowledge and information to apply to particular problems; they have the ability to recognize similarities and differences.

2. *Sagacity.* Wise persons have a good understanding of a variety of people. They show a number of virtues, above all, self-honesty—they are people who know themselves well. They are considerate of others and have a genuine concern for them; they are fair and listen to all sides of an issue; they are modest, and so they feel they can always learn from others, while not being afraid to admit to making a mistake; they are willing to correct their mistakes, learn, and then go on; they seek the counsel of others.

3. *Learning capacity.* Wise persons attach importance to ideas and are very perceptive; they learn from other people's mistakes.

4. *Judgment.* Wise persons are sensible and have good judgment; they think before they act, speak, or make decisions; they are able to take the long view versus seeking only short-term outcomes.

5. *Expeditious use of information.* Wise persons have maturity and experience; they seek out detailed information; they learn and gain information from past mistakes and successes and change their mind on the basis of experience.

6. *Perspicacity.* Wise persons have good intuition and offer solutions that are on the side of right and truth; they are able to see through things and read between the lines.

If these studies are accurate, when we think of the exceptionally sagacious, such as Socrates, Confucius, Buddha, Solomon, Jesus, and Mohammad, we think of people with most of the following characteristics: good decision-making capacity (Sternberg 1985; Holliday and Chandler 1986; Baltes et al. 1991); the uncanny ability to choose the right course of action in a highly complex moral situation; exceptional deliberative talent, discernment, and good judgment; savoir-faire

> "The prudent man will lead a moral life when he considers it has four rewards: a sense of virtue gives him peace, his body is not overtaxed, at night he sleeps a happy sleep, and when he wakes, he wakes with joy."
>
> —Dharmapada

based on worldly experience (Labouvie-Vief 1982; Perry 1970; Csikszentmihalyi and Rathunde 1991: 35); a sophisticated folk psychology that allows for proper interaction and communication with others (Csikszentmihalyi and Rathunde 1991: 45ff.); a powerful self-directed reflective capacity (Holliday and Chandler 1986); and a strong moral vision or direction brought on by an integrated understanding of the order of things (Csikszentmihalyi and Rathunde 1991: 28ff.). The sagacious have a strong vision of the way things should be, a deep understanding of what is truly fine, and a clear sense of the good life.

4.3 HOW WISDOM IS ACQUIRED

To be counted as wise, one must have a good character, especially a virtuous disposition (Aristotle, *Nic. Ethics* 1107a1–2; Aquinas, *Summa* Pt. I–II Q. 58 Art. 5). But although one cannot be practically wise without moral virtue, one cannot be morally virtuous without practical wisdom (*Nic. Ethics* 1144a: 36, 1144b30–32; cf. Richard Sorabji 1980: 212). "There is a close mutual connection between prudence and excellence of character, since the fundamental principles of prudence are determined by the virtues of character, while prudence determines the right standard for the moral virtues" (*Nic. Ethics* 1178a15–19; cf. also Sowardka 1987; Baltes and Smith 1991: 107). Without temperance, for example, a person is susceptible to moral blindness and, hence, bad judgment when it counts. If a person is overcome by passion or desire, his deliberation is bound to be flawed. As Epimarchus writes, "No one deliberates rightly about anything in anger" (485 B.C.: 23: 44). Daniel Goleman suggests that when emotions overwhelm concentration, what is being swamped is the mental capacity cognitive scientists call "working memory" (1995: 79). Working memory is the executive function par excellence for mental life, and without the right sort of temperament and character, working memory will not function properly, and prudent wisdom will be difficult to achieve. For this reason, only people with certain types of virtuous disposition will tend toward wisdom. Also, virtuous habits engender a certain sense of the good life, necessary for proper moral vision. Temperance, again, allows one to see higher beyond immediate pleasures to the possibility of a broader sense of life than the mere satisfaction of pleasure. As Cicero said, "A man of courage who considers pain the greatest evil, or a temperate man who declares indulgence to be the greatest good, is surely an impossible contradiction" (*De officiis* 5). Those capable of controlling passions, desires, and appetites are able to make clear judgments (cf. *Summa* Pt. I–II Q. 57 Art. 4), and those capable of overcoming fear and enduring hardship also contribute to the development of good moral judgment or prudence. Furthermore, without a degree of moral strength, decisions will be flawed and judgments impaired. Consequently, the acquisition of wisdom requires good moral character.

Although necessary, character is not sufficient for moral wisdom. Aristotle makes it clear that experience is also required: The young may easily acquire mathematical skill, but rarely would they be counted as morally wise (*Nic. Ethics* 1141b18; cf. Clayton and Birren 1980; Baltes and Smith 1991: 88; Labouvie-Vief 1991: 52)— although some have questioned this claim (cf. Orwoll and Perlmutter 1991: 172; Meacham 1991: 181). Aristotle suggests that, precisely because of their experience, we ought to heed the advice and counsel of older people (*Nic. Ethics* 1143b12–15). Experience allows us to become familiar with the particulars of life and to acquire a certain folk psychology concerning human character and behavior, a grasp of cases, models, and paradigms of decision making, in general, what Aristotle calls *synesis*, a sort of understanding of the way things are (*Nic. Ethics* 1143aff.). Experience also provides the opportunity to test our decision-making capacity; trial and error often lead to better judgment as well (*Nic. Ethics* 1143a20ff.).

However, it is not the experience as such that makes one wise, but the manner in which we apprehend and learn from it. The wise person must have the right sort of intelligence and cognitive processes to learn from experience and to rightly apprehend the information we receive through the course of our lives. Clearly, there are older people who have had experience, yet are not what we consider sagacious. As the saying goes, "There is no fool like an old fool." Experience alone is not sufficient for sagacious understanding, and wisdom is a relatively rare acquisition (Baltes and Smith 1991: 96). This requires the special talent of reflection, especially self-reflection. Socrates had thought that the most important thing was "to know thyself." Without self-knowledge it is difficult to learn from mistakes, and thus, experience would lose its utility. Being deluded about who you are and what you've done would dull the ability to gain some insight from experience. Sagacious understanding also requires other intellectual talents pertinent to experience: a keen sense of observation, understood as the ability to notice patterns in those experiences and connect them with others; discernment, the talent for subtle perception of nuances and differences in situations that allows you to distinguish them from other ones; intuition, the ability to grasp the gist of an experience; and insight, a moment when, through an expanded awareness, one recognizes the limitations of a previous perspective.

In general, then, *moral wisdom is something acquired over time for those with a certain virtuous disposition who have the intellectual talent to learn from experience.*

4.4 REASONING WISELY

Moral reasoning is thought to be different from theoretical or logical reasoning (Kitchener and Brenner 1991: 226). As we saw earlier in the Introduction to this book, theoretical versus practical accounts of moral reasoning help to define the difference between the sagacious tradition in ethics and the modern theoretical one. The theoretical account sees the job of moral reasoning as the discovery of rationally justified principles that can then be applied to particular cases, much in the way physical laws would be determinate for any single case to which they apply. For this reason, the modern tradition has been focused on discovering these ethical principles. On the other hand, according to the practical account of moral reasoning, its function is to persuade ourselves and others why we should do one thing rather than another in this particular situation; theoretical reasoning is concerned to show us why we should believe one thing rather than another (Aristotle, *De Motu* 701a8–12), that is, why we should believe in a particular law or principle. Moral reasoning results in decision and action rather than belief (*De Motu* 701a8–12). To be persuaded to act, a person must be convinced that this action is the right thing to do in order to attain a worthy goal. The core of wisdom is a kind of intelligence that involves making judgments about what the right thing to do is in a given situation. The commonly understood features of wisdom previously discussed are all conducive to this talent. A morally wise person must have a certain level of intelligence and education, good sense, discernment, experience, self-knowledge, a good folk psychology, and the rest.

When people are making deliberate judgments, that is, reasoning about what to do in a certain situation, they are performing an intentional or goal-directed action. Since wisdom is generally concerned with such intentional or goal-directed actions, we might be able to clarify the investigation of its peculiar kind of reasoning by focusing on each of the principal aspects of any intentional act. The philosopher Georg von Wright (1979), who has studied such behavior in great detail, argues that intentional action can be divided into the following three aspects:

1. the *end* of the action, that is, the short- or long-term reason why an action is done;
2. the *means* of the action, that is, the strategy, plan, or course of action thought by the agent best to achieve that goal;
3. the *execution* of an action, understood as the result of the decision to do what an agent believes is necessary to accomplish the goal.

In making deliberate judgments about what to do in certain situations, we often encounter various aspects of intentional action, expressed by the following questions:

1. What sort of goals should I pursue in life, and how should they be ranked? What should be my priorities in life—what is the good life after all?
2. What are the best moral means by which to attain these goals? What life plans should I make to achieve the good life?
3. What is my present situation?
4. What is the best plan to follow, given that situation?
5. Should I resolve to do it now?

The sort of reasoning found in wisdom can then be more specifically characterized as the proper connection among act, means, and end (cf. *De Anima* 433a15). As Aristotle claims, for us to light upon the correct course of action, the end must be worthy, the means to the end morally right, and the action done at the right time in the right way (*Nic. Ethics* 1142b16–35). The distinctive capacity of the wise person is being able to find, in a given particular situation, what should be done as part of the good life (Engberg-Pedersen 1983: 218). In general, a wise person possesses "the unique ability to look at a problem or situation and solve it" (Sternberg 1985) in a morally satisfactorily way. *Moral reasoning is concerned with the process of connecting end, means, and decision in a way that preserves the moral integrity of the outcome.* Moral reasoning must show why a certain goal or way of life is desirable, why this course of action is better than others in attaining or realizing this goal or this way of life, and that, given the present situation, this sort of action is in our power to do. It is concerned to show that there is a concordance between means and end and between action and end that is morally adequate.

If wise moral reasoning is concerned specifically with the ends, means, and the execution of action, then it can be divided into three concerns for the purpose of analysis:

> *Moral vision,* which is concerned with an evaluation of the ends of action, including the sense of the good life.
>
> *Deliberation,* which is concerned with evaluating the best moral means to attain ends.
>
> *Judgment,* which is concerned with coming to a decision about what to do in a particular situation relative to the ends desired and the means deliberated.

In this light, wisdom can be seen as the perfection of the other features of moral competence discussed so far. It perfects the desire to do the good by developing a robust sense of the good life, a moral vision. It perfects virtuous behavior by guiding it deliberately toward the proper ends defined by that moral vision—by telling us when, where, with whom, and how to act virtuously. For example, according to Aristotle, courage is not facing any danger for any reason, but facing the right danger for the right reason (*Nic. Ethics* 1115b15–20); thus, we cannot know what courage requires of us now without knowing what the good life in general requires. Whatever other roles practical wisdom may play, it enables people, in light of their conception of the good life in general, to perceive what virtue requires of them and thereby to save them from making the wrong choices in life. Practical wisdom also constrains strength of will to act on the right decisions in the right context (cf. Aquinas, *Summa* Pt. I–II Q. 57 Art. 6). To use a well-worn metaphor, moral sentiment makes us desire a worthwhile destination, but moral vision tells us where to look. Moral strength gives us the power to do what is necessary to go the distance, but judgment tells us when it is best to exercise that resolve. Virtue keeps us going on the path and straying from it, but deliberation shows us how to use the path to get there.

4.5 MORAL VISION

Visions can be understood in one sense as predictions. In these cases we talk about the visionary, or the soothsayer, who claims to see as Apollo did the shape of things to come. This word is also used in the context of religious or spiritual visions (cf. Moreira 1996), in which the divine is said to appear to the devotee, or the manner in which a mystic is said to attain special access to the divine (cf. Miller 1990). Vision quests are cases where the young warrior must make a solitary journey until a personal totem appears. Vision is also used more ordinarily as a term for an imagined

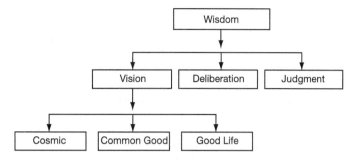

Vision is part of wisdom, and is concerned with the ends of action. Cosmic vision is an understanding of the moral order of the world; the common good is concerned with the good community; while the good life is a vision of our personal happiness.

result of a certain plan, as in the case of Martin Luther King's dream of a fully integrated society or a political leader's vision of this country for the 21st century. René Descartes claimed that "he was visited by three consecutive dreams in a single night" in which his future intellectual work was revealed.

But vision also has a broader meaning than any of these. The metaphor of the vista and horizon can help us understand vision in this sense. To use the language of the philosophers Martin Heidegger (1928: 416) and Hans-Georg Gadamer (1975: 269), a horizon is the limit of what we see, and the vista is where we see it from, the window through which we see through all other windows. Persons with vision in this sense are individuals who have ordered everything and made the picture of the world coherent for themselves. For that reason, they see which way to go. The world that once was a "blooming, buzzing confusion," in William James's famous words, is now consolidated into a coherent picture. As Csikszentmihalyi and Rathunde remark, a strong moral vision or direction is brought on by an integrated understanding of the order of things (1991: 28ff.). In fact they are coincident. All beliefs get their final import from their relation to a vision, and so no belief is understood in its full import until one understands the vision to which it belongs. A vision of this sort rises above disparate pieces of information, specific beliefs, particular theories, and personal experiences into a story of the way the world is. In *War and Peace*, the Mason, one of Tolstoy's characters, argues with Pierre that "the highest wisdom is not founded on reason alone, nor on those worldly sciences of physics, chemistry, and the like, into which intellectual knowledge is divided. ... The highest wisdom has but one science—the science of all, the science of explaining all creation and man's place in it" (1968: 429; in Csikszentmihalyi and Rathunde 1991: 32). The sage is someone who has a profound insight into the human condition and into the order of things and, on the basis of that understanding, has a certain moral vision (cf. Engberg-Pedersen 1983: 223).

The great philosophers exemplify vision in this sense. Plato, Aristotle, Aquinas, Kant, Hegel, and Nietzsche each believed that he had reached a point where his particular horizon had given order to the world and everything in it. According to Aristotle, the morally wise person has a sense of the good life (*Nic. Ethics* 1140a25–31), a view of the best (*Nic. Ethics* 1141b13), or an idea of happiness (*Rhet.* 1366b20). In this sense it can be said that a *moral vision is an answer to the questions "What is the good life?" and "How should one live?" It is concerned with the course, variations, conditions, conduct, and meaning of life* (Baltes and Smith 1991: 87). Moral wisdom involves knowledge of the highest good, and it serves as the point from which moral (practical reasoning) starts (*Nic. Ethics* 1151a16–17). Plato insists that for virtue not to collapse simply into a means to the satisfaction of lower needs, we must find something higher to look up and be dedicated to, something more enduring than ourselves. Without moral vision one is directionless, caught up in a world of trying to attain immediate and transitory goods. As Plato sees it, the behavior of God, when properly understood, could serve as this ultimate vision (whose behavior incidentally looks like the perfect philosopher) (*The Laws* 716c–718a). In fact, Kant insists that to make sense out of morality, we must postulate that there is a highest good (1788: 128–130).

But visions do not have to be as systematic and sophisticated as the great philosophers; they can also be relatively unsystematic and simple. This is the sense of vision expressed by Thomas Sowell (1987: 3): Unsystematic visions are cognitive but preanalytic maps of the world; they are silent shapers of thought (1987: 8), so they guide our systematic reasoning about the world. Conflicts of visions are more fundamental than conflicts of beliefs, since changes of vision require a change in the entire framework or outlook a person has about the world and so affect the systems of beliefs in a dramatic way. According to Sowell (1987: 13), visions are like maps that guide us through a tangle of bewildering complexities about reality. They should not be confused with interests. When interests are at stake, parties know clearly what is to gain or lose, but when there is a conflict of visions, the parties are often unaware of its underlying assumptions simply because it forms a background to most decisions concerning our interests (1987: 7). Visions should not be confused with goals such as getting a home, a college degree, or getting married; such goals, however, may constitute some part of the vision. Visions are also not simply emotional drives; they have a remarkable conceptual structure (1987: 7).

If we continue with the metaphors of horizon and vista, it is clear that they have both a temporal and a spatial dimension. In the metaphor of the vista, we are presently at a point to which we have come from some other point and look out at a distant horizon. We attain a vista by an arduous climb up the peak, and the past—what is behind us—marks the struggle to attain the vista. On the other hand, the vista is seen in the present, and the vista itself is a distant future. By analogy a vision addresses the past, present, and future by giving an answer to three specific questions: How did we come about? (the past). How is it that we came to be the way we are? (the present). What will become of us? (the future). Walter Lippman notes perceptively that

> at the core of every moral code there is a picture of human nature, a map of the universe, and a version of history. To human nature (of the sort conceived), in a universe (of the kind imagined), after a history (so understood), the rules of the code apply (1965: 80).

The metaphor of the vista also involves a sense of purposefulness and direction. The vista gives us a direction in which to go, but from a place found in the present and rooted by what we have done in the past. The past, present, and future each carry different senses of purposefulness (Heidegger 1928: 416). The future is associated with one kind of purpose, "for the sake of"—what is it that we hope to attain? The present is associated with "the in order to"—given where we are, how do we get to where we want to go? The past is associated with "in the face of"—given where we have come from, what we must overcome or endure to get where we want to be?

In providing us with a vista and a purpose, a vision gives us an understanding of the way in which the world works—that is, world in the sense of the cosmos and the order of things. It also frames the way in which we see others in our communities, societies, and nations as we each strive, individually, for some sense of the good life which that vision also provides. Thus, we can think of vision as having three aspects: cosmic, communal, and individual. In the cosmic vision, we acquire sense of the moral tenor of the order of things; in the communal vision, we look for a sense of the common good; and in the individual vision, we strive for some sense of the good life for ourselves.

4.5.1 Cosmic Vision

A cosmic vision is a picture of the world that conveys a certain sense of the moral order of things. It also tells us how we should understand ourselves as moral agents within that world. Although it can take the form of a sophisticated system of thought and beliefs, it is ordinarily expressed for most people in story form, especially in the basic myths of a culture. Why stories? Philosopher Martha Nussbaum explains that well:

> certain truths about human life can only be fittingly and accurately stated in the language and forms characteristic of the narrative artist. ... A view of life is *told*. The telling itself–the selection of genre, formal structures, sentences, vocabulary, of the whole manner of addressing the reader's sense of life–all of this expresses a sense of life and of value, a sense of what matters and what does not ... of life's relations and connections. (1990: 4–5).

There are good reasons for the fit between stories and moral visions. As we saw in Chapter One, in our discussion of moral education (Section 1.4.4), stories appeal to the imaginative parts of our brain (Vitz 1990). This approach is more delightful than a reasoned approach (Kilpatrick and Wolf 1994: 21; Vitz 1990). Telling stories is a form of enchantment that draws our attention better than any other mode of discourse (Bettelheim 1977). Moreover, it is easy to identify with the story, to become involved in the story, because there is a parallel between the way in which narratives organize events and the way in which we organize our lives (Scheibe 1986; Sarbin 1986; Robinson and Hawpe 1986; Vitz 1990). There is simply a storied nature to our lives. As Mark Johnson notes,

> narrative characterizes the synthetic character of our very experience, and it is prefigured in our daily activities and projects. The stories we tell emerge from, and can then refigure, the narrative structure of our experience. Consequently, the way we understand, express, and communicate our experience is derived from and dependent on that prior narrative structure of our lives (1993: 163).

In other words, since our lives are narratively organized, it is much easier to place ourselves in a story than to identify with a logically arranged system of beliefs. The drama of the story helps to incorporate us into an imaginative process of participation and identification. This is perhaps the reason why storytelling is a more universal form of discourse than any other type, and nearly every culture has a repertoire of stories. A story is a way to express something that can't be said with a series of factual statements.

Second, stories easily convey a certain moral view. If a picture is worth a thousand words, a story is worth a hundred propositions. All stories have a moral or normative character. In fact, it could be reasonably argued that the very act of telling a story carries with it a certain moral view. We saw in Chapter One how moral emotions could be thought of as generated from "little stories." The emotion of moral outrage, for example, requires a scenario in which we perceive someone as violating a rule or norm which leaves a victim and sets up a drama of opponents, one of which we consider to have wronged the other. By telling even the simplest story—for example, the king died and then the queen died of grief—the storyteller also gives those events a moral ascription. The simple declaration of those two events implicitly suggests that the events were somehow terrible or tragic, that we should sympathize with the queen because her relationship with her husband was loving, that losing a loved one is always a terrible thing, and that it is indeed a harsh world that allows such things. If a fairytale is told where the dragon kidnaps a princess who is rescued by a young lad, the story defines opponents—those who are counted as good and those who are bad. It also imputes a kind of justice over these events so that the good prevail and the vicious do not.

If we put these two theses together—that stories inherently convey moral outlooks and that we can easily identify with them—then it follows why moral visions are often linked with stories. We are able to give moral meaning to our lives through the comparison of our life story and the stories we are told; by that means stories can provide models of visions and outlooks. Thus, if we tell stories about the origins of things, the way things came to be—as origin myths do—we are giving that origin and our present condition a certain moral outlook at the same time. To the extent that we believe those stories in some sense of the term, then we also buy-in to the moral picture it presents. Such stories answer the three questions posed by any grand moral vision: How is it that we came to be? How is it that we came to be the way we are? What will become of us?

Plato, more than any other philosopher, certainly recognized this and busied himself with composing stories which captured nicely the sort of moral vision that he elaborated in the longhand of systematic reasoning. Plato relates a myth—the story of Er (*Republic* 614-621)—which is similar to reincarnation theories in many respects, but which emphasizes the importance of acquiring wisdom concerning the best life. Er, a soldier killed in battle, escaped the usual process of forgetfulness that is required of all the souls that pass from this life and reenter it at a later date. Consequently, he was able to tell others the nature of the world hereafter. According to Er, when a soul dies it undergoes a judgment. If it has led a decent life, then it is moved to the right to pleasant circumstances; if not, it is led to the left to rather unpleasant conditions. In any case, after a while, both left and right populations are required to take a new life. They can choose a wide variety of lives. Each of these lives is outlined in its general characteristics, and each appears to have advantages. There will be three sorts of styles of selection, however. Those who have suffered from a bad life will, of course, not choose the same life again even though it appears to have certain advantages; however, they may still choose another bad life since they may lack wisdom about what constitutes the best sort of life. Those on the right may wish to choose the same sort of life that led them to good circumstances, but if theirs was simply the result of the moral luck of living conventionally in a good community and they have not acquired any wisdom or understanding of the good life, then they, too, may be tempted to choose the wrong sort of life, given its appearances. If they choose badly, then their circumstances in the next afterlife are worse. Only those who have gained knowledge of the best life, and so consistently choose the good life, end the cycle of reincarnation and judgment; the person is allowed to dwell pleasantly in a heaven well suited to the life of the mind.

What Plato's cosmic vision tells us is how the order of things generally operates, whether it is just or unjust, and what sense of justice it has. At the same time, on the basis of that account, it defines the role for the moral agent: It tells us what an agent must do to flourish and prevail. The only person who is safe from mistake, then, is someone who knows, who has wisdom, concerning the nature of the good life. Plato has arranged a story of the nature of things so that it promotes wisdom as the means to salvation.

Consider the Genesis stories (Gen 2: 1–25; 3: 1–24), common to Judaism, Christianity, and Islam. Yahweh creates a world out of the void which is geometrically well-ordered. It begins with a division of light and dark, of days and nights, of heaven and earth, and on earth divisions between land and water and types of plants, animals, and humans. Everything that is created is pronounced good. In second Genesis, Yahweh creates a perfect paradise for Adam and Eve in which all their needs are taken care of. They need only obey the fundamental rule of paradise, not to eat the fruit of the tree of the knowledge of good and evil, and all will remain well for them. However, they are tempted and violate the command. As a result, Adam and Eve are expelled from paradise into a world which is imperfect, a world in which they must now labor and suffer. Compare this to a myth from the Tlingit, a native people from the northwest coast of North America:

> Raven goes to a place where there's some dirt and rocks. He tries to put them together, but they don't stick. That Raven, he's got a temper, so he kicked the rocks and swore because he hurt his toes. But then he had another idea. This time he mixed in some water with the rocks and dirt. He worked hard, that Raven did, and had an awful time of it. The mountains dropped off. The oceans spilled over. Sometimes he got so mad he just kicked the whole thing to pieces. Raven's world was lumpy and bumpy, and it sure didn't look like what he had in mind. But he was good and tired of working on it. So he said the hell with it. And that's the way it stayed (in Klouda 1993: 27).

The tenor of the two stories is remarkably different. As opposed to the well-ordered, perfect world created by a perfect God for Adam and Eve, Raven is an ill-tempered, disorganized creator. The world reflects a certain chaos, imperfection, and incompleteness in the Tlingit vision. Also, Raven as portrayed in other myths is a trickster god who has many uncomplimentary features. The world is imperfect because it was created in an imperfect fashion by an imperfect creator whose character is suspect. On the other hand, as reflected in the account of the creation in *Genesis* (1: 1–31), the world is created through a very ordered process of division and partition. The creator, Yahweh, is a rational creator who creates for the good, and the order of the world reflects this goodness. But it is human beings with their flaws and imperfections who create a world now full of suffering, death, and misery. In the Tlingit vision the imperfection of the world is already present, and the world is created more or less by happenstance. In such a world human beings must work within the confines of the way things are and do the best they can.

Each of these stories addresses the three fundamental questions of any vision. For the Adam and Eve myth we have lost paradise, and that is the reason why we are presently in our condition of labor, suffering, and death; but it also engenders the possibility of regaining paradise, and indeed, the remainder of biblical literature–Hebrew, Christian, and Islamic (to the extent that the Genesis myths are incorporated into the literature of the Koran and The New Testament)—is devoted to the various ways in which this might be done. The Tlingit myth suggests a permanent imperfection in the order of things, which accounts for the present state of affairs, and although it is less hopeful than the Adam and Eve vision, it appears more tolerant and understanding of our moral makeup.

A person's vision of the world understood in this manner frames the way in which that person sees the world morally, but also how she sees herself as a moral agent. A teacher had a discussion with a student who had a particular interpretation of reincarnation and the law of karma. She argued that the accumulation of rewards and punishments for good or bad deeds is a perfect principle of justice. This meant, in her view, that a person's suffering is due to some bad karma in a previous life, and not only that, but those responsible for the person's suffering may have been victims of the person in some previous life. She even argued that if a woman is raped, then it was the result of some action in a previous life, and the rapist was someone involved in that previous life as well. She felt that only under this view could the true meaning of suffering be revealed so that we could learn from our past mistakes and move on to a higher form of life the next time around. This particular cosmic outlook undoubtedly frames her moral one. First, any harm or suffering she endures is justly deserved, and similarly for others. This engenders certain attitudes that would not be present, for instance, in a typical Christian view, which argues that many cases of suffering are undeserved and the result of vicious persons or intentions. The attitudes toward victims and perpetrators would be remarkably different than hers.

In typical Christian or Muslim metaphysics, the understanding is that God gives humans free will and judges them on the basis of what sorts of actions they choose. They are given one chance in this earthly life, and on the basis of their performance, they are rewarded or punished in an eternal afterlife. Under the Christian–Muslim view, the moral agent is situated in the framework of a test or trial and is placed in the role of a combatant who must struggle against temptations and vicious forces to prove themselves to the ultimate judge. Under this person's interpretation of the law of karma, it acts more like a natural law, inexorable in its consequences, rather than like a judge. Thus, the consequences of bad decisions will force one into a worse sort of life, and so the role one plays as a moral agent is more of an apprentice who must learn from life's mistakes until they can evolve—through that understanding—to a higher form, eventually falling out of the cycle of life and suffering altogether. Her cosmic vision gives her a framework by which to assess the character of the world and role that she should play in it as a moral agent.

Thus, our cosmic visions often depend on the kinds of stories we tell ourselves about the origin and nature of things. Although each story conveys a certain uniqueness, most stories can be classified under generally recognized patterns, each with a peculiar *ethos*. Some of the more common ones are tragedy, comedy, romance or melodrama, irony, and satire (cf. Frye 1957). *Romances* or *melodramas* are some of the most frequently told stories. Common fairytales and nearly every Hollywood action film are examples of melodramas. Movies such as *Star Wars, Independence Day, Armageddon, The Terminator*, and other popular films are clear cases. A melodrama typically has a plot that involves a conflict between opponents clearly defined as good and evil. It does not usually take much for the audience to distinguish the good from the bad and identify with the good moral agents. Although there are many subtle nuances *in melodramas, the plot usually allows the good agents victory over the bad ones, and in the process victims are rescued or in some manner saved from harm.* The implicit norm in a melodrama is what might be called a *perfect principle of justice.* There is a right order (as understood by the story), and that right order prevails, such that

1. Reward should be given to those who deserve it.
2. No reward should be given to those who do not deserve it.
3. Punishment or harm should not be directed to those who do not deserve it.
4. Those who perpetrate harm against the undeserving of harm are deserving of punishment and our outrage.
5. Those who punish those who perpetrate harm against the undeserving of harm, or protect or prevent harm to the undeserving of harm, deserve our admiration and gratitude.

These norms express a sort of moral tautology, nicely said by the writer Anthony Trollope: "If I could do this, then I thought I might succeed in impregnating the mind of the novel-reader with a feeling ... that things meanly done are ugly and odious, and things nobly done beautiful and gracious" (quoted in Booth 1988: 211).

The melodrama works by first establishing for the audience those who are deserving of reward and punishment and those who are not. It then carries out a story in which the deserving of reward are rewarded, the undeserving of reward are not rewarded, perpetrators are punished, and victims are revenged, saved, or successfully protected from harm. Melodramas or romances have a tendency then to define the opponents in the conflict as the case where one side threatens this perfect principle of justice, while the other seeks to realize or defend it. Along with this tendency is another one that typically portrays the antagonist or the Other as outside the group associated with the story's intended audience, or if he is within the group, then someone whose foul character and deeds warrant punishment. Almost by necessity the opponent in the romance must be a subscriber to an immoral universe; the hero, even if he is of lowly or outlaw status, expresses a moral order. A pure romance, of course, can be adulterated by some of the other genres: It may express tragic, ironic, or comedic tones so that it involves martyrdom of the hero or attenuations to the destruction of the opponent.

This melodramatic or romantic vision is a popular and hopeful one, and it is one generally found in several different religions. The great Christian thinker Augustine, for example, argued that the eternal law by which God governs the cosmos is "that by which the wicked deserve misery, the good, a life of blessedness" (*De lib. Arb.* I.6). Paul (10–67 C.E.), considered by many the principal formulator of Christian doctrine, expresses the sense of agency well in this vision (Philippians 1: 27–30):

> I shall know that you are unanimous in meeting the attack [of your enemies] with firm resistance, united by your love for the faith of the gospel and quite unshaken by your enemies. This would be the sure sign that they will lose and you will be saved. It would be a sign from God that he has given you the privilege not only of believing in Christ, but of suffering for him as well. You and I are together in the same fight as you saw me fighting before and, as you will have heard, I am fighting still.

Indeed, the moral agent in the romantic vision is the one who rises to the defense of the good order, whose faith does not waiver in the goodness of the order they are defending, and whose efforts to defeat the opponent do not weaken. As Paul writes, "My one hope and trust is that I shall never have to admit defeat, but that now as always I shall have the courage for Christ to be glorified in my body, whether by my life or by my death" (Philippians 1: 19–20). Clearly, then, the image of the faithful and trustworthy warrior is the dominant image of moral agent in the romantic vision.

In many regards the romantic or melodramatic pattern is considered the default one: Most people want to see the right order prevail. *Ironies* play against that expectation. *In* a strong *irony*, such as George Orwell's *1984, the right order does not prevail.* The protagonist, Winston Smith, struggles against the oppressive regime of Big Brother, with its pervasive attempts at thought control. In the end his attempts are foiled, and Big Brother is shown to have been in charge all along, despite Smith's apparent escape from its purview. Needless to say, ironies present a bleak picture of things. Instead of focusing on the loss of right order, some ironies may suggest that there is no order or, if there is, that it is unknowable. Kafka's *The Trial* is a good example of this. The protagonist, K, is awakened one morning to be told that he has been accused of a crime for which he must stand trial. The remainder of the book charts his attempt to find out who is accusing him, why, and who are these people who plan to bring him to trial. The reader simply witnesses K's march through this labyrinth of inquiry without finding an answer. Some ironies, such as Anton Chekhov's *The Cherry Orchard* or Arthur Miller's *Death of a Salesman* focus on decay—the decay of a culture, a family, or a person. In a related way some ironies center on people's illusions. In Henrik Ibsen's the *Wild Duck*, the inventor is working on an invention that will never happen. In Samuel Beckett's *Waiting for Godot*, the characters are waiting for someone who will never show. In Chekhov's *Uncle Vanya*, the title character works under the illusion that the professor is an esteemed scholar, when he is not. Some ironies show futility: Despite effort, people find themselves in the same position or even worse. In the recent film *A Simple Plan*, small town brothers happen across a cache of stolen drug money. In their efforts to conceal the money from authorities, their friend is killed, a brother dies, they lose the money, and the true character of one man's wife is revealed.

One feature that is consistent through these variations of irony is the depiction of the protagonist as weak, flawed, and otherwise unadmirable. The Protestant reformationists Luther and Calvin had a strong ironic vision of human beings, believing that their natures were essentially weak and depraved: "man, being fallen and abandoned by God, cannot will good. ... [God] finds them [man] to be ... perverted and evil. ... they cannot but do what is perverse and evil" (Luther 1525: 129). The American Puritan philosopher and preacher Jonathan Edwards (1704–1758) expresses this vision very well. In his famous sermon "Sinners in the Hands of an Angry God," he says,

> Your wickedness makes you as it were heavy as lead, and to tend downwards with great weight and pressure towards hell; and if God should let you go, you would immediately sink and swiftly descend and plunge into the bottomless gulf, and your healthy constitution, and your own care and prudence, and bent contrivance, and all your righteousness, would have no more influence to uphold you and keep you out of hell, than a spider's web would have to stop a fallen rock (1741: 162).

Unlike the romance or melodrama, irony blends the dichotomies of good and bad, and the apparently good is as likely to be as flawed as the apparently bad. In Clint Eastwood's *The Unforgiven*, the sheriff and townsfolk are as vicious and vile as the bounty hunters. In the end there is no good person to anchor into the story. In irony conflict is a constant part of the human landscape, and resolutions—although desirable—only assuage temporarily or generate new sources of conflict. The best one can do is manage them.

Whereas romance or melodrama emphasizes the conflict between opposing groups, or opposing normative structures, *tragedy focuses on the conflicts and violations of norms within the group.* Tragedies show what happens when alliances falter, families fall apart, friends betray one another, or subjects prove disloyal. Gloster in *King Lear* says it most succinctly: "Love cools, friendship falls off, brothers divide: in cities, mutinies; in countries, discord; in palaces, treason; and the bond cracked between son and father" (Act I Sc. II). The implicit normative structure which tragedy appeals to can be expressed by the following:

> Parents ought to love their children and children their parents.
> Husbands ought to love wives and wives husbands.
> One should remain loyal to the group.
> Harmony and goodwill should be present within the group.

What is so horrifying about tragedy, as 19th-century philosopher Georg Hegel notes, is the violation of these norms and the self-destruction of the group which is seen as the concrete manifestation of ethical life (1962: 47). Conflict leads to destruction, out of which a new hope for harmony must begin. Still, tragedies share implicitly the norm of romance—that right order ought to prevail, but it does so indirectly by showing how a sense of justice sweeps over those who violate these norms. As opposed to romances or melodramas, where we see a noble hero who exemplifies the virtues and good qualities which the culture's story admires, in classic tragedies we see a character who is noble in many respects but seriously flawed in at least one way. For Othello, it is jealousy; for Macbeth and Richard III, it is ambition; for Hamlet, indecision; for Oedipus, curiosity.

Classic comedy shares the same implicit normative structure as tragedy but, of course, involves the realization of these norms rather than the consequences of their violation. Classic comedy shouldn't be confused with slapstick, stand-up comedy, or the sitcoms on TV, although these share some of it patterns. To avoid the modern connotation of the word *comedy,* we might call this a *thalian* vision, after the Greek muse of comedy, Thalia. In comedy, or the thalian vision, incest is avoided, lovers are reconciled, and the foolish are made to see the folly of their ways before it is too late. In general, comedy, such as Dickens's *A Christmas Carol,* reincorporates the other into the community and reinforces the good will of the group toward one another. *A Midsummer Night's Dream* is a true comedy precisely because in the end it puts true lovers together and prevents the artificially proposed arrangements of Hermia's father, Egeus. Comedies are successes at upholding the norms which both tragedies and comedies share. The key to that success is the cleverness or prudence that prevails in the hero, as in *A Midsummer Night's Dream, Much Ado About Nothing,* or Plautus's comedies, and that involve success at enlightening those key figures or blockers who would rend the family or community apart.

Comedies frame opponents in a different light than do melodramas: not as Other, but as potentially One—a blocker, who through misunderstanding or some other flaw puts obstacles in front of their own happiness and harmony with others. In agreement with romance, comedy argues that conflicts are resolvable—however, not in terms of destruction of the Other, but in reconciliation with the Other. Harmony is the goal and, unlike irony, it is thought to be achievable.

The philosophy of Gandhi (1869–1948) is a good illustration of the thalian vision. Gandhi held to the doctrine of *satyagraha,* which he used effectively against the British in winning national independence for India in the 1940s. British punitive aggressions against those who challenged its jurisdiction were not met by force in kind, but a "steadfast communal holding to truth." The grip of this force would loosen the grip of the tyrant; its own inner lawlessness would be its own undoing, and one had only to wait for it to fall apart. The immoral agent in this case is the one who falls into the trap of violence and force to achieve her aims and loses the good heart that sees a basic decency in the human race.

Satires share the view with melodramas that the right order should prevail, but they *attempt to show that the prevailing order is far from the right one.* Satires, such as Voltaire's *Candide* or Jonathan Swift's *Gulliver's Travels*, expose and undermine the hypocrisy and absurdity that exists and attempt to restore a more honest and truer one. In the classic satire the hero runs into conflict with the existing order and in the process realizes its hypocrisy, masks, foolishness, and false airs. In light of this discovery, the hero resolves to be true to himself, and pledges a simpler life.

Henry David Thoreau (1817–1862) illustrates this vision. As argued in *Walden*, it is the ethic of the established way of life that actually enslaves humans rather than frees them as promised. People must recognize this irony and hypocrisy to free themselves from the burdens imposed on their lives and live a simpler, truer way of life. For example, he urges them to throw off the yoke of the work ethic which, rather than improving their lives, forces them into a strained, striving life with limited yield. Some of Thoreau's sentiments are famously expressed in the following passages:

> I am convinced, both by faith and experience, that to maintain one's self on this earth is not a hardship but a pastime, if we will live simply and wisely. ... (1854: 49).

> Simplicity, simplicity, simplicity! I say, let your affairs be as two or three, and not a hundred or a thousand. ... (1854: 63).

> I said to myself, I will not plant beans and corn with so much industry another summer, but such seeds, if the seed is not lost, as sincerity, truth, simplicity, faith, innocence, and the like, and see if they will not grow in this soil, even with less toil and manurance, and sustain me, for surely it has not been exhausted for these crops (1854: 113).

Sometimes the recognition of hypocrisy and absurdity can lead people to a very cynical view of life. The cynic (as opposed to the skeptic) believes that human society is essentially corrupt and incorrigible. They often cast doubt on efforts to change things and distrust those who might have good intentions in this respect. Some cynics decide to join the hypocrisy rather than resist or change it, and they do it a way that's to their benefit. Consider the following life story:

> I was about fifteen, going on sixteen. I was sitting in a coffee shop in the Village, and a friend of mine came by. She said, "I've got a cab waiting. Hurry up. You can make fifty dollars in twenty minutes." Looking back, I wonder why I was so willing to run out of the coffee shop, get in a cab, and turn a trick. It wasn't traumatic because my training had been in how to be a hustler anyway.
>
> I learned it from the society around me, just as a woman. We're taught how to hustle, how to attract, hold a man, and give sexual favors in return. The language that you hear all the time, "don't sell yourself cheap." "Hold out for the highest bidder." "Is it proper to kiss a man good night on the first date?" The implication is it may not be proper on the first date, but if he takes you out to dinner on the second date, it's proper. If he brings you a bottle of perfume on the third date, you should let him touch you above the waist. And go on from there. It's a market place transaction.
>
> Somehow I managed to absorb that when I was quite young. So it wasn't even a moment of truth when this woman came into the coffee shop and said, "Come on." I was back in twenty-five minutes and I felt no guilt (in Johnson 1993: 155).

Since society deals with human relations in economic terms, then why not exploit that for one's own benefit? The person who buys into the order of things is fooled by the hypocrisy; the person who understands it and uses it is nobody's fool.

Each of these narrative visions prescribes a certain role to the hero of the tale; for romance the moral agent must be prepared to fight the villainous opponent to the death, and the only way she can achieve her goal is by defeating that opponent. The hero must prove herself worthy of the goal and must have virtues that allow her to prevail. For tragedy the hero must exhibit the greatest sort of courage in that he must risk all without regard to the consequences of the action. Like the model of Prometheus, he must prove himself noble, even if it brings on the wrath of the gods and great suffering. In irony the hero must first become aware, through trial and tribulation, that the powers that be are not necessarily for the best and that attempts to change or overcome his condition will most likely lead to destruction. He must learn what is in his power to do and what is not and act accordingly. In satire the hero must eliminate her naïveté and recognize the duplicity and hypocrisy of the powers that be. She must be wary and distinguish the false from the true. This requires that, above all, she be true to herself. In comedy the hero serves to enlighten his opponent and to make his opponent see the folly of his ways; the goal is to achieve worthy ends in a way that incorporates everyone into what the hero knows is the best form of life.

Each of these narrative types also prescribes a certain outlook toward the opponent. In the romance the opponent is someone who embodies the opposite values of the hero and who must be defeated or subordinated for the hero to prevail. The opponent, however, may be equal or greater in power than the hero. In tragedy the opponent is someone (or something) whose power is so formidable that there is probably no hope of defeating it. But it must be shown that one will not be willing to forgo one's honor or nobility in the process. In comedy the opponent is viewed as someone who is misled or ignorant and needs to be changed, to be made to see the light, but eventually to be incorporated into a certain way of life. In satire the opponent is someone to be exposed for who he really is, to be scorned for the pretense, and left to face the consequences of living a lie.

A cosmic vision provides a general framework for moral agency. How people see the order of things—romantically, tragically, comedically, ironically, satirically— and how they see themselves in this regard—as leader, champion, martyr, underdog, outsider, rebel, misfit, outlaw—will generate the larger sense of moral agency.

4.5.2 The Common Good

One aspect of vision has to do with our relation to the cosmos and the order of things as such; another has to do with how we envision our relations with others. Societies are inherent features of the human condition, and they form for obvious reasons: mutual protection and security; social bonding, including marriage and procreation; economic advantage; and a myriad of other benefits that would be hard to derive from a singular existence. Many believe that societies generate a *common good in the sense that a cumulative and cooperative effort by generations over time creates the sorts of institutions and infrastructure that allow each member to tap into a wealth of benefit that could not be achieved by individual effort.* How we envision society figures greatly in the pursuit of our own sense of the good life.

Just as cosmic visions are often articulated by stories, interestingly, many modern theories of the state—starting in the 17th century—also used stories of an "original contract" to articulate their particular visions of the state and its purposes. The community may be seen as the means by which conflicts are resolved or the source of perennial struggle. The community can be thought of as the means by which progress is made toward a greater good, or it may be something that must be avoided before individuals can achieve happiness. We can think, as 18th-century philosopher Jean-Jacques Rousseau (1712–1778) did, that societies corrupt our basically good nature (1755) or, on the contrary, as 17th-century philosopher Thomas Hobbes (1651) thought, set aright our corrupted nature. Hobbes had a basically *ironic view* that human beings are essentially corrupt, selfish, ignorant, and prone to vicious disposition; it is only through the employment of strong and vital institutions, combined with a strong hierarchical organization of society, that these dispositions can be directed to some level of collective good.

A *thalian vision*, on the other hand, politically speaking, has confidence in the basic virtue of human nature. The purpose of institutions is to avoid obstacles to attainment of full realization. In this vision there is an emphasis on individuals' basic good-heartedness and their capacity for self-governance and wisdom in regulating their own affairs. Indeed, Rousseau's vision has this thalian theme. In his speculative account of prehistory, he tells a story of how the "state of nature" was governed by a sense of equality among members of communities. As these small communities progressed by means of art, technology, and science to become more complicated societies, inequalities begin to emerge. It is precisely these inequalities which corrupt the original nature of human beings and lead to the atrocities and horrors common to modern human society. Consequently, an understanding of this original equality, this original social contract, is needed to reestablish legitimate bases of power in our society. We must remove those false bases of power, those blockers, which prevent us from realizing our more genuine, peaceful, and compassionate natures.

Modern thinkers such as Gandhi and Martin Luther King have public visions that share these thalian themes to some degree. Consider Martin Luther King's famous "I Have a Dream" speech:

> I still have a dream. It is a dream deeply rooted in the American dream. I have a dream that one day this nation will rise up and live out the true meaning of its creed: "We hold these truths to be self-evident; that all men are created equal." I have a dream that one day … sons of former slaves and the sons of former slave-owners will be able to sit together at the table of brotherhood. … I have a dream that one day … little black boys and black girls will be able to join hands with little white boys and white girls and walk together as sisters and brothers (King, August 28, 1963).

In this vision the community is seen as a place where conflicts can be resolved, where opponents and enemies can be incorporated into a higher communal life already implicit in the existing one. It is a vision based on an implicit trust in the willingness of opponents to recapture the basic goodness and virtues in their characters. It is the institutions and the organization of society that have corrupted this basic goodness. In this vision there is a view of an original, more fundamental sense of equality among the members of a community. Indeed, instead of viewing the opponent as someone who must be destroyed to gain victory, the methodology of nonviolent resistance shared by Gandhi and King views the opponent as someone who is defeated by showing the fundamental immorality of their oppression and by awakening them to an understanding they already have of good behavior and of sound, moral vision. The opponents are not treated as enemies to be vanquished, as the romantic vision would suggest, but as blockers who, through their own ignorance and folly, cannot see the error of their ways. The goal is to eventually incorporate them into the new order of things.

As mentioned, it could be argued that Thomas Hobbes and Adam Smith have an ironic vision. Both view human nature as essentially flawed, a nature that cannot be transcended. For Hobbes (1651) the natural state of human beings is one of egoism and rampant violence; for Smith (1759), as mentioned previously, human beings are essentially egoistic as well. Both thinkers argue that it is only by means of the right sort of institutions and political organization that the flaws in such nature can be arranged so that they can prove to be beneficial for most. For Hobbes this requires that individuals forgo their natural sovereignty and autonomy over themselves in favor of a higher sovereign who can then use that power to preserve peace and security among them. For Smith measures can be less severe. Even though human beings are egoistic, it is when a socioeconomic system is based on that sort of motivation that good results often occur. A market economy based on egoistic interests can often promote collective goods.

**Hitler's Social Vision
from *Mein Kampf:***

"Without the possibility of using lower human beings, the Aryan would never have been able to take his first steps toward his future culture; just as without the help of various suitable beasts which he knew how to tame, he would not have arrived at a technology which is now gradually permitting him to do without these beasts. ... Thus, for the formation of higher cultures the existence of lower human types was one of the most essential preconditions. ... It is certain that the first culture of humanity was based less on the tamed animal than on the use of lower human beings. ... Hence it is no accident that the first cultures arose in places where the Aryan, in his encounters with lower peoples, subjugated them and bent them to his will. ... Thus, the road which the Aryan had to take was clearly marked out. As a conqueror he subjected the lower beings and regulated their practical activity under his command, according to his will and for his aims" (1924: 294–95).

Notice how Hitler employs a certain account of history in his vision and a certain view of human nature, both of which clearly forebode his actions and his future vision for Germany.

The 17th-century philosopher John Locke (1689) promotes a blend of the thalian and ironic visions, somewhere between Hobbes and Rousseau. Like Rousseau, Locke argues for a state of nature characterized by egalitarianism and harmony, but instead of being corrupted by a progressively complex society, it is set into disorder by errant individuals, much in the way paradise is destroyed by the disobedience of Adam and Eve. Consequently, like Hobbes but not to the degree of oppression required by him, Locke argues that civil society comes into existence precisely to protect the rights and property of good-living individuals against its transgressors. The state exists solely for the sake of the protection of these basic rights and does not have its legitimacy independently of its citizens' approval. As a result, when the state oppresses these rights, citizens may legitimately rebel against it. Locke recognizes a basic human nature that is decent and good, but is subject to deviation and transgression. Consequently, a society must be so designed that it encourages the former while repressing the latter. Civil society for Locke has more of a negative than positive function; it serves the purpose of adjudicating conflicts and ensuring basic rights. Rather than determining the sense of the collective good, the state exists only to allow enough freedom for individual pursuit of happiness.

Montesquieu (1689–1755) also expresses this tension between the ironic and thalian vision. The classical form of the republic, as understood by Montesquieu, is rule by the virtuous. Here virtue is understood not only as excellence of character but nobility of birth, education, and wealth—in other words, characteristics of the aristocratic class. Given a choice between a democratic and an aristocratic republic, Montesquieu argues for the latter because it will prove to be not only more stable but also will be governed better. Because the few in this case would rule the many, there was a need for a more centralized government. To avoid the concentration of too much power in the hands of the few and, therefore, the possibility of tyranny, this centralized government required a balance of powers so that the various branches of government could serve as safeguards against the usurpation of power by one part of the government or the consolidation of power by a few (1737–1743).

American political vision also expresses variations of this tension between the thalian and the ironic vision that continue presently in somewhat different guises; it is heavily influenced by the thinking of Locke, Montesquieu, and Hume. This tension is manifest in the differences between Jefferson and Madison in their debate on the Constitution and the best form of government.

On the one hand, there is Jefferson's hope for a democratic republic—to use Montesquieu's language as expressed in the Declaration of Independence. The document argues for a fundamental belief in human beings as equal in sovereign power (although actually qualified as pertaining to male freemen with some property), capable of self-governance, with the right of people to rebel against those governments which seek to oppress these basic rights. This translated into a desire for less centralized governments and institutions in favor of self-governance.

In a letter to Madison (December 20, 1787), although Jefferson makes it clear that he agrees with Madison's Montesquieu-inspired balance of powers in the Constitution, he believed it was for the sake of restraining state power rather than preventing the concentration of power by the few. This is verified by his strong advocacy of what was to become the Bill of Rights. He insists on most of the matters that are later formulated in that doctrine, all of which pertain to the protection of the ordinary citizen from state intrusion: freedom of religion and press, habeas corpus laws, trials by jury, and the like. "A bill of rights is what the people are entitled to against every government on earth, general or particular, and what no just government should refuse. ... " (1787: 476). In other words, to the degree that there was confidence in the basic virtue of the ordinary citizen, then the need for more central control was lessened. Jefferson later theorized about "wards," smaller units even than counties, that would engage people at a root level. He distrusted the grant of great power to a governing group at the top of the hierarchy and, for this reason, greatly admired the New Englanders' concept of the town meeting.

But whereas Jefferson saw danger in a strongly centralized government, Madison saw it in its weakness. A strong central government was needed precisely because of the tendency of local and special interest groups to break into factions and to be disposed to real and political warfare. He was especially afraid of the ability of a large majority of the people to wield their power over smaller groups (particularly like the propertied and wealthy classes). The difference with Jefferson was also manifest in their differing opinions of Shays' Rebellion, an armed rebellion of indebted Massachusetts farmers and war veterans against farm foreclosures, and rebellion in general. Jefferson not only tolerated such rebellions but encouraged them as the necessary reestablishment of democratic power (letter to Madison, January 30, 1787). Madison, on the other hand, viewed it as leading to anarchy and reinforced his belief in a strong, centralized, and well-administered government. Although both believed in the ideals of the republic—understood as having its ultimate power in the mass of citizens whose representatives are elected by them—

Madison leans to the more aristocratic view of the Montesquieu republic and Jefferson to its democratic sibling.

But if Madison leaned toward a more aristocratic republic, his friend and coauthor of *The Federalist Papers,* Alexander Hamilton (who argued for a lifetime term of appointment for the president), leaned even closer to Montesquieu's ideal. In a speech given in Philadelphia in 1787, Hamilton said:

> All communities divide themselves into the few and the many. The first are the rich and wellborn, the other the mass of the people. ... The people are turbulent and changing; they seldom judge or determine right. Give therefore to the first class a distinct, permanent share in the government. They will check the unsteadiness of the second, and as they cannot receive any advantage by change, they therefore will ever maintain good government.

But as *The Federalist Papers* show, Hamilton, Madison, and Jay were constrained by the democratic principles already set forth in the revolution. Their compromise was a Constitution which paid homage to democratic republicanism but which also established a highly centralized form of representation by election from the masses. Hence, their emphasis on federalism as opposed to the loose confederation of states that was in place at that time. As Madison writes,

> The first question that offers itself is whether the general form and aspect of the government be strictly republican. It is evident that no other form would be reconcilable with the genius of the people of America; with the fundamental principles of the Revolution; or with that honorable determination which animates every votary of freedom to rest all our political experiments on the capacity of mankind for self-government (1787–1788: No. 39).

Tensions between Different Senses of the Common Good in the Twentieth Century

In their book *Habits of the Heart,* Bellah et al. show with some clarity how this tension between the thalian and ironic vision of the common good still animates our 20th-century political outlook. They outline what they call the "six visions of the public good" that have arisen over the last century. The six can be articulated as three contrastive pairs. The first and most enduring is populism versus the establishment, the second is neocapitalism versus welfare liberalism, and the third is administered society versus economic democracy (1996: 257). What's clear is that each of these contrastive pairs articulates a persistent tension that has existed in American society between the ironic and the thalian, one which is articulated more specifically as the tension between individualism and communalism and between egalitarianism and elitism. Individualism holds generally that a good society is one that maximizes individual liberty with the least amount of interference from the state as a whole, whereas communalism stresses the values of association, family, neighborhood, community, and the common good. Egalitarianism is a belief in the capability of ordinary people for self-government and a general confidence in their wisdom in such matters. Elitism is the view that select individuals or leaders of institutions are required to bring the masses toward some level of social justice. Let's look at the first two pairs for the sake of illustration.

According to the authors of *Habits of the Heart,* populism versus the establishment rose at the end of the 19th century as a reaction to the closing of the Western frontier and the simultaneous expansion of large industry. Now that the territory had been settled and consolidated, there needed to be an effort to achieve a certain level of national stability and social justice. The establishment vision was primarily associated with the industrial and financial elites who thought the way to fix the social order was through large institutions, universities, hospitals, churches, museums, schools, clubs, and associations working together alongside the large corporations and industries to establish proper social order (1996: 258–259). The philosophy of Andrew Carnegie, the

Continued

Tensions between Different Senses of the Common Good in the Twentieth Century, *Continued*

19th-century steel magnate, was partly reflective of this position. He spoke of the need for industrial leaders to think of themselves not just as owners of corporations but as trustees of the nation's wealth and thus as administrators of its use for the collective good (1996: 259–260).

Opposed to this vision was the populist one. It accented the Jeffersonian egalitarian ethos rather than the elitist one. It claimed that "the people," ordinary citizens, had sufficient wisdom to govern their own political affairs rather than having to appeal to the leaders of elite institutions (1996: 259). In other words, both visions aimed at working toward a collective good, but they differed strongly on who should determine that good. In its simplest form, the establishment vision emphasized social engineering as a way of moving the country toward its struggle for social justice, whereas the populist movement thought that social justice should occur in the context of face-to-face communities, where self-government was the dominant ideal.

With the crisis of the Great Depression in 1929 and the failure of large business institutions, two other related yet significantly different visions

emerged. Both began to focus more on social justice in terms of economic well-being. Welfare liberalism, as exemplified by Roosevelt, aimed to solve the economic and social hardships that the Depression brought through massive government-administrated programs and plans (1996: 262). The aim was to achieve a public good through the sharing of the benefits of economic growth, on the one hand, and constant regulation of the business world, on the other. The latter was for the purpose of abating unfair competition and promoting equal opportunity in economic life. Neocapitalism, as exemplified by Ronald Reagan, on the other hand, held that the role of government should be reduced so that individuals, families, neighborhoods, and small communities could have more freedom to pursue their own particular sense of the good life and self-sufficiency. In neocapitalism the self-sufficient business serves as the paradigm of self-sufficiency in citizens, and the welfare of citizens is tied to the liberty of the market, necessary for its growth and development. These two visions still dominate the current American political scene, and clearly, they still retain the tensions present in the original visions for this country.

4.5.3 Happiness and the Vision of the Good Life

In the Declaration of Independence, Thomas Jefferson proclaims his famous list of inalienable rights: "life, liberty, and the pursuit of happiness." A large part of a person's moral vision is bound up with this pursuit of happiness and some sense of the good life. Often it is their most immediate concern in life. It is thought that happiness is something that is desired by most if not all (cf. Mill 1861: 35). Happiness, according to Aristotle, is the intransitive end for human life (*Nic. Ethics* 1197b20). It is not a means to some end but is an end in itself. Things are done ultimately to be happy, and one is not happy to be anything else. All plans find their fruition in happiness.

The difficulty is that it is not entirely clear what is meant by happiness (see figure). Nevertheless, it is worthwhile sorting out its complexity because it is so central to most people's lives. As a start we can make a distinction between the sense of happiness as *well-being* and as *living well. Well-being is a term used in the psychological literature to describe one's inner, affective, subjective state and is usually associated with sanguine mood and a certain level of contentment.* It should be distinguished from the emotion of joy, which we all feel on the occasion of very positive events in our lives. *Sanguine mood* is one that is usually associated with a feeling of comfort (versus anxiety), pleasantness (versus depression), enthusiasm (versus boredom), vigor (versus tiredness), and placidity (versus anger) (cf. Warr 1990). *Contentment* is a feeling of satisfaction with one's current state of affairs as measured by the lack of desire for more than one has; contentment may also result from the satisfaction of the progress toward goals or plans.

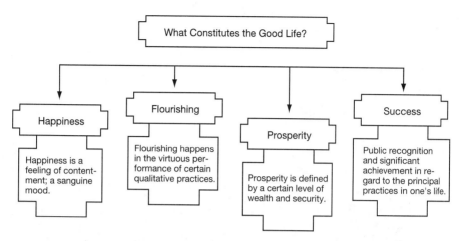

The question of what constitutes the good life is a perplexing one. Happiness is often thought of as the goal of the good life, but what is meant by happiness is a difficult problem.

Living well, on the hand, is not related to one's inner state of mind but to active living and doing, as the term implies. Philosopher Richard Brandt defines it as the case where a pattern of life, a way of being, develops which realizes a certain sense of the good life (1972: 414). *Living well is the result of the right sort of activity within the sorts of practices that constitute human being and the human condition*: personal relations, such as friendships, marriage, family; social and civic functions; work or professional activities; and one's intellectual life. Living well is living the good life as it is realized in these various kinds of activities. Aristotle uses the word *eudaimonia* (literally, having a good demon or spirit) to describe this sense of happiness. Some translators have preferred the terms *flourishing* to "happiness," which we will also adopt here. Thus, *living well is a flourishing that results in the activity of living the good life.*

Well-being has been studied a great deal by psychologists and is often the subject of the self-help literature. One of the most interesting current theories on well-being is developed by David Lykken and Auke Tellegen in a 1996 article in *Psychological Research.* The study involved over 2000 twins born between 1936 and 1955. Their conclusion was that happiness is governed by a congenitally determined neurochemical "set point" or "thermostat" (1996). According to them, the normal, everyday vicissitudes of life have an impact on one's happiness, but it doesn't seem to last very long. This is a conclusion confirmed by psychologists Edward and Carol Diener of the University of Illinois, who argue that events like being promoted or losing a lover affect a person's mood over a period of about 3 months, and after 6 months the effect seems to be gone, at which point one returns to whatever steady-state mood one is wired for. This is true even for lottery winners and victims of terrible car accidents. Frank Fujita at Indiana University, South Bend, argues similarly: "The things that occur in your life affect your momentary, weekly or monthly mood, but they don't change you forever. You will get back to your basic personality" (in Perkins 1996). The Dieners qualify this by saying that terrible things can certainly have long-term affects and change one's view of the world. Other studies make further qualifications by showing that daily fluctuations of well-being may have more to do with noncongenital factors (cf. Reis et al. 2000).

Lykken and Tellegen conclude that the feeling of happiness is genetically based but randomly distributed and probably has its physical basis in levels of dopamine in the brain. There is no strong statistical correlation of the feeling of happiness to education, income, professional achievement, marital status (1996; cf. also Valiant 1993; but cf. Veenhoven 1994 for a challenge to these claims). If Lykken and Tellegen are correct, then whether one feels content or sanguine is unrelated to how one is living. In other words, it's quite possible to feel happy yet have no objective basis for feeling so and, conversely, to feel unhappy and have no basis for feeling so.

This impression is somewhat confirmed in a study, "Illusion and Well-Being," by two psychologists, Shelley Taylor and Jonathan Brown (1988; cf. Flanagan 1991: 318ff.). Generally speaking, their conclusion is that those who are happy (1) have more of a tendency to be unrealistic in their positive views of self, (2) are more likely to have illusions of control over chance events in their lives, and (3) are often more unrealistically optimistic.

In regard to the first characteristic, for example, happy people will rate themselves overwhelmingly as having more positive than negative traits; they rate their performance on a task more positively than observers do; they will judge the group to which they belong as better than other groups; their abilities are seen as rare and disabilities as common; they think their abilities have improved when, in fact, they have remained unchanged; and whatever they do poorly they judge it as less important than things at which they are accomplished. In regard to the second characteristic, the happy personalities feel they have more control over situations that appear to be governed by chance. Third, happy people will often feel that their chances of experiencing negative events—car accidents, job loss, illness, and so on—are less likely than others. Their predictions of events are more likely to reflect what they wish for than what is more objectively likely (1988: 197).

Conversely, Taylor and Brown found that individuals who are moderately unhappy, as indicated by moderate depression and low self-esteem, tend to be more balanced in self-perception. They are able to recall both positive and negative information about themselves with equal frequency; they show greater evenhandedness in their attributions of responsibility for actions; and they display greater congruence between self-evaluations and ratings of objective observers (1988: 196).

This suggests that well-being, rather than based on an external set of events, may be internally projected upon them. If we pair this study with the previous ones on happiness, this suggests that happier people have a tendency to be subject to more illusions about themselves and the world around them. It is quite possible, then, that subjectively happy persons may be happy without any real reason for being so.

As mentioned earlier, well-being should be distinguished from living well or flourishing. Well-being is a subjective state, but living well is the result of activities, of living a life in a certain way. Flourishing or living well should be distinguished from notions such as prosperity and success. *Prosperity may be defined as the attainment of a certain level of security and wealth.* Prosperous people live within a certain economic comfort zone which allows them to provide for themselves and their families in a manner that certainly satisfies their needs, if not many of their wants as well. Success has more to do with status than security and comfort, but it may certainly result in prosperity depending on what sort of success is achieved. *To be a success means that a person has achieved a certain level of recognition, status, and position relative to the sort of practice or occupation in question.* This suggests that success is dependent on how others view a person, rather than how he may view himself. A person might feel personally buoyed by climbing a 2000-foot peak, and it may have been especially difficult for him given his fear of heights, or some particular disability or disadvantage, yet that would not achieve much recognition in mountain climbing circles. A doctor might feel that she is successful just by being able to finish medical school; yet if her patient roster is empty because of her incompetence, then most people would not count her as a success. Status or recognition is usually something that can be conferred on a person by others; personal successes may feel good, but they are just that—personal. Success can, of course, come in degrees and is also relative to a certain category. We might count a politician successful if she has been elected to the state legislature, but perhaps more successful if elected to the Congress. The president of the United States could, in many respects, be counted as the most successful of politicians, although relative to other presidents, he may not be as successful.

The difference between flourishing and success or prosperity can be articulated by the difference between the intrinsic and extrinsic goods of any practice, a distinction made by philosopher Alasdair MacIntyre in his book *After Virtue* (1981: 181). Flourishing is more the result of the intrinsic goods of one's activities and practices; success and prosperity have to do with their extrinsic goods. When a person is aiming at the intrinsic goods of a practice, there is something about the doing of the activity itself that one finds rewarding and worthwhile. Obvious examples can be found in personal relations, such as best friendships. Being good friends is pleasurable and rewarding in itself, whatever external goods it may incidentally bring. External goods, on the other hand, are found as a consequence of the activity. A job may be done precisely because of the money, seen as its external good, as opposed to one that is done because a person simply enjoys the work. Of course, an activity can be done for both reasons—an occupation will always afford the possibility of both intrinsic and extrinsic goods. A person seeking an education can be doing it simply as a means of getting its extrinsic rewards: a living wage, job security, and some status in the community; others may do it simply because they find learning itself to be a worthwhile activity. Others, in turn, may be doing it for both reasons. In an interview in *The New Yorker*, William Gills, who is president of the University of Phoenix, touted the institution as the future of higher education, since it catered to the interests of a certain type of student. He said: "The people who are our students don't really want the education. They want what the education provides for them—better jobs, moving up in their careers ... that kind of stuff" (Traub 1997). In a similar vein, Picasso said about artists that

> success is an important thing. It has often been said that an artist should work for himself, for the love of art, and scorn success. It's a false idea. An artist needs success. Not only in order to live, but primarily so that he can realize his work (Ashton 1974: 86–87).

Yet it seems that this relation between the external and the inner goods of a practice must be balanced delicately to ensure the excellence of the practice. It is quite possible to corrupt a practice, such as art, by aiming at success rather than the quality or excellence of art. As psychologist Mihaly Csikszentmihalyi points out in his study of 200 artists 18 years after they left art school, it was those who in their student days had savored the sheer joy of painting itself who had become the serious painters. Those who had been motivated in art school by dreams of fame and wealth for the most part drifted away from art after graduating:

Painters must want to paint above all else. If the artist in front of the canvas begins to wonder how much he will sell it for, or what the critics will think of it, he won't be able to pursue original avenues. Creative achievements depend on single-minded immersion" (in Goleman 1995: 93).

This points out another essential characteristic of flourishing, at least as Aristotle understood it. Flourishing has to do with living *well*. That means that whatever practices one does, they must be done well with excellence. The Greek word for excellence is *arētē*, which also means virtue, and in his classic definition of flourishing, Aristotle plays on this word:

> the good of man is the active exercise of his soul's faculties in conformity with excellence or virtue, or if there be several human excellences or virtues, in conformity with the best and most perfect among them. Moreover this activity must occupy a complete lifetime; for one swallow does not make spring, nor does one fine day; and similarly one day or a brief period of happiness does not make a man supremely blessed and happy (*Nic. Ethics* 1198a10–20).

For Aristotle, then, *flourishing is the result of the virtuous exercise of the best human practices over the course of one's life, leading to a perfection or fulfillment of the person as a human being*. It is a fulfillment that entails a certain kind of enjoyment. He likens this enjoyment to the enjoyment often found in sense perception:

> All sense perception is actively exercised in relation to its object, and is completely exercised when it is in good condition and its object is the best of those that can be perceived by the senses. ... From all this it follows that in any sense perception that activity is best whose organ is in the best condition and whose object is the best of all the objects that fall within its range, and this activity will be the most complete and the most pleasant. For each sense, and similarly all thought and study, has its own pleasure and is pleasantest when it is most complete; but it is most complete when the organ is in good condition and the object worthiest of all that fall within its range; pleasure completes the activity (*Nic. Ethics* 1174b15–23).

Is There a Similarity between Aristotle's Notion of Flourishing and Maslow's Concept of Self-Actualization?

According to psychologist Abraham Maslow (1968), self-actualization is a process by which one is able to develop a potential that lies in the inner core of the person (1968: 197):

> To make growth and self-actualization possible, it is necessary to understand that capacities, organs and organ systems press to function and express themselves and to be used and exercised, and that such use is satisfying, and disuse irritating. The muscular person likes to use his muscles, indeed, has to use them in order to feel good and to achieve the subjective feeling of harmonious, successful, uninhibited functioning which is so important an aspect of good growth and psychological health. So also for intelligence, for the uterus, the eyes, the capacity to love. Capacities clamor to be used, and cease their clamor only when they are well used (1968: 201).

Is it in the activity of practices that we realize ourselves, or are practices triggers for what we are?

Pleasure or enjoyment results from the activity of seeing something of worth and seeing it in the best way possible; similarly, a certain kind of pleasure or enjoyment results when a practice which is worthy is performed well. It completes the activity and is its correlate. Assuming no temperamental or situational peculiarities, then a person who is flourishing should also have a certain subjective correlate, a certain qualitative enjoyment to her life. This pleasure is different from any sorts of extrinsic pleasures that the activity may afford. Aristotle seemed to believe that the highest kind of flourishing results from contemplation (*theoria*), understood as the activity of the mind for its own sake as applied to the study of the order of things (*Nic. Ethics* 1177a11–18). Aristotle reasons that since the mind is that which is highest in human beings, then its excellent exercise should result in the highest form of flourishing (*Nic. Ethics* 1177a20). But although a life of contemplation may result in the highest form of flourishing, such a life pursued exclusively is impossible for human beings since, in order to live, we must supply ourselves with the necessities of life; in fact, such an exclusively contemplative life seems only possible for the gods (*Nic. Ethics* 1177b26–30). Human beings are only capable of a secondary kind of flourishing associated with the proper exercise of virtue.

> "Don't aim at success—the more you aim at it and make it a target, the more you are going to miss it. For success, like happiness, cannot be pursued; it must ensue ... as the unintended side-effect of one's personal dedication to a course greater than oneself."
>
> —Viktor Frankl

These claims by Aristotle suggest that flourishing is the product of two variables: the qualitative good of the practice and the degree of its virtuous exercise. This supposes there are grades of flourishing. If one could virtuously pursue the highest practices exclusively, then that would lead to the highest sort of flourishing; yet one can still be counted as flourishing although one is engaged in the more ordinary practices of life, with the qualification that they are pursued virtuously. Following the opinion of Solon, Aristotle argues that one need not be counted as a great success in order to flourish:

> It is possible to perform noble actions even without being ruler of land and sea; a man's actions can be guided by virtue also if his means are moderate. That this is so can be clearly seen in the fact that private individuals evidently do not act less honorably but even more honorably than powerful rulers. It is enough to have moderate means at one's disposal, for the life of a man whose activity is guided by virtue will flourish. Solon certainly gave a good description of a flourishing man, when he said that he is a man moderately supplied with external goods, who had performed what he, Solon, thought were the noblest actions, and who had lived with self-control. For it is possible to do what one should even with moderate possessions. Also Anaxagoras, it seems, did not assume that a flourishing man had to be rich and powerful (*Nic. Ethics* 1179a1–15).

Aristotle emphasizes that flourishing still can be a fragile attainment. The flourishing person is someone who can bear better the vicissitudes of life but cannot entirely escape them:

> If activities are, as we said, what gives life its character, no flourishing man can become miserable; for he will never do the acts that are hateful and mean. For the man who is truly good and wise, we think, bears all the chances of life becomingly and always makes the best of circumstances, as a good general makes the best military use of the army at his command and a good shoemaker makes the best shoes out of the hides that are given him; and so with all other craftsmen. And if this is the case, the flourishing man can never become miserable—though he will not reach blessedness, if he meet with fortunes like those of Priam [the king of Troy whose city is ransacked by the Greeks and whose son is killed by Achilles] (*Nic. Ethics* 1100b33–1101a8).

Peak Experiences

According to psychologist Abraham Maslow, many persons have a peak experience in the context of certain activities or events. These are "felt as a self-validating, self-justifying moment which carries its own intrinsic value with it" (1968: 79).

Maslow's Hierarchy of Needs

Psychologist Abraham Maslow developed a hierarchical arrangement of needs such that the lower needs served as more powerful motivators than those higher up; we will be weakly motivated by higher needs until our lower needs are met:

transcendence
self-actualization
esteem
belongingness and love
safety and security
physiological

Could this hierarchy serve as an indication of which practices are necessary for flourishing?

If Aristotle is correct, flourishing depends on the right sense of the good life. The obvious questions, then, are what are the right practices and what is the best sense of the good life? Some popular views suggest that it is the life of wealth; some understand the good life to be the life of pleasure; for others it is a life of comfort and security. Still others will proclaim the life of fame, recognition, or power to be the most desirable. Let's consider each of these candidates, examine their strengths and flaws, and at the end return to a reexamination of the best sense of the good life.

Query: Flow and Flourishing

University of Chicago psychologist Mihaly Csikszentmihalyi has collected a number of accounts of peak or optimal performance. Athletes know this as "the zone," the point at which excellence becomes effortless, crowd and competitors disappear into a steady absorption of the moment (Goleman 1995: 90). One typical account of this feeling is given by a composer:

> You yourself are in an ecstatic state to such a point that you feel as though you almost don't exist. I've experienced this time and again. My hand seems devoid of myself, and I have nothing to do with what is happening. I just sit there watching in a state of awe and wonderment. And it just flows out by itself (Csikszentmihalyi 1975; cf. Goleman 1995: 90).

Csikszentmihalyi claims that there are certain cross-cultural characteristics of flow: (1) it arises out of certain sorts of activities or practices that have clear goals and immediate feedback and which have tasks that are completable, (2) the participant is able to concentrate on the activity and enjoys a certain level of mastery, which results in (3) an intense enjoyment marked by egolessness, effortlessness, and an impression that the duration of time has been altered (1990: 49ff.). Games are common examples of such phenomena. A person who has mastered chess to a certain degree experiences most of this while playing; chess is a game that has clear goals and immediate feedback.

Flow makes such activities autotelic (what we have called endotelic). One does the activity for the sake of the activity: "flow ... [is a] state in which people are so involved in an activity that nothing else seems to matter; the experience itself is so enjoyable that people will do it even at great cost, for the sheer sake of doing it" (1990: 4). Csikszentmihalyi seems to claim that there are certain kinds of practices that are conducive to flow but also that one is capable of creating flow in activities not so disposed by certain inner adjustments to the perception of the activity (1990: 2).

Csikszentmihalyi wants to make a stronger claim, however, that happiness is—in a certain sense—flow; that to become happy one must be occupied with those sorts of practices and activities that have a tendency to result in flow or to transform activities that do not into ones that do. However, by identifying happiness with flow, Csikszentmihalyi is characterizing it as a psychological state rather than in its objective sense:

> Happiness, in fact, is a condition that must be... cultivated... privately by each person. People who learn to control inner experience will be able to determine the quality of their lives, which is as close as any of us can come to being happy (1990:2).

Query: Flow and Flourishing, *Continued*

For Aristotle, flow might be considered the result of the mastery of certain qualitatively good practices; but it's the practice rather than the enjoyment that constitutes flourishing. Csikszentmihalyi's position, on the other hand, has certain unwelcome ethical consequences: the reasons activities or practices are done are for the enjoyment they might create. But if one does something for the sake of flow or the enjoyment, then whatever one enjoys one will do. The activity itself is not evaluated except as whether it produces flow or not; the moral quality of the activity, then, is not a reason for doing it. "The purpose of flow is to keep on flowing" (1990: 54). He soon begins to recognize the consequences of his position. He realizes that it's quite possible to generate flow from a number of morally questionable activities and practices:

The Marquis de Sade perfected the infliction of pain into a form of pleasure and in fact, cruelty is a universal source of enjoyment for people who have not developed more sophisticated skills.... Gladiatorial combat amused the Romans.... Spaniards approach the killing of bulls with reverence, and boxing is a staple of our own culture. ... Criminals often say things such as: "If you showed me something I can do that's as much fun as breaking into a house at night, and lifting the jewelry without waking anyone up, I would do it" (1990: 69).

The paradox for Csikszentmihalyi is that if happiness is constituted by flow, yet flow can be achieved by a number of various practices regardless of their moral quality, then it is quite possible for the vicious or the immoral to be happy in that sense of the term. If happiness is flow and if flow can result from a number of activities, both moral and immoral, then the choice for being moral cannot lie in happiness.

By identifying the goal of the practice with the flow that may result from it, Csikszentmihalyi is making the same mistake as the hedonists. Aristotle insists on that delicate relation between practice and pleasure. It is not so much that pleasure or enjoyment should be the goal in doing something as in the moral quality of the doing, in which case an appropriate enjoyment can result. By identifying happiness with its subjective version, Csikszentmihalyi promotes the idea that all there is to happiness is generating flow regardless of the quality of the activity. To illustrate this point consider the following passage:

The sense of security can be improved by buying a gun, installing strong locks on the front door, moving to a safer neighborhood, exerting political pressure on city hall for more police protection, or helping the community to become more conscious of the importance of civil order. All these different responses are aimed at bringing conditions in the environment more in line with our goals. The other method by which we can feel more secure involves modifying what we mean by security (1990: 43).

If you achieve security by taking ordinary precautions and also organize the community in citizen patrols, community councils, and police–community liaisons, this not only will achieve some measure of security for you but also for others; consequently, you have achieved a greater collective good through these activities and practices. But if all you do instead is modify your subjective sense of security, then not only have you failed to create some security for others but you may also be promoting a kind of illusion for yourself.

Still, Csikszentmihalyi's concept of flow makes for some interesting speculation about what sort of enjoyment or pleasure might accompany genuine flourishing. If we think of flourishing as an optimal life, then it should have a certain kind of flow to it. It could be argued that it might generate a kind of "superflow." A good word for it would be affluence, if it didn't already have connotations associated solely with wealth.

4.5.4 The Life of Pleasure, Adventure, and Entertainment

The 18th-century philosopher and legislator Jeremy Bentham (1748–1832) defined happiness in terms of the degree of pleasure it creates subjectively in the practitioner. This is often measured in quantitative terms: intensity, duration, certainty, propinquity, fecundity, purity, and extent (*Principles*, Chap. 4). The worth of an activity, then, is the sort of pleasure it brings. (For more on Bentham, see Section 5.4.3.) Many people understand the good life as a life dominated by pleasure, replete with entertainment and enough adventure to keep it from being too dull. In this vision of the good life, one's aim is to maximize those pleasures which life

"I thought to myself, 'very well, I will try pleasure and see what enjoyment has to offer.' And there it was: vanity again! ...I did great things: built myself palaces, planted vineyards. ...I had too, more than anyone in Jerusalem before me. I amassed silver and gold, the treasures of kings and provinces. . . .I then reflected on all that my hands had achieved and on all the effort I had put into its achieving. What vanity it all is, and chasing of the wind! There is nothing to be gained under the sun."

—Ecclesiastes 2:1–13

affords. To promote this way of life, a person should choose an occupation that affords both the wealth necessary to sustain such a lifestyle and, at the same time, provides time and opportunity for its pursuit. This is perhaps why occupations in the entertainment industry are sought by so many people. When successful, being a Hollywood actor or rock musician can be very attractive to many people. The occupations do not have the weighty responsibilities characteristic of many positions of power or importance, yet they do have all the fame and recognition those might bring. One is able to live a frivolous, playful life which is quite suitable to this sense of the good life. Fame is pursued as a means to enhance one's pleasure in life. Recognition does not have to be deserved, under this view, as long as the recognition provides the means for the pursuit of pleasure and entertainment. This would be expressed by the difference, for example, between a musician who strives to be the best musician he can be and so seeks recognition among his peers and one who simply seeks popular recognition as such; the first pursues excellence in his craft, which may then afford genuine recognition, while the latter seeks fame first and so would gladly mold his talent toward popular appeal.

Aristotle remarks that "it would be strange if our end [that is, our goal in life] were amusement, and if we were to labor and suffer hardships all our life long merely to amuse ourselves. ... Obviously, it is foolish and all too childish to exert serious efforts and toil for purposes of amusement" (*Nic. Ethics*, 1176b27–32). But Aristotle did not live in our entertainment-driven society, where such a life is frequently lived and culturally promoted. However, despite the attractions of this way of life, persons living this lifestyle must still endure the same kinds of problems as ordinary folk: bad marriages, drug and alcohol addiction, depression and psychological maladies, anomie, problems

"In the late 19th century a shift started from self-control to self-realization, from the world of the producer, based on the values of self-denial and achievement, to the consumer culture that emphasized immediate satisfactions and the fulfillment of the self through gratification and indulgence."

—Daniel Horowitz, *The Morality of Spending* (Johns Hopkins University Press, 1985, p. 149)

"By the 1950s American culture had become primarily hedonistic, concerned with play, fun, display, and pleasure."

—Daniel Bell, *The Cultural Contradictions of Capitalism* (Basic, 1976, p. 70)

with children, health problems, social and political concerns, and so on. In other words, a purely sybaritic or hedonistic lifestyle is probably impossible to maintain, either because its full-blown pursuit leads to self-destruction or because there are kinds of pain and suffering in life that are unavoidable. Unless people divorce themselves from all relations, they risk the difficulties that make the pursuit of pleasure difficult, but it is hard to imagine a person separated from society in that sense as happy (*Nic. Ethics* 1097b9–11; 1099b).

One person thought to exemplify this way of life is Hugh Hefner, founder of *Playboy* magazine and a large entertainment industry, who seemed able to accomplish this sense of the good life in the fullest terms. A documentary of his life, *Hugh Hefner: Once upon a Time* (1995, directed by Robert Heath), reveals some interesting insights about this paragon of hedonism. As ironic as it sounds, it is clear that

The Happiest Place on Earth?

These are the words (without the question mark) on the sign which greets visitors to Disneyland in Anaheim, California. Disneyland is considered by many to be the icon of American culture. The theme of most rides in the park expresses an interesting pattern of adventure. The Pirates of the Caribbean illustrates this. The visitor is ushered onto a boat which floats peacefully through a re-creation of the backways of the Louisiana bayous. Suddenly, the boat slides down a hill and into the midst of sea battle between pirate ships and a fort defending a town. As the boat moves along, one witnesses the pillage of the town by the pirates, remarkably re-created by the use of mechanical dummies: There is looting, arson, the harassment and torture of the townsfolk, and several pirates lustfully chasing women (a scene that has been apparently removed in the newer versions). These events would normally be horrifying, but here they are all portrayed comically and in the spirit of "good fun." The Pirates of the Caribbean ride simulates danger and for that very reason does not place the rider in any real danger. It allows the rider to witness these dangerous actions and events safely and, because of the power and effectiveness of the simulation, produces a kind of thrill for the rider. Thrill, like the experience of a roller coaster, occurs when a person is brought to the brink of danger and pulled back. It could be argued, then, that if this is the happiest place on earth, happiness is defined in terms of entertainment, thrill, and adventure.

Do you agree? Do you think that Disneyland is the happiest place on earth?

In Disney's classic movie *Pinocchio*, there is a segment in which Pinocchio is seduced and tricked into accompanying a number of other boys to "Pleasure Island." There they are allowed all possible entertainments: There are amusement rides, games, they can smoke, fight, tear up the place—just about anything they find amusing. The problem is that the more they indulge in these entertainments, the more they begin to acquire the physical properties of jackasses, until at last they are literally transformed into the beasts of burden.

Do you think this might serve as an allegory about Disneyland? (Walt Disney World in Florida indeed has a part of its facility called "Pleasure Island.")

Hefner could not have done what he had done without certain character virtues, and his life in fact illustrates some of the points made earlier. First, Hefner had great industry, without which he could not have started his magazine from scratch; he was daring and ambitious, developing a concept few others would develop in the very Puritan climate of the 1950s. Also, outside of his sexual life and a bout with dexedrine, Hefner showed a remarkable amount of temperance and self-control, given the number of temptations around; he avoided serious drug and alcohol addiction and the sort of disease and decline that avid partying might bring on. He seemed amicable and good-tempered. Although one could certainly criticize his way of life and the sort of values he promoted, especially in regard to women, nonetheless, he was stalwart in the sense that he had to defend his beliefs and way of life against constant attack by the media, various church leaders and organizations, government attempts at censorship, the feminist movement, and other sundry attacks. He also had to endure a number of usual and not so usual tragedies and difficulties in his life. His organization came under scrutiny by the Drug Enforcement Agency for what now appears to be trumped-up charges of cocaine trafficking. The investigation lasted several years and was finally dismissed. It led to the suicide of his dear friend and secretary and involved a great deal of pressure from surveillance and the possibility of informants within his organization. In the 1980s a friend, the director Peter Bogdanovich, publicly attacked him and his organization after the murder of Dorothy Stratton by her ex-husband. Stratton was playmate of the year and Bogdanovich's lover. Hefner also suffered a minor stroke later on. What also becomes clear in the context of the documentary is that Hefner strove to make *Playboy* a legitimate and serious magazine and became himself a

Query: How Much of Your Life Is Occupied with Entertainment?

Consider for a moment the amount of time you spend on entertainment. Consider the following activities in your calculation: watching TV, including watching sports events; watching videos; playing computer games, Nintendo games, board, and card games; doing crossword and jigsaw puzzles; hobbies; playing sports and outdoor recreation (baseball, skiing, hiking, biking, etc.); listening to music; going to the movies; going to bars and nightclubs; dancing; eating out; attending concerts; taking vacations, drives, and so on. *What would be your average amount of time spent on entertainment per week? Do you think that amount of time is appropriate?*

The entertainment industry, including the Hollywood movie, sports, and music industries, plays an enormous role in the lives of Americans and other advanced industrialized countries. These are extremely profitable businesses. Successful film actors and sports figures make enormous salaries, sometimes much more than CEOs of large corporations and certainly much more than those responsible for running our society, including the president of the United States. They make much more than doctors and surgeons who save lives everyday or researchers who find cures for disease. Often Americans are more knowledgeable about the lives of film stars and sports figures than they are about the historical figures who founded and shaped our culture. Consider for a moment how many magazines are devoted to the entertainment industries just listed and you'll get a sense of how much interest there is in entertainment as opposed, let's say, to politics.

strong advocate of different political causes. Many good writers and social and political commentators were recruited and published by Hefner. He even managed to recruit some of his most vocal opponents, such as William Buckley. Also, as his manifesto on the "playboy philosophy" indicates, he was intent on defending the sort of life he exemplified. This demonstrates that he was not just interested in the hedonistic lifestyle but wanted also to achieve a certain status or recognition in the community, which could only be achieved by promoting the social value of his enterprise and his way of life. It is clear that without the personal virtues, recognition, social status, and wealth he acquired, he would not likely live the kind of hedonistic lifestyle he did, nor did this particularly seem to be his goal in life, strictly speaking. It was not just the pleasure, but the money, fame, work, and power that constituted living well for him. What is interesting and ironic, of course, is that in the end he found a greater sense of well-being in a lifestyle remarkably different from the one he promoted most of his life: "I thought I could find happiness in a series of relationships but I found it in marriage, home and family." But with a double twist of irony, his wife filed for divorce a few years after that statement.

4.5.5 The Life of Security and Comfort

Where the thrill of pleasure and adventure can be a wild ride down the road of life, many people prefer a life of security and comfort, a prosperous life devoted to the comforts of home and hearth, family, friends, and the good life in the Rockwellian sense of the term. This is certainly one meaning of what is often called "the American Dream." In this sort of life, a person seeks occupations that make good provision for such goals, which also afford the opportunity and time to maximize the enjoyment of family life and friends. Wealth is for the sake of security, the maximization of such interpersonal relations, and the enjoyment of life.

But if security, comfort, and good personal relationships are the essence of this good life, often these pursuits can conflict with one another and create a level of tension inherent in this way of life. To achieve financial security, for example, people have to be successful at their careers or occupations. This may require long hours at work, which detract from the time that can be spent with family and friends; work may limit time spent with children and the involvement in their lives necessary to establish the sort of emotional connectedness essential in parent–child or spousal relations. But whatever time is devoted to family relations, the stress involved in long hours of hard work may also affect the tenor of relations at home. Success at work can generate personal ambitions at the cost of the family good. It may lead to the narrowing of focus of one's role in the family as simply being an economic provider rather than a provider of emotional support. Consider the case of Brian Palmer, who is profiled in *Habits of the Heart* (Bellah et al. 1996), a book written by a group of sociologists, philosophers, and theologians on the matter of the good life in America. Palmer is a successful businessman who lives comfortably in a San Jose suburb and works as a top-level manager for a large corporation. He was married with three sons, but got divorced, remarried, and now lives with his three children and his new wife's children. During his first marriage, he would typically stay in his office until midnight. He was proud of the fact that he had moved from the sybaritic life of his early youth, but his present singular pursuit of career came at a certain cost:

> What was my concept of what constituted a reasonable relationship? I guess I felt an obligation to care for materially, provide for, a wife and my children, in a style to which I'd like to see them become accustomed. Providing for my family materially was important. Sharing wasn't important. Sharing of my time wasn't important. I put in extremely long hours, probably averaging 60 to 65 hours a week. I'd work almost every Saturday. Always in the office by 7:30. Rarely out of the office before 6:30 at night. ... That was numero uno. But I compensated for that by saying, I have this nice car, this nice house, joined the Country Club. Now you have a place you can go, sit on your butt, drink, go into the pool. I'll pay the bills and I'll do my thing at work (1996: 4).

Soon his wife announced her plans to divorce him. This led to a dramatic reevaluation of his sense of the good life, especially since his three boys chose to live with him:

> Well I think I just reestablished my priorities. ... That exclusive pursuit of success now seems to me not a good way to live. That's not the most important thing to me. I have demonstrated to myself, to my own satisfaction, that I can achieve about what I want to achieve. So the challenge of goal realization does not contain that mystique that it held for me at one time. I just have found that I get a lot of personal reward from being involved in the lives of my children (1996: 6).

Now he is bound by a husband-and-wife type of relationship that he believes is founded on mutual respect, admiration, affection, and the ability to give and receive freely. Industry without attention to the other important aspects of one's life—especially if industry is leaning toward workaholism—can be destructive to the very relations which industry is meant to serve. Yet at the same time, stress on relations may go the other way if there is economic insecurity. The stress of an economically substandard quality of life is well-established. The conflict between providing a secure economic base for one's family and attention to the emotional life of those you love becomes a persistent part of the landscape of family life.

The pursuit of comfort can also lead to certain conflicts in this sense of the good life. American culture is a largely consumer-oriented culture whose economy runs on providing an indefinite number and variety of goods for a population whose desire for such goods increases indefinitely as well. The desire for goods drives production of such goods, and the proliferation of such goods drives desire for them. As the famous economist John Galbraith puts it:

> if production creates the wants it seeks to satisfy, or if the wants emerge *pari passu* with the production, then the urgency of the wants can no longer be used to defend the urgency of the production. Production only fills a void that it has itself created (1984: 121–122).

Comfort becomes defined as a nice home, plenty of electronics, two cars and a garage, the latest recreational vehicles, yearly vacations, fashionable clothes, plenty of toys (for both children and adults), etc., etc. But there can always be nicer homes, better electronics, more vacations, better equipped RVs, etc., etc. This leads to what Mihaly Csikszentmihalyi calls the "paradox of rising expectations" (1990: 10): As each level of wealth and comfort satisfies certain desires, new desires arise. Without the temperance of contentment, greed and envy can drive consumers to ever spiraling heights of consumption for the materials of life (see Section 3.3.6). Americans already consume thirty times more than the average Indian consumer and ten times more than the average Mexican. This spiraling consumption is called "affluenza" by John de Graaf and Vivia Boe in a documentary of the same title. In a seminar entitled "Money and the Meaning of Life," taught by the philosopher Jacob Needleman, one of his students wrote him the following description of herself as she shopped:

> I am not exaggerating when I say that I saw a person under the influence of a drug. I saw a hungry animal. I saw a person in a hypnotic trance. It's not that I actually bought so many things—it's the way I was. ... When I came home with a dozen packages and started opening them ... I realized an extraordinary thing—I saw that each article of clothing was like a little dream. I felt like someone waking up from sleep. The dresses, the belt, the shoes, even the sweater I had bought for my husband, even the cookbook, were bought in a dream, a little dream. ... I dreamed the dresses would make me happy, beautiful, sexy ... each little dream was accompanied by physical sensations of pleasure. ... I felt it as happiness and future happiness! I realized all this in the middle of quarreling with my husband about money. ... (1991: 174).

Not only does affluenza require money to feed it, which can then lead to the strong conflict between making money and family life discussed earlier, but the proliferate use of consumer goods can in and of itself also negatively affect the fabric of family relations. For example, consider the effects of TV alone on the modern family. Viewing TV by both children and adults has caused a change in family interaction patterns which many have argued has diminished the sort of interaction necessary to tie families together. If each child has a TV in his or her own room and the parents have theirs, this can increase the negative effects even more. If there is only one TV, at least the family is in the same room together, sharing at least copresence. Combine this with the effects of stereos, computers, hobbies, and other isolating activities and the result could be quite profound. If the parents are both busy working to maintain this level of consumption, then even the ritual of family dinners may be passé.

There is also a third source of conflict that exists in the American Dream in this sense, and that is the conflict between the private and public good. The American Dream is essentially the pursuit of private goods in the context of a certain economic, social, and political arrangement. One obvious source of tension between this private pursuit of the good life and the public realm is felt when the public arrangements directly interfere or conflict with one's private pursuits. To secure private goods, one must acquire a certain amount of power in the public realm. Thus, to maintain security for the American Dream, participation in public life must also occur. The isolating pursuit of the American Dream can only succeed if public arrangements are consistently ordered to permit it; the American Dream is one that is necessarily integrated into the public sphere. Education is an obvious place where family life meets public concerns; neighborhood is another. If one's neighborhood is drug- and crime-ridden, it's hard to imagine a secure and comfortable family life. Even though the American Dream may be privately experienced, it is publicly achieved.

If one can negotiate around these various conflicts inherent in the American Dream, still the core of the dream—family life—is not an easy practice. To maintain a good family life, one needs to establish good relations in the family between spouses, between spouses and children, among children, kin, and so forth. To be a good parent alone requires one to draw on many of the virtues: patience above all, endurance, perseverance, industry, frugality, temperance, courage, kindness, and just about every other one. Good friendships, marriages, and family life really depend on being with good persons. To seek out comfort and security also requires the exercise of the virtues. A lying, abusive husband is unlikely to make a good companion; irresponsible parents are unlikely to have the sort of children who add to a flourishing family life.

4.5.6 The Life of Wealth

Ask people if they'd like to be wealthy and their typical reaction indicates that you're asking a stupid question. People often dream of a life of wealth with all its luxury and promise. People who have the ambition of being millionaires seek occupations and lifestyles that are conducive to maximizing wealth. According to Angus Campbell, most people felt more money would improve their life, and four-fifths of the people he surveyed would like to be rich (1981: 41).

One classical objection to the pursuit of wealth as the best sense of the good life is something like the following: Clearly, unless people are interested in acquiring money for the sake of money, money is inherently instrumental; that is, money is almost always accumulated for the sake of something else, such as power, enjoyment or pleasure. So it's really not the goal of one's life because it is always used as a means for some other goal. Consider the following statements by Donald Trump, the real estate magnate, from his book, *The Art of the Deal*:

> I don't do it for the money. I've got enough, much more than I'll ever need. I do it to do it. Deals are my art form. Other people paint beautifully on canvas or write wonderful poetry. I like making deals, preferably big deals. That's how I get my kicks (1987: 3; cf. Needleman 1991: 31).

But if money is a means to some goal—"money is the means of means" Georg Simmel says (1990: 485)—can it be the means to the things we need to be happy? In his book *The Loss of Happiness in Market Democracies* (2000), Robert Lane argues that more money can't buy more happiness, at least for those above the poverty line (a sign in a shop window disagrees—"You can buy happiness, just don't pay retail"). More money is not the means toward happiness, nor can it get what most people need, which is warm interpersonal relations, close neighbors, and solidarity in family life. These are things which many people claim money cannot ordinarily buy. The things that it can buy, such as pleasure, may also lead to the sybaritic lifestyle with its tendency for self-destruction. A recent study by psychologist David Myers in his book *The Pursuit of Happiness* confirms this. He argues that although money can certainly buy more material goods and create less stress and anxiety in life, it apparently does not make the rich happier than the less rich in the context of their family lives or friendships. Ed Diener, a psychologist at the University of Illinois, found that very wealthy persons report being happy on the average 77 percent of the time, while persons of average wealth say they are happy only 62 percent of the time (Diener et al. 1985). As Mihaly Csikszentmihalyi notes, although this difference is statistically significant, it is not as large as one would expect, given that the 400 richest Americans were selected for the "very wealthy" group (1990: 45). What is interesting is that no one in Diener's "very wealthy" group thought that money alone would guarantee happiness. A comprehensive study on the quality of American life (Campbell et al. 1976) reports that a person's financial situation is one of the least important factors affecting overall satisfaction with life (cf. Csikszentmihalyi 1990: 45). When it comes to love, friendship, and kinship, whatever problems or felicities exist cannot be fixed or bought with money. In Diener's study of the very wealthy, one young woman he interviewed had this to say about life with her mother and wealthy but abusive stepfather:

> He drives a BMW and just bought a Mercedes. They gave me a Mazda 626. He shops at Bloomingdale's and bought me a Gucci watch. One year he gave me a sailboard. Our house has 2 VCRs and 3 Hitachi TVs. Do these things make me happy? Absolutely not. I would trade all my family's wealth for a peaceful and loving home (1985).

Moreover, the rich are not immune from personal tragedies which, like the less rich or poor, they must bear as well; although money may buy the best healthcare, even the best healthcare cannot cure all. And of course, everyone, rich or poor, must die. Those who have money seem to concur. Ted Turner—who recently gave $1 billion to the United Nations—gave the following advice to Larry King (of the CNN interview show): "never make a decision based on money—if you're choosing between jobs, don't let money be the deciding factor" (interview with David Frost 1997).

Will Winning the Lottery Make You Happier?

Before answering that question, consider the case of Buddy Post who won $16.2 million in the Pennsylvania lottery in 1988. Since then he was convicted of assault, his sixth wife left him, his brother was convicted of trying to kill him, and his landlady successfully sued him for one-third of the jackpot. The crumbling mansion he bought with his winnings is half-filled with paperwork from bankruptcy proceedings and lawsuits; the gas has been shut off. "Money didn't change me," Post said reflectively, "it changed people around me that I knew, that I thought cared a little bit about me. But they only cared about the money." His landlady sued him because she claimed they shared the winning ticket. His brother plotted to kill him to get access to the money. He fired a warning shot to scare off his stepdaughter's boyfriend who was demanding money for some business venture; that landed him in jail. He has about $500,000 in debts, not counting legal fees and taxes. He hopes to auction off the rest of his $5 million in winnings to pay off those debts. "After winning that kind of money, there's always going to be some kinds of problems. But I didn't know it was going to escalate into some kind of nightmare." His final comment? "Money draws flies" (Kapsambelis 1996).

"'I've been rich and I've been poor,' Sophie Tucker has said, 'and believe me, rich is best.' As many other values are weakened, the question for Americans becomes not 'Is there anything that money ... can buy?' but, 'How many of the things that money will not buy are valued and desired more than what money will buy?' Money is the one unambiguous criterion of success, and such success is still the sovereign American value."

—C. Wright Mills, *The Power Elite*

The pursuit of money corrupts practices and so can destroy what nonmonetary values and benefits it may have.

In that interview with David Frost in 1997, broadcast on PBS, Larry King made a claim that "money can only solve money problems." In one sense this seems to be correct. Getting the sort of house you would like is a money problem and money would solve it; having a loving relation with your spouse doesn't seem to be solvable by giving him or her money—if anything it might exacerbate whatever problems existed. What he or she would be attracted to would be the money, not the money giver. As the old adage goes, "Money can't buy love." But in another sense the claim that "money can't buy you everything" might be wrong, as Jacob Needleman points out. In a class he was giving, entitled, Money and the Meaning of Life (written about in his book of the same title), he asked his students to perform a little thought experiment. Think of a current problem you have and ask yourself how much money it would take to fix (1991: 112). A few students volunteered examples.

One argued that if he had a few thousand dollars, he wouldn't have to put up with the insults from an old friend from whom he had borrowed money. If he didn't have to borrow the money, he could be more candid with him; he wouldn't have to be silent in the face of those verbal cuts.

What Needleman seems to point out is that although money could solve many problems, it is the manner in which it solves them that may be questionable. If he had money, he wouldn't have to borrow, and if he didn't have to borrow, he wouldn't have to demean himself. But this lets him off the hook; if he would be willing not to demean himself for the few thousand that he's borrowed from his friend, then would he not gain something that would be more lasting and valuable? If he had a few thousand to solve this problem, yet did not have the character, wouldn't his lack of character still make him vulnerable to other situa-

---

Wealth in America

When Microsoft stock went up 8 points over one weekend, it added $2 billion to founder Bill Gates's net worth. Gates is not only the richest man in America, but in the world—his estimated worth is currently $36.4 billion. According to a United Nations report released in July 1999, the combined wealth of the world's three richest families is greater than the annual income of 600 million people in the least developed countries, and the world's 200 richest people have doubled their wealth to more than $1 trillion. In the same period the number of people living on less than $1 a day has remained unchanged at 1.3 billion. Ten percent of all American households now make $100,000 or more; at least 3.5 million American households had net worths of more than $1 million in 1995. Tiger Woods gets $60 million in promotional fees, Jerry Seinfeld got $1 million per TV episode, and John Walter departed AT&T on a golden parachute worth $30 million after just 9 months of work. As Donald Trump put it: "You can't be too greedy." *Forbes Magazine* had to come up with a new definition for billionaire to pare its annual list of the world's money elite down from 445 to 200.

Despite the fact that the rich are getting richer, the wealth gap in the United States is growing even faster. The average wealth of the richest 1 percent increased from $10 million to more than $14 million from 1989 to 1997. But wealth at the low end is actually shrinking, as the use of credit cards, debit cards, and home-equity loans pushes many middle-income families and lower-income families further into debt, out of the home-buying market, and even into bankruptcy. The median family wealth in the United States has remained relatively unchanged at $52,000 for the last 15 years.

Surprisingly, those in the middle-class show little resentment toward the wealthy: "Americans very much admire people who have more money than they do; secretly they wish they could be more like Bill Gates or Donald Trump, even while they give lip service to Mother Teresa," said Robert Wuthnow, a professor of sociology at Princeton (cf. *Amassing Wealth.* Reprinted in *Anchorage Daily News,* August 3, 1997).

tions? For example, couldn't it be possible that somewhere down the line he needs to borrow $10,000; wouldn't he still be vulnerable to demeaning himself in that case? Money wouldn't solve the problem of his deficiency in this regard, although it could help him avoid certain situations in which he would be called upon to demean himself—of course, depending on how much money he had. As one of Needleman's students, an accountant, commented,

> A lot of wealthy people use money to soften all the edges of life, to avoid working through difficulties. It's like cotton batting. But not only wealthy people. I've seen this in many of my clients. The rich ones sometimes use money in this way, the not-so-rich ones dream of using it like that (1991: 113).

If the results of the study by Ronald Ingelhart are correct, "income has a surprisingly weak effect on happiness. When we have basic human rights, secure food and shelter, meaningful activity, and enriching relations, our happiness is unaffected by whether we drive a BMW or, like those in so many societies, walk or ride a bus" (1990: 242).

Still, as sociologist C. Wright Mills argues

> whenever the standards of the moneyed life prevail, the man with money, no matter how he got it, will eventually be respected. A million dollars, it is said, covers a multitude of sins. ... In a society in which the money-maker has had no serious rival for repute and honor ... [the] pursuit of the moneyed life is the commanding value, in relation to which the influence of other values has declined, so men easily become morally ruthless in the pursuit of easy money. ... (1956: 346).

But power or recognition gained through wealth may be suspect after all. Unless you live in an oligarchy, the political power gained from wealth is considered illegitimate. Although making money takes certain talents, abilities, and characteristics, you are often more recognized for your wealth than for those characteristics. Thus, people will honor or respect the wealth rather than the person.

4.5.7 The Life of Fame and Power

In the 1970s Andy Warhol made his famous remark: "in the future everyone will have 15 minutes of fame." Indeed, attempting fame by any means possible seems to be the pastime of a number of people who will do a number of bizarre, odd, and often degrading things just to get a few minutes of airtime. Fame is thought to bring a certain amount of benefit and pleasure derived from adulation or at least recognition by a large number of people. Sociologist Leo Braudy writes, "the urge for fame mingles one's acceptance of oneself with the desire for others ... to recognize that one is special. It is the most immediate effort individuals make to reach beyond themselves, their families, and their place in a[n] ... order to claim a more general approval of their behavior and nature" (1986: 585). Put more simply, fame is an "intangible urge to be someone" (1986: 591). Consequently, the world is populated by wannabes and successful wannabes.

In 1978 a murderer complained in a letter to Wichita authorities: "How many times do I have to kill before I get a name in the paper or some national attention?" (Associated Press, February 11, 1978). This kind of lust for renown is an indication of the principal difficulty with this sense of the good life. If the aim in a person's life is to become famous, then that alone is not sufficient to guarantee how one will become famous. Leo Braudy has claimed that this is exactly what has happened:

Particularly since WWII, the increasing number and sophistication of the ways information is brought to us have enormously exploded the ways of being known. In the process the concept of fame has been grotesquely distorted (1986: 3).

The Guinness Book of Records is an exemplar of this phenomenon. As Braudy writes, this document "demonstrates that everything humans can do has been turned into something that humans can compete to do" (1986: 8). A perusal of the "records" shows the most bizarre and grotesque accomplishments imaginable. There are the endless ways in which people attempt to reach the North Pole, circumnavigate the globe, or some other such venture: the first person to solo to the North Pole, the first to sled dog to the North Pole, the first to walk to the North Pole, the first woman to walk to the North Pole, etc., etc. There is really no goal in these activities other than the fame they achieve (or the product endorsement contracts they might garner). As Daniel Boorstein defined it, "a celebrity is someone who is famous for being famous." One might ask: "What purpose does it serve to have somebody be the first to walk to the North Pole?" Why couldn't the time, energy, money, and effort be spent on some goal that has more collective benefit? In this frenzy for fame, activities are not measured by their moral worth or collective good but by their potential for renown. The quest for fame has also distorted our sense of what counts as heroic, according to Dick Keyes, author of *True Heroism*. When young people are asked for their heroes, most respond with the names of well-known sports or entertainment figures. "Celebrity and ability seem to have replaced courage and character as most qualification for respect" (1995).

Another difficulty with fame—as many have noted, even as early as Aristotle— is the fickleness of the public in regard to the famous (*Nic. Ethics* 1095a20ff.). Since fame depends on recognition by the public, then as the public changes its regard, so go the fortunes of the famous. Achievement and success are defined primarily in terms of what other people think is worthy of admiration (Braudy 1986: 587). It seems that Hollywood, the music industry, or the sports world offers us somebody new every week to worship or admire. Musical groups come and go, and those who remain become the subject of ridicule if they persist too long. But some have noted a darker side to this fickleness, a sort of ambivalence in the public toward the famous, alternately wishing to put them up on a pedestal, but then to knock them off (cf. Braudy 1986: 8). Clark Gable said to David Niven:

> We all have a contract with the public—in us they see themselves in what they would like to be. ... They love to put us on a pedestal and worship us. ... But they've read the small print, and most of us haven't. ... So, when we get knocked off ... the public feels satisfied (Niven 1975: 22; cf. Braudy 1986: 8).

Those who seek power, on the other hand, strive for positions that enable them to transcend the ordinary environments of ordinary people; they are in positions to make decisions having major consequences on a large number of people (Mills 1956: 3). As a result, they are alternately admired or feared by the people who suffer the consequences of those decisions.

> They are in command of the major hierarchies and organizations of modern society. They rule the big corporations. They run the machinery of the state and claim its prerogatives. They direct the military establishment. They occupy the strategic command posts of the social structure, in which are now centered the effective means of the power and the wealth and the celebrity which they enjoy (Mills 1956: 4).

Genuine power is the ability to get others to do one's will because they believe in the legitimacy of that person's authority to do so (cf. Arendt 1970: 44ff.). As Voltaire puts it, power "consists in making others act as I choose." For those who do not recognize such authority, a person in power can utilize the instruments of force available to his or her position. Force is the application of violence to ensure that others conform to the directives of those in power. Because of that power and their ability to draw on the instruments of force, people in power are consequently sought out by others who feel that the quality and character of their own lives are dependent on the decisions of the authorities, who become centers of influence, favor, and prestige. All of this creates a certain intoxicating buoyancy for many people in power. Bertrand de Jouvenal calls it an "incomparable pleasure" (1952: 110). Being powerful also has the advantage of being able to increase one's own advantage: Whatever decisions the powerful are capable of making that also affect their lives, they can make them so that they themselves become thereby advantaged.

As anyone who has power knows, there are two major difficulties with this way of life: getting power and keeping it. Because power is so coveted, and the vicious often want it, getting and holding power may require being immoral. Those who are willing to do this may already have a lowered moral sensibility, or any moral sensibility they had may be worn away by the rigors of such a pursuit:

> the most important question, for instance, about the campaign funds of ambitious young politicians is not whether the politicians are morally insensitive, but whether or not any young man in American politics, who has come so far and so fast, could very well have done so today without possessing or acquiring a somewhat blunted moral sensibility (Mills 1956: 343).

The paradox of power is that even those with the best intentions—those who seek power for the sake of some collective good—must compete for it with the vicious and with those who seek it for their particular interests. The vicious will prevail if the good-intentioned do not act as viciously, but when the well-meaning prevail in that manner, then the good is lost. Machiavelli, more than any other thinker, realized this basic paradox. Here is his recommendation to the power ambitious:

> how we live is so far removed from how we ought to live, that he who abandons what is done for what ought to be done, will rather learn to bring about his own ruin than his preservation. A man who wishes to make a profession of goodness in everything must necessarily come to grief among so many who are not good. Therefore it is necessary for a prince who wishes to maintain himself, to learn how not to be good, and to use this knowledge and not use it, according to the necessity of the case (*The Prince*, Chap. 15).

4.5.8 The Virtuous Life: Does Virtue Lead to Happiness?

One thing that has been noted in the various accounts of the good life is that all require the exercise of some virtue to avoid the pitfalls that each sort of life contains. Paradoxically, a life of pleasure and enjoyment requires temperance to succeed; security and comfort require one to be frugal and industrious, not greedy or covetous; to be a good parent or spouse, one has to be kind, patient, and courageous. The acquisition of wealth not only requires temperance, frugality, industry and the like but also some direction.

But second, each of these senses of the good life falls short in various ways of a genuine sense of flourishing. Those who pursue pleasure exclusively, like Hugh

Hefner, end up pursuing many other things as well. For these various reasons, Aristotle argues that the virtuous life is the most accurate sense of happiness in the sense of flourishing. A life is most complete, and a person can be counted as flourishing, when she can enjoy each of these senses of the good life as a person with a virtuous character. A good person will enjoy the right sort of pleasures, which life can afford at the right amount, in the right way, and with the right people; a person with virtuous character makes for a good partner, parent, and friend, has goodwill towards others, is a safe companion and good neighbor. Wealth is pursued without greed or ruthlessness. Those with virtuous character can be trusted with power to be fair-minded and to perform roles and execute duties in a fair and just way. Aristotle sees flourishing as consonant with virtue. Virtue is the perfection of the person's character, and a person with good character is more capable of flourishing than one without good character. Flourishing is achieved by acting virtuously in every important aspect of your life. Flourishing is the excellent exercise of oneself in all respects. Just as the harpist who plays excellently produces beautiful music, so the person who acts in accordance with virtue produces the best life (*Nic. Ethics* 1098a10ff.). For this reason, Aristotle, as we saw, defines flourishing as "an activity of the soul (*psychē*) in conformity with excellence or virtue" (*Nic. Ethics* 1098a15–17). But just as even the virtuoso cannot make good music from a bad composition, so good persons must be careful about the quality and worthiness of the practices they choose to constitute the most significant part of their lives. A flourishing life is one that allows you to enjoy the real pleasures of life, to engage in highly qualitative relations with others, to attain a certain amount of wealth in a respectable way, and to reach a certain well-deserved status and recognition, but all within the context of virtuous living. Virtuous living should generate the right sort of pleasures, should set the parameters for the best kinds of relations, allow genuine recognition, and exercise power justly, and not at the cost of what is the right thing to do.

Should we believe Aristotle? Does the life of virtue lead to happiness? The Greek Stoic philosopher Epictetus echoes Aristotle's promotion of the life of virtue by claiming that "virtue promises happiness, prosperity and peace" (*Moral Disc.* Chap. iv). This is also a claim repeated by 18th-century philosopher David Hume: "Inward peace of mind, consciousness of integrity, a satisfactory review of our own conduct; these are very requisite to happiness" (1777: 283). This is contemporarily advocated by Philippa Foot (1978), who argues that there is a necessary connection between virtue and happiness and that only the virtuous person is truly happy (cf. Flanagan 1991: 316).

This claim is challenged by contemporary philosopher Bernard Williams, who suggests a number of counter circumstances (1985: 45–46). There are certainly people who are unhappy because of their viciousness, but there are also those who are vicious because they are unhappy and from conditions not necessarily tied to ethical circumstances: misery, rage, loneliness, despair. Moreover, there are some people who are not vicious and who try hard to be virtuous, yet are miserable from their virtuous state. There are also a few who are vicious but not miserable and in fact may be happy. Also, Williams notes that it may be the case that there are those who are vicious and miserable, yet prosperous, and so can enjoy its associated pleasures, but if they were less vicious, they would also be less successful. Finally, there are the unremarkably vicious people who, for whatever reason, may feel perfectly happy and content.

Bernard Williams is a contemporary British philosopher. His best known work is *Ethics and the Limits of Philosophy*.

Being Good for Goodness' Sake?

If we hope to be happy by being virtuous—that is, strictly speaking, "flourishing"—then it is clear that virtue is instrumental and a means to some end; it is not done for its own sake, but for the sake of flourishing. Immanuel Kant questions such motives. In his way of thinking, the person who acts virtuously to be happy is less of a moral agent than the one who acts virtuously because it is the right thing to do. We discussed in Sections 1.5 and 3.32 how Kant felt that not only the inclination to do the good should not serve as a basis for morality, but also why an inclination or sentiment to do the good is not a morally praiseworthy motive for an action. After all, if one is inclined to do acts of kindness, then there is no effort or struggle in doing it, so no special praise should be given (1785: 15ff.). A person who acts well out of inclination is therefore less of a moral agent than one who acts well despite disinclination. This holds true for the other end of the action—the consequence: Those who act well for the sake of something else, some reward or benefit, are less true moral agents, or less praiseworthy, than those who act for the sake of the good, without regard to its consequence, either in terms of its benefit or harm (1785: 17).

This distinction between doing good for the sake of something else and doing good for its own sake is again captured by Kant's distinction between acting from duty and acting according to duty. The example which Kant gives is that of the shopkeeper who charges his customers an honest price simply because cheating would be bad for business, as opposed to one who charges honestly because that is the right thing to do and does so even in cases where cheating would have no detection or consequences (1785:13). As far as Kant is concerned, then, the only truly good person is the one who wills the good for the sake of the good, and not for any of its possible consequences—even happiness. What do you think of this claim?

Williams's challenge might be attenuated if we employ some of the distinctions made earlier among well-being, flourishing, and prosperity. First, since psychological evidence suggests that the subjective feeling of well-being, understood as a mood or feeling of contentment, is not mainly the result of one's state of affairs, then it's quite possible that there are those who are not virtuous, not flourishing, or not prosperous, who nonetheless feel content and generally happy.

Second, it is also the case that success at certain practices requires that one must be vicious to some degree, and one can often succeed at any practice by vicious means. As Alasdair MacIntyre stresses, "the possession of the virtues may perfectly well hinder us in achieving external goods ... notoriously, the cultivation of truthfulness, justice and courage will often, the world being what it contingently is, bar us from being rich or famous or powerful" (1981: 183). The claim that cheaters never prosper may not be entirely true. Such persons may be able to enjoy whatever pleasures are associated with success. However, it may be questionable whether persons so situated can be counted as flourishing. Certainly, there are practices, such as extortion, that are inherently corrupt and so require viciousness to succeed. But among those practices that are not inherently corrupt, it would seem that vices such as dishonesty, ruthlessness, unfairness, and the like would prevent participants from gaining whatever contribution that practice would make to their flourishing. As MacIntyre has emphasized, virtues achieve whatever goods are internal to a practice (1981: 178). To the extent that virtues promote the good internal to a practice, then it can be truly said "to be its own reward." For example, if a scientist stole another person's work or cheated or lied about the results of experiments—even though that might lead to fame and success—those vices would deprive that scientist of the sense of accomplishment, the joys of discovery, the achievement of understanding, the "flow" resulting from the synchrony of hard work done well, and its positive results. In that case it may be more correct to say that cheaters never flourish—or at least never flourish within that practice. It is also hard to imagine certain sorts of practices, such as marriage, friendships, child-rearing, and the like, in which vicious behavior would cause participants to flourish. Flourishing within such practices would seem to require a predominance of honesty, fairness, kindness, respect, and other virtues.

In the end Williams's solution to his own dilemma is to propose that, although it is not necessarily so, for the most part, virtuous behavior and moral upbringing are advantageous to both individual and society:

> we have little reason to believe that they [children] will be happier if excluded from the ethical institutions of society. Even if we know that there are some people who are happier, by the minimal criteria, outside those institutions, we also know that they rarely become so by being educated as outlaws. As a result of all that, we have much reason for, and little reason against, bringing up children within the ethical world we inhabit, and if we succeed they themselves will see the world from the same perspective (1985: 48).

4.6 DELIBERATION

Recall that there are three aspects to moral reasoning: concern with the ends of actions, or moral vision; address of the best moral means to an end, or deliberation; and finally, concern for the best choice, or judgment. If the good life can be thought of as a plan for life, with its various goals, then deliberation involves the question of how that plan is best achieved and how those goals should be accomplished.

4.6.1 Rational Calculation

Some argue that deliberation is simply a matter of rational calculation of means to an end. *The term rational here is usually used in the economic sense, that is, a person who is self-interested and interested in maximizing her good or utility, generally speaking* (cf. Gauthier 1990: 209). More specifically, a rational person is one who "acts to bring about that outcome which he prefers, among those which he believes are open to him" (Gauthier 1990: 214). In this regard he is a person who, under proper conditions of knowledge and reflection, understands which outcomes are possible or likely, prefers one outcome to another because it does maximize his good or utility, and then seeks the most efficient means of attaining it (Gauthier 1990: 211). Conversely, then, we can infer that a person is *irrational* and not engaged in proper rational calculation if he (1) seeks that which is impossible or unlikely, (2) chooses among possible outcomes that which he prefers less, (3) chooses among possible outcomes that which does not maximize what he prefers, or (4) chooses inefficient means of attaining what he prefers when he is knowledgeable of the best alternatives. Thus, if a person prefers the life of pleasure to the life of virtue, then she will attempt to determine which pleasures are possible for her, relative to her situation and means, and then maximize pleasure in her life by the most efficient means possible.

In maximizing his good, a rational person would always choose the most efficient means for attaining it. John Rawls outlines some of the process involved in efficiency (1971: 411–416). The first consideration is what he calls *the principle of effective means.* This suggests that we should adopt that plan which realizes the end with the least expenditure of means or, given the equal expenditure of means, choose the one that fulfills the objective to the fullest possible extent (1971: 412; cf.

Gauthier 1990: 211). If there are two financial plans that involve roughly the same risk, yet the first would yield $2000 profit in 1 year and the second the same amount in 2 years, then the first choice is the clear one. If, on the other hand, there are two plans, both of which yield $2000 in 2 years, but the first only requires a $500 investment, while the second $1000, then the choice is clear. Assuming the same risk and the same outcome, choose the one that requires the less expenditure of means, or where there is the same expenditure of means, choose that one that yields more of the good preferred. This principle can also be applied to negative outcomes. If all the possible outcomes are bad, the principle of effective means suggests that you should choose the least worse. If a person using tax strategy A is going to pay $20,000 in taxes to the IRS, while plan B will have him paying $30,000, then plan A is the more efficient.

The second principle associated with efficiency is what Rawls calls *inclusiveness*. This suggests that one plan is preferred to another if its execution would achieve all of the desired aims of the other plan and one or more further aims in addition (1971: 412). If a visit to a friend accomplishes both social obligations and allows one to accomplish business ends as well, then that would be preferred to one that accomplishes just one or the other.

Given this general account of rational calculation, the question is whether it is the best means of *moral* deliberation. Some philosophers, such as David Gauthier, argue that it is. As we'll see in Section 4.8.3, he claims that starting from the standpoint of rational calculation, we assume a self-interested agent who is simply interested in maximizing her good and may have no desire to be constrained by ethics in this pursuit. In his work, he attempts to show how even under those conditions such an agent will be forced by concerns of maximizing her good to act with interest toward the interests of others. Simply put, he shows that a purely selfish, egoistic pursuit of goals will not in the end maximize them; rather one will find cooperation always in one's best interest when others cooperate. But to achieve some level of cooperation, one's pursuit of ends must be constrained by a legitimate recognition of the right of others to pursue their own ends (1986: 17)—otherwise others will fail to cooperate with you, and you will lose the advantage. This strategy—often called the tit-for-tat strategy—suggests that we are most advantaged when we cooperate with others who cooperate and don't cooperate with those who don't cooperate with us (see Section 5.4.8).

There may be some reasons to argue against using rational calculation as the paradigm for moral deliberation. For one thing, it frames moral deliberation from the framework of a "least moral agent," as someone who is a pure self-interested calculator when in fact many people are already morally robust, meaning that they have moral sentiments, virtues, and habits which dispose them toward moral constraints. To start with the lowest common denominator, so to speak, yields a result that might require moral agents to act less morally than they are inclined. Second, the framework of self-interest assumes a background of competition with other individuals also self-interested; yet many of our decisions are made in the context of cooperative arrangements, such as families or professional relationships, where we have the interests of others in mind. If a doctor is offering a treatment plan based on his preferences or calculations, then that may not be morally appropriate in the doctor–patient relationship that has informed consent as a norm. Third, rational calculation is articulated in terms of preferences, yet the moral limitation on preferences is not part of the notion of rational calculation. Some concept of the good is needed to adjudicate among those preferences that are morally worthwhile. One could imagine a scenario in which a person's preference is for murdering opponents, and who could gain the cooperation of others in such a way that he achieves his goals in the most efficient manner; that person would be counted as rational, but we would hardly count him moral, intuitively speaking.

4.6.2 Cunning

Joseph Fouché was a cunning man. He gained power and prospered during a period of great tumult in late 18th–early 19th-century France. During the French Revolution he was a radical Jacobin. After the terror he became a moderate republican, and under Napoleon he became a committed imperialist. Napoleon appointed him his minister of police and made him the Duke of Otranto. Napoleon often had him do his dirty work, especially digging up scandal on people. But Napoleon could never trust the man himself, was often suspicious of the slippery character, and kept a large contingent of people spying on him. Yet, although he at one time or another fired all of his ministers for treason or betrayal, he could never prove anything about Fouché. After his escape from Elba in 1815, he had to once again rely on Fouché since, given his cunning, he was the only former minister who remained from the old regime. After a few weeks back in power, Napoleon's spies reported the suspicion that Fouché was collaborating with the Austrian minister, Metternich. Napoleon's spies managed to intercept a courier who confessed that he had given a letter to Fouché from Metternich and revealed the location of a special meeting with his agents in Basel. But when one of Napoleon's spies infiltrated the meeting, he came back with the impression that the Austrian agents felt Fouché was double-crossing *them*. Later when Fouché met with Napoleon, he produced a letter from Metternich, saying that he could not read it since it was written in an invisible ink, but the courier had failed to supply the powder necessary to make it visible. Napoleon flew into a rage, believing that Fouché had betrayed him, but he could not give the proof. Once again Fouché had used his cunning to escape ruin. Fouché had managed to use his spies to spy on Napoleon's and knew of their infiltration. He managed to have his agents convince them that he was in fact spying for Napoleon (cf. Greene 1998: 379–380).

    Cunning is another form of calculation or deliberation concerned with maintaining one's advantage, especially in the context of power relations or politics. Classic models of cunning are found in Niccolo Machiavelli's (1469–1527) *The Prince* and Sun Tzu's *The Art of War*. For Machiavelli wisdom understood as cunning is simply a set of rules, advice, and strategies meant to maintain whatever advantage you presently have and to get those advantages you want. Machiavelli's understanding of prudence is based on a dark, ironic vision of human beings and human affairs, which is typical of those who see prudence as only cunning. But rather than suggesting means for compensating for such flaws in political life, Machiavelli promotes ways in which the prince can take advantage of them for the sake of self-advantage:

> how we live is so far removed from how we ought to live, that he who abandons what is done for what ought to be done, will rather learn to bring about his own ruin than his preservation. A man who wishes to make a profession of goodness in everything must necessarily come to grief among so many who are not good. Therefore it is necessary for a prince who wishes to maintain himself, to learn how not to be good, and to use this knowledge and not use it, according to the necessity of the case (*The Prince*, Chap. 15).

The goal in cunning is to do those things that maintain and secure one's power and advantage. Virtue and vice are simply means to that end, and one is preferred to the other only when it achieves this goal: "If one considers well, it will be found that some things which seem virtues would, if followed, lead to one's ruin, and some others which appear vices result in one's greater security and wellbeing" (*The Prince*, Chap. 15). For example, in regard to generosity, although Machiavelli suggests that the appearance of liberality is beneficial, in truth stinginess is to be preferred among princes: "For spending the wealth of others will not diminish your reputation, but increase it, only spending your own resources will injure you. There is nothing which destroys itself so much as generosity, for by using it you lose the power of using it, and become either poor and despicable, or, to escape poverty, rapacious and hated" (*The Prince*, Chap. 16). Similar advice is given in other matters. Cunning rulers are those who ought not keep their promises when it would be against their interest. "If men were all good, this precept would not be a good one; but as they are bad, and would not observe their faith with you, so you are not bound to keep faith with them" (*The Prince*, Chap. 18). It is better to be feared than loved, since humans have less scruple in offending people who make themselves loved than those who make themselves feared; love is held by a chain of obligation which, "men being selfish, is broken whenever it serves their purpose; but fear is maintained by a dread of punishment which never fails" (*The Prince*, Chap. 17). But still people have to make themselves feared in such a way that if they do not gain love, they at any rate avoid hatred. On the matter of revenge, Machiavelli advises us that persons will revenge themselves for small injuries, but cannot do so for great ones: "The injury therefore that we do to a man must be such that we need not fear his vengeance" (*The Prince*, Chap. 3). In general, if the virtues are to your advantage, then it is not necessary to have them, "but it is very necessary to seem to have them" (*The Prince*, Chap. 18).

Similarly, Sun Tzu's *Art of War* (ca. 500 B.C.E.) is a manual of strategy for those who aim at victory in battle, but it is often used as sage advice for any adversarial situation and has been used in business, sports, and law. "When doing battle," Sun Tzu advises, "seek a quick victory. A protracted battle will blunt weapons and dampen ardor" (Chap. 2). Rather than wasting one's own resources, "a wise general will strive to feed off the enemy" (Chap. 2). The true art of war is victory without doing battle: "To subjugate the enemy's army without doing battle is the highest of excellence. Therefore, the best warfare strategy is to attack the enemy's plans, next is to attack alliances, next is to attack the army, and the worst is to attack a walled city" (Chap. 3). So when should one attack? Sun Tzu advises that "invincibility lies in the defense; the possibility of victory in the attack. One defends when his strength is inadequate; he attacks when it is abundant" (Chap. 4). How should one attack? "If ten times the enemy's strength, surround them; if five times, attack them; if double, divide them; if equal, be able to fight them; if fewer, be able to evade them; if weaker, be able to avoid them" (Chap. 3). How can one be assured of victory?

> There are five factors of knowing who will win: One who knows when he can fight, and when he cannot fight will be victorious; one who knows how to use both large and small forces will be victorious; who knows how to unite upper and lower ranks in purpose will be victorious; one who is prepared and waits for the unprepared will be victorious; one whose general is able and is not interfered by the ruler will be victorious. One who knows the enemy and knows himself will not be in danger in a hundred battles. One who does not know the enemy but knows himself will sometimes win, some-

times lose. One who does not know the enemy and does not know himself will be in danger in every battle (Chap. 3).

In a recent book entitled *The 48 Laws of Power* (1998), Robert Greene writes in the spirit of Machiavelli and elaborates the maxims that are needed to maintain power and retain advantage. These include:

Never put too much trust in friends, learn how to use enemies.
Conceal your intentions.
Always say less than necessary.
Get others to do the work for you, but always take the credit.
Avoid the unhappy and unlucky.
Use selective honesty and generosity to disarm your victim.
Pose as a friend, work as a spy.
Crush your enemy totally.
Do not commit to anyone.
Discover each man's thumbscrew.
Assume formlessness.

It is clear that if people are to be cunning and take these "laws" to heart, then they must be vicious, ruthless, and brutish. So corrupted, the possibility of flourishing in Aristotle's sense may have disappeared. Yet those who engage in power for good ends may be forced to heed Machiavelli's warning of the virtuous person in the midst of corruption—if not for their own sake, at least for the sake of the good cause they may represent. Because the vicious often seek power, those who use power for the good are often placed into ruthless combat. Power and politics, therefore, become a place where cunning seems to be the norm. It is what Bernard Williams calls the problem of "dirty hands" (1978: 55). There are simply some political acts which have good political reasons, and without which worthy political projects might fail, yet would not be done by honorable and scrupulous people (1978: 57). Williams sees the solution as finding the middle ground between Plato's question, "How can the good rule?" and Machiavelli's, "How to rule the world as it is?" with the question "How can the good rule the world as it is?" (1978: 72). From the inside, the good politician is one who has an active sense of moral costs and limits, who for every act that must be done at some moral cost, there is a corresponding sense of regret and remorse. From the outside, the political system must be structured to place constraints on ruthlessness and cunning, all the while knowing that such acts do take place. To the degree that a system is publicly scrutinized, avoids control of power by a few, has clear and formal processes for political positions, and minimizes the amount of corruption needed to ascend to these positions of power, then a political system can constrain the amount of Machiavellianism needed (1978: 71). Machiavelli's advice may be more appropriate for those political systems structured on absolute rule than on democratic, publicly scrutinized systems. But even in the latter, cunning may be a necessary art for even the best among us.

4.6.3 Aristotle's Account of Deliberation

For Aristotle *deliberation* is more than just rational calculation, and its purpose and method are different from cunning (*Nic. Ethics* 1142b23–24). For Aristotle deliberation (*eubolia*), unlike rational calculation, is more than just determining the necessary and efficient means to an end. It is concerned with the proper *moral* means to a *good* end. Unlike cunning, deliberation is not just concerned with one's advantage but also with what is understood as good, generally speaking. Wisdom is an ability that not only allows you to accomplish things but to accomplish good things in a morally acceptable way. Consequently, good deliberation must be opposed to cunning (*Nic. Ethics* 1144a25). Cunning and clever people, although smart and often able to get ahead, are not necessarily good persons. They are very adept at getting things and advantages for themselves or for others, but often at the price of bad character. The good deliberator, as Aristotle insists, must choose the noblest means (*Nic. Ethics* 1142b23–24), that is, must choose not only the means that are most effective but also the means that are right (*Nic. Ethics* 1142b23–24). In this regard deliberation is concerned to measure the means to some concept of the good life, moral vision, or right desire. Cleverness is to practical wisdom as natural virtue is to genuine virtue (*Nic. Ethics* 1144b1–5). That is to say, a person with raw or natural courage can use it effectively for good or evil, whereas a person with genuine virtue is disposed to use it for good only. Similarly, a cunning person has a natural cleverness that could be used to succeed at any purpose, while the wise person is one who directs deliberation to the good. Aristotle writes,

> A man of deficient self-restraint or a bad man may as a result of calculation arrive at the object he proposes as the right thing to do, so that he will have deliberated correctly, although he will have gained something extremely evil; whereas to have deliberated well is felt to be a good thing. Therefore it is this kind of correctness in deliberation that is Deliberative Excellence, namely being correct in the sense of arriving at something good (*Nic. Ethics* 1142b16–22).

According to Aristotle, deliberation is concerned with things that happen in a generally indeterminate way (*Nic. Ethics* 1112b9–10). We don't deliberate about the motion of the planets, since that is fixed, but we can deliberate about whether a certain set of means will best achieve an end within the context of human action. Experience rather than scientific knowledge is what is relied on in these matters (*Nic. Ethics* 1112a24), and that is why in especially important matters we often rely on the counsel and wisdom of others (*Nic. Ethics* 1112b11). We also deliberate about things that are in our power to do or can be done; there is no sense in deliberating about the impossible or the necessary (*Nic. Ethics* 1112a30). We don't, strictly speaking, deliberate about ends, just means to the end (*Nic. Ethics* 1112b13). A doctor, Aristotle says, does not deliberate about whether he shall heal, only the way in which he shall if possible (*Nic. Ethics* 1112b12–14). As Aristotle suggests, deliberation is limited on one side by desire for the end or goal but on the other by the discernment and choice of a particular thing to be done (*Nic. Ethics* 1113a1–2). The territory of deliberation is between moral vision and choice; it lies between end and the act that must be done to accomplish it.

For Aristotle calculation is something embedded within and guided by good deliberation. If several morally acceptable ways are possible to a goal, only then does one employ the principles of rational calculation (cf. *Nic. Ethics* 1112b15–25; *Meta.* 1032b15–25). In this regard deliberation is an investigation that works backward from the end to what must first be done to accomplish that end (*Nic. Ethics* 1112b20–24). It determines which of the means is in the person's power to do or not to do (*Nic. Ethics* 1112b25). As primarily a process by which we determine the necessary means to an end, it takes the form of what he calls a "practical syllogism" (*De Motu* 701a10–25):

> I need a covering
>
> A cloak is a covering
>
> What I need I ought to make
>
> I ought to make a cloak

It is, in accordance with the principles of rational calculation, a step-by-step determination of the best, or at least the necessary, means to an end *(De Motu* 701a20–25). I want or need this; this is what I must do to get it; consequently, I should do it. The general sense of this sort of practical syllogism is neatly expressed by von Wright (1979: 19):

> An agent, A, wants to attain some end, E
>
> A believes that unless he does P he will not attain E
>
> Therefore A resolves to do P

But as already emphasized, calculation is embedded within the larger framework of moral deliberation. As Aristotle articulates it, "Excellence in deliberation will be correctness with regard to what conduces to the end of which wisdom is the true apprehension" (*Nic. Ethics* 1142b34–35).

4.6.4 Cicero's Model of Deliberation

Cicero's account of deliberation draws on the insights of Aristotle as well as the ancient Stoic master Panaetius. Cicero accepted Aristotle's general characterization of deliberation and practical reasoning as something distinct from the rigorous forms of theoretical reasoning found in science and mathematics. Deliberation had to do with what was probable, provisional, and within our power to do. He also seems to agree with Aristotle that calculation is embedded within deliberation, and seeking one's advantage is constrained by a larger sense of the good or the honorable. With Panaetius, he seems to agree with the old master's acceptance of the adage "do not let the quest for the perfect destroy the good." Responding to the strong criticisms of Carneades against the early Stoics, whose doctrines aimed at the perfect exercise of virtue in ideal lives, Panaetius conceded his point that the particulars and nuances of concrete moral situations muddied the waters of ideal moral laws or principles. Panaetius's aim was to apply best principles and best reasoning practices to particular situations with the hopes of discerning what was morally preferable as opposed to what was morally perfect. The task of moral deliberation was to identify what was the appropriate or fitting action in any particular situation to the best of one's ability, while still adhering to general principles and the moral order of things (cf. Jonsen and Toulmin 1988: 77–78).

Cicero translated Panaetius's view to the idea that what was important in moral deliberation is the present situation before us and that we determine what the right thing or the right duty is for that situation. The fulfillment of duties is always addressed to a particular situation, but those decisions must be guided by a strong moral vision of the order of things and moral principle. In this regard Cicero—like all the Stoics—believed in an eternal natural law or order: "right reason in conformity with nature, present in all men, unchanging, eternal, commanding all to the performance of duty, prohibiting evil" *(De rep.* III.33) (For a discussion of natural law, see Section 5.5.) Our highest duty then is toward moral goodness (*honestas*) or the honorable (*De officiis* III.8). But how a duty is to be performed or

Cicero (104–43 B.C.E.) was Rome's greatest orator and philosopher. Throughout his career he allied himself with the Roman republic against those Romans, such as Cataline and Caesar, who sought to replace that form of government. Exiled and often threatened with assassination, he returned twice to champion various causes with his amazing oratory. In his retirement he wrote several books on philosophy, his most important being a handbook on Stoic morality, *De officiis*. After Caesar's death he came out of retirement to defend Octavius and to descry Antony. But Octavius turned against him. He tried to flee Rome, but he was overtaken by a mob of bounty hunters and killed.

interpreted is always a matter of deliberating within the context of a particular situation: "These different circumstances should be scrutinized in every instance of duty, so that we may become skilled evaluators of duty and by calculation perceive where the weight of duty lies, so that we may understand how much is due to each person" (*De officiis* I.59). In deliberating in a particular situation, one's duty is often in conflict with what appears to be advantageous or useful. Extrapolating a bit from Cicero's remarks, we can say that, for him, deliberation involves a series of questions rising from the merely calculative to the moral. In regard to some action or set of actions, we must ask the following questions:

1. Is it something that is necessary to do for some other thing? (*De officiis* 171)
2. Can it be done? If so, is it something that can't be helped? If it is something that can be otherwise, is it easy or hard? (*De officiis* 171)
3. Is it something that should be done given the particulars of the situation? (*De officiis* 176)
4. Does the thing for which it is to be done have value or worth? (*De officiis* 171)
5. If so, is it advantageous? (*De officiis* 9)
6. If so, does it conflict with what is good and honorable? (*De officiis* 9, 125)

Questions 1 and 2 are part of what Cicero calls *necessity* in deliberation (*De officiis* 170) and are comparable to what we have called rational calculation. This is simply the determination of what is necessary to attain some end with an eye toward its possibility and convenience (*De officiis* 169). Deliberation must end with a determination of what can be done and what can easily be done, that is, accomplished in the shortest possible time with the least exertion, expense, or trouble (*De officiis* 169). If the actions are not convenient, then it should be at least determined whether they are possible: Although they require exertion, expense, and trouble, still, if these difficulties are faced, can it be accomplished? (*De officiis* 169). Otherwise, they must be determined to be either impossible or something that cannot be helped.

Question 3 concerns what Cicero calls *affection* (*De officiis* 176). It is apprehension, discernment, and acuity in regard to the changing nature of things. Affection is a change in the aspect of things due to time, or the result of actions or their management, or to the interests and desires of men, so that it seems that things should not be regarded in the same light as they have been or have generally been regarded (*De officiis* 176). There are certain matters that must be considered with reference to time and intention and not merely by their absolute qualities (*De officiis* 176). Lying is wrong, but lying to the Nazis with the intention of saving many lives is not wrong. In all these matters one must think what the occasion demands and what is worthy of the persons concerned, and one must consider not what is being done but with what spirit anything is done, at what time, and how long it has been going on (*De officiis* 176).

Questions 4 and 5 are concerned with *advantage*, and so if deliberation ended with these two questions, it would be the same thing as cunning or cleverness. But question 6 ensures that both calculation and advantage are constrained by moral deliberation, and it becomes the final arbiter as to what to do. The good and honorable are what have an inherent value (*De officiis* 159); the advantageous involves security and power (security is safety; power is the possession of resources sufficient for preserving oneself and weakening another) (*De officiis* 169); and calculation is concerned with what is necessary, possible, and efficient to do.

The greatest necessity is that of doing what is good and honorable, and if it is not honorable, it should not be done, even if it appears to be disadvantageous. Cicero writes,

> when we encounter advantage in some plausible form we cannot help being impressed. But close examination may reveal something morally wrong with this apparently advantageous action. In such a case the question of abandoning advantage does not arise, since it is axiomatic that, where there is wrong, there can be no true advantage: for Nature demands that all things be right and harmonious, consistent with Nature and therefore with each other (*De officiis* III.35).

If it is honorable, then, its advantage can be considered. If it is honorable and advantageous, convenience should be considered (*De officiis* 173). It is often necessary, then, to weigh these against each other (*De officiis* 174) (see figure), but in

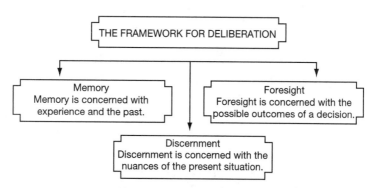

According to Cicero, deliberation has a temporal framework: memory helps us access the past; discernment aids in the perception of the present situation, while foresight helps us to imagine what could happen.

Cicero's thinking, ultimately, there is no conflict between the good and the advantageous: The good is always advantageous (*De officiis* III.38). Still, Cicero insists that there can be no universal rules in this regard: Although honor is to be preferred to security, one should prefer security in a case in which, though honor is lost for the moment while gaining security, it may be recovered in the future by courage and diligence. In this case we are able to say truthfully that we were pursuing honor, since without security we could never attain honor. In such circumstances it will be proper to yield to another, to meet another's terms, or to keep quiet for the present and await the right opportunity. If this is not possible, one should prefer honor (*De officiis* 174).

Cicero also contributes another interesting dimension to the understanding of deliberation. According to him, deliberation has three aspects (*De inventione* 160): *memory, discernment,* and *foresight*—which correspond to the past, present, and future—all of which work together to create the best decision (see figure). This is usually articulated in the understanding that prudence applies past experience to the present with due consideration of the future. *Memory, therefore, is the ability to draw from past experience, and that means learning lessons from the past when things have gone wrong as well as recalling those things that have gone right. Discernment is a perception of the details of the present situation, its nuances and particulars, and the understanding of the characters of those involved. Foresight is the ability to imaginatively grasp the consequences of one's possible actions and its affects on others, given who they are.* Foresight is the heart of wisdom since it is the place where moral considerations come into play the most. Foresight involves an estimation of the moral worth of the various courses of action and a determination of whether the means conforms to your moral rules, standards, and principles. This particular understanding of deliberation as connected to the past, present, and future became a standard way of think-

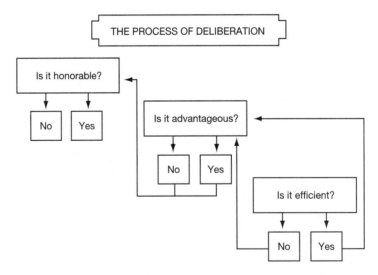

Cicero's Model of Deliberation. The decision to perform an action must be weighted by its efficiency, its advantage, and its goodness. Honor outweighs advantage, and advantage efficiency. If an action is dishonorable, it shouldn't be done, even if it is advantageous; if an advantageous action is honorable but hard to do, it still might be worth doing.

ing about prudence and wisdom throughout the Middle Ages and the Renaissance. Christian iconology, for example, often portrayed Prudence as a figure wielding three mirrors, each inscribed with the temporal references, or as a three-headed figure, one an aged face, the other youthful, and the third middle-aged. One of the more famous paintings about Prudence is Titian's *Allegory of Prudence* done in the 16th century. Keeping with this last tradition, he allegorizes Prudence as a three headed-figure, an old man facing left toward the past, a young man profiled right looking to the future, and a middle-aged man looking straight ahead. Titian, however, superimposes these three human heads over three corresponding animal heads: the old man over a wolf, the middle-aged over a lion, and the youth over a dog. These three animal figures hark back to Hellenistic Egypt, where the god Serapis was worshiped. Old icons showed him enthroned with a three-headed monster at his feet with the wolf, the lion, and the dog composing each head. We are not clear about the meaning of the monster, although some interpretations ally Serapis with the sun, the latter being the creator of time for the Egyptians. Under this view advocated by interpreters such as Macrobius in the 5th century and Petrarch in the Renaissance, the lion's head stands for the present, whose position between past and future is strong and fervent. The wolf's head represents the past because the memory of things belonging to the past is devoured and carried away. The image of the dog, trying to please, denotes the future of which hope always paints a pleasant picture.

4.6.5 Memory

A story was recently told about a man who had wandered too far from his village near Bethel in western Alaska just as a winter storm came up. Soon he became disoriented and lost. He wasn't adequately prepared for the weather and started to become quite cold. As he looked around him, not knowing which way to go, he thought surely he would die—but he remembered a story his grandfather had told him about a man who had gotten lost in a storm and began to freeze. The man had gathered up a bunch of winter dried grass that stood above the snow and stuffed it under his clothes and into his boots. In that way he was saved from certain death. The lost man decided to do the same thing, and when rescuers found him the next day, he was hungry but still alive.

"The great thing, as the old people have told us," Odili says in Chenua Achebe's book *A Man of the People*, "is reminiscence; and only those who survive can have it" (1967: 145; cf. Siebers 1992: 178). In the context of deliberation, memory is the means by which we can access stored wisdom to aid us in making the right moral decisions. Memory serves as a repository of all sorts of relevant and pertinent knowledge pertaining to moral decision making. Baltes and Smith (1991: 100) claim that in long-term memory we have an extensive database about life matters that is analogous to a cross-referenced encyclopedia. Schank and Abelson (1977) characterize this encyclopedia as having both general and specific knowledge:

> General knowledge enables a person to understand and interpret another person's actions simply because the other person is a human being with certain standard needs who lives in a world which has certain standard methods of getting those needs fulfilled. ... Specific detailed knowledge about a situation allows us to do less processing and wondering about frequently experienced events (1977: 37; Baltes and Smith 1991: 100).

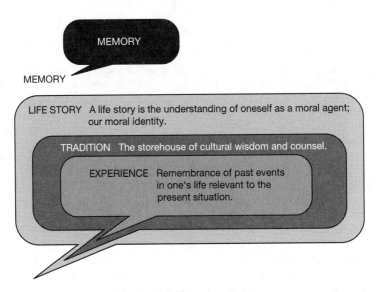

Memory is an essential part of deliberation; it serves as an access to past experience, traditional wisdom, and a sense of ourselves as moral agents, all of which aid in deciding what to do in a certain situation.

This wisdom is not only our own, but the wisdom of our cultures and traditions. Wisdom is accessed in this manner through a number of ways: the recollection of past, relevant experiences; narratives, such as histories, stories, allegories, and parables; proverbial wisdom; and well-known cases which may have special prominence in our culture or tradition and often serve as paradigms for doing the right or avoiding the wrong thing (see figure).

Just as the preceding story illustrates, personal experiences are one way in which memory helps us make the right decisions. Experience is often remembered narratively, as a significant event in our lives that had either a positive or negative outcome. We use the former to help continue our good fortune and the latter to avoid past mistakes. Often, if we are asked for advice in this regard, we search our memories for our own relevant experiences, relate the story, and then attempt to draw inferences pertinent to the situation at hand.

Stories and histories are often used to convey wisdom since, as was discussed earlier in the context of moral education (Section 1.4.4), stories and lives have parallel structures: Stories have a lived quality, and lives have a storied character. That parallel allows us to identify more easily with the characters of the story and so adopt the content of the story to our own lives. Applying the story to the present situation becomes easier. The story also conveys information on how to behave or how not to behave and thereby allows us to compare those paradigms with present comparable situations. This perhaps accounts for the common practice of many peoples of telling relevant myths, folktales, legends, fables, parables, or biographical stories as a response to dilemmas, hardships, or situations that call for a decision or an answer to a query. Aesop, of course, is famous for his fables, each of which contains a gem of wisdom. The flea standing on the axle of a moving chariot looks backward down the dirt road which the chariot has traveled, proclaiming, "What dust I raise!" The fable tells us succinctly the folly of false pride, how persons may confuse their own minuscule part with the larger effects of something grander than themselves. It is easy to remember this story and it is easier to remember its lesson. Often the wisdom of the wise is conveyed in story form. The *Analects* have a storied, anecdotal character which allows for more readability, easier recollection, and better understanding. In that way Confucius's wisdom is conveyed in succinct form. Plato understood this as well and so tried to convey his complex philosophical thought through stories of Socrates, who engaged in thoughtful dialogue with his fellow citizens and students. The dialogues are more than just recorded exchanges between thinkers; they convey a certain drama, tension, and pathos which help us digest some of the more difficult philosophy. Socrates is more than just a thinker who said certain things; he is portrayed as someone who lives, suffers, and dies, who feels conviction and curiosity, and lives a life that exemplifies the sort of wisdom he promulgates. Not only is the wisdom of Jesus conveyed by means of telling the story of his life, but the story often uses parables to explain his thought. The Parable of the Good Samaritan, for example, warns us against the stereotype and allows us to consider the hypocrisy of those who claim to be better than others. The philosopher Jacob Needleman (1991) recounts a remarkable legend that grew up in Jewish culture around the figure of Solomon the wise (cf. Ginzberg 1909). Here's a summary of the story:

> God commands Solomon to build a grand temple. But according to Mosaic law he cannot cut the stones to the temple with any earthly (i.e., lower) instrument. He calls his advisors for counsel. They mention the existence of a remarkable being that was created by God at the twilight of creation—the shamir. The shamir is the smallest of creatures yet has the power to cleave rocks easily. They believe that it may be in the possession of the demons. By this time Solomon had conquered all the demons and enslaved them—except for the king of the demons, the devil himself, Asmodeus. He summoned the demons and demanded that they reveal the whereabouts of the shamir. They testify that they do not know its location—that information is known only by their king, Asmodeus. Solomon knows that Asmodeus would not voluntarily give the information; he also knows that Asmodeus is especially susceptible to wine. He discovers where he dwells and sends a servant to secretly pour wine in his well. Asmodeus tries to avoid drinking from the well, but becomes so thirsty he cannot resist. Solomon's servant captures him easily at this point and returns him to Solomon bound in chains. Solomon promises that he will release him if he gives him information about the shamir, and Asmodeus complies. He tells Solomon that the shamir is entrusted to the hoopoe bird. As the shamir splits rocks the hoopoe bird plants seeds from various trees and plants into the cracks, and so vegetation eventually grows from the barren wastelands. Solomon sends his soldiers to capture the shamir from the bird. The soldiers eventually locate the hoopoe and capture it by trickery, relieving the bird of its charge—the shamir. Failing in its duty, the hoopoe commits suicide. The shamir is given to Solomon and the temple is built.

One can mine this legend for many lessons and insights—the grandest project may require the smallest thing to succeed; to do good things, one must know how to deal with evil; even the highest goods may come at the cost of what is essential to life—along with an indefinite number of other bits of wisdom.

Proverbial wisdom is another means of employing memory in the aid of good decision making. "In addition to the indirect learning one may get from stories, wisdom may be directly stored in memory by means of proverbs, saws, and sayings that often serve this purpose as summaries of significant information about life and its management (Smith et al. 1989; Baltes and Smith 1991: 97). Proverbs can represent a distillation of personal and cultural knowledge about life (Berger and Luckmann 1967). The recollection of a wise saw in the proper context can help a person remember both the things to do and things to avoid in a certain situation. Proverbs are also a concise way to convey a complex bit of information and persuasion to others who share some understanding of the meanings which it conveys. Oral cultures engaged in counsel or debate often employ proverbial ways of argument. The contemporary African writer Chinua Achebe conveys this tradition well in his books *Things Fall Apart* and *Anthills of the Savannah*. Achebe links memory and story: "the storyteller creates the memory that the survivors must have—otherwise their surviving would have no meaning" (1989). "Proverbs are stories that survive in the life of memory; and for Achebe, wisdom in life comes with the recollection of proverbs and their successful use in place where people live" (Siebers 1992: 178). Achebe creates a good example of their use in *Anthills of the Savannah*, a story of the rise to power of three friends, one of whom becomes head of state, known as His Excellency. The Abazon, a regional people, do not vote to give His Excellency the title of President-for-Life, which he has requested. He takes revenge on them by refusing to develop a system of wells for the region, which results in a devastating water shortage. A delegation goes to the capital to plead with him. But the delegation is seen as a mob of agitators. Ikem, one of His Excellency's childhood friends, and who is from this region, attends one of these meetings, but is met with skepticism by the group because of his friendship with His Excellency and his absence from meetings and ceremonies of the group. An old man stands up to defend Ikem by use of proverbial wisdom:

> Going to meetings and weddings and naming ceremonies of one's people is good. But don't forget that our wise men have said also that a man who answers every summons by the town-crier will not plant corn in his fields. ... But leave this young man alone to do what he is doing for Abazon and for the whole of Kangan; the cock that crows in the morning belongs to one household but his voice is the property of the neighborhood. ... " (1987: 112).

Later His Excellency uses Ikem's attendance in this meeting as an excuse to have him executed for treason. But as Tobin Siebers points out, the use of proverbial wisdom in this context draws on the recollection of what everyone knows as part of their culture and tradition (1992: 185), "they permit an economical access to a body of shared knowledge and narratives ... " (1992: 189).

Yet some complain that the use of proverbial wisdom verges on the use of platitudes and worn clichés in the place of thoughtful reflection (cf. Siebers 1992: 179). Richard Whately, an influential 19th-century logician, notes this problem: "Considering that proverbs have been current in all ages and countries, it is a curious circumstance that so much difference of opinion should exist as to the utility, and as to the design of them. Some are accustomed to speak as if proverbs contained a sort of concentrated essence of the wisdom of all Ages, which will enable any one to judge and act aright on every emergency. Others on the contrary represent them as fit only to furnish occasionally a motto for a book, a theme for a school-boy's exercise, or a copy for children learning to write" (1828: 393–394). Moreover, as he points out, in many cases proverbs contradict one another. "That proverbs are not generally regarded, by those who use them, as, necessarily, propositions of universal and acknowledged truth ... is plain from the circumstance that many of those

The Counsel of Aesop

Aesop, a Greek fabulist and author of *The Fables*, is thought to have lived from 620–540 B.C.E.

Fine weather friends are not worth much.

Birds of a feather flock together.

No arguments will give courage to the coward.

The tyrant will always find a pretext for his tyranny.

One story is good, till another is told.

If men had all they wished, they would be often ruined.

Look before you leap.

Don't make much ado about nothing.

Honesty is the best policy.

There is no believing a liar, even when he speaks the truth.

Notoriety is often mistaken for fame.

Whatever you do, do with all your might.

Those who seek to please everybody please nobody.

Evil companions bring more hurt than profit.

Pride goes before destruction.

Example is more powerful than precept.

Everyone is more or less master of his own fate.

Evil wishes, like chickens, come home to roost.

Fine feathers don't make fine birds.

Those who assume a character which does not belong to them only make themselves ridiculous.

Necessity is the mother of invention.

A willful person will have his way to his own hurt.

Contentment with our lot is an element of happiness.

It is easy to kick a man that is down.

Persuasion is better than force.

---

most in use, are ... opposed to each other; as e.g., 'Take care of the pence, and the pounds will take care of themselves;' to 'Be not penny-wise and pound-foolish;' ... " (1828: 394). We may say "a stitch in time saves nine," but "if it ain't broke, don't fix it"; "haste makes waste," but "you better make hay while the sun shines." Whately concludes, "It seems, I think, to be practically understood, that a proverb is merely a compendious expression of some principle, which will usually be, in different cases, and with or without certain modifications, true or false, applicable or inapplicable" (1828: 394). Thus, proverbs should be seen as tools which are applied correctly by the wise person to help justify or support a correct action or position.

The study of cases is another way we draw on memory understood as tradition. Cases as they are remembered or stored in historical records serve as a means by which people can draw on situations from the past that may be similar to or different from present circumstances. It provides examples of similar situations, how they were decided, and what was their outcome. For example, one of the principal investigators in the O.J. Simpson case, Detective Thomas Lang, ruled out the possibility that the murders of Nicole Simpson and Ron Goldman were drug motivated. As he argued, in his experience as a detective for a number of years, drug-related murders typically involved guns; in this case a knife was used. Also, such murders take place in more secluded areas, but this happened in a middle of a respectable residential area. Finally, there is usually strong evidence of drug transaction in the place of residence, but no such evidence was present at Nicole Simpson's home. Given this, Lang thought it would be fruitless to pursue that line of investigation. Case study is an important process in medicine and law. Medical students study cases to become aware of errors or successes in good clinical diagnosis and treatment. Lawyers study cases to draw out certain legal inferences, but also to apply that consequence to their own cases. There are very famous legal cases—the case of *Roe v. Wade*, the Dred Scott decision, the O.J. Simpson case, and so on—which serve as both precedent and guides for certain other similar cases. *Casuistry* is the study of

---

The Counsel of Confucius

Confucius lived from 551 to 479 B.C. and is said to have been the one responsible for molding Chinese civilization more than any other person.

Is one not a superior man if he does not feel hurt even though he is not recognized?

The superior person does not seek fulfillment of his appetite nor comfort in his lodging. He is diligent in his duties and careful in his speech. He associates with others of moral principles and thereby realizes himself.

A person who reviews the old so as to find out the new is qualified to teach others.

He who learns but does not think is lost; he who thinks but does not learn is in danger.

Wealth and honor are what everyone desires. But if they have been obtained in violation of moral principles, they must not be kept. Poverty and humble station are what everyone dislikes. But if they can be avoided only in violation of moral principles, they must not be avoided.

A superior person is not for anything or against anything. He follows righteousness as the standard.

If one's acts are motivated by profit, he will have many enemies.

Someone wishing to establish his own character, also establishes the character of others, and wishing to be prominent himself, also helps others to be prominent.

Repay hatred with uprightness and virtue with virtue.

The superior person seeks room for improvement in himself; the inferior seeks it in others.

Only the most intelligent and the most stupid do not change.

Exercise

Pick one or two of these and evaluate their wisdom.

———

Source: *The Analects of Confucius.* Translated by A. Waley. New York: Vintage, 1938.

---

past cases to determine what to do in a present situation or the awareness of circumstances that might arise in a present similar situation.

But besides providing the means of accessing personal, cultural, and traditional wisdom, memory affects deliberation in another important way. Memory also appears to be a necessary condition for the continuity of our lives and our identity as a person. If a person could not remember from one day to the next whether previous experiences were part of his life, it would be difficult for that person to maintain any sense of identify and, consequently, any sense of a life story. There is the famous case of Clive James who, stricken with an organic brain disease, lost all long-term and short-term memory. He lived in a perpetual world of "nows." He could not recognize his wife or his friends, and each time they visited, even if they had just come the previous day, he would have to be introduced to them all over again. Interestingly, he was still able to retain skills, such as language, writing, and nearly every other thing he had learned in his life, but he could not remember from day to day. Each experience for him was novel: It was the first time he had seen the sky, the first time he had tasted steak, and so forth. He wrote in his diary profusely, but when he read it, he did not recognize it as his writing or any events he had experienced. Thus, memory enables us to acquire an identity over time, a life story which we claim as our own, and a past that accumulates and adds or burdens us in several ways. Such a life story prepares the ground for how the present situation is going to affect or fit into that life history. It allows us to make decisions in terms of an understanding of ourselves as moral agents, as the sorts of persons we are or would want to be. Memory centers our sense of ourselves as moral actors in the world as we understand it. Memory allows us to see how this decision we are about to make will affect our self-understanding. Memory sets the framework for the coordination of life story and moral vision. Charlotte Linde writes:

The Counsel of the Swahili

Swahili proverbs constitute an unwritten wisdom shared by many east African ethnic groups.

A person becomes what he wants to become.

What one cultivates is what one harvests.

The area covered by your life is not as important as what you build on it.

One who throws mud gets himself soiled as well.

He who does good to people does it also to himself.

Goodness and kindness are stronger than harshness.

Wisdom creates well-being.

Whether you have little or much, be content.

A beginning is a beginning, there is no beginning which is bad.

He who does not see his own vices should not take notice of the faults of his companions.

An unpleasant truth is better than a pleasant false-hood.

It is you yourself who stepped on the thorns which are on the road.

The bad craftsman quarrels with his tools.

He who laughs at a scar has not received a wound.

He who does not know how to forgive, let him not expect to be forgiven.

He who does not harm you, do no harm to him.

It is better to build bridges than walls.

A boat doesn't go forward if each one is rowing his own way.

Avarice is the root of all evil.

If you can't build a hut, build a shack.

He who wants everything loses everything.

Exercise

Pick one or two of these proverbs and evaluate their wisdom.

——

Source: Scheven, 1981.

---

life stories express our sense of self: who we are and how we got that way. They are also one very important means by which we communicate this sense of self and negotiate it with others. Further we use these stories to claim or negotiate group membership, and to demonstrate that we are in fact worthy members of those groups, understanding and purposefully following moral standards (1993: 3).

Life stories help us to incorporate the present situation into the whole of our life and to see the affects of certain decisions on that continuity: "having a private life story ... organizes our understanding of our past life, our current situation, and our imagined future" (1993: 11). A person may have perceived herself as honest and loyal to her friends; yet in this situation, she may be called upon to be both dishonest and disloyal to a friend. How will that affect her vision of the good life, her sense of self, and the sense of her friend's life? It may not be simply a matter of continuity with the past, but also a break with it. Given past mistakes and dissatisfactions with her way of life, a certain decision in the present situation may mean a fresh beginning, a new direction. This idea is nicely expressed by John Dewey (1859–1952):

Now every such choice sustains a double relation to the self. It reveals the existing self and it forms the future self. That which is chosen is that which is found congenial to the desires and habits of the self as it already exists. ... The resulting choice also shapes the self, making it, in some degree, a new self. ... In committing oneself to a particular course, a person gives a lasting set to his own being. Consequently, it is proper to say that in choosing this object rather than that, one is in reality choosing what kind of person or self one is going to be. Superficially, the deliberation which terminates in choice is concerned with weighing the values of particular ends. Below the surface, it is a process of discovering what sort of being a person most wants to become (1960: 149).

A person, for example, may have had the experience of a close friend dying. The manner in which his friend approached the imminence of his death was one of avoidance and denial. Whenever this person was around his friend, he treated him very gingerly and monitored his conversation for anything that might offend his friend. As a result, the conversations were always sober and focused on his friend's problems. The outcome, he soon realized, was very unsatisfactory. His friend felt cut off from the real world; the conversations were depressing; they really never talked about his impending death; and so many things were left unresolved. He finds himself now in a similar situation—a close relative is dying—and he vows not to repeat the mistakes of the past. Thus, even though the situations are not identical, they are close enough to invite comparison and to apply the lesson of the past. In general, access to memory is access to experience which in turn allows us to draw on lessons from the past to situate the present in the continuity of our life. This aids us in precluding or promoting certain courses of action.

4.6.6 Discernment

Deliberation without discernment would make us into moral incompetents. It is one thing to deliberate about the means to an end, but to apply a plan without attention to the nuances—the "affection" of the situation as Cicero would have it— is simply foolish. As Elizabeth Anscombe noted in her analysis of Aristotle's practical syllogisms, if you were to mechanically follow a practical syllogism that recommends that "everything sweet ought to be tasted" and the recognition that "this is sweet" (*Nic. Ethics* 1147a28–30), then your health would be at serious risk if you mechanically went about tasting everything you could find that was sweet (cf. Anscombe 1976: 59ff.). Discernment allows us, in part, to recognize that rules or generalities do or do not apply to particular situations. As Aristotle notes, although it may be good for people to walk, it may not be good to walk in a certain situation (as in a blizzard) (*De Motu* 701a10–25).

Discernment could be defined more precisely as a kind of discrimination concerned with apprehending the whole from its parts, analyzing the whole into its parts, determining which parts are most salient to the whole, comparing and contrasting one thing with another, and thereby being able to recognize one thing as an instance of another. People talented with discernment are able to grasp the sense of a situation quickly; they are then able to analyze its critical elements. They can compare them to similar circumstances in their memory's repertoire, yet note the critical differences in order to apply correctly any generalities from past circumstances to the present one. Aristotle likened discernment to the ability of a geometer to recognize that a complex geometrical figure was composed of triangles (*Nic. Ethics* 1142a23; 1112b22), that is, showing the relation between part and whole and among wholes and parts. The first step in discernment is to be able to grasp the present situation in both its entirety, as a whole, but also to be able to recognize the parts which make up that whole. Once that is in place, comparisons allow us to say that a past experience is similar to the present one; contrasts allow us to determine how they are different. When we are drawing on our memory and experience to the present situation, we want to be sure how they are similar and how they are different before we apply the one to the other. By being able to show that two cases are similar, we are able to apply a generality to it as gained from our experience with similar cases. The differences, on the other hand, show us where to qualify that generalization. We may have had experience with volatile situations, and we may have learned how to diffuse them, but we must also understand the parts and particulars of the situation to apply that knowledge to the present situation. There may be a difference in how to handle the situation if the two opponents are children as opposed to adults or a man and a woman as opposed to two men. We might also have to understand different kinds of anger: Handling a hot-tempered person may require a somewhat different strategy than a person known to be vengeful and bad-tempered.

How might these various processes work together? Let's suppose you're walking down a relatively isolated dirt road. In the distance you can see an animal; you come a bit closer and identify it as a dog. What should you do? Should you continue walking ahead? Run away? Retreat and find a new route? Discernment aids in the deliberation of an appropriate plan. For instance, discrimination helps you focus on the dog's barking. You discern the bark as hostile or threatening. Discrimination also allows you to notice other things about the dog: Is the tail wagging or not? Is the stance of the dog threatening? What about its mouth—is it foaming? Is the nose wrinkled? Are the ears flat? Generalizations from both your past experience and your storehouse of knowledge suggest that dogs disposed as this dog is might be dangerous. Yet you also know from your past experience that not all dogs that bark aggressively are necessarily hostile—sometimes after you approach them they become friendly. Is this the case here? You notice, however, that this particular bark seems more hostile than the usual kind of greeting or warning bark that you've experienced with dogs. You decide, then, to walk slowly backward, since you've learned from experience that running only causes the dog to chase you. Discernment and memory work together to suggest an appropriate course of action that provides safety for you and lack of harm to the dog.

However, discernment is not simply a cognitive organization of present events; it is also the proper valuative and affective assessment of those fine discernments. It can be as simple as the recognition that this is a dangerous situation or that it is a situation in which one should show remorse or be apprehensive. For example, in the previous discussion of cowardliness, Glenn Gray noted that "constitutional" cowards often perceive danger where there is none; Aristotle seems to agree with this view. Cowardliness is in part due to affective misperception. Understood as a valuative assessment, discernment helps determine what is important to consider or notice in the situation, but also the importance of the situation relative to a larger scheme of things. In other words, discernment determines what is salient and, therefore, prepares the ground for proper judgment. This is a situation that is dangerous; in fact, it is one in which there could be physical harm. Is it significant enough to warrant facing that danger? Not only must we consider what is important to pay attention to in a situation, but also how important is the situation overall: What are the things that are at stake here that are of significant value? As John Dewey writes:

> Perception involves having a sense of the relative indicative or signifying values of the various features of the perplexing situation; to know what to let go as of no account; what to eliminate as irrelevant; what to retain as conducive to the outcome; what to emphasize as a clew to the difficulty. This power … in important affairs [is called] insight, discernment (1933:123).

Discernment, according to philosopher Martha Nussbaum, is also bound up with an emotional assessment of the situation (1990: 76ff.). Discernment involves an affective component which serves to differentiate and organize. It is the affective component which allows us to appreciate the particulars in their richness (Nuss-

---

Case Study in Discernment

*Was There a Difference between the Actions
of Lt. Kelly Flinn and Gen. Joseph Ralston?*

In 1997 Air Force Lt. Kelly Flinn, the first female pilot to fly a B-52 bomber, was accused of adultery, fraternization with an enlisted man, disobeying a direct order, and lying to her commander, when she had an affair with Marc Zigo, the civilian husband of a military friend, and a second enlisted man. Rather than being brought to trial, Flinn was dismissed from the Air Force but without a dishonorable discharge. Shortly thereafter, Air Force Gen. Joseph Ralston was nominated by Secretary of Defense William Cohen for the position of chairmanship of the Joint Chiefs of Staff. When he admitted that he had an affair after he had separated from his first wife 13 years ago, there was a public outcry to remove his name from nomination. This was in the wake of a number of sex scandals that had already rocked the armed forces. Moreover, there were claims of inequity and double standards from many quarters in the different treatment of Flinn. Because Ralston was a man, a general, and a friend of the Secretary of Defense, some claimed that he was being given preferential treatment while Kelly, who was a lieutenant and a woman, was being especially picked on and punished.

In her defense Flinn claimed that because of her own loneliness and frustrations, she was swept up into a relationship with Zigo, who later proved to be an abusive liar. She tried to quit the relationship for fear of her safety; however, after his suicide attempt, she reestablished the relationship, and he moved in with her. She lied about the affair with Zigo initially on his prompting but was caught in the lie when he admitted the affair to Air Force investigators. When Flinn was ordered not to have any contact with Zigo,

he was already living with her, and she was afraid that if she broke off the relationship, he might attempt suicide again. She felt that the Air Force was singling her out because she was a woman, that the trial was set against her, and that the Air Force leaked materials to the press that prejudiced her case. As a result, she was forced to take the general discharge rather than serve jail time (cf. Flinn 1997).

Some, such as Gen. Ron Fogleman, Air Force Chief of Staff, argued that Flinn was disciplined not because of the adultery nor because she was a woman, but because she had lied to official inquiries and disobeyed a direct order to stay away from Zigo. As a pilot for B-52s armed with nuclear weapons, it was imperative to trust and good order that an officer remains honest and obeys orders. He argued that the record shows that men who lied under similar circumstances were treated the same way. As an example, Gen. John Longhouser, head of the Aberdeen Training Center (where most of the sex scandals took place), was forced into early retirement.

Article 134 of the military code states that "adultery is punishable when directly prejudicial to good order and discipline and not to acts which are prejudicial only in a remote or indirect sense. … It is confined to cases in which the prejudice is reasonably direct and palpable." One interpretation of this suggests that adultery is not inherently punishable but only when it directly affects good order.

Questions for Discussion

1. Were the cases of Flinn and Ralston different or were they the same?
2. Were they different enough to warrant the different forms of punishment?
3. Should Ralston's candidacy have been withdrawn?

---

baum 1990: 77). When we are engaged in a situation that requires a moral decision, this affective aspect of discernment allows us to become connected to the situation in a way that disallows treating it as an instance of a general kind. It makes us more attuned and finely aware of what is at stake in the situation.

In sum, discernment is a cognitive, affective, and valuative perception of the parts (or aspects) of a situation in relation to other parts and parts to the whole, including the situation in relation to wider considerations. In this way discernment is necessary for allowing what is deliberated to be addressed to this situation. For example, in regard to assigning blame, Aristotle says that it is not easy to determine by means of a principle or rule at what point and how much someone is blameworthy for some action. This sort of decision rests on perception (*Nic. Ethics* 1109b18–23). The subtleties of a complex situation must be addressed in the situation itself and cannot be handled beforehand by means of some general rule (cf.

Nussbaum 1990: 69). Prior formulations lack both concreteness and flexibility. Rules and principles are correct insofar as they do not err with regard to particulars, but it is not possible for a formulation intended to cover many different particulars to achieve a high degree of correctness (Nussbaum 1990: 69). Experience, judgment, and understanding—in the context of discernment—must come into play at this point and serve to both correct and supplement any general rule or principle (cf. *Nic. Ethics* 1137b13ff.). A principle or rule may serve as a vague summary of wise decisions, and so it is appropriate to supplement it with situational corrections, but it must be the particular judgment that makes the corrections (Nussbaum 1990: 69). The result of applying rules and principles inflexibly and mechanically to variable situations is often either imprudent or absurd. Discernment allows us to apply the rule properly to the shape of the situation (cf. *Nic. Ethics* 1137b30–32). Good deliberation accommodates itself to the shape that it finds, responsibly and with respect for complexity (Nussbaum 1990: 70).

4.6.7 Foresight

Foresight is the use of the imagination to determine the likely consequences of certain actions. As Epimarchus writes, "The wise man should think beforehand, not afterwards" (485 B.C. 23: 41). Foresight is similar to what Mark Johnson calls imaginative deliberation, that is, an ability to imaginatively work out various possibilities for acting within a given situation and to envision the potential help and harm that are likely to result from a given action (1993: 202).

As with memory, foresight can also be understood narratively. In fact, we can liken foresight to the task of an author. Suppose that an author has already laid down the general features of the character of the players in a story; suppose also that the author has set up a certain situation that the actors are involved in. The talented author then must construct a scenario for their actions and reactions, feelings and emotions, that is consistent with their character and plausible, given their circumstances. With such constructed scenarios, a person can see more vividly the consequences of certain courses of action. This is why, as mentioned earlier, many ethics educators believe that storytelling is a good tool for ethics training. Following the consequences of bad decisions or seeing the results of folly and the fallout of bad character, a person can vividly simulate a way of life without having to undergo the live-and-learn consequences of real life.

Consider, for example, the case of Maggie Tulliver in George Eliot's *The Mill on the Floss*. In the course of the story, she is confronted with the possibility of running away with Stephen Guest, for whom she feels strong passion, but who is engaged to her cousin, Lucy. Moreover Maggie is engaged to Philip Wakem. At first her deliberations take on the following form:

> there was a fierce battle of emotions, such as Maggie in all her life of struggle had never known or foreboded: it seemed to her as if all the worst evil in her had lain in ambush till now and had suddenly started up full-armed with hideous, overpowering strength. There were moments in which a cruel selfishness seemed to be getting possession of her: why should not Lucy—why should not Philip suffer? She had to suffer through many years of her life, and who had renounced anything for her? And when something like that fullness of existence—love, wealth, ease, refinement—all that her nature craved was brought within her reach, why was she to forgo it, that another might have it—another, who perhaps needed it less? But amidst all this new passionate tumult there were the old voices making themselves heard with rising power till, from

> time to time, the tumult seemed quelled.... Where, then, would be all ... the deep pity for another's pain which had been nurtured in her through years of affection and hardship, all the divine presentiment of something higher than mere personal enjoyment which had made the sacredness of life? She might as well hope to enjoy walking by maiming her feet, as hope to enjoy an existence in which she set out by maiming the faith and sympathy that were the best organs of her soul (1860: 582).

Eliot depicts her deliberation as a struggle between two alternative plans, one to refrain from further pursuit of Stephen and the other to move headlong into a romantic relation with him. Maggie struggles with the two plans and tries to envision how she would live with each choice and who she would be in the process. Even though the affair with Stephen would be a selfish and cruel act, still she feels she deserves the "fullness of existence." Still, since that would require her to cast away all those qualities she values, she doubts she could go through with it—would that full existence be "the full existence she dreamed"?

But despite her qualms, she agrees to a boat trip down the river with Stephen. Due to a number of circumstances, they must spend the night on the boat, which was a scandalous prospect for this time. With Stephen's prompting, Maggie finds herself more and more drawn to the prospect of the affair. But despite that fact, she steps back to contemplate the matter:

> she had brought sorrow into the lives of others—into the lives that were knit up with hers by trust and love. The feeling of a few short weeks had hurried her into the sins her nature had most recoiled from—breach of faith and cruel selfishness.... And where would that lead her?—where had it led her now?... She felt it now—now that the consequences of such a fall had come before the outward act was completed.... And a choice of what?... not a choice of joy—but of conscious cruelty and hardness; with their murdered trust and hopes? Her life with Stephen would have no sacredness: she must for ever sink and wander vaguely, driven by uncertain impulse.... (1860: 597).

Given who she is, her values, and her beliefs, she imagines a life with Stephen under the circumstances of breaking the trust of her cousin and fiancé. She doesn't like what she sees; her life with Stephen, even though it would be one that fulfills her romantically, would have "no sacredness." To her that seems more important to the integrity of her character, her life.

As Maggie's deliberations illustrate, foresight can not only allow us to think through the particular consequences of certain actions, but to imagine how such consequences would fit in with our individual moral vision and sense of the good life. Through foresight you can imagine the affects of actions on the people involved. How will your decision affect your friend in this case? How will he react? Knowing him, you can see how he will be affected, how he will suffer. Foresight allows us to see the bigger picture in the consequences of our actions. How would it be if you did plan A rather than plan B? Would doing plan A contradict those things about yourself that you admire most? Would they be consistent with your moral vision and sense of the good life?

Lack of foresight in this sense can have serious consequences for individuals, but it has grave consequences for those who must make decisions that affect thousands or even millions of lives. In *The Tragedy and Lessons of Vietnam*, former Secretary of Defense Robert McNamara detailed the folly of his decision making during the Vietnam War (1995). McNamara noted, first, a failure in discernment, that the civilian and military leaders involved were wrong in failing to recognize the nature of the conflict in Vietnam. But also they failed to have the foresight to see that the strategy they were following would not accomplish the objective of winning the war. McNamara now finds it "incredible" that they failed to consider the political, military, financial, and human costs of deepening U.S. involvement. Of course, this is now little consolation to the thousands whose lives were ruined by untimely death, maiming, and psychological trauma to combatants, as well as those who lost loved ones during the war.

4.6.8 Methods of Moral Deliberation: Casuistry and Narrative Ethics

If the elements of deliberation are memory, discernment, and foresight, there is still the question of how these are integrated into a form of practical reasoning that allows for good moral outcomes. Case study, or *casuistry*, provides one such model. As we noted earlier, Cicero, in his book *On Duties (De officiis)*, outlines the essentials of such a method. In explaining to his son—to whom his book is dedicated—how a person should go about fulfilling his duties, he shows how the study of cases and stories can be useful in determining one's duty in a particular situation. Cases and stories draw on memory and the wisdom of the past, and applying them to the present situation allows us to foresee both good and bad outcomes of the alternative choices we may have. What is important in the present situation, morally speaking, is that we do the proper duty. Case study is a means of discerning what those proper duties are. Of course, this deliberation has to be constrained by appeal to the natural law, commanding that we should do good and avoid harm; our highest duty is always toward the good, although what that may be for a particular situation has to be determined case by case.

As Cicero develops it, casuistry is closely linked with the classical art of rhetoric, understood then as the art of persuading others to the truth. Rhetors were often used as lawyers in both ancient Greece and Rome. The orator, like a good lawyer or debater, is concerned with showing something is true in a particular case—that this person is innocent in this situation or whether or not this law should be passed. In doing so, the good orator had first to show the issue or general principle involved in the case. Next the orator had to employ justifications for or against the case based on a set of arguments that has been associated with this issue in the past. In doing so, the orator had to rely on the conventional wisdom and understanding that his audience shared. However, the orator had to adjust those to the nuances of the situation at hand.

Modern casuistry was developed in the 16th century by Jesuit moral theologians, who were also inspired by rhetorical models. One of these founders, the 16th-century Italian Jesuit Matteo Ricci, created a method that integrated memory, discernment, and foresight. Casuistry begins with memory, and Ricci developed a memory model, which he called a "memory palace" (cf. Spence 1984; Jonson 1995: 240–241). A memory palace is a mental device for storing and recalling images and ideas; mnemonic devices were the means by which rhetors could amass quotations, arguments, and images for their use. The memory palace was an imaginary building of ample proportions divided into many rooms, large and small, into which the data of memory were placed like furniture and decoration. In search of an idea, the orator would enter the memory palace and search for the appropriate image or idea with his visualized imagery of the palace (Jonson 1995: 241). In this way an abstract idea, image, or argument could be visualized as a piece of furniture or sculpture in a room.

Using memory as the background, casuistry (again following classical rhetorical strategy) begins, first, with determining the topoi or "places" of the case. The topics are comparable to the rooms within the memory palace. Different subject matter has different palaces or different rooms within the palace. The topics for political issues might be different than the topics for education. For example, a particular ethical case might involve topics such as a sense of the good life, conflicts of interest, best interests, and so on. General arguments in favor or against the topic could be drawn from the memory palace in the room associated with it. Thus, all arguments for or against an appropriate course of action could be rehearsed.

The second step is to discern the particulars of the case. The circumstances become the furniture and decoration of the rooms of the memory palace (Jonson 1995: 243). These are the who, what, why, when, and where of the case. In dealing with the particular case, we need to know who are the principal agents, what is their character and life story, are they young, old, married, single, and so forth? Thus, along with general arguments about the topics of the case, modified or qualified arguments can then be applied to the particulars of the case. For example, in general, where there is a conflict of interest, one might apply the argument that conflicts should be resolved by consensus or agreement of the parties; yet because one of the agents involved in this particular case is young or immature, then we might have to apply a different argument, such as the case should be resolved in favor of the best interests of the immature person or a substituted judgment on behalf of the agent should take place.

The final step in this process is the comparison of cases (Jonson 1995: 245) to determine what should be done. One looks for those precedents that resemble the current case. These then serve as paradigms for a solution to this particular case. In comparing the cases, one must be aware of their similarities and differences and their possible outcomes. In the end casuistic reasoning is like walking back and forth between the rooms of the memory palace, inspecting with care their contents. The appropriate resolution of the case arises from the converging impression made by all of the relevant facts and arguments. In the casuistic method one confronts a case in all its particularity and peculiarity and attempts to develop persuasive arguments to support a right judgment about it. It takes seriously the nature of the practice or institution in which the case takes place, and it scrutinizes the circumstances that make this a particular instance of some practice (Jonson 1995: 246).

Casuistry is currently being revived by a number of ethics thinkers (cf. Jonson and Toulmin 1988; Arras 1994; Kirk 1927), and it is a method that is used productively in the areas of medicine, law, public administration, engineering, and other "practical" sciences. These practical fields deal with concrete cases and are concerned with immediate facts about specific situations and individuals. They are concerned with general principles only indirectly, as they bear on the case. Using the clinical situation as a paradigm, Jonson and Toulmin give some general characterizations to the casuistic method that show similarities with its historical origins and which can serve to exemplify moral reasoning. For example, we may have some general knowledge about bacterial infection. When it is treated with a suitable antibiotic agent, the multiplication of the bacteria is checked and the body's immune system fights the infection quickly. When the infection is not so treated, the bacteria multiply unchecked and the immune system takes longer to overcome the infection. Administration of an appropriate antibiotic is thus an effective therapy for such infections. However, as it stands, this general rule does not tell us how bacterial infection can be identified in practice or which antibiotics are effective against which infections. Even in clinical contexts, these rules are detached from the details of actual experience (Jonson and Toulmin 1988: 32–33). A physician may report the following on the condition of an individual patient:

> The patient displayed typical symptoms of a bacterial infection, and initial laboratory tests showed streptococci in the blood. After a week of anti-streptococcal antibiotics, however, there has been no significant improvement. Further tests are required, to determine if the first lab tests were incorrect or incomplete, and other bacteria were masked by the streptococci; or if we are here faced with a new strain of streptococci, which calls for the use of different antibiotics. While this is being checked out, the patient should continue to rest, take plenty of fluids, and give the existing treatment the best chance of working (Jonson and Toulmin 1988: 33).

In this approach the case is described as completely and accurately as possible; suggestions for possible solutions are made, but generally, it is unclear what is going on here. The clinical case involves a wider range of factors than the bit of general knowledge given above. The clinical case involves the outcomes of previous experience and compares the present one with these. It also considered the possibility of novel situations. Comparison with previous cases serves as a warrant for trying certain resolutions, but all resolutions are held presumptively, that is, with a wait-and-see attitude.

In clinical diagnosis the starting point is the current repertory of diseases, injuries, and disabilities for which definitions exist in the medical literature and are so stored in the medical memory, so to speak. Given the taxonomy of known conditions and the paradigmatic cases that exemplify the various types, diagnosis becomes a practice of discernment using analogy with past cases. As new cases present themselves for examination, the physician collects details from each patient's history, his own immediate observations, results from lab tests, and then uses these to place a particular patient's condition into a type, much in the way the rhetor would classify arguments or types. Forced to choose among alternative diagnoses, the physician then must make the best presumption, keeping in mind all the possible outcomes and side-effects that might result (Jonson and Toulmin 1988: 40). What medical students learn in clinical training is what to look for as indicative of a specific condition and how to recognize it if it turns up again. This process relies heavily on analogy with past cases, requires discernment of pattern recognition, and treats all decisions for treatments as provisional and presumptive (Jonson and Toulmin 1988: 41). As Kenneth Kirk writes,

> Casuistry is a process of applying old illustrations to new problems to discover when the new corresponds to the old in its essential features, so that the same principle will cover both. The more we collect valid illustrations of each particular principle, the less room for doubt there will be about its applicability in normal circumstances... (1927: 108–109).

Another currently developed method of moral deliberation that shares many assumptions with casuistry is called *narrative ethics*. In fact, since case studies can be viewed as narratives, then it might be plausible to suggest that casuistry is a special case of it. What we have seen in our analysis of memory, discernment, and foresight is how they are narratively structured. Memory and experience can be recalled in narrative fashion, one's identity is narratively articulated, and foresight can be likened to the authorship of a story. Moreover, moral vision is often cast in story form. Consequently, understanding deliberation and moral decision making narratively may prove to be a helpful paradigm.

As Adam Zachary Newton writes, the basic thesis of many of these theories is that "ethical discourse often depends on narrative structures" (1995: 8). The implication is that there can be strong parallels between the moral assessment of our storied lives and the stories we tell, between a morally good story and a moral life. In this regard Alasdair MacIntyre argues that, first, we understand ourselves and attain our identity narratively: "How natural it is to think of the self in a narrative mode?" (1981: 192). "In what does the unity of an individual life consist? The answer is that its unity is the unity of a narrative embodied in a single life. ... The unity of a human life is the unity of a narrative quest" (1981: 203). Second, our understanding of others is narratively centered: "it is because we all live out narratives in our lives and because we understand our own lives in terms of the narratives that we live out that the form of narrative is appropriate for understanding the actions of others" (1981: 197; cf. 194). Third, all understanding of self and others is mediated through the fundamental narratives of the traditions in which they are embedded (1981: 207): "there is no way to give us an understanding of any society, including our own, except through the stock of stories which constitute its initial dramatic resources" (1981: 201). Practical or moral reasoning, then, is a process of deciding—within the context of self-narratives and narratives of the traditions to which we belong—what to do: "I can only answer the question 'What am I to do?' if I can answer the prior question 'Of what story or stories do I find myself a part?'" (1981: 201). "We enter human society ... with one or more imputed characters—roles into which we have been drafted—and we have to learn what they are in order to be able to understand how others respond to us and how our responses to them are apt to be construed" (1981: 201). As Booth writes, "we all are equipped, by a nature (a "second nature") that has created us out of story, with a rich experience in choosing which life stories, fictional or "real," we will embrace wholeheartedly. Who we are, who we will be tomorrow depends thus on some act of criticism, whether by ourselves or by those who determine what stories will come our way. ... " (1988: 482).

How, then, can narratives help us make better moral decisions? David Burrell and Stanley Hauerwas suggest the better narrative is one that avoids destructive alternatives, violence, and distortion (1977: 137). In other words, we want stories whose endings and outcomes are "happy" or thalian, ones that resolve the conflict without resorting to violence. We want to avoid tragedy and above all irony. But is that enough to help us decide what to do in a certain situation?

Consider the following case that may illustrate some of its uses and some of its problems. Elizabeth Bouvia was the center of a controversy in the 1980s around what is now commonly called physician-assisted suicide. Afflicted all her life with severe cerebral palsy and degenerative arthritis, she admitted herself into Riverside General Hospital in 1985, declaring that she no longer wanted to live. Her cerebral palsy was such that she was confined to a wheelchair and had use only of her right arm. She wanted to be allowed to refuse food and to die in comfort in the hospital. The hospital resisted her request, she was force-fed, and she brought the hospital to court to allow her relief from the force-feeding and to be permitted to die. When she lost the case in court, she left the hospital and went to Mexico, hoping that the doctors there would assist in her request. When they refused, she gave up her quest and hired a private nurse to help take care of her. There is more to the story, but consider the ethical question of whether the doctors should have assisted in her request. Consider, for a moment, some facts in this part of the story:

1. Elizabeth Bouvia leaves Riverside General Hospital, April 7, 1985.
2. Elizabeth Bouvia travels to the Hospital del Mar at Playease de Tijuana, Mexico.
3. Elizabeth Bouvia leaves the hospital 2 weeks later and returns to California.
4. Elizabeth Bouvia enters a private care center.

Consider, now, a narrative as written in the *Archives of Internal Medicine* by two physicians involved with Bouvia's case at Riverside General Hospital, which uses these basic facts:

> The standoff continued until April 7, [1] when Ms. Bouvia unexpectedly checked herself out of the hospital. [2] The hospital bill for the 217 days, excluding physicians' fees, was more than $56,000, paid by Riverside County and the State of California. Ms. Bouvia went to the Hospital del Mar at Playease de Tijuana, Mexico, [3] known for amygdalin (laetrile) treatments for cancer. She believed the staff would help her die. [4] Her new physicians, however, became convinced that she wanted to live. Two weeks later, Ms. Bouvia left the hospital, hired nurses, and moved to a motel. Three days later, with her friends, [5] a reporter, and an intern from the Hospital del Mar at her side, she gave up her plan to starve herself to death and took solid food. Ms. Bouvia said that she wanted treatment, including surgery to reduce muscle spasms. As of August 1985, Ms. Bouvia's location and plans were not known. [6] Her case was complicated further by the revelation that the newspaper reporter who covered the case most closely had a contract with Ms. Bouvia for a book, television, and movie rights to her story (cf. Pence 1990: 32–33).

The implication of the narrative is clear. The choice to leave the hospital was unexpected and perhaps erratic [1]. This ascribes somewhat irrational or unbalanced motives for her decision. This is further reinforced by the fact that she believed that the physicians at the Hospital del Mar would accede to her wishes to assist in her suicide. The aside here is that since they sanctioned the use of laetrile treatments [3] which, at that time, was not approved for cancer treatment in the United States on the basis of its ineffectiveness. The implication by the authors is that they might help her commit suicide since they seemed unscrupulous for that reason. But when even they thought she wanted to live, that could serve as vindication for their belief that she really wanted to live all along, and it validated their judgment not to allow her to die. This was reinforced by her own statements after the refusal of the Mexican doctors to help her. To add to the suspicious nature of her motives, they mention that a reporter had contacted her with an offer to write her story, and there was the promise of television and movie rights to her story.

The explanations that are used to account for the sequence of events already lend themselves to certain valuative direction. Her leaving Riverside General Hospital shows something of an erratic character, while ultimately her decision to give up her campaign for physician-assisted suicide is because of a book deal. This is meant to cast doubt on Elizabeth Bouvia's character. Her decision making may seem flighty and unreliable, and the motives surrounding her desire to die by physician assistance are suspect and perhaps insincere, given that she suspended them when given the possibility of a book and movie deal.

Like a melodrama, the manner in which the story is told places the physicians and Elizabeth Bouvia in antagonistic roles. The goal of the physicians is to disassemble sympathy for Bouvia to the point of showing her at least as an undeserving victim, if not an antagonist in a real-life melodrama. The physicians in turn wish to hold up their roles as professional defenders of good medical practice, assaulted by a woman with questionable motives and somewhat psychologically unbalanced.

Consider, on the other hand, a second narrative using the same basic facts, given by George Annas, a law professor and known advocate for Elizabeth Bouvia:

> Two years ago this column dealt with Elizabeth Bouvia's unequal and doomed struggle. … After losing both in the hospital and in the courtroom, Ms. Bouvia fled to Mexico on April 7, 1985 to seek her death. She was soon persuaded that Mexican physicians and nurses would be no more sympathetic to her plan than those at Riverside, and so returned to California. Because of the brutal forcefeeding she had endured at Riverside, she was afraid to return there. Since no other facility would admit her unless she agreed to eat, she resigned herself to eating and entered a private care location. There she remained, without incident, for more than a year (cf. Pence 1990: 33).

In this case the explanation of the same events is quite different. She left Riverside General Hospital not because of a whim, but because of the force-feeding that she was undergoing. Second, her move to Mexico was one of desperation, but even the Mexicans were unsympathetic. Her decision to return to feeding was not because of a supposed book deal, but because no other facility would admit her unless she agree to eat. Thus, she had to resign herself to eating, but rather than revisit a public facility, she entered a private care location. In this narrative Annas is attempting to place Elizabeth Bouvia into an even more sympathetic position: Not only is she the undeserving victim of disease, misfortune, and human unkindness, but now she is also the undeserving victim of these physicians, who use their position and authority to thwart her efforts for a more dignified and humane ending to her suffering, thereby defining them in the roles of persecutors in a tragedy. If more facts were known, this could make her even more sympathetic. For example, we might include her parents' divorce at the age of 5, her institutionalization at the age of 11, her father's financial abandonment at the age of 18, her miscarriage, her brother's drowning, and her divorce.

So which narrative are we to prefer? If we use the first, we may be prone to accept the decision of the physicians not to assist her since they seem to be upholding professional ethics against a patient with questionable or unstable motives. If we accept the second narrative, we may be moved to sympathy for Elizabeth Bouvia and so argue that it would be right to assist her in her death. As John Arras writes, "the proponent of narrative ethics not only must ask which story should control her actions in a given situation but eventually must confront the ultimate question of what makes any story morally compelling and worthy of our allegiance. How, in other words, are we to know that the story with which we begin is a 'good story' or a better story than the available alternatives?" (1997: 76). If as Arras points out we use Burrell and Hauerwas's criteria for a good story, "then it would appear that the criteria themselves, and not the narratives are fundamental to the critical function of ethics" (1997: 77).

The narratives in and of themselves do not make the recommendation: Each has what Paul Lauritzen calls "the persuasive power of a coherent narrative" (1996: 8). Each draws our sympathy in a certain direction and each, if true, could make strong justifications either for or against Bouvia's request. Given the events and the imputed character of Elizabeth Bouvia in the first narrative, the thematic unity of the story makes sense; similarly for Annas's narrative. No matter how detailed the narratives become, the detail alone will not help decide. There is also no apparent reason why we should accept the narrative framing of the authors. Both aim at melodramatic positioning, but with contrary results. Annas attempts to make the doctors oppressors in a melodrama with Bouvia the victim, while the physicians attempt to stamp themselves with the seal of integrity in their struggle to uphold professional ethics against a patient whose motives and stability are suspect. We may question this positioning and imagine, instead, a more ironic story in which the moral quality of all the agents involved is suspect or at least as not as pure as the stories make it out to be. In this sort of reading, we must fight the urge to take sides, as the stories want us to do, and manage the conflict to a point somewhere in the area between the posturing of the narrators. Or could this not be a comedy? The real problem is in misunderstanding among blockers; the real goal is to overcome the misunderstandings between opponents and try to find a solution that leaves both sides in agreement.

Narratives in themselves do not tell us how a story should end; they are a framework for helping us make better moral decisions. Narratives, like casuistry, help concretize and give rich, living detail to the situations in which we must make moral decisions. Telling the situation as a story helps to give us an important sense and feel for all the moral nuances that may arise. But narratives do not seem to supply us with the criteria by which we can then make our moral judgments and decisions. Where does Cicero, for example, find justification for the natural law or the ranking of the good and honorable over the advantageous? It cannot be the cases themselves, since it is these imperatives which guide the decision making in those particular cases. Thus, it would seem that both casuistry and narrative ethics must make an appeal to some general rules, principles, or larger moral vision, as a larger guide for making the right decision.

4.7 JUDGMENT AND DECISION

At the end of deliberation, alternatives must be weighed and a decision made. According to Aristotle, judgment is concerned with the thing to be done (*Nic. Ethics* 1143a34) and is more or less the act of weighing; choice is the decision to follow through: "choice [is] one of the things in our power which is desired after deliberation" (*Nic. Ethics* 1113a10) (see figure on page 284). Choice must be distinguished from wish. We can wish for the impossible, but we can choose only what is in our power and what can be brought about by our own efforts; we wish to be healthy, but we choose the acts that will make us healthy (*Nic. Ethics* 1112a1–2). Judgment is the decision of what to do, given the plans deliberated, and when to do it, given the discernment of a particular situation. Choice, on the other hand, is commitment to an action in the context of a judgment. The deliberation ceases when we reach the point where the decision must be made, and we recognize that what we have deliberated is in our power to do (*Nic. Ethics* 1113a3–14).

According to John Dewey, judgment only arises from something doubtful. If there is no doubt, then the decision is merely a matter of perception and recognition; on the other hand, if the issue is too mysterious, then also no judgment can occur (1933: 121). In general, Dewey argues that judging is the act of selecting and weighing acts as they present themselves (1933: 119). A person of sound judgment is one who can estimate, appraise, and evaluate with tact and discernment, and it is analogous to the procedure of a judge on the bench. On this model there are three features (1933: 120):

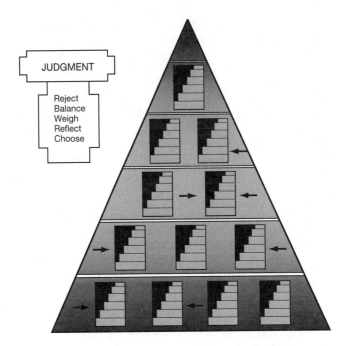

Judgment is a process of weighing, rejecting,
and balancing deliberations, ending in a choice.

1. a conflict, consisting of opposite claims regarding the same objective situation;
2. a process of defining and elaborating these claims;
3. a final decision closing the particular matter.

When making a final judgment there are two things to consider: (1) matters of fact and whether the information that pertains to them is accurate and reliable and (2) matters of principle, that is, whether the actions or plans will conform with good moral sense (cf. 1933: 122). Conflicts occur and, hence, uncertainty about what to do arises when there is inadequate information or when moral principles appropriate to the situation conflict.

4.7.1 Kidder's Paradigms of Moral Judgment

Rushworth Kidder, founder of the Institute for Global Ethics, addresses some of the issues concerning conflict of principles in moral judgment. He argues that judgments about what to do in a particular situation fall into two broad types: (1) right versus wrong, which he calls moral temptations, and (2) right versus right, which he calls moral dilemmas. We should probably add a third category, which might be called tragic choices. This is usually the case of wrong versus wrong or the choice of the perceived lesser evil. William Styron's book *Sophie's Choice* illustrates this sort of decision. In the book Sophie, a Polish survivor of the Holocaust, recounts the horrifying choice she had to make. As she and her two young children, a boy and a girl, entered Auschwitz, the Nazi officials divided the victims into groups of those who were to work in the camp and those who were to be put to death immediately. The

In her essay "Personal Responsibility Under Dictatorship" (1964), Hannah Arendt condemns the logic of tragic choices, of choosing "the lesser of two evils." Her focus is the many Jews who collaborated with the Nazis in their actions in the Jewish ghettos. Many of these leaders defended themselves precisely on that basis—that collaborating with the Nazis to put the Jews in the ghetto or to send some to the concentration camps was a means of saving many more lives. Although it was a tragic choice, it was a choice that had to be made. Arendt condemns this sort of reasoning because it works as part of the machinery of terror and crime imposed on people by totalitarian regimes. The choice of the lesser evil is a false choice because it leads the individual to conform to a criminal state. Its great weakness is that those who choose the lesser evil soon forget that they have chosen evil. They make their choices from those offered by the cruel and inhumane. *Do you agree with Arendt?*

commandant gave Sophie a clear choice: She must choose which of her children is to be put in the group designated for immediate death. If she does not choose, then the entire family will be placed in the group. Sophie chooses the life of the older child, her son, over the daughter. The horror of watching her little girl being dragged away, screaming, leaves an unbearable psychological scar; in the meantime her boy also dies in the camp. After surviving the Holocaust, she moves to America, but living with the heaviness of her choice becomes so haunting that she commits suicide. Circumstances were such that no matter what she chose a horrible outcome would result.

Moral temptations are easier to resolve than the other two types because one is making a judgment between the right thing and the wrong thing to do, and one should choose the right thing. The difficulty arises in the execution of the plan precisely because the alternative may be so appealing in some sense of the term. Consider a temptation which philosopher Jacob Needleman writes about. He gave a seminar to professionals called "Money and the Meaning of Life." In this seminar he promoted a certain thesis about our relation to money which mediated between the two extremes of spiritual asceticism and crass materialism. In doing so, he felt he had an appropriate answer to the question of the proper role of money in our lives. During the seminar he had befriended two students, Alyssa, who was an accountant, and Bill, who happened to be a millionaire (in fact his wealth was estimated to be something like $65 million). Even after the seminar their relationship persisted and was tied to the themes of the course, a genuine and honest pursuit of the meaning of money in their lives. One night as they were discussing some aspect of this problem over wine, Bill suddenly presented Needleman with a small mahogany box. When Needleman opened it, it was full of gold, perhaps as much as a half-million dollars worth. He describes what follows:

> my mind there was pure chaos and bewilderment, and the muscles in my shoulders were … tensions of every kind. … The radiance of the gold blazed into my brain. … My legs started trembling as though filled with nervous little sparrows. My breathing became rough and coarse like the panting of a hungry wolf. … I was being torn apart by warring, all-consuming impulses. … "Take it! Take the gold!" a strong, euphoric voice urged me. "A half million dollars! And to him it's nothing! He's worth sixty-five million! He wants you to have it. He appreciates you. Accept the gift! Don't be a fool. Think of the good things you can do. … All your problems are over. … You owe it to him to accept it. … You deserve it. … " I started fingering the gold coins like some comic-strip miser and my body thrilled to the feel and weight of them. … At the same time a stern voice was shouting at me, "You must not! You haven't earned it! It's not yours! He's drunk! … You must not take advantage of him. And besides, Alyssa is watching. What will she think of you? Word will get out. What will people think of you? Don't do it! It's immoral, it's only money. Don't sell yourself!" (1991: 244–245).

Shortly, Needleman handed the box back to Bill, "I can't accept this Bill. ... Thank you." Bill took back the box.

Moral dilemmas are often more difficult to resolve than moral temptations. In moral dilemmas one is faced with a situation in which conflicting virtues, values, or principles may be operative. According to Kidder, moral dilemmas take the form of four broad paradigms: truth versus loyalty, the individual versus community, short-term versus long-term, and justice versus mercy (1995: 112–113). These paradigms illustrate clearly how wisdom must direct virtue to the better outcome and why, therefore, virtue is not sufficient to guarantee good moral judgments.

Truth versus loyalty is typically a quandary in which one must choose between the virtue of truthfulness and the virtue of loyalty. Judgment is concerned to make the right choice in the matter. Truth telling is, as we have seen, the presentation of information which you believe to be accurate; loyalty involves allegiance to a person, an institution, or a set of beliefs. This is a common enough dilemma. For example, a business colleague is asked by another for a letter of reference (cf. Kidder 1995: 123–124). The two have been good friends and associates, but Cal knows that Harry has had ethical lapses in the past. Should Cal write a confidential letter to a potential employer mentioning some of the more serious lapses, or should he remain loyal to his friend and overlook these in his recommendation, stressing instead the many strong business qualities the man has? In this case the conflict is between two "honorable" courses, to use Cicero's terms—loyalty to friends is admirable, but so is honesty. Which is to be chosen in this case?

The individual versus the community defines another familiar dilemma and concerns conflicts of fairness or justice. Often we are called upon to make decisions that will benefit a number of people at the expense of a special sacrifice by one person, or conversely, there is the case where the promotion of the good for an individual requires diminishing some collective good. Promoting collective goods and promoting the good of deserving individuals are both honorable courses to take, but sometimes these maxims will recommend opposed choices. In this dilemma we are really asking a question of fairness or justice for whom. Kidder illustrates this with the following true story, which happened to an ethics instructor when he was a young man (1995: 131–132):

> Shot down over Germany during World War II, he was taken to a prison camp and interrogated by the Nazis. He endured painful physical torture but revealed nothing because he happened to have no strategic information. Some weeks later a new prisoner arrived, one of his close friends. The friend asked about the nature of the interrogation and torture. At that point his friend confessed that he had a low tolerance for pain and that he would most likely reveal his extensive knowledge about troop movements and planned raids. If he talked, the Nazis would put that knowledge to good use; the probable result would be numerous casualties on the U.S. side. He could see no other alternative than his own death. Yet so great was his aversion to pain that he lacked the will to commit suicide. Instead, he asked his good friend to kill him before morning.

What should he have done? Sacrifice the individual or the community? Some of the noblest actions involve individual self-sacrifice for the sake of the group, but how can it be moral to take the life of a friend?

Short-term versus long-term goods is one of the most familiar of the dilemmas and involves a proper adjudication of temperance. These occur in all areas of life (Kidder 1995: 133ff.). Economic choices easily fall into this category: Should I buy

---

Case Study: What Would You Do?

In *How Good People Make Tough Choices*, Rush-worth Kidder relates the following true incident (1995: 57):

> An auto mechanic was called early one morning to the scene of a wreck on a state highway in Ohio. Arriving at the isolated, wooded spot, he could see immediately what had happened: a large flatbed truck had gone off the highway and hit a tree head-on. On impact, its load of steel had torn loose and slid forward through the back of the cab, pinning the driver helplessly inside. The cab was on fire, in danger of exploding at any minute. As he arrived, so did a state police car. As the trooper ran to the open cab window,

the mechanic could hear the driver inside screaming, "Shoot me! Shoot me!" It was obvious the trooper could not lift off that load of steel and free the driver.

What would you do in this situation? Think about it for a while before you read what the trooper did.

As the flames became more intense, the trooper slowly removed his gun from his holster, but paused and put it back. When the driver started to scream more, he removed it again, but put it back. Running back to his cruiser, he grabbed a small fire extinguisher, not big enough to put out the fire. However, he sprayed it in the face of the driver, putting him to sleep. Shortly after that the cab exploded.

---

a car now and have the enjoyment of its use, even though I don't have enough savings to make a cost-efficient down payment, or should I wait until I have enough savings to make a down payment and so deprive myself of a year's worth of enjoyment? Often environmental choices have this character: Should we advance the economy by mineral or natural resource extraction, which will yield large profits for corporations and have immediate economic benefits for local populations, or should we preserve the integrity of the environment for future populations and long-term environmental cleanliness?

Justice versus mercy is also a commonly encountered dilemma of right versus right. Kidder's example—mentioned in the Case Study: What Would You Do?—of the truck driver pinned in a burning cab by steel girders, illustrates this dilemma. The state trooper realizes that, as a matter of justice, he has no right to shoot the man, yet the motivation to be merciful and shoot the man before he begins to suffer horribly is also great. Often this dilemma takes the form of a decision whether or not to punish someone for a mistake or a wrong. Justice and fairness demand that if one violates a rule, then punishment should be impartial and across the board. Yet often the offender is under unique circumstances that may require special consideration. Kidder gives the following case, which is summarized here (1995: 21):

> A newspaper editor hired a young woman for the food page of the paper. She had great credentials and progressed to the point where, as assistant editor, she wrote regularly. One day she wrote a piece on Maine blueberries, which the editor thought was a fine article. However, the next day the food editor, a woman with decades of experience, came to the editor and held a copy of an old cookbook with an account of Maine blueberries that was word-for-word the story the young writer had written. Plagiarizing is, of course, a serious affair no matter what the business, but especially so for journalism. Whereas the young woman had made a choice between right and wrong, the editor—who happened to be Kidder himself—felt he had an ethical dilemma between justice and mercy. On the one hand—and out of a sense of justice—he wanted to fire the woman on the spot; on the other hand, he wanted to find out the source of the problem, why a woman with such a promising career would make such a false move and see if the circumstances warranted exception to the rule that justice would dictate.

Kidder decided on the side of mercy; he discovered that she indeed had serious personal problems. Because the piece had not yet been published, he had some latitude to act: he moved her to an editing slot, with the understanding that she was to do no more writing. She remained in that position several years, eventually leaving to take a job outside journalism.

4.7.2 Bad Judgment

Bad judgment usually occurs under one or more of the following circumstances. First, it can occur when someone chooses to do something in spite of the fact that a little deliberation would show its undesirable or immoral consequences. In this sort of bad judgment, a person can be blamed for not having deliberated when they should have and simply going with impulse or unreflective intuition. Of course, there are many situations in which there is no time for deliberation—one must act quickly and decisively. There are many anecdotes of people who simply acted instinctively to an emergency without giving it the least thought. Even in this case, however, people may anticipate certain emergencies or critical situations and may have already thought how they might respond. One example of this process is mentioned by philosopher Charles Peirce:

> [my mother] spilled some burning spirits on her skirt. Instantly, before the rest of us had had time in order to think what to do, my brother, Herbert, who was a small boy, had snatched up the rug and smothered the fire. We were astonished at his promptitude, which, as he grew up, proved to be characteristic. I asked him how he came to think of it so quickly. He said: "I had considered on a previous day what I would do in case such an accident should occur" (*Collected Papers*, 5.532; cf. Andacht 1996).

A second type of bad judgment occurs when someone chooses to do something without complete deliberation, including when someone chooses to do something before alternative plans have been fully deliberated. In this case the person can be blamed for judging hastily and not making an informed decision, but acting on partial information. Sometimes people may act on the first plan that comes along if it sounds good enough; yet more information might show that it is a less than adequate choice.

A third sort of bad judgment occurs when someone makes a judgment while their judgment is impaired. Someone could be blamed for choosing to make an important decision while intoxicated, confused, or otherwise not mentally competent.

A fourth kind of bad judgment occurs when, despite what deliberation has suggested, someone chooses the morally undesirable path nonetheless; rather than going with what is morally satisfactory, they choose to go ahead with the option that satisfies desires, passions, or has risky consequences. This was discussed in Section 2.3 on moral weakness. It may be characterized as a case where moral weakness impinges upon good judgment. A temptation or some immediate reward may be a powerful enough motivator for action that it distorts or corrupts good judgment; a person may rationalize the action until it conforms with giving in to the temptation. It is only when the action leads to undesirable consequences that people may become puzzled as to why they acted against their better judgment.

Flying accidents illustrate these various types of bad judgment. Sometimes pilots will fly without really examining the route, the weather conditions, or other factors necessary for a safe trip. Also, as in the tragic accident of 7-year-old pilot

---

Case Study: Bad Judgment

Consider this letter to Ann Landers:

> Dear Ann Landers: I am an 18-year-old single mother of twins. My parents threw me out of the house when I told them I was pregnant. Three months after the twins were born, I got herpes from a magazine salesman. The guy lied to me and said he had eczema. None of this has anything to do with my problem, but I thought I'd give you some background. The real trouble is I am having an affair with a married man. He is 26 and unemployed, and his wife is a professional wrestler. She is one tough lady, and I don't want to tangle with her. She walked in on us one afternoon in their apartment. Fortunately, I had my clothes on (most of "Rick's" were off). He is a very fast thinker, introduced me as a chiropractor and said I was giving him an adjustment. She then told me she was having trouble with her back and asked me to give her an adjustment too. I faked it as best I could. She was very pleased, said I had helped her more than any chiropractor who had ever worked on her, and asked for an appointment the next day. Ann, I have been going over there regularly. Yesterday was her sixth adjustment. She pays me $20 a visit. Can I get in trouble for practicing medicine without a license? Please give me some advice right away. I can't ask anybody else for help, and I sure do need it. —Depending on You in Corning, N.Y.

Questions for Discussion

1. How does the way in which she phrases the request help show a lack of discernment and good judgment?
2. What are some of the different types of bad judgments made here?

Jessica Dubroff, a decision was made to fly despite what reasonable deliberation suggested—bad weather and an overloaded plane in thin atmosphere were not good conditions for flying. Sometimes, even when good deliberation dictates against a plan, some will act on impulse or completely ignore what they know best.

4.7.3 Decision

A decision closes or concludes the question at issue. This determination not only settles that particular case, but it also helps fix a rule or method for deciding similar matters in the future (Dewey 1933: 126). Choice occurs when we have been persuaded to do something by means of our deliberation and judgment. Judgment—when it can take place in a relatively leisurely way—spirals upward to a resolution among possible plans or sets of actions. We can think of it as a conical helix that circles recursively over the various aspects upward toward a single decision; with each recursion the area of the spiral becomes smaller until we focus on the best course of action. Decision is a commitment to act on one choice rather than another.

Choices are not always easy to make; they are fraught with temptations and doubt. A decision to do A rather than B may have immediate consequences that weaken your resolve. If anywhere, it is here that moral strength proves important. Maggie in *The Mill on the Floss* meets the most resistance when she confronts Stephen with her choice not to continue the affair:

> "I will not begin any future, even for you," said Maggie tremulously. ... "What I told you at Basset I feel now:—I would rather have died than fall into this temptation."
>
> "We will not part," Stephen burst out, instinctively placing his back against the door. ... "I will not endure it. You'll make me desperate—I shan't know what to do."
>
> Maggie trembled. She felt that the parting could not be effected suddenly ... she must be prepared for a harder task than that of rushing away while resolution was fresh. ... Her heart beat like the heart of a frightened bird; but this direct opposition helped her—she felt her determination growing stronger. ... (1860: 601).

Case Study: The Tragedy on Mt. Everest

On May 10, 1996, eight people died climbing Mt. Everest and one was severely frostbitten. That made twelve people altogether who died on the mountain for that climbing season. Jon Krakauer, a journalist and mountain climber, was on the fatal ascent. He wrote an account of the tragedy in his book *Into Thin Air* (1996).

Krakauer's recounting of the events leading to the tragedy illustrates a number of issues in moral judgment and decision making, as well as a number of other ethical issues. Krakauer was hired by the magazine *Outside* to do a story on climbing Mt. Everest. It had always been a dream of his to summit the formidable peak, but despite his many climbing experiences, he had never tackled this one. Krakauer joined a team led by Rob Hall, an experienced climber and guide from New Zealand. Hall ran a guiding company called Adventure Consultants and charged $65,000 per client to guide an ascent. He waived Krakauer's fee in exchange for the advertising for his company that Krakauer's piece would bring. There happened to be three other expeditions on the mountain at the same time: Scott Fischer, owner of Mountain Madness, a Taiwanese group headed by Gau Ming Ho, and a South African expedition led by Ian Woodall.

Because of the large number of climbers on the mountain (thirty-three altogether), Rob Hall tried to coordinate with the other expeditions to create an efficient climb once they had all moved to the higher elevation camps. Assuming the weather cooperated, there would be a window of opportunity for going through the Death Zone (25,000 feet and higher) and reaching the summit at 29,028 feet, after which it would become very dangerous to ascend or descend. Exposure on or near the summit would mean certain death. Fischer and Gau were willing to cooperate, but Woodall refused (he also refused to lend out his radio to call for help when many of the climbers were later stranded and dying on the mountain; after his return Woodall became the center of a national scandal in South Africa when the Johannesburg *Sunday Times*—which was sponsoring the group—discovered that he lied about his mountaineering qualifications and military experience).

However, despite the fact that Gau had agreed to the scheduling, when it came to start for the summit he moved out at the same time as Hall. As a result, a terrible bottleneck was created near the summit which contributed greatly to the tragedy. In addition, although all four expeditions agreed that their Sherpas would cooperate in fixing the lines necessary to attach safety tethers (these provided stability on the steep, windy route to the summit), both Gau and Woodall failed to keep up their end of the bargain. This failure also contributed to the disaster. In fact, Gau had done a number of questionable things before. It was claimed that he was reckless and had little real experience. His last venture on Mt. McKinley required a dangerous high-level rescue. On the May 10 ascent, he started for the summit when he said he would not—only hours after he had learned by radio that one of his teammates, Chen Yu-Nan, had died (Chen had earlier fallen 70 feet down an ice slope, and Gau left him to recover in a tent). When he heard the news, Gau said, "O.K. Thank you for the information," and moved toward the summit as if nothing had happened.

Despite the untrustworthy behavior of Gau and Woodall, both Hall and Fischer made plans to summit the mountain. Hall was strongly motivated to succeed because of the presence of Krakauer: If the article in *Outside* depicted his expedition's failure, that would hurt his business and reputation. Fischer was motivated for a different reason, by the presence of Sandy Hill Pittman in his party. Pittman was a rich New York socialite; she wanted desperately to succeed at Everest, since it would be the last of the seven summits, the highest peak on each continent, she needed to conquer. Her goal was to complete her book, *Summits of My Soul*. She was filing daily accounts of the climb for NBC. This put a great deal of pressure on Fischer. In fact, Fischer worked very hard to accommodate his client. She brought two laptop computers, several cameras, tape recorders, a satellite telephone, coffee, and an espresso maker to base camp, where she also received regular deliveries of *Vogue* via DHL. Fischer made sure that his Sherpas brought her hot tea each morning as she awakened and rolled her sleeping bag for her. Fischer's lead Sherpa, Lopsang Jangbu, had to carry Pittman's satellite telephone up to one of the higher camps the day before the summit attempt; the day of the disaster, she was "short-roped" to him, meaning basically that he had to pull her up the mountain. This left Fischer's best and most experienced guide exhausted and useless the day he was needed the most. Lopsang had to make a momentous decision that day: When he and Fischer were stranded under severe weather conditions near the summit and Fischer had become delirious from cold and tiredness, Lopsang was too exhausted from his struggles with Pittman to assist his boss. He stayed with Fischer for an hour, but decided to leave him, hoping to send another guide up to rescue him.

There were other decisions and consequences that led to the disaster. Despite Hall's and Fischer's warnings to their clients that the window of opportu-

Case Study: The Tragedy on Mt. Everest, *Continued*

nity for the summit would close by the afternoon, the leaders themselves and some of their clients would ignore those warnings. When one of the clients, Beck Weathers, started to suffer from snow blindness, Hall made him promise to wait below the summit until his return. As climbers who took the window-of-opportunity warning seriously passed Weathers on their way down, he was nearly blind. He remained stranded since Hall never returned. Because of that, as the weather escalated later in the afternoon, Weathers wandered around blindly along with other stragglers. When he was found later by one of Hall's guides, he was unconscious and left for dead. His hands and face were covered with ice. Miraculously, as he lay there in the snow half-frozen, he regained consciousness and wandered by accident into the nearest camp (with his severe frostbite Weathers—who is a surgeon—lost his right hand, all his fingers on his left hand, and his nose).

Because of all the tension between the rival expeditions and the failure of Gau to stick to his agreements, Ang Dorje, Hall's head Sherpa, and Lopsang Jangbu, Fischer's head Sherpa, feuded over who should fix the safety lines for the last part of the ascent to the summit. After waiting in a bottleneck near the summit for nearly an hour for the lines to be set, some of the other guides fixed the lines themselves. The wait wasted oxygen which was necessary at this altitude. For some reason, Anatoli Boukreev, one of Hall's guides, didn't use oxygen (the speculation is that ever since the ascent of Everest without oxygen by the climber Messner, this has been a special goal for the more experienced climbers). This made it impossible for him to stay with the slower climbers; he had to descend rapidly to get back to the nearest camp before the effects of oxygen deprivation set in. The bottleneck also forced climbers who made the summit and were descending to wait, again wasting more oxygen. Krakauer was in such a position, panicking as his oxygen ran out. Krakauer became hypoxic as he came across his friend and one of Hall's guides, Andy Harris. Harris was standing over a pile of oxygen bottles; Krakauer desperately asked him for a fresh bottle, but Harris insisted they were all empty. Because of his own hypoxic state, Krakauer did not recognize that Harris was in a similar condition and delusional. As it turned out, some of the bottles were full. Later Krakauer thought he saw Harris with some other climbers; it was only later that he realized that he had left Harris behind on the mountain and in that state without assisting him down. Harris was one of the eight who died that day.

Because of the bottleneck, many of the climbers who chose to continue to the summit did not make it

until two or three in the afternoon, past the window of opportunity predicted by the guides. Rob Hall broke his own rule and insisted on reaching the summit, dragging his client Doug Hansen with him. Hansen had climbed the year before with Hall and had failed to reach the summit and had gotten frostbitten toes. Hall had reduced his fee to entice Hansen back the following year. He wanted Hansen to reach the summit; but after they made it, nearly 4 o'clock in the afternoon, Hansen collapsed (as he had done the previous year). Hall made the decision then and there not to leave Hansen. As the storm grew Hall became more debilitated and frostbitten. In desperate conversations with him on the radio phone, members of the base camp tried to talk him down. But Hall was too weak to try. Two Sherpas tried to reach Hall but failed because of the intense cold and wind. In one final call he did talk to his wife in New Zealand. He told her of the impossibility of being rescued from the summit ridge. His last words: "Don't worry too much."

Although the two Sherpas could not reach Hall and Hansen, two others did manage to find Fischer and Gau. When he was found Fischer was near death: He was barely breathing, his eyes were fixed in their sockets, and his teeth were tightly clenched. Gau was in better condition. The Sherpas, who could only carry one person between them, chose Gau and left Fischer behind. A similar decision was made by Anatoli Boukreev. If you recall, he had to descend from the summit rapidly because he didn't use oxygen. This forced him to pass his slower clients. But after the storm struck the mountain, he managed to get out during a lull and came across Sandy Hill Pittman, Beck Weathers, and Yasuko Namba, among others. Both Weathers and Namba were unconscious, covered in ice. Boukreev made the decision to leave them behind. He rescued Pittman and the others. Weathers, as mentioned, managed to regain consciousness and return to camp. Yasuko Namba had hoped to be the first Japanese woman to do what Pittman hoped to do— to conquer the highest peaks of the seven continents. On the next day, several other expeditions at base camp helped bring Weathers and Gau down. They were flown to safety in a dramatic high-altitude helicopter evacuation.

The storm had also taken the lives of three members of a Tibetan expedition attempting the summit from the Tibetan side of the mountain. When they were discovered in serious trouble by a Japanese team that was following them, they simply passed them by. One of the Japanese climbers later told a journalist, "We didn't know them. No, we didn't give

Continued

Case Study: The Tragedy on Mt. Everest, *Continued*

them any water. We didn't talk to them. They had severe high-altitude sickness. They looked as if they were dangerous." Another said, "Above 8000 meters is not a place where people can afford morality."

Questions for Discussion

1. Consider the following critical decision-making points in this tragic event. Evaluate them in terms of the categories discussed so far. Were they good judgments, bad judgments, well or poorly deliberated? How much foresight was present? Was discernment a factor in the decision making? How did memory play a role?

   a. Hall's and Fischer's decision to summit the mountain despite the unreliability and lack of cooperation of Gau and Woodall.
   b. Fischer's decision to have Lopsang Jangbu, his most experienced guide, short-rope Sandy Pittman and carry her equipment.
   c. Hall's decision to leave Beck Weathers below the summit and having him promise to stay there until his return; Weathers's decision to stay with the promise.
   d. Boukreev's decision not to use oxygen as he climbed the mountain.
   e. Krakauer's encounter with Andy Harris at the oxygen bottles.
   f. Rob Hall's decision to summit with Doug Hansen after the window of opportunity.
   g. Rob Hall's decision not to leave Doug Hansen after he collapsed.
   h. Lopsang Jangbu's decision to leave Scott Fischer.
   i. The Sherpas decision to rescue Gau and leave Scott Fischer.
   j. Boukreev's decision to leave Beck Weathers and Yasuko Namba.
   k. The Japanese team's decision not to help the Tibetan team.

2. Krakauer describes the process of climbing in detail: "walking … left me wheezing for several minutes. If I sat up too quickly, my head reeled and vertigo set in. The deep, rasping cough … worsened day by day. Sleep became elusive, a common symptom of minor altitude illness." He'd lost 20 pounds, developed crippling headaches, and coughed so violently that he tore thoracic cartilage. When he reached the summit on May 10, his first time, and a dream he had since childhood, he described it in the following way:

"Plodding slowly up the last few steps to the summit, I had the sensation of being underwater, of life moving at quarter speed. And then I found myself atop a slender wedge of ice, adorned with a discarded oxygen cylinder and a battered aluminum survey pole, with nowhere higher to climb. … Reaching the top of Everest is supposed to trigger a surge of intense elation; against long odds, after all, I had just attained a goal I'd coveted since childhood. But the summit was really only the halfway point. Any impulse I might have felt toward self-congratulation was extinguished by overwhelming apprehension about the long, dangerous descent that lay ahead."

After the disaster was reported there were a number of debates on the Internet and in the op-ed pages of newspapers. Although there were many critics who called the climb "foolhardy" and "stupid," at least one writer defended the climbers' actions, saying that they knew the risks and died doing something they loved. What is your estimation of the worthiness of the goals involved in this adventure?

   a. Krakauer's goal of using the climb for writing a story about climbing Mt. Everest.
   b. Pittman's goal of climbing Mt. Everest so she could finish her book about climbing all seven highest continental peaks.
   c. Hall's and Fischer's goals of getting their clients to the summit.
   d. Yasuko Namba's goal of being the first Japanese woman to climb the seven continental peaks.
   e. The general idea of climbing Mt. Everest.

3. Krakauer points out a number of consequences of the Everest expeditions. First, there was a dramatic change in Sherpa culture, introducing hard currency and lethal hazards. The Sherpas are a minority in Nepal who worship the mountain—Sagarmatha, as they call it—as goddess of the sky; but despite this, they seem to welcome these changes. The Sherpas are necessary to the expeditions. They carry the equipment, and their experience and acclimation at high altitudes make them hardy, life-saving guides. But of course, the work is very dangerous. Several weeks before the May 10 disaster, Ngawang Topche, a Sherpa working for Scott Fischer, showed weakness and fatigue at Camp One on the mountain. He disobeyed Fischer's order to descend to a safer altitude because he was afraid that he wouldn't be hired for future expeditions. Soon Ngawang was delirious and developed pulmonary edema (fluid in the lungs). It is often fatal unless the victim is immediately

Case Study: The Tragedy on Mt. Everest, *Continued*

evacuated to a lower altitude. Krakauer claims that owing to Fischer's inadequate planning, there was a delay in bringing the Sherpa down the mountain and in hiring a helicopter to transport him to Katmandu. Before reaching the hospital Ngwang stopped breathing for a while; he was left brain-damaged and eventually died some weeks later in June.

Do you think the Sherpas are being exploited for the sake of the adventure and thrills for well-to-do clients?

4. Krakauer also points out the effect on the ecology of these expeditions. He described the mountain as a garbage dump, littered with empty oxygen

canisters, shredded tents, human feces, and corpses. Rob Hall had organized a cleanup operation in 1990 that removed 5 tons of garbage from Base Camp, and Scott Fischer had removed 5000 pounds of trash from the mountain. There is also deforestation in the surrounding areas due to the high demand for firewood for hydroelectricity to support some of the medical clinics paid for by international relief groups and supported by the climbers. Are the goals of climbing Mt. Everest worth the ecological damage?

5. Do you agree with the Japanese team member's statement that "Above 8000 meters is not a place where people can afford morality"?

Case Study: The Decision to Drop the Atomic Bomb on Hiroshima

On August 6, 1945, the Enola Gay dropped the first atomic bomb ever used in combat on the city of Hiroshima with a population of 280,000. Along with the bomb dropped on Nagasaki, these have so far been the only atomic bombs used in combat. Approximately 70,000 men, women, and children, most of them nonmilitary, died instantly in the Hiroshima explosion. An additional 50,000 died within months from radiation poisoning and burns.

The principal decision makers were Harry Truman, president of the United States at this time; Henry Stimson, Secretary of War; John McCloy, Stimson's assistant; Gen. Leslie Groves, who headed the Manhattan Project responsible for the building of the bomb; and Jimmy Byrnes, Secretary of State. (Harry Truman had succeeded President Roosevelt when he died unexpectedly in April 1945.)

Gen. Leslie Groves was in charge of the Manhattan Project, the concerted effort by the military and the nation's scientists to develop the atomic bomb. By the time Truman became president, the Manhattan Project was near completion, and there was hope that the bomb would soon be tested in the Nevada desert. Gen. Groves had a lot at stake in the project. Nearly $2 billion had been spent in the effort (today's equivalent of $26 billion). Groves felt that if the project was stopped or failed to produce a viable bomb, his career would be ended. For this reason, he needed to convince Truman to continue the project. Known as an arrogant and manipulative man, Groves bragged to his colleagues and subordinate that he played on Truman's insecurities and admira-

tion of Roosevelt to get him to go along with the project. The second thing Groves needed to do was to demonstrate to his bosses, Congress, and the nation that the amount of money spent on the bomb was worth it—that the bomb was a powerful and amazing new weapon. He believed that the best way to demonstrate the power of the bomb would be to explode it over a city that had not already been damaged by bomb attacks so that its destructive capability could be fully appreciated. By March 1945 B-29 sorties had wiped out over 32 square miles of the four largest Japanese cities, killing at least 150,000 people. In May a raid on Tokyo had created a huge firestorm. The only cities that seemed to be pure targets worth bombing were Hiroshima and Kyoto. It was clear that neither one was a military target; otherwise they would have been bombed like the other cities. Hiroshima had some geographical features that might inhibit the full impact of the blast. Groves originally wanted to bomb Kyoto because, as the cultural center of Japan, its destruction would have a bigger impact on the Japanese. But eventually, Groves settled on Hiroshima as the best target.

Henry Stimson, Secretary of War and Groves's boss, had more ambivalence about the weapon's use. He thought it might be a means to world peace, but he clearly realized its potential for creating even greater horrors. Stimson saw himself as a gentleman and a soldier from upper-class stock and steeped in Christian values. He felt that he had been a good soldier, taking field combat during World War I rather than a safe desk job. As a lawyer, he had tried to be

Continued

Case Study: The Decision to Drop
the Atomic Bomb on Hiroshima, *Continued*

honest and avoided taking sleazy clients. He had always been concerned with the right thing to do, not just the expedient; still, he knew what politics was all about and realized the compromise. During the decision process, Stimson was 77 and showing signs of fatigue.

With the atomic bomb almost ready for testing, Stimson convinced Truman to set up an interim committee to advise him what to do with the bomb should it become ready for use. Truman was cordial and respectful to Stimson, but felt that he could not confide in him or show him weakness or indecision. The committee was composed of Stimson and Harrison, his deputy secretary; Jimmy Byrnes, Secretary of State; Ralph Bar, Undersecretary of the Navy; Karl Compton, president of MIT; and a scientific advisory panel, including Robert Oppenheimer, who was the scientific head of the Manhattan Project, and famous physicists such as Enrico Fermi. The task of the interim committee was given by Stimson: "Our great task is to bring this war to a prompt and successful conclusion. We may assume that our new weapon puts in our hands overwhelming power. It is our obligation to use this power with the best wisdom we can command."

It seemed that the interim committee had no doubts that the bomb should be used. The first question, however, was whether to use the bomb in non-military demonstration in such a manner that the Japanese would be so impressed that they would see the uselessness of the war or to use it in a secret military operation that would have such devastating effects as to achieve the same end. Various possibilities for nonmilitary demonstration were proposed, and arguments were brought against them. If a bomb was exploded in Japan with previous notice, the Japanese air power was still adequate enough to interfere with it. Such interference or attack might cause the bomb to fail, and such an end to an advertised demonstration of power would be much worse than if the attempt had not been made. If there was an invited demonstration, but the bomb proved to be a dud, the interval between the next one would be too great to be effective in the meantime. If the test were made on some neutral territory, it was hard to believe that Japan's more fanatic and militarist leaders would be impressed. If such an open test were made first and failed to bring surrender, the chance of shock and surprise would be gone. It was also feared that, if the Japanese were told the bomb was going to be exploded in a certain location, they would bring American prisoners of war into the area. The committee eventually decided unanimously that

the atomic bomb should hit Japan without warning and that it should be dropped on a combined military and residential target to produce the maximum psychological shock.

The scientific advisory panel agreed with the committee, even though they were aware of dissension among their scientific colleagues. Most scientists polled by Compton wanted a military demonstration in Japan to be followed by a renewed opportunity for surrender before full use of the weapon was employed. James Franck and Leo Szilard had drafted a memorandum in June arguing against the use of the bomb. In the memorandum they wrote, "If the United States were to be the first to release this new means of indiscriminate destruction upon mankind, we would sacrifice public support throughout the world, precipitate the race for armaments, and prejudice the possibility of reaching an international agreement on the future control of such weapons. Much more favourable conditions for the eventual achievement of such an agreement could be created if nuclear bombs were first to be revealed to the world by a demonstration in an appropriately selected and uninhabited area." Oppenheimer thought that the two overriding considerations were the saving of lives in the war and the effect of actions on the stability of the postwar world. He wasn't at the time convinced that exploding an atomic bomb like a firecracker over the desert would likely be very impressive. It was only after that was actually done in the first test that he changed his mind, but by then the committee had already made its recommendation to the president.

In the meantime the debate among the military chiefs had yielded the following options. Gen. Hap Arnold was convinced that conventional bombing plus a naval blockade would succeed. The Japanese would find it difficult to endure more "fire raids" like the one over Tokyo in May. However, intelligence reports collected by Stimson in early July showed that although Japan's economic position had deteriorated greatly, their determination was still strong. Many of the Japanese leaders believed that unconditional surrender would be the equivalent of national extinction. The report recommended heavy bombing followed by an invasion of the Japanese mainland.

Invasion was also the recommendation of the army. Gen. Marshall believed that an invasion would succeed if Russia helped with an attack launched from Siberia. He told Truman that it might eventually cost as many as a half million lives to force the Japanese to surrender unconditionally. Stimson thought that the figure was overly optimistic

Case Study: The Decision to Drop
the Atomic Bomb on Hiroshima, *Continued*

and that there would be many more casualties. He reasoned that the operation following the landing would be a very long and costly struggle and that the going would be like the last ditch defense efforts of the Japanese on Iwo Jima and Okinawa. Stimson thought the price would be too high and advised Truman against this option. Nonetheless, a plan for invasion was devised. The invasion was to be under the joint command of Gen. Douglas MacArthur and Adm. Chester Nimitz. Thirteen divisions of the U.S. Sixth Army—approximately 650,000 troops, 2500 ships, and 5000 planes—were to be used in opening up three fronts on Japan's southernmost island, Kyushu. The invasion was scheduled for November 1, 1945. Apparently, Japan had anticipated such an invasion in that location and in the meantime had amassed some 540,000 men to defend Kyushu and planned to use 5000 kamikaze planes, which had been used to great effect at Okinawa, to force Washington to accept a negotiated settlement rather than unconditional surrender.

Stimson believed that neither bombing nor invasion would end the war swiftly and that invasion would be very costly in terms of American lives. Despite the evidence that Stimson brought to bear against bombing and blockade, there was apparently counter evidence to support its probable success. A strategic-bombing study done after the war concluded that under relentless bombing, the Japanese would have surrendered before the scheduled invasion, November 1. Of course, although this strategy would have saved innumerable American lives, it would have had led to a terrible devastation of the Japanese civilian population depending on how long the Japanese militarists would resist. Recall that just 10 days of bombing in March had killed nearly 150,000 people (the Hiroshima bomb killed 120,000). But there were political and strategic reasons for rejecting both the blockade and the invasion. Military leaders were worried about the morale of the troops, especially those who had fought and just won in Europe. They had no desire to now fight Japan; they felt that they had won their war and had a right to return home right away. American families were also tired of the sacrifice. With the victory in Europe, they wanted the war with Japan over as soon as possible.

The other option to invasion or blockade—besides using the bomb—was negotiation. Stimson's assistant, John McCloy, urged this on his boss: He thought it would be crazy not to consider a political solution. There was an indication of a peace-minded contingent in Japan, headed by the Foreign Minister

Togo, who had the Emperor's ear. The Japanese had approached the Russians with the possibility of a negotiated peace, but a clear indication that Japan was still strong enough to reject an unconditional surrender. McCloy thought that if Japan was made to surrender but with the right to keep their Emperor, this would ease them into surrender by saving face. But in a June 17 meeting McCloy's proposal was rejected for a number of reasons. Apparently, there was evidence that suggested that rather than making overtures of peace to the United States through the Russians, the Japanese hoped to ally themselves with the Russians. Ever since Yalta, the United States and England realized the real possibility that Stalin would replace Hitler as the new threat to world peace. Stalin was not to be trusted; if he was capable of forming a pact with Hitler to suit his purposes, he was certainly capable of doing it with Japan. A pact between Russia and Japan would be a serious threat to American security. Alternately, there was evidence to suggest that Stalin had no intentions of making peace with the Japanese and that he was intent on invading Manchuria shortly. Just as he had grabbed territory in Eastern Europe, he was likely to do the same in the Asian theater. On the other hand, if Truman tried to negotiate a separate peace with Japan, he would be denounced by the Russians and the Allies. The Allies had long agreed that there would be nothing less than unconditional surrender. In any case the Japanese were not to be trusted in negotiations, and their surprise attack on Pearl Harbor demonstrated this. Moreover, the American public had sacrificed so much during the war and was not in a merciful mood, Secretary of State Byrnes argued. A recent poll had shown that, because of Pearl Harbor and the Bataan death march, the public was not kindly disposed toward the Japanese. A sizable number wanted to execute the Japanese emperor. Most people wanted unconditional surrender from Japan, and Truman had a great deal of popular support when he demanded it. Even though Stimson personally lobbied Truman for the negotiated solution after the June 17 meeting, he apparently had his own doubts about it. He urged Truman on July 2 to give a carefully timed warning to the Japanese before using the bomb in the hope that the Japanese would be reasonable and call for surrender. In the meantime on July 4, the interim committee came with its recommendation that the bomb should be dropped without warning on a combined military and civilian target.

In early July Truman met with Stalin and Churchill at the Potsdam Conference. During that conference he became even more convinced of the

Continued

Case Study: The Decision to Drop
the Atomic Bomb on Hiroshima, *Continued*

danger of Stalin; it was clear about his postwar ambitions in Eastern Europe, and he could see clearly that the Soviet Union would quickly change status from ally to rival. Truman wanted to show the Russians that he could not be easily intimidated and that he could stand up to them and not back-off. He told Stalin of the atomic bomb partly to threaten and intimidate him. His Secretary of State, Jimmy Byrnes, suggested that, if the Russians knew the United States had an atom bomb and the willingness to use it, they would be more manageable.

While at Potsdam on July 16, news came from Groves in the Nevada desert that the bomb had tested successfully. Groves was jubilant, and Stimson, who had approved the $2-billion expenditure, was also relieved by the news. It was reported that the success of the bomb seemed to give Truman new confidence, and thereafter he took more of a leading role at the conference according to Churchill. Stalin reacted coolly to the news.

On July 31, gathering together all the recommendations, Truman gave the order to bomb Hiroshima as soon as weather permitted after August 2, with Nagasaki as a second target. Truman noted in his diary that he instructed Stimson to use the bomb only against military personnel, but he had to know that Hiroshima was primarily a civilian target. Groves was put in charge of the operation, and the bomb was dropped on August 6 at 8:15 in the morning. Stimson had a heart attack on August 8 and was forced to resign. Because Groves wanted to show that a new $400-million trigger device was worth the money, he wanted to bomb a second target, Nagasaki, even though Emperor Hirohito had decided to surrender before Nagasaki. The Nagasaki bomb killed an additional 70,000 people. With the second bomb and the Russians invading Manchuria, the Japanese militarists had no choice but to go along with the Emperor's wishes.

Although initially there was strong, widespread public support for the Hiroshima decision, especially since it ended the war quickly, doubts began to rise after some of the horrifying details of the bombing became clear. Even though Truman lost some of his early enthusiasm about the decision and seemed to worry about the matter, he still claimed in published documents as late as 1955 that he made the right decision and would do the same thing again. In his public testimony Groves argued that the bomb was not a cruel instrument of war, but in fact a quick and relatively painless way to die. Stimson wrote a piece justifying the decision, although some important details which could place some doubt on the decision were left out.

Questions for Discussion

1. Using Cicero's terms, how does efficiency, advantage, necessity, affection, and honor come into play in some of the decision making here?

2. Consider any of the decisions made. How is calculation played against advantage in some of these decisions? How is advantage played against honor or morality in these decisions?

3. Consider any of the decisions made. How is memory used? Deliberation? Foresight? What are some of the flaws or strengths in their use?

4. Would you consider the decision to drop the bomb a tragic choice, a moral dilemma, or a moral temptation?

5. How did the character flaws of the various decision makers influence their judgment?

6. Who among the decision makers, if any, do you find admirable and why? Who seems to be the least moral decision maker?

7. Given the hindsight of more than 50 years, which course of action would you consider to have been the wisest to take? What do you think of the claims made in the Franck and Szilard memo?

8. Some have claimed that the atomic bomb would never have been dropped on a Caucasian population and that some racism was present in the decision. Discuss this issue and how prejudice could lead to bad judgment.

9. If it is assumed that the Hiroshima decision was necessary, was the Nagasaki decision simply punitive and cruel?

10. Can wartime decisions against an aggressive enemy afford to be moral ones? Are there limits to what one group can do to another even if they are bitter enemies? Why would it be important for victors to maintain a modicum of morality in their victory? Would the same hold for the defeated or for those whose survival is at stake?

11. Paul Fussell, author of *The Great War and Modern Memory*, wrote an article on Hiroshima for *The New Republic* in 1981 praising the decision to drop the atomic bomb. At the time Fussell was a soldier who was about to be transferred to the Pacific after years of fighting in Europe. He argues that the critics of the decision are often too remote from the original experience. For those soldiers facing death for who knew how many more years, the bomb was a welcome relief. *What do you think of Fussell's view?*

Sources: Lee 1995, Lifton and Mitchell 1996, Stimson 1947, Takaki 1996, Truman 1955, Weintraub 1995, and Yass 1972.

Other Cases for Deliberation

The following cases are based on real-life situations.

1. You live in a nice, pleasant neighborhood. You've known your neighbors, Bob and Alicia, for 3 years. They've been friendly and helpful to you, and you have socialized on occasion. They're both professionals and hold excellent jobs. Their 5-year-old boy comes over occasionally to play with your child of the same age. One day you notice a couple of big bruises on the boy's thigh. "How'd you get those bruises on your legs?" you ask. "My mommy bumped me hard when I wouldn't listen to her. One day she burned me too." What do you do?

2. You're a single parent struggling to make ends meet. You've taken your kids to a video game arcade, when you notice a $20 bill lying on the floor. You pick it up and assume that it belongs to a young, obviously married couple occupied with a video game. Just as you ask them if they dropped a $20 bill, you realize that you should've asked them if they lost some money and what the denomination was just to make sure it was their money. They claim that it is their money, and the man turns to the woman and says, "Have you been losing our money again?" What do you do or say?

3. Kathy's sister, who's 17, has a boyfriend, Tom, who's 19. Kathy, who is 15, is infatuated with him. They start seeing each other behind her sister's back and then start sleeping together. In a few months Kathy discovers she's pregnant. She has an abortion, encouraged by Tom. Tom decides to stop seeing Kathy a month after the abortion. A month after that he breaks up with Kathy's sister and moves to California. Two years later, Kathy hears that he's married there and now has a child. Should she tell her sister what happened? Since she was underage at the time of the affair, should she tell the police?

4. Harry is a top executive at a major corporation that is presently being attacked for its alleged lack of hiring of women and minorities. He is called to a meeting of other top executives in the company—all white men—to address this issue. Much to his chagrin, the meeting is full of satire, rude, and racist remarks about African Americans, affirmative action, and the official policies of the company against discrimination and for affirmative action. Since the meeting was arranged by Harry, he had the session tape-recorded. What should he do with those tapes?

5. A couple runs a small cleaning service. After they hired an employee, they begin to notice small things missing around the office such as a roll of stamps, a Dictaphone, and some cash out of a purse. After the problem continued, they brought the employee in for questioning. She acted indignant and quit. The employee had access to their customers' keys. Should they tell their customers to change their locks and risk losing their business?

6. On his return from a visit to North Korea, Ohio Congressman Tony Hall asked, "Should the world allow North Koreans to starve because their Stalinist government denies them freedom?" Some argue that helping North Korea through its famine will simply help an oppressive and dangerous regime survive and continue on its course. What do you think?

4.8 WISDOM AND THE QUESTION OF MORAL KNOWLEDGE

Wisdom is concerned with moral know-how. It aims to discern the best sense of the good life and make possible sound moral judgments on the appropriate moral means to attain it. The question that arises, however, is whether we can be assured that the visions, deliberations, and judgments that make up the core of wisdom are morally correct. Can wisdom alone give us such assurance?

4.8.1 Aristotle's Dispute with Socrates and Plato

In *The Meno* Socrates makes the claim that "virtue is knowledge" (*Meno* 87d). The reasoning behind this position is the following. Whatever virtuous dispositions a person might have, such as self-control in regard to pleasure, even though we consider these dispositions good to possess, they can still be hurtful without the use of reason to direct them toward the good (*Meno*, 88a). In other words, Socrates's

Plato (428–348 B.C.E.) and **Aristotle** (384–322 B.C.E.) are considered to be the greatest of Western philosophers. Although Aristotle was a student of Plato's for many years, Aristotle developed a philosophy that disagreed with Plato's in many respects. Aristotle's most important work on ethics is *The Nicomachean Ethics.*

position reflects the instrumental theory of the virtues, that virtue without the guide of wisdom can lead to immoralities. But since what makes virtuous dispositions genuinely good is knowledge of the good or rational principle, then virtue is knowledge. Given the axiom that all people desire good things (especially understood as that which will positively benefit them) (*Meno* 77a–e), then it is a simple inference to the claim that all people will act upon what they know to be the good whenever it is possible for them to do so. As we saw in Section 2.2 this is the explanation for moral weakness: People are morally weak to the degree that they are not sure of the moral or factual information they have. We've already addressed the difficulties with this position. First, you may question the axiom that all persons desire that which will positively benefit them; this seems to deny genuine wickedness or self-destructiveness. Second, it does not directly follow from the fact that you desire to do something that is good for you, and from the fact that it is possible to do, that you will do it. In many cases it may require certain character traits such as temperance or courage which, if lacking, would inhibit or prevent you from doing what you know you should do.

But these criticisms aside, Plato is interested in showing what follows from his claim in regard to the acquisition of virtue. In *The Meno* Socrates addresses the question of whether virtue can be taught, whether it can be acquired by training and enculturation (*asketon*), or whether it is inborn (*Meno* 70a). Plato's answer to this is not only in *The Meno* but also in *The Republic* and *The Laws* (cf. Taylor 1956: 131). The argument that virtue is knowledge suggests that it can be taught. Yet, as pointed out in *The Meno*, it seems from observation, at least of Athenian culture, that those who are considered virtuous have not been entirely successful at teaching virtues to their children. If virtue were teachable, then surely, virtuous fathers could teach their sons. This leads Socrates to suggest that perhaps those who are virtuous are lucky in the sense that they've come across virtue by right opinion rather than knowledge. This would explain why even though they are virtuous themselves they are unable to convey that to their offspring. This allows Plato to imply still that virtue can be taught if there is knowledge of it. This is a position taken up in *The Republic.* Here the view is that only those who have acquired genuine knowledge of virtue are able to teach virtue and, moreover, are able to prescribe a course of training and enculturation that ensures proper virtue in others. We need not teach the knowledge of virtue to everyone, only the leaders of the community; participants in the community need only be enculturated with right opinion. Learning the knowledge about virtue is for the few leaders or statespeople of a culture, while training is for the masses; consequently, trust in and loyalty to traditions set down by the learned are what is needed for the majority of people, but true wisdom is required only of the few.

Aristotle clearly agrees with the first part of Plato's contention, that virtue requires the guidance of wisdom to be genuine virtue (*Nic. Ethics* 1144b8–10), but ultimately disagrees with Plato's vision of transmittable and scientific-like ethical knowledge. Aristotle makes a distinction between natural and perfected or genuine virtue. Dispositions toward self-control and bravery can be there from birth, "but we seek for the presence of such qualities in another way," that is, the good in the strict sense. "For both children and brutes have the natural dispositions to these qualities, but without reason these are evidently hurtful." We may be "led astray by them, as a strong body which moves without sight may stumble badly ... still, if a man once acquires reason, that makes a difference in action; and his state, while still like what it was, will then be virtue in the strict sense." Therefore, just as there is a difference between cleverness and practical wisdom, "so too in the moral part there are two types, natural virtue and virtue in the strict sense, and of these the latter involves practical wisdom" (*Nic. Ethics* 1144b8–10). Simply put, naturally virtuous dispositions need the guidance of reason to become genuinely and consistently virtuous dispositions.

However, despite their agreement that virtue needs wisdom to become genuine virtue, Plato and Aristotle disagree about the inferences from that position. Socrates and Plato argue that, therefore, virtue is nothing other than knowledge or wisdom, while Aristotle argues that virtues *involve* rational principle (*Nic. Ethics* 1144b28–29); that is, rational principle alone is not sufficient to produce virtue. But moreover, Socrates and Plato want to argue that virtue is a matter of scientific-like knowledge (*episteme*) (*Meno* 87d), whereas Aristotle insists that ethics cannot be a science like physics, for example (*Nic. Ethics* 1094b11–27). In addition, given the character of human action, the use of practical wisdom for ethical decision making cannot be precise, even if it could be counted as scientific knowledge. For Aristotle reason in this context can hope at best to be practical reasoning, which for him, as we saw, is a complex of various processes that address the indeterminacy of contextualized human action. The process itself is indeterminate given the nature of what it deals with. Wisdom is not teachable because it is not exact knowledge that involves algorithmic or formulaic knowledge. Wisdom requires experience, perceptual acuity, and judgment, which are not teachable but simply must be acquired over time. That's why it is easy to teach the young mathematics, but the study of ethics will not benefit the young (*Nic. Ethics* 1095a1–10). This is nicely illustrated in a story told by John Stuart Mill (in Dewey 1933: 123):

> A Scotch manufacturer procured from England, at a high rate of wages, a working dyer, famous for producing very fine colors, with the view of teaching to his other workmen the same skill. The workman came but his method of proportioning the ingredients, in which lay the secret of the effects he produced, was by taking them up in handfuls, while the common method was to weigh them. The manufacturer sought to make him turn his handling system into an equivalent weighing system, that the

general principles of his peculiar mode of proceeding might be ascertained. This, however, the man found himself quite unable to do, and could therefore impart his own skill to nobody. He had, from individual cases of his own experience, established a connection in his mind between fine effects of color and tactual perceptions in handling his dyeing materials; and from these perceptions he could, in any particular case, infer the means to be employed and the effects which would be produced.

Similarly, wisdom requires the sort of learning from experience that is not teachable scientifically, exactly, or algorithmically.

Plato's overarching vision for ethics is nicely expressed by A.E. Taylor (1956: 144): the search for a guide to permanent and continuous virtuous disposition. And this requires a sound traditional code of conduct grounded in genuine knowledge. The hope here is to avoid the vagaries of personal opinion and the variety of traditions in favor of a form of moral knowledge that can guarantee, when properly applied, consistently good moral outcomes. Martha Nussbaum expresses Plato's ideal similarly. The controversy between Plato and Aristotle—the idea of rational choice as the measurement of all alternatives by a single quantitative standard of value, a science of measurement (cf. Plato, *Protagoras* 356a–e)—was motivated by a desire to simplify and render tractable the bewildering problem of choice among heterogeneous alternatives. "Plato, for example, argues that only through such a science can human beings be rescued from an unendurable confusion in the facade of the concrete situation of choice, with its qualitative indefiniteness and its variegated plurality of apparent values" (1990: 56).

For Aristotle the reason why rules and principles cannot be strictly applied to situations is that practical matters are inherently indeterminate (*Nic. Ethics* 1137b17–19). It is difficult to envision Shakespeare's advice literally: "never a borrower or lender be." Nor is it easy to catalogue a set of rules for borrowing, since lending money to your children or to an acquaintance will involve different precautions and conditions. For this reason, "every statement about matters of practice ought to be said in outline and not with precision. … Such cases do not fall under any science … but the agents themselves must in each case look to what suits the occasion, as is also the case in medicine and navigation (*Nic. Ethics* 1103b34–1104a10). Using this analogy to medicine, it is clear, however, that Aristotle does not intend to say that ethical decisions are purely situational and variable, for medicine has generalized rules and procedures and is backed up by science and information; but the art of medicine requires the subtle perception and discernment of the particular situation and, consequently, the right application of those rules. People of practical wisdom must meet the new with responsiveness and the variable with imagination (Nussbaum 1990: 71). At the same time, those who are practically wise are not awash at sea with no moral guide or principle whatsoever: "practical wisdom," as Aristotle says, "is not concerned with universals only; it must also recognize particulars, for it is practical, and practice concerns particulars" (1141b4–16). But in saying that, he is saying that it is also concerned with universals. Rules and general procedures can be aids in moral development for those, on the one hand, too young for practical wisdom, but also even for those with experience, as an aid in summary or standardized decision procedure (Nussbaum 1990: 73). If rules are not sufficient, they may be highly useful, frequently even necessary (Nussbaum 1990: 75). But it is clear in any case that Aristotle argues against the idea of rational choice being captured in a system of general rules or principles which can then simply be applied to each new case (Nussbaum 1990: 66). Good moral decisions cannot be generated from any scientific-like knowledge, but must be grasped with insight through experience (*Nic. Ethics* 1142a11ff.).

The issue here is plain and harks back to the discussion in the Introduction between the sagacious tradition in ethics and the modern theoretical one. If Aristotle is correct, there can be no moral knowledge in the scientific or systematic sense of the term, and even if there can be, its application is tenuous given the indeterminacy of human affairs. On the other hand, if there is moral knowledge in the scientific sense, then the question of its application is still remaining. (For a related discussion, see Section 5.2.6.)

4.8.2 Kant's Notion of Practical Reason as Opposed to Aristotle's

For Aristotle practical reason is a concrete process that deals with the morally adequate connection of means to end and is opposed to the merely calculative, which seeks only the most efficient and expedient means to an end. Practical reason for Aristotle is distinct from theoretical reason, mainly because it is about human affairs, which makes it inherently indeterminate.

Immanuel Kant, on the other hand, has a different, more elaborate concept of practical reason. Practical reason is simply a certain application of what he calls "pure" reason to the human will; by "pure" reason he means the character of reason in its attempt to grasp the ultimate, systematic, and absolute understanding of all things (1781: 319). It is in a sense similar to Plato's understanding of theoretical knowledge or "science." This will result in ultimate, underlying principles and ideas concerning the nature of things (1781: 58). He often calls pure reason the search for the unconditioned, that is, knowledge which is not conditioned by, dependent on, or justified by something else but is self-justifying and serves to ground or justify all else (1781: 319). When pure reason addresses human action, specifically the human will, then it is pure practical reason (1788: 15). By this he means that it determines the will in an unconditioned way, without regard to anything that a person may desire, any plan a person may have, or any reward for doing something. It is simply the will to do the good for the sake of the good. It is similar to the idea of unconditional love—love for its own sake without ulterior motive. Even in Aristotle's account, acting virtuously is for the sake of happiness, and so the virtuous acts are conditioned by the goal of happiness or the good life, as opposed to the fact that one may act virtuously simply for the sake of doing so, that is, because that is the right thing to do. If someone does the right thing because she wants to be happy, then her will to do the right thing is conditioned by the goal of happiness; but if she wills to do the right thing simply because it is the right thing to do, then she is acting in an unconditional way. As mentioned, Kant argues that acting from duty expresses this idea (1785: 13) (see Sections 1.5, 2.6, 3.3.2). For example, a salesman may charge a customer an honest price for the merchandise simply because it is the honest thing to do, or may do it because he believes it's good for business to maintain the appearance of integrity. In the last case the person is motivated by the consequences of acting honestly rather than the "pure" and unconditioned quality of the honest act.

This is a different solution than Plato's. Plato sees the question of ethics as a theoretical question. That is, we can treat the question of what is the "good" as if it were a scientific problem that could be solved by means of theoretical reason. Kant is not saying that pure theoretical reason can be used to discover what is good. Instead, when what is inherent in the character of "pure" reason is applied to justifying or directing human action, the only reasons or justifications that are unconditioned are those that are not determined by the ends or consequences of the action. All other reasons or justifications, then, are conditioned by some goal or consequence derived from those human actions. The willingness to determine one's actions purely on the basis of something other than a goal or consequence of the action is the proper use of pure practical reason.

If you act to accomplish some end, then your actions are subordinate to that end and determined by that end; in that case you are controlled by the goal rather than yourself, although certainly it may require self-control to attain that end. But even in that case, the self-control is for the purpose of attaining the goal or end (although it is better to have at least that sense of self-control than not). True freedom, according to Kant, is just the power of control over oneself for the sake of nothing other than that control. Some argue that freedom is the ability to do what you want, but a want is a desire or a goal, and what that really suggests is that you are being controlled by that "want." Freedom in the true sense is self-determination or autonomy (literally "self-legislation") (see Section 2.5). As paradoxical as it may sound, the true test of freedom is when you don't do what you want. If you are determined to act in a certain way regardless of desires, wants, ends, or the consequences, then you are self-determined and thus free of any external influence other than your self-determination.

The difference between the Aristotelian sense of practical reason and Kant's leads to a difference in the framework in which moral agents are trying to make the right decisions. From Aristotle's view moral agents are, first of all, persons who have a certain sort of character and experience. They are living in a community composed of certain kinds of practices and institutions, which have a certain tradition and way of being. In this context they make moral decisions on the basis of who they are relative to the traditions and ways of being of their community and on the basis of some sense of the good life. For Kant, on the other hand, the highest form of practical reason involves moral agents capable of transcending the interests and roles of the community in which they live, indeed, transcending any personal interests they may have. The ideal moral agent is one who is impartial in this regard. When this impartiality is achieved in Kant's way—by a principle that does not consider the consequences of actions, systems of reward, or preferences of individual plans—but simply what a person should do as a matter of obligation, then such a principle is called *deontological* (coming from the Greek word *deon* meaning "duty" or "obligation"). On the other hand, some ethical thinkers, such as the utilitarians, argue that such impartiality can be achieved by incorporating the consequences and ends of actions in an impartial way. In that case the ethical principle that is developed is called *teleological* (from the Greek word *telos* meaning "end" or "purpose") or *consequentialist.*

4.8.3 The Unity of the Different Senses of Practical Reason

Kant's sense of practical reason is different from both Plato's and Aristotle's. As opposed to Plato, it is not simply the application of theoretically (i.e., scientifically) discovered ethical principles and concepts to human affairs, nor as opposed to Aristotle, is it simply the deliberation of the best way to the good life. Instead, practical reason is literally reason turned practical in the sense of applying the form of reason—the search for the unconditioned—to the determination of the will. The will becomes unconditioned only when it is self-determined independent of any desire, goal, or end.

From the Kantian perspective, there are at least three senses of practical reason (cf. Habermas 1993: 8ff.). In one sense practical reasoning is technical reasoning or what we've called rational calculation, the determination of the most efficient and expedient means to an end. Wisdom fills out the second sense of the term. It is the delivery of moral ends by moral means. In other words, only those deliberations are prudent which contribute to the good life, understood in the framework of some moral vision. The third sense of practical reason is as pure practical reason, understood as an unconditioned principle of action, that is, a principle not based on desire, goals, or consequences.

One way to resolve the conflict between these different types of practical reasoning is simply to prefer one to the other. The other way is to suggest that their work is complementary but hierarchical; that is, they should also involve a certain rank order. First, clever calculation, as Aristotle insists, is not wisdom since it pays no attention to the goodness of the means, but simply the attainment of the end. Calculation is then subordinate to wisdom in the sense that the guides of wisdom serve as a higher-order evaluation and selection of calculated plans or actions. However, although wisdom is a higher-order deliberation than calculation, it is still deliberation of a means to an end—deliberation to determine the best way to attain the good life. Thus, it is conditioned by some end. Pure practical reason, then, can serve as a higher-order evaluation of deliberated plans and actions since it is not conditioned by some end. This makes the goal of moral knowledge to be the establishment of a higher-order criterion by which to judge the moral quality of actions and plans; practically speaking, it seems to be simply an attempt to articulate an algorithm for higher-order deliberation. The principle which moral knowledge seeks serves as an algorithm or formula for the most comprehensive form of moral deliberation or judgment. What we find in Kant's sense of moral knowledge is a relatively justified decision procedure for best moral outcomes.

The alternative to this hierarchical arrangement is to suggest that one or the other of the senses of practical reason is to be preferred to the exclusion of the others. If technical reasoning is to be preferred to the other forms, then practical reasoning is simply rational decision making in the sense of choosing those outcomes which maximize the best interests of the agent. Moral deliberation is then reduced to the model of economic rationality, best expressed by models such as game theory and decision theory (cf. Gauthier 1986: 8) (see Section 5.4.8). From this view moral constraints on decisions are justified only if they contribute to the maximization of interests.

One current thinker who argues in this sense is David Gauthier (1986). He wants to develop "a theory of morals as part of the theory of rational choice ... rational principles for making choices, or decisions among possible actions, include some that constrain the actor pursuing his own interest in an impartial way" (1986: 3). This has the convenience of showing that even a completely egoistically oriented agent, interested only in his own welfare, may still have to adopt more impartial constraints on his behavior. Gauthier begins describing the situation of the agent as follows:

> from an initial presumption against morality, as a constraint on [the] ... person's pursuit of his own interest. A person is conceived as an independent centre of activity,

endeavoring to direct his capacities and resources to the fulfillment of his interests. He considers what he can do, but initially draws no distinction between what he may and may not do. How then does he come to acknowledge the distinction? How does a person come to recognize a moral dimension to choice ... ? (1986: 9).

Of course, from Kant's perspective this is analogous to doing what one should do because of some advantage it yields rather than for its own sake, just as the store owner recognizes that honesty is good for business. Indeed, Gauthier recognizes exactly this: "Practical reason is linked to interest, or ... to individual utility, and rational constraints on the pursuit of interest have themselves a foundation in the interest they constrain. Duty overrides advantage, but the acceptance of duty is truly advantageous" (1986: 2). As he says clearly elsewhere, the theory "enables us to demonstrate the rationality of impartial constraints on the pursuit of individual interest to persons who may take no interest in others' interests" (1986: 17). Of course, the advantage of this position is that the motivation for abiding by any moral constraints so discovered would be very strong since it would simply appeal to the individual interests of the moral agent. In a certain sense the claim would not be unlike Plato's—that getting people to do the right thing is simply a matter of their knowing what is best for themselves, since everyone desires that.

But this also reveals the difficulty with this position because it still implicitly appeals to a sense of the good life, even if that is individually determined. When it is said that the moral agent is seeking to maximize her interests, those interests we assume are based on some sense of what is good; mere technical reason, thought of as procedures for decisions which will maximize the interests of the agent, will not really determine whether those interests are themselves conducive to the genuine good of the agent; they will only suggest how those ends are to be maximized. It allows one to maximize the individual's preferences "but disclaims all concern with the ends of action" (Gauthier 1986: 26). For example, we may say that assuming that wealth is a good and then those decision procedures (which may include certain moral constraints) which maximize wealth are to be preferred; but how wealth and how much wealth fit into a genuine sense of the good life is left unanswered. Paradoxically, then, we may maximize a person's interests (in terms of their subjectively conceived interests), yet minimize their overall good. Technical reasoning still needs a theory of wisdom; specifically, calculation may not help articulate a moral vision.

Practical reason in the sense of wisdom does not define moral agency in the way that calculation does. Rather than a separate individual guided by subjectively conceived preferences, moral agents are thought to be persons who are acting within a family, a group, a community, or a nation with which they are connected. These institutions and practices have traditions and normative structures which work to generate the preferences and values of its individual members. This shared tradition and life with others serve as the source of the sense of the good life. Rather than practical reason being merely instrumental, as devising the most efficient means to a preferred end, practical reason as wisdom seeks to find a concordance between good ends and good means, a way of life that best generates the good life. This preference for wisdom is advocated contemporarily by a theory called communitarianism (cf. Sandel 1982; Walzer 1981).

Under the communitarian view, any attempt at pure practical reason in Kant's sense presupposes a certain concept of the good as derived from sense of community. Moral agents stripped of all communal values could not make moral decisions, only arbitrary ones (Sandel 1982: 21). The very sense of rational and moral agency is embedded in the structure of certain communities (Sandel 1982: 175). Morality is something rooted in the particular practices of actual communities, so the idea of looking to discover abstract principles of morality by which to evaluate or redesign existing societies is an implausible one. Instead, evaluation should be based on implicit understanding of our social institutions and their traditions. For these reasons we should not look to universal, abstract principles but to a common good as understood by those very members of a certain community (Walzer 1983: 314). This view gets expressed in the claim that some concept of the good must precede any concept of the right, the latter understood as a principle that is impartial to any sense of the good and is used to adjudicate among conflicting goods. Indeed, this point seems to be confirmed by John Rawls's attempt to follow the Kantian model, that is, to generate a principle of right independent of some concept of the good, so that the right is seen as something prior to the good (1971: 396) (see Section 5.3.4). But in doing so, Rawls admits that he must employ some sense of the good (1971: 396).

Is morality, then, just "local" as Walzer suggests (1983: 314)? This would suggest that the evaluation of moral behavior cannot extend beyond a particular community's sense of the good life. The true test of whether an ethical principle, a principle of pure practical reason in Kant's sense, could be achievable would be if the procedural application of the principle alone is sufficient for generating morally satisfactory outcomes; that is, are character, vision, and other such things also necessary, or are they rendered irrelevant by the principle? One way to formulate the issue would be the following: Could a clever person with no particularly great moral sentiment be constrained by these principles in their deliberation such that moral outcomes would result? This is an issue to be decided in the next chapter. But the provisional thesis here is that, although any ethical principle may not be successful in passing such a test, still that principle and moral knowledge in general play a vital role in the generation of moral competence. This position suggests an integrated view of the variety of senses of practical reason: that their interrelation is the most satisfactory outcome. Moral knowledge has a specifiable function within the framework of moral competence so organized here. Moral knowledge is to provide justification for a principle which will aid in the evaluation of means–ends deliberations. Its goal is to find a reliable principle which, when used consistently, can generate good moral outcomes for the most part. The hallmark of a truly rational decision procedure would be that it should remove some of our ethical perplexity and vulnerability, putting us more securely in control of the more important things. Consequently, it serves nearly the same function as judgment, under the sense of wisdom; yet it is but one component of moral competence. Principles of pure practical reason are not sufficient to generate moral competence; not only is moral character needed, but prudent deliberation is a prior requirement.

REVIEW QUESTIONS

1. Define some of the commonly understood characteristics of moral wisdom. What is involved in acquiring wisdom? Why do you think experience is necessary for acquiring wisdom? Is experience alone sufficient for moral wisdom? Could a person with a vicious character or someone with serious vices be morally wise? What sort of intelligence do you think is necessary for learning from experience? How does wisdom enhance each of the other features of moral character?

2. How is moral or practical reasoning different from theoretical reasoning?

3. What is meant by moral vision? What is a cosmic vision, a public vision, a sense of the good life? How are they interrelated?

4. Discuss the valuative differences between the origin myth found in Genesis and the Tlingit origin myth.

5. What are some of the general characteristics of romance, tragedy, irony, satire, and comedy? What sort of conflicts are involved in each? What sort of relations between opponents are involved in each type of narrative?

6. Which type of narrative most characterizes your moral vision? Which of the types of heroes do you most admire?

7. What is meant by success? What is the difference between being a success and accomplishing goals? What is prosperity? Does success always lead to prosperity?

8. What is happiness? What is flourishing? What is Lykken and Tellegen's theory of happiness?

9. What are some of the difficulties with the sense of the good life understood as adventure and entertainment? Comfort and security? The pursuit of wealth? Fame and power? Is Aristotle's account of the good life as the virtuous life adequate in your estimation?

10. What is rational calculation? What are some of its principles? Why does Aristotle argue that deliberation is not calculation?

11. What is cunning? Why does Aristotle believe that deliberation should not be confused with cunning?

12. What are some of the general features of Aristotle's model of deliberation?

13. What are some of the general features of Cicero's model of deliberation?

14. What is the relation among necessity, convenience, advantage, and honor in Cicero's model?

15. Give an account of how memory functions in the context of deliberation.

16. What is meant by the memory palace?

17. What is meant by discernment? What role does it play in deliberation?

18. What is meant by foresight? What is meant by imaginative deliberation? What is the analogy between storytelling and foresight? Is the analogy accurate and useful?

19. What is casuistry? What are some of its difficulties? What is narrative ethics? How does it help or hinder deliberation?

20. What are some of the general features of judgment? What role does it play in practical reasoning? What's the difference between decision and judgment? What are Kidder's three paradigms of judgment? Under what conditions does bad judgment usually occur?

21. What is the nature of the dispute between Aristotle and Plato in regard to the relation of virtue and knowledge? Who in your estimation gives the better account?

22. What is Aristotle's notion of practical reason? How does Kant's notion of practical reason differ from Aristotle's? What are some other senses of practical reason? What are some suggestions for the various ways in which the different senses of practical reason might be resolved?

23. What is meant by impartiality? What's the difference between deontological or autonomy-based principles and consequentialist ones? How are deontological principles impartial? How are consequentialist ones impartial?

QUESTIONS FOR DISCUSSION

1. In many cultures elders are given special status, honor, and respect, and often young members of the family and group must defer to their judgment. Do you think this is a good practice? What problems might arise? What do you think of the prevalent attitude of the younger generation in the 1960s, who argued "don't trust anyone over 30"?

2. If Socrates, Solomon, Jesus, Confucius, Buddha, and Mohammad are all considered wise, yet disagree with one another in certain respects, is wisdom sufficient for understanding what is truly the right thing to do? Shouldn't it be the case that the wise could at least agree on the best sense of the good life?

3. Which of the various conditions for acquiring moral wisdom is the most important in your opinion? Which is the least important? Do you think that studying ethics academically would help make you wise?

4. Take each of the five cosmic visions discussed in the text—the tragic, the romantic, the comedic, the ironic, and the satiric—and list what you believe to be their truths or benefits. Compare these with what you believe to be their falsehoods and harms. Of the moral visions discussed, which appeals to you most and why?

5. Do you think you can flourish without being happy? If you had to make a choice between happiness, flourishing, or success, which would you choose? What do you think of Lykken and Tellegen's theory of happiness?

6. Why do you think the entertainment industry has such a power over our lives?

7. Which of the following devil's bargains would you be willing to make?

   a. a life of wealth but with little pleasure;

   b. a life with a loving family but little money;

   c. a life of pleasure and adventure but no family or long-term relationships;

   d. a life of fame but one plagued with misfortunes;

   e. a life of power but with the great enmity of others.

8. Do you believe those who say that only the virtuous will be truly happy?

9. What sort of life would result for someone who was consistent and efficient in rational calculation?

10. Does Machiavelli make a good point: In a world that is less than perfect, is it folly to act morally? When dealing with the vicious, must not one be as cunning if not more cunning than they?

11. Why should someone forgo personal benefit and advantage for the sake of what is good?

12. Which of the three aspects of deliberation—memory, discernment, and foresight—do you consider the most important and why? If you could be especially adept at one, which would you choose?

13. Why do you think people become irresolute sometimes when making decisions?

14. Do you think ethics can become a science? Would it be a good thing if it were?

CASE STUDIES FOR DISCUSSION

1. Slavery is still a practice in parts of the Sudan, where it is practiced mostly by the northern peoples against the southern Dinka tribes. Recently, some charitable groups, such as the Swiss-based Christian Solidarity International, have gone to the Sudan and pioneered the practice of buying the freedom of Sudanese slaves from their owners. They claim to have freed nearly 9000 slaves by this practice. In response to this effort, some schools and groups in America have raised money to help the Swiss organization. Others, such as the Human Rights Watch, criticize this practice. They say that buying slaves only encourages more slavery, since the owners will be paid for existing slaves and then have more motivation to continue their raids to acquire more slaves. What is the best thing to do? Should you raise money to free slaves, knowing that it may encourage more slave trade or should you not encourage Christian Solidarity to continue its practice?

2. Cicero relates the story of Regulus who, by a trick, was captured by Hannibal's father in Africa. They sent Regulus to the Roman senate under oath, the condition being

that Regulus himself should return to Carthage unless the Romans agreed to return certain captive nobles to the Carthaginians. When he came to Rome, however, he argued against returning the captives, since he believed that it was not to Rome's advantage. Yet he kept his oath and returned to Carthage and certain death. Do you think Regulus was bound by his oath to the Carthaginians? Or was he foolish to keep such an oath made to his enemies and under duress?

3. Mary is best friends with a married couple, Susan and John. She is equally friendly with both the husband and wife. Her problem is the following. Susan invited her to lunch one day, and in the course of the meal, she revealed to Mary that she was having an affair with another man. Mary was shocked, but Susan got Mary to promise that she would not say anything to John. John would be devastated, and it probably would mean the end of the marriage if he found out. Susan doesn't want the marriage to end, but is strongly drawn to her lover. She's hoping that she can move past this relationship and dedicate herself to her primary one. A week later, Mary is invited to lunch with John who, during the meal, expresses his feelings that Susan may be having an affair with someone. He asks Mary point blank whether she knows anything about an affair. Keeping in mind her promise to Susan, she tells him no. But afterward she feels terribly guilty about the lie. At the same time she knows if she tells John the truth the marriage will probably fall apart, and Susan may simply need some time to get herself together enough to save the marriage. The whole matter is complicated by the fact that Mary has always had an attraction for John. Although she is not very comfortable with the thought, she knows that this might be her opportunity to start a relationship with John by revealing the affair. On the other hand, their marriage has been a very good one, at least up to now, and to see it destroyed would be a tragic thing, she believes. These are, after all, her good friends, and she should want what is best for them. At the same time, she is offended by Susan's infidelity and feels that John should be told. What advice would you give her?

4. A man, Tom, comes to you with the following situation. He has a lovely, intelligent, and attractive daughter, Sharon, who has been doing well in college. They have had a fairly close relationship most of their lives. In the past her boyfriends have been generally decent, attractive men, and she has almost always seemed to have good relationships with them. The break-ups were for ordinary reasons. However, now she has taken up with a married man, Larry. He has seen the man in question and thinks very little of him. He has expressed his disdain for the entire situation to his daughter who has resisted his arguments and pleas. He wants to contact the husband's wife to inform her of the situation, but he knows that his daughter will view this as strong interference in her personal life. He realizes that as a result of this action he may cause estrangement between him and his daughter, and he dreads the thought of that outcome. At the same time, he does not want to see his daughter get caught up in what he sees as a self-destructive relationship. What should he do?

5. Cicero poses the following questions: May a person of moral quality who is starving to death take food from a person who is of no account? May an honest man, freezing to death, steal the clothes of a vicious man? Cicero argues that in principle it is immoral to rob even a completely useless person merely for one's personal advantage. But if the starving man's qualities are such that, should he survive, he will render great service to humankind, then there is nothing blameworthy in taking the food for that reason. Do you agree with Cicero?

6. The ancient Roman Stoics also debated about real estate. Should an honest man, when selling a house, reveal to the buyer that the house is not really as good as it looks? Antipater argued that he should. Diogenes argued that as long as the owner does not claim that the house is perfect, he has no obligation to reveal its specific faults. Cicero sides with Antipater. He supports his position by stating that concealment depends not merely on keeping silence but also on the desire to keep interested parties ignorant so as to profit by their ignorance. With whom do you side?

7. Charles Loring Brace, founder of the Children's Aid Society of New York, started what came to be known as "Orphan Trains" in the 1850s. The trains ran until 1929, when the practice was stopped. Brace's idea was to save children from the squalor of life in New York City, where they often had to beg for food or live in overcrowded orphanages. He hoped to send them out to a wholesome life on farms out in the midwest. The trains, loaded with children, would stop at various towns; the children would line up, and some would be selected by local families. In some cases the children were treated kindly, in others they were no more than indentured servants, and in some cases they were sent back to New York City after living with the families for a few months. Do you think Brace did the right thing?

SUGGESTED READINGS

On the Nature of Wisdom and Practical Reasoning

Ackrill, J.L. 1973. *Aristotle's Ethics.* New York: Humanities Press.

Aquinas, Thomas. *Summa Theologica.* First Part, Questions 57–61. New York: Benzinger Brothers, 1947.

Aristotle. *Nicomachean Ethics. Book VI. The Basic Works of Aristotle.* Edited by R. McKeon. New York: Random House, 1941.

Blackburn, Simon. 1999. *Ruling Passions: A Theory of Practical Reasoning.* Oxford, England: Oxford University Press.

Bradley, G.H. 1962. *Ethical Studies.* Oxford, England: Oxford University Press.

Charvet, John. 1995. *The Idea of an Ethical Community.* Ithaca, NY: Cornell University Press.

Cicero. 1974. *On Duties.* Translated by H. Edinger. Indianapolis, IN: Bobbs-Merrill.

Confucius. c. 350 B.C.E. *The Analects.* Translated by A.Waley. New York: Vintage, 1938.

Foot, Phillipa. 1978. *Virtues and Vices.* Berkeley: University of California Press.

Gracian, Balthasar. 1637. *The Art of Worldly Wisdom.* Boston: Shambala, 1993.

Johnson, Mark. 1993. *The Moral Imagination.* Chicago: University of Chicago Press.

Jonson, Albert, and Toulmin, Stephen. 1988. *The Abuse of Casuistry: A History of Moral Reasoning.* Berkeley: University of California Press.

Kekes, John. 1992. *The Examined Life.* University Park: Penn State University Press.

———. 1997. *Moral Wisdom and Good Lives.* Ithaca, NY: Cornell University Press.

Kidder, Rushworth. 1995. *How Good People Make Tough Choices.* New York: William Morrow.

Kirk, Kenneth. 1927. *Conscience and Its Problems: An Introduction to Casuistry.* London: Longman's Green.

Machiavelli, N. 1513. *The Prince.* New York: Modern Library, 1950.

MacIntyre, Alasdair. 1981. *After Virtue.* Notre Dame, IN: University of Notre Dame Press.

Meilander, Gilbert. 1984. *The Theory and Practice of Virtue.* Notre Dame, IN: University of Notre Dame Press.

Miller, Richard. 1996. *Casuistry and Modern Ethics.* Chicago: University of Chicago Press.

Milo, Ronald. 1966. *Aristotle on Practical Knowledge and Weakness of Will.* The Hague, the Netherlands: Mouton.

Nussbaum, Martha. 1990. *Love's Knowledge.* Oxford, England: Oxford University Press.

O'Neill, Onora. 1996. *Towards Justice and Virtue: A Constructive Account of Practical Reasoning.* Cambridge, England: Cambridge University Press.

Pieper, Josef. 1966. *The Four Cardinal Virtues.* Notre Dame, IN: University of Notre Dame Press.

Richardson, Henry. 1994. *Practical Reasoning about Final Ends.* Cambridge, England: Cambridge University Press.

Rorty, A., Editor. 1980. *Essays on Aristotle's Ethics.* Berkeley: University of California Press.

Sun Tzu. *The Art of War.* Translated by Samuel Griffith. Oxford, England: Oxford University Press, 1984.

Veatch, Henry. 1962. *Rational Man.* Bloomington: Indiana University Press.

Von Wright, Georg. 1963. *The Varieties of Goodness.* London: Routledge and Kegan Paul.
———. 1979. *Practical Reason.* Ithaca, NY: Cornell University Press.
Williams, Bernard. 1981. *Moral Luck.* Cambridge, England: Cambridge University Press.
———. 1985. *Ethics and the Limits of Philosophy.* Cambridge, MA: Harvard University Press.

On the Psychology of Wisdom

Baltes, P., Smith, J., Staudinger, U., Sowarka, D. 1991. Wisdom: One Face of Successful Aging? *Late-Life Potential.* Edited by M. Perlmutter. Washington DC: Gerontological Society of America.
Baltes, P., and Smith, J. 1991. Toward A Psychology of Wisdom and Its Ontogenesis. *Wisdom: Its Nature, Origins and Development.* Edited by R. Sternberg. Cambridge, England: Cambridge University Press.
Clayton, V., and Birren, J.W. 1980. *The Development of Wisdom across the Life-Span. Life-Span Development and Behavior.* Edited by P. Baltes et al. Vol. 3. New York: Academic Press.
Csikszentmihalyi, M., and Rathunde, K. 1992. The Psychology of Wisdom: An Evolutionary Interpretation. *Wisdom: Its Nature, Origins and Development.* Edited by R. Sternberg. Cambridge, England: Cambridge University Press.
Holliday, S., and Chandler, M. 1986. *Wisdom: Explorations in Adult Competence.* Basel, Switzerland: Karger.
———. 1991. Wisdom as Integrated Thought. *Wisdom: Its Nature, Origins and Development.* Edited by R. Sternberg. Cambridge, England: Cambridge University Press.
Kitchener, K., King, P., Wood, P., and Davidson, M. 1989. Consistency and Sequentiality in the Development of Reflective Judgment: A Six Year Longitudinal Study. *Journal of Applied Developmental Psychology* 10: 73–95.
Kitchener, K., and Brenner, H. 1991. Wisdom and Reflective Judgment. *Wisdom: Its Nature, Origins and Development.* Edited by R. Sternberg. Cambridge, England: Cambridge University Press.
Labouvie-Vief, G. 1982. Dynamic Development and Mature Autonomy. *Human Development* 25: 161–191.
Meacham, John. 1991. The Loss of Wisdom. *Wisdom: Its Nature, Origins and Development.* Edited by R. Sternberg. Cambridge, England: Cambridge University Press.
Orwoll, L., and Perlmutter, M. 1991. The Study of Wise Persons: Integrating a Personality Perspective. *Wisdom: Its Nature, Origins and Development.* Edited by R. Sternberg. Cambridge, England: Cambridge University Press.
Perry, W.I. 1970. *Forms of Intellectual and Ethical Development in College Years.* New York: Holt, Rinehart and Winston.
Sowarka, D. 1987. Wisdom in the Context of Persons, Situations and Acts. Common Sense Views of Elderly Women and Men. Unpublished manuscript. Federal Republic of Germany: Max Planck Institute for Human Development and Education.
Sternberg, R. 1985. Implicit Theories of Intelligence, Creativity and Wisdom. *Journal of Personality and Social Psychology* 49(3): 607–627.

On the Notion of Practical Reason

Beck, Lewis White. 1960. *A Commentary on Kant's Critique of Practical Reason.* Chicago: University of Chicago Press.
Brandt, R.B. 1979. *The Right and the Good.* Oxford, England: Oxford University Press.
Habermas, Jurgen. 1993. *Justification and Application.* Translated by C. Crioin. Cambridge, MA: MIT Press.
Kant, Immanuel. 1785. *Foundations of the Metaphysics of Morals.* New York: Bobbs-Merrill, 1959.
———. 1788. *Critique of Practical Reason.* New York: Bobbs-Merrill, 1956.
Williams, Bernard. 1985. *Ethics and the Limits of Philosophy.* Cambridge, MA: Harvard University Press.

CHAPTER FIVE

Moral Knowledge

One who loves humanity but not learning will be obscured by ignorance. One who loves wisdom but not learning will be obscured by lack of principle. One who loves faithfulness but not learning will be obscured by heartlessness. One who loves uprightness but not learning will be obscured by violence. One who loves strength of character but not learning will be obscured by recklessness.

—Confucius

Man's dignity rises from his ability to reason and thus to choose freely the good in preference to evil.

—Walter Lippmann

Our moral sentiments motivate us to do the good. Moral strength is the power to do what is right. Virtues create dispositions toward the good. Wisdom provides us a vision of the good and shows us how to accomplish it. Moral knowledge gives us *assurance* of *what* is right and wrong. It does so by providing us with general rules and principles of moral conduct—algorithms of wisdom. Moral knowledge can assure us that murder is wrong or that, if we follow a certain principle correctly, it would help us do the right thing. When moral principles are justified, they give us a *warrant* to criticize, encourage, constrain, prevent, and facilitate the behavior of ourselves and others. As such, they can serve as aids to deliberation; however, they are unlikely to substitute for wisdom completely. Rules and principles are general by their very nature; moral actions and choices are particular and must be made in consideration of the nuance and subtlety of a complex situation. Following rules mechanically makes for moral idiocy.

Moral knowledge is acquired over time through learning, study, and reflection. We need something else to rely on in the meantime. Moral intuitions usually play this role. *Moral intuitions are our unreflective, initial, and usually enculturated sense of what is right or wrong.* We feel that murder, incest, or child abuse is horribly wrong; yet we may not have articulated to ourselves why it is wrong other than our strong feeling that it is. Moral intuitions are enculturated by family, religion, and civic institutions. If intuitions are firmly inculcated, they provide for strong and decisive moral action and direction. But that is also precisely their danger because intuitions without justification may lead us to choose the wrong things. Great harm can result from false intuitions that are nonetheless acted upon in an assured way. The danger of moral knowledge, on the other hand, is that by opening intuitions to criticism, people may lose their moral compass and decisive character. However, should it prove successful, moral knowledge can provide security for our moral beliefs.

It must be kept in mind that no matter how important moral knowledge is, character and wisdom are also needed to retain moral competence. Moral knowledge alone is not sufficient to generate consistently moral behavior. Some psychological studies seem to bear this out. Krebs (1968) argued that although intellectual ability and cognitive development are necessary for good decisions, they are not sufficient for higher moral development. In addition, James Rest's work seems to suggest that there is not much correlation between moral character and higher levels of moral reasoning (1979). Indeed, IQ and intellectual ability are not very good predictors of life success, generally speaking, including moral and emotional competence (cf. Vaillant 1977; Felsman and Vaillant 1987; Sternberg 1985; Gardner 1993; Block 1995).

5.1 MORAL INTUITION

However we may come to moral knowledge, we start with our basic moral intuitions—fundamental convictions acquired since childhood that certain things are right or wrong. Robert Fulghum (1986) does an entertaining job of making some of these explicit: play fair, tell the truth, don't fight, clean up after yourself, take turns, don't blame others for what you've done, share. Some thinkers have suggested we have a special ability or "faculty" to sense right or wrong. This position was especially popular among a group of 18th-century British moralists. Anthony Shaftesbury (1711), Francis Hutcheson (1725), Joseph Butler (1726), and Thomas Reid (1788) all argued for something like a moral instinct or moral sense. Reid perhaps says it best: "the abstract notion of moral good and ill would be of no use to direct our life, if we had not the power of applying it to particular actions, and determining what is morally good, and what is morally ill. Some philosophers, with whom I agree, ascribe this to an original power or faculty in man, which they call the *Moral Sense*, the *Moral Faculty, Conscience.* … " (1788: III. Pt. III, Chap. 6). Shaftesbury, who is thought to be the original thinker in this regard, believed that such a sense was innate or instinctive (1711: II, 135). Yet he also seemed to think that this sense was corruptible, so that people could fall away from their natural ability to discern right from wrong.

The flaws with this approach are obvious. Given that we have different or corrupted intuitions, how are we to discern the right ones from the wrong if our moral sense is the only means of doing so? Moreover, if we have such an innate ability, then why are there differing intuitions and why do intuitions seem to change over time? Our cognitions are not infallible and our perceptions are not infallible, so why should any other faculty or sense we have be infallible? There is certainly sufficient evidence to suggest that we have a capacity for internalization and acquiring moral emotions and sentiments. The fact that everyone, other things being equal, is able to acquire some moral emotion, such as guilt or shame, does not also infer that every person will feel guilt or shame over the same things. Intuitions are inculcated by parents, teachers, peers, and religious and civic leaders. They reflect the ethos of the culture, the general set of beliefs and norms concerning proper moral behavior; they are often summary expressions of what is considered virtuous behavior. Just like the virtues, they can vary from culture to culture so that a warrior society might emphasize certain rules or virtues over others or a particular culture may see its intuitions change slowly over time. Although there may be relatively common intuitions among cultures—prohibitions against incest, dishonesty, murder of kin, and the like—the commonality may not be due to an innate capacity but simply to the fact that incest avoidance, promise keeping, and the like are essential for a flourishing society.

There are two competing views concerning the acquisition of intuitive moral intuitions. The first, which is the received view, argues that such rules are acquired typically through cultural transmission, that is, through direct tutoring or instruction by authority figures such as parents, teachers, clergy, and so on (cf. Whiting 1967). The second, called the *self-construction view,* argues that children develop standards through a rational or cognitive construction based on interpersonal interactions that allow them to notice the inherently harmful consequences of moral transgressions (Turiel 1983). There are, of course, intermediate positions, such as that expressed by Carolyn Edwards (1987). She argues that transmission and self-construction are complementary and coexistent processes; that is, children do not construct moral standards for themselves independently of cultural assistance but neither do they passively receive such standards from authorities. Rather, with increasing age and experience, children apply progressively more complex and logical analysis to cultural distinctions and categories; they transform what they are told and what they experience into their own self-organized realities.

Both the self-construction and the transmission theories assume that children adopt moral rules and standards on the model of learning behavior. In the case of the latter, it is a matter of the transmission of information; in the case of the former, it is a question of inference and observation. However, as Jerome Kagan (1987: xii) points out, the motivations for the acquisition of these standards and rules are more complex and may involve several noncognitive determinants: (1) a desire to retain a close emotional tie with authority figures, (2) a desire to avoid adult disapproval, and (3) an identification with another. Indeed, rather than tutoring being understood as the passive acquisition of information, it is more accurate to view learning as the acquisition of a pertinent exemplar. Instead of authority figures telling children what the rules of honesty are, children have an easier time assimilating real-life or story examples of honesty. A morally suitable role model may be didactically more effective than a set of behavioral maxims. Ordinary moral thinking may consist more in comparing contemplated actions with stored exemplars of good and bad behavior than with the formulation and deduction of consequences from abstract principles.

5.1.1 The Conflict between Moral Intuition and Moral Knowledge

Moral beliefs grounded in moral intuitions are acquired differently than those acquired from moral knowledge. Suppose you were asked your opinion about a very divisive issue, such as abortion. Most likely you would take one side or the other based on what you intuitively feel about the question. But if you were pressed further for reasons, justifications, and the like, soon you would be reaching for relatively formulated rules or principles which represent those intuitions. So you may argue that it is wrong to kill an innocent human being, and the zygote, embryo, and fetus are human beings; or you may argue that it is wrong to violate the liberty of a woman on such basic issues as matters of reproduction. But in both cases, you are now relying on moral knowledge rather than moral intuition. Moral knowledge is a more systematic and reflective acquisition of moral insight.

Some thinkers, however, believe that moral intuitions are a more reliable guide to right conduct than the reflective and systematic process typical of moral knowledge. The 20th-century economist and philosopher F.A. Hayek argued that intuitions evolve from patterns and habits of conduct which persist over time precisely because they promote collective goods (Sowell 1987: 51). For him moral intuitions are adaptations to past experience which have grown up by selective elimination of less suitable conduct. They are as much an indispensable foundation of successful action as is our conscious knowledge. We don't rationally choose the behavior, but the competition of institutions and societies leads to a general survival of the most effective collection of cultural traits. "Man has certainly more often learnt to do the right thing without comprehending why it was the right thing, and he is still better served by custom than understanding." There is "more intelligence incorporated in the system of rules of conduct than in men's thoughts about his surroundings" (Hayek 1960: 26). Individual reflection on these norms does little to benefit the system and may in fact harm it to some extent. Moral wisdom is most likely found in the collective evolution of norms through its actual governance of human affairs, rather than through any reflective process that might advance it. Similarly, laws, rules, and principles ought to follow tradition rather than leadership by highly reflective individuals or some elite intelligentsia. "The life of the law," according to Oliver Wendell Holmes, "has not been logic; it has been experience." Judgments express "an intuition of experience which outruns analysis and serves up many tangled impressions, impressions which may lie beneath consciousness without losing their worth." According to Holmes, "The development of our law has gone on for nearly a thousand years, like the development of a planet, each generation taking the next step ... obeying a law of spontaneous growth" (1952: 26).

This traditionalist, evolutionary account argues that intuitions are the product of wiser forces than either individuals or groups; they are the result of the interaction of forces in the institutions and practices out of which they emerge. The most dangerous stages in the growth of civilization, according to Hayek, are precisely when people come to regard all the traditional beliefs as superstitions and refuse to accept or to submit to anything which they do not rationally understand (1979: 162–163). In general, the historic and systemic wisdom expressed inarticulately in moral intuitions of the culture is more likely to be correct than the special insights of the few.

The opposite view is usually associated with Enlightenment-inspired thinking. Under this view, tradition is thought to be a source of prejudices and bias which must be overcome if there is to be genuine moral progress. True moral knowledge must begin with a foundation that is agreeable to reason, rather than historically based in custom. Progress has been made precisely through the few who, armed with great moral insight, have progressed humanity to higher levels of moral life. William Godwin (1756–1836), an 18th-century philosopher, argued that virtue is promoted when persons can "avow their actions, and assign it reasons upon which they are founded." If we could only make ultimate principles of morality and justice clear to each person, "we may expect the whole species to become reasonable and virtuous" (1793: I, 66).

The traditionalist view suggests that the individual's best contribution to the collective good is to adhere to the special duties of his institutional role and let the systemic processes determine outcomes. Yet it seems that history has shown that great, important, and sweeping changes in history—changes which have led to moral improvement—have come from individuals who step outside of their traditional roles and who develop systems of thought that are exactly contrary to the ones in which they are steeped. The traditionalist account of change makes it a passive affair. The Enlightenment account, though it cannot seriously sweep aside all intuitions, allows an element of reflection that seems essential to the possibility of change. A more reasonable position, then, is to suggest that intuitions and knowledge are both present in individuals and that any person's moral growth is a process of the reasonable and reflective use of both. Intuitions form the stable basis of our moral convictions but are subject to revision as we encounter their criticism and elaboration. At the same time any process of moral knowledge cannot begin in a vacuum, or absent some tradition, but must be based to some extent on these intuitions. Intuitions are the means by which we may initially test and revise any moral knowledge we propose. Revision of intuitions in light of knowledge and a test of knowledge in light of intuitions are the more ordinary processes by which moral thinking progresses.

5.2 STAGES OF MORAL KNOWLEDGE

Acquiring moral knowledge usually involves various steps or stages. The first step is to clarify our basic intuitions. Reflection and analysis can help us make explicit the moral rules that may be underlying them. Once we understand the rules that underlie our moral intuitions, we can then attempt to systematize them into a coherent body of thought. Finally, reasoning provides the means by which we can justify the various rules and principles that operate in our lives. For this reason, moral knowledge can be said to consist in at least three stages: *clarification*, *systematization*, and *justification* (see figure). Reflection, analysis, and reasoning can help us organize our moral beliefs systematically and enable us to develop a set of relatively justified rules that can be used to guide our behavior—a code that we can live by. A simple way of expressing the differences among the purposes of each stage is to suggest that the first is engaged in articulating the various moral rules which form the basis for a moral code, whereas the stage of systematization is concerned with developing and expressing that moral code, while the stage of justification functions to *validate* that code.

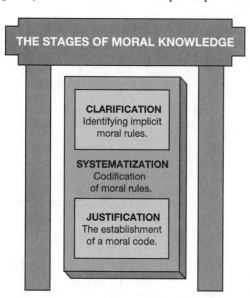

THE STAGES OF MORAL KNOWLEDGE

CLARIFICATION
Identifying implicit
moral rules.

SYSTEMATIZATION
Codification
of moral rules.

JUSTIFICATION
The establishment
of a moral code.

5.2.1 The Stage of Clarification

In the first stage of moral knowledge, we are concerned with the organization, expression, and clarification of our basic intuitions. Certainly, before we can evaluate and justify what we believe, we must know what it is we do believe. "Values clarification" (cf. Raths et al. 1966) has been maligned lately by a number of ethics educators (cf. Kilpatrick 1992; Lickona 1991). Their general complaint is that values clarification doesn't teach values, but promotes whatever values a person does in fact have. It leaves a person with the impression that beliefs are justified by the mere fact that a person holds them. This confuses the question of what one's values are with the question of whether they are worth holding. Certainly, if moral knowledge consisted only in clarification of one's moral beliefs and values, then it would be lacking as a source of moral justification and standards. Simply to affirm what you believe is no justification for that belief. Also, if part of the pedagogy of values clarification is to promote the idea that all moral rules and beliefs are equally valid, then it can be argued that this is a serious mistake. This promotes an especially bad form of relativism, a topic we'll take up shortly. It can be argued that, although a variety of moral beliefs may be healthy for a culture, since it promotes growth and correction for a culture, and although it may be healthy for a culture to be tolerant of opposing moral beliefs, still where there is the possibility of serious conflict among opposing beliefs, recourse to discourses that weigh standards for proper moral conduct must be available to avoid violence. Such discourses require relatively objective, or at least intersubjective, standards of procedure and evidence. It is not enough to have a moral value or rule; it must also be defended and justified.

However, despite some of the legitimacy of these complaints, if values clarification is viewed as one among several interconnected stages of moral knowledge, then its necessity is obvious. This is an important part of justifying one's moral code. At the stage of clarification, people seek an understanding of the basic rules that implicitly guide their decisions about what is right or wrong. This may involve a balancing process that goes back and forth between moral intuitions and rules until there is a match. The test of this would be whether or not the strict following of the rules yields those intuitions in each case.

For example, recall the discussion of sexual continence in Section 3.3.7. The aim of the virtue was to determine the who, how, what, when, and why of sexual practices. To formulate a rule concerning such practices, you could first begin with a list of all known sexual practices and your moral intuition regarding each of these practices. Consider the following:

> heterosexual intercourse, masturbation, sodomy, fellatio, cunnilingus, premarital sex, adultery, homosexuality, troilism, orgyism, sadomasochism, incest, fetishism, voyeurism, necrophilia, pedophilia, exhibitionism

You may intuitively label some of these moral practices repugnant, others tolerable, and some permissible. The goal of clarification is to show that this intuitive division between the repugnant and the permissible follows from a certain rule, which would then be part of an implicit moral code you may have about sexual behavior. One rule might be "only heterosexual sex with a married partner, exclusively for the purposes of procreation" is permitted. That would exclude every sort of sexual act except vaginal intercourse in the context of procreation. Consider a different rule: "Anything between consenting, competent adults is permissible." That rule would exclude pedophilia, incest, adultery (assuming it is secretive and without approval of the other spouse), but would permit premarital

Antioch College's Sexual Offense Policy

According to this policy, "all sexual contact and conduct on the Antioch College campus and/or occurring with an Antioch community member must be consensual." Consent is defined as "the act of willingly and verbally agreeing to engage in specific sexual contact or conduct." The following is a summary of the rules for sexual conduct:

1. If sexual contact is not mutually initiated, then the person who initiates it must get the verbal consent of the other individual(s) involved.
2. Obtaining consent is an on-going process that must be obtained at each new level of physical or sexual contact.
3. The person with whom sexual contact is initiated is responsible for expressing verbally his or her consent or lack of consent.
4. If someone has initially consented but stops consenting, then the other individual(s) must stop immediately.
5. To knowingly take advantage of someone who is under the influence of alcohol, drugs, and/or prescribed medication is not acceptable behavior.

This policy seems to adhere to the rule that any sort of sex between consenting adults is permissible, with a strong emphasis on the "consent." *What do you think of this rule? What do you think of Antioch's policy? Why would trying to get an intoxicated person's consent violate this rule?*

sex, homosexuality, sadomasochism, and so forth as long as it was between consenting adults. Finally, consider a third rule: "A person is permitted to engage in any sexual practice with anybody for the purpose of getting pleasure of some sort from it." This, of course, would permit just about anything on the list. In general, the rule is an accurate expression of your intuitions to the extent that, if mechanically followed, it would make the same sorts of divisions between the morally permissible and impermissible that your intuitions did. However, there might be some need for adjustment to make the match perfect. For example, the "consenting, competent adult" rule would make incest among adults permissible. If that is an intolerable intuition, then one must either adjust the rule so that it excludes the possibility or forgo the intuition to maintain consistency.

5.2.2 The Stage of Systematization

Systemization is concerned with articulating a consistent and coherent code that pertains to the various compartments of moral life—ethics concerning sexuality, marriage, raising children, the environment, business, profession, capital punishment, abortion, euthanasia, and so on. For example, a person might be against abortion because she believes that it is wrong to kill human beings (in which case you also assume that the fetus is a human being), but she is not against war in principle nor is she against capital punishment. In that case the rule "it is wrong to kill human beings" must either be qualified or changed to address apparent inconsistencies. One might qualify the rule by saying that "it is wrong to kill innocent human life," "it is permissible to kill in the case of self-defense," or some other formulation.

The process of moving back and forth between one's moral intuitions and the rules in a manner that achieves a general concordance between them is called *reflective equilibrium* by John Rawls and others (Rawls 1971: 20, 48–50; Daniels 1979; Nielsen 1991). Reflective equilibrium incorporates the kind of matching discussed in the clarification stage of moral knowledge between moral intuitions and rules, but here it is concerned with this process at a much more comprehensive level. As the "reflective" aspect of reflective equilibrium implies, it is concerned to establish a general coherence and consistency among intuitions and rules. Establishing an exact concordance between intuitions and rules seems unlikely; consequently, there will always be some element of adjustment going on either in terms of the intuitions or in terms of the rules. This will be complicated by the continual addition of new cases and topics to consider as they arise in one's moral culture. To take a case in point, cloning may not have been considered before, but now that it is a real possibility, reflection on its moral character becomes morally urgent. Yet reflection may require the revision of initial intuitions. To incorporate it in a systematic way with other rules and intuitions may require some overall adjustment to the system, and a back-and-forth process is continued until a reasonable equilibrium is established between intuitions and rules. However, given the continual addition of new ethical issues, and the sorts of changes in beliefs that come with personal growth, this may turn out to be a lifelong, ongoing process. Still, with a good foundation and understanding of one's code in hand, the reflective equilibrium process becomes more manageable.

Pushing for consistency and coherence among rules usually leads to the search for some overall moral principles for the system. *Principles* can serve as a higher-order expression of those rules, which in turn express the various moral compartments of one's life. Reflective equilibrium at this level is at once easier and more difficult, and it often requires more adjustment. It is easier since the principle is a condensed expression of a set of rules, but more difficult since it is more abstract, general, and consequently, more vague. Rawls describes the process at this level in the following way:

> When a person is presented with an intuitively appealing account of his sense of justice … he may well revise his judgments to conform to its principles even though the theory does not fit his existing judgments exactly. He is especially likely to do this if he can find an explanation for the deviations which undermine his confidence in his original judgments and if the conception presented yields a judgment which he finds he can now accept. From the standpoint of moral philosophy, the best account of a person's sense of justice is not the one which fits his judgments prior to his examining any conception of justice, but rather the one which matches his judgments in reflective equilibrium. As we have seen, this state is one reached after a person has weighed various proposed conceptions and he has either revised his judgments to accord with one of them or held fast to his initial convictions. … (1971: 48).

Together the rules and principles are the expression of one's moral code. The relation between rules and principles can be clarified in the following way, although there is some disagreement about these matters (cf. Shafer-Landau 1997; Nussbaum 1990; Hare 1972; Gert 1970). Moral rules prescribe or proscribe for certain actions: You shouldn't steal, you shouldn't lie, you should help a friend in need, and so forth. Moral rules have a certain *generality* (Shafer-Landau 1997: 584); that is, they intend to cover a wide range of actions of a certain type. The *scope* of a rule is a determination of that type of action or practice. For example, in regard to direct inquiries of all sorts, one shouldn't lie. The rule applies to all cases of lying, which defines its generality and scope. Its generality has to do with discursive practices of inquiry and not property relations, and its scope pertains to all cases of direct inquiry. The scope of rules might be attenuated to various degrees, for example, "never lend money to a friend," which specifies a subtype of lending; it concerns the practice of lending, but its scope is restricted to a certain situation—lending to someone you know. There may be no proscription against lending, just against lending to a friend.

Rules also imply a certain normative *universality;* that is, "no one" should lie (cf. Gert 1970: 66; for a contrasting view see Nussbaum 1990: 68). Typically, a moral rule does not say that men should lie and women shouldn't or that everybody must tell the truth except the king. However, the universality may also be attenuated. There are moral rules that may hold only for certain types of people, for example,

American Association of University Professors
Statement on Professional Ethics

I. Professors, guided by a deep conviction of the worth and dignity of the advancement of knowledge, recognize the special responsibilities placed upon them. Their primary responsibility to their subject is to seek and to state the truth as they see it. To this end professors devote their energies to developing and improving their scholarly competence. They accept the obligation to exercise critical self-discipline and judgment in using, extending, and transmitting knowledge. They practice intellectual honesty. Although professors may follow subsidiary interests, these interests must never seriously hamper or compromise their freedom of inquiry.

II. As teachers, professors encourage the free pursuit of learning in their students. They hold before them the best scholarly and ethical standards of their discipline. Professors demonstrate respect for students as individuals and adhere to their proper roles as intellectual guides and counselors. Professors make every reasonable effort to foster honest academic conduct and to ensure that their evaluations of students reflect each student's true merit. They respect the confidential nature of the relationship between professor and student. They avoid any exploitation, harassment, or discriminatory treatment of students. They acknowledge significant academic or scholarly assistance from them. They protect their academic freedom.

III. As colleagues, professors have obligations that derive from common membership in the community of scholars. Professors do not discriminate against or harass colleagues. They respect and defend the free inquiry of associates. In the exchange of criticism and ideas professors show due respect for the opinions of others. Professors acknowledge academic debt and strive to be objective in their professional judgment of colleagues. Professors accept their share of faculty responsibilities for the governance of their institution.

IV. As members of an academic institution, professors seek above all to be effective teachers and scholars. Although professors observe the stated regulations of the institution, provided the regulations do not contravene academic freedom, they maintain their right to criticize and seek revision. Professors give due regard to their paramount responsibilities within their institution in determining the amount and character of work done outside it. When considering the interruption or termination of their service, professors recognize the effect of their decision upon the program of the institution and give due notice of their intentions.

V. As members of their community, professors have the rights and obligations of other citizens. Professors measure the urgency of these obligations in the light of their responsibilities to their subject, to their students, to their profession, and to their institution. When they speak or act as private persons they avoid creating the impression of speaking or acting for their college or university. As citizens engaged in a profession that depends upon freedom for its health and integrity, professors have a particular obligation to promote conditions of free inquiry and to further public understanding of academic freedom.

Questions for Discussion:

1. Often professional codes are lists of statements of what is expected of a professional with little reflection in terms of its underlying principles or justification. What harm do you possibly see in that?
2. What do you think a professor should do if he or she disagrees with any of these general rules?
3. Is it better for a group of experienced professionals to set standards of conduct for the profession, or should individuals reflectively develop their own codes? What would be a better arrangement and why?

"thou shall not covet thy neighbor's wife" applies, we presume, to men only. The universality of a rule tells us who or what sort of person it applies to, its scope tells us what sort of practice or situation it applies in, while the generality tells us the range of actions within a certain practice to which it applies. In other words, a rule attempts to address in a formulaic way some of the questions that arose as early as our discussion of virtue: the what, where, when, and with whom of moral conduct. A moral rule, such as "thou shalt not steal," is really saying something like the following: For all persons, in relation to matters of property, you shouldn't take what another owns. It applies to *all* persons in *every* situation of practices of a certain *type*. *Principles*, on the other hand, can be considered higher-order rules. "Thou shalt not steal" and "thou shalt not kill" are instances of rules, but to continue with the biblical reference, the golden "rule," "do unto others as you would have others do unto you," is actually a good example of a principle. Like rules, principles have the properties of being universal and general, and they have a certain scope. However, they usually exemplify these to a higher degree. Principles are usually intended to apply to everyone and to every situation in practices of all sorts. "Do unto others as you would have others do unto you" applies to stealing, killing, adultery, lying, and so on. Because of this greater generalizability, principles can serve as reasons for rules, just as rules can serve as reasons for actions. Consequently, the business of moral knowledge is in part to provide a reasonable catalogue of principles, which can then serve to justify rules, which can then serve to guide particular actions.

5.2.3 Integrity and Moral Codes

Having integrity is often associated with having a moral code, so this might be a good place to discuss this particular moral notion. One of the better definitions of *integrity* is given by contemporary theologian Stephen Carter (1996: 7):

> Integrity ... requires three steps: (1) discerning what is right and what is wrong; (2) acting on what you discern, even at personal cost; and (3) saying openly that you are acting on your understanding of right from wrong.

It can be argued that simply discerning what is right or wrong may not be sufficient for integrity; what is needed is a more comprehensive and systematic sense of right and wrong, something which a moral code can provide. In addition, there is a difference between simply adopting a code ready-made and engaging in a process of reflective equilibrium that helps to establish that code more genuinely for oneself. Most professions have moral codes. The adoption of a moral code by a professional might be simply a pledge to adopt a set of conventions which the person does not fully understand or has rightly considered. Contemporary philosopher Shelly Kagan, for example, argues that integrity is based on the possession of a coherently justifiable moral code (1989: 93). Without a well-organized code, one's behavior can be inconsistent or incongruent, even if there is some discernment of right from wrong; a code helps establish this consistency of behavior, and without such consistency, integrity seems unlikely.

The second feature of Carter's definition also seems to be essential to integrity. Part of having integrity is acting on what you believe to be right, even when that might sacrifice your advantage. As philosopher Robert Solomon notes, integrity is the will to do what one knows one ought to do (1992: 168). This is echoed by the late French novelist, Paul Bourget: "one must live the way one thinks or end up thinking the way one has lived." American revolutionary Thomas Paine insisted that integrity is a form of mental faithfulness to oneself and that infidelity in this regard consists in professing to believe what he does not believe (1794). This aspect of integrity ensures the congruence of behavior, a consistency between thought and action, which is also often emphasized in characterizations of integrity. Of course, it may be easy to have integrity if no personal sacrifice or disadvantage occurs in following one's moral code. It is only when such an act incurs risk or danger in some sense of the term that the true test of integrity is made. For this reason, Solomon calls integrity, in part, "moral courage" (1992: 168).

The third important feature of integrity is public avowal of the code upon which one acts. A person with integrity is someone who expresses such a code openly and without shame. Those who act on the basis of a secretly held code really can't be said to have integrity because without public knowledge of the code there is no way to test the congruence between code and action. An open avowal of the code also suggests that one is not ashamed to follow it and that it is worthy of espousal by others.

Assuming these conditions to be some of the more important characteristics of integrity, still there is the issue of whether integrity is sufficient for consistently moral behavior or even if the code is something that should be always admired. One obvious problem with relying on integrity as a sign of moral behavior is the fact that the code that one adheres to may be morally suspect. Certainly, many criminals have codes, and it could be argued that criminals have integrity to the extent that there is congruence in their lives between their codes and their actions. If part of a criminal code is not to rat on fellow criminals, it is still immoral behavior since it is used to protect criminal behavior which unjustly harms others. For example, there is the "Universal Code of Laws for the Almighty Black Disciple Nation," a gang to which 11-year-old Robert Sandifer belonged. He shot and killed a 14-year-old girl and wounded a 16-year-old boy on the orders of his gang in 1994, but then was executed himself by his own gang. The gang's rules include:

1. I pledge my soul, heart, love and spirit to the Black Disciple Nation and will be part of it even in death.
2. All soldiers regardless of rank or position must strive to help each other.
3. No soldier shall consume any addictive drugs.

In and of themselves, the rules seem worthwhile, although the absolute loyalty promoted by the first rule can be questionable. When it is discovered that the gang makes its money by selling drugs, then the import of rule 3 becomes clearer. It's all right to sell drugs to others, but not to take them yourself. Also there are no proscriptions against killing, obviously, since Robert was directed to kill by the leaders of the group. The practice to which the code belongs must also be morally evaluated before we can say that the code is worthy of loyalty and obedience. As Samuel Johnson notes, "Integrity without knowledge is weak and useless, and knowledge without integrity is dangerous and dreadful" (1759).

5.2.4 The Stage of Justification

Precisely because of Samuel Johnson's point, many consider *justification* the most important function of moral knowledge, since it *is concerned with providing the grounds or reasons for principles and codes*. Once moral principles have been formulated, the next step is to find some justification for the principles. In this case a certain hierarchy of justification results: Actions are justified by appeal to rules, rules are justified by appeal to principles, and principles are justified by inherent rational appeals.

As one ascends from clarification through systematization to justification, the question changes from what moral rules you have to whether your moral rules are worthy of being followed; that is, given your rules, can they be justified to yourself and others? This aspect of moral knowledge is of special interest to moral philosophers, and it is what primarily occupies much of moral thinking, particularly since Kant. Moral knowledge ultimately deals with the validity of principles. As we will see, this is a difficult task to accomplish, but one that can be reasonably attempted.

5.2.5 Kohlberg's and Gilligan's Stages of Moral Reasoning

A fair and honest evaluation of moral rules and principles requires that persons be able to distance themselves somewhat from their own conventions, traditions, and authorities. Without that possibility of impartiality, a genuine and fair evaluation

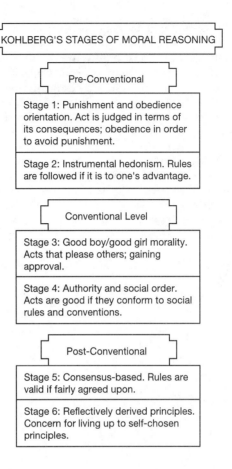

KOHLBERG'S STAGES OF MORAL REASONING

Pre-Conventional

Stage 1: Punishment and obedience orientation. Act is judged in terms of its consequences; obedience in order to avoid punishment.

Stage 2: Instrumental hedonism. Rules are followed if it is to one's advantage.

Conventional Level

Stage 3: Good boy/good girl morality. Acts that please others; gaining approval.

Stage 4: Authority and social order. Acts are good if they conform to social rules and conventions.

Post-Conventional

Stage 5: Consensus-based. Rules are valid if fairly agreed upon.

Stage 6: Reflectively derived principles. Concern for living up to self-chosen principles.

cannot take place. The stage of justification, then, requires a certain kind of moral reasoning that is often difficult to consistently practice. It requires that one attain a certain level of objectivity and impartiality. This includes the ability to abstract one-self from one's own interests, not to be biased toward one's own traditions, and to appeal to reasons rather than authority. To understand what is involved in this type of reasoning, we might contrast it with other ways of moral reasoning as catalogued by Lawrence Kohlberg (1966; 1981) and Carol Gilligan (1982).

Kohlberg argues that there are three levels of moral reasoning: *preconvention-al, conventional,* and *postconventional,* each of which is subdivided into two stages and can be summarized as follows (see figure above). At the *preconventional level,* Stage 1 is the punishment and obedience orientation; it is guided by the precept that "you do what you're told," mostly because if you don't the result is punishment and if you do the result is reward. In this stage, one is justified in an action if you can find a rule justifying it as dictated by some authority; it is based on the belief that pun-ishment inevitably follows disobedience, and anyone who is punished must have been bad. Stage 2 is justification in terms of instrumental hedonism; that is, you should act morally since it is a means of attaining certain personal goals. Thus, the precept is "an act is right if it serves your desires and interests"; the rule is good to the extent that it is successful in accomplishing certain legitimate interests, that is, if "there's something in it for me."

At the *conventional level*, Stage 3 is the stage of good-boy/good-girl orientation, that is, maintaining good relations and the approval of others. This is expressed by the precept that "if you're considerate, nice, and kind, you'll get along with people." Stage 4 is reasoning based on social authority. It is expressed by the precept that "everyone in society is obligated and protected by the law," or "the law is the law and it should be obeyed." Rules and actions are justified because they maintain social order, or rules should be obeyed out of respect for social authority.

At the *postconventional level*, Stage 5 is reasoning based on the idea of contract or agreement. This is expressed by the precept that "you are obligated by whatever arrangements are agreed to by due process procedures." Stage 6 is justification based on purely rationally conceived principles.

To illustrate these stages further, we might look at typical responses to the so-called "Heinz dilemma," which Kohlberg posed to his various subjects. In this example the subjects are given a case where a man's wife is dying of a disease. The man cannot afford the cost of the drug which will enable her to be cured, and the druggist will not lower his price. The question posed is whether the man should steal the drug. Responses pro and con corresponding to the various stages are as follows:

Stage 1: "If you let your wife die, you will get in trouble."
"You shouldn't steal the drug because you'll be caught and sent to jail if you do."

Stage 2: "It wouldn't bother you much to serve a little jail term, if you have your wife when you get out."
"He may not get much of a jail term if he steals the drug, but his wife will probably die before he gets out, so it won't do him much good."

Stage 3: "No one will think you're bad if you steal the drug, but your family will think you're an inhuman husband if you don't."
"It isn't just the druggist who will think you're a criminal, everyone else will too."

Stage 4: "If you have any sense of honor, you won't let your wife die because you're afraid to do the only thing that will save her."
"You'll always feel guilty for your dishonesty and lawbreaking."

Stage 5: "If you let your wife die, it would be out of fear, not out of reasoning it out."
"You would lose your standing and respect in the community and break the law."

Stage 6: "If you don't steal the drug, you would have lived up to the rule of the law but you wouldn't have lived up to your own standards of conscience."
"If you stole the drug, you'd condemn yourself because you wouldn't have lived up to your own conscience and standards of honesty."

The preconventional level is a level at which people are directed externally by punishment and reward; they have not quite matured into the internalization process. This is almost a premoral way of justifying or judging action. The conventional level seems to rest on moral intuition and appeals to authority; it is not entirely a reflective way of justifying and judging action. It is only at the postconventional stage that we see a genuinely reflective manner of judging and justifying. Presenting systematic reasons for positions at this stage is crucial for either persuading yourself or others.

Although Kohlberg's levels do seem to reflect familiar types of moral reasoning, there have been a number of criticisms of his work. Some have addressed the lack of cross-cultural confirmation, although some of that has been remedied of

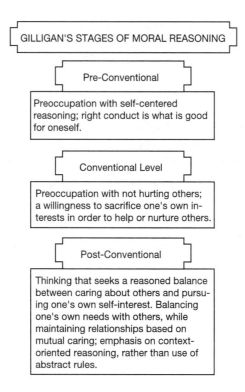

GILLIGAN'S STAGES OF MORAL REASONING

Pre-Conventional

Preoccupation with self-centered reasoning; right conduct is what is good for oneself.

Conventional Level

Preoccupation with not hurting others; a willingness to sacrifice one's own interests in order to help or nurture others.

Post-Conventional

Thinking that seeks a reasoned balance between caring about others and pursuing one's own self-interest. Balancing one's own needs with others, while maintaining relationships based on mutual caring; emphasis on context-oriented reasoning, rather than use of abstract rules.

late. Another source of criticism is its claim of gender bias. Carol Gilligan has argued that women and girls often were placed in the lower stages of moral reasoning (most often in Stage 3), when in fact they have a style of reasoning not reflected in Kohlberg's list. Gilligan argues that women are more often motivated by care or concern for disputants in moral conflicts and act to resolve the problems through mediation rather than judgment. All of the stages and the setup of problems in Kohlberg assume an attitude of judgment rather than mediation; in other words, Kohlberg assumes a rather judicial model of moral reasoning, which might not always be appropriate for certain situations or reflective of moral reasoning in general, especially among women. Martin and Schinzinger (1989) summarize Gilligan's ethic of caring in three levels analogous to Kohlberg's (see figure above).

Under this model, moral conflicts are not resolved on the basis of adjudication of rights or sorting out of duties; rather, compromises are sought which can accommodate everyone in the dispute. Philosopher Rita Manning gives a good illustration of this approach (1992: 44ff.). She gave three different variants of one of Aesop's fables to a number of students and asked them to make a resolution of the problem. This one concerned a porcupine who entreats a group of moles to share their burrow with him for the winter. In one scenario the porcupine is homeless because he was too lazy to prepare his own burrow ahead of time, and now it is too late. In a second scenario, although he had prepared a burrow, it was destroyed through no fault of his own. In a third scenario there is a stress on the fact that the porcupine will die if the moles do not admit him. On the other hand, the moles complain that if they admit the porcupine, they'll be less comfortable because the burrow will be overcrowded and the porcupine's sharp quills will jab them.

Some of the solutions are based on moral principles or rules. Those who argued that the porcupine should not be admitted based their decision on claims that, for example, laziness should be penalized and hard work rewarded or that one should respect property rights or that people should help themselves first. Those who thought the porcupine should be admitted used some of the following justifications: one should alleviate suffering, one should protect life, people should help one another, or one should help those who will be in a position to return the help someday. Those who responded from a care perspective, on the other hand, argued that one should try to construct a compromise that will allow you to accommodate everyone; there was an attempt to use their creativity and intelligence to find a way that meets the needs of all those in conflict. Rather than seeing two alternatives of either admitting or excluding the porcupine, a care-based strategy would seek a way to alter things so that the moles' discomfort is limited while still permitting the porcupine to live with them for the winter (e.g., perhaps the porcupine can help expand the burrow).

The dispute between Gilligan and Kohlberg is far from settled. Whereas a study by Norma Haan (1975) argued that the moral judgments of women differ from those of men when women's judgments are tied to feelings of empathy and compassion, a later study by Walker et al. (1984) argued that there were no statistically significant gender differences as measured within Kohlberg's moral stage framework. A more recent study by the same group (1987) found that women are more likely to choose personal over impersonal dilemmas as problems to talk about, and personal dilemmas were more likely to elicit a care response rather than a rights framework, but controlling for dilemma content, sex differences were not found to be significant.

The work of the psychologists Kitchener et al. (1989) on epistemic cognition lends support to the general character of Kohlberg's stages of moral development by showing a parallel in how people attempt to justify their beliefs. According to their developmental model, there are seven changes in epistemic assumptions that can occur in an individual:

1. Beliefs need no justification since there is an absolute correspondence between what is believed and what is true.

2. Beliefs are unjustified, unexamined, or justified via authority. Subjects assume there is a right answer to most issues.

3. In areas in which answers exist, beliefs are justified via authorities. In areas in which answers do not exist, there is no rational way to justify beliefs. Beliefs are justified strictly intuitively.

4. Beliefs are justified by giving idiosyncratic reasons (e.g., choosing evidence that fits the beliefs). Decisions appear as partially reasoned and somewhat arbitrary.

5. Beliefs are justified within a particular context via the rules of inquiry for that context. Justifications are assumed to be context specific; thus, choosing between competing interpretations is often difficult and resisted.

6. Beliefs are justified by comparing evidence and opinion on different sides of an issue or across contexts and then constructing solutions that are evaluated by personal criteria (e.g., by values or the pragmatic need for action).

7. Beliefs are justified probabilistically via evidence and argument using generalizable criteria (e.g., which argument offers the most complete or compelling understanding of an issue).

Combining the features of Kohlberg's and Gilligan's postconventional level of reasoning and Kitchener's higher stages of epistemic cognition, it is possible to give a more specific characterization to the type of moral reasoning needed at the level of justification. The kind of reasoning at this stage assumes some internalization so that justification of principles is not based purely in terms of personal reward and punishment. Second, there is an attempt to justify moral principles without regard to self-interest and personal benefit. There is an avoidance of popular appeal or social approval; there is a capability of looking beyond existing law for the approval or disapproval of a principle. At this level there is an attempt to justify the principle in terms of its objective rational merit rather than its conventional or authoritative approval; indeed, the claim shared by Kohlberg, his predecessor, Piaget, and others is that the capacity for moral reflection bears a general relation to an individual's capacity for abstract and complex reasoning (Evans 1982).

5.2.6 Subjectivism, Dichotomous Thinking, Relativism, and Other Roadblocks to Inquiry

Kohlberg's stages of moral reasoning or judgment show the level of maturity needed in a person to begin genuine inquiry into the underpinnings of their norms and behaviors. Those who reason at the preconventional level are constrained by a kind of thinking that wants to know the punishments and rewards involved in the behavior and "what's in it for me." A person thinking at the conventional level has a tendency to believe that whatever their culture, conventions, or laws say is in fact right, if not something natural and obvious. It is only in postconventional thinking that people attempt to step outside of their own personal interests, the external rewards or punishments for acting in a certain way, and the biases of their own conventions to seek a genuine justification for ethical behavior. In other words, people at the postconventional stage are prepared for genuine moral inquiry.

However, regardless of the sort of reasoning stage people find themselves in, there are certain kinds of beliefs and attitudes which act as roadblocks to inquiry. In conversation or debate with others about ethical matters, we often come across these kinds of remarks: "Well, I don't know about that, but that's your opinion, and this is mine—everyone's entitled to their opinion." Or you might hear: "You can't prove that for sure; there's no way to prove that that's right." You might also hear people say: "It's all relative; one group believes this, another believes that—there doesn't seem to be any truth in ethics." The attitude expressed by the first position is called subjectivism; the second is a case of dichotomous ("black or white") thinking; and the third is often called relativism.

Subjectivism is the belief that all ethical judgments are simply personal opinions that can't be based in fact or in truth. It is comparable to a claim that a belief is justified merely by the fact that a person holds it. An opinion is just what people happen to believe in, and since there's no way to adjudicate between these opinions, then there's really no sense in arguing about them. It's simply how people feel. It is rather like a question of taste, so that the old Latin proverb, *de gustibus non est disputandum* (of taste there is no dispute) also holds for ethical debate.

But when persons say, "It's all a matter of opinions, and there are as many opinions as there are people" or "Who's to say what is right?" what these really imply is an unwillingness to defend or justify their own opinion or to place their opinions under scrutiny. By giving you the right of your opinion, such a person feels free to advocate his or her own opinion without interference from you. Since it's all opinion, you're entitled to yours and I'm entitled to mine, and we don't have to bother with defending them because there's no way to settle opinion anyway. Since there's no way to justify a belief, then that person doesn't have to worry about defending her beliefs. But by labeling beliefs as "mere" opinion, such a position implies that anyone's belief is as good as another. Although this is very democratically generous, it disallows the possibility that some beliefs or opinions may be more worthy or credible than others. Surely one would not want to put Hitler's beliefs and Mother Teresa's beliefs on the same moral footing or the opinions of someone who has carefully studied a matter over years with someone who has no knowledge of it whatsoever. This attitude short-circuits any genuine effort to enter into serious conversation and dialogue about moral issues and matters and is a way to allow people the security of their beliefs without the responsibility of their defense.

In many respects subjectivism is understandable in the case where people have a great deal of life investment in their beliefs. What they believe may help them deal with the difficulties of life, or they may have sacrificed certain things for their beliefs, and there may be a great deal of investment in them. Threats to these beliefs in the form of questioning, criticism, and evidence may create anxiety, especially among those who are not adept at articulating and defending their beliefs. But unless one hopes to remain cloistered and has the energy and purpose to continually set up such defenses around those beliefs, they will inevitably be subject to criticism and review, and it may even be from the believer himself as he matures or encounters different beliefs. Yet without recourse to discourse, there are few alternatives to violence or force to resolve issues. It would be ideal, of course, if all opinions were tolerable or did not conflict, but neither is the case in the real world. By encouraging dialogue and treating reason-giving discourse seriously, there are fewer roads to force.

Dichotomous thinking also leads to resignation concerning ethical debate. *A dichotomous thinker thinks in terms of absolutes: Either a claim is absolutely true or absolutely false.* If it can't be proven absolutely, then it's not worthy of consideration. But this is making unrealistic demands and setting high expectations for what can be proven or justified ethically. Such demands and expectations are bound to be disappointed, and the result can contribute to a cynicism about the resolution of ethical issues and problems. Such cynicism and doubt discourage inquiry. Even our best model of knowledge, science, cannot prove things absolutely. Science works with a method that can give us confidence in the credibility of certain hypotheses, but it is hardly able to assure us that something is true once and for all. What we see in the history of science is a struggle for better hypotheses and theories. Science is not satisfied with what it has and continues to improve. It is better at showing why a hypothesis or theory is no longer credible than why one is true. What good, mature scientists know is that hypotheses are tentative claims that may undergo qualification or refutation in the future. Yet most scientists are not skeptical or cynical about the methodology of science precisely because they can see success and improvement. Scientists go with best knowledge and information, not with absolute truth. The methodology of science allows them to select the best among a number of plausible hypotheses, but it does not allow them to determine which ones are absolutely true. We should not expect anything better in the arena of ethical inquiry. From a superficial point of view, the history of ethics looks like a continual change of opinion, but a deeper understanding of that process can discern a great deal of improvement in our understanding of ethical life. Just as in science, ethical agents must go with their best knowledge and information, realizing full well that it is by no means perfect or complete. Reasons and arguments given for why murder is wrong can be shown to outweigh those that claim it is right and, although "murder is wrong" cannot be proven absolutely or without qualification, there can be enough confidence in its credibility to warrant following it as a maxim. A dichotomous thinker is also less tolerant of gray areas in moral judgments and decisions. A dichotomous thinker may believe that lying is absolutely wrong, and that's the end of the story. However, as most mature ethical thinkers know, ethics is replete with ambiguities and nuances, and it is a wise person who can discern the differences between cases without compromising the integrity of his ethical principles.

The third roadblock to inquiry is a position commonly referred to as *relativism*. Not only do many people feel that ethics is mostly a matter of opinion, but also that all moral beliefs are relative to a culture, a group, a historical period, or individuals. *Relativism generally argues that the justification for a moral belief is a matter of convention; that is, what is right is what is held to be right by most if not all of the culture in which one lives.* There are thought to be three types of relativism: *empirical, cultural,* and *normative* relativism (cf. Taylor 1975). Empirical relativism suggests that because, as a matter of empirical fact, there are no universally held norms, then there are no universal justifications for moral beliefs that we can appeal to. Cultural relativism argues that the ultimate justification for a belief lies in the ethical conventions of a culture. Finally, normative relativism suggests that because cultures differ in their ethical codes, no standard of objective adjudication can be appealed to in cases where they conflict.

Empirical relativism is a common position. The Latin poet Ovid said, "there is nothing in which the world is so varied as in customs and laws. A given thing is abominable here, which brings commendation elsewhere." The 16th-century philosopher and essayist Michel de Montaigne thought that "the murder of infants, the murder of fathers, sharing of wives, traffic in robberies, license for all sorts of sensual pleasures, nothing in short is so extreme that it is not accepted by the usage of some nation" (1572–1588). This is also a view promoted by many anthropologists; Ruth Benedict claimed that "morality differs in every society, and is a convenient term for socially approved habits" (1954).

One wonders how true this claim actually is and how strictly this claim must be held. For example, if we could find rules common enough, although not universal, would that be sufficient to disprove this claim? Is it also possible that some variations in a rule or code might still qualify something as commonly held? For example, take the case of incest; if Ovid and Montaigne are correct, then there should be cultures which permit incest; still there is enough evidence to suggest that incest prohibition is common enough and that many of the examples of incest may often be understandable qualifications (cf. Shepher 1980). Incest may be qualified because of certain conventional characterizations of kinship relations. To take a case in point, in many matrilineal cultures (where descent is through the mother), the uncle (mother's brother) and nephew relation is very important. In addition, as in the ancient Tlingit culture, an ideal marriage was between the uncle's daughter and his nephew. This, of course, in most modern Western kinship systems is a first-cousin marriage and treated as an incestuous union. Still within Tlingit culture any marriage or sexual relations between siblings or parents' offspring were strictly forbidden. Other cases that are often suggested as counterexamples to incest prohibitions often turn out to be exceptions or qualifications. Incest among ancient Egyptian royalty was common, but even then, this was only allowable between siblings, although not with the youngest sister. This was prohibited for all other Egyptians were prohibited; the justification for the exception was that since the Egyptian royalty were divine, they were exempted from human laws. In any case incest prohibitions are present enough in all cultures to warrant a claim to their commonality. To use an analogy, there are a few exceptions to head gestures for yes and no; most cultures signal yes with an up and down shake of the head and not by left to right. Should we disregard the commonality of such a gesture because there are some exceptions?

There are good reasons to suggest that most cultures would hold certain common proscriptions against incest, murder of kin, lying, and theft. Without such proscriptions the fabric of a culture would be very thin indeed. Because the preservation of a society depends on such normative practices, one would imagine that such norms are fairly common. How could a society thrive if it did not in some way value its young? Even though infanticide may be practiced in some cultures, still the care and protection of the young seem to be a very common norm. Without a propensity for truth telling, communication would break down; consequently, honesty also has to be a fairly common norm. As philosopher James Rachels argues, "there are some moral rules that all societies will have in common, because those rules are necessary for society to exist" (1986).

Cultural relativism is another matter. Its argument is something like the following: The justification for a norm lies in its predominant practice in the culture. This suggests that because most in a particular culture practice something, then that is what justifies the practice. But if one thinks this through, the argument may be a very weak one. It would suggest, for one thing, that normative change is unlikely or that normative change is in some sense arbitrary. In pre-Civil War America slavery was a common practice, but in post-Civil War America it was not; the change that occurred was, of course, a violent one, but it was motivated in part by moral arguments, many of which were accepted initially only by a minority. Hardly anyone today advocates slavery; the change was not like simply switching a light on or off, but involved strong public debate and ultimately tragic warfare. Some people died for such beliefs; it's hardly likely that people were willing to die for arbitrary ones.

In its more extreme form, cultural relativism leads one to accept the greater force in the culture or to accept whatever is the most popular belief as the right belief. In empirical fields the folly of this is clear. If most people felt at one time that the earth is flat, does that make it so? A more serious problem results in the area of ethics. If Nazism was the most popular belief in post-Weimar Germany, did that make it right? One can also see the serious consequences of this position if it comes to a matter of conflicting beliefs. If most people in Freedonia believe in peaceful coexistence but if most people in neighboring Unfreedonia believe in the right of the mighty to take whatever they can, then under the view of relativism, who is to say who is right? There is no way to adjudicate between these conflicting beliefs except by means of the greater force. This is somewhat ironic because many people who advocate relativism do so as an antidote to imperialism and colonialism, but their view could logically condone it. There are also other more conceptual inconsistencies with relativism. Relativism makes a claim, it makes a claim, that relativism is "true," and it says it is true of all cultures. But on the other hand, relativism claims that nothing is absolutely or universally true. So if it is consistent, it cannot claim that it is true and it does not make any sense for it to make such claims.

The third type of relativism is *normative relativism*. This suggests even more radically that not only do cultures differ from one another, morally speaking, but it is impossible or nearly impossible for one culture to understand the moral norms and life of another. The concepts by which we understand our moral life and the criteria we use to judge it are incommensurable with those in other cultures. But this infers that there is no way to resolve conflicting disputes other than by elimination of the opponent, since there is nothing in common to appeal to. Because it assumes a skepticism from the start—that there are no common norms or ways of understanding norms different than our own—then where serious conflict arises, there is no other recourse. Second, there is an inconsistency in this position. To claim that one culture cannot understand another culture's norms already implies that we do understand that they do not understand. In other words, it is possible to understand another culture's misunderstanding. Why is it not possible, then, to understand another culture's understanding of itself? Third, one wonders if this claim is empirically true. An analogy with languages can illustrate the point. There is nothing more varied than languages; yet despite these differences, it is possible to speak another language, and many people become quite fluent. Often a foreign speaker may know the mechanics of a language better than a native speaker. In addition, it is clear that there is no reason why some child, although born into one language, cannot be raised in another. There is no congenital reason why an English-born baby could not, under the right conditions, become a native Hungarian speaker. Similarly, we suppose that learning another culture's ways likewise could be done. In principle, then, the skepticism of this claim may be doubted.

5.2.7 Ways of Justifying Ethical Principles and Their Problems

Having discussed the sort of maturation needed to engage in the genuine justification of moral principles and the kinds of attitudes to be avoided in its pursuit, it's time to turn to the problem of justification itself. How do we go about justifying an ethical principle or norm? Science, for example, justifies its claims by means of experimental testing: If a hypothesis has credibility, then it should predict a certain outcome. If the outcome occurs, then that adds to its credibility; if it fails, then it is discredited accordingly. If we have a certain hypothesis about the orbit of Mars, then that hypothesis—if credible—should be able to predict where Mars will be in its orbit at any one time. If it fails at doing that, then it's time to go back to the drawing board. Mathematics proceeds somewhat differently. Relative to a certain set of axioms or assumptions, it demonstrates by strict reasoning standards what necessarily follows from those assumptions. The proof that x has a value of either 2 or -3, if $x^2 + x - 6 = 0$, follows from a very strict process of reasoning that is irrefutable relative to the axioms of the system.

So how should ethics proceed in its justification of principles? This is one of the most difficult issues ethical theory has to face, and it produces some of the most complicated thought and theory. As we saw earlier in the Introduction of this book, although ethical theory employs empirical findings and uses logical inferences and definitions in its inquiries, it is concerned primarily with norms, understood as a category distinct from these. Thus, the methodology that is appropriate to empirical sciences, such as physics, or logical sciences, such as mathematics, may not be entirely helpful here, although this has to be qualified somewhat. Certainly, we could not justify an ethical principle that flew in the face of known empirical laws or theories, nor could we justify one that was inconsistent or violated the norms of logic. Showing that an ethical principle is inconsistent or that it leads to absurdities could help in evaluating that principle. If it is inconsistent or self-contradictory, then we know that it is fundamentally flawed no matter what other problems it might have. But still there is the problem of evaluating those that do not have such logical problems. The core issue of a principle's normativity—that is, why, in some sense of the term, it is what we *ought* to do—is not addressed by logical consistency. If one adheres to some version of the golden rule—do unto others as you would have others do unto you—then why should we abide by that principle? *Justifying a norm, then, is a matter of showing why we ought to adhere to it.* So how do we determine the root of obligation to a principle?

One of the most common and simplest ways to justify an ethical principle is by appeal to authority. We are obligated to obey the commands of legitimate authority. If such an authority is the source of an ethical principle, then the obligation to adhere to it is rooted in our obligation to obey that authority. A popular bumper sticker expresses this idea exactly: "God said it, I believe it, and that's all there is to it." In religious matters we appeal to the authority of sacred scripture, to the authority of some religious leader, or directly to a divine authority. But as we have seen in regard to Kohlberg's analysis, appeals to authority are thought to involve lower-stage moral reasoning. Why is such reasoning thought to be inadequate? Arguing that something is justified because an authority, such

---

In his *Autobiography* Benjamin Franklin made the following claim:

"Revelation had indeed no weight with me as such; but I entertained an opinion that tho' certain actions might not be bad because they were forbidden by it, or good because it commanded them, yet probably those actions might be forbidden because they were bad for us or commanded because they were beneficial to us, in their own natures.... "

---

as God, tells us it is the right thing to do is often thought to be a weak argument. As Plato noted long ago, no matter how impeccably good and virtuous the authority, the fact that such an authority issues something does not make it good; rather one should think conversely—it is good and that is why a virtuous authority would issue it. Unless a divine authority chooses the principles arbitrarily, then it must have some good reason for choosing the ones it does. Consequently, the reasons why something is the right thing to do are independent of who issues it. For example, if divine authority issues the Ten Commandments, did it matter what they said? Would they have been just as valid if what was issued were Ten Commandments contrary to the existing ones? Instead of being forbidden to kill, we were permitted to, or instead of being forbidden to bear false witness against our neighbor, we were encouraged to. Obviously, there is something about the particular content of the Ten Commandments which gives them their credibility to many people. It is not just the claim that they were the issue of divine authority that does so.

There are other problems with using authority as a means of justification. One difficulty is relying on the infallibility of the authority. Unless you are in direct communication with God, God's commands are issued through representations and documents. There are plenty of people who pose as authority or who may claim that they are speaking through the authority of a divine source, but the history of such pronouncements shows many charlatans afoot. In our culture there are thousands of religions with leaders who claim direct communication or understanding of the word of God, yet many of whose pronouncements contradict one another. It may also be questionable whether we are hearing the pronouncement of that authority accurately. This is especially a problem for commands passed down through a tradition. The Torah, Bible, and Koran all have things in common, but they also have important differences. Yet each of these traditions proclaims these books to be the exact and direct word of God. The Christian Bible also has a history of editorial decision as well. For example, the Gospel of St. Thomas has been left out of its canon. Why are certain books canonical and others not? The example of the Torah, Bible, and Koran also demonstrates an additional problem with using authority to justify things. A person does not want to rely on just any authority but must recognize the authority as an authority somehow. If an authority is not recognized by a group as such, his or her pronouncements are not going to have much weight. Thus, there must be a way to determine that someone is worthy of authority, and that adds an additional problem to the mix. The only way to avoid that problem is to appeal to an universal authority, but it is not clear if such an authority exists. But even if we could get around all of these problems and be guaranteed that a pronouncement is a direct and unadulterated command from an infallible divine authority, we would only be assured that it *is* good. We would not know *why* it is good. The entire purpose of moral knowledge is to determine *why* something is right, and so appeals to authority would ultimately not satisfy this goal.

The ethical tradition offers a second way to justify a principle. Some thinkers argue that there is something like a *natural law,* which expresses fundamentals about our moral natures and is inherent in the order of things. We are obligated to heed this law since we should follow our natures. Natural law often has a religious edge to it as well because a divine being is often thought to be the source of this law. However, there are some who believe that an appeal to a divine origin is not necessary and that it is something that can be made understandable through the use of reason alone. But in either case the natural law tradition avoids some of the difficulties associated with appeals to authority. Even if the natural law has a divine origin, the arguments of natural law theorists are that this natural law is the product of reason nonetheless. It is not justified by the fact that it is issued by an authority but by the fact that its divine creator uses reason to form it. Consequently, there are reasons for accepting it other than the brute fact of its divine origins.

Our theory of natural rights derives from this natural law tradition. Natural right theory, as it is developed by John Locke and others, argues that there is a state of nature for human beings that is characterized by certain natural rights, and those governments are good and justified to the extent that the form of government upholds these natural rights. Various thinkers from the 18th-century English, American, and French traditions have articulated these as a right to life, liberty, property, and the pursuit of happiness. The Bill of Rights adds several to these more basic ones, including the right of religion, free expression, assembly, and so on. The United Nations' Declaration of Universal Human Rights adds a number of others. Although these lists of rights show commonalities, they also seem to reflect changes and differences. The concept of human nature is thought to be something that is invariant over time. If they were truly a reflection of an invariant human nature, then it would seem that such rights or natural moral laws would also be invariant. The difficulty with this approach is that, empirically speaking, the biological and psychological sciences have moved away from a concept of a basic "nature" to the idea of a biologically and culturally evolving human being, and for good reason. It is difficult to prove that there is a basic human nature when biology shows so much variability in life. A simple glance at the last 2000 years of human history shows a remarkable difference in traditions and cultures.

A third strategy that has been employed to justify ethical principles is one that simply suggests we have a special ability or "faculty" to sense right or wrong, as discussed briefly in the opening section of this chapter on intuition. We are then obligated to listen to this voice of moral authority, or "conscience," precisely because it directly and intuitively gives us access to what is right and wrong. This position was especially popular among a group of 18th-century British moralists. Anthony Shaftesbury, Francis Hutcheson, Joseph Butler, and Thomas Reid all argued for something like a moral instinct or moral sense. Reid perhaps says it best: "the abstract notion of moral good and ill would be of no use to direct our life, if we had not the power of applying it to particular actions, and determining what is morally good, and what is morally ill. Some philosophers, with whom I agree, ascribe this to an original power or faculty in man, which they call the *Moral Sense*, the *Moral Faculty, Conscience*. ... " (1788: III, Pt. III, Chap. 6). But as we noted earlier, the flaws with this approach are obvious. For one thing, if we have such a faculty, then why are there differing intuitions, and why do intuitions seem to change over time? Our cognitions are not infallible and our perceptions are not infallible, so why should any other faculty or sense we have be infallible? There is no empirical support for such a moral sense, although there is certainly sufficient evidence for acquiring moral emotions and sentiments. The fact that everyone, other things being equal, is able to acquire some moral emotion, such as guilt or shame, does not also infer that every person will feel guilt or shame over the same things.

A fourth strategy is to measure the worth of a principle by measuring the worth of its consequences. This follows the advice of the old adage "by their fruits you shall know them." Thus, to the extent that the consequences of following a principle are desirable, then we are obligated to adhere to that principle. If happiness is desirable and the principle is a means of happiness, then obligation to the principle is clear. This methodology produces a class of principles called *consequentialist* or *teleological*, the latter derived from the Greek word *tēlos*, meaning "end" or "purpose." In some ways this approach is analogous to the method science employs to justify its hypotheses. A scientist looks to the consequences of a hypothesis to test its predictability; similarly, by looking at what sorts of things follow from the consistent and persistent employment of a principle can help justify it. For example, people might argue that a principle is justified in following because it can lead to a good in some sense of the term. If consistently followed, it might make a person happy in the long run or it may be something that is conducive to the good life. Or it may be something that, should everyone follow it, would produce the greatest possible good. This is indeed the manner in which the utilitarians argued. The utilitarian principle stated that every action should be calculated so as to produce the greatest good for the greatest number. Consequently, almost by definition, it could be justified since—if followed consistently—it would lead to the greatest happiness for the greatest number.

Consequentialist methodologies also have their problems. What is clear from this approach is that people do not follow the principle because it is right; they follow it because in doing so they are promised something good from it. For example Epicurus argued that one should be virtuous because it will bring you some degree of happiness and peace of mind. To some extent Aristotle argues the same way by suggesting that it is through virtue that one flourishes. Yet, if we have Kohlberg's stages of moral reasoning in mind, this seems to be a lesser form of moral reasoning. This is comparable to the way in which children or even some adults are enticed into abiding by the rules of a certain religion—if you obey these rules, you will be rewarded with heaven, and if you disobey, you will spend eternity in hell. In this case people are obeying the norm not because they believe it is right, but because they believe it will get them to heaven. From the interest of ethical theory, this doesn't justify the principle; it only shows what might motivate people to follow it. Saying that it will reward us does not address the issue of why it is right; what it says is that if you want something good for yourself, this is what you ought to do. There may be an even more serious methodological flaw with this approach. The methodology may involve circularity. If you are going to measure the goodness of a principle by means of the goodness of its consequences, then you must be able to identify what counts as good consequences. For example, if a consequence of following a principle is that it would prohibit slavery, then we must already know somehow that slavery is a wrong. Thus, to evaluate the principle in this manner, we must rely on our moral intuition that slavery is wrong. Yet as we have seen, intuitions are not always reliable and may change over time. The purpose of a principle, as we argued, is to serve as a means of evaluating our intuitions, not the other way around. Consequentialism, then, is involved in a circularity that states principles justify intuitions and intuitions justify principles.

A fifth approach is somewhat analogous to mathematical methodology, and it is one of the more difficult approaches to understand. The attempt here is to identify those things that must be assumed or are axiomatic for the possibility of morality. What is it without which morality could not be possible? Once we have identified that, then the goal is to deduce a principle from that assumption. Obligation to this principle follows from the fact that it is a necessary result of what makes morality possible to begin with. Violate the principle and you violate the conditions of morality. This is a methodology most associated with the philosopher Immanuel Kant, and it produces a class of principles called *deontological.* Deontological derives from the Greek word *deon* meaning "duty." Here duty connotes the idea of something that "must" be done, that has an ethical necessity to it, and so is normative in that sense. For Kant and for most deontologists, the condition that is necessary for morality is freedom or free will. Without freedom, morality would not be possible. If our behaviors were completely determined, it would make absolutely no sense to talk about normativity, or what we ought to do, since we could not do other than what we actually do. But as we saw in Chapter Two, a usual interpretation of freedom is in terms of autonomy, that is, self-legislation and self-direction. Self-legislation involves giving oneself a law or law-like principle to live by. Now what is the nature of a law? A law, especially a physical law, is something that is both universal and necessity. All water boils at 100° Celsius is a law that holds for all water under normal atmospheric conditions. Kant argues, then, that from this concept of autonomy, understood as self-legislative, we can derive an ethical principle, which he calls the categorical imperative. The categorical imperative demands that all our actions conform to the very form of a law, that is, that whatever we are about to do, it should be something that *everyone* would *have to* do. If under those conditions we cannot find any inconsistency in the result, then the action is morally appropriate. For example, if I intend to lie in a certain situation, then if it were the case that everyone were forced to lie, then the meaning of truth telling and lying would make no sense any longer. Since the categorical imperative is the expression of self-determination, which in turn is the concept of freedom, then in order to be free one's actions have to abide by this principle. Violating this principle is not acting morally, since the action is not self-determined.

The difficulty with this approach, as we will see, is that there can be various interpretations of the concept of autonomy, producing varieties of principles of this sort. One suspects, then, that the derivation process involved in this methodology does not involve the same rigor and necessity as true mathematics might. It does assume freedom, and a certain interpretation of freedom as self-determination—which is an assumption after all. But even if these interpretations could be granted, the methodology is still flawed in the sense that it relies on assumptions. As we know from mathematics, a deductive system is as strong as its basic assumptions or axioms. However, the axioms themselves cannot be proven without recourse to some other axioms, which in turn would have to be proven ad infinitum.

The purpose of principles is to help us evaluate our moral intuitions. Yet all these approaches to their justification seem to make an appeal to intuitions in some form or another—as authority, conscience, natural law, natural desires, and basic axiomatic assumptions. This problem can be expressed in a rather abstract argument. First, we can try to justify an ethical principle by either moral or nonmoral reasons; if we use moral reasons, then we're led into circularity or regression, since we have to justify those moral reasons in turn. If we use nonmoral reasons (e.g., pleasure, utility, or self-interest), then we fail to give *moral* justification for the principle (cf. Williams 1985: 55).

Is there any way to escape some appeal to intuition in justifying moral principles? Some argue that there is not. It seems nearly impossible to escape some intuition in formulating and defending an ethical principle—and we may not want to do this because moral intuitions are valuable to us for real reasons. Consequently, such thinkers (Gadamer 1975; Rorty 1979; Nielsen 1991) argue that, given the limits on moral justification, the best we can hope for is something like *reflective equilibrium*, discussed earlier. Reflective equilibrium is a way of adjusting our intuitions in light of principles, and principles in light of intuitions, without really claiming one or the other as foundational. This involves what is called a *hermeneutic* process, understood as a method of interpretation in which a part is understood in its connection to a whole, and the whole is understood better as new parts are integrated with it. For example, understanding the first chapter of a book may be limited until we see how it fits into the whole story. Yet the whole story gets known as its parts become integrated with one another. Similarly, our intuitions help us to formulate and test a principle which can be seen as a larger picture of those intuitions; yet that larger picture may help us to rethink our intuitions. In this process the biases, prejudices, and infelicities of our system get addressed and worked out in relating part to whole and whole to parts. Just as the legal system works on the basis of a given tradition that gets more refined and adjusted as new cases arise and are incorporated into the general understanding of the law, so should it be with regard to moral rules and principles. This process has more the character of a serious conversation than a rational demonstration. Richard Rorty characterizes some of this in the following way:

> This holist line of argument says that we shall never be able to avoid the "hermeneutic circle"—the fact that we cannot understand the parts of a strange culture, practice, theory, language, or whatever, unless we know something about how the whole thing works, whereas we cannot get a grasp on how the whole works until we have some understanding of its parts. This notion of interpretation suggests that coming to

understand is more like getting acquainted with a person than like following a demonstration. In both cases we play back and forth between guesses about how to characterize particular statements or other events, and guesses about the point of the whole situation, until gradually we feel at ease with what was hitherto strange. The notion of culture as a conversation rather than as a structure erected upon foundations fits well with this hermeneutical notion ... (1979: 319).

The purpose of moral knowledge is not to give an ultimate foundation to some ethical code or principle, but to keep the conversation about ethics going and in the process to come to a greater understanding and refinement of these matters.

Indeed, some thinkers want to abandon the idea of a search for moral foundations altogether. As Bernard Williams suggests, "The moral philosopher in search of justifications sometimes overestimates the need for justification or overestimates its effect" (1985: 29). "It is not obvious what a justification of the ethical life should try to do, or why we should need such a thing" (1985: 23). The argument is that searching for foundations does not play as important a role in our moral lives as some thinkers have thought. The inability to find, in principle, a justification for moral rules and principles will not destroy the moral fabric of a culture and its people. After all, we are already steeped in a moral tradition surrounded by authority which provides the basis of our action. We do not easily reject or exchange our more basic intuitions because our way of life and our essential practices and institutions are constituted by them. Just because we cannot reasonably justify the claim that murder is wrong doesn't mean that we're going to go out and kill someone. Our moral sentiment and intuition keep us in place in that regard. If we had to wait for rational justification to assure us, then there would be a great deal of moral deviance.

Still there is something unsatisfying about an ethics based on continual conversation. It raises more questions than it answers. What are to be the parameters of such conversation? Does the conversation itself have principles or guidelines? Why should conversation be heralded as the best form of moral discourse? Why should we prefer conversation to just plain dogmatic authority? The conversation and its outcome may simply mirror whatever prejudices, biases, and infelicities exist in our implicit moral codes; rather that mollifying these, conversation may simply perpetuate them. As a result, despite these formidable limitations imposed upon the search for justifications for ethical principles, many philosophers have continued the search—and some with interesting and clever strategies, as we'll see.

5.2.8 Feminist Criticisms of the Principle Approach

Feminist theory has placed in question the need for foundational justifications for ethical principles. It has also questioned the entire framework of principle-and-rule thinking. The latter, as we have seen, hopes to establish foundations for ethics by means of justified principles and rules, which are then applied to the evaluation of particular actions. Under this view, ethics is a matter of formal procedure and argumentation on the basis of reasons and rules that can be used in the abstract to resolve particular conflicts. Nel Noddings writes,

> It has been traditional in moral philosophy to insist that moral principles must be, by their very nature as moral principles, universifiable. If I am obligated to do X under certain conditions, then under sufficiently similar conditions you also are obligated to do X. But the principle of universifiability seems to depend ... on a concept of "same-

ness." In order to accept the principle, we should have to establish that human predicaments exhibit sufficient sameness, and this we cannot do without abstracting away from concrete situations those qualities that seem to reveal the sameness. In doing this, we often lose the very qualities or factors that gave rise to the moral question in the situation. That condition which makes the situation different and thereby induces genuine moral puzzlement cannot be satisfied by the application of principles developed in situations of sameness (1984: 85).

"The moral problem" in the care approach, as Carol Gilligan notes, is "a problem of care and responsibility in relationships rather than as one of rights and rules" (1982: 73). "Thus the logic underlying an ethic of care is a psychological logic of relationships, which contrasts with the formal logic of fairness that informs the justice approach" (1982: 73).

The care approach does at least two things differently than the rule-and-principle approach. It is first finely attuned to the situation and the relations of those who face a conflict or moral dilemma. At the same time it avoids relativism by adhering to a fundamental position with regard to every situation: maintenance or establishment of caring relations of the persons in those situations (Noddings 1984: 85). The goodness of decisions in these situations is measured by how it lends to the dynamic growth of existing relations toward more mutually reciprocal and caring ones (Noddings 1984: 86). As Carol Gilligan writes, the ethic of care "reflects a cumulative knowledge of human relationships [and] evolves around a central insight, that self and other are interdependent. ... The fact of interconnection informs the central, recurring recognition that just as the incidence of violence is in the end destructive to all, so the activity of care enhances both others and self" (1982: 74).

The principle-and-rule approach to ethics implicitly uses a judicial model for decision making. It assumes there are basic conflicts of interest or principle and that these should be resolved in favor of one or the other. It relies heavily on a hierarchical ordering of principles and rules, such that what is right or wrong can be determined in the abstract, separate from the context of particular situations. In the ethic of care, as Carol Gilligan points out, judgments shift away from the hierarchical ordering of principles and formal procedures of decision making. There is an insistence on the particular. To take a case in point, women contemplating Kohlberg's Heinz dilemma (see Section 5.2.5) resist the hypothetical dilemma it poses; instead they insist that substance be given to the skeletal lives of the people in the dilemma. Only when their particularity is fleshed out, when their relationship to one another is established, where it is possible to consider how decisions will affect them meaningfully are women then posed to address the dilemma (1982: 100–101). From a care perspective, the issue in the Heinz dilemma is not between the priority of life over property rights, but in terms of the actual consequences stealing would have for a man of limited means and little social power who loves his wife. From the care perspective, mature moral judgments work toward the issues of responsibility and care and avoid their polar opposites, *irresponsibility*, that is, a turning away from one's commitment to care, and *cruelty*, that is, not caring what happens to others (Gilligan 1982: 99).

Earlier in the discussion of moral judgment (Sections 4.6.7 and 4.7), the example of Maggie Tulliver in George Eliot's *The Mill on the Floss* was used to illustrate the process of deliberation and decision. Maggie's choice was not to continue an affair with her cousin's fiancé. But in her process of deliberation, we see no resort to a set of principles to decide between what is right and wrong in the abstract and then apply it to her situation; instead there is a strong, emotionally embedded voyage through the complexities of the situation. In the end her decision is not based on principles of utility, of weighing costs or benefits, or some version of the golden rule; instead it is a struggle between selfishness and responsibility in the context of her relationships with those affected. In the end she makes her decision on her refusal "to take a good for myself that has been wrung out of misery." Indeed, the minister in the novel, Mr. Kenn, remarks that "the principle upon which she acted [was] a safer guide than any balancing of consequences." George Eliot playing the role of narrator tells her audience, "the mysterious complexity of our life cannot be laced up in formulas," that it cannot be bound by general rules, but must be guided "by a life vivid and intense enough to have created a wide, fellow-feeling with all that is human."

The principle-and-rule approach has as one of its goals the development of a general and universal guideline that can be reasonably justified. Feminists argue that such justification is misplaced. But from the care perspective, the justification for caring comes from being embedded in caring relations; rational justification justifies rationally, caring justifies with one's emotional life, one's whole way of being: "we can see there can be no justification for taking the moral viewpoint— that in truth, the moral viewpoint is prior to any notion of justification" (Noddings 1984: 95). For example, killing is not wrong because it follows from the libertarian principle, which in turn is justified by arguments from autonomy; rather, under the care perspective, killing is wrong when it destroys the possibility of caring, removes all possible connectedness, as the random murder of another illustrates. Yet it can also be something that enhances the caring relation, as when a loving spouse requests removal of the ventilator to stop the suffering of her husband (cf. Noddings 1984: 107–108). "The test of my caring is not wholly in how things turn out; the primary test lies in an examination of what I considered, how fully I received the other, and whether the free pursuit of his projects is partly a result of the completion of my caring in him" (1984: 81). Caring is measured by one's receptivity to the other. Martin Buber relates the story of a student who came to him ostensibly with some matter other than the one that he wanted to really talk about—committing suicide. Later the student did do exactly that. Buber faulted himself not so much for not preventing the suicide, but for not being open and receptive to the student. The receptivity is what really mattered in this case (1966: 17–18; cf. Noddings 1984: 114).

But if caring engagement with others is to replace ethical principles as a determination of the right thing to do, there are some questions that arise. First, the disposition of caring in and of itself does not tell us how much to care, with whom, and for what purposes. For example, Rita Manning writes,

> My day-to-day interactions with other persons create a web of reciprocal caring. In these interactions, I am obliged to be a caring person. I am free, to a certain extent, to choose when and how to care for these others. My choice is limited by my relationships with these others and by their needs. A pressing need calls up an immediate obligation to care for; roles and responsibilities call up an obligation to respond in a caring manner. In the first case, I am obligated … to respond; in the second, I can choose, within limits, when and how to care (1992a: 46).

But what are these limits and how are they determined? Can a person care for everybody in every degree? The vague imperative to care may be unproblematic for a small circle of caring obligations, but if one's role extends to larger populations, how is caring to be managed? The assembly person in the large city, the mayor, the governor, the senator, the administrator must make decisions that affect thousands or millions of people. A decision based on care for people who one has no real connection with, and who are engaged in several conflicts with others, demands an abstract solution. Manning argues that "often we don't need to appeal to rules in deciding whom to care for and how to care for them. A creature's need and our ability to meet it identifies it as a candidate for caring for. We decide how to care for by appeal to the need, the strategies for meeting it, and the desires of the one in need about how best to meet the need. But when I am not in direct contact with the objects of care, my actions cannot be guided by the expressed and observed desires of those cared for, and hence I might want to appeal to rules" (1992a: 50–51). But if we might want to appeal to rules, which rules do we appeal to? And if we have to appeal to rules in the long run, what purpose does the care ethic serve? If everybody should be cared for, that alone doesn't tell the decision maker who should get what in a system of scarce resources.

In discussing the limits on caring, Manning writes,

> I don't think that we are obligated to be like Mother Teresa. ... We can limit our obligation to care. ... First, I have a prima facie obligation to care for when I come across a creature in need who is unable to meet that need without help, when my caring is called on as part of a reciprocal relationship, or when indicated as part of my role responsibility. ... But I must also recognize that I am a person who must be cared for and that I must recognize and respond to my own need to be cared for (1992a: 49).

But the balance between caring for others and caring for oneself sounds here like the ordinary consideration of cost and benefit. But whereas principles, such as the utilitarian principle, suggest a less vague account of the proper relation between the two, the caring ethic leaves it solely up to the individual caregiver. The arbitrariness in the model could be disturbing to some. The utilitarian principle starts exactly where the care ethic leaves off.

The critical issue for the care approach is the same as the principle-and-rule one: Why are we obligated to care? It could be answered that to the extent that we are in caring relations we cannot help but care. But what of the situations in which we are not? Some feminist theorists, such as Nel Noddings and Rita Manning, claim that caring is a natural disposition. But this claim places them in the same jeopardy as many of the principle-and-rule approaches. That is a contention that must be proven. Caring is not a universal sentiment; many moral agents operate on the basis of duty or honor rather than the caring sentiment. Moreover, even a natural disposition is no guarantee that we are doing the right thing.

Third, the dismissal of rules and principles and their substitution by the ethics of care could lead to some undesirable consequences. The ethic of care emphasizes connectedness and often emphasizes the family and mother–child relations as paradigms. But clearly, some institutions and practices seem disanalogous to family models. In fact some practices, such as the legal system, may become corrupted under such models. If the legal system was modeled on partiality rather than impartiality and relied on the kinds and degrees of connectedness of judicial officials with the offenders, serious corruption could result. Similarly with political decision makers, a practice based on connectedness to others could lead to nepotism in a large sense. In general, a society based on these ideas of emotional connectedness sounds like a form of tribalism. The entire edifice of rights and principles of justice, which treat individuals abstractly but equally, was one of the important means by which the modern state was developed and continues to be an effective means of government.

Thus, despite some of the limitations in discovering an ultimate justification for ethical principles or some of the questions raised about their use in moral life, an inquiry into their character, kind, and proof is a worthy enterprise. Even if a process of reflective equilibrium is the best we can hope for, it is still important to examine those principles—their strengths and weaknesses. Before we can determine the manner in which they can best serve us in our ethical lives, we need to understand them, their proofs, and justifications. With the assumption of the worth of their inquiry in mind, let's examine some of the more basic and classical principles.

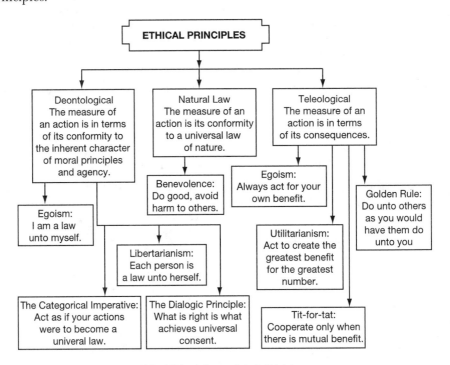

Ethical Principles and their Divisions

5.3 DEONTOLOGICAL PRINCIPLES

As mentioned in Section 4.8.3, *deontological theories attempt to develop ethical principles on the basis of obligation, on what is the right thing to do, without recourse to the interests or plans of moral agents or the consequences actions may have on those agents.* Teleological or consequentialist theories attempt to establish impartial principles on the basis of the interests of the moral agents and the consequences of their actions.

The justification of deontological principles is complex and difficult. These sorts of principles cannot appeal to particular interests, consequences, or senses of the good life, but must come from the formal or conceptual character of obligation itself. The dominant strategy in this regard is to show how the concept of autonomy generates certain principles. The reason this approach is used was made clear by Kant (1785). As we saw in Section 2.1, morality without freedom of the will is impossible. Without the possibility of blame or praise and the ability to correct our behavior, morality makes absolutely no sense. If as argued in Section 2.5 freedom of the will is understood as autonomy or self-legislation, then the very possibility of morality lies in autonomy. Given that autonomy is necessary for morality, then any principle that follows from the nature of autonomy would have the same necessity. How that idea of autonomy is best interpreted, and which principles are generated thereby, is the subject of the next sections. The list of deontological principles in this regard include the following: the principle of egoism, the libertarian principle, the categorical imperative, contract ethics, and the principle of discourse ethics.

5.3.1 The Principle of (Deontological) Egoism

The principle of egoism interprets the notion of autonomy in the following sense: *I am a law unto myself*. If freedom entails self-legislation, then the very essence of autonomy defines a person as a law unto herself. Thomas Hobbes expresses the idea of egoism most vividly as the claim that "every man has the right to everything" (*Leviathan*, Pt. I, Chap. 14). This suggests that you may act on any plan that you have determined for yourself, regardless of its harm to others.

In the early part of Plato's famous dialogue *The Republic*, Socrates is confronted by Thrasymachus who claims that Socrates's espousal of noble moral motivations is naive and irrational. In an abusive exchange, Thrasymachus claims that human beings naturally pursue power and pleasure. They may, rationally speaking, have to constrain that pursuit because of other people's power over them. Some may even be fooled into thinking that they should respect the interests of others, but this is usually the result of cultural conventions and enculturation—it is certainly to the benefit of those in power to make others think that it is right to uphold those very conventions that keep the powerful in power. But again, this is where naiveté is harmful to the naive. Justice, Thrasymachus declares, "is nothing but the advantage of the stronger." *Is Thrasymachus right?*

Max Stirner (1806–1856) can be counted as one of the few philosophers who is a genuine advocate of deontological egoism. Stirner was a student of Hegel's who eventually revolted against his teacher's philosophy. He is often seen, in contrast to Marx, to be a "right" Hegelian rather than on the "left." His philosophy is more harmonious with anarchism and advocates a basic antagonism to the state and collective institutions. Stirner's first and only major book is entitled *Der Einzige und sein Eigentum* (1845) (translated as *The Ego and Its Own* in 1907). He contended that each individual is a law unto himself. All political or ethical concepts that invoke some common or collective nature or good are false; rights and duties do not exist. The only thing that justifies an action is the might of the individual ego. As far as Stirner was concerned, one's goal in life was the expression of one's unique individuality; this typically required rebellion against larger powers, such as institutions, religions, the

Max Stirner (1806–1856) was a German philosopher and student of Hegel's. His real name was Johann Schmidt. He was one of the few true advocates of egoism. He spent a number of years at the university, associating with the so-called "right" or "free" Hegelians, including Bruno and Edgar Bauer. After graduation he lived in poverty until he got a job at a Berlin academy for girls. There he lived a double life, one as a respectable teacher at the academy and a second as Max Stirner, radical writer. In 1845 he published his only important book, *Der Einzige und sein Eigentum* (1845) (translated as *The Ego and Its Own* in 1907). He was married briefly, and in his later years he engaged in a number of unsuccessful economic ventures that left him hounded by creditors to the end of his days. He died in poverty and obscurity in 1856.

state, or any abstract moral law. Such fictitious entities weakened one's own sense of uniqueness.

Rebellion was advocated rather than revolution because revolution aimed simply to restore one government or institution with another. Rebellion was simply a fight against any authority, institution, or power that would limit the individual. It was the truest expression of the individual's power. Stirner actually viewed crime as one form of rebellion in this sense. Crime can be seen as the assertion of the individual over and against the sacred and the collective. It is also clear that the essence of rebellion is violence, and Stirner imagined, like Hobbes, that true egoism would lead to "a war of all against all." However, Stirner thought that eventually a sort of balance of power between remaining egoists would prevail, ending with a so-called "union of egoists." This would replace the state and involve no laws or set organization. In this condition individuals would withdraw into their uniqueness which would lessen chances of conflict, since less commonalities would reduce divisiveness.

Despite Stirner's hopefulness for a peaceable union of egoists, since each person has self-sovereignty, that is, is a law unto herself, then each one can make no claims against another, and everyone has a claim to anything they have determined autonomously. The results of such a permission would be obvious, "a war of all against all"—to use Hobbes's own language (*Leviathan*, Pt. I, Chap. 13), in which life would be "nasty, brutish and short" in the end. Clearly, if I have a right to do anything to anybody, and others have the same, then any hope for a secure or happy life would be out of the question. But of course, should we lose the struggle or live in a constant struggle, which is Hobbes's view, then we are hardly heeding the command to act in one's own benefit. It is clear that even the strongest, given the right sort of opposition, will fall.

Thomas Hobbes (1588–1679) was an English political philosopher whose best known work is *The Leviathan.*

Nietzsche attempts to solve this problem by assigning this permission only to persons of a certain nobility or higher form of life (the so-called *Übermensch*, or superman). In this case the common run of persons is free to engage in a sort of "herd morality" which provides restrictions on the will of its members for the sake of the security and benefit of the community. But noble people are free to will what is generated out of their sense of nobility, and so engage in a form of "master morality" (1886: 213ff.). Thus, noble people may do as they will, while the herd must serve the will of others. Of course, this solution makes the principle of egoism greatly partial, and it is not clear why someone, especially among the herd, would be commanded by it other than threat of force. In other words, if there is a double standard which allows one

---

Ayn Rand (1905–1982) is another thinker whose views are associated with this sort of egoism, but her views are closer to the libertarian principle. Objectivism, as she calls it, is the view that one should hold one's own life as one's ultimate value and one's own happiness as one's highest purpose (1964: 29). The objectivist advocates rational selfishness which holds that human good does not require sacrifices and cannot be achieved by the sacrifice of anyone to anyone (1964: 31). How then does it adjudicate between individuals? There will be no conflicts in principle if each person understands the other as pursuing their own interests rationally (1964: 31). First, no one has a right to take something from another by force (1964: 32). Each must treat the other as equals in a free, voluntary, and uncoerced exchange. To this end she advocates laissez-faire capitalism as the paradigm of such interaction. The role of government is simply to ensure against the use of physical force by others; otherwise it is not to interfere with the freedom of individuals. Her ethical writings are more statements of views than arguments, but her fiction has a very popular following, including *Atlas Shrugged* and *The Fountainhead.*

---

to be egoistic yet others not, it is not clear why the herd would freely adopt such a double standard. The only recourse of the noble person is to impose his will on others; but, of course, one is back to the initial problem which this was supposed to resolve—the war of all against all. Hobbes's own solution grants that the members of the community should subordinate their will to another, a sovereign, but implicitly through consent and contract, and in their best interests (*Leviathan*, Pt. II, Chap. 17).

5.3.2 The Principle of Nonmaleficence (the Libertarian Principle)

The principle of nonmaleficence, often called the libertarian principle, interprets autonomy somewhat differently than the principle of egoism. The dominant metaphor used in this framework is that of the self as territory or sovereign domain, which then has a certain inviolability to it. Under this view, it is true, as egoism suggests, that everyone is a law unto themselves, but what that means is that I must respect the other's inherent autonomy. Whereas egoism allows you to use another for your own benefit, under the principle of nonmaleficence, respect for the autonomy of another makes it the case that no one is obliged to become a means for someone else's plans or goals without a consent. This is Kant's claim (1785: 47), but that is interpreted by libertarians as meaning that I cannot be used to benefit another, not even for some collective good (cf. Nozick 1974: 33). Any contribution I might make to another's good or benefit is purely voluntary and not a matter of obligation; any mutual benefit must also be voluntary. But because others have this right also not to be used for another's good, the only thing I am obliged to do is to refrain from using them for my benefit without their consent, in a way that harms them, or even in the case where it might benefit them. The only prima facie duty I have to others, then, is to do them no significant harm; hence, nonmaleficence is the *only prima facie duty*.

Rousseau expresses well the sense of the *principle of nonmaleficence: "Do what is good for you with the least possible harm to others"* (1755: 133). The consistent employment of such a principle promotes the maximization of one person's pursuit of the good life compatible with another's. For any given community, it seeks the compatibility of individual plans in a way that allows

Jean-Jacques Rousseau (1712–1778) was a French political philosopher best known for his work *The Social Contract*.

each person to maximize her sense of the good life. The arrangement should allow people to apply their talents and abilities in a competition for goods which permits them to pursue their individual plans for happiness and the sense of the good life. This general idea is expressed by John Locke (1689: 22) in the context of the acquisition of property:

> Though the earth and all inferior creatures be common to all men, yet every man has a property in his own person; this nobody has any right to but himself. The labour of his body and the work of his hands we may say are properly his. Whatsoever, then, he removes out of the state that nature hath provided and left it in, he hath mixed his labour with, and joined to it something that is his own, and thereby makes it his property. For this labour being the unquestionable property of the labourer, no man but he can have a right to what that is once joined to, at least where there is enough, and as good left in common for others.

You are free to apply your labor and talent to the acquisition of those things that will promote your sense of happiness with the proviso that such acquisition allows others a similar opportunity, that is, that their pursuit of happiness is not significantly harmed by yours. David Gauthier interprets this "Lockean proviso" in the following way: "We interpret the Lockean proviso so that it prohibits worsening the situation of another person, except to avoid worsening one's own through interaction with that person. Or, we may conveniently say, the proviso prohibits bettering one's situation through interaction that worsens the situation of another" (1986: 205). In a general sense, this solves the problem of what would count as significant harm. In a trivial sense of harm, the fact that I am breathing the air means I am harming you, since I am depleting the oxygen supply to some degree. Should I stop breathing? Under the proviso, although I am using the air, the air is not soiled enough by my breathing in a way that would worsen your quality of air. Consequently, through my own use I have still "left in common" the air "as good for others." I have not significantly worsened your situation. However, if someone creates a factory that pollutes the air in a way that seriously affects the health of the local residents, then it is an obvious violation of the principle of nonmaleficence.

John Locke (1632–1704) was an English philosopher and political thinker whose works *An Essay Concerning Human Understanding* and *Of Civil Government* were highly influential for thinkers in the 18th century, including the framers of the American Constitution.

The libertarian principle interprets individual autonomy as the right of self-determination. It suggests that we should not violate the integrity of a person by interfering with that person's power to make decisions in situations where potential harm from that action would affect only that individual. It therefore creates a large sphere of privacy, that is, the sphere in which the individual is free to pursue her sense of happiness without interference from others. John Stuart Mill, although not usually identified as a moral libertarian, expresses this sentiment nonetheless:

> The only purpose for which power can be rightfully exercised over any member of a civilized community, against his will, is to prevent harm to others. His own good, either physical or moral, is not a sufficient warrant. ... The only part of the conduct of anyone for which he is amenable to society is that which concerns others. In the part which merely concerns himself, his independence is, of right, absolute. Over himself, over his own body and mind, the individual is sovereign (1859: 9).

Besides recognizing and maximizing a sphere of individual privacy, the libertarian principle also implies that all decisions which affect a person (either harmfully or positively) must have the consent of that person as well. The libertarian principle, then, justifies a cooperative arrangement that emphasizes the consent of the governed.

Clearly, the principle of nonmaleficence is a step above the principle of egoism, since it does take into consideration the interests of others. However, this consideration is minimal because libertarians do not aim at a maximum of cooperation with others, but only seek the fulfillment of their own interests with the minimum of interference from them. The libertarian principle creates a kind of negative reciprocity: Do not harm me and I will not harm you. It does not actively seek mutual advantage in a positive sense. At the basis of a libertarian morality is a mutual recognition of fundamental interests, but the goal of such morality is weighted toward the individual pursuit of interests rather than any collective goals. The result is a rather thin sense of community. But of course, for some people that is a plus rather than a minus.

The tenor of the libertarian ethic suggests that institutions and practices are meant to maximize the liberty of individuals rather than to engage in a collective effort to produce a collective good. Again, this is an ethos well received in a number of quarters in American culture. However, although that expresses well the ethic of certain competitive practices, it doesn't express the ethos present in other sorts of practices, such as family life or other formative or nurturing institutions. Some critics, such as the communitarian theorists (cf. Sandel 1982), argue the idea that the role of an ethical principle to maximize individual liberties in a collective arrangement assumes that all collective goods should be subordinate to the pursuit of individual plans for happiness. Such an arrangement makes for a very thin sense of community indeed.

In addition, if taken strictly, the principle of nonmaleficence leads to some ethically counterintuitive behaviors. One way in which the test of harm has been formulated is the following: If my absence would better your situation, then I am doing you harm; if not, then I am not doing you harm. If I shot you with a gun, then my absence would better your situation (you would be alive if it weren't for me). But consider the following scenario. We're leaning on the rail of a boat, perfect strangers. Suddenly, the boat lurches and you fall over the rail. Although the libertarian principle bids me to do you no harm, it does not obligate me to do you any good. Because I would be put out by calling for help (I'm more interested in finishing my drink), I don't feel an especial need to assist you. Because I am not the cause of your harm (whether I was there or not, had the boat lurched while you leaned on the rail, you would've fallen overboard), then I do nothing wrong in not aiding you. Your situation would not change in my absence. This, of course, goes against any decent inclination we have, and a good community would be one that goes beyond simple nonmaleficence to helping those in need. Everyone needs help sometime in their life with problems that they cannot solve on their own. A community that does not respond to those who suffer in natural disasters, for example, is a mean-spirited community indeed. Libertarians can defend themselves by arguing that the principle does not forbid someone to help another in that situation. Certainly, that is true but the point also shows that such help would be supererogatory, that is, beyond the ordinary duty of the principle, and so makes many morally decent actions voluntary. The libertarian principle is a step above egoism because it requires mutual recognition, but it obligates us to a minimal, negative reciprocity.

5.3.3 The Categorical Imperative

For the egoist, autonomy means being a law unto oneself. But if each person is a law unto himself, then the libertarian principle is more consistent in that respect, since we must recognize the autonomy of each individual. The recognition of each person as a sovereign being means that all actions done to another or along with another must have that person's consent. The libertarian principle emphasizes the compatibility of such sovereign beings, so that in such an arrangement the liberty of each individual is maximized and harm to others minimized. The result is that the libertarian principle permits you to do whatever you wish as long as it does not significantly harm another.

Imagine, however, a more radical reflection on this reasoning. What the libertarian is saying is that if everyone were to follow this principle strictly, that is, if

Immanuel Kant (1724–1804) is considered to be one of the most influential and important thinkers in the Western ethical tradition. His most important works on ethics include *Foundations of the Metaphysics of Morals* (1785) and *The Critique of Practical Reason (1788)*. It is in these works that Kant develops the notion of the categorical imperative.

everyone acted not to harm another, then the outcome would be a life of peaceful coexistence. On the other hand, if everyone were to follow the principle of egoism strictly, and anyone did anything they wished to anybody, the result would be a war of all against all. As we saw, for the principle of egoism to be an advantage to its advocate, only a few can practice it. Consequently, its universalization cannot be made without inconsistency. What this suggests is that a test of a principle's worth rests on its ability to be universalized without inconsistency: "What if everybody were to do that?" Consider, for example, the case of stealing. If stealing were universalized and everyone stole, then not only would no one be safe in terms of their person and possessions, but what would eventually remain to be stolen if everything was gained by stealing? In order to create possessions, one must produce them, but if one comes into possession of things only by stealing, then nothing would be made to steal. There is an inherent inconsistency in stealing; possession by stealing would not be possession, since anyone could steal what you have stolen. The entire concept of property or possession would disappear. Stealing works only when there are people who produce, buy, and sell things. For that reason, stealing cannot be universalized, but certainly, the practice of producing, buying, and selling can without inconsistency. Consider another practice commonly called "free-riding." A free-rider is someone who takes the benefits from a particular cooperative practice without contributing anything to it. If everyone acted as a free-rider, there would be no cooperative practices because no one would be willing to contribute what it would take to yield a certain benefit from them. Suppose someone were to borrow some money from another with no intention of paying it back. If that were universalized as an activity, clearly lending money would become foolish, and no one would believe what anyone promised (Kant 1785: 40).

Based on these considerations, Kant comes to the conclusion that what justifies a principle is whether or not what it recommends conforms to the very nature of a principle as such, that is, what it recommends is justified if it can be universalized without inconsistency. Kant calls this test the categorical imperative. The categorical imperative expresses the very form of a principle. As such it becomes the means of testing the morality of any action by showing that when that action is universalized it produces a consistent or inconsistent result. *One of the most familiar formulations of the principle is as follows: Act as if the maxim (the rule that would express the action) were to become a universal law* (1785: 39). The procedure that is involved in the categorical imperative can be outlined as follows:

1. Form a "hypothetical" imperative: I am to do X to bring about Y. In other words, one's deliberation about or plan for a particular end can be formalized in this way. This constitutes the "maxim" of your action.
2. Generalize the maxim: Everyone is to do X to bring about Y.
3. Imagine the generalized maxim in (2) as a law of nature, that is, a law that must be followed.
4. Consider the result when (3) is combined with other existing natural laws and human dispositions.
5. If the result is inconsistent or absurd, then you should not act on (1).

The beauty of the categorical imperative is that it relies only on the primitive logical notion of inconsistency to evaluate an action. As we noted in Section 5.2.6, this was the least controversial way to evaluate a principle but, at the same time, seemed to have very limited scope and application. Here Kant has managed to work out a more fruitful way of using it. Another advantage of the categorical imperative is that it expresses well the legislative aspect of autonomy. The goal of the libertarian principle, for example, is to maximize individual freedom—but freedom understood as doing whatever one wishes to do, which as we saw in Section 2.5 doesn't capture the genuine sense of autonomy. Kant's categorical imperative seems to express it more fully, since what it demands of persons is that they legislate for themselves a principle in the genuine sense of the term, that is, one that can be universalized.

Kant presents an interesting justification for the categorical imperative that can be summarized succinctly here (cf. 1785: 64–74). First, morality presupposes autonomy (1785: 66). We made it clear in Chapter Two that without freedom morality would make no sense. Without freedom there can be no blame or praise or any way to change or modify our behavior accordingly. Consequently, without freedom morality is impossible. But freedom, properly understood, is autonomy; that is, it is the capability of self-legislation or self-government. If freedom is understood as the freedom to do anything we wish, then this is not self-governed behavior, but behavior governed by our desires, urges, wants, and needs. Self-governance is governing ourselves by means of some law or principle. If we chose otherwise (e.g., if we chose to be governed by our desires), then we are not truly autonomous. The very concept of a principle entails essentially the idea of universalization, that is, something that applies to all persons in similar cases. The categorical imperative expresses the form of a principle. Hence, the categorical imperative is derived from the very idea of freedom or autonomy (1785: 72ff.). The argument can be summarized even more succinctly:

Morality presupposes autonomy.
Autonomy presupposes self-legislation.
Self-legislation presupposes the notion of moral law.

Moral law presupposes the idea of universal application.
The categorical imperative expresses the very form of a moral law.

Ultimately, the categorical imperative expresses a very simple truth about the justification for acting on a moral principle: The reason to act on principle is the only reason that is a truly moral one. This is why Kant uses the notion of acting from duty again and again as an exemplar of moral behavior (see Section 1.5). Acting for the sake of principle is the only purely moral motive for action, and it is also why Kant proclaims the good will, that is, the will to be governed by principle, as the only thing that is good in an absolute sense (1785: 9) (see Section 2.6).

Despite the ingenuity of Kant's argument, there are a number of problems that have been noted with the categorical imperative. One criticism can be expressed through the example of lying. The categorical imperative would seem to condemn lying as a practice. If everybody lied then no one could be trusted, and indeed, the distinction between lying and truth telling would no longer have any meaning. But is this entirely true? If everybody lied and everybody knew that everybody lied, then for all practical purposes, it would also be easy to determine the truth. If you asked someone who consistently lies whether they've stolen something of yours, and they say they have not, then you would know they did. From this point of view, then, it wouldn't matter whether everybody consistently lied or consistently told the truth; there would still be a way of finding the truth. Lying is harmful when it is in the context of a predominance of truth telling, not when it is universalized. The inconsistency test may not always work against practices we intuitively feel are wrong.

Eichmann's Account of the Categorical Imperative

Adolf Eichmann was responsible for deaths of millions of Jews during the Holocaust. In *Eichmann in Jerusalem* (1963), Hannah Arendt recounts Eichmann's defense of his actions in terms of Kant's categorical imperative. Eichmann claimed that he had lived his whole life according to Kant's categorical imperative; that he had done his duty, and now he was being prosecuted for doing what was right. "I meant by my remark about Kant that the principle of my will must always be such that it can become the principle of general laws." *Is this a distortion of Kant's categorical imperative, or is it a good rendering?* Arendt claimed that it was a distortion since the way Eichmann interpreted it was to act as if the maxim of your action was the same as that of the law of the land. *Do you think Arendt is right?*

There is a second problem with the categorical imperative that also becomes clear in the example of lying. Let's assume that the categorical imperative would prohibit lying because of a basic inconsistency in universalizing its practice. However, would we say the same of the case where a German citizen during World War II, hiding Jews in her attic, lies to the Gestapo at the door? Most people would want to argue that lying is morally permissible in this case. For this reason, we might want to qualify our maxim by reducing its scope: Should someone be in the situation exactly similar to this, then it would be permissible to lie. Universalizing that would not necessarily lead to any inconsistencies. If everybody who was hiding Jews in their attic lied to the Nazis, it is hard to see the inconsistency. The problem is that if we allow such qualifications of lying, cheating, or stealing in certain circumstances, then we could justify many actions to suit our particular needs. Would there be an inconsistency in permitting every spouse to lie about his or her adulterous affair? In other words, qualifications could be easily used under these circumstances to justify what a person might feel are reasonable exceptions to a rule, and consequently, the process could become a very subjective evaluation of action. If, on the other hand, we cannot qualify the categorical imperative in such a way, then we can end up condemning such morally prudent acts as lying to the Nazis in order to save innocent lives.

However, the case of lying to the Gestapo brings up another problem with the categorical imperative that may be more difficult to address by this example. One might say that the reason a person is justified in lying to the Gestapo is that the liar is trying to protect the innocent from unjust harm. Since lives are at stake, that should take priority over truth telling. We owe more to the innocent than we do to vicious killers. It would seem that the universalization of the maxim to protect the innocent from unjust harm would not involve any inconsistency. If everyone protected the innocent from unjust harm, that is a practice that would certainly be consistent, if not welcome. Assuming also that truth telling would pass the categorical imperative test, then the person answering the questions of the Gestapo would have two conflicting imperatives: not to lie and not to allow the innocent to be harmed. The categorical imperative itself does not seem to address this conflict, and moral judgments are full of such conflicts.

There is yet another criticism of the categorical imperative. It may be the case that the principle is not purely deontological at all, but implicitly consequentialist. It could be argued that the categorical imperative implicitly imparts some sense of the good life and employs some consequentialist considerations in its estimation of a particular action. After all, the toleration of an inconsistent practice itself involves some sense of the good life—it assumes that a society constituted by a set of consistent practices is a good society. But if the categorical imperative employs some sense of the good life, some sense of what is morally tolerable, then it violates its original intent to serve as an evaluation of various senses of the good life without recourse to any particular sense of the good life. As John Stuart Mill argues, "when [Kant] begins to deduce from [the categorical imperative] any of the actual duties

---

Should We Tell the Truth No Matter What?

Kant has been criticized for claiming that truth telling is an absolute duty regardless of the consequences. It would seem to suggest that, for example, we should tell the Nazis that we are hiding Jews in the attic if they ask us. But Kant would say that it would be even wrong to lie to the Gestapo. What is his reasoning for this? The only pure moral motive for acting is for the rightness of the principle, not for the goodness or badness of its consequences. Jean-Paul Sartre's story "The Wall" illustrates this idea. The story takes place during the Spanish Civil War. Pablo Ibbieta is captured by the fascists, and they interrogate him to find the whereabouts of one of his best friends, who is also one of the more important republican leaders. As a lesson they execute two of his comrades, captured along with him. However, over time Ibbieta begins to acquire a certain psychological attitude, in which he begins to view everyone—the fascists, his comrades, and his best friend—as vermin and not worthy of his concern. He loses his fear for his own life at this point and decides that he will tell the fascists the whereabouts of his friend, the republican

leader. But just as he is about to disclose this, he decides that they are not worthy of the truth, and he wants to play a joke on them. He will tell them a lie—and direct them to a cemetery nearby the house where his friend is hiding. He then waits for them to return, knowing full well that he will be executed, but satisfied that he had made them search in vein. Much to his surprise he is not brought out to the wall to be shot the next morning. He peers out into the courtroom to see his friend against the wall instead. He hears the shots. As it turns out, his friend, having an argument with his cousin, decided to leave the safety of his house and go to the cemetery in question. There the fascists discovered him and returned him to prison to be executed. Kant's point would be that because we are never assured of the consequences of our actions, we should not use them as the moral basis for our actions. We should always do the right thing regardless of what we believe will be the consequences.

What is your impression of this story? Does it illustrate Kant's point?

of morality, he fails, almost grotesquely, to show that there would be any contradiction, any logical impossibility, in the adoption by all rational beings of the most outrageously immoral rules of conduct. All he shows is that the consequences of their universal adoption would be such as no one would choose to incur" (1861: 6). Indeed, J.J.C. Smart notes that a certain form of utilitarianism, called rule-utilitarianism, comes very close to the sense of the categorical imperative (1973: 199). Rule-utilitarianism argues that it is not whether a particular act produces good consequences that should serve as a measure of whether it is good or bad, but whether a rule based on the act, if followed by all or almost all, would produce better consequences than not.

5.3.4 Contract Ethics and Discourse Ethics

Autonomy as self-governance literally means that one adopts for oneself the law which will govern one's moral life, and thus it suggests two aspects to that concept: a law or moral principle and consent to that principle. The libertarian ethic focuses on the consensual aspect of autonomy while the categorical imperative focuses on the nature of principles.

In the libertarian view each person is an autonomous moral agent, and so each person's sovereignty must be respected. This generates an indefinite number of individual spheres of sovereignty. The difficult problem then becomes one of negotiating a compatibility among these different spheres of self-governance. What is universal under the libertarian principle is individual autonomy; how the individual self-governs may not be and can vary to a large degree—as long as it does not include significant harm to others—which then defines the minimum of compatibility in this arrangement. Any law, or any action for that matter, that is imposed on any individual sphere of autonomy must have each person's consent, even if it is consonant with the person's own self-legislation. The only common morality that can occur, then, is that which is universally consented to by these autonomous individuals, and of course, the claim that each individual should be treated as an autonomous agent, and the no-harm principle—these must already be implicitly consented to. Thus, consent seems to be the fundamental aspect of the libertarian interpretation of autonomy, and the idea of a contract in which equally autonomous individuals come together to consent to a set of principles which will govern their behavior serves as a model of the libertarian ethos.

Consider the categorical imperative in this regard. The universalization test which the principle employs is really a thought experiment in which we imagine everyone acts as if they have accepted a certain rule of behavior and follows it strictly and mechanically. If everyone could adopt that rule under those conditions, then the rule is morally worthy; otherwise it is not. Universal consent to a rule could also be a test of a principle's moral worth.

The recognition that universal consent is at the center of autonomy-based principles forms the fundamental insight of contract and discourse ethics. In fact, the idea of universal consent is a more radical account of autonomy, and it brings together its two essential aspects: governance by universalizable principles and consent to those principles. Because consent is at the basis of these principles, a principle based on conditions for consent would seem to be the most fundamental principle: what is right is what everybody can agree is right.

In *A Theory of Justice,* John Rawls develops this argument in an interesting way. If the model of contract is at the basis of ethical principles, what would such a contractual process look like, especially if its aim is to bring about an impartial principle that could gain universal consent? To achieve this Rawls uses an imaginary device which he calls the *veil of ignorance* (1971: 136–142). He asks us to imagine a situation in which persons are in an *original position* in which they must decide the basic principles that will govern their cooperative arrangements, institutions, and practices. But he asks us to imagine that they "forget" who they are in a particular society, their gender, status, wealth, race, and so on. At the same time they still retain their abilities as rational agents to reason and deliberate and to understand the basic sense of what it requires for humans to live together. In essence the original position expresses exactly the idea of a deontological principle—a principle that is freely chosen without regard to self-interest or situation.

Given the original position and its conditions, Rawls argues that agents so situated would consent to what he calls *the greatest liberty principle, the idea that a cooperative arrangement should involve the equal distribution of liberty, compatible with a like liberty for all* (1971: 60). Since no one knows what his or her particular gender, status, or level of wealth is, each person would assign equal shares of liberty to each individual no matter what their status or position. Equal shares are always a rational choice when it is not clear whether you will be the least advantaged in a certain arrangement. For example, if you are to divide a pie into pieces for eight people, all of whom want to get as much pie as they possibly can and in a way that allows each person to take whatever piece she wants, then you might choose the following arrangement: Let the last person to take a piece of pie decide on how the pie should be cut. The least advantaged person would most likely argue that the pie should be cut in eight equal parts. That way she can be assured that she gets as much as anybody else. Equality always advantages the least advantaged in a collective arrangement. Under the greatest liberty principle, collective arrangements of persons should maximize their liberty not only to participate in the governance of such arrangements, but in the pursuit of their own senses of happiness.

So far this outcome is similar to a libertarian position. The difference between libertarianism and Rawls's position is expressed by a second principle that Rawls argues would be adopted by rational agents in the original position. This is called *the difference principle. It suggests that for the same reason that participants in the original position would choose equal shares of liberty for each other, they would also choose equal shares of all other goods, including wealth, status, roles, recognition, and so forth* (1971: 62). However, since inequalities in these goods may be more advantageous to those affected by it—for example, an unequal distribution of roles in a particular practice or institution based on differences in ability may make that practice more excellent, and so its products more beneficial for those who participate in it—then it can be agreed that such inequalities are justified if they are to everyone's advantage. More specifically, the least advantaged in a certain practice or institution should be better off with whatever unequal arrangement he or she has than without it (1971: 76ff.). Inequalities, then, are not morally right if they are not to the benefit of the least advantaged in the group.

There are several theoretical criticisms of Rawls's argument. The first set of criticisms comes from utilitarians who claim, for example, that rational agents in the original position would choose the utilitarian principle over the greatest liberty principle (cf. Harsanyi 1982). Some argue it is not clear why rational agents would not take risks in the sense that given, for example, they may have a one-in-ten chance of being some ethnic minority or a one-in-twenty chance of being disabled, they would choose principles that would inherently disadvantage those groups at the price of greater advantage to more likely group categories.

A second set of criticisms comes from feminist ethics. Virginia Held (1993) argues that the entire framework of the contract model and the emphasis on autonomous individuals is itself the problem. Such a model presupposes a certain kind of relation—actually, a lack of relation—among those decision makers in such an arrangement. The model imposes a certain framework that is unrealistic, but also excludes other genuine alternatives that are real forces in our cultural lives. There is simply a large segment of cultural practices—family life, especially—that is not contractual and cannot be placed in this mold (1993: 200). Held contrasts the model of mothering to the contractual model. In the contractual model, one has distinct individuals who have their own interests and are disinterested in the interests of others; they compete for whatever goods are made available through general cooperation. What constitutes such a society is competition and conflicts of interest. In the mothering model, on the other hand, there is a strong sense of nurturing, trust, and emotional bonds with others, as exemplified in a good mother–child relation; what motivates improvement in arrangements and practices is not competition but concern to improve the lot of those dependent on others for their well-being. More particularly, the mothering model would encourage a cultural ethos that is measured by how actions affect children—understood as the least advantaged members of a group—rather than whether it maximizes liberty of competing individuals (1993: 201–202).

A third set of criticisms comes from communitarians, such as Michael Sandel (1982), who in some respects agree with the feminist critique. He argues that the way in which Rawls designs the contractual situation, each of us must be viewed as persons independent of our particular interests and attachments, capable of abstracting ourselves enough to evaluate them (1982: 175). But in actuality we cannot detach ourselves from our interests and attachments, since these are exactly what establish our identities. Not only would we lose our identity in this regard but also our capacity to be moral agents and so choose a principle (1982: 19). Sandel argues that in the original position, there is really only one moral agent because all agents in the decision process are abstracted to the same level and type. Rawls's position presupposes that there is something like a self prior to the interests and purposes that it has. Such a conception of a person amounts to nothing more than an abstraction, a radically disembodied subject which is the opposite of real persons who are radically situated in their lives (1982: 21). A disembodied, decultured person would have no real motivation nor any capacity for deliberation, but would choose arbitrarily, which is hardly the best decision-making model (1982: 21). In fact, the agents described in the original position are incapable of choice since they don't really choose those principles. Their situation is so designed that they are guaranteed to select the greatest liberty principle and no other (1982: 127). The point that the communitarians stress in their critique of contract ethics is that it attempts to establish the constituting principles for a community prior to any sense of community; yet it seems that the very existence of individuals capable of agreeing to such principles already presupposes some such sense of community. What is fundamental to moral life is community, a community understood as being heavily invested in certain interests, common goods, and ways of life. The attempt to search for a principle independent of some such community will be fruitless if not impossible. (For a discussion of communitarianism, see also Section 4.8.3.)

A fourth set of criticisms comes from those who share Rawls's contractual approach to ethics. These go deeper toward some of the theoretical difficulties with Rawls's position. It is not clear whether Rawls's approach is purely deontological in the sense of a principle that is prior to all interests and ends. Although the original position is intended to express this deontological requirement, it also illustrates how it seems impossible to escape some sense of the good life, as Sandel points out. After all, the rational agents participating in the original position must have a sense that it is good to decide on principles in this way, they must also employ some sense of a good society, and they must have some sense of what is to their advantage. Thus, the original position implicitly contains some sense of the good life and, consequently, cannot fulfill its function as a pure deontological principle. The original position, then, is a reflection of a type of community, composed of agents of a certain type, with a certain sense of the good life. Based on that design, the greatest liberty principle would be the one chosen in that situation, as Sandel also points out. But suppose we were to adjust these conditions and, for example, change the nature of the agency involved or some of the conditions for agreement; in that case we would end up with a different principle being chosen. In other words, a strong circularity is detectable in Rawls's reasoning here. Given a principle, one can design an original position that would generate it; consequently, the original position presupposes some of the characteristics of the principle it is supposed to justify. For example, David Gauthier, who shares the contractual approach to ethics along with Rawls, nonetheless derives a much different principle precisely because the agents are differently designed in the original position. His moral agents are self-interested and egoistically acting persons; they would choose—purely on the basis of self-interest—a libertarian, no-harm principle as their ethical basis for cooperation (cf. Gauthier 1986).

Discourse ethics, as developed by German philosophers Jürgen Habermas (1990, 1993) and Karl-Otto Apel (1980), tries to eliminate some of the many difficulties associated with contract ethics. First, it avoids some of the feminist and communitarian criticisms by suggesting that participants in consensual agreements about ethical principles and collective behavior should not have to forget their particular interests, their connectedness to others, or their particular sense of the good life in the process. Instead, discourse ethics aims to show that the essential characteristics of such an

Jürgen Habermas is a contemporary German philosopher who helped develop critical theory and the notion of discourse ethics. His most important books are *Communication and the Evolution of Society* (1979), *Moral Consciousness and Communicative Action* (1990), and *Justification and Application* (1993). Karl-Otto Apel is also a contemporary German philosopher. His work on discourse ethics is developed in *Towards a Transformation of Philosophy* (1980).

effort, of a discourse that aims at such a consensus—and regardless of the interests participants bring to bear—contain an ethical principle which participants have already implicitly consented to. The principle, which could be called *the dialogic principle, claims that the measure of what is right is what can be agreed to by those affected by such decisions in a discursive practice that aims at genuine consensus. The principle could be expressed somewhat more simply: Do unto others what all of you, together, could agree should be done to each other.*

What is meant by a genuine consensus? More specifically, what is it that people do when they attempt to justify a principle? Simply put, they are engaging in a reason-giving discourse with others in an effort to come to an agreement about some principle. It might be suggested, then, that since all attempts at justification require this kind of generic-looking discourse, the necessary conditions for that discourse would also be the very presuppositions the participants would have to agree to even before they agreed to any principle discussed. In other words, the presuppositions of such a discourse already bind people together in their search for an ethical principle. If it so happens that the presuppositions of such a discourse have an ethical character to them (which they do), then our problem is solved; the matter is already settled.

What do these ethical principles or rules look like? First, to reach a genuine consensus and agreement, people must freely accept the contents of such an agreement. To freely accept means that it is something that accords with one's own will rather than another's; no coercion can be used to force someone to accept something else. In fact, to force someone to agree to something is not really an agreement, but simply a sham agreement. If in a debate a teacher threatens a student with a bad grade unless she agrees with her, it is not the case that the student actually agrees with the teacher, but rather a situation in which the student pretends to agree for the sake of preserving her grade for the course.

Second, let's also suppose that a principle which will now govern the institutions and practices that make up your life has been chosen in a discourse that excluded you in principle from participating in the deliberation; in that case it is also unlikely that you would consent to such a principle. Discourses that exclude participants who may especially disagree with the result of the discourse do not achieve a genuine consensus, only mock ones.

Finally, if the discourse were so structured that you could not properly participate in it, then you would also not likely be in agreement with the result. For example, if certain people were not given the same opportunities as others to defend and critique various proposals and related matters—to the point where they felt that their questions or considerations had not been fully addressed—then surely such persons would have difficulty consenting to whatever the result of the deliberations might be. Indeed, if they were treated unequally in the process, with less powers of membership than other deliberators, then in principle they might have difficulty agreeing with the result.

These three rules of discourses that aim at genuine consensus can be succinctly stated in the following way: (1) *the rule of equality*—all participants have equal power in the process of determining the best ethical principle; each has as much right as the other to make claims and criticize them; (2) *the rule of noncoercion*—force or coercion cannot be used against any participant in the process; (3) *the rule of nonexclusion*—participants cannot be excluded in principle from a discursive process that will result in a rule that affects them. A rule is morally right when there is a consensus about it under these conditions.

Because these rules are necessary for any consensus, they form the necessary constituents of any ethical principle because they are already implicitly agreed to by the agents in the practice of trying to reach consensus. In addition, by the very practice of trying to reach a consensus on an ethical principle, participants have implicitly consented to consensus, specifically universal consensus as the test of the principle. This can easily be shown by imagining a thought experiment in which there is an attempt to exclude another's principle from such a consensual process. In that case one would have two choices: (1) to treat the principle as pertaining only to you or your group's ethical life, in which case you are saying that it is not worthy of being followed by others; that is, it is not worthy or even capable of being universalized; and (2) to proclaim its universal worthiness and simply impose it upon others by force (since you are restricting the basis of its consent). Neither alternative would qualify it as a principle in the genuine sense of being universalizable. There is another cleverer proof of these rules: Suppose you wanted to deny the rules of discourse ethics; you would have to employ those very rules in disproving it. What this shows is the rules underlying consensus-based discourses are intractable—meaning that they cannot be eliminated discursively, although they can certainly be ignored. However, if they are ignored, then you are no longer trying to achieve consensus.

Discourse ethics seems to solve the problem of the ultimate justification of an ethical principle in an interesting way. As mentioned earlier, any attempt to justify or ground an ethical principle without appealing to moral intuitions will end up in circularity (the principle justifies results which justify the principle), regress (the principle requires another to justify it, which in turn requires another, ad infinitum), or dogmatism (one simply accepts the principle as intuitively clear or based on authority). By showing that the presuppositions of consensus-based discourses are intractable, the principle does not resort to dogmatism since it is the very means by which one persuades another without imposing authority. It does not involve regress because there is no appeal to any other more fundamental principles; an attempt to refute the principles requires their employment. Discourse ethics is not circular since the rules do not justify results that justify the rules, but the rules are themselves the defining conditions for justification. (For a simpler presentation of this argument, see The Allegory of the Convention which follows.)

Although discourse ethics addresses some of the difficulties with contract ethics, it does generate its own problems. For one thing, since it requires universal consensus of actual people as a test of the rightness of a rule, it is hard to imagine how such a test could be practically applied. The universalization in the categorical imperative can be performed by a single agent in a thought experiment and so yield a relatively immediate judgment on what to do. But to attain a consensus of some degree is a real-time process, and so judgment about what to do in certain situations may be a prolonged affair. In general, the practical question that arises is how extensive must the consensus be? The principle could require an indefinite consensus extending to future generations. Discourse ethics may work well in situations in which there are a finite and definite number of decision makers or where decisions are made by consensus to qualify consensus—for example, a consensus to allow majority vote. However, it may not work very well otherwise. In response to this criticism, defenders of discourse ethics argue that the point of the principle is to generate a decision-making process based on the consensus of those who will be affected by such decisions. To the degree that the process achieves consensus, then to that degree will we have assurance of the moral quality of the results. There will never be an absolute or universal consensus, but the principle works to color practices and institutions with the notion of consensus, and to that extent, it has a certain effect on how we make moral decisions.

Although this first criticism is concerned more with the practical application of discourse ethics, a second criticism addresses an apparent inherent inadequacy. With its emphasis on discursive processes, it assumes a certain level of competence in its participants. This would exclude from the process those who do not meet this level of competence such as children, the mentally disabled, the infirm, the mentally incompetent, and so forth. In many cases decisions must be made about them, yet in principle they are excluded from the decision-making process that will affect them. Discourse ethics would seem to violate its own principle in this regard. Yet to include them in the process somehow would seem impossible because they cannot reasonably participate in the process as designed. Indeed, this is a problem not only for discourse ethics, but all the varieties of deontological principles, since they rely so much on the notion of autonomy and consent. If decision makers can only be those who have risen to a certain level of competence in giving consent and in making decisions, then those who have not reached that level seem to be inherently disadvantaged.

The Allegory of the Convention
(Told in the Spirit of Borges)

You may recall the events central to Plato's story of the cave. He told of a story of men raised in a cave all their lives, who are chained in such a way that they mistake the shadows on the walls for everything that is. When one is freed and sees the causes of the shadows, and then is forced outside to see the sun, he realizes the true nature of things. But when he reenters the cave to reveal this truth to his comrades, he is rebuffed—even threatened with death. But Plato failed to tell the whole story, leaving out certain details. The entire story was first recorded by Hermogenes, an Athenian storyteller, historian, philosopher, and contemporary to both Socrates and Plato. It was his account of the trial and death of Socrates that the historian and adventurer Xenophon used in his own recollections of Socrates. Plato's version, of course, was much different. Apparently, there was some rivalry between Hermogenes and Plato, and as Plato's prestige grew with the formation of the Academy, Hermogenes's own work fell into the shadows of obscurity and historical neglect. But as recent manuscript discoveries make clear, a comparison of the two versions shows that Hermogenes's is far superior, of greater length and depth, and shows more storytelling talent than Plato's. For some reason Plato did not mention that the story took place in Atlantis, nor did he mention the historical circumstances of the events recounted in that tale.

It seems that on Atlantis, in darker times long ago, men thought it natural to enslave other men, women, and children. Some were used domestically, others as laborers in the fields, but the most unfortunate were made to work the large mines. To maximize their effort, they were made to spend their whole lives in the mines. Accommodations for an entire community were, in fact, provided for them beneath the earth. The masters knew that to maintain order a certain amount of ritual and mystery about their lives had to be maintained. They were also left ignorant about life outside of the caves. So it was, after a few generations of living in the caves, that a whole culture with certain fundamental beliefs developed.

Confident that their plan had worked, the masters decided to perform an experiment. They would release one of the cave dwellers, a man by the name of Pellior, to the outside world and return him to see what effect his revelations would have on the populace. It was at that point that Plato's story began, using the man's rough ascent of the cave, his viewing of daylight, and return to the cave for his own illustrative purposes. But as Plato recounted the story, the man's return and his attempt to reveal the existence of an outside world to the cave dwellers failed. In fact, the cave dwellers so firmly believed in their world that they nearly killed Pellior. The masters were now satisfied that the cave dwellers' beliefs were so solidified that even the power of truth would not dissuade them. The offending cave dweller was freed, not only for his own safety, but to ensure against any corrupting influence he might have on the others. And he lived as a free man with others above. But he never forgot the true lesson of his near encounter with death that day, that it was one thing to be the bearer of truth and another to get others to believe it. This problem he passed on to his children as a sacred trust, and they passed it on to theirs, as a problem to be contemplated and solved.

In the meantime Atlantis had changed greatly. Eventually, the cave dwellers were reincorporated into the daylight world. Atlantis became a loose confederation of a wide variety of groups with differing beliefs and religions. Conflicts and disputes began to be resolved more agreeably, and a kind of spontaneous avowal toward nonviolence arose. And so it was settled that communities would resolve their difference through dialogue for fear of edging back into a more barbaric age. But as the various communities settled into the ordinariness of life, differences arose among them in terms of their ethical principles. Beyond the common agreement that no blood was to be shed over any conflict—and given certain similarities among the various principles—there was not much agreement otherwise. And so each group hardened its views, and each view was broadcast through every other group so that those views less

The Allegory of the Convention, *Continued*
(Told in the Spirit of Borges)

coherent or credible soon lost followers, while those more potent remained in vogue. The island soon settled on those principles that were the fittest. Those principles which perished were among those whose leaders could not make them understandable or intelligible. Those who could not understand would change to those they could. Soon those who were insincere about their beliefs, who believed only artificially or halfheartedly about the principle or believed it as a means to continue their position of power, were either exposed or adopted principles they could truly believe. And every group that was settled so proclaimed their principle as the right one, that it was a principle worthy of universal recognition, that it was something that everyone would do best to believe.

By the end of this process, the member of any group had a good understanding of their principle, so that they were able to present good reasons for accepting it and could present it in a relatively clear and intelligible way. Each believed sincerely in their principles, and each proclaimed them fit for universal recognition. But the fact of the matter was that there were now several such principles, and there seemed to be no further change of resolution among them. This disturbed many leaders, and so many of them agreed to meet to resolve the matter.

A meeting was held in the Great Hall. There was an auditorium in the hall that had at its center a place for addressing everyone. There were speakers who were assigned the task of keeping order, and soon that was established, so that in no time speakers took their turn addressing the matter. Shortly, Corintha, great-great-granddaughter of Pellior, took her turn. She was tall and wearing mostly blue; she made quite an impression upon everyone. She looked round, waiting for any noise and distraction to disappear. There was some indirect conversation on what the previous speaker had said. Finally, she spoke.

"Friends. The matter is already settled, and I'm amazed you don't see it."

Everybody was surprised by this remark and puzzled, too. Several laughed, thinking that she was hoping simply to lighten the mood of the meeting. But many, somewhat irritated, shouted out that she should explain what she meant, and this was echoed elsewhere, so that, finally, there was an uproar among the participants. Algirdas, the Chair, saw fit to ring the bell which quieted most and allowed him their full attention.

"It seems, Corintha, that there is a request to clarify what you mean. Perhaps you should proceed." He stepped back from the Chair's stage, and every-

one focused on Corintha as she stood, her eyes closed, deep in thought, calling upon the wisdom of her family's special duty.

Corintha seemed calm despite the general irritation displayed by others. She lifted her head back slightly, adjusting her blue attire more comfortably. She began again.

"Since we all pledge to nonviolence, then our only hope is to call for a universal convention in which delegates from each position would enter into dialogue in order to resolve the matter. Now what would prevent any delegates from participating? Well, for one thing, if they were not going to be treated equally with other delegates—then they would be at an inherent disadvantage. If they were restricted in their opportunity to present their position or respond by criticism to others, surely they would not want to participate. Or if they were afraid that they would be coerced in some fashion, that other delegates would join forces against them, or engage in other such strategic actions. But who among the other delegates would wish that to happen? If each understands her beliefs, and can defend them, making them intelligible to others, and each is sincere in her beliefs, and feeling them worthy of universal approval, then each would have no fear in having them opened to debate and criticism. In fact, each would welcome the opportunity. They would have no need to make alliances with others in order to ensure victory in the debate, since that would be a sign of weakness of their own beliefs. And who among the delegates would not participate in the convention, knowing that there would be equality of participation and no coercion? Only those who were not confident in their beliefs, those who held back some insincerity and who could not defend them. So you see, my friends, that the principle we seek, the one upon which we could agree, is in fact the one we've already agreed to; it is the one that expresses what is necessary for the convention to take place. But because that is clear we need not even hold the convention—the matter is settled and here is our principle: that upon which we can agree to in a fair, noncoercive deliberation, where all parties affected by the matter are equal, and their power to defend and criticize are the same, is morally right."

She stepped back momentarily from the center of speaker's stage, and wiped her face with a long kerchief removed from her neck. She was so involved in her speech that only then did she notice the local conversations and remarks that started immediately after she was finished.

After some time had passed, one man, Merced, gained the comment stage. Bearded, lean, he spoke

Continued

The Allegory of the Convention, Continued
(Told in the Spirit of Borges)

with a strong voice and without the niceties most expected.

"I can't see this as something that everyone would agree to before agreeing to it. Here are my reasons. ..."

But just then Corintha violated custom and spoke out of turn, not allowing Merced to finish.

"If I could say just one thing before you say anything, I promise that you will need to say no more, and we'll all save time. If for some reason you are not satisfied with what I have to say, then, of course, I will gladly hear what you have to say." Corintha ended by looking directly at her interlocutor across the way.

Merced bowed toward her, "Go ahead, then. I'll wait."

She returned the gesture and faced him while she spoke.

"In denying my principle you are affirming it; and what that means is that in order to maintain the virtue of consistency, you must recognize it as necessary for any dialogue, including ours."

"Go on," Merced said, standing back from the center of the comment stage, his face perplexed, but also looking as if its fire had been drawn from it.

"If you aim to convince me, to have me accept freely what you believe is wrong with this principle, then, you must accept the conditions stated in that principle. You cannot refute it without, at the same time, admitting it; and if you do not accept it, then you cannot be really aiming to convince me." She stepped back and looked down near the front of the stage.

There was no comment from Merced and the audience broke out again in discussion. She was addressed several times, and she attempted to accommodate all critics. Some left still unconvinced, but many left satisfied, and she returned to her community confident that all would see as she did now.

5.4 TELEOLOGICAL PRINCIPLES

Deontological principles measure the goodness of actions in terms of their conformity to the formal characteristics of autonomy. Acting morally is acting autonomously, and thus, those conditions necessary for autonomy are also the basis for deciding on the right thing. Deontological principles derive their impartiality by being based on something that should be chosen by every moral agent prior to choosing anything else.

Teleological principles, on the other hand, measure the goodness of actions in terms of the consequences they entail for that moral agent. Impartiality is achieved not by ignoring the interests of particular moral agents but by arranging the consequences of choices so that they maximize benefit for moral agents. For this reason, teleological principles focus on the notion of what counts as benefit, who should receive these benefits, how much, and in what proportion to others. The principal theories in this regard include egoism (its consequentialist version), utilitarianism, and game theory.

5.4.1 The Principle of (Consequentialist) Egoism

There are versions of egoism other than the type discussed in Section 5.3.1. Rather than egoism being applied to the noble man, who through the power of his will and the nobility of his spirit has a right to impose his will on the world, there is the more ordinary sense of egoism as a person who lives within a cooperative community, but seeks benefits without real consideration of the harm or benefit to other members of that community. He is someone who seeks a gain with as little cost to himself as possible. For this sort of egoist, *one should act in a way that benefits you, regardless of the harm or benefit to others.*

Now it must be understood that most people are self-interested, but having interests doesn't necessarily make one an egoist. The world is not divided between egoists and altruists; just because persons are not self-sacrificing does not mean they're egoists. It is not so much having interests that make persons egoists as it is whether or not, in considering their interests, they also consider the interests of others. Egoists consider only their interests in deciding what to do and want gain without the consideration of cost to others.

The egoist in this sense is often a cynic and more likely to hold a negative satirical vision of the community—someone who downplays cooperative schemes or goals. Often the weapon of the egoist is the accusation of hypocrisy: "Everyone is an egoist, but I'm one of the few who admits it." According to this view, everyone is an egoist because even if she does good, she gets some pleasure out of it, and that's why she does it. Mother Teresa helped all those people because it made her feel good. Yes, but doesn't that say something about the moral character of Mother Teresa—that she derived pleasure from this rather than from beating and robbing the infirm? If what the egoist says is true, then everybody is an egoist, and so there's no moral distinction between Hitler and Mother Teresa—after all, they each took pleasure in what they did. This, of course, goes against our common intuitions that recognize moral differences among such people. This is nicely illustrated with a story about Abraham Lincoln (cf. Sharp 1928: 75; Rachels 1971).

It seems Lincoln and a companion were riding a coach and discussing this very topic, Lincoln claiming to be an egoist, his companion supporting altruism. Suddenly, in the midst of this discussion, Lincoln, distracted, banged loudly for the driver to stop. As they were near a stream, Lincoln could see that some piglets had wandered too near the muddy shore, had become entrapped in it, and so were in peril of drowning. Lincoln got out of the coach and went to their aid. The price of extracting them from the mud was a very dirty set of good clothes. Upon his return, his companion gloated, thinking that Lincoln's actions surely provided the proof against Lincoln's own position. But the future president persisted in calling the act selfish and egoistic: "I couldn't sleep tonight knowing that those pigs might have drowned, and so I saved their lives for the sake of a good night's sleep."

But clearly, this is a refutation of Lincoln's self-ascription. It is a remarkable and kind person, indeed, who would lose sleep over the fate of little piglets; that is certainly superior to the person who would simply ignore the situation and not lose sleep over it and far superior to the one who would take advantage of the pigs' dangerous situation to have a fine meal that night (cf. Rachels 1971).

There are other more formal difficulties with egoism. It is simply inconsistent to advocate it publicly as a principle (cf. Medlin 1957). Perhaps it could be expressed in the following way: "Everyone should act in her own best interest without regard to the interests of others." But as a prescription for everyone it violates the content of the principle. If I advise you to be an egoist, then I am thinking of your best interest. To be consistent, I must forgo espousing a principle which claims egoism as the best form of behavior.

If that is so, a certain consequence follows which happens to conform to the way things are as well. The egoist, in order to be an egoist, must never publicly admit it. A world full of egoists would soon devolve into a Hobbesian state of nature, where life is "nasty, brutish, and short." Egoists can only be egoists when there are many reciprocists, or even altruists, to hold things together. If a number of people are paying taxes to maintain the road they all use, yet an egoist comes across a scheme which enables him not to contribute to its upkeep, this will only work if some others contribute. If no one contributes, then the road deteriorates. The egoist is parasitic upon a cooperative institution or practice, and if the practice dissolves, then so does any advantage for being an egoist. Moreover, if we discover that the egoist is not paying her fair share, then we will generally seek sanctions against her until she does. For this reason, the egoist cannot publicly announce that she is acting egoistically, but must feign cooperation to remain at an advantage. This is another reason why the egoist cannot publicly advocate or recommend egoism as a principle.

These arguments should be enough to dismiss egoism as an adequate principle for a public, impartial morality. But even if it did serve as a principle of justice, institutions and practices based on it would soon become corrupt. A judge acting on egoistic principles, strictly speaking, could only decide on cases which personally benefited her. For example, in a child custody case, the judge would not decide on the basis of what was in the best interest of the child, and if there was no particular benefit to the judge in deciding one way or the other, the decision would be purely arbitrary. Certainly, a bribe could change the decision from an arbitrary one. The idea of just institutions or practices is that they do, in principle, take into consideration the interests of the accused, of the victim, or of the ward of the court. These kinds of roles are fiduciary ones; that is, we entrust our welfare to judges, juries, police, physicians, firefighters, educators, all of whom could not do, in principle, what they should do if guided by the principle of egoism.

5.4.2 The Tit-for-Tat Principle

Tosca was faced with a moral dilemma. Her lover, Cavaradossi, has been condemned to death by Scarpia, the police chief. Scarpia, however, has offered her a deal. If Tosca will sleep with him, he will save her lover's life by telling the firing squad to use blanks. In Tosca's culture and time, steeped as it was in strong sexual mores and sexism, this was tantamount to complete dishonor for a woman. She even risked the rejection of her lover, should he find out. Nonetheless, she tells Scarpia that she will do the deed. But after he has given the order to use blanks, she stabs him dead. She discovers—much to her dismay—that Scarpia chose to deceive her too. The firing squad uses real bullets, Cavaradossi dies, Tosca commits suicide, and Scarpia is murdered (cf. Ridley 1996: 53). In Puccini's *Tosca*, Scarpia and Tosca are involved in a situation typically described by game theory. Opponents try to press their advantage against one another in the hope of winning big. If Tosca had been successful in her deception, she would have saved the life of her lover, all the while keeping her honor; if she had cooperated without deception, she would have saved the life of her lover, but would have lost her honor—that is, if Scarpia were also willing to cooperate—and that is the rub. If Scarpia had cooperated, he would have had his way with the beautiful Tosca, although he would have allowed his enemy Cavardossi to live. But if he deceived Tosca, he would have both the things he wanted—again, assuming Tosca would cooperate. The real difficulty in such strategic situations is to figure out whether it is to your advantage to cooperate or to defect from cooperation, that is, to deceive the opponent.

The tit-for-tat principle attempts to give an answer to the question. *It argues that you should cooperate when others do, and not cooperate when others don't.* It is a principle that has gained recent prominence with certain developments in the theory of games and figures centrally in what is now being called *evolutionary ethics*. The goal of game theory is to devise the best strategies for interacting with others to accomplish certain beneficial goals. It assumes rationally economic agents, who (as we discussed in Section 4.6.1 on rational calculation) are self-interested and will always seek what is in their best interest, choose the action which maximizes their gain, or seek those actions which will minimize their loss. For this reason, it could be considered within the camp of consequentialism, since it is used as a means for advantage.

In game theory you face an opponent who has her own goals and interests, some if not all of which may be opposed to yours. You interact with the opponent in a way that yields the most gain or minimizes loss to you. In this context, if you are faced with a choice between a cooperative venture with another or a venture antagonistic to others, there are four possibilities in principle (keeping in mind that cooperation requires you to constrain your interests, while in antagonism you press your advantage to the disadvantage of the opponent). The figure below illustrates these possibilities: (1) both could act antagonistically, in which case there would be immediate losses for both; (2) you could act antagonistically, while your opponent does not, in which case there is gain for you and loss for your opponent; (3) you could expect to act cooperatively, yet your opponent does not, in which case there is great loss for you and great gain for the opponent; (4) both of you could act cooperatively, in which case there would be moderate gains for both.

This is often illustrated by what is called the prisoner's dilemma. Two prisoners are interrogated separately by police for a crime. If both cooperate with one another and do not implicate the other in the crime, then they are both likely to go free. But if either one implicates the other, then the accuser will get off or get reduced charges, but the accused will do serious prison time. If both implicate each other, both will do time. If you are one of the prisoners, should you cooperate or should you rat? It would seem that if you were to act rationally (that is, seek the action that would yield the greatest gain), then you should be a rat. Yet if the other is also a rat (as is most likely), then that would lead to a worse outcome for both. However, if you cooperate, there is a chance your opponent might not, in which case you would lose even more.

There seems to be only one way out of this dilemma, so formulated, according to political scientist Robert Axelrod (1981): a tit-for-tat strategy. In 1979 he set up a tournament to explore the logic of cooperation. He asked people to submit a computer program to play the prisoner's dilemma game 200 times against each other program submitted, against itself, and against a random program. At the end

TIT-FOR-TAT STRATEGY

		AGENT 1			
		Cooperate		Defect	
A G E N T 2	Cooperate	+5	+5	-10	+10
	Defect	+10	-10	-5	-5

The outcomes of a tit-for-tat strategy.

of this contest, each program would have scored a number of points. Much to everyone's surprise, the "nicer" programs won; that is, those programs which maximized cooperation were the clear winners. Anatol Rapoport, also a political scientist, submitted the tit-for-tat program that was the clear winner. It simply began by cooperating and then did whatever the opponent did the last time (cf. Ridley 1996: 60).

The prisoner's dilemma assumes a one-time choice, but of course, life offers a continual number of choices among opponents who live within striking or cooperative range of one another. It is more likely that if you act antagonistically toward another, the other will retaliate; therefore, it is not to your advantage to act antagonistically. But neither is it to your advantage to act cooperatively in the expectation that your opponent won't. The most rational course over time is to act cooperatively when your opponent does, but meet antagonism with antagonism; as soon as hostilities cease, then cooperate again. Thus, you make it clear that you are willing to cooperate but will meet any antagonism with antagonism. Axelrod explains why the principle is so effective:

> What accounts for tit-for-tat's robust success is its combination of being nice, retaliatory, forgiving and clear. Its niceness prevents it from getting into unnecessary trouble. Its retaliation discourages the other side from persisting whenever defection is tried. Its forgiveness helps restore mutual cooperation. And its clarity makes it intelligible to the other player, thereby eliciting long-term cooperation (1984).

This happens, of course, to be a strategy prevalent among foreign policymakers: Extend cooperative gestures, but retaliate in kind should the opponent prove antagonistic. It seemed to be the basis of America's M.A.D. (mutually assured destruction) policy concerning nuclear warfare during the Cold War: American policymakers let it be known to their Russian counterparts that America would not engage in any first strike policy, but should the Russians strike first, then America would engage in a counterstrike that would ensure the massive destruction of Russia. The old standard father's advice to his son is illustrative of the tit-for-tat rule: "I don't ever want to catch you starting a fight, but I also never want to catch you not finishing one."

The tit-for-tat principle has figured prominently in recent developments of evolutionary ethics. The basic axiom of evolutionary ethics is what Richard Dawkins has famously called "the selfish gene" (1976). This is the idea that, from an evolutionary point of view, all organisms aim at self-preservation, and the transmission of its genes into future generations. Why is it, then, that if this selfish impulse is at the core of every organism's being, we see so much cooperation, reciprocity, and even altruism in both animal and human societies? How is it possible

---

Case Study: Would Game Theory Justify Michael Milken's Actions?

Junk-bond king Michael Milken was a money-making wizard. It turns out that much of his talent was for dishonesty. During his heyday at Drexel Burnham Lambert, he probably stole more money than anyone in American history. He was sentenced to 10 years in prison for his crimes and is now out on parole. Milken and Drexel settled more than 150 securities and other civil lawsuits with companies and individuals who charged Milken wronged them. The agreement stipulated that Milken must pay $500 million—80 percent of his personal net worth—into the $1.3 billion settlement fund. Still Milken was left with $125 million of his own money and access to the $300 million his wife, children, and brother were permitted to keep. Does game theory suggest that, at least in this case, crime is the right thing to do?

The futurist Marvin Cetron asked ten deans of the nation's business schools to pose to 100 of their students the following question: If you do an illegal deal, get caught and tried and convicted, serve a 3-year prison sentence, and emerge with $500 million from the deal, would you still do it? Three in five of the business students said they absolutely would (cf. in Kidder 1995: 51).

to get from the selfish gene to cooperative relations? The answer is the tit-for-tat strategy. The tit-for-tat strategy assumes purely self-interested beings, yet over a period of time, players learn that it is in their self-interest to cooperate with others when they also cooperate. Consequently, cooperation becomes an evolved strategy for maximizing self-interest. Geneticists John Maynard Smith and G. Price (1973) showed how the tit-for-tat strategy did not have to be a rationally conscious principle, but could be understood as an evolutionary mechanism based on selection, which created "stable strategies," so that no animal using it would be worse off than an animal playing some different strategy. Axelrod himself collaborated with biologist William Hamilton to draw attention to the usefulness of the tit-for-tat strategy in describing animal behavior. Additional support came from research done by Robert Trivers (1971; cf. also Sigmund 1993) and the research of Gerald Wilkinson showing tit-for-tat behavior in vampire bats (1984).

Although the tit-for-tat strategy has some empirical support, there is also clear evidence of animal behavior that does not exhibit tit-for-tat strategies, as Heinsohn and Packer had shown in the behavior of lionesses (1995). Some economists have also criticized the theory on several grounds: (1) that the evidence is based on simulations rather than real life and (2) even under those conditions of simulation, the tit-for-tat strategy doesn't prevail, but rather gets its high marks by consistently scoring on draws (cf. Martinez-Coll and Hirshleifer 1991; Binmore 1994; Ridley 1996). In general, it is a highly restrictive strategy that is only appropriate for certain idealized, competitive practices, but not all practices are competitive. It is a strategy that is not appropriate among members of a family, where antagonisms should be met with attempts by parents, for example, to forgo personal benefit to ensure eventual harmony. In addition, consensual activities are at the basis of many communities. As opposed to competitive practices, consensual ones aim at some agreement or understanding which can then serve as a basis for governance. Establishing the constitution is a consensual rather than a competitive practice (although, of course, it's naive to think that competition did not take place). In other words, game theory frames all moral action as if it were competitive when, in fact, consensual and fundamentally cooperative activities constitute a great deal of communal life.

5.4.3 The Golden Rule

In its positive form *the principle states, "All things whatsoever you would that men should do to you, do you even so to them"* (Matthew 7:12). Also it is often expressed negatively: "Do to no one what you would not want done to you" (Tobit 4:15). Besides its use in Hebrew and Christian texts, this venerable principle is found in the Torah, Babylonian texts such as "The Story of Ahikar," in the Hindu tale "Mahabharata," Taoism, Buddhism, in Christian texts (Matthew 7:12 and Luke 6:31), in the Koran, and in Confucius (*Analects* V.11; XV.23). The negative version stresses refraining from harm; the positive version includes both avoiding harm and doing another good.

The interpretation of the positive version varies somewhat: Some interpret it as saying that you should do unto others as you would have others do unto you regardless of what they actually do to you. This interpretation of the golden rule makes it appear very altruistic. A second interpretation suggests that you should do unto others as you would have others do unto you to promote a level of reciprocity—a sort of "what goes around comes around" attitude. In the first case you should do unto others what you wish others would do to you, while in the second you should do unto others what you want done to you because it will, ideally, promote reciprocal behavior on their part. In either case the principle could be interpreted consequentially—it is right because of the results that follow from its consistent and universal use.

Either interpretation yields certain problems. First, the application of the principle is very subjective. Widely varying results could occur depending on the character of the person doing the deliberation. Imagine a vicious or self-destructive person applying the golden rule. In these cases people don't care what you do to them as long as they get to do it to you. If one doesn't mind being killed, then killing might be permitted. "It authorizes the quarrelsome person who loves to be provoked, to go about provoking others, and the person who hates friendliness and sympathy, to be cold and unsympathetic in his dealing with others" (Russell 1942: 110). As Richard Whately pointed out many years ago, people could use it to justify any action that might benefit them unjustly. For example, a guard using the golden rule might be obligated to release his prisoner since, if he were a prisoner, he would not want to be imprisoned (1857: Chap. IV). Use of the golden rule could lead to contradictory results depending on a person's own inclinations or desires. A request from someone for euthanasia could be justified if one reason is that it is what one would want in that situation, or the opposite could result, if it is not what you would want if you were in that situation. A person could use the principle to justify heroic measures in keeping a terminally ill person alive or use it to justify hastening their death. Consequently, it is an inconsistent guide for making the right choices.

But the golden rule is also very paternalistic. Because what you do to another is determined in terms of your own sense of what is good for you, you may impose an unwelcome action on the other person. To take a simple example, if you like to be tickled, then the golden rule would justify tickling another; but if the other person doesn't like to be tickled, then you are doing them harm rather than good. George Bernard Shaw, in *Maxims for Revolutionists,* said, "Do not do unto others as you would they should do unto you. Their tastes may not be the same." As L.J. Russell points out, "What I should wish others to do to me is often quite different from what they would wish me to do to them; and the latter is often much more important than the former" (1942: 109). The golden rule takes away the obligation to get another's consent when actions affect them; it contains no provision for that. You are permitted to do something to another solely on the basis of what you deem good for yourself. What is good for one may not be good for another, and so you cannot impose your sense of the good on another without some consideration of what the other wants. It makes the assumption that there is a relative uniformity of desire and want among others and, of course, in a complex society this is certainly not true (cf. Lippmann 1922: 121–122).

Although Bishop Whately points out the problems with the golden rule, in the end he defends it by suggesting that rather than being an algorithm for making specific decisions it is simply a reminder to do what you would regard as fair, right, just, and reasonable if you were in the other person's place (1857: Chap. IV). With some qualification, Marcus Singer argues similarly. If the rule is interpreted as saying that "one should do unto others what you would want others to do unto you," then the classic criticisms apply. But if the rule is interpreted more generally to say that "one should do unto others as you would have others do unto you," then the classic objections do not hold (1963: 299). As Singer explains, "Here what I have to consider is the general ways in which I would have others behave in their treatment of me. And what I would have them do, in abstraction from any of my particular desires, and all that I am entitled to expect them to do, is to take account of my interests, desires, needs and wishes—which may well be different from theirs—and either satisfy them or else not willfully frustrate them" (1963: 300). The golden rule demands that whatever standards you expect from others you should also apply to them.

The difficulty with Singer's interpretation is that it makes the principle somewhat useless as a procedural algorithm, which in part is the purpose of formulating a principle. Singer's formulation is more or less a restatement of the principle in slightly different, more general language, but which removes the procedure implicit in the rule. The procedure involves (1) determining what sort of action you're about to do that will affect another; (2) considering the effect; (3) determining whether you would want to be affected similarly in the same situation; (4) if yes, then do it, and if not, then don't. But saying that the golden rule means that you should simply act fairly (without specifying which rules to employ in that effort) takes the utility out of the golden rule. Under Singer's and Whately's interpretation, at its best, the golden rule simply gives us an imperative to act fairly. I shouldn't claim special treatment or exemption for myself. If I'm in a practice with certain known rules, then I should act toward others on the basis of those rules. But that doesn't say what the rules should be or whether the rules that are in place are necessarily good ones. The problem of which standards to apply is still not resolved by the formulation. Singer recognizes this when he notes that "the Golden Rule by itself does not unambiguously and definitely determine just what these 'standards or principles' should be. ... " (1963: 313). In this case George Bernard Shaw might be right: "The golden rule is that there are no golden rules" (*Maxims for Revolutionists*).

5.4.4 The Utilitarian Principle

The utilitarian solution to the problem of establishing an impartial ethical principle is very simple. *The best actions are those which maximize the amount of happiness for those individuals affected by a decision, given their sense of happiness.* What better outcome could there be for a group of people cooperating with one another than the overall increase in their happiness? Utilitarianism looks to the collective outcome of the actions rather than the autonomy of the individual agents as a source of evaluation. The utilitarian principle is formulated in the following way: *Of several actions, the one that promotes the greatest happiness for the greatest number is to be preferred, where happiness is defined as pleasure in some sense or another.* Utilitarianism, more than any other ethic, lends itself to a kind of calculus for decision making. It is allied with cost–benefit analysis, decision theory, and game theory.

5.4.5 Bentham's Account of Utilitarianism

Although certainly Jeremy Bentham (1789) had predecessors (including Shaftesbury, 1711, Hutcheson, 1725, David Hume, 1739, Adam Smith, 1759), he is considered one of the earliest proponents of utilitarianism. He defined it as follows: "By the principle of utility is meant that principle which approves or disapproves of every action whatsoever, according to the tendency which it appears to have to augment or diminish the happiness of the party whose interest is in question: or, what is the same thing in other words, to promote or to oppose that happiness" (*Principles*, Chap. 1). As he notes, a better formulation is the so-called *"greatest happiness or*

Jeremy Bentham (1748–1832) was a political philosopher and legislator and is considered to be the founder of utilitarianism.

greatest felicity principle": "the greatest happiness of all those whose interest is in question, as being the right and proper, and only right and proper and universally desirable, end of human action" (*Prin.*, Chap. 1). This same principle is stated earlier by Hutcheson: "that action is best, which procures the greatest happiness for the greatest numbers; and that, worst, which, in like manner, occasions misery" (1725, Sec. III, par. 8). By utility, Bentham meant "that property in any object, whereby it tends to produce benefit, advantage, pleasure, good, or happiness ..." (*Prin.*, Chap. 1). However, as far as he was concerned, these were all names for the same thing, namely, pleasure (*Prin.*, Chap. 1). For this reason, Bentham's (as well as Mill's) version of utilitarianism is rightly called hedonistic utilitarianism.

Since happiness is identified with pleasure, then applying the utilitarian principle is a matter of calculating properly the pleasure involved in acts among those affected by that action. This calculation requires taking into consideration the following aspects of pleasure (*Prin.*, Chap. 4):

1. its intensity
2. its duration
3. its certainty
4. its propinquity
5. its fecundity, by which Bentham meant its chance of being following by a similar chain of pleasures or pain
6. its purity, by which Bentham meant its chance of not being followed by sensations of the opposite kind
7. its extent

Calculating whether an act was good or bad, then, involved a relatively simple procedure, a sort of hedonic calculus (*Prin.*, Chap. 4):

1. Begin with an identification of those in a community most immediately affected by the action.

2. For each person determine each distinguishable pleasure that is initially produced by it.

3. For each person determine each distinguishable pain that is initially produced by it.

4. For each person determine the fecundity of the pleasures and the impurity of the pains.

5. For each person determine the fecundity of the pains and the impurity of the pleasures.

6. For each person sum up the pleasures on one side and the pains on the other. The balance, if it be on the side of pleasure, will give the good tendency of the act for each individual; if on the side of pain, the bad tendency of it for each individual.

7. Take an account of the number of persons involved. Sum up the numbers for whom the act has a good tendency; sum up the numbers for whom the act has a bad tendency. Take the balance, which, if on the side of pleasure, will give the general good tendency of the act; if on the side of pain, then its evil tendency.

Bentham mentions a mnemonic verse that reflects the calculation here (*Prin.*, Chap. 4 n.):

Intense, long, certain, speedy, fruitful, pure—
Such marks in pleasures and in pains endure.
Such pleasures seek if private be thy end:
If it be public, wide let them extend.
Such pains avoid, whichever be thy view:
If pains must come, let them extend to few.

Bentham's method of calculation here is often called the *total principle* (cf. Parfit 1990: 136) because it involves the addition of all positive utility minus negative utility for each individual. This is consonant with three axioms which Bentham proposes in regard to this view: (1) that every person has a right to happiness (where happiness is pleasure), (2) that each person is to count for one, and (3) that what is to count as pleasurable for the person is determined by the individual's standard (*Prin.*, Chap. 1, Sect. 4). Under this last rubric, Bentham uses the motto, "poetry is as good as pushpin" (those homey embroidered sayings). By that he meant, at least within the same category of pleasure, that any pleasure is as good as another as determined by individual experience. If one person enjoys going to the opera but another disdains it in favor of drinking a bottle of gin, then each is worth the same within the hedonic calculus. Thus, Bentham advocates a strong egalitarian version of utilitarianism.

5.4.6 John Stuart Mill's Version of Utilitarianism

John Stuart Mill agrees with *the general formulation of the utilitarian principle: "Actions are right in proportion as they tend to promote happiness; wrong as they tend to produce the reverse of happiness"* (1861: 10). He also, like Bentham, identifies happiness with pleasure (1861: 10). However, he disagrees in great measure with Bentham's egalitarian version of utilitarianism. As opposed to the view which suggests that "poetry is as good as pushpin," Mill counters with the claim that it is "better to be Socrates dissatisfied than a fool satisfied" (1861: 14). By that he meant that not all pleasures are equal just because they are enjoyed by someone. Rather the measure of the worth of a pleasure is in terms of the character or worth of the person doing the

John Stuart Mill (1806–1873) was one of the most influential of the English philosophers in the 19th century. He is best known for his work on utilitarianism. His writings include *Utilitarianism* (1861), *On Liberty* (1859), and *The Subjection of Women* (1869).

enjoying. If a pig enjoys a certain pleasure, yet Socrates does not, then it is worth less; if Socrates enjoys a pleasure, yet a pig does not, then it is worth more. Thus, in calculating the greatest happiness, one must make qualitative distinctions among the pleasures being produced by the various actions.

According to Mill, the standard for this qualitative measure would be made by those who have met two conditions: (1) they are persons of a certain character who are capable of nobler feelings and desires (1861: 14) and (2) they have knowledge and experience of the pleasures to be compared (1861: 15). In that case, among those judges, their preferences or the majority of their preferences are to be the preferences for the whole (1861: 15). As opposed to Bentham's egalitarian version of utilitarianism, Mill proposes an elitist one.

In addition, as opposed to Bentham's "total principle" of calculation, Mill seems to have advocated what is now called the *average principle of utilitarianism* (cf. Myrdal 1953: 38ff.). This is where one takes the sum of utilities for each action multiplied by the number of people who have it and divided by the total population. The difference between the total and average principle can be expressed as follows:

Total Principle

$$\sum n(p_i)$$

where p_i is the degree or kind of pleasure and n is the number of persons receiving that pleasure.

Average Principle

$$\frac{\sum n(p_i)}{t}$$

where p_i is the degree or kind of pleasure, n is the number of persons receiving this pleasure, and t is the total population.

The differences between these two principles will be discussed shortly along with some of their perceived shortcomings.

5.4.7 The Preference versus Happiness Versions of Utilitarianism

Many criticisms have been directed to the classical account of happiness as pleasure, and how pleasure is to be defined and measured. The argument, as discussed in Section 4.5.3, is that if pleasure is happiness and pleasure is merely a psychological state, then people should be just as happy to experience a sort of faux-pleasure without recourse to actual experience, a sort of "experience machine" as contemporary philosopher Robert Nozick calls it (1974: 42ff.). The experience machine would allow you to experience a state of pleasure without really being engaged with those things that are pleasurable or desirable. All utilitarian calculations, then, would be reduced to producing and maintaining such machines; in other words, to put it more strikingly, a society on pleasure-producing drugs would be the best society. Clearly, then, it is not just a state or feeling of pleasure that makes one happy, but the attainment of something that is truly desirable. To avoid some of these difficulties, several philosophers (cf. Ayer 1954) have argued that the concept of pleasure should be replaced by the idea of *desire-satisfaction*, or as economists prefer, the notion of *preference* in the utilitarian account. According to Ayer, one should identify the happiness of a person not with some measurable psychological state but the class of ends that the person in fact pursues; happiness then would be the satisfaction of these ends or desires. Put differently, happiness for a person would be the attainment of what goals, goods, or ends a person prefers to attain. Ayer proposes that, in replacing desire-satisfaction (or preference) with pleasure, Bentham's version of the utilitarian principle becomes the following: We are always to act in such a way as to give as many people as possible as much as possible of whatever it is they want (1954: 49).

R.B. Brandt defends *the happiness version* against the desire-satisfaction account (1979). The difficulty with the preference version is that if the goal in utilitarianism is happiness, then mere satisfaction of desires may not reach that goal. There is an important difference between the satisfaction of a desire and the achievement of happiness: The first may be accomplished without achieving the latter simply because some people desire what will make them unhappy; in addition, what people desire may change over time. What else does the policy maximize if not happiness? The most important difficulty with Brandt's account, however, is that it does assume an implicit form of paternalism or at least some objective account of happiness. That is to say, Brandt's argument supposes that not all desire-satisfaction will lead to happiness, that some desires, if attained, will whereas others will not independently of whether persons desire them or not. Consequently, we should strive to maximize the satisfaction of those desires that will lead to happiness independently of whether even the majority of people does not desire them. As we will see this is a problem that faces most Mill versions of the utilitarian principle.

5.4.8 Act- versus Rule-Utilitarianism

In utilitarianism there is a division among those who argue for an act version of the theory, while others promote what is called rule-utilitarianism. According to *act-utilitarianism, the principle of utility is to be applied to particular actions in particular circumstances*. That is, regardless of whether the rule against lying is generally a good one, the act-utilitarian asks whether it is good in this situation to lie based on the utilitarian consequences (cf. Smart 1973). What act-utilitarianism asks is: What good and evil consequences will result directly from this action in this circumstance? It then uses that response to measure the goodness of the action. Since the act-utilitarians do not think that the observance of a general rule always promotes the general good, they would seem to advocate the violation of such a rule if it would lead to the greatest good for the greatest number.

Rule-utilitarianism, on the other hand, *argues that instead of measuring the consequences of particular actions, one should measure the utility of following an action on the basis of the utility of its rule* (cf. Brandt 1967). The rule against lying has great utility, and for that reason one should not lie, even in this particular circumstance where it might have great benefit. Some rule-utilitarians emphasize an entire system of rules or moral codes rather than just the individual evaluation of a moral rule. In this case one should seek those systems of rules for moral life which would have the effect of maximizing utility for that population.

Rule-utilitarianism turns out to be similar in some ways to the categorical imperative. Both are concerned with the universal application of a rule. But whereas the categorical imperative measures the goodness of a rule in terms of its consistency or lack of consistency, rule-utilitarianism considers the goodness of a rule in terms of the consequences it has for the community as a whole.

5.4.9 Justification and Criticism of the Utilitarian Principle

So far we've looked at the main proponents of utilitarianism and its varieties. A question remains concerning its justification. Of course, if one tries to justify it by appealing to its consequences, this involves a fallacy of circularity. Mill takes a different strategy. His justification of the utilitarian principle is based on a rather simple claim: "Nothing is good to human beings but in so far as it is either pleasurable or a means of attaining pleasure or averting pain" (1861: 51). In other words, the utilitarian principle is justified because it maximizes pleasure, and pleasure is what everyone considers desirable. This relatively simple argument is severely criticized by early 20th-century philosopher G.E. Moore. Moore

---

G.E. Moore (1873–1958) was an English philosopher and one of the founders of modern analytic philosophy. Moore argued that moral concepts of the good were fundamental and unanalyzable, but were nonetheless intuitable. Of two states of affairs, any normal human adult could "cognize" which was better than the other. Disagreements occur only because the states are not clearly analyzed or specified. The idea of moral intuition is discussed in Section 5.1.

---

argues that Mill, among others, commits what he calls the "naturalistic fallacy" (1903: 66). Mill's proof is flawed because the good is not the desirable but what ought to be desired, just as the detestable ought to be detested. If the desirable means what it is good to desire, then it is no longer plausible to say that our only test of that is what is actually desired. Bad desires are also possible. Thus, although it may be true that most or all people desire pleasure, it does make pleasure, thereby, the good. By trying to base something moral on something natural or nonmoral, Mill is telling us that we ought to desire something because we actually do desire it. Mill's logic is flawed: Because the good means the desirable does not mean that what is desirable is always what is good. Because Mill offers this as the primary justification for the principle, then the foundations for the principle are questionable even though, of course, it is widely used both in individual lives and in general public policymaking.

Some have criticized the utilitarian calculus. Derek Parfit (1990) has made an interesting argument showing how the total utility principle can easily yield counterintuitive results. Without showing much of the calculation, one can devise the following scenarios. Suppose we have an opportunity to control the population of a certain community, which in turn will dictate the quality of life for each individual in it. Let's suppose that as we increase the population, the quality of life decreases; in this case the quality of life might decrease, loosely speaking, from one in which there are nice creature comforts, good education and work opportunities, entertainment, arts, and general enhancements in life to one that is relatively mediocre, gray, and dull and finally to one that is a bare maintenance of life. It's quite possible, under arguments by Parfit, that as the population greatly increases, the total utility principle would warrant that increase, since its formula allows numbers to count favorably toward the total amount of pleasure experienced by a population. Thus, the total principle would favor large populations with very low qualities of life over smaller ones with more average or even superior qualities of life. The average principle seems to avoid this dilemma.

Another difficulty with the total principle becomes clearer if we combine it with the preference version of utilitarianism. In this case it easily could lead to the tyranny of the majority. The preferences of the few, whose preferences might in fact be worthier, would be swept away under the more powerful interests of the majority. This could result in the progressive homogenization and mediocritization of the society as well. As the majority's preferences become favored, the preferences of the few have less chance of survival so that the majority's values eventually permeate society. By treating all pleasures the same (evaluatively speaking), Bentham's version really reduces moral decision making to a question of quantity: how much of a certain pleasure will be distributed over a population that prefers it versus the quantity of a competitive pleasure. This proposal may also reduce the overall quality of the pleasure depending on what sorts of pleasures the majority prefers. It may turn out that pushpin pushes fine poetry into obscurity.

To take a morally neutral example, suppose you are the director of the National Endowment for the Arts (NEA); suppose also that your decision procedures for the distribution of funds are set by the preference version of the Bentham total principle of utilitarianism. Since all preferences in art are equally valuable, then this would suggest that no applicant should be judged on artistic merit but simply on the presence of an application. In that case the fairest way to distribute the funds would be either through a lottery system or first come first served or some other similar device. In this case an artwork by Picasso would be as worthy as velvet Elvis paintings. Now suppose also that economic conditions were such that the only way an artist could make a living creating art was by funding through the NEA. Chances are very good that since great talent is rarer than not, the artworks of more talented artists would soon become very rare indeed, mediocrities would become more predominant, and an argument could be made that the quality of art in the world would suffer as a whole.

Although the average principle might escape some of these difficulties, John Rawls (1971: 167) has a strong criticism of it. Under Rawls's view the average principle could allow scenarios where the quality of life vastly improves for a majority precisely on the backs of a small minority who are deprived of very fundamental goods (e.g., their basic rights). Rawls argues in this case that the average principle could justify slavery. For example, suppose an autonomous locality has a major industry that suddenly goes bankrupt, and one-eighth of the population is suddenly jobless. The average principle could (among other possibilities) justify an arrangement in which the jobless are taken in as indentured servants by some of the employed on the basis of a time period suitable to the new masters. Since the economic conditions of most are improved and the average utility would not decline by much, then the arrangement could be justified, even though it violates basic liberties of many of the individuals involved. To avoid such a possibility, Rawls argues that the utilitarian principle must be supplemented by a deontological one, which guarantees that certain basic rights and liberties cannot be transgressed. The utilitarian principle lends itself to expediency for the sake of average happiness, and this could allow it to violate fundamental rights in that regard. Modern democracies, on the other hand, are especially interested in guaranteeing individual rights, even at great cost or inconvenience. Thus, the utilitarian principle does not seem entirely consonant with rights-based communities.

As opposed to Bentham's utilitarianism, Mill's version would tend toward elitism. If it is combined with the happiness version of utilitarianism, then happiness is to be defined by the preferences of those who have the wisdom and experience of those various pleasures; the collective good is to be guided by the decisions of a few. The goal here is to maximize genuine happiness on the basis of the wisdom of the few. Even though this is often how things work, so that a minority of those in power run the legislature, the judiciary, business, education, and religious institutions, it can lead to a strong form of paternalism that many find unpalatable, and it is actually inconsistent with Mill's own strong political libertarianism. To use the foregoing NEA example, in Mill's case, because elite artists would be deciding who got funding, it is true that the quality of art would most likely improve. However, the tastes of those other than the few would not be represented. Thus, what is to be enjoyed or represented artistically would be determined by an elite minority in this case.

Another problem with both algorithms of the utilitarian principle is that they often require a comparison of what many consider to be incommensurable values or utilities. Wherever it is the case that you are dealing with the same utility, let's say money, the algorithms work fairly well. If you have a choice between two actions, A_1 and A_2, and A_1 produces X amount of money for population P_1 and A_2 produces Y amount of money for population P_2, and if X is greater than Y and P_1 greater than P_2, then it is clear that one should prefer A_1 by utilitarian principles:

$\text{Action}_1 \rightarrow X$ for Population_1

$\text{Action}_2 \rightarrow Y$ for Population_2

where $X > Y$, and $\text{Population}_1 > \text{Population}_2$

However, the matter becomes more complicated when X and Y represent different values, for example, life, health, and money. If the decision is whether to save 1 million utility customers a few dollars on their electric bills every month by building a nuclear power plant versus the health of 1000 powerplant workers, the measures become more difficult to make. Often a common medium, such as money, is used to make the comparison. This requires that we assign a monetary value to life or health. Some find this unpalatable, but it is done in public policymaking, risk management, and engineering all the time. The engineer has to calculate the cost of straightening a curve in the road versus the number of deaths caused by the degree of curvature; risk managers have to decide between the cost of a car design and the number of lives that may be lost due to its limitations. Consider the following case.

The beaches in Anchorage, Alaska, are very silty in many places; at low tide these cause mud flats which are extremely dangerous to be on should the tide come back in. Because the tide reenters so quickly, the mud acts like quicksand and draws an unsuspecting person into a concretelike hold. Such was the fate of a woman who recently arrived from out of state. Her four-wheeler got stuck on the flats, and her

Case Studies: The Sacrifice of a Few for the Benefit of Many

According to *The Age Newspaper* in Melbourne, Australia, children in orphanages were used to test experimental vaccines for diphtheria and whooping cough for several decades after World War II. An infectious disease expert, Dr. David Vaux of the Walter and Eliza Hall Institute of Medical Research at the University of Melbourne, argued that the testing was necessary to save lives in the orphanages. The children lived in close quarters and contagious diseases were rampant. "Many children's lives were saved," he said. "I think the scientists, the medical profession and the sisters running the orphanages could be congratulated for doing their utmost to protect their children." "It shouldn't have happened then," federal Health Minister Michael Wooldridge said. "It couldn't happen now." Vaux said the vaccines were first tested on animals for any toxic effects before being given to humans. "At the time, there were all sorts of infectious epidemics going through children, especially where children were crowded together," Vaux said. Many of the diseases either caused paralysis or were lethal (Associated Press, July 15, 1997).

Vaux seems to be using a utilitarian justification for the action here, namely, that since many more lives would be saved by experimenting with the vaccines on the children, then it was justified. Assuming that living is more pleasurable than dying, there was more benefit created for more people by this action. Wooldridge, on the other hand, seems to argue more deontologically, namely, that there was no right for the experimenters to use the children as guinea pigs, even if it meant that many other children's lives would be saved.

Questions for Discussion

1. With whom do you agree and why?
2. Is it possible, on the basis of the utilitarian principle, to justify immoral acts if everyone benefits from them?

Suppose it could be argued that car theft creates more happiness than not. For example, car thieves employ a number of people: men to deliver the cars, work on the license numbers, paint them, give them papers, drive them out of state, and find customers for them. The underground economy in stolen cars also allows many working people to own cars they couldn't normally afford. Car owners are ultimately happy too because they get a new car from the insurance company. The only people who lose are insurance companies, but such losses are part of the reason they are in business.

Question for Discussion

Do you see a flaw in this reasoning? Using utilitarian criteria, could this be an agreeable argument?

---

legs in turn became anchored in the mud. As the tide came in, all the rescuers could do was hold her while she drowned in the rising tide. After this horrible incident, a call was made to post signs throughout the area. After some consideration the city office that handled such affairs decided against it for the following reasons: (1) the high initial cost of designing, making, and placing the signs; (2) the added cost of maintenance of the signs; (3) the liability to the city of Anchorage because of the posting of signs and the increased cost of insurance as a result; (4) the low incidence of deaths of this type. In other words, if one person dies every 10 years on the mud flats, then it is not worth the cost in money to the city to prevent it. For many, of course, this seems like a reasonable decision; however, it still shows that one must often pit incommensurable values against one another, something which requires a common denominator, to make a decision.

The problem with incommensurability is that a utilitarian decision framework often forces such incommensurable measures: jobs versus the environment, cost versus lives, and so forth. In this case our decision making gets locked into a win–lose or no-win situation. Other decision frameworks might argue for a more holistic approach in which values are not measured one against the other but systematically as paradigms or models. For example, instead of asking if we want a cleaner environment or better jobs, perhaps it would be more fruitful to discuss larger systems of organization that maximize all of what we consider valuable to life. The very character of utilitarianism lends itself to the incommensurability

Williams's Paradox

Philosopher Bernard Williams presented the following paradox about utilitarianism (1973: 116–117). George, who has a wife and two children, is out of work when a friend offers him a job that would involve studying ways to conduct chemical and biological warfare. George believes that he cannot accept this particular job because of his moral code against the use of chemical weapons in warfare. Yet he needs the money desperately for his family, especially for his children's needs. George also happens to know that if he doesn't take the position, there is another one who has absolutely no qualms about using chemical weapons and would, most likely, zealously and obediently conduct such research. George now has an opportunity to help his family and to prevent a fanatic from obtaining a powerful position that, if misused, could have dangerous consequences. In addition, it seems the public would benefit if George accepted the position: He would be more responsible than the other candidate. Still, George is very bothered by violating his own principles and conducting such immoral research. On the basis of utilitarian calculations, it seems that George should take the job. But since that requires him to violate his own integrity, it would suggest that utilitarianism can often demand a compromise to integrity.

Question for Discussion

Do you agree with Williams?

---

problem because it seeks to balance different values, interests, and preferences rather than addressing what is right or wrong. Often, then, the result is a trade-off between antagonistic value claims.

Another difficulty with the utilitarian algorithms is that they tend toward the bureaucratization of moral decision making and thus place the power of directing the good in the hands of those not always affected by the outcomes. The utilitarian calculus seems to lend itself to manipulation from above, by those in power making decisions, rather than from within, by those affected by such decisions. It is imaginable, as John Rawls has proposed, that the utilitarian principle could demand self-sacrifice by a few (or at least the altruism of some) for the sake of the collective good as part and parcel of the ethical picture it paints. Thus, if the enslavement of a few benefited the whole greatly, such an arrangement could be justified under such a calculus.

5.5 THE NATURAL LAW THEORY AND RIGHTS-BASED ETHICS

The natural law theory takes a different approach to establishing an ethical principle than either the deontological or consequentialist ones. Yet it holds similarities with both. There are various views of this theory, however. Some argue for a purely naturalistic account, while others, such as medieval theologian and philosopher Thomas Aquinas suggest a more religious grounding for the natural law. It is a theory which was formative in the development of the concept of natural rights, so influential to the idea of the modern state in the 18th century. It is a theory that is found in Aristotle and has continued to the modern day. Natural law theory argues that an ethical principle can be derived from a naturally existing law, which is universal, and can be discerned by the proper application of reasoning. Since it is formed by reason, it can be discovered by it.

5.5.1 History of Natural Law Theory

The Greek Sophists made a distinction between nature (*physis*), with its invariable order, and laws (*nomos*), which were thought to be the result of human convention and society. For them all morals and political laws had no other basis than the agreements and conventions of human beings in the context of their particular groups and cultures. There was nothing beyond this to appeal to. Thus, the notion of a natural law would seem self-contradictory to them. One of the earliest thinkers to argue against this view and articulate the notion of a natural law was Aristotle:

> Particular law is that which each community lays down and applies to its own members: this is partly written and partly unwritten. Universal law is the law of nature. For there really is, as every one to some extent divines, a natural justice and injustice that is binding on all men, even on those who have no association or covenant with each other. It is this that Sophocles' Antigone clearly means when she says that the burial of Polyneices was a just act in spite of the prohibition: she means that it was just by nature (*Rhet.* 1373b4).

The Stoics were instrumental in the formative development of the notion of natural law, although their particular conception takes on a fatalistic and religious air. Natural law is that which will exert itself over the order of things. Reason urges us to obey it willingly, but it will be forced upon us nonetheless. Cicero expresses this view well:

> There is truly a law, which is right reason, fitted to our nature, proclaimed to all men, constant, everlasting. It calls to duty by commanding and deters from wrong by forbidding, neither commanding nor forbidding the good man in vain even when it fails to move the wicked. It can neither be evaded nor amended nor wholly abolished. No decree of Senate or people can free us from it. No explainer or interpreter of it need be sought but itself. There will not be found one law at Rome and another at Athens, one now and another later, but one law, everlasting and unchangeable, extending to all nations and all times, with one common teacher and ruler of all, God, this law's founder, promulgator, and enforcer. The man who does not obey him flees from himself and, even if he escapes other punishments normally incurred, pays, the supreme penalty by the very fact that he despises the nature of man in himself (*De republica* Bk. III, xxii, 33).

For Cicero this natural law is "right reason in conformity with nature, present in all men, unchanging, eternal, commanding all to the performance of duty, prohibiting evil" (*De rep.* III.33). In his book *On Duties,* he states it more simply as "to refrain from harm and serve the common good" (*De officiis* I.31). Cicero also stresses the theme of equality that is to become the hallmark of natural law theory and, later, the theory of natural rights:

> And so, however we may define man, a single definition will apply to all. For those creatures who have received the gift of reason from nature have also received right reason, and therefore they have also received the gift of law, which is right reason applied to command and prohibition. And if they have received law, they have received Justice also. Now all men have received reason; therefore all men have received justice (*De legibus* I.x.29; xii.33).

Since all human beings are rational, and reason is the means by which to apprehend the natural law, then all human beings are equal in their command and prohibition under that law.

Christianity contributed greatly to the development of natural law theory. Thomas Aquinas's work was especially influential. The Stoic concept of the natural law as a divinely ordered process of creation was translated into the Christian view of the creator God ordering all things for the good. This *eternal law*, as Aquinas articulated it, was not simply an expression of the arbitrary will of God, but it originates in the mind of God and so is a product of divine reason (*Summa* Q. 91. art. 1; Q 93. art. 4). *The eternal law is that all things are directed toward some good, and so the order of things is highly purposive and rational.* In attributing this order to the quality of God's rational mind, Aquinas avoids many of the traditional criticisms directed to appeals to authority for justifying moral principles. It is not based on the arbitrary will of a powerful divine being, but on its divine intel-

---

Thomas Aquinas (1225–1274) was an Italian-born theologian and philosopher and the student of Albert the Great (1206–1280). Aquinas set out to make Aristotle respectable and acceptable to Catholic doctrine at this time. He was quite successful and is considered the most central source for official theological doctrines of the Catholic Church. He agreed with Aristotle that the end of human beings, understood as natural beings composed of body and soul, is flourishing. However, the highest end was knowledge of God, which could lead to a perfection of the human being and a state that would develop a "divine likeness."

---

lect. Thus, the moral law is rationally chosen, but by a divine being. *Aquinas argues that the natural law is derived from this eternal law. Since all things are directed toward some good, then the natural law commands us to do good and avoid evil* (*Summa* Q. 94. Art 2). Clear expressions of the natural law in this regard include self-preservation, acting for the good of our kin, and to live peaceably, and to avoid harm to others in the societies and groups in which we live (*Summa* Q. 94. Art 2). All good political laws are in turn derived from this natural law.

5.5.2 The Natural Law Expressed as a Principle of Benevolence

The natural law, which commands us to do good and avoid evil, can be expressed as a *principle of benevolence* or, as Christian thinkers are want to say, a principle of love. In Romans 13: 8–10 Paul writes that "all the commandments: You shall not commit adultery, you shall not kill, you shall not steal, you shall not covet, and so on, are summed up in this single command: *You must love your neighbor as yourself.* Love is the one thing that cannot hurt your neighbor; that is why it is the answer to every one of the commandments." Paul is suggesting that the principle underlying many of the ordinary moral rules is the principle simply to love another, that is, to treat them benevolently. *The principle of benevolence expresses the simple sense of goodwill: Do good and don't do harm* (Frankena 1973: 45). It expresses a basic axiom of moral decision making: In all choices aim for the good and avoid harming others. Philosopher William Frankena breaks this down

---

Herbert Simon's Theory of Altruism

Herbert Simon is a professor at Carnegie-Mellon University and an authority on psychology, computer science, and economics, for which he won a Nobel Prize in 1978. In a 1991 article in *Science*, Simon argued that acts of altruism, the sacrificing of one's own interests for others, are maladaptive from the perspective of evolutionary theory, specifically sociobiology. Sociobiology argues that individuals only help others who are closely related to them or who can bestow some benefit on them in return. Why, then, would cases of altruism be fairly common? Simon argues that altruism is a by-product of docility, understood as "receptivity to social influence." Docility is adaptive because by going along with others one gets along. Societies often exploit this trait by teaching people to do things which diminish individual fitness but benefit the greater good. According to Simon, societies that foster this sort of altruism will thrive as long as the costs of altruism to individual fitness do not exceed the benefits from docility. Simon infers that docility allows those who are a bit more cunning and intelligent to use the trait of docility in others to their advantage

into the following considerations (1973: 47): The principle of benevolence enjoins us not only (a) *to refrain from doing harm to another* (the principle of nonmaleficence) but also, more positively, (b) *to prevent harm befalling another,* (c) *to remove or remedy harm,* and (d) *to do another good.*

One difficulty with the principle of benevolence is that it is rather vaguely formulated. Most of the other principles entail algorithms or procedures for determining the good; the principle of benevolence just tells you to do the good and not to do harm and for that reason is not very helpful as stated. Granted that nearly all of the principles assume the axiom that you are to do the good, the principles suggest the manner in which the good is to be attained. All sorts of questions arise in this context: To whom are we to do good? To how many? How often? How much? In addition, are we just as obligated to prevent harm as we are not to harm? Is doing another good always an obligation or only under certain circumstances? If someone wants my theater ticket, should I give it to him, since it will do him good? Should I constantly strive to do good for others? Is that an ordinary obligation or supererogatory?

We might try to remedy this by specifying the kinds of goods and harms we have in mind. For example, consider the medical profession. Assuming that one of the goods which medical practice can offer is curing disease, then that practice would translate the four directives of the principle of benevolence in the following way: The physician is obligated not to cause disease, to prevent disease, to remedy disease, and to restore health. But besides listing what a physician is obligated to do, the principle of benevolence does not really say what the constraints on the pursuit of these goods should be. Although we can specify the goods to be achieved in the context of some practice, the principle of benevolence doesn't really help us any further.

Random Acts of Kindness

In 1994 Gavin Whitsett, professor of communications at University of California, wrote a little pamphlet called *Guerilla Kindness.* He advocated doing a number of random and anonymous kindnesses for others as a way of generating more of the behavior in others. The phrase "practice random acts of kindness and senseless acts of beauty" was coined by Anne Herbert, a San Francisco-area writer.

Allan Luks, author of *The Healing Power of Doing Good,* compares the euphoria that volunteers experience when helping others to the endorphin-induced "runner's high." He claims that this feeling relieves stress and raises self-esteem.

Question: If we act altruistically because it benefits us in this way, are we really acting altruistically?

Another possibility is to qualify the four directives in a way that answers some of the questions just posed. These may be listed in a convenient mnemonic:

1. *ability:* Do you have the skill, knowledge, and ability to do (a), (b), (c), and (d) above? Certainly, neither a drowning man nor the would-be rescuer is benefited if the latter cannot swim.

2. *availability:* Is the person in need accessible to you?

3. *avocation:* Are there present those who are specially trained for such aid? If not, then you have a duty to notify them, but if unavailable, then you have a duty to aid the person in need to the best of your ability.

4. *accountability:* To what extent has the mature victim been responsible for the need of aid? To what extent are you responsible for the victim's need?

5. *autonomy:* Does the person want help?

6. *allocation:* Are we aiding the person in terms of their needs versus their preferences or wants (i.e., in terms of their welfare instead of their well-being)?

7. *adversity:* What are the risks involved to the benefactor?

But these are rough-and-ready qualifiers. It's not entirely clear why such qualifications should be made other than on the basis of common moral intuitions: The idea is to adjust the principle so that it meets the ordinary sense of what it means to be benevolent. But the job of the principle is to give us clearer formulation of what to do.

5.5.3 The Beginnings of Natural Rights Theories

The Reformation theory of both Luther and Calvin had proposed the basic depravity of human nature; consequently, the use of a natural law that claimed a disposition in human nature toward the good seemed incompatible with this theology. But whereas Protestant Christianity during this period dropped interest in natural law theory for the most part, and with some notable exceptions, the Enlightenment thinkers and their predecessors revitalized it, and in doing so, it underwent a number of important changes. First, it moved from a concern with natural law to that of natural rights. "The modern theory of natural law was not, properly speaking, a theory of law at all. It was a theory of rights" (*D'entreves* 1957: 59). As Hobbes argues

> though they [the Romans] that speak of this subject use to confound *ius* and *lex*, *right* and *law*: yet they ought to be distinguished; because RIGHT consisteth in liberty to do, or to forbear: whereas LAW determineth, and bindeth to one of them: so that law and right differ as much, as obligation and liberty (1651: Pt. I, Chap. 14).

Thus, for modern theory, natural law is not only a source of command and obligation but a means of establishing entitlement. *Rights declare a default condition of liberty to act and whose exercise must be respected so that such a right is not interfered with.* For John Locke, the natural law becomes translated as an obligation not to harm others in their life, liberty, and possessions precisely because these things are natural rights and so are not to be interfered with (1689: I.6–7).

Second, the modern theory attempts to give a more naturalized account of the natural law without reliance on the theologically based notion of an eternal law. The emphasis in the Enlightenment was on the discovery of this natural law by the use of reason and the assumption that what makes human beings unique and what they all hold in common is their rational natures. Thus, the natural law is derived from the very nature of being a rational being and is evident to them in their capacity as rational beings. Whereas Aquinas had declared the natural law as the command "to do good and to avoid evil," Hugo Grotius (1583–1645), often thought to be the founder of the modern theory of natural law, claimed that "the law of nature is a dictate of right reason which points out that an act … has in it a quality of moral baseness or moral necessity" (1625: I. 1.10). Thus, natural law was to be understood as a power of reason based purely on reason, and not on the divine, eternal law. In some sense Grotius took Aquinas's claim that the eternal law was not a dictate of the will of God but the exercise of God's reason one step further. For Grotius, natural law would retain its validity even if God did not exist (1625: Sect. 11). Although he himself was a pious Christian who believed that God had implanted this natural law in human beings, nonetheless his aim was to show, in the troubling times of the Reformation and its aftermath, how such a law could be proved without reference to any theological underpinnings. To this end he emulated the methodology of mathematics of his time, which believed that the basic axioms of mathematics were self-evident. Axioms such as "equals added to equals are equal" or "the shortest distance between two points is a straight line" or a whole is greater than any one of its parts" were self-evident and did not require any proof:

> I have made it my concern to refer the proofs of things touching the law of nature to certain fundamental conceptions which are beyond question; so that no one can deny them without doing violence to himself. For the principles of that law, if only you pay strict heed to them, are in themselves manifest and clear, almost as evident as are those thing which we perceive by the external senses (1625: Sect. 39).

Thomas Jefferson's famous words in the Declaration of Independence, "we hold these truths to be *self-evident*, that all men are created equal," echo the claim that such rights could be discerned through the use of reason alone. Thus, the justification of rights was not based on theological underpinnings—although Jefferson, just as Grotius, acknowledged that these rights are bestowed on human beings by their Creator—but on the basis of what was inherently rational and subject to reason.

For modern natural rights theorists, the device of the "state of nature" becomes a clever means of providing a clearer account of natural rights and their priority in the matter of moral and political affairs. In the state of nature, theorists imagine the human condition prior to the existence of any political state or organization. In this state of nature, one finds human beings living by the terms of these natural rights, as if they were living by the natural law, and the formation of the state or any political organization is constrained by this natural condition. The

---

The Universal Declaration of Rights

There are thirty articles to this particular Declaration of Rights adopted by the United Nations in 1948. These include a number of rights recognized in the American Constitution, such as equality, life, liberty, property, free speech, religion, and certain protections of the law. But it also adds a number of others. Some of these include:

Article 14: Everyone has the right to seek and to enjoy in other countries asylum from persecution.

Article 15: Everyone has the right to a nationality.

Article 16: Everyone has a right to marry and to found a family.

Article 22: Everyone has a right to the free development of his personality.

Article 23: Everyone has a right to work.

Article 24: Everyone has a right to rest and leisure.

Article 25: Everyone has a right to a standard of living adequately for the health and well-being of himself and his family.

Article 26: Everyone has a right to education.

Article 27: Everyone has a right to participate in the cultural life of the community, and to enjoy the arts.

In commenting on this document, Jeane Kirkpatrick, the conservative ambassador to the United Nations under Ronald Reagan, argued that the proliferation of rights was due to a fundamental confusion between rights, goals, and wants. She argued that such rights take on the character of a "Letter to Santa Claus" (1980). They can multiply indefinitely because there does not seem to be any clear standard that informs them. For every goal toward which human beings have worked, these now seem to be cast as rights rather than as aspirations. Rights, she argues, are vested in persons; goals are achieved by efforts of persons. Such "rights" then vest the responsibility in others rather than in oneself.

Questions for Discussion

1. Do you agree with Kirkpatrick's claims?
2. Is it possible to imagine additional rights that have as much claim as these?
3. What might be the difference between wants and rights?
4. If a right is a claim upon another, to whom are these claims addressed?
5. Which of these, if any, would you not count as rights?

device shows the hierarchical order of things—that rights exist prior to any laws of a state, and it is these basic rights which constrain any formation of government. The difficulty with this approach is that the numbers and kinds of rights that are deemed natural vary in relation to the constitution and character of the state of nature. For Thomas Hobbes, as we saw earlier (Section 4.5.2), the state of nature is constituted by a life that is nasty, brutish, and short, since there is only one right which all human beings share equally, namely, the right to everything. Consequently, the purpose of the state is to ensure security away from this state of nature. But for John Locke, as we also saw earlier (Section 4.5.2), the state of nature is differently constituted. Here the natural rights include life, liberty, and property, and the purpose of government is simply to ensure that these rights are freely exercised and properly adjudicated when they conflict in a population of citizens. For Jefferson, the basic rights are life, liberty, and the pursuit of happiness, and the Bill of Rights adds several more. The French Constitution of 1789 also includes the right to fight oppression. The Universal Declaration of Human Rights, adopted by the United Nations in 1948, has thirty rights listed, some of which are further subdivided.

This variety and increasing volume of rights suggest one of the more fundamental difficulties with the natural rights approach. The claim that natural rights are self-evident has been shown to be a weak criterion for evidence. This is even the case in mathematics which, as we saw, served as an inspiration for modern theories. Prior to the 19th century, it was thought that there was basically only one geometry—Euclidean geometry—and its basic axioms were self-evident. Who could dispute that the shortest distance between two points is a straight line, that there are parallel lines, or that two lines intersect at only one point? But with the development of non-Euclidean geometries after the 19th century, the self-evidence of these axioms was placed into question. It was quite possible to develop perfectly consistent geometries whose axioms contradicted some of the Euclidean ones. Thus, the whole standard of self-evidence had to be thrown out. We see a similar problem here in the notion of natural rights as self-evident. Their self-evidence is a sub-

---

Is the Claim That "The Whole Is Greater Than Any of Its Parts" Self-Evident?

For most people, this would seem like an obvious truth. How could it be otherwise? It does not seem possible that a part could be greater than or equal to the whole of which it is a part. Yet a mathematics developed by Georg Cantor, called transfinite arithmetic, seems to refute this apparently self-evident claim. Consider the set of all natural counting numbers, 1, 2, 3, 4, 5 ... This class is certainly infinite. For any natural counting number you provide, one larger can also be provided. Consider now the class of even counting numbers, 2, 4, 6, 8, ... This set is also infinite. For any even number, a person can also provide the next largest one. Now the even numbers are a subset, that is, a part of the set of natural counting numbers. In fact, it would seem to be exactly half the number of that set. Yet they are both infinite sets. Consequently, a part is equal to the whole, and the axiom you thought self-evident no longer seems so. Self-evidence proves to be a weak criterion for counting something as true.

---

jective criterion, depending on whether or not the person being addressed sees them as self-evident. If the person does not, then there is not much recourse to claim that he in fact does see them as self-evident or should see them as self-evident. J.B. Mabbott clearly states the difficulty with this approach:

> Natural rights must be self-evident and they must be absolute if they are to be rights at all. For if a right is derivative from a more fundamental right, then it is not natural in the sense intended; and if a right is to be explained or defended by reference to the good of the community or of the individual concerned, then these "goods" are the

ultimate values in the case, and their pursuit may obviously infringe or destroy the "right" in question (1958: 57–58).

The second strategy of explaining rights—by devising a state of nature and showing how certain rights are recognized in it—also fails on the face of it. It is not clear why one is to prefer Locke's rights of life, liberty, and property to Hobbes's right of everybody to everything. Of course, depending on which rights are adopted in the state of nature, the character of that state, the reasons why government will be formed, and the reasons why they should be dissolved will differ. The problem of which rights are natural rights has not been solved by this conceptual device—these rights are still presupposed, not proven. It could be argued that the thirty or so rights listed in the Universal Declaration of Human Rights appear to be just that—a list of someone's proposal for what should count as a right, but it seems to exist without justification. This is perhaps why, as Richard Wasserstrom notes, many in the 20th century believed that the doctrine of natural rights had been thoroughly discredited through the vagueness of their formulation, the failure of agreement as to what they are, and the lack of any ground or argument for them (1991: 257).

5.5.4 Rights-Based Ethics

Rights-based ethics attempt to show that the notion of right is essential for morality and that societies based on rights are far better than those based solely on obligation or utilitarian notions such as happiness or pleasure. Thinkers usually associated with this theory include Richard Wasserstrom, Joel Feinberg, J.L. Mackie, and Ronald Dworkin. They are aware of the faults and limitations of the traditional natural rights theories and endeavor to develop a concept of right that is not based on self-evidence or appeals to the inherent nature of human beings. Whereas deontological theories focus on what we are obligated to do on the basis of what is inherent in our features as moral agents, and whereas teleological or consequentialist theories focus on what should be done to further certain goals, such as happiness, advantage, or a common good, rights-based theories focus instead on what moral agents are fundamentally entitled to (Mackie 1992: 169). *Entitlements* then serve as the basis for the most fundamental obligations we have toward others. Thus, rights-based theories attempt to show that our more fundamental obligations depend upon our rights rather than suggesting, as deontologists do, that fundamental obligations generate rights. Rights-based ethics also attempt to show that consequentialist principles, utilitarianism in particular, implicitly appeal to some notion of right and so presuppose it. Thus, rights-based theories claim that both deontological and consequentialist principles rely on some notion of right.

The first task of rights-based theory is to give an account of rights that avoids some of the pitfalls and difficulties of the natural right theories. Richard Wasserstrom does an interesting job of outlining some of these essential characteristics. For Wasserstrom, rights are entitlements which allow persons to make certain claims against others. To claim something by right is different than obtaining it through the grant of a privilege, the receipt of a favor, or the presence of a permission (1991: 258–259). Generally, rights constitute the strongest of all moral claims that can be asserted. They serve to define and protect those things which all human beings are entitled to have. They indicate those areas which every human being is entitled to act without securing further permission or assent, and they function to put certain matters beyond the power of anyone else to grant or to deny. They provide ready justification for acting in certain ways and ready grounds upon which to condemn any interference (1991: 260). For example, a right to life is one that a person need not justify to others. A person can secure it, protect it, and ensure its health without permission from others. At the same time, it is something which is not in any one else's power to destroy.

Using the arguments of Gregory Vlastos (1992), Wasserstrom also points out that only those entitlements that can be considered universal, that is, equally assigned to all human beings without distinction, can be counted as rights. To suggest that rights hold only for some violates the sense of right as a default condition; partial allotment of rights would characterize it as a privilege that some have and others don't. Being president of the United States is possible for only a few and so could never be counted as a right. Similarly, being a billionaire is also a rarity. But having the liberty to choose and attempt to be president or a billionaire is something that can be allotted to all persons. Thus, either all human beings have rights or none do.

Rights-based theorists argue that goal-based ethics requires some notion of right to ensure the prevention of ends-justify-the-means sorts of abuses and the proliferation of undesirable or morally counterintuitive consequences. In this regard it makes the same sort of criticism of consequentialist theories as deontological ones do, and its solution seems similar. Without some notion of right, they argue, utilitarianism lends itself to expedient solutions to problems in the distribution of goods. For example, as we saw, it could justify slavery on the basis of greatest good for the greatest number. An inviolable right to freedom would constrain such solutions. Of course, Mill understands this well and attempts in both *Utilitarianism* and *On Liberty* to account for the notion of right and basic obligations purely on utilitarian grounds. Obligations would arise to enact whatever means are appropriate for achieving the end. Rights could also be derived in similar fashion as conditions that are critical to the greatest good for the greatest number. Indeed, this is how Mill argues the case in *Utilitarianism:*

> Justice is a name for certain classes of moral rules which concern the essentials of human well-being more nearly, and are therefore of more absolute obligation, than any other rules for the guidance of life; and the notion which we have found to be of the essence of the idea of justice—that of a right residing in an individual—implies and testifies to this more binding obligation (1861: 73).

In other words, since well-being or happiness is the end of human action and notions of right are essential to secure well-being, then we are obligated to respect them precisely because they are necessary means to well-being. But the difference between a rights-based approach and a utilitarian one becomes clear on this point. Since rights are ultimately dependent upon well-being for their justification if, as it turns out, well-being demands their dismissal, then such dismissal would be warranted. On a rights-based or a deontological account, rights are the fundamental obligations, and well-being must be subordinate to them. In other words, no matter how many people will benefit by a certain action, rights cannot be violated in achieving it. A collective body should not be able to limit the free speech of any of its members, even if there is good reason to believe that it will produce a greater good, such as security or better cooperation (cf. Scanlon 1992: 137).

Second, it is clear, as rights-based theorists point out, that utilitarianism implicitly assumes certain rights. For example, both Bentham and Mill argue that each person's happiness is to count as much as any other's. After all, the principle does not state the greatest happiness for the smallest number. Thus, equality is an essential feature of utilitarianism. Since equality directs how the utilitarian calculations are to be made and so defines the very essence of the utilitarian principle, the utilitarian principle cannot be used to determine that equality is justified by utilitarianism—except in an ad hoc way. If utilitarianism were to assume instead that men's happiness is worth more than women's, then the calculation of benefit would be different than if it assumed, conversely, that women's is worth more than men's, and differently again if it assumed that both are equally worthy of happiness. But if it did not assume equality, then it would seem to violate its own principle, namely, the greatest happiness for *the greatest number*. Thus, utilitarianism must presuppose equality in some form. The derivation of the utilitarian principle as it is seems to depend on the presumption of equality and not conversely.

This argument is also one made by deontology. Thus, both rights-based theories and deontology are in agreement on their criticisms of utilitarianism. The real issue, then, for rights-based theorists, is not only to distinguish themselves from deontological theories of obligation, but to show how obligations are dependent upon, or derived from, some notion of rights. Rights-based theorists are interested in showing that rights and obligations are not the same thing. If that were the case, then deontology would be sufficient to articulate the notion of right.

S.I. Benn and R.S. Peters argue that "right and duty are different names for the same normative relation, according to the point of view from which it is regarded" (1959: 89). That is, rights and duties are two aspects of a relation of obligation. This is certainly Kant's view. Rights are nothing more than "moral capacities to bind others ..." (1797a: 43), and "all rights as well as duties are derived only though the moral imperative, which is a proposition commanding duties; the capacity to obligate others to a duty, that is, the concept of a right, can be subsequently derived from this imperative" (1797a: 45). Thus, obligation is expressed in the categorical imperative, and both rights and duties are derived from it. Rights are the power to obligate, and duties are the requirement of those obligations. This is often called the "logical correlation doctrine" (Feinberg 1991: 268): Rights and duties are correlates.

J.L. Mackie concedes that rights could be viewed as nothing more than a certain set of duties. If someone has the moral right to do *X*, then she does not have a duty not to do *X*, meaning that she is not obligated to refrain from doing *X* and can do it if she chooses. But others are morally obligated not to interfere or prevent her from doing *X*. For example, a right to liberty means that she is not obligated to constrain her own liberty, and others are obligated not to interfere with it. But Mackie argues that this should be viewed the other way around: The fact that she has a right to do *X*, if she so chooses, obligates others not to interfere with that choice. The obligation comes from respect for the right, not from another obligation. Second, as both Richard Wasserstrom and Joel Feinberg point out, rights and duties do not always correlate. For example, it would be reasonable to assume that persons have a duty to be charitable to others, but it is not the right of any one person to demand charity without the consent of the beneficiary. That is, all rights correlate with obligations, but not all obligations correlate with rights.

Wasserstrom and Feinberg also argue that a social arrangement based solely on duties would be more morally impoverished than one that included both rights and duties. The answer to the question, "Why ought anyone have a right to anything?" is that such a system would prevent persons from asserting exactly those

kinds of claims that rights allow us to make. We ought to be able to claim as entitlements those minimal things without which it is impossible to develop one's capabil-
ities and to live as a human being (1991: 263). Feinberg concurs. People in a society
without rights would not be able to make claims on others and have no notion of
what is their due. If a person does not have a right to liberty, then such a person
cannot make a claim against another to refrain from interfering with that liberty.

What are some of the responses to this position? Actually, Kant makes a similar, but more striking, point to the one made by both Wasserstrom and Feinberg.
He imagines an arrangement of permutations between duties and rights (1797a:
47). A society in which there are neither duties nor rights would pertain to a sub-
human culture. One having only duties but no rights would be equivalent to a slave
or serf culture in which one is obliged but not the subject of obligation. In such a
society, the slave owes everything to the master, and the master owes nothing to the
slave. A fourth would be one in which there are only rights but no duties. This Kant
believes would describe a supreme being, such as God. God as creator has a right to
make claims upon human beings, and no duties to them as such. The best arrangement for human society is one in which there are both duties and rights. Having
both aspects of obligation makes reciprocity possible or, as Kant says, "a relationship of men to men" (1797a: 47). That arrangement is certainly more desirable
than a master–slave one. If everyone can be both the subject of obligation and do
what is obliged, then each person can demand that others fulfill their obligations
and themselves be subject to such demands. Without such an arrangement there is
only hierarchy, where a few are owed and the many are obligated to the few. Thus,
Kant would agree that both duties and rights are desirable in a social and political
arrangement precisely because they promote reciprocity.

However, this is not an argument for the priority of right over duty, nor necessarily duty over right, but appeals to an implicit consequentialism—a society
would simply be better off in some intuitive way if it had both rights and duties (cf.
Scanlon 1992: 137). However, as Kant understands it, the point here is to show the
priority of *obligation*, from which both duty and right flow. For Kant, duties and
rights are simply two facets of a complete sense of obligation, so that it is this complete sense of obligation that is generally preferable for Kant. Obligation, according to Kant—and as we have seen earlier—is a requirement of an action that
conforms to the categorical imperative (1797a: 23). Obligation is generated by the
fact that people have willed for themselves a certain law, a law being something that
can be consistently required of everyone. You should only will for yourself that
which you would require for everyone. Obligation is generated through
autonomous, self-legislative acts. A duty, on the other hand, is the content of such
an obligation. Thus, an obligation both commands and requires, that is, makes
claims on ourselves and others, and so requires us to do or not to do something.

This can be illustrated by a couple of examples. If a person is indebted to
another, then the lender can make a claim on the borrower for repayment. The
duty of the borrower is to repay the lender. But both the claim and the duty stem
from an obligation generated by the mutual recognition of the norm that "debts
should be paid." Kant would argue that the mutual recognition stems from the fact
that each realizes that it conforms to a categorical imperative; that is, it is a claim
that one could make on everyone and anyone, including the person across the
table. If, on the other hand, it would only hold for a few, then repayment might not
be required, depending on if that person were one of the lucky few. In that case,
however, a lender would be foolish—unless he was coerced—to lend money to that

person. What holds the relationship together is a mutual sense of obligation, not just the right, nor just the duty, but that these roles could be interchanged for both persons.

Thus, the difficulty with both Wasserstrom's and Feinberg's arguments lies in the confusion of duty with obligation. It could be argued that it is this same confusion on which the discrediting of the correlation thesis relies. It is the case that not all duties entail rights, although all rights entail duties. But all rights involve obligations and so do duties. Thus, the more common concept at the heart of both is that of obligation.

What ethical principle does a rights-based ethic ultimately generate? Interestingly, rights-based theorists seem relatively mute on this. It may be said that it implicitly generates an obligation not to interfere with basic rights, so that it generates something similar to a libertarian principle. Thus, one has an obligation not to harm another's life, liberty, property, or whatever rights fill in the blank. A more specific way to think of this rights-based principle is suggested by Ronald Dworkin. What he argues is that rights act as trumps over collective goods. Thus, even if someone believes that the suppression of a speech or a movie is for the better good of the community, to the extent that people are entitled to liberty of speech, then such actions should not take place (1992: 153). What rights-based ethics tries to guarantee, then, is that individual entitlements are not sacrificed for the sake of the greater good. Thus, a rights-based principle might be expressed in the following way: *act in a manner that does not violate the rights of any individual affected by your decision.*

5.6 USING PRINCIPLES IN MORAL DECISION MAKING

From the perspective of moral knowledge, the best principle is one that is more fully justified, that is, one that shows why it is normative for us and entails a clear obligation to follow. Each principle we've examined, however, has flaws, yet most have strengths. Still the flaws can be graded. The principle of egoism is by and large the most flawed: It is not consistent to advocate it to others, nor can it be publicly advocated without losing its advantage for the egoist. It fails the most minimal standard for a principle—that it at least be consistent. On the other side of the coin, the principle of benevolence is also weakly justified. It is not clear why we have an obligation to benefit others (to whom we have no special duties, such as we do to our spouse or children), especially if it may entail harm to ourselves. Certainly, we may want to help others, but why we have an obligation to do so is unclear under this principle. In general, consequentialist principles, such as the utilitarian, are weak because they inherently involve a circularity. Since the measure of the goodness of an act lies in its consequences, the measure of the consequences determines the goodness of the principle; yet how do we measure the consequences by means of the principle? That is rather circular. The measure of the consequences is typically based on certain moral intuitions. For example, if we followed this principle, it could justify slavery, but slavery is morally repugnant from an intuitive point of view; yet principles justify our intuitions, and we can't use intuitions to justify the principles without being accused of circular reasoning. Deontological principles avoid the circularity of consequentialist reasoning and rely instead on derivations from the logical character of autonomy. But this is also their weakness because there can be subtle differences in the interpretation of that concept which, nonetheless, have important consequences. Still, of all the deontological principles, the dialogic has a justification that may escape some of the more ordinary difficulties with justifying ethical principles.

But even if it is argued that the dialogic principle contains the best justification, we have seen that it has several flaws. Moreover, even if deontological principles are better justified, the cost–benefit analysis, typical of utilitarianism and game theory, is a common and valuable form of deliberation. Indeed, it is hard to imagine moral decision making without some appeal to consequences in this regard.

The question, then, is how to resolve the conflict among these principles, some of which are better justified than others, yet all of which have certain flaws. As it turns out, this question has been studied by a number of moral theorists with the following results: (1) *single-principle theories* suggest that we simply choose the best-justified principle to the exclusion of others (cf. Gert 1988) and basically live with its limitations; (2) *balancing principles*—one balances the competing claims of the principles by scaling each claim relative to the decision context, and weighing the results (cf. Ross 1930); (3) *lexical ordering* suggests that there is a priority among principles such that the conditions for one principle must be completely satisfied before another is allowed to come into play (cf. Rawls 1971: 42ff.); (4) *mixed strategies* are a combination of lexical ordering with balancing (cf. Veatch 1995).

The difficulty with the single-principle theory is that every principle we've examined has flaws so that even the adoption of the best-justified principle will promote inherently problematic choices.

Balancing principles can be a suspect practice. This implies assigning scaling to each principle specific to some context, and then assigning some weight to the result. It is unclear what criterion is used to assign the various weights. As philosopher Robert Veatch (1995: 208ff.) argues, balancing theory can be nothing more than an elaborate rationale for letting prejudices rise to the surface or justifying the choice a person really wants to make anyway. A person can always argue that one principle or another is more weighty in a given situation so that it matches the outcome he wants.

The *mixed approach*, which Veatch himself advocates, argues for a combination of lexical ordering and balancing. It is based by analogy on Talmudic ethics (cf. 1995: 211). The idea is that certain obligations always have priority in Jewish law, specifically, laws that proscribe against idolatry, murder, and certain sexual offenses. The law requiring preservation of life takes next priority, requiring suspension of even dietary laws and laws proscribing against travel on the Sabbath (cf. Rosner and Bleich 1979: 19). Veatch proposes the following strategy: first, balance the consequentialist principles, assigning equal weights; second, balance the deontological principles, likewise giving them equal weights; third, lexically rank the aggregate effect of the deontological principles over the consequentialist ones. It is not clear, however, why, if balancing is suspect—even by Veatch's own remarks—in this case it is less suspect. Even if it is involved in only half the strategy, then that half is suspect. It is not clear why we should assign equal weights to the various principles or why the deontological principles are to have lexical ordering over the consequentialist ones. Furthermore, it is unclear what is meant by the "aggregate" of two principles balanced against each and which are likely contrary to one another.

Lexical ordering appears to be a stronger alternative in many respects. First of all, the rank of principles is based on the quality of their justification, which is as it should be in the case of moral knowledge: The principle with the best justification is first in lexical order. Second, the manner in which each principle is addressed is

Balancing Principles

Principle	Scale					Weight	Total
1. How much will I be benefited by this action? [egoism]	1	2	3	4	5	_____	_____
2. Are the undeserving of harm unharmed by this action? [libertarianism]	1	2	3	4	5	_____	_____
3. How much benefit does this create for how many? [utilitarianism]	1	2	3	4	5	_____	_____
4. Have all those who should be involved in the decision making been involved? [dialogic]	1	2	3	4	5	_____	_____
5. Will the action enhance or maintain present cooperation among those affected by action? [tit-for-tat]	1	2	3	4	5	_____	_____
6. Would I want this action to become something that should apply to everyone in a similar situation? [categorical imperative]	1	2	3	4	5	_____	_____
7. Would I want this action to happen to me? [golden rule]	1	2	3	4	5	_____	_____
8. Does the action protect basic rights of individuals over benefit to the group?	1	2	3	4	5	_____	_____
Total						_____	_____

This checklist might serve as a model for balancing principles. Each principle's conditions are represented in the table by a question, followed by a scale which measures how much the proposed action satisfies the requirements of that principle. A weight (positive or negative) can be assigned to each question, depending on the importance of the principle. A high total score would assign a certain degree of confidence to the decision, whereas a low score would suggest the action is morally questionable.

clearly specified: The conditions for the first principle must be satisfied before satisfying the conditions for the second.

To illustrate how this works, let's suppose that the deontological principles employ stronger justifications than rights-based, which in turn have stronger ones than consequentialist principles, and among the deontological ones, the dialogic principle is the strongest in this sense. The dialogic principle satisfies the sense of the categorical imperative without the subjective imperialism it entails. It also satisfies much of the libertarian principle without the strong individualism it involves. If there are cases in which an individual's actions do not significantly harm another, then actions without strong effects on others need not have their consent, in which case the dialogic principle does not come into play. In regard to the consequentialist principles, we can think of the tit-for-tat and the utilitarian principles as cost–benefit calculations, the first concerned with individual benefits and the second with collective goods.

Putting this all together suggests the following results. There should be a lexical ordering such that the conditions for the dialogic principle be satisfied before we engage in any cost–benefit estimation of the plans and choices involved in an ethical situation. If you notice, this particular outcome actually parallels Cicero's

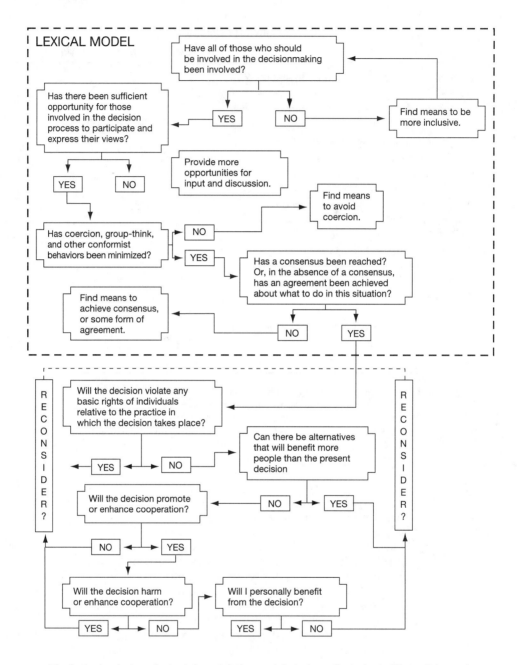

The lexical ordering of principles might be modeled after a flow chart. All conditions of the highest ranked principle must be met before the conditions of the lower ranked ones. Suppose for example, that the dialogic principle is ranked highest. Its conditions are organized within the dotted box. All other principles are ranked outside the box.

deliberative strategy: The honorable choice has priority over the advantageous, but among the honorable choices, choose the one most advantageous and, among those, the plan that is most efficient. Of course, in this case what is "honorable" is spelled out by the dialogic principle, and what is advantageous and efficient is spelled out by the utilitarian or tit-for-tat principle. In a sense Cicero's strategy also involves a lexical ordering as well.

Let's end with an example that illustrates how such lexical ordering works. Consider the case of a kidney transplant specialist who has a number of patients, all of whom require kidney transplants to continue living. For the sake of simplicity, let's assume that all the patients are competent adults, but let's grant that they vary otherwise in terms of age, sex, race, wealth, and other socioeconomic factors. Let's also suppose that the number of organs available is smaller than the number of patients who need them. What sort of moral guideline should the physician use in the decision-making process? The lexical ranking of the principles suggest that, first, all the conditions for the dialogic principle or rights-based principles must be satisfied before any cost–benefit calculations are made. This would suggest, first of all, a determination of whether each patient desires the kidney transplant. To avoid the paternalism or subjectivism of the other deontological principles, the patients must be asked under ideal conditions of information whether they would desire such a procedure. Let's say the result is that most want such a procedure, but there are a few who don't. Assuming they have been properly informed, there has been no violation of the dialogic principle in excluding them from the donation list of available organs. Since everyone who has been affected in this context has been addressed, and no one has been excluded because of who they are—that is, no one has been excluded because of age, sex, or race and because no one has been given special consideration because of who they are (e.g., in terms of wealth, status, or fame)—in other words, because everyone has been treated equally and fairly in the consideration, then the physician can proceed with a cost–benefit analysis of the situation purely on the basis of medical criteria. For example, a patient might have a number of other medical anomalies which would not make a kidney transplant viable. Even if the patient wants the transplant, the transplant would not be medically feasible either because the patient would die or the other conditions would prevent the new kidney from functioning. Or, for example, although age was not a factor in determining whether a person should be excluded from consideration, the advanced age of this particular patient has made him so frail that, again, such a procedure would not be medically viable. Another medical factor for consideration might be the original causes of the kidney disease. If it is the result of chronic alcoholism and the patient is currently alcoholic, exclusion might be warranted purely on the basis of cost–benefit analysis, unless the patient showed genuine indications of movement toward sobriety. Among the remaining patients, assuming that medical cost–benefit ratios are about the same, then which ones would get the donated organs must be determined in a fair and equitable manner (e.g., in terms of the order of request or the degree of urgency, which is the usual practice).

To the degree that a principle can be properly justified, it can assure us in our personal deliberations that actions or rules which conform to it would yield morally satisfactory outcomes. In this respect principles can serve as algorithms of wisdom, and often this is the form they take. They operationalize deliberation. To use the golden rule as an example, it says that when making a moral decision, do that thing to another which you would want done unto you. Familiar principles such as the golden rule or the utilitarian principle serve as general frameworks for moral decision making. However, it must be cautioned that such principles cannot serve as a substitute for wisdom. Because they are general and have wide scope, they cannot be easily applied to every particular situation. In this respect they are unlike scientific laws which tell us that all things of a certain sort behave in the same way under the same specified conditions. In moral situations the conditions vary widely, and the principle can only serve as a guideline. Because they must be applied, wisdom must be involved in any case—even if we can be assured of the moral accuracy of the principle.

But in addition to their personal use, moral principles generate a certain *ethos,* that is, a certain understanding of moral decision making and a framework for understanding the broad constitution of institutions and practices that would be based on them. Depending on the principle, each one will create a frame: a frame for understanding the nature of moral agency and relations among such agents; how we should design practices and institutions; and how they are best served. This generates something comparable to a moral vision, but rather than being the result of a general cosmic vision, it attempts a more systematic account of that vision, as it is drawn logically from the implications of a principle.

Case Study: Using Ethical Principles to Decide Moral Issues—Euthanasia

One of the most controversial moral issues of recent times is euthanasia. Euthanasia in its most general sense is the practice of withholding or withdrawing medical treatment to allow someone with a terminal illness or debilitative condition to die. It can also include acts which hasten death under those circumstances. Withdrawing or withholding treatment is called passive euthanasia, while hastening death is called active euthanasia. The classification is complicated by the fact that the disposition of the patient also needs to be taken into consideration. If the patient is competent and consents to the active or passive euthanasia, then it is a case of voluntary euthanasia. But if the dying person is unconscious, comatose, or otherwise incompetent, then it is a case of nonvoluntary euthanasia. The contemporary controversy centers on whether we should allow euthanasia to be practiced and, if so, what forms of it are morally acceptable.

Although passive voluntary euthanasia is a relatively standard practice in hospitals and clinics, it was the center of a large debate a few decades ago. The issue of whether the withdrawal of nutrition and hydration should be allowed was the focus of much of this debate. Today every state has what are called living wills, which provide a public record of a competent patient's wishes in this regard—wishes that must be legally respected (although apparently they are not always followed in practice). The question of passive euthanasia for incompetent patients is more controversial. A recent Supreme Court decision (*Cruzan v. Director, Missouri Dept of Health* 110

S.Ct. 2841, 1990) made it clear that competent patients have a right to refuse or withdraw medical treatment, but it left the matter of incompetent patients undecided. In the meantime the issue of active euthanasia remains extremely controversial. Jack Kevorkian is at the center of this debate and, to date, he has assisted well over thirty people with terminal illnesses and debilitative conditions in their deaths. For 20 years, Holland has decriminalized the practice of physician-assisted dying and other forms of active euthanasia. Recently, Oregon voters narrowly passed Measure 16, which permits physicians to prescribe lethal doses of medication for the competent terminally ill. A recent Supreme Court decision on that matter (*Washington et al. v. Glucksberg* 1997 NL 348094) argued that, although there is no constitutional right to physician-assisted suicide, states may decide this issue for themselves.

The difficulties with the various ethical principles become more manifest when they are applied in the sort of concrete decision making required here. Consider, first, a feasible use of the libertarian principle to solve this moral issue. The libertarian principle argues that any action should be permitted by an individual so long as it does not cause significant harm to others, or if there is any harm, it is incurred primarily by the individual herself. Based on that understanding, many libertarians argue that a dying person not only should be permitted to refuse or withdraw medical treatment, but should also be allowed—with the consent of the doctor—physician assistance in dying. Since dying affects the dying per-

Case Study: Using Ethical Principles
to Decide Moral Issues—Euthanasia, *Continued*

son primarily, then any harm or good that comes from a speedy death would affect that person primarily. Consequently, such persons should have full liberty to make those sorts of decisions. One difficulty with this account is the measure of significant harm. Although it is true that dying affects the dying person primarily, how people die could have a bearing on the larger society as a whole. As some argue, a society that permits physician-assisted suicide creates a number of harms to the larger fabric of the culture. First, it affects the practice of medicine, since it changes its norms from preserving life to destroying life. This could have a number of unforeseen ramifications. Second, allowing the terminally ill or severely debilitated to be killed could seriously weaken the moral fabric of the culture. If a culture moves away from norms that promote care and concern for the dying and suffering, some argue that would push us closer to a barbarous, unfeeling society. Also, the libertarian principle does not really address the issue of incompetent patients. Since they cannot decide for themselves, how are we to use the libertarian principle in this case to make decisions about their welfare? Although these arguments can be countered, the point is that they legitimately raise the issue of how far to extend significant harm. If these arguments are legitimate and the harm is extensive, then by the logic of the libertarian principle, the decision of physician-assisted suicide is not an individual one, but a culture-wide one.

Proponents of the utilitarian principle might feel perfectly comfortable with that outcome. After all, according to that principle, actions are good to the extent that they promote the greatest happiness in a society. Decisions to permit the practice of physician-assisted suicide would be determined on the basis of whether it promotes more happiness than not. One difficulty is trying to figure the appropriate pleasure calculus. If it is based on the individual measure of pleasure and pain, then an argument could be made for case-by-case permission when the suffering is much greater than any pleasure gained by prolonging the death. At the same time, if more collective calculi are used, then the previous arguments concerning the affect of such a practice on the collective norms of a culture would have some bearing on the decision, along with other intangibles and incommensurables. For example, it might be determined that physician-assisted suicide has a very strong positive economic impact. It might be the case that, because a large number of medical resources, beds, and monies are used to prolong the dying process, such economic values could be measured against these other normative values. On the other hand, it could be the case that physician-assisted suicide has a strong negative economic impact, since it adversely affects profits for the medical industry. The difficulty with collective calculi in either case is that if it is determined that physician-assisted suicide does promote the greatest collective good, then there is the danger that many who do not wish it will have it imposed upon them; and if it does not promote the collective good, then there will be many who will be forced to endure suffering they see no reason to endure. What if the collective calculus determines that there is overwhelming economic benefit to actively euthanizing the poorest patients, since funds for keeping them alive come from the public coffers? There is also an additional danger with collective calculi, especially in the case of incompetent patients. In one sense, by relieving every patient of individual choice, it solves the problem of how to make decisions about incompetent patients; but that is precisely the danger of such a practice because it allows people to make decisions about other people's fate when they are helpless and incapable of making their own.

Using the golden rule also has difficulties. Although this appears to promote an individual choice, there are a number of players in the decision process. Who is the golden rule directed to—the physician or the patient? If the patient chooses a speedy death over prolonged suffering, how does the formula of the golden rule apply since it is a harm or help that applies to the individual and not others? If it is directed toward the physician—even if the request comes from the patient—contemplating assisting in the death of that suffering patient, then the result will be clearly subjective. The decision would be based on whether or not the physician would personally want physician assistance in dying if she were in that position; if she does, then she should act accordingly, and if not, then she shouldn't. But this really doesn't factor in the patients' own wishes, strictly speaking. It might be a criterion used on incompetent patients with some effect, but it is a paternalistic judgment because you are deciding for others on the basis of what you would want. It is not even the case that you may be deciding on the basis of the patient's best interests, but only what you would want in such a situation.

The categorical imperative also has problems. If we are to universalize the practice of euthanasia, it is not clear how far to specify the scope of the universalization in order to measure its absurdity or consequences. If we were to hasten the death of everyone who was terminally ill or severely debilitated, this might be an unpalatable result for a number of peo-

Continued

Case Study: Using Ethical Principles
to Decide Moral Issues—Euthanasia, *Continued*

ple; but if this is specified enough, it might not be considered so. For example, in many people's thinking, hastening the death of someone with a terminal illness whose death is imminent and who is suffering in great pain seems neither contradictory, absurd, nor even with undesirable consequences.

The dialogic principle suggests that a decision is right if it is made by those primarily affected by that decision in a fair and deliberative process. The question here is how to delimit the participants in the decision, since the effect of that decision is somewhat vague. Should it just be the immediate decision makers—the dying person, of course, the physician, the family? Should the nurses be included? What about the hospital? In general, to the extent that the practice itself affects the general moral tenor, should the culture as a whole be part of the process? In addition, there is the problem of incompetent patients; since they are incapable of discourse, yet a decision must be made about their situation, it would seem that the dialogic principle would not inherently have any means to make such decisions.

Another way to address the problem of the application of these principles is to think of them as the basis for different sorts of decision models. What kinds of decision models does each principle generate? First, the principles can be divided into those which have the individual at the center of the decision making, as opposed to those that emphasize collective deliberation. The libertarian principle and the golden rule are prime examples of the first. Although the categorical imperative individualizes the decision, it is based on a universalization of that decision. On the other hand, the utilitarian and the dialogic principles are prime examples of collective deliberation.

The libertarian principle argues for a decision model in which the individual moral agents are the primary decision makers. To the extent that their decisions do not have significant harm on others, it is their determination of harm or benefit to themselves that will be the deciding factor in decisions about euthanasia. This sort of decision model promotes the idea that the dying person is the lone agent who must decide her own fate, especially if some decisions restrict harm to that person. This model also illustrates one of the problems with the libertarian principle—namely, that it promotes a very thin sense of connectedness and community. Dying people, except in relatively rare circumstances, are connected with spouses, children, friends, and family. They often have emotional attachments to others; yet the tendency of the libertarian principle is to abstract the person from these attachments. In many respects

this attitude is promoted by legal mechanisms, such as the living will, or the legal system, which as in the Cruzan case treats a dying person not as a family member, but actually as an individual whose interests may in fact conflict with the interests of his family. What is interesting is that—at least in the case of competent persons—the courts have generally recognized this decision model as the most appropriate one. The Cruzan decision legitimates the idea that the consent of the competent dying person to treatment or lack of treatment is fundamental, even if such decisions are contrary to the wishes of family or physician.

But whereas the libertarian principle concentrates the power of decision making in the individual, the utilitarian model would dispose it more toward administrative decision making. Under the utilitarian model, decisions would be made on the basis of a cost–benefit calculus that would be relatively standard and therefore could be employed by any person or group of persons so qualified. For example, the philosopher Richard Brandt proposes a utilitarian model for making decisions in the very difficult and thorny cases of infant euthanasia. Often decisions in these cases to make heroic efforts to keep premature or anomalous infants alive are inconsistent precisely because they are contrary to parents' wishes and physician concerns. Brandt (1987) argues that infants should be grouped into three classes: (1) those whose condition (e.g., anacephaly) is so anomalous that at best they will have a short and unpleasant life; in this case they should be allowed to die; (2) marginal conditions in which the infants' lives are only marginally beneficial to them, but at a high economic and psychological cost to others; in this case the infant should be aggressively treated only if the parents or society is willing to bear the burden of caring for the infant; and (3) those infants who have conditions which stand a good chance of survival with aggressive treatment and whose consequences would result in a reasonably decent life. In this case either the family or society should provide the necessities for them to develop this capacity. The advantage of such a decision model is that it promotes some consistency on the basis of relatively objective criteria, but that is also its disadvantage because it imposes criteria for decision making on those most affected by the decisions (the parents and infants) without necessarily getting their consent or even their input. Brandt argues for the use of "systematic statistical information" on survival rates and so on to help in these decisions. In other words, a decision could be made rather objectively in terms of percentages: What are the chances

Case Study: Using Ethical Principles
to Decide Moral Issues—Euthanasia, *Continued*

that the baby will survive, and if it survives, what are the chances for a meaningful life?

The dialogic principle, in contrast, promotes decisions based on dialogue among those affected by such decisions. Not only is the patient involved in the decision making, but so are the family, the physician, and other health professionals related to the case. The goal is to reach a decision that has consensus among these participants. The advantage of such a model is that, like the libertarian principle, it stresses the importance of consent, but unlike that model, it treats the person more realistically as someone connected with others. Also, unlike the utilitarian principle, it does not promote administrative criteria for decisions, but the decision is the result of the dialogue among the participants. Its disadvantages, however, are clear. It does not address those cases where the dying person may be incompetent. In those situations it leaves the person most affected by the decision out of the dialogue. Second, it doesn't seem to set any criteria for the limits of the dialogue. How many are to be included and how far should the dialogue extend?

Questions for Discussion

1. Can you think of any additional advantages or disadvantages to the various models considered here?
2. Which model, in your opinion, is the best? Why?

REVIEW QUESTIONS

1. Why is moral knowledge an important aspect of moral competence?
2. What is moral intuition? How is it contrasted with moral knowledge?
3. What are the various psychological theories concerning the acquisition of moral intuition? Which one is more accurate in your estimation?
4. Discuss Hayek's position in regard to moral intuition. What is the source of the conflict between moral intuition and moral knowledge?
5. What are the various levels of moral knowledge? What is involved in value clarification? What is meant by systematization? What is meant by justification?
6. What are the general characteristics of moral rules? Principles? What's the difference between moral rules and principles?
7. What are the various stages of moral reasoning according to Kohlberg? What is Gilligan's criticism of Kohlberg? What is Gilligan's alternative to Kohlberg's analysis?
8. What are some of the problems in justifying ethical principles?
9. What are some of the difficulties in justifying a principle by means of authority?
10. What is the difference between deontological and consequentialist principles?
11. What is the deontological version of egoism? The consequentialist version? What are the difficulties of each?
12. What is the principle of nonmaleficence? What are some of its limitations?
13. What is the categorical imperative? What are some of its limitations?
14. What is meant by contract ethics? Discourse ethics? What are their limitations?
15. What is the utilitarian principle? How does Mill's version differ from Bentham's? What is the difference between the preference and pleasure version? What is the difference between act- and rule-utilitarianism? What is the difference between the total and average principle? What are some of the difficulties with the utilitarian principle? How does Mill justify the utilitarian principle? Is he successful?
16. What is the tit-for-tat strategy? What are its limitations?
17. What is meant by the golden rule? What are its difficulties?
18. What is the natural law theory? What is rights-based ethics? How does it differ from the deontological approach?

19. What is meant by the principle of benevolence? What are its problems?

20. What are the various strategies for deciding among competing principles? Which one in your opinion is the best strategy and why?

QUESTIONS FOR DISCUSSION

1. What are the dangers that lie in Hayek's conservatism? What are the dangers present in the Enlightenment ideology? Is there a middle ground?

2. What is the danger of relying on moral intuitions for doing the right thing? What is the danger in not relying on moral intuitions?

3. Do you think that the process of clarifying one's moral intuitions inherently leads to their revision?

4. Can systematization of moral beliefs be completely achieved? What are the consequences of living with inconsistencies? Does our society operate with inconsistent moral beliefs?

5. Are you convinced by arguments against subjectivism and relativism? If moral beliefs cannot be settled by reason, what alternatives are there?

6. Comment on the feminist critique of the principle-and-rule approach.

7. What in your opinion is the better type of principle: deontological or teleological?

8. Which among the deontological principles gives the best interpretation of autonomy?

9. Which of the two versions of utilitarianism, Bentham's or Mills's, is preferable?

10. Which of the principles considered seem the best in your opinion? How would you incorporate the other principles, if at all?

SUGGESTED READINGS

On Moral Education

Dunn, Judy. 1987. The Beginnings of Moral Understanding: Development in the Second Year. *The Emergence of Morality in Young Children*. Edited by J. Kagan and S. Lamb. Chicago: Chicago University Press.

Edwards, Carolyn. 1987. Culture and the Construction of Moral Values. *The Emergence of Morality in Young Children*. Edited by J. Kagan and S. Lamb. Chicago: Chicago University Press.

Eisenberg, Nancy. 1986. *The Altruistic Emotion, Cognition and Behavior*. Mahwah, NJ: Erlbaum.

———. 1992. *The Caring Child*. Cambridge, MA: Harvard University Press.

Gilligan, Carol et al. editors. 1990. *Mapping the Moral Domain: A Contribution of Women's Thinking to Psychological Theory and Education*. Cambridge, MA: Harvard University Press.

Hutcheon, Pat. 1999. *Building Character and Culture*. New York: Praeger.

Kagan, Jerome. 1987. Introduction. *The Emergence of Morality in Young Children*. Edited by J. Kagan and S. Lamb. Chicago: Chicago University Press.

Leming, James. 1983. *Foundations of a Moral Education*. Westport, CT: Greenwood Press.

Lickona, Thomas. 1991. *Educating for Character*. New York: Bantam Books.

McClellan, B. Edward. 1999. *Moral Education in America: Schools and the Shaping of Character since Colonial Times*. New York: Teacher's College Press.

Natale, Samuel, and Wilson, John. 1991. *Central Issues in Moral and Ethical Education*. Washington, DC: University Press of America.

Riemer, Joseph. 1990. *Promoting Moral Growth: From Piaget to Kohlberg*. Prospect Heights, IL: Waveland Press.

Sommers, Christina. 1993. Teaching the Virtues. *The Public Interest* Spring: 3–11.

Turiel, E. 1983. *The Development of Social Knowledge Morality and Conventions*. Cambridge, England: Cambridge University Press.

Windmiller, M., Lambert, N., and Turiel, E., editors. 1980. *Moral Development and Socialization*. Boston: Allyn and Bacon.

On Values Clarification

Beek, Clive. 1977. Developing Curriculum for Value Education in the Schools. *Counseling Psychologist* 6(4): 30–32.
Bennett, William, and Delattre, E. 1978. Moral Education in the Schools. *The Public Interest* 50.
Eger, Martin. 1981. The Conflict in Moral Education. *The Public Interest* 81.
Lockwood, Alan. 1978. The Effects of Values Clarification and Moral Development Curricula on School-age Subjects. *Review of Educational Research* 48.
Simon, Sidney, Howe, L., and Kirschenbaum, H. 1978. *Values Clarification*. New York: Hart.
Sommers, Christina-Hoff. 1984. Ethics without Virtue: Moral Education in America. *American Scholar* 53(3): 381–389.

On Integrity

Carter, Stephen. 1996. *Integrity*. New York: Basic.
Fleischacker, Samuel. 1992. *Integrity and Moral Relativism*. Leiden: Brill.
Gaita, Raimond. 1981. Integrity. *Proceedings of the Aristotelian Society*. Suppl 55: 161–176.
Kerr, Donna. 1984. *Barriers to Integrity*. Boulder, CO: Westview Press.
Ramsay, Hayden. 1997. *Beyond Virtue: Integrity and Morality*. New York: St. Martin's Press.
Solomon, Robert. 1992. *Ethics and Excellence*. New York: Oxford University Press, pp. 168–174.
Taylor, Gabriele. 1981. Integrity. *Proceedings of the Aristotelian Society*. Suppl. 55: 143–159.
Tyler, W.S. 1857. *Integrity, the Safeguard of Public and Private Life*. Springfield, IL: Samuel Bowles.
Winch, Peter. 1968. *Moral Integrity*. Oxford, England: Basil Blackwell.

On Kohlberg and Gilligan

Blum, L. 1988. Gilligan and Kohlberg: Implications for Moral Theory. *Ethics* 98: 472–491.
Brook, R. 1987. Justice and the Golden Rule: A Commentary on Some Recent Work of Lawrence Kohlberg. *Ethics* 97: 363–373.
Duska, Ronald, and Whelan, Mariellen. 1975. *Moral Development: A Guide to Piaget and Kohlberg*. New York: Paulist Press.
Gibbs. 1977. Kohlberg's States of Moral Judgment: A Constructive Critique. *Harvard Educational Review* 47: 42–61.
Gilligan, Carol. 1982. *In a Different Voice*. Cambridge, MA: Harvard University Press.
Kohlberg, Lawrence. 1981–1984. *Essays on Moral Development. The Psychology of Moral Development*. 2 vols. New York: Harper and Row.
Kurtines, W., and Grief, E.B. 1974. The Development of Moral Thought. *Psychological Bulletin* 81: 453–470.
Langford, Peter. 1995. *Approach to the Development of Moral Reasoning*. Mahwah, NJ: Erlbaum.
Power, Clark. 1991. *Lawrence Kohlberg's Approach to Moral Education*. New York: Columbia University Press.
Rest, James, et al. 1999. *Postconventional Moral Thinking: A Neo-Kohlbergian Approach*. New York: Erlbaum.
Shweder, R. et al. 1987. Culture and Moral Development. In *The Emergence of Morality in Young Children*. Edited by J. Kagan and S. Lamb. New York: Basic.

On Egoism

Clark, John. 1976. *Max Stirner's Egoism*. New York: Left Bank Books.
Gauthier, David. 1970. *Morality and Rational Self-Interest*. Upper Saddle River, NJ: Prentice Hall.

Medlin, Brian. 1957. Ultimate Principles and Ethical Egoism. *Australasian Journal of Philosophy* 35: 111–118.

Nagel, Thomas. 1970. *The Possibility of Altruism.* New York: Oxford University Press.

Osterberg, Jan. 1988. *Self and Others: A Study of Ethical Egoism.* Dordrecht, the Netherlands: Kluwer.

Rachels, James. 1976. Egoism and Moral Skepticism. In *Philosophy: Paradox and Discovery.* Edited by A. Minton. New York: McGraw-Hill.

Rand, Ayn. 1961. *The Virtue of Selfishness.* New York: Signet.

Shaver, Robert. 1998. *Rational Egoism: A Selective and Critical History.* Cambridge, England: Cambridge University Press.

Stirner, Max. 1995. *The Ego and Its Own..* Translated by David Leopold. Cambridge, England: Cambridge University Press.

Van Ingen, Jack. 1994. *Why Be Moral? The Egoistic Challenge.* New York: Peter Lang.

On Libertarianism

Friedman, Milton. 1962. *Capitalism and Freedom.* Chicago: University of Chicago Press.

Hayek, Friedrich. 1976. *The Mirage of Justice.* London: Routledge and Kegan Paul.

Hospers, John. 1971. *Libertarianism.* Los Angeles: Nash.

Jeffrey, Paul, editor. 1981. *Reading Nozick.* Totowa, NJ: Rowman and Littlefield.

Nozick, Robert. 1974. *Anarchy, State and Utopia.* New York: Basic.

On the Categorical Imperative

Allison, Henry. 1996. *Idealism and Freedom: Essays on Kant's Theoretical and Practical Philosophy.* Cambridge, England: Cambridge University Press.

Aune, Bruce. 1979. *Kant's Theory of Morals.* Princeton, NJ: Princeton University Press.

Beck, Lewis White. 1960. *A Commentary on Kant's Critique of Practical Reason.* Chicago: University of Chicago Press.

Carnois, Bernard. 1987. *The Coherence of Kant's Doctrine of Freedom.* Translated by David Booth. Chicago: University of Chicago Press.

Felicitas, Munzel. 1999. *Kant's Conception of Moral Character.* Chicago: University of Chicago Press.

Guyer, Paul. 1992. *The Cambridge Companion to Kant.* Cambridge, England: Cambridge University Press.

———. 1997. *Kant's Groundwork of the Metaphysics of Morals.* New York: Rowman and Littlefield.

Hoffe, Otfried. 1994. *Immanuel Kant.* Translated by M. Farrier. Albany: State University of New York Press.

Kant, Immanuel. 1775–1780. *Lectures on Ethics.* Translated by L. Infield. New York: Harper and Row, 1963.

———. 1785. *Foundations of the Metaphysics of Morals.* Translated by L. W. Beck. New York: Bobbs-Merrill, 1959.

———. 1788. *Critique of Practical Reason.* Translated by L. Beck. New York: Bobbs-Merrill, 1956.

———. 1797. *The Metaphysical Principles of the Virtues.* Translated by J. Ellington. New York: Bobbs-Merrill, 1964.

Korsgaard, Christine. 1996. *Creating the Kingdom of Ends.* Cambridge, England: Cambridge University Press.

Nell, Onora. 1975. *Acting on Principle. An Essay on Kantian Ethics.* New York: Columbia University Press, 1975.

———. 1990. *Construction of Reason: Explorations of Kant's Practical Philosophy.* Cambridge, England: Cambridge University Press.

Paton, Herbert. 1999. *The Categorical Imperative: A Study in Kant's Moral Philosophy.* Philadelphia: University of Pennsylvania Press.

Rawls, John. 1980. Kantian Constructivism in Moral Theory. *The Journal of Philosophy* 88: 515–572.

Ross, W.D. 1930. *The Right and the Good.* Oxford, England: Oxford University Press.

———. 1954. *Kant's Ethical Theory.* Oxford, England: Clarendon Press.

Schott, Robin May, editor. 1997. *Feminist Interpretations of Immanuel Kant.* State College: Pennsylvania State University Press.

Sullivan, Roger. 1994. *An Introduction to Kant's Ethics.* Cambridge, England: Cambridge University Press.

Velkley, Richard. 1989. *Freedom and the End of Reason: On the Moral Foundation of Kant's Critical Philosophy.* Chicago: University of Chicago Press.

Wike, Victoria. 1994. *Kant on Happiness in Ethics.* Albany: State University of New York Press.

Wood, Allen. 1999. *Kant's Ethical Thought.* Cambridge, England: Cambridge University Press.

On Rawls and Contract Ethics

Alejandro, Roberto. 1998. *The Limits of Rawlsian Justice.* Baltimore, MD: Johns Hopkins University Press.

Daniels, N. 1978. *Reading Rawls: Critical Studies of a Theory of Justice.* Oxford, England: Basil Blackwell.

Gauthier, David. 1986. *Morals by Agreement.* Oxford, England: Oxford University Press.

Kukathas, C., and Pettit, P. 1990. *A Theory of Justice and Its Critics.* Stanford, CA: Stanford University Press.

Larmore, Charles. 1987. *Patterns of Moral Complexity.* Cambridge, England: Cambridge University Press.

Mulhall, Stephen, and Swift, Adam. 1996. *Liberals and Communitarians.* New York: Blackwell.

Pogge, T.W. 1989. *Realizing Rawls.* Ithaca, NY: Cornell University Press.

Rawls, John. 1951. Outline of a Decision Procedure for Ethics. *Philosophical Review* 60: 177–197

———. 1971. *A Theory of Justice.* Cambridge, MA: Harvard University Press.

———. 1999. *Collected Papers.* Edited by S. Freeman. Cambridge, MA: Harvard University Press.

Reaths, Andrew, Herman, Barbara, and Korsgaard, Christine. 1997. *Reclaiming the History of Ethics: Essays for John Rawls.* Cambridge, England: Cambridge University Press.

Wolff, R.P. 1977. *Understanding Rawls.* Princeton, NJ: Princeton University Press.

On Discourse Ethics

Apel, Karl-Otto. 1980. *Towards a Transformation of Philosophy.* Translated by G. Adey and D. Frisbe. Boston: Routledge and Kegan Paul.

———. 1996. *Selected Essays: Ethics and the Theory of Rationality.* New York: Humanity Books.

Bernstein, J.M. 1995. *Recovering Ethical Life: Jurgen Habermas and the Future of Critical Theory.* London: Routledge.

Dews, Peter 1999. *Habermas: A Critical Reader.* New York: Blackwell.

Habermas, Jürgen. 1990. *Moral Consciousness and Communicative Action.* Translated by C. Lenhardt and S. Nicholsen. Cambridge, MA: MIT Press.

———. 1993. *Justification and Application.* Translated by C. Cronin. Cambridge, MA: MIT Press.

———. 1998. *Between Facts and Norms.* Translated by W. Rehg. Cambridge, MA: MIT Press.

Hahn, Lewis. 2000. *Perspectives on Habermas.* Chicago: Open Court.

Howe, Leslie. 1999. *On Habermas.* New York: Wadsworth.

Joas, Hans, and Honneth, Axel. 1991. *Communicative Action: Essays on Habermas's Theory of Communicative Action.* Cambridge, MA: MIT Press.

McCarthy, Thomas. 1981. *The Critical Theory of Jürgen Habermas.* Cambridge, MA: MIT Press.

Outhwaite, William. 1995. *Habermas: A Critical Introduction.* Stanford, CA: Stanford University Press.

Rehg, William. 1997. *Insight and Solidarity. A Study in the Discourse Ethics of Jürgen Habermas.* Berkeley: University of California Press.

White, Stephen, editor. 1995. *The Cambridge Companion to Habermas.* Cambridge, England: Cambridge University Press.

On Utilitarianism

Adu-Amankwah, Patrick. 1997. *The Moral Philosophy of R.M. Hare: A Vindication of Utilitarianism?* London: Peter Lang.
Albee, Ernest. 1999. *History of English Utilitarianism.* New York: Thoemmes Press.
Ayer, A. J. 1954. *The Principle of Utilitarianism. Philosophical Essays.* London.
Bayles, Michael, editor. 1968. *Contemporary Utilitarianism.* Garden City, NY: Doubleday.
Bentham, Jeremy. 1789. *Introduction to the Principles of Morals and Legislation.* Oxford, England: Hafner Press, 1948.
Blanshard, Brand. 1961. *Reason and Goodness.* London: George Allen and Unwin.
Brandt, R.B. 1979. *The Right and the Good.* Oxford, England: Oxford University Press.
———. 1992. *Morality, Utilitarianism, and Rights.* Cambridge, England: Cambridge University Press.
Crisp, Roger. 1997. *Routledge Guidebook to Mill on Utilitarianism.* London: Routledge.
Feldman, Fred. 1997. *Utilitarianism, Hedonism and Dessert: Essays on Moral Philosophy.* Cambridge, England: Cambridge University Press.
Frey, R.G., editor. 1984. *Utility and Rights.* Minneapolis: University of Minnesota Press.
Glover, Jonathan, editor. 1990. *Utilitarianism and Its Critics.* New York: Macmillan.
Hayri, Matti. 1994. *Liberal Utilitarianism and Applied Ethics.* London: Routledge.
Jackson, Julius. 1993. *A Guided Tour of Mill's Utilitarianism.* New York: Mayfield.
Lyons, David. 1965. *Forms and Limits of Utilitarianism.* Oxford, England: Clarendon Press.
———. 1991. *In the Interest of the Governed: A Study of Bentham's Utility and Law.* Oxford, England: Clarendon Press.
———. 1997. *Mill's Utilitarianism: Critical Essays.* New York: Rowman and Littlefield.
Mill, John Stuart. 1861. *Utilitarianism.* New York: Bobbs-Merrill, 1957.
Quinton, Anthony. 1988. *Utilitarian Ethics.* LaSalle, IL: Open Court.
Scarre, Richard. 1996. *Utilitarianism.* London: Routledge.
Scheffler, Samuel. 1982. *The Rejection of Consequentialism.* Oxford, England: Clarendon Press.
———, editor. 1988. *Consequentialism and Its Critics.* Oxford, England: Oxford University Press.
Sen, A. and Williams, B., editors. 1982. *Utilitarianism and Beyond.* Cambridge, England: Cambridge University Press.
Shaw, William. 1998: *Contemporary Ethics: Taking Account of Utilitarianism.* New York: Blackwell.
Sidgwick, Henry. 1963. *The Methods of Ethics.* London: Macmillan.
Smart, J.J.C., and Williams, B. 1973. *Utilitarianism: For and Against.* Cambridge, England: Cambridge University Press.
Smith, James, and Sosa, E., editors. 1969. *Mill's Utilitarianism: Text and Criticism.* Belmont, CA: Wadsworth.
Stephen, Leslie. 1940. *English Utilitarians: Jeremy Bentham.* London: Peter Smith.
Tansjo, Tornbjorn. 1998. *Hedonistic Utilitarianism.* Edinburgh, Scotland: Edinburgh University Press.

On Natural Law Theory

Aquinas, Thomas. *Summa Theologica.* Questions 90–97. New York: Benzinger Brothers, 1947.
Dworkin, Ronald. 1978. *Taking Rights Seriously.* Cambridge, MA: Harvard University Press.
Finnis, John. 1991. *Natural Law.* New York: New York University Press.
George, Robert, editor. 1995. *Natural Law Theory: Contemporary Essays.* Oxford, England: Clarendon Press.
———. 1999. *In Defense of Natural Law.* Oxford, England: Clarendon Press.
———, and Wolfe, Christopher. 2000. *Natural Law and Public Reason.* Washington, DC: Georgetown University Press.

Haakonssen, Knud. 1996. *Natural Law History: From Grotius to the Scottish Enlightenment.* Cambridge, England: Cambridge University Press.

Hall, Pamela. 1999. *Narrative and the Natural Law: An Interpretation of Thomistic Ethics.* Notre Dame, IN: University of Notre Dame Press.

Hittinger, Russell. 1994. *A Critique of the New Natural Law Theory.* Notre Dame, IN: University of Notre Dame Press.

Hurlbut, E.P. 1996. *Essays on Human Rights and Their Political Guarantees.* New York: Rothman.

Lisska, Anthony. 1998. *Aquinas's Theory of Natural Law.* Oxford, England: Oxford University Press.

McLean, Edward, editor. 2000. *Common Truths: New Perspectives on Natural Law.* New York: ISI Books.

Rhonheimer, Martin. 2000. *Natural Law and Practical Reason: A Thomistic View of Moral Autonomy.* Translated by G. Malsbary. New York: Fordham University Press.

Rommen, Heinrich. 1998. *Natural Law: A Study in Legal and Social History and Philosophy.* Indianapolis, IN: Liberty Fund.

Rothbard, Murray. 1998. *The Ethics of Liberty.* New York: New York University Press.

Simmons, A. John. 1992. *The Lockean Theory of Rights.* Princeton, NJ: Princeton University Press.

Strauss, Leo. 1999. *Natural Right and History.* Chicago: University of Chicago Press.

Traina, Cristine. 1999. *Feminist Ethics and Natural Law.* Washington, DC: Georgetown University Press.

Weinreb, Lloyd. 1990. *Natural Law and Justice.* Cambridge, MA: Harvard University Press.

Westerman, Pauline. 1997. *The Disintegration of Natural Law Theory: From Aquinas to Finnis.* New York: Brill.

EPILOGUE

Moral Competence

Without moral sentiment, moral competence is hardly possible. To be morally competent, it is necessary to have a desire to do the right thing. As we have seen, moral sentiment can be expressed in a number of ways, but all the ways begin with the process of internalization and socialization, where norms, standards, models, rules, and paradigms become incorporated into the self and later expand to become part of how we understand ourselves as moral agents. The internalization of these norms means that we are willing to modify our behavior without the necessity of external controls. Not in every case, but in general, there is now a change between someone whose behavior has been controlled externally and one who is beginning to exercise internal controls. At this point we feel that we are a dutiful person, or a caring one, someone with a strong sense of honor or nobility. Our thinking rises from the preconventional stage of moral reasoning to at least the conventional stage in Kohlberg's analysis. Rather than evaluating behavior solely in terms of external rewards or punishments, we begin to think in terms of what is the right thing to do—even if it is only as conventionally understood.

The norms we internalize become our moral intuitions; they provide us with initial moral content. They tell us what is right and wrong: It is wrong to lie, to murder, to steal. These are acquired in the practices and institutions that make up one's life. First, and above all, is the family, where the care and love of our parents nurture empathy and sympathy in us. These emotional connections facilitate the adoption of the various norms taught by our parents and are supplemented by other authority figures in our lives. We learn how our actions affect others by observation and inference. Soon we learn to rely on these intuitions for answers to our questions about the right thing to do.

As we mature, we move from a being more or less controlled by the biology and psychology of the body to a person who begins to take control of those processes. If internalization makes us willing to modify our behavior, this power of control gives us the strength to do it. Moral strength becomes an empowerment, the ability to self-direct despite the inner resistance of emotion, passion, desire, and the external resistance in our environment of obstacles and difficulty.

Out of autonomy our moral dispositions are formed; these dispositions work on the structure of our character already provided by temperament and trait. By learning to control our passions and desires internally, we learn to become temperate; by controlling fear, we become brave. We begin to develop projects and plans for life, learn dedication to causes, and develop purposes that may involve sacrifice, risk, and danger. We mature into public roles and practices; we learn to be fair, kind, and respectful. We acquire a sense of justice.

Autonomy and virtuous disposition work together to generate greater self-direction and self-control. What we seek now is a moral direction that can be affirmed and articulated; a direction which assures us about the right thing to do. The quest for wisdom and moral knowledge begins.

Autonomy understood as self-direction demands that we form projects and plans for life. We soon learn that our projects, plans, and purposes must be tied together by some moral vision. A moral vision expresses a certain moral character in the order of things. Our plans for life become more formulated, and we begin to envision a sense of the good life for ourselves. At first, this may be provided by the conventions of our culture, but through trial and error, experience, we want to discover a more authentic sense of the good life. Our deliberative talents become better tuned as we attempt to progress closer to our goal of the good life. We learn a folk psychology; we make mistakes that teach us moral lessons. In the meantime our sense of ourselves as moral agents gathers a history; it becomes more and more the framework of our moral decisions. It becomes clearer who we want to be, morally speaking, and where we are presently. Our judgment matures; we learn to be resolute in our choices.

Moral vision feeds on our moral sentiment and in so doing makes it more robust. Deliberation enhances our moral strength; getting a clearer picture of what should be done enables us to direct our moral energy to its accomplishment. Determination becomes hardier. With the power of vision, deliberation, and choice, virtuous dispositions are put to better use for well-defined moral purposes. As our moral wisdom grows the other aspects of moral competence benefit.

As wisdom develops so does the quest for moral knowledge. Moral knowledge aids wisdom, refines moral intuition, and provides us with some assurance of the right thing to do. It helps refine our moral intuitions by making explicit the rules that implicitly underlie them; it modifies them by providing some criteria for their evaluation. It tries to organize these rules into higher-order principles, and at its highest stage it seeks to justify principles. The product of moral knowledge is assurance—assurance that in some measure there are general rules for moral conduct that can withstand reasonable scrutiny. With such assurance, ethical principles can then come to serve as algorithms for deliberation. Although they cannot substitute for moral wisdom, they can provide general frameworks for our deliberations.

Moral competence is desirable for what it is and for what it can bring. It helps to form desirable character. It is clear that a person who is temperate, courageous, fair, honest, kind, and respectful is someone you want to be around; these characteristics make for a valuable citizen, a model parent, a sterling spouse, and a safe

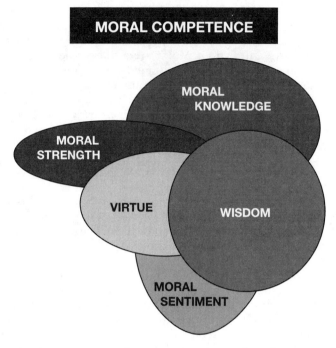

Moral competence is the integration of a number of important abilities: moral sentiment, the desire to do the right thing; moral strength, the power to do it; virtue, the disposition to keep on doing it; wisdom, knowing how it's done; and knowledge, knowing what the right thing to do is.

companion. One obviously suspects that the more morally competent persons in a community, the better the community; it is the morally competent who strive to be fair and to see justice done. Moral competence helps us in our search for the best life not only in terms of providing us with a sound, authentic vision, but with discovering the best means to its attainment and the strength to pursue it. Although the morally competent may not prosper and do not always flourish, moral competence helps us bear tragedy and misfortune, endure hardship, and be patient and hopeful. But even if it does not have these uses, moral competence has a value in itself. It is the sign of excellence in the person whose behavior is a value simply because of its beauty and design.

APPENDIX

Writing Ethics Term Papers

THE PURPOSE OF WRITING PHILOSOPHY PAPERS

Traditionally, the purpose of writing philosophy papers is to explore a particular topic or issue and to critically assess any claims made about it. The result is, ideally, some well-supported and reasoned conclusion about the matter. The paper allows one to exercise reasoning skills and to practice critical thinking. It provides an experience in rational discourse, understood as a model of resolving conflicts. It gives one a deeper and more profound understanding of an issue or topic, and it allows one to provide either more justification or criticism of an issue or topic.

CHOOSING A SUBJECT FOR THE PAPER

There are basically two types of ethics papers: theory or position papers. Position papers have to do with moral issues. A moral issue is a matter of public importance, which concerns a moral evaluation of past, actual, or potential practices that are (currently) in dispute. Examples include voluntary active euthanasia, physician-assisted suicide, capital punishment, abortion, pornography, medical paternalism, confidentiality, the ethics of drug testing in the workplace, sexual ethics, what children owe their parents, environmental ethics, the ethics of international aid, affirmative action, animal rights, neonatal euthanasia, birth control, business ethics, and so on.

Theory papers, as the name implies, are concerned with certain aspects of moral theory. Topics may include general ones such as the nature of temperance, moral deliberation, the principle of egoism, and the like. Biographical topics have to do with a particular philosopher's theory or view, for example, "Aristotle's Doctrine of the Mean" or "Cicero's Account of Deliberation."

1. Choose a Subject of Interest to You

It is much easier to write about something that you have concern and passion about than about something that is simply perfunctory. Try to choose a subject that you may have had some personal experience or familiarity with in some regard. If you're not entirely sure of your interests, look for an anthology in ethics. Usually, the anthologies are organized by topics; browsing through these might give you an idea for your topic.

2. Choose a Controversial Subject

If the subject you have chosen concerns an issue, then it should be a relatively controversial issue rather than a settled one. Refrain from selecting obscure topics which may be the interest of only a few.

3. Choose a Manageable Subject

A manageable subject is one that has a reasonable amount of research material available. Unless one has special access to information, if there is too little research material available, then it will require an exhaustive search that may simply take too much time. In this case find a different topic with more information available. On the other hand, if there is too much material available, then reading all the relevant material and incorporating it into your paper may require more time than is available. In this case narrowing your topic to some specific aspect of the more general topic might help.

4. Make Sure the Subject Is Approved by the Instructor

Sometimes students will choose topics that marginally fall within the area of ethics. Certain subjects may be more appropriate for psychology or sociology than philosophy. Having the instructor review the subject may avoid this difficulty.

FINDING SOURCES

1. Start with references in the text. Next look at general anthologies (anthologies are collections of articles by a variety of authors on a particular subject) that deal with your issue or topic. Usually the editors will have some of the classic articles on the subject matter with more references supplied. Compare several anthologies for best results.

2. Look under subject in your library holdings or on-line catalogue. Look for titles with your subject. Also refer to the collected bibliographies.

3. Look at your library's on-line databases. See what is current in the last 2 years.

4. Look at indices. Ask the reference librarian. *The Philosopher's Index* and the *Humanities Index* are two places to begin. Look for specialty indices too (e.g., biomedical indices).

5. Look at reference works. *The Encyclopedia of Ethics, A Companion to Ethics, The Encyclopedia of Philosophy, The Routledge Encyclopedia of Philosophy, The Encyclopedia of Religion and Ethics, The Bibliography of Bioethics, Encyclopedia of Values, Dictionary of the History of Ideas, Internet Encyclopedia of Philosophy* (http://www.utm.edu/

research/iep/) are the most common. For further reference, see *Directories in Print*, edited by C. Montgomery (Detroit: Gale Research).

6. Look in current issues of relevant philosophy journals. These may not have yet been indexed in the *Philosopher's Index*. Here is a list of relevant ethics journals:

Bioethics
Bioethics Forum
Bioethics Quarterly
Bioethics Update
Business and Professional Ethics Journal
Business and Society Review
Business Ethics Quarterly
Business in the Contemporary World
Christian Bioethics
Corporate Confidentiality and Disclosure Journal
Corporate Ethics Digest
Criminal Justice Ethics
Environmental Ethics
Environmental Values
Ethica
Ethics
Ethics and Animals
Ethics and Behavior
Ethics and International Affairs
Ethics and Medicine
Ethics and Medics
Ethics Digest

Ethics: Easier Said Than Done
Ethics in Education
Ethikos: Examining Ethical Issues in Business
Euthanasia Review, The
Faith in Ethics
Foundations
Georgetown Journal of Legal Ethics
Hastings Center Report, The
Humane Medicine
International Journal of Applied Philosophy
International Journal of Moral and Social Studies
International Journal of Value-Based Management
IRB: A Review of Human Subjects Research
Issues in Law and Medicine
Journal of Applied Philosophy
Journal of Business Ethics
Journal of Clinical Ethics
Journal of Ethical Studies
Journal of Ethics

Journal of Information Ethics
Journal of Mass Media Ethics
Journal of Medical Ethics
Journal of Medical Humanities and Bioethics
Journal of Medicine and Philosophy
Journal of Moral Education
Journal of Religious Ethics
Journal of Value Inquiry
Kennedy Institute of Ethics Journal
Law and Philosophy
Law and Society Review
Making the Rounds in Health
Medical Humanities Review
Medicine and Law
Notre Dame Journal of Law, Ethics, and Public Policy
Philosophy and Public Affairs
Privacy Journal
Professional Ethics
Professional Liability Today
SOUNDINGS
Theoretical Medicine
Values and Ethics in Health Care

The following newsletters might also be helpful:

BioLaw: A Legal and Ethical Reporter on Medicine, Health Care, and Bioengineering
Business Ethics Resource
COGEL Guardian
Corporate Crime Reporter
Corporate Examiner
Criminal Defense Ethics: Law and Liability
Ethics and Policy
Ethics in Government Reporter

Ethics Newsgram
EthNet
Fineline
Government Regulation of Business Ethics
Human Research Report
Issues in Ethics
Managing Ethics Newsletter
Media Ethics Update
Medical-Moral Newsletter
National Reporter on Legal Ethics and Professional Responsibility

Organizational Ethics Newsletter
Perspectives on the Professions
Professional Ethics Report
Professional Monitor
QQ: Report from the Center for Philosophy and Public Policy
Reporter on the Legal Profession
Tough Questions
Western Bioethics Network

7. Look in nonphilosophy journals relevant to your topic; for example, if you're dealing with an issue in medical ethics, you might want to look in prominent medical journals, such as *The New England Journal of Medicine* or *Lancet*, for articles which might address your ethical issue.

8. Look on the Web. There are over 100,000 sites on the Web that deal with ethical topics or issues. To help sort through these, you might link to:

Ethics Resources on the Net http://condor.depaul.edu/ethics/resource.html

Philosophy in Cyberspace http://www-personal.monash.edu.au/~dey/phil/

Philosophers' Web Magazine http://www.philosophers.co.uk

The Window: Philosophy on the Internet http://www.trincoll.edu/depts/phil/
philo/index.html

American Philosophical Association http://www.udel.edu/apa/

Peter Suber's Guide to Philosophy on the Internet http://www.earlham.edu/
suber/philinks.htm

Yahoo's list of Philosophy Links http://www.yahoo.com/Arts/Humanities/
Philosophy/

A few of the better ethics Websites include:

Ethics Updates http://ethics.acusd.edu/index.html

Applied Ethics Resources   http://www.ethics.ubc.ca/resources/

Centre for the Study of Ethics in the Professions   http://www.iit.edu/~csep/

Ethics Connection http://scuish.scu.edu/Ethics/homepage.html

DOING THE RESEARCH

1. After selecting the subject, reflect on the issue and organize your thoughts; if it's
a topic, then determine your belief in its credibility.
2. Initiate research and gather as much material as you feel appropriate. One book
or a few articles are likely not sufficient, unless the subject is very specific.
3. Read the material; take notes, copy, and order quotations.
4. Organize your notes into categories of related matters.
5. Revise and refine your initial intuition about the matter.

CONSTRUCTING THE PAPER

For an issue:

1. Show why the issue you are considering is interesting and important.
2. State the thesis you are defending.
3. Present the initial arguments in support of your thesis.
4. Present the major possible objections to your thesis.
5. Reply to those objections.
6. Examine honestly whether your thesis meets the objections and refine it accordingly.

For a topic:

1. Show the importance and significance of the topic.
2. Give some background to the topic.
3. State clearly what you intend to show in the paper and give a summary or outline of the strategy or procedure.
4. Clearly define the concepts involved.

5. Give an explication and interpretation of the topic, with reference to various scholarly opinions (either historical, current, or both).

6. Present a critical evaluation of the interpretations and explications.

7. End with a summary of the outcome and an assessment of the topic in light of your research.

WRITING THE PAPER

1. Consider your audience and write clearly, as if you were explaining the matter to someone who was unfamiliar with the subject but sophisticated and intelligent enough to understand its finer points. Obfuscation is usually considered to be a sign of confusion or lack of understanding on your part of the subject matter.

2. Define your principal terms. These do not necessarily have to be formal definitions, but some explication of their meaning might be appropriate. For example, if you're discussing euthanasia, what is meant by euthanasia, are you speaking of a particular type, and so on.

3. Make sure your spelling, grammar, and diction are correct. Bad spelling is distracting for the reader; bad grammar makes statements unclear and often diminishes the quality of your work in the mind of the reader; bad diction, especially the use of sophisticated words inappropriately, will also have a negative impact on the reader. Read for typos; too many typos show that you did not review the text carefully enough.

4. Do not make gross, hasty generalizations or unsupported factual claims. Avoid fallacies, ad hominem attacks, circular reasoning, appeals to the popular or traditional character of beliefs, strongly emotional appeals, or rhetorical arguments. Always be fair to your opponents and offer the strongest versions of their claims you can make. The refutation of a fair and well-formulated position is always more effective than one that distorts or exaggerates a position.

5. It may be helpful, especially with a position paper, to imagine yourself in the role of an expert in regard to the subject matter, who is to bring this matter to public scrutiny or to a public panel for consideration. Write the paper accordingly.

6. If using sacred texts (the Bible, Torah, Koran, Bhagavad Gita, etc.), use them as if your audience does not subscribe to the authority of that text. In other words, don't assume that these are authoritative for everyone, but use whatever arguments or claims they make as rationally supportive of your position.

ETHICAL USE OF SOURCE MATERIAL

1. Quote sparingly unless your paper involves a close reading of an original text; the purpose of the paper is to see your work—not somebody else's.

2. Quote accurately; if you are adding missing words to make the passage coherent, indicate this with brackets around the words supplied by you. Use ellipses when you have purposefully left out words, phrases, or sentences in the quotation. Indicate if you have added emphasis.

3. When paraphrasing what an author has said, make sure you credit your source nonetheless, even if you don't quote directly.

4. Avoid dishonesty, intentional inaccuracy, and nondisclosure of information relevant to your paper; treating your opponent cynically and disrespectfully only has the effect of preaching to the choir, while motivating your opponents to dismiss your arguments.

5. Avoid plagiarism, which is considered by many to be one of the worst actions of a writer. Plagiarism occurs when a writer knowingly uses the exact or nearly exact words of another without crediting the author. This also goes for the practice of buying ready-made term papers. Pretending that another's work is one's own is still plagiarism, even if that person wrote the paper for your use. Seeking out such sources and paying them is planned deception.

SOURCES FOR WRITING PHILOSOPHY PAPERS

Barry, Vincent. 1983. *Good Reason for Writing.* Belmont, CA: Wadsworth.

Bedau, Hugo. 1996. *Thinking and Writing about Philosophy.* Boston: St. Martin's Press.

Graybosch, Anthony, Scott, Gregory, and Garrison, Stephen. 1998. *The Philosophy Student Writer's Manual.* Upper Saddle River, NJ: Prentice Hall.

Seech, Zachary. *Writing Philosophy Papers.* Belmont, CA: Wadsworth.

Soccio, Douglas. 1995. *How to Get the Most Out of Philosophy.* Belmont: Wadsworth.

Weston, Anthony. 1987. *A Rulebook for Arguments.* Indianapolis, IN: Hackett.

REFERENCE AND BIBLIOGRAPHY STYLE

The following are standard reference style manuals:

Gibaldi, Joseph. 1999. *MLA Handbook for Writers of Research Papers.* 5th edition. New York: Modern Language Association.

Publication Manual of the American Psychological Association. 1994. 4th edition. Washington, DC: American Psychological Association.

Turabian, Kate L. 1996. *A Manual for Writers.* 6th edition. Chicago: University of Chicago Press.

Glossary

Accountability: an obligation to answer for something on the basis that one's actions were bound by a norm, rule, law, directive, or expectation.

Act-utilitarianism: a type of utilitarianism that assumes an action to be the basic unit in the evaluation of behavior; contrasted with rule-utilitarianism.

Acting in ignorance: Aristotle's term for cases where one is either acting unaware or with loss of self-control; for example, acting while intoxicated.

Acting out of ignorance: Aristotle's term for cases where one is acting without knowledge of general or particular information that applies to the situation at hand; for example, not knowing that fatty foods are unhealthy or not knowing that this particular food is fatty; or being ignorant of particular circumstances, for example, that a car has broken down in the middle of a curve one is about to negotiate.

Admiration: a positive feeling toward the behavior or character of other persons, which characterizes them as an ideal worthy of emulation.

Alexithymia: a psychological condition marked by a lack of understanding or recognition of one's own emotional states and feelings.

Altruism: acting for the good of another without consideration of harm or benefit to oneself.

Ambition: self-control in regard to goals and ends in life. Its vices include ruthlessness and directionlessness. A high-minded person is one with especially noble goals or pursuits.

American Dream: a vision of the good life characterized by the pleasures of home and hearth, economic comfort, and good family relations.

Asceticism: a view which involves the radical denial of pleasure, especially bodily pleasures, in favor of a life free from earthly desires, as the surest way to inner peace or the elimination of vice.

Attachment: a bonding relation; significant emotional connection with another, such as parent to child or child to parent.

Authoritarian parenting: a style of parenting which involves severe physical punishment and strong use of authority in establishing moral rules of conduct.

Authoritative parenting: a style of parenting which involves mild physical punishment coupled with mild withdrawal of love; the encouragement of independence within well-defined limits and a willingness to explain reasons for rules, giving permission to children to express verbal disagreement.

Autism: a congenital condition marked by withdrawal from social interaction; symptoms include an inability to recognize and feel more complex emotions.

Autonomy: self-determination or self-governance. A state in which one has freely adopted a set of moral rules to guide one's behavior; mastery of self.

Average principle: a version of the utilitarian calculus which considers the relation between the numbers of people affected by certain pleasures and the total population.

Benevolence, the principle of: the claim that, above all, one ought not to harm another, but also ought to remedy distress, prevent harm, and do another good.

Blame: attributed to persons whose actions have violated some norm, rule, or law for which they can be held accountable.

Calculation: the ability to determine the most efficient means to an end.

Caring: a sentiment based on sympathy that involves a general regard for the welfare of others and distress over their suffering, with an emphasis on connectedness to others.

Casuistry: a technique of deliberation which focuses on the case; it uses a comparison and contrast with past cases to discover the best course of action for the present one.

Categorical imperative: a principle developed by Immanuel Kant which, in one version, claims that one should act so that the maxim of that action would become a universal law.

Clarification, stage of: a stage of moral knowledge concerned with the formulation of moral intuitions under specific rules.

Comedic vision: a vision that supposes that most people are good and the vicious behavior is due to ignorance; a belief in a fundamental order to things which realizes happiness.

Comedy: a type of story in which a clever and wise hero of low social status succeeds in overcoming obstacles placed by an opponent of high social status. In the end the conflict is resolved happily and in a way that incorporates both hero and blocker.

Communitarianism: a theory that suggests that the notion of the good is known prior to the notion of the right; the good is derived from the sense of the tradition within a community rather than independently or prior to it.

Compassion: a species of sympathy that usually involves a sudden "softening of the heart" when present to the suffering of others.

Compatibilism: the position that any behavior is free to the extent that it lacks external or internal coercion; more positively, it is the claim that an action is free to the extent that the self or higher cortical functions determine the behavior. Also known as soft determinism.

Compelled behavior: behavior caused by circumstances that are psychologically or physically overpowering or life threatening.

Consequentialist: moral principles based on the kinds of consequences their performance entail; a primary example of a consequentialist principle is utilitarianism; also called teleological.

Contentment: satisfaction with what one has and self-control in regard to the desire for what others possess. Its vices include covetousness.

Contract ethics: a theory attributed to John Rawls in which it is claimed that the foundation of ethics lies in the outcomes of fair decision-making processes.

Cosmic vision: a sense of the moral order of the cosmos.

Courage: self-efficacy in regard to risky or dangerous actions which have as their goal something larger than personal interest. Bravery is the control of fear. Fearlessness is lack of fear in typically dangerous situations. Cowardliness and foolhardiness are considered the vices in regard to courage.

Cunning: the ability to determine successful means to a particular goal, but without consideration of its moral quality; calculation concerned with maintaining one's advantage.

Curiosity: along with docility and studiousness, considered variously as vice or virtue, but generally defined as self-control in regard to the acquisition of information or knowledge. Meddling and allotrioepiscopia are the corresponding vices.

Decision: a formed judgment; the end process of practical reasoning which results when we are persuaded to do something by our deliberation and judgment.

Deliberation: a part of practical reasoning concerned with determining the best moral means to a goal.

Deontological: moral principles that derive their legitimacy from a certain interpretation of autonomy; the justification for an action lies in its character independent of any consequences it might have; a primary example of a deontological principle is the categorical imperative.

Determinism: the position that there is no free will; the claim that all human behavior is fixed by some combination of physical, biological, psychological, and social laws; also known as hard determinism.

Dialogic principle: the claim that one ought to do to others what all can agree, in a fair deliberative process, to do to one another.

Dichotomous thinking: a form of absolutist thinking that suggests that if something cannot be proved to be absolutely true, it must be false.

Dilemma, moral: a kind of moral judgment concerned with the choice between two right actions that are incompatible.

Discernment: a part of deliberation concerned with the determination of the nuances and particularities of one's present moral situation.

Discourse ethics: a theory developed by Jürgen Habermas and Karl-Otto Apel which argues that the foundations for ethics lies in the inherent structure of consensus.

Disgust: a feeling of revulsion toward the behavior or character of another.

Duress, acting under: nonvoluntary actions due to highly constraining events outside of the agent's control.

Duty: the sentiment that one is to do certain things, or to refrain from doing certain things, as a matter of obligation to oneself or others relative to a role one plays.

Effective means, the principle of: a principle of calculation that suggests we should adopt that plan which realizes the end with the least expenditure of means.

Egoism, the principle of: the claim that one ought to do what is best for oneself without regard to the harm or benefit to others (the consequentialist version); the claim that I am a law unto myself (the deontological version).

Emotion, moral: an emotional reaction to an action or event which has some moral import or evaluation to it; for example, outrage, disgust, admiration, sympathy, etc.

Emotivism: the theory which suggests that all moral claims and judgments are nothing more than expressions of ethical feelings or sentiments, which have the purpose of getting others to feel similarly.

Empathy: the ability to read the emotional state or feelings of others based on the experience of one's own feelings, emotional states, and suffering.

Empirical propositions: claims made about natural processes, such as the motion of the planets, the behavior of gases, genetic behavior, and the psychology of human beings.

Endotelic: having its own purpose or end.

Epicureanism: a view associated with the Greek philosopher Epicurus which is a version of hedonism that argues for the pursuit of only those sorts of activities, such as contemplation and the like, which yield higher-order and longer lasting forms of pleasure.

Eudaimonism: happiness defined as flourishing; flourishing is defined as a condition constituted by the virtuous performance of certain qualitative practices, which results in a special form of enjoyment.

Exotelic: being for the purpose of something else.

Fair-mindedness: a disposition in a person to be fair; someone is fair-minded if inclined to correct unfair practices toward fairness or is capable of being impartial and unbiased in judgment.

Fairness: the character or quality of practices which creates mutual advantage for its participants and engenders equal, impartial, and unbiased treatment.

Fame, life of: a vision of the good life in which the predominant goal is to attain public recognition and power.

Feminist ethics: the view that trust, sympathy, and other moral feelings are the basis of morality; an emphasis on caring, mediation, and connectedness as a means of making ethical judgments, rather than a hierarchical ordering of principle and rule.

Flourishing: a translation of Aristotle's eudaimonia; the sense of happiness found in the excellent or virtuous performance of the best practices which human life has to offer.

Flow: an enjoyment one gets from mastery of a practice, as marked by a feeling of loss of self-awareness and condensation of time.

Foresight: a part of moral deliberation concerned with the use of the imagination to determine the likely consequences of certain actions.

Forgiveness: a virtue that involves the disposition to forgo those trespasses made against you by others; its vices include vengefulness and softness.

Free will: the ability of human beings to act in a way that is not determined or fated to be.

Frugality: self-control in regard to saving and spending money. Its vices include extravagance and miserliness.

Game theory: a mathematically based theory of behavior that suggests the best strategies for maintaining an advantage in competitive practices.

Generality: a feature of moral rules and principles that delimits the kinds of practices to which the rule applies.

Generosity: a virtue involved with the disposition to give more than what is expected in certain circumstances; its vices include prodigality and stinginess.

Golden mean: Aristotle's account of virtue as a mean between two extremes, the one characterized by excess and the other by lack or deficiency in an emotion, feeling, or desire.

Golden rule: the claim that you should do unto others as you would have others do unto you.

Good life: a definition of happiness; a sense of what an individual should strive for as the ultimate set of goals in his or her life.

Good-temper: self-control in regard to anger. Its vices include bad-temper and apathy. There are, in addition, several species of bad-temper, including hot-temper, choleric, and sulkiness. Anger mixed with disgust produces, scorn, disdain, and contempt.

Good will: Kant's notion which involves the idea that the will which wills the good regardless of consequence is the only thing that can be counted as good in the absolute sense.

Goodwill: a positive fellow feeling toward others.

Guilt: a self-generated feeling of anxiety resulting from the violation of an internalized norm that has caused harm to others.

Happiness: well-being, usually defined subjectively as the feeling of contentment and joy; compare flourishing and prospering as other senses of happiness.

Hedonism: the view that pleasure defines the sense of the good life.

Heteronomy: control of one's behavior by something other than oneself; contrasted with autonomy.

Honesty: a virtue that involves the disposition to abide by the conventional or contractual rules of a practice; its vices include dishonesty and legalism.

Honor: a sentiment which involves the emphatic feeling that a moral person is one who does or does not engage in certain types of acts.

Incompetence: a person can be considered incompetent under one or more of the following conditions: (1) someone who cannot exercise judgment, as in the case of a comatose person; (2) someone who cannot form judgments, as in the case of young children or mentally disabled persons, or (3) someone who makes impaired judgments, either due to self-imposed intoxication, drug addiction, disease, mental illness, or pathology.

Industry: temperance in regard to leisure time; its vices include workaholism and sloth.

Instrumental theory of virtue: the claim that the virtues are necessary but not sufficient means for moral action.

Integral theory of virtue: the claim that the virtues when practiced as a whole lead to consistently moral action.

Integrity: consistent and public adherence to a moral code, even when it is personally disadvantageous to do so.

Internalization: a psychological process by which norms and standards are adopted as one's own; a willingness to correct behavior without the incentive of external reward or punishment.

Intuition, moral: inculcated moral convictions.

Ironic vision: a vision that supposes human beings are inherently weak and disposed to vice, living in an order beyond their comprehension; the moral agent is one who understands this and constrains his or her tendency toward viciousness.

Irony: a story marked by an unremarkable hero's attempt to overcome an especially oppressive order, resulting in his or her disillusionment, death, or breakdown.

Judgment: a part of practical reasoning concerned with weighing alternatives, a process which usually occurs at the end of deliberation.

Justice: principles concerned with the proper distribution of benefits and costs, rights and duties, and punishments and rewards in practices and institutions.

Justification, stage of: a stage of moral knowledge concerned with establishing the validity of certain moral principles.

Kindness: a virtue that involves the disposition to treat those under one's power with consideration; its vices include cruelty and softness.

Knowledge, moral: justified moral content, usually expressed in terms of a rule or principle.

Liability, tort: a legal determination of responsibility for compensation of harm done to another in cases of civil law.

Libertarianism: the view that there is free will. The claim that there is an aspect of the self associated with the will which serves as a decision maker between competing courses of action, which is not determined by the causes of those actions. It is also associated with the view that some human behavior, specifically goal-directed or intentional behavior, is not subject to causal determination the way in which other more obvious behaviors are. The existence of goal-directed behavior is an indication of "free will."

Libertarianism, the principle of: See *Nonmaleficence, the principle of.*

Lockean proviso: a test for significant harm to others: Does my absence improve their condition? If so, then I am doing them significant harm.

Love: an intense emotional bond with another in which the suffering of one creates suffering in another.

Memory: an important part of the process of deliberation in Cicero's model; deliberation, in part, employs the past in determining the best course of action; the past is represented by our life story and identity, experience, and cultural wisdom.

Memory palace: a mnemonic technique developed by 16th-century Jesuit philosopher Matteo Ricci to help deliberate about particular moral cases; one uses the metaphor of a palace, with its particular rooms, as a means for remembering certain topics in regard to the comparison and contrast of particular cases.

Minimum psychological realism, the principle of: the claim that all moral theory should be limited by a realistic appraisal of the character, behavior, and decision-making processes of human beings.

Modesty: a virtue that involves an accurate appraisal of one's talents and abilities; its vices include shamelessness, boastfulness, and mock modesty.

Moral competence: the character, ability, knowledge, and know-how to do the right thing consistently.

Moral emotion: an emotional reaction to an action or event which has some moral import or evaluation to it; for example, outrage, disgust, admiration, sympathy, etc.

Moral intuition: inculcated moral convictions.

Moral knowledge: justified moral content, usually expressed in terms of a rule or principle.

Moral luck: aspects of human action which are out of one's control yet serve to determine its moral quality.

Moral psychology, laws of: developed by John Rawls to characterize the development from being loved to the stage of loving and trusting others.

Moral reasoning, stages of: an account developed by Lawrence Kohlberg concerning the typical moral stages through which human beings advance in their judgment of the rightness or wrongness of actions.

Moral sentiment: a certain configuration of moral feelings which establishes in a person a certain style of inclination toward the good.

Moral strength: the power of self-control in the face of immoral choices, as directed to some moral end or behavior.

Natural law: the claim that there is an inherent moral law in human nature, accessible by reason, and having either a divine or natural origin; often it is formulated as: do good and avoid evil.

Naturalistic fallacy: an argument developed by G.E. Moore which points out a confusion between what is natural or naturally desirable and what is good.

Negligence: an omission or failure to perform ordinary safety procedures for a certain practice.

Nobility: a sentiment which views oneself as aspiring toward a certain model of excellence in behavior and perfection in character; pursuit of something greater or more valuable than self.

Nondisclosure: withholding information that one believes to be true and would be pertinent to a person's interests.

Nonmaleficence, the principle of: claims that one is free to do whatever one wishes as long as it does not significantly harm another; also called the libertarian principle.

Norm: a mutually recognized standard of behavior.

Normative propositions: claims made about what people ought to do.

Obligation: a recognition of commitment to the performance or omission of an action or to the adherence of a standard.

Outrage, moral: a feeling of anger usually directed toward the perpetrator of a wrong.

Patience: the ability to delay or wait for what is desired. Perseverance is the ability to endure a number of hardships for the sake of a goal that is desired.

Permissive parenting: a style of parenting characterized by lax parental control, little participation, and little observation of children's conduct; often involves a wide permission of behavior with few or no limits set.

Perseverance: the ability to endure in achieving some goal; its vices include doggedness and resignation.

Pity: a form of sympathy that involves distress over the suffering of another, yet also includes a patronizing element or feeling of superiority.

Pleasure: an attractive positive feeling marked by a sense of satiation or anticipation.

Pleasure, life of: a vision of the good life whose primary goal is to maximize the amount of pleasure and enjoyment in one's life.

Polite virtues: virtues that are proper for social interaction; these include charm, wittiness, politeness, unpretentiousness, and friendliness.

Practical reason: Kant's term for the application of pure reason to the human will; the character of pure reason is its attempt to grasp the ultimate, systematic, and absolute understanding of all things; when applied to the will it seeks an underlying, universal moral principle for human behavior.

Practical reasoning: a reasoning process concerned with the connection of ends, means, and act in a way that preserves the moral integrity of the outcome.

Preference utilitarianism: a view within utilitarianism that argues that people's preferences ought to be the definition of happiness rather than some objective account of happiness as pleasure.

Pride: the virtue of self-respect; its vices are arrogance, vanity, and self-deprecation.

Principle, moral: a higher-order moral rule which is marked by universality and generality but has wider scope than moral rules; it is used to justify lower-order rules.

Principle of effective means, the: a principle of calculation that suggests we should adopt that plan which realizes the end with the least expenditure of means.

Principle of responsibility, Aristotle's: the claim that responsibility should be assigned according to the proportion of voluntariness in the action.

Prospering: financial and public success in a particular practice or set of practices.

Proximate cause: that cause which is closest in the causal nexus responsible for an outcome or event; the salient and relevant cause of an event.

Prudence: a form of practical reasoning concerned with choosing the best means and ends for a moral life.

Psychopathy: a congenital condition marked by the absence of moral feeling, difficulty in forming attachments, and a high threshold for fear and anxiety.

Recklessness: criminal negligence; a gross deviation from commonly prescribed rules of caution pertaining to a certain practice.

Reflective equilibrium: a process of adjustment between principles and moral intuitions, which assumes a basic circularity in trying to justify principles.

Regret: a feeling occasioned when persons have done something imprudent or inadvertent that resulted in harm to themselves.

Relativism: a view that all moral rules and principles have no objective or universal validity, but have validity only to the culture in which they are practiced; *empirical relativism* is the claim that as a matter of empirical fact there are no universally held norms; *cultural relativism* is the view that we cannot understand the norms of another culture; *normative relativism* is the view that there are no objective criteria to appeal to in the adjudication of conflicts.

Remorse: a feeling of sorrow or sadness occasioned by doing something morally imprudent in a way that results in harm to others; usually felt after a person recognizes the full impact of what he or she has done to others.

Respect: a virtue that involves the disposition to recognize the basic worth of another person.

Responsibility: an assignment made to someone who is accountable for voluntary actions that have caused a certain outcome.

Right: an inherent entitlement which others are obligated to respect and not to interfere with.

Righteousness: an emotion felt when justice has been done.

Rights-based ethics: the view that all obligation stems from rights, understood as fundamental claims which a person can make against another.

Romance: a particular kind of story defined by a strong sense of good versus evil. A story in which a villain causes a crisis, and a hero, who exemplifies a number of virtues, resolves it by vanquishing the villain; also called melodrama.

Romantic vision: a vision that sees the world as divided between good and evil; the moral agent is one that proves him- or herself in defense of the good order.

Rule, moral: a proscription or prescription for behavior characterized by universality, generality, but restricted in scope to certain types of behaviors; rules are generally used to justify or recommend certain actions.

Rule-utilitarianism: a view within utilitarianism that argues that rules rather than acts ought to be the basic unit in the evaluation of behavior; contrasted with act-utilitarianism.

Satire: a kind of story in which a naive hero comes to recognize, by means of many misadventures, the hypocrisy and falsehood of an existing order.

Satiric vision: a basic distrust of the existing order of things; a tendency to value simpler, more natural ways of life, as opposed to the pretense and hypocrisy of the conventional way of life.

Schadenfreude: feigned sympathy; secret delight in the suffering of others.

Scope: the specification of a moral rule in the context of a certain practice.

Security: a virtue of self-control in regard to what one possesses or in regard to lovers or friends. Its vices include jealousy and complacency.

Self-control: mastery over feelings of pleasure and positive emotions; temperance is the primary virtue of self-control.

Self-direction: the ability to give oneself a set of rules and principles to guide and limit behavior.

Self-efficacy: mastery over external circumstances which may constrain or limit accomplishment of goals; mastery over more negative emotions, such as fear; courage is the primary virtue of self-efficacy.

Self-mastery: the ability to exert control over one's inner life.

Sexual continence: a virtue concerned with moderation in sexual behavior; its vices include lust and prudishness.

Shame: a group-generated feeling of anxiety directed toward one's own failings in comparison to an internally adopted group norm or standard of behavior.

Socialization: a process by which one acquires norms, habits, and desires consonant with one's culture at large.

Sociopathy: a condition marked by an absence of moral feeling, a tendency toward cruel behavior, and a proclivity toward violence.

Stoicism: a view associated with the Greek philosopher Epictetus, which advocates a life of virtue over a life of pleasure and an acceptance and endurance of those things in our life that we are powerless to change. It promotes an indifference to both pleasure and pain.

Subjectivism: the belief that all ethical questions are matters of personal opinion; ethics is a matter of taste and cannot in principle be decided.

Sybaritism: a kind of hedonism which argues for the unbridled and indiscriminate pursuit of pleasure.

Sympathy: the feeling of distress that may occur when we witness the suffering of another.

Systematization, stage of: a stage of moral knowledge concerned with the hierarchical organization of moral rules into a well-formulated code.

Teleological principles: principles which measure the goodness of actions in terms of how they benefit the agents involved; also called consequentialist.

Temperance: a virtue concerned with self-control in regard to pleasure. Its vices include self-indulgence and insensitivity.

Temptation, moral: a kind of moral judgment that involves a choice between right and wrong.

Tit-for-tat principle: a claim developed by game theory which suggests that one ought to cooperate when others do and avoid cooperation when others don't cooperate.

Tolerance: a virtue concerned with the willingness to allow another to lead a vision of the good life that contrasts with one's own; its vices include intolerance and liberality.

Total principle: a version of the utilitarian calculus the makes decisions on the basis of the sum of the number of people affected by a certain kind of pleasure.

Tragedy: a story marked by a crisis created by an admirable although flawed hero. The story resolves by means of the death or defeat of the hero by an inexorable force.

Tragic choice: a kind of moral judgment in which one must choose between the lesser of two evils.

Tragic vision: a vision that supposes that the order of things is fixed and indifferent if not hostile to human beings; the moral worth of an agent is shown by his or her desire to do the right thing even though it will not necessarily bring contentment.

Trust: a global feeling resulting from a certain degree of connectedness to others; confidence in the goodwill of others.

Truthfulness: a virtue concerned with the disposition to tell what one believes to be true in the context of a direct inquiry; its vices include lying and bluntness.

Universality: a feature of a moral rule or principle that specifies the number or kind of people to which the rule applies.

Utilitarian principle: a principle developed by Jeremy Bentham and John Stuart Mill which claims that one ought to choose that action which creates the greatest happiness for the greatest number.

Utilitarianism, act: See *Act-utilitarianism.*

Utilitarianism, preference: a view within utilitarianism that argues that people's preferences ought to be the definition of happiness rather than some objective account of happiness as pleasure.

Vice: failure at self-mastery in regard to certain feelings, emotions, and desires.

Virtue: success at self-mastery in regard to feelings, emotions, and desires.

Virtue, life of: as characterized by Aristotle, it is a life dedicated to the virtuous performance of the essential practices that constitute a good life.

Vision, moral: cognitive but preanalytic sense of the good life; a sense of the moral order of the cosmos and the social world.

Voluntariness: the degree of inner and external control over actions.

Voluntary action: action done with deliberation or action done knowingly.

Weakness, moral: lack of self-control in the face of immoral choices.

Wealth, life of: a vision of the good life in which the predominant goal is the accumulation of money.

Wickedness: a desire to harm others motivated by a sense of the loss of good in oneself.

Will to power: Nietzsche's concept defined as the instinctive desire for growth and the accumulation of power.

Wisdom: the ability to consistently choose morally right actions; having deliberative talent, discernment, good judgment, and savoir-faire.

References

Achebe, Chinua. 1959. *Things Fall Apart*. New York: Fawcett Crest.
———— 1967. *A Man of the People*. New York: Anchor.
———— 1987. *Anthills of the Savannah*. New York: Anchor.
———— 1989. Interview with Bill Moyers. *A World of Ideas*. Edited by B. Flowers. New York: Doubleday.
Ackrill, J.L. 1973. *Aristotle's Ethics*. New York: Humanities Press.
Adorno, T.W., et al. 1950. *The Authoritarian Personality*. New York: Harper.
Ainslie, George. 1992. *Picoeconomics*. New York: Cambridge University Press.
Alexander, Shana. 1979. *Anyone's Daughter*. New York: Viking Press.
Allinsmith, G. 1968. The Learning of Moral Standards. *Inner Conflict and Defense*. Edited by D.R. Miller, G. Swanson et al. New York: Holt, Rinehart and Winston.
Amato, P.R. 1986. Emotional Arousal and Helping Behavior in a Real-life Emergency. *Journal of Applied Social Psychology* 16: 633–641.
Ambrose. Concerning Virgins. *Nicene and Post-Nicene Fathers*. Vol. X. Edited by P. Schaff. Grand Rapids, MI: Eerdmans, 1979.
Andacht, Fernando. 1996. The Ground of the Imagination in the Semiotic of C.S. Peirce. Unpublished manuscript.
Anscombe, Elizabeth. 1976. *Intention*. Ithaca, NY: Cornell University Press.
Apel, Karl-Otto. 1980. *Towards a Transformation of Philosophy*. Translated by G. Adey and D. Frisbe. Boston: Routledge and Kegan Paul.
Aquinas, Thomas. *Summa Theologica*. New York: Benzinger Brothers, 1947.
Arendt, Hannah. 1963. *Eichmann in Jerusalem*. New York: Penguin, 1994.
———— 1970. *On Violence*. New York: Harvest.
Aristotle. *Nicomachean Ethics. The Basic Works of Aristotle*. Edited by R. McKeon. Translated by W.D. Ross. New York: Random House, 1941.

————. *Prior Analytics. The Basic Works of Aristotle.* Edited by R. McKeon. Translated by A.J. Jenkinson. New York: Random House, 1941.

————. *The Rhetoric. The Basic Works of Aristotle.* Edited by R. McKeon. Translated by W. Roberts. New York: Random House, 1941.

————. *The Metaphysics. The Basic Works of Aristotle.* Edited by R. McKeon. Translated by W.D. Ross. New York: Random House, 1941.

————. *De Anima. The Basic Works of Aristotle.* Edited by R. McKeon. Translated by J. Smith. New York: Random House, 1941.

————. *De Motu. The Complete Works of Aristotle.* Edited by J. Barnes. Translated by A. Farquhanson. Princeton, NJ: Princeton University Press, 1984.

Aronfreed, Justin. 1968. *Conscience and Conduct.* New York: Academic Press.

————. 1969. The Concept of Internalization. *Handbook of Socialization Theory and Research.* Edited by D.A. Goslin. Chicago: Rand McNally.

Arras, John. 1994. Principles and Particularity: The Role of Cases in Bioethics. *Indiana Law Journal* 69: 983–1014.

————. 1997. Nice Story, But So What? *Stories and Their Limits.* Edited by Hilde Nelson. New York: Routledge.

Asch, S.E. 1946. Forming Impressions of Personality. *Journal of Social Psychology* 41: 258–290.

Ashton, Dore. 1974. *Picasso on Art.* New York: Penguin.

Associated Press. 1991. Robbers Test Walker's Faith. May 6.

Athanasius. *Life of Anthony. Nicene and Post-Nicene Fathers.* Vol. IV. Edited by P. Schaff. Grand Rapids, MI: Eerdmans, 1979.

Aufrecht, Steven. 1996. Toward a Model for Determining Appropriate Corrective Action in Public Employee Discipline. *Journal of Collective Negotiations* 25(3): 171–197.

Augustine. 399–419. *De Trinitate. Nicene and Post Nicene Fathers of the Christian Church.* Vol. III. Edited by P. Schaff. Grand Rapids, MI: Eerdmans, 1979.

———— 401. *The Confessions. Nicene and Post Nicene Fathers of the Christian Church.* Vol. I. Edited by P. Schaff. Grand Rapids, MI: Eerdmans, 1979.

Averill, J.S. 1980. On the Paucity of Positive Emotions. *Advances in the Study of Communication and Affect. Assessment and Modification of Emotional Behavior.* Vol. 6. Edited by K. Blankstein, P. Pliner, and J. Polivy. New York: Plenum.

Axelrod, Robert. 1981. The Emergence of Cooperation Among Egoists. *American Political Science Review* 75: 306–318.

———— 1984 *The Evolution of Cooperation.* New York: Basic.

Ayer, A.J. 1952. *Language, Truth and Logic.* New York: Dover.

———— 1954. The Principle of Utilitarianism. *Philosophical Essays.* London: Macmillan.

Bacon, Francis. 1625. The Essayes or Counsels, Civill and Morall. *Selections.* Edited by S. Warhaft. New York: Bobbs-Merrill, 1965.

Bacon, M., Child, I., and Barry, H. 1963. A Cross-Cultural Study of Correlations of Crime. *Journal of Abnormal and Social Psychology* 66: 291–300.

Bahadur, Mahomed. 1898. *Mahomedan Law.* Vol. 3. Calcutta: Thacker, Spink and Co.

Baier, Annette. 1985. *Postures of the Mind.* Minneapolis: University of Minnesota Press.

———— 1986. Trust and Antitrust. *Ethics* 96: 231–260.

———— 1987. Hume, the Women's Moral Theorist? *Women and Moral Theory.* Edited by E. Kittay and D. Meyers. Totowa, NJ: Rowman and Littlefield.

———— 1991. *The Progress of Sentiment.* Cambridge, MA: Harvard University Press.

Baier, Kurt. 1972. Types and Principles of Responsibility. *Individual and Collective Responsibility.* Edited by Peter French. New York: Schenkman.

Bain, Alexander. 1859. *The Emotions and the Will.* London: John Parker and Son.

Baltes, P., et al. 1991. Wisdom: One Face of Successful Aging? *Late-Life Potential.* Edited by M. Perlmutter. Washington, DC: Gerontological Society of America.

————, and Smith, J. 1991. Toward a Psychology of Wisdom and Its Ontogenesis. *Wisdom: Its Nature, Origins and Development.* Edited by R. Sternberg. Cambridge, England: Cambridge University Press.

Bandura, Albert. 1965. Influence of Model's Reinforcement Contingencies on the Acquisition of Imitative Responses. *Journal of Personality and Social Psychology* 1: 589–595.

————— 1971. *Social Learning Theory.* New York: General Learning Press.

————— 1986. *Social Foundations of Thought and Action: A Social-Cognitive Theory.* Upper Saddle River, NJ: Prentice Hall.

—————, Reese, L., and Adams, N. 1982. Microanalysis of Action and Fear Arousal as a Function of Differential Levels of Perceived Self-Efficacy. *Personality and Social Theory* 13: 173–199.

Barbour, Tracy. 1995. Tearful Driver Gets Nine Months for Robbery. *Anchorage Daily News,* March 9.

Barnett, M. 1987. Empathy and Related Responses in Children. *Empathy and Its Development.* Edited by N. Eisenberg and J. Strayer. Cambridge, England: Cambridge University Press, 146–162.

Baron-Cohn, Simon, et al. 1993. Do Children with Autism Recognize Surprise? *Cognition and Emotion* 7(6): 507–516.

Batson, D., et al. 1981. Is Empathic Emotion a Source of Altruistic Motivation? *Journal of Personality and Social Psychology* 40: 290–302.

—————, Bolen, M., Cross, J., and Neuringer-Benefiel, H. 1986. Where Is the Altruism in the Altruistic Personality? *Journal of Personality and Social Psychology* 50: 212–220.

—————, Fultz, J., and Schoenrade, P.A. 1987. Adults' Emotional Reactions to the Distress of Others. *Empathy and Its Development* edited by N. Eisenberg and J. Strayer. Cambridge, England: Cambridge University Press, pp. 163–184.

—————, Dyek, J. Brandt, J. Batson, J., Powell, A., McMaster, M., and Griffith, C. 1988. Five Studies Testing Two New Egoistic Alternatives to the Empathy Altruism Hypothesis. *Journal of Personality and Social Psychology* 55: 52–77.

—————, et al. 1989. Negative-state Relief and the Empathy-altruism Hypothesis. *Journal of Personality and Social Psychology* 50: 212–220.

—————, C., Batson, J., Griffith, C., Barrientos, S. Brandt, J., Sprengelmeyer, P., and Bayly, M. 1989. Relation of Sympathy and Personal Distress to Prosocial Behavior: A Multimethod Study. *Journal of Personality and Social Psychology* 57: 55–66.

—————, and Sager, Karen. 1997. Is Empathy-induced Helping Due to Self–Other Merging? *Journal of Personality and Social Psychology* 73(3): 495–505.

————— 1997. Self-Other Merging and the Empathy-Altruism Hypothesis: Reply to Neuberg et al. *Journal of Personality and Social Psychology* 73(3): 517–523.

Baumrind, D. 1980. New Directions in Socialization Research. *Psychological Bulletin* 35: 639–652.

————— 1986. *Social Foundations of Thought and Action: A Social-Cognitive Theory.* Upper Saddle River, NJ: Prentice Hall.

————— 1983. Rejoinder to Lewis's Reinterpretation of Parental Firm Control Effects: Are Authoritative Families Really Harmonious? *Psychological Bulletin* 94: 132–142.

————— 1991. The Influence of Parenting Style on Adolescent Competence and Substance Use. *Journal of Early Adolescence* 11: 56–95.

BBFC. (1995). British Board of Film Classification: Annual Report 1995–1996. London: Author.

Beck, Lewis White. 1960. *A Commentary on Kant's Critique of Practical Reason.* Chicago: University of Chicago Press.

Bekker, Scott. 1997. Reckless Driver Causes Pileup on Pa. Highway; 7 Die. Associated Press, March 22.

Bellah, Robert, et al. 1996. *Habits of the Heart.* Berkeley: University of California Press.

Beller, Jennifer, and Stoll, Sharon. 1992. A Moral Reasoning Intervention Program for Student Athletes. *The Academic Athletic Journal* 45–57.

Benedict, Ruth. 1954. *The Chrysanthemum and the Sword.* Tokyo: Tuttle.

Benn, S. 1985. Wickedness. *Ethics* 95: 795–810.

Benn, S.I., and Peters, R.S. 1959. *Social Principles and the Democratic State.* London: Routledge.

Bennett, Jonathan. 1974. The Conscience of Huckleberry Finn. *Philosophy* 49: 123–134.

Bennett, William. 1993. *The Book of Virtues.* New York: Simon and Schuster.

Bentham, Jeremy. 1789. *Introduction to the Principles of Morals and Legislation.* Oxford, England: Hafner Press, 1948.

Berger, P., and Luckmann, T. 1967. *The Social Construction of Reality.* Garden City, NY: Doubleday.

Berkowitz, L., and Rawlings, E. 1963. Effects of Film Violence on Inhibitions Against Subsequent Aggression. *Journal of Abnormal and Social Psychology* 66(5): 405–412.

Berkowitz, Marvin. 1998. Fostering Goodness: Teaching Parents to Facilitate Children's Moral Development. *Journal of Moral Education* 27(3): 371–392.

Berry, Mike, and Gray, Tim. 1999. Cutting Film Violence: Effects on Perceptions, Enjoyment, and Arousal. *Journal of Social Psychology* 139(5): 567–583.

Bettelheim, Bruno. 1977. *The Uses of Enchantment.* New York: Vintage.

Bing, Leon. 1991. *Do or Die.* New York: HarperCollins.

Binmore, K. 1994. *Game Theory and the Social Contract.* Cambridge, MA: MIT Press.

Black, Henry Campbell, et al. 1980. *Black's Law Dictionary.* 6th edition. St. Paul, MN: West.

Blair, R., et al. 1995. Emotion Attributes in the Psychopath. *Personality and Individual Differences* 19(4): 431–437.

Blesius, R. 1989. The Concept of Empathy. *Psychology, A Journal of Human Behavior* 26: 10–15.

Block, J. 1995. Unpublished manuscript. University of California at Berkeley.

Bloom, Alan. 1987. *The Closing of the American Mind.* New York: Touchstone.

Bloomfield, Harold, and Kory, Robert. 1980. *Inner Joy.* New York: Wyden Books.

Blum, Deborah. 1995. Scientists Say Psychopaths Born—Not Made. *The Sacramento Bee,* November 19.

Blum, Lawrence. 1980. *Friendship, Altruism and Morality.* London: Routledge and Kegan Paul.

——— 1980a. Compassion. *Explaining Emotions.* Edited by A. Rorty. Berkeley: University of California Press, pp. 507–517.

Bohart, A.C. 1991. Empathy in Client-centered Therapy: A Contrast with Psychoanalysis and Self Psychology. *Journal of Humanistic Psychology* 31: 34–48.

Bok, Sissela. 1979. *Lying.* New York: Vintage.

Booth, Wayne. 1988. *The Company We Keep.* Berkeley: University of California Press.

Boren, H. 1992. *Roman Society.* Lexington, MA: Heath.

Bowers, L.B. 1990. Traumas Precipitating Female Delinquency: Implications for Assessment, Practice, and Policy. *Child and Adolescent Social Work Journal* 7: 389–402.

Bowlby, J. 1988. *A Secure Base: Parent–Child Attachment and Healthy Human Development.* New York: Basic.

Bradburn, N. 1969. *The Structure of Psychological Well-Being.* Chicago: Aldine.

Bradley, F.H. 1962. *Ethical Studies.* Oxford, England: Oxford University Press.

Brandt, R.B. 1967. Some Merits of One Form of Rule-Utilitarianism. *University of Colorado Studies.* Boulder: University of Colorado Press.

——— 1972. Happiness. *Encyclopedia of Philosophy.* Edited by P. Edwards. Vol. 3. New York: Macmillan.

——— 1979. *The Right and the Good.* Oxford, England: Oxford University Press.

——— 1987. Public Policy and Life and Death Decisions Regarding Defective Newborns. *Euthanasia and the Newborn.* Edited by R. McMullin et al. Dordrecht, the Netherlands: Reidel.

Braudy, Leo. 1986. *The Frenzy of Renown.* Oxford, England: Oxford University Press.

Braund, Susan. 1995. Story Medicine. *Anchorage Daily News,* February 16.

Braungart, Richard G. 1972. Family Status, Socialization, and Student Politics. *American Journal of Sociology* 77: 108–130.

Brehm, John, and Rahn, Wendy. 1997. Individual-Level Evidence for the Causes and Consequences of Social Capital. *American Journal of Political Science* 41: 999–1023.

Brown, Roger. 1965. *Social Psychology.* New York: Praeger.

Buber, Martin. 1966. *The Way of Response.* Edited by N. Glatzer. New York: Schocken Books.

Burrell, David, and Hauerwas, Stanley. 1977. From System to Story: An Alternative Pattern for Rationality in Ethics. *The Foundations of Ethics and Its Relationship to Science.* Edited by H. Engelhardt and D. Callahan. Hastings-on-Hudson, NY: Hastings Center.

Burton, R. 1963. The Generality of Honesty Reconsidered. *Psychological Bulletin* 70: 481–499.

Buschke, A., and Jacobsohn, F. 1948. *Sex Habits.* New York: Emerson Books.

Butler, Joseph. 1726. *Fifteen Sermons upon Human Nature.* New York: Lincoln-Rembrandt, 1986.

Butterworth, G., 1991. The Ontogeny and Phylogeny of Joint Visual Attention. *Theories of Mind.* Edited by A. Whiten. Oxford, England: Basil Blackwell, pp. 223–232.

———, and Cochran, E. 1980. Towards a Mechanism of Joint Visual Attention in Human Infancy. *International Journal of Behavioral Development* 19: 253–272.

Buzzuto, J.C. (1975). Cinematic Neurosis Following *The Exorcist. Journal of Nervous and Mental Disease* 161: 43–48.

Byrnes, James. 1947. *Speaking Frankly.* New York: Greenwood.

Campbell, A., et al. 1976. *The Quality of American Life.* New York: Russell Sage.

Campbell, Angus. 1981. *The Sense of Well-Being in America.* New York: McGraw-Hill.

Campbell, C.A. 1957. *On Selfhood and Godhood.* New York: Macmillan.

Cantor, J., and Reilley, S. 1982. Adolescents' Fright Reactions to Television and Films. *Journal of Communications* 32(1): 87–99.

Carlson, Richard. 1997. *Don't Sweat the Small Stuff... and It's All Small Stuff.* New York: Hyperion.

Carter, Jimmy. 1996. *Living Faith.* New York: Times Books.

Carter, Stephen. 1996. *Integrity.* New York: Basic.

Carver, C., and Scheier, M. 1995. *Perspectives on Personality.* Boston: Allyn and Bacon.

Cattell, R. 1946. *Description and Measurement of Personality.* Yonkers, NY: World Book.

Chisholm, R.M. 1964. *Human Freedom and the Self.* Lawrence: University of Kansas Press.

Cialdini, R.B., Darby, B., and Vincent, J. 1973. Transgressions and Altruism: A Case for Hedonism. *Journal of Experimental Social Psychology* 9: 502–516.

———, et al. 1987. Empathy-based Helping: Is It Selflessly Motivated? *Journal of Personality and Social Psychology* 52: 749–58.

Cialdini, R.B., and Fultz, J. 1990. Interpreting the Negative Mood-Helping Literature via "Mega-"Analysis: A Contrary View. *Psychological Bulletin* 107: 210–214.

Cialdini, Robert B., and Brown, Stephanie L. 1997. Reinterpreting the Empathy–Altruism Relationship: When One into One Equals Oneness. *Journal of Personality and Social Psychology* 73(3): 481–495.

Cicero. *De inventione.* Translated by H.M. Hubbell. Cambridge, MA: Harvard University Press, 1960.

——— *De officiis.* Translated by H.G. Edinger. Indianapolis, IN: Bobbs-Merrill, 1974.

——— *De finibus.* Translated by H. Rackham. Cambridge, MA: Harvard University Press, 1914.

——— *De republica.* Translated by G. Sabine and S. Smith. New York: Bobbs-Merrill, 1929.

——— *De legibus.* Translated by Clinton Walker. Cambridge, MA: Harvard University Press.

Clark, David, and Fawcett, J., editors. 1987. *Anhedonia and Affect Deficit States.* New York: PMA Publishing Co.

Clark, R.D., and Word, L.E. 1974. Where Is the Apathetic Bystander? Situational Characteristics of the Emergency. *Journal of Personality and Social Psychology* 29: 279–287.

Clarke, Randolph. 1996. Agent-Causation and Event-Causation in the Production of Free Action. *Philosophical Topics* 24: 19–48.

Clayton, V., and Birren, J.W. 1980. The Development of Wisdom across the Life-Span. *Life-Span Development and Behavior.* Edited by P. Baltes et al. Vol. 3. New York: Academic Press.

Cleckley, Hervey. 1982. *The Mask of Sanity.* St. Louis, MO: Mosby.

Coleman, John. 1987. Conclusion: After Sainthood. *Saints and Virtues.* Edited by J. Hawley. Berkeley: University of California Press.

Coles, Robert. 1986. *The Moral Life of Children.* New York: Atlantic Monthly Press.

Comstock, G., and Paik, H. 1991. *Television and the American Child.* New York; Academic Press.

Comstock, G., and Strasburger, V. C. 1990. Deceptive Appearances: Television Violence and Aggressive Behavior. *Journal of Adolescent Health Care* 11(1): 31–44.

Confucius. c. 350 B.C.E. *The Analects.* Translated by A. Waley. New York: Vintage, 1938.

—— (attributed). *The Doctrine of the Mean. Source Book in Chinese Philosophy.* Translated by Wing-Tsit Chan. Princeton, NJ: Princeton University Press, 1963.

—— c. 200 B.C. *The Great Learning. Source Book in Chinese Philosophy.* Translated by Wing-Tsit Chan. Princeton, NJ: Princeton University Press, 1963.

Corey, Gerald, and Corey, Marianne. 1997. *I Never Knew I Had a Choice.* Albany, NY: Brooks/Cole.

Coverdale, Miles. 1550. *A Spiritual and Most Precious Pearl.* New York: Walter Johnson, 1979.

Csikszentmihalyi, Mihali. 1975. Play and Intrinsic Rewards. *Journal of Humanistic Psychology* 15(3).

—— 1990. *Flow.* New York: Harper.

——, and Rathunde, K. 1991. The Psychology of Wisdom: An Evolutionary Interpretation. *Wisdom: Its Nature, Origins and Development.* Edited by R. Sternberg. Cambridge, England: Cambridge University Press.

Cyprian of Antioch. 357. *De Bono Patientiae.* Translated and edited by M. George Conway. Washington, DC: University Press of America, 1957.

Damasio, Antonio. 1994. *Descartes' Error: Emotion, Reason and the Human Brain.* New York: Grosset/Putnam.

Damon, W. 1988. *The Moral Child.* New York: Free Press.

Daniels, Norman. 1979. Wide Reflective Equilibrium and Theory Acceptance in Ethics. *Journal of Philosophy* 76:15–32.

Davidson, Art. 1990. *In the Wake of the Exxon Valdez.* San Francisco: Sierra Books.

Davidson, Donald. 1980. How Is Weakness of the Will Possible? *Essays on Actions and Events.* Oxford, England: Oxford University Press.

—— 1982. The Paradox of Irrationality. *Philosophical Essays on Freud.* Edited by R. Wollheim and J. Hopkins. Cambridge, England: Cambridge University Press.

Davies, Paul. 1983. *God and the New Physics.* New York: Touchstone.

Davis, Maxine. 1958. *Sex and the Adolescent.* New York: Dial Press.

Davis, M.H. 1983. Empathic Concern and the Muscular Dystrophy Telethon: Empathy Concern a Multidimensional Construct. *Personality and Social Psychology Bulletin* 9: 223–229.

Dawkins, Richard. 1976. *The Selfish Gene.* Oxford, England: Oxford University Press.

Deigh, John. 1995. Empathy and Universalizability. *Ethics* 105: 743–763.

D'Entreves, A.P. 1957. *Natural Law.* London: Hutchinson University Library.

Derstine, C.F. 1943. *Manual of Sex Education.* Grand Rapids, MI: Zondervan.

—— 1944. *Paths to Beautiful Womanhood.* Grand Rapids, MI: Zondervan.

DeSousa, Ronald. 1980. The Rationality of Emotions. *Explaining Emotions.* Edited by A. Rorty. Berkeley: University of California Press, pp. 127–152.

Devlin, Patrick. 1965. *The Enforcement of Morals.* Oxford, England: Oxford University Press.

De Vos, George. 1973. *Socialization for Achievement: Essays on the Cultural Psychology of the Japanese.* Berkeley: University of California Press.

Dewey, John. 1933. *How We Think.* Lexington, MA: D.C. Heath.

—— 1960. *Theory of the Moral Life.* New York: Holt, Rinehart and Winston.

Didion, Joan. 1968. *Slouching Towards Bethlehem.* New York: Farrar, Straus and Giroux.

Diener, E., et al. 1985. Happiness of the Very Wealthy. *Social Indicators Research* 16: 263–274.

Doi, Takeo. 1977. *The Anatomy of Dependence.* Tokyo: Kodansha International.

Dominguez, Joe, and Robin, Vicki. 1992. *Your Money or Your Life.* New York: Penguin.

Doogan, Mike. 1995. A Very Determined Woman Looks for Money for a Special Trip. *Anchorage Daily News,* June 10.

Donnerstein, E., Slaby, R., and Eron, L. 1994. The Mass Media and Youth Violence. *Violence and Youth: Psychology's Response.* Edited by J. Murray, E. Rubinstein and G. Comstock. Vol. 2. Washington, DC: American Psychological Association, pp. 185–256.

Duan, C., and Hill, C.E. 1996. The Current State of Empathy Research. *Journal of Counseling Psychology* 43: 261–274

Dunn, Jerry. 1996. *Tricks of the Trade for Kids.* New York: Houghton Mifflin.

Dunn, Judy. 1987. The Beginnings of Moral Understanding: Development in the Second Year. *The Emergence of Morality in Young Children.* Edited by J. Kagan and S. Lamb. Chicago: Chicago University Press.

Durbin, D.L., et al. 1993. Parenting Style and Peer Group Membership Among European-American Adolescents. *Journal of Research on Adolescence* 3: 87–100.

Dworkin, Ronald. 1992. Rights as Trumps. *Theories as Rights.* Edited by Jeremy Waldron. Oxford, England: Oxford University Press.

Edwards, Carolyn. 1987. Culture and the Construction of Moral Values. *The Emergence of Morality in Young Children.* Edited by J. Kagan and S. Lamb. Chicago: Chicago University Press.

Edwards, E. 1984. *The Relationship Between Sensation-seeking and Horror Movie Interest and Attendance.* Unpublished doctoral dissertation, University of Tennessee, Knoxville.

Edwards, Jonathan. 1741. Sinners in the Hands of an Angry God. *Jonathan Edwards.* Edited by C. Faust and T. Johnson. New York: Hill and Wang, 1962.

Eisenberg, Nancy. 1986. *The Altruistic Emotion, Cognition and Behavior.* Mahwah, NJ: Erlbaum.

———, McCreath, H., and Ahn, R. 1988. Vicarious Emotional Responsiveness and Prosocial Behavior: Their Interrelationships in Children. *Personality and Social Psychology Bulletin* 14: 298–311.

———, and Miller, P.A. 1987. Empathy, Sympathy and Altruism: Empirical and Conceptual Links. *Empathy and Its Development.* Edited by N. Eisenberg and J. Strayer. Cambridge, England: Cambridge University Press, pp. 292–316.

———, et al. 1989. The Role of Sympathy and Altruistic Personality Traits in Helping. A Reexamination. *Journal of Personality* 57: 41–67.

Eisenberg-Berg, N., and Geisheker, E. 1979. Content of Preachings and Power of the Model/Preacher: The Effect on Children's Generosity. *Developmental Psychology* 15: 168–175.

Ekman, P. 1993. Facial Expression and Emotion. *American Psychologist* 48: 384–392.

Eliot, George. 1860. *The Mill on the Floss.* Edited by A.S. Byatt. New York: Penguin, 1982.

Elms, A., and Milgram, S. 1966. Personality Characteristics Associated with Obedience and Defiance Towards Authoritative Command. *Journal of Experimental Research in Personality* 1: 282–289.

Engberg-Pedersen, Troels. 1983. *Aristotle's Theory of Moral Insight.* Oxford, England: Clarendon Press, 1983.

Enomoto, Carl. 1999. Public Sympathy for O.J. Simpson: The Roles of Race, Age, Gender, Income, and Education. *American Journal of Economics & Sociology* 58(1): 145–162.

Epictetus. *Moral Discourses.* Translated by E. Carter and T. Higginson. Edited by T. Gould. New York: Washington Square Press, 1964.

——— *The Manual. The Essential Works of Stoicism.* Edited by M. Hadas. Translated by G. Long. New York: Bantam, 1958.

Epicurus. *Letter to Menoeceus. Epicurus: The Extant Remains.* Translated by C. Bailey. Oxford, England: Clarendon Press, 1926.

Epimarchus. 485 B.C. *Fragments. Ancilla to the Pre-Socratic Philosophers.* Translated by K. Freeman. Cambridge, MA: Harvard University Press, 1978.

Erikson, Eric. 1991. *Childhood and Society.* New York: W.W. Norton.

Etzioni, Amitai. 1993. *The Spirit of Community.* New York: Touchstone.

Evans, C. 1982. Moral Stage Development and Knowledge of Kohlberg's Theory. *The Journal of Experimental Education* 51: 14–17.

Eyesenck, H. 1960. *The Structure of Human Personality.* New York: Macmillan.

Federman, J.1996. Film and Television Ratings: An International Assessment. Unpublished report. Studio City, CA: Mediascope.

Feinberg, Joel. 1991. The Nature and Value of Rights. *Introduction to Moral Theory.* Edited by Kenneth Rogerson. Chicago: Holt, Rinehart and Winston.

Feldman, R. 1968. Response to Compatriot and Foreigners Who Seek Assistance. *Journal of Personality and Social Psychology* 10: 202–214.

Felsman, J.K., and Vaillant, G. 1987. Resilient Children as Adults: A 40 Year Old Study. *The Invulnerable Child.* Edited by E. Anderson and B. Cohler. New York: Guilford Press.

Festinger, Leon. 1957. *A Theory of Cognitive Dissonance.* Evanston, IL: Row, Peterson.

Finkelstein, Norman, and Birn, Ruth. 1998. *A Nation on Trial.* New York: Metropolitan.

Fischer, John. 1999. Recent Work on Moral Responsibility. *Ethics* 110: 93–139.

Flack, Richard. 1967. The Liberated Generation: An Exploration of the Roots of Student Protest. *Journal of Social Issues* 23: 52–75.

Flanagan, Owen. 1991. *Varieties of Moral Personality: Ethics and Psychological Realism.* Cambridge, MA: Harvard University Press.

Flinn, Kelly. 1997. *Proud to Be.* New York: Random House.

Foot, Phillipa. 1978. *Virtues and Vices.* Berkeley: University of California Press.

Fortenbaugh, William. 1969. Aristotle: Emotion and Virtue. *Arethusa* 2: 163–185.

Fortune, Reo. 1963. *The Sorcerers of Dobu.* New York: Dutton.

Frankena, William. 1973. *Ethics.* 2nd ed. Upper Saddle River, NJ: Prentice Hall.

Frankfurt, Harry. 1969. Alternate Possibilities and Moral Responsibility. *Journal of Philosophy* 45: 829–839.

––––––– 1994. An Alleged Asymmetry between Actions and Omissions. *Ethics* 104: 620–623.

Franklin, Benjamin. 1771–1790. *Autobiography.* Edited by L. Lemisch. New York: New American Library, 1961.

Friedman, Marilyn. 1989. Feminism and Modern Friendship: Dislocating the Community. *Ethics* 99: 275–290.

Frye, Northrop. 1957. *Anatomy of Criticism.* Princeton, NJ: Princeton University Press.

Fulgum, Robert. 1986. *Everything I Know I Learned in Kindergarten.* New York: Ivy.

Fukuyama, Francis. 1995. *Trust.* New York: Free Press.

––––––– 1999. *The Great Disruption. Human Nature and the Reconstitution of Social Order.* New York: Free Press.

Gadamer, H.G. 1975. *Truth and Method.* New York: Seabury Press.

Galbraith, John. 1984. *The Affluent Society.* 4th edition. New York: American Library.

Galloni, Allesandra. 1997. Following Orders Defense. Associated Press, April 5.

Gambetta, Diego. 1988. Can We Trust Trust? *Trust: Making and Breaking Cooperative Relations.* Edited by Diego Gambetta. Oxford, England: Blackwell.

Gardner, Howard. 1983. *Frames of Mind.* Cambridge, MA: Harvard University Press.

––––––– 1993. *Multiple Intelligences: The Theory in Practice.* New York: Basic.

Gates, Henry Louis, Jr. 1998. In Praise of Hypocrisy. *The Atlantic Monthly,* January.

Gauthier, David. 1986. *Morals by Agreement.* Oxford, England: Oxford University Press.

––––––– 1990 *Moral Dealing.* Ithaca, NY: Cornell University Press.

Geach, Peter. 1977. *The Virtues.* Cambridge, England: Cambridge University Press.

Gearan, Anne. 1996. Silencing the Scream. Associated Press, September 25.

Gert, Bernard. 1970. *The Moral Rules.* New York: Harper.

––––––– 1988. *Morality. A New Justification of the Rules.* New York: Oxford University Press.

Gill, Misty. 1999. The Changed Face of Liability for Hostile Work Environment Sexual Harassment: The Supreme Court Imposes Strict Liability in *Faragher v. City of Boca Raton,* 118S.Ct. 2275 (1998), and *Burlington Industries, Inc. v. Ellerth,* 118 S.Ct. 2257 (1998). *Creighton Law Review* 32(5): 1651–1720.

Gilligan, Carol. 1982. *In a Different Voice.* Cambridge, MA: Harvard University Press.

Ginet, Carl. 1990. *On Action.* Cambridge, England: Cambridge University Press.

Ginzberg, Louis. 1909. *The Legends of the Jews.* Philadelphia, PA: The Jewish Publication Society of America.

Gladding, S.T. 1988. *Counseling: A Comprehensive Profession.* Columbus, OH: Merrill.

Gleich, James. 1987. *Chaos.* New York: Penguin.

Godwin, William. 1793. *Enquiry Concerning Political Justice.* Toronto: University of Toronto Press, 1969.

Goldhagen, David. 1996. *Hitler's Willing Executioners.* New York: Knopf.

Goldman, Alvin. 1993. Ethics and Cognitive Science. *Ethics* 103: 337–360.

Goldman, Rene. 1995. Moral Leadership in Society: Some Parallels between the Confucian "Noble Man" and the Jewish Zaddik. *Philosophy East & West* 45(3): 329–366.

Goldstein, K., and Scheerer, M. 1941. Abstract and Concrete Behavior. *Psychological Monographs* 53: 2.

Goleman, Daniel. 1995. *Emotional Intelligence.* New York: Bantam.

Golzius, Hendrik. 1584. *Patientia and Fortitude*. Rouen.

Gordon, R. 1995. Sympathy, Simulation, and the Impartial Spectator. *Ethics* 105: 727–742.

———, and Baker, J. 1995. Autism and the "Theory of Mind" Debate. *Philosophical Psychopathology: A Book of Readings*. Edited by G. Graham and L. Stephens. Cambridge, MA: MIT Press.

Gracian, Balthasar. 1637. *The Art of Worldly Wisdom*. Boston: Shambala, 1993.

Grandin, Temple. 1996. *Thinking in Pictures*. New York: Vintage.

Gray, Glenn. 1967. *The Warriors: Reflections on Men in Battle*. New York: Harper and Row.

Greenberg, B.S., and Gordon, T. E. 1971. Social Class and Racial Differences in Children's Perceptions of Televised Violence. *Television and Social Behavior: Television's Effects—Further Explorations*. Edited by G.A. Comstock, E.A. Rubenstein, and J.P. Murray. Washington, DC: U.S. Government Printing Office, pp. 55–82.

Greene, Robert. 1998. *The 48 Laws of Power*. New York: Viking.

Greenspan, Patricia. 1988. *Emotions and Reasons: An Inquiry into Emotional Justification*. New York: Routledge.

Grim, P.F., Kohlberg, L., and White, S. 1968. Some Relationships Between Conscience and Attentional Processes. *Journal of Personality and Social Psychology* 8: 239–252.

Grotius, Hugo. 1625. *Laws of War and Peace*. Translated by Francis Kelsey. Oxford, England: Clarendon Press, 1925.

Grych, J.H., and Fincham, F.D. 1990. Marital Conflict and Children's Adjustment: A Cognitive-Contextual Framework. *Psychological Bulletin* 108: 267–290.

Gunter, B. 1994. The Question of Media Violence. *Media Effects*. Edited by J. Bryant and D. Zillmann. Hillsdale, NJ: Erlbaum, pp. 247–272.

Gunter, B., and Furnham, A. 1983. Personality and the Perception of TV Violence. *Personality and Individual Differences* 4(3): 315–321.

——— 1984. Perceptions of Television Violence: Effects of Programme Genre and Type of Violence on Viewers' Judgments of Violent Portrayals. *British Journal of Social Psychology* 23: 155–164.

——— 1991. *Television Violence and Programme Appreciation*. Unpublished manuscript. University of Sheffield, England.

Gyekye, Kwame. 1987. *An Essay on African Philosophical Thought: The Akan Conceptual Scheme*. Cambridge, England: Cambridge University Press.

Haan, Norma. 1975. Hypothetical and Actual Moral Reasoning in a Situation of Civil Disobedience. *Journal of Personality and Social Psychology* 32: 255–270.

Habermas, Jürgen. 1990. *Moral Consciousness and Communicative Action*. Translated by C. Lenhardt and S. Nicholsen. Cambridge, MA: MIT Press.

——— 1993. *Justification and Application*. Translated by C. Cronin. Cambridge, MA: MIT Press.

Hallie, Philip. 1997. *Tales of Good and Evil, Help and Harm*. New York: HarperCollins.

Hamilton, Alexander, Madison, James, and Jay, John. 1787–1788. *The Federalist Papers*. New York: New American Library, 1961.

Hamilton, W. 1964. The Genetical Evolution of Social Behavior. *Journal of Theoretical Biology* 7: 1–52.

Hammurabi. 1792–1750 B.C.E. The Code of Hammurabi. *Ancient Near Eastern Texts Relating to the Old Testament*. Edited by J. Pritchard. Princeton, NJ: Princeton University Press, 1969.

Hare, R.M. 1972. Principles. *Proceedings of the Aristotelian Society* 73: 1–18.

Hare, Robert. 1970. *Psychopathy*. New York: Wiley.

——— 1999. *Without Conscience: The Disturbing World of the Psychopaths Among Us*. New York: Guilford Press.

———, and Schalling, D. 1978. *Psychopathic Behavior*. New York: Wiley.

Harlow, Harry, and Zimmerman, R. 1959. Affective Responses in the Infant Monkey. *Science* 130.

Harsanyi, J.C. 1982. Morality and the Theory of Rational Behavior. *Utilitarianism and Beyond*. Edited by A. Sen and B. Williams. Cambridge, England: Cambridge University Press.

Hart, H.L.A. 1959. Immorality and Treason. *The Listener,* July 30.

——— 1968. *Punishment and Responsibility.* Oxford, England: Oxford University Press.

Hartshorne, H., and May, M. 1928–1930. *Studies in the Nature of Character.* 3 vols. New York: Macmillan.

Hawking, Stephen. 1994. *Black Holes and Baby Universes.* New York: Bantam.

Hawkins, Henry. 1633. *Parthenia Sacra.* London: Ashgate.

Hayek, F.A. 1960. *The Constitution of Liberty.* Chicago: University of Chicago Press.

——— 1979. *Law, Legislation and Liberty.* Chicago: University of Chicago Press.

Hegel, Georg. 1962. *On Tragedy.* Edited by Anne Paolucci and Henry Paolucci. New York: Harper.

Heidegger, Martin. 1928. *Being and Time.* Translated by John Macquarrie and Edward Robinson. New York: Harper and Row.

Heil, John. 1989. Minds Divided. *Mind,* October.

Heinshon, R., and Packer, C. 1995. Complex Cooperative Strategies in Group-Territorial African Lions. *Science* 269: 1260–1262.

Heisler, G.H. (1975). The Effects of Vicariously Experiencing Supernatural-Violent Events: A Case Study of *The Exorcist's* Impact. *Journal of Individual Psychology* 31(2): 158–170.

Held, Virginia. 1990. Feminist Transformation of Moral Theory. *Philosophy and Phenomenological Research* (Supplement): 321–344.

——— 1993. *Feminist Morality.* Chicago: University of Chicago Press.

Heller, Scott. 1998. Emerging Field of Forgiveness Studies Explores How We Let Go of Grudges. *Chronicle of Higher Education* July 17.

Herman, Barbara. 1993. *The Practice of Moral Judgment.* Cambridge, MA: Harvard University Press.

Higgins, G. 1994. *Resilient Adults: Overcoming a Cruel Past.* San Francisco: Jossey-Bass.

Hitler, Adolf. 1924. *Mein Kampf.* Translated by R. Mannheim. Boston: Houghton Mifflin, 1943.

Hirsch, Samson Raphael, editor. 1978. *The Hirsch Siddur and Psalms.* Translated by Samson Hirsch. Jerusalem: Feldheim Publishers.

Hobbes, Thomas. 1651. *Leviathan.* Oxford, England: Clarendon, 1964.

Hoffman, M.L. 1977. Moral Internalization: Current Theory and Research. *Advances in Experimental Social Psychology.* Edited by L. Berkowitz. Vol. 10. New York: Academic Press, pp. 85–133.

——— 1980. Moral Development in Adolescence. *Handbook of Adolescent Psychology.* Edited by J. Adelson. New York: Wiley-Interscience.

——— 1984. Interaction of Affect and Cognition in Empathy. *Emotions, Cognition, and Behavior.* Edited by C. Izard, J. Kagan, and R. Zasonc. New York: Cambridge University Press, pp. 103–131.

——— 1984. Empathy, Its Limitations, and Its Role in a Comprehensive Moral Theory. *Morality: Moral Development and Moral Behavior.* Edited by J. Gerwirtz and W. Kartines. New York: Wiley.

———, and Saltzstein, H.D. 1967. Parent Discipline and the Child's Moral Development. *Journal of Personality and Social Psychology* 5: 45–57.

Holliday, S., and Chandler, M. 1986. *Wisdom: Explorations in Adult Competence.* Basel, Switzerland: Karger.

——— 1991. Wisdom as Integrated Thought. *Wisdom: Its Nature, Origins and Development.* Edited by R. Sternberg. Cambridge, England: Cambridge University Press.

Holmes, Oliver Wendell. 1952. *Collected Papers.* New York: Peter Smith.

Holmgren, Margaret. 1993. Forgiveness and the Intrinsic Value of Persons. *American Philosophical Quarterly* 30(4): 341–353.

Hornstein, H., Fisch, E., and Holmes, M. 1968. Influence of a Model's Feeling about His Behavior and His Relevance as a Comparison Other on Observer's Helping Behavior. *Journal of Personality and Social Psychology* 10: 222–226.

Hume, David. 1739. *Treatise of Human Nature.* Edited by L.A. Selby-Rigge and P.H. Nidditch. Oxford, England: Clarendon Press, 1978.

——— 1777. *An Enquiry Concerning the Principles of Morals.* Edited by L.A. Selby-Rigge. 3rd ed. Oxford, England: Oxford University Press, 1975.

Hutcheson, Francis. 1725. *An Inquiry Concerning Moral Good and Evil.* New York: Touchstone.

Ingelhart, E. 1990. *Culture Shift in Advanced Industrial Society.* Princeton, NJ: Princeton University Press.

Jacobsen, Neil, et al., 1994. Affect, Verbal Content, and Psychophysiology in the Arguments of Couples with a Violent Husband. *Journal of Clinical and Consulting Psychology* 48(4).

James, William. 1890. *The Principles of Psychology.* 2 Vols. New York: Dover, 1980.

Jefferson, Thomas. 1787. Letter to James Madison, December 20. *The Papers of Thomas Jefferson.* Edited by J. Boyd. Princeton, NJ: Princeton University Press, 1950.

Jimenez, Janey. 1977. *My Prisoner.* New York: Sheed Andrews and McMeal.

Johnson, B.R. 1980. General Occurrence of Stressful Reactions to Commercial Motion Pictures and Elements in Films Subjectively Identified as Stressors. *Psychological Reports* 47: 775–786.

Johnson, Mark. 1993. *The Moral Imagination.* Chicago: University of Chicago Press.

Johnson, Samuel. 1759. *The History of Rasselas.* Edited by J. Enright. London: English Library, 1977.

Jonson, Albert. 1995. Casuistry: An Alternative or Complement to Principilism. *Kennedy Institute of Ethics Journal* 5(3): 237–253.

———, and Toulmin, Stephen. 1988. *The Abuse of Casuistry: A History of Moral Reasoning.* Berkeley: University of California Press.

Jouvenal, Bertrand de. 1952. *Power: The Natural History of Its Growth.* London: Greenwood.

Kagan, Jerome. 1987. Introduction. *The Emergence of Morality in Young Children.* Edited by J. Kagan and S. Lamb. Chicago: Chicago University Press.

——— 1994. *Galen's Prophecy.* New York: Basic.

———, and Lamb, S. 1987. *The Emergence of Morality in Young Children.* Chicago: University of Chicago Press.

Kagan, Shelly. 1989. *The Limits of Morality.* Oxford, England: Oxford University Press.

Kane, Robert. 1996. *The Significance of Free Will.* New York: Oxford University Press.

Kant, Immanuel. 1775–1780. *Lectures on Ethics.* Translated by L. Infield. New York: Harper and Row, 1963.

——— 1781. *Critique of Pure Reason.* Translated by N. Smith. New York: St. Martin's Press, 1965.

——— 1785. *Foundations of the Metaphysics of Morals.* Translated by L.W. Beck. New York: Bobbs-Merrill, 1959.

——— 1788. *Critique of Practical Reason.* Translated by L. Beck. New York: Bobbs-Merrill, 1956.

——— 1797. *The Metaphysical Principles of the Virtues.* Translated by J. Ellington. New York: Bobbs-Merrill, 1964.

——— 1797a. *The Metaphysical Elements of Justice.* Translated by John Ladd. New York: Bobbs-Merrill, 1965.

Kapsambelis, Niki. 1996. Big Jackpot Draws Misery. Associated Press, August 26.

Kaufman, J., and Cicchetti, D. 1989. Effects of Maltreatment on School-age Children's Socioemotional Development: Assessments in a Day-camp Setting. *Developmental Psychology* 25: 516–524.

Kawachi, Ichito, et al. 1997. Long Live Community: Social Capital as Public Health. *The American Prospect,* November/December, 56–59.

Keeble, John. 1991. *Out of the Sound* . New York: HarperCollins.

Kekes, John. 1992. *The Examined Life.* University Park: Pennsylvania State University Press.

Kenny, A. 1963. *Action, Emotion and Will.* London: Routledge and Kegan Paul.

Keyes, Dick. 1995. *True Heroism.* Colorado Springs, CO: New Press.

Kidder, Rushworth. 1995. *How Good People Make Tough Choices.* New York: William Morrow.

Kilpatrick, William. 1992. *Why Johnny Can't Tell Right from Wrong.* New York: Touchstone.

Kilpatrick, W. Gregory, and Wolf, Suzanne. 1994. *Books That Build Character.* New York: Touchstone.

King, Martin Luther. 1963. I Have a Dream. Speech delivered at the March on Washington, August 28.

Kirk, Kenneth. 1927. *Conscience and Its Problems: An Introduction to Casuistry.* London: Longman's Green.

Kirkpatrick, Jeane. 1980. Establishing a Viable Human Rights Policy. *World Affairs* 323: 334.

Kitchener, K., and Brenner, H. 1991. Wisdom and Reflective Judgment. *Wisdom: Its Nature, Origins and Development.* Edited by R. Sternberg. Cambridge, England: Cambridge University Press.

———, King, P., Wood, P., and Davidson, M. 1989. Consistency and Sequentiality—the Development of Reflective Judgement: A Six Year Longitudinal Study. *Journal of Applied Developmental Psychology* 10: 73–95.

Klausner, Samuel. 1965. A Colligation of Concepts of Self-Control. *The Quest for Self-Control.* Edited by S. Klausner. New York: Free Press.

Klein, Donald. 1987. *Depression and Anhedonia. Anhedonia and Affect Deficit States.* New York: PMA Publishing.

Klimes-Dougan, Bonnie, and Kistner, Janet. 1990. Physically Abused Preschoolers' Response to Peers' Distress. *Developmental Psychology* 26.

Klineberg, Otto, et al. 1979. *Students, Values and Politics.* New York: Free Press.

Klouda, Naomi. 1993. Songs of the Raven. *Alaska,* October, 27–31.

Knack, S., and Keefer, P. 1997. Does Social Capital Have an Economic Payoff? A Cross Country Investigation. *Quarterly Journal of Economics* 112: 1251–1288.

Kohlberg, Lawrence. 1966. *Essays on Moral Development: The Psychology of Moral Development.* New York: Harper and Row.

——— 1981. *Essays on Moral Development.* New York: Harper and Row.

Kornet, Allison. 1997. The Truth about Lying. *Psychology Today* 30(3): 52–57.

Korsgaard, Christine. 1996. *Creating the Kingdom of Ends.* Cambridge, England: Cambridge University Press.

Krakauer, John. 1996. *Into Thin Air.* New York: Villard.

Kramer, Peter. 1993. *Listening to Prozac.* New York: Viking.

Kristof, Nicholas. 1996. Japanese Serious about Fairy Tales. *New York Times,* December 9.

Labouvie-Vief, G. 1982. Dynamic Development and Mature Autonomy. *Human Development* 25: 161–191.

——— 1991. Wisdom as Integrated Thought: Historical and Developmental Perspectives. *Wisdom: Its Nature, Origins, and Development.* Edited by R. Sternberg. Cambridge, England: Cambridge University Press.

Lactantius. *The Divine Institutes.* The Ante-Nicene Christian Library. Edited by A. Roberts and J. Donaldson. Volume VII. Grand Rapids, MI: Eerdmans, 1979.

Laplace, Pierre. 1814. *A Philosophical Essay on Probabilities.* New York: Dover, 1951.

LaPorta, R., Lopez-de-Silanes, F., Shleifer, A., and Vishny, Robert. 1997. Trust in Large Organizations. *American Economic Review Papers and Proceedings* 87: 333–338.

Latane, B., and Darley, J. 1968. Group Inhibition of Bystander Intervention. *Journal of Personality and Social Psychology* 10: 215–224.

Lauritzen, Paul. 1996. Ethics and Experience: The Case of the Curious Response. *Hastings Center Report* 26: 6–15.

LeDoux, Joseph. 1992. Emotion and the Limbic System Concept. *Concepts in Neuroscience* 2(1).

——— 1995. Emotion: Clues from the Brain. *Annual Review of Psychology* 46: 209–235.

Lee, Bruce. 1995. *Marching Orders.* New York: Crown.

Levenson, R., Ekman, P., and Friesen, W.V. 1990. Voluntary Facial Action Generates Emotion-Specific Autonomic Nervous System Activity. *Psychophysiology* 27(4): 363–384.

———, et al. 1992. Emotion and Autonomic Nervous System Activity in the Minangkabau of West Sumatra. *Journal of Personality and Social Psychology* 62(6): 972–988.

Lewis, C.S. 1955. *The Magician's Nephew.* New York: Macmillan.

Lews, Linda. 1997. *Teach Your Kids the Consequences of Poor Sportsmanship.* Scripps-Howard News Service, July 4.

Lickona, Thomas. 1991. *Educating for Character*. New York: Bantam Books.

Lifton, Robert Jay, and Mitchell, Greg. 1996. *Hiroshima in America: Fifty Years of Denial*. New York: Putnam.

Linde, Charlotte. 1993. *Life Stories*. Oxford, England: Oxford University Press.

Lippman, Walter. 1922. *Public Opinion*. New York: Free Press, 1965.

Liszka, James. 1990. *The Semiotic of Myth*. Bloomington: Indiana University Press.

———— 1996. *A General Introduction to the Semeiotic of Charles S. Peirce*. Bloomington: Indiana University Press.

Lloyd, Genevieve. 1984. *The Man of Reason: "Male" and "Female" in Western Philosophy*. Minneapolis: University of Minnesota Press.

Locke, John 1689. *Second Treatise of Civil Government*. Chicago: Gateway, 1971.

Lorenz, Konrad. 1997. *On Aggression*. New York: Fine Communications.

Lucretius. *On the Nature of the Universe*. Translated by J. Mantineband. New York: Friedrich Ungar, 1968.

Luther, Martin. 1525. *The Bondage of the Will*. Translated by E. Winter. New York: Ungar, 1973.

Lutz, Catherine. 1988. *Emotion, Thought and Estrangement: Western Discourses on Feeling. Everyday Sentiments in a Micronesian Atoll and Their Challenge to Western Theory*. Chicago: University of Chicago Press.

Lykken, David. 1995. *The Antisocial Personality*. Mahwah, NJ: Erlbaum.

———— 1996. Psychopathy, Sociopathy and Crime. *Society* 34(1): 29–38.

————, and Tellegen, Auke. 1996. Happiness Is a Stochastic Phenomenon. *Psychological Research* 7(3): 186–194.

Lynd, Helen. 1973. *On Shame and the Search for Identity*. Cambridge, MA: Harvard University Press.

Mabbott, J.B. 1958. *The State and the Citizens*. London: Arrow.

MacDonald, Margaret. 1992. Natural Rights. *Theories of Rights*. Edited by Jeremy Waldron. Oxford, England: Oxford University Press, pp. 21–40.

Machiavelli, N. 1513. *The Prince*. Translated by I. Ricci. New York: Modern Library, 1950.

MacIntyre, Alasdair. 1981. *After Virtue*. Notre Dame, IN: University of Notre Dame Press.

Mackie, J.L. 1992. Can There Be a Right-Based Moral Theory? *Theories of Rights*. Edited by Jeremy Waldron. Oxford, England: Oxford University Press, pp. 168–181.

Magid, Ken, and McKelvey, Carole. 1989. *High Risk: Children without a Conscience*. New York: Bantam.

Main, Mary, and George, Carol. 1985. Responses of Abused and Disadvantaged Toddlers to Distress in Agemates: A Study in the Day-care Setting. *Developmental Psychology* 50: 953–962.

Manickam, L.S.S. 1990. Empathy: A Comparative Study of Professionals and Trained Lay Counselors Using Hypothetical Situations. *Indian Journal of Psychiatry* 32: 83–88.

Mann, Lee, et al. 1994. Alexithymia, Affect Recognition, and the Five-Factor Model of Personality in Normal Subjects. *Psychological Reports* 74(2): 563–567.

Manning, Rita. 1992. *Speaking from the Heart: A Feminist Perspective on Ethics*. Lanham: Rowan and Littlefield.

———— 1992a. Just Caring. *Explorations in Feminist Ethics*. Edited by E. Cole and S. McQuin. Bloomington: Indiana University Press.

Maris, Peter, et al. 1995. Knowledge of Basic Emotions in Adolescent and Adult Individuals with Autism. *Psychological Reports* 76(1): 52–54.

Martens, Willem. 2000. Antisocial and Psychopathic Personality Disorders: Causes, Course, and Remission—A Review Article. *International Journal of Offender Therapy and Comparative Criminology* 44(4): 406–430.

Martin, Mike, and Schinzinger, R. 1989. *Ethics in Engineering*. New York: McGraw-Hill.

Martinez-Coll, J., and Hirshleifer, J. 1991. The Limits of Reciprocity. *Rationality and Society* 3: 35–64.

Maslow, Abraham. 1968. *Toward a Psychology of Being*. New York: D. Van Nostrand.

Mathai, J. 1983. An Acute Anxiety State in an Adolescent Precipitated by Viewing a Horror Movie. *Journal of Adolescence* 6: 197–200.

May, Larry. 1983. Vicarious Agency and Corporate Responsibility. *Philosophical Studies.*

McCord, W., and McCord, J. 1956. *Psychopathy and Delinquency.* New York: Grune and Stratton.

McNamara, Robert 1995. *The Tragedy and Lessons of Vietnam.* New York: Times Books.

McPherson, James. 1997. *For Cause and Comrades.* New York: Oxford University Press.

McWilliam, Candida. 1990. Vanity. *Vogue,* March.

Meacham, John. 1991. The Loss of Wisdom. *Wisdom: Its Nature, Origins and Development.* Edited by R. Sternberg. Cambridge, England: Cambridge University Press.

Medlin, Brian. 1957. Ultimate Principles and Ethical Egoism. *Australasian Journal of Philosophy* 35: 111–118.

Medred, C. 1994. You Have to Learn to Deal with Fear. *Anchorage Daily News,* August 16.

Meilaender, Gilbert. 1984. *The Theory and Practice of Virtue.* Notre Dame, IN: University of Notre Dame Press.

Melden, A.I. 1961. *Free Action.* London: Routledge and Kegan Paul.

Mele, Alfred. 1987. *Irrationality.* Oxford, England: Oxford University Press.

Meltzhoff, A., and Moore, A. 1977. Imitation of Facial and Manual Gestures by Human Neonates. *Science* 198: 75–78.

——— 1983. Newborn Infants Imitate Adult Facial Gestures. *Child Development* 54: 702–709.

Melzer, Bruce. 1992. The Politics of Lies. *Anchorage Daily News,* October 5.

Mencius. *The Book of Mencius. A Source Book in Chinese Philosophy.* Translated by Wing-Tsit Chan. Princeton, NJ: Princeton University Press, 1963.

Meyerowitz, R. 1995. Boarder Hurt on Denali. *Anchorage Daily News,* July 16.

Milgram, Stanley. 1974. *Obedience to Authority.* New York: Harper and Row.

Mill, John Stuart. 1859. *On Liberty.* Edited by E. Rapaport. Indianapolis, IN: Hackett, 1978.

——— 1861. *Utilitarianism.* New York: Bobbs-Merrill, 1957.

Miller, Clyde. 1990. The Icon and the Wall: *Visio* and *Ratio* in Nicholas of Cusa's *De Visione Deo. Proceedings of the Catholic Philosophy Association* 64: 86–98.

Miller, William. 1992. *The Anatomy of Disgust.* Cambridge, MA: Harvard University Press.

Mills, C. Wright. 1956. *The Power Elite.* Oxford, England: Oxford University Press.

Milton, John. 1644. *Areopagitica. Complete Prose Works.* Edited by E. Sirluck. 8 vols. New Haven, CT: Yale University Press, 1959.

Mischel, Walter, Shoda, Y., and Peake, P. 1990. Predicting Adolescent Cognitive and Self-Regulatory Competencies from Preschool Delay of Gratification. *Developmental Psychology* 26: 978–986.

Mitchell, Derek, and Blair, James. 2000. State of the Art: Psychopathy. *Psychologist* 13(7): 356–364.

Montaigne, Michel de. 1572–1588. *Essays.* Edited by D. Frame. New York: St. Martin's Press, 1963.

Montesquieu, Charles-Louis de. 1737–1743. *The Spirit of the Laws.* Edited by David Carrithers. Berkeley: University of California Press, 1978.

Moore, G.E. 1903. *Principia Ethica.* Cambridge, England: Cambridge University Press, 1960.

Moriera, Isabel. 1996. Augustine's Three Visions and Three Heavens in Some Early Medieval *Florilegia. Vivarium* 34(1): 1–14.

Morgan, Kathyrn Paul. 1990. Strangers in a Strange Land: Feminists Visits Relativists. *Perspectives in Relativism.* Edited by D. Odegaard and C. Stewart. Toronto: Agathon Press.

Mundorf, N., Weaver, J., and Zillmann, D. 1989. Effects of Gender Roles and Self Perceptions on Affective Reactions to Horror Films. *Sex Roles* 20: 655–673.

Murphey, Jeffrey. 1972. Moral Death: A Kantian Essay on Psychopathy. *Ethics* 82: 284–298.

Murphy, Jeffrie. 1982. Forgiveness and Resentment. *Midwest Studies in Philosophy* 7: 503–516.

Myrdal, Gunnar. 1953. *The Political Element in the Development of Economic Theory.* Translated by P. Streeten. London: Routledge and Kegan Paul.

Nagel, Thomas. 1976. Moral Luck. *Proceedings of the Aristotelian Society* Supp. Vol. 50.

——— 1979. *The Possibility of Altruism.* Princeton, NJ: Princeton University Press.

——— 1987. *What Does It All Mean?* Oxford, England: Oxford University Press.

Needleman, Jacob. 1991. *Money and the Meaning of Life.* New York: Doubleday.

Neuberg, Steven L., and Cialdini, Robert B. 1997. Does Empathy Lead to Anything More Than Superficial Helping? Comments on Batson et al. (1997). *Journal of Personality & Social Psychology* 73(3): 510–517.

Newton, Adam Zachary. 1995. *Narrative Ethics.* Cambridge, MA: Harvard University Press.

Nicholson, Peter. 1985. Toleration as a Moral Ideal. *Aspects of Toleration.* Edited by J. Horton and S. Mendis. Oxford, England: Oxford University Press.

Nielsen, Kai. 1973. *Ethics without God.* Buffalo, NY: Prometheus.

——— 1991. *After the Demise of the Tradition.* Boulder, CO: Westview Press.

Nietzsche, Friedrich. 1881. *Dawn. Complete Works.* Edited by O. Levy. 18 vols. New York: Russell and Russell, 1964.

——— 1882. *The Gay Science.* Translated by W. Kaufmann. New York: Vintage, 1964.

——— 1883–1888. *The Will to Power.* Translated by W. Kaufman. New York: Vintage, 1968.

——— 1886. *Beyond Good and Evil.* Translated by W. Kaufman. New York: Vintage, 1966.

——— 1887. *The Genealogy of Morals.* Translated by W. Kaufman. New York: Vintage, 1968.

——— 1888. *The Antichrist.* The Portable Nietzsche. Translated by W. Kaufman. New York: Viking, 1954.

——— 1888. *The Twilight of the Idols.* Translated by W. Kaufman. New York: Viking, 1954.

Niven, David. 1975. *Bring on the Empty Horses.* New York: Bantam.

Noddings, Nel. 1984. *Care: A Feminist Approach to Morals and Education.* Berkeley: University of California Press.

Nozick, Robert. 1974. *Anarchy State and Utopia.* New York: Basic.

Nussbaum, Martha. 1990. *Love's Knowledge.* Oxford, England: Oxford University Press.

Oakley, Justin. 1991. *Morality and the Emotions.* London: Routledge.

O'Connor, Timothy. 1966. Why Agent Causation? *Philosophical Topics* 24: 143–151.

Ohlms, David. 1988. *The Disease of Alcoholism.* Cahokia, IL: GWC.

Oliner, Samuel, and Oliner, Pearl. 1988. *The Altruistic Personality.* New York: Free Press.

Orwoll, L., and Perlmutter, M. 1991. The Study of Wise Persons: Integrating a Personality Perspective. *Wisdom: Its Nature, Origins and Development.* Edited by R. Sternberg. Cambridge, England: Cambridge University Press.

Paine, Thomas. 1794. *The Age of Reason. The Complete Writings of Thomas Paine.* 4 vols. Edited by P. Foner. New York: Library of America, 1945.

Palmer, E.L., Hockett, A.B., and Dean, W.W. (1983). The Television Family and Children's Fright Reactions. *Journal of Family Issues* 4: 279–292.

Parfit, Derek. 1990. Overpopulation and the Quality of Life. *Utilitarianism and Its Critics.* Edited by J. Glover. New York: Macmillan.

Park, K.A., and Waters, E. 1989. Security of Attachment and Preschool Friendships. *Child Development* 60: 1076–1081.

Patterson, James, and Kim, Peter. 1991. *The Day America Told the Truth.* Upper Saddle River, NJ: Prentice Hall.

Payne, M.A. 1993. Barbadian Adults' Perceptions of Eighteen Popular U.S. Television Programs. *Perceptual and Motor Skills* 77: 771–775.

Peirce, Charles. 1965. *The Collected Papers of Charles S. Peirce.* 8 vols. Edited by P. Weiss, C. Hartshorne, and A. Burks. Cambridge, MA: Harvard University Press.

Peloquin, S.M. 1995. The Fullness of Empathy: Reflections and Illustrations. *The American Journal of Occupational Therapy* 49: 24–31.

Pence, Gregory. 1990. *Classic Cases in Medical Ethics.* New York: McGraw-Hill.

Perkins, K. 1996. Happiness a State of Mind, Not Events, Research Says. McClatchy News Service, May 14.

Perry, W. I. 1970. *Forms of Intellectual and Ethical Development in College Years.* New York: Holt, Rinehart and Winston.

Philips, Natalie. 1999. Years Later Oil Spill's Toll Still Rising. *Anchorage Daily News*, March 22.

Piaget, J. 1932. *The Moral Judgment of the Child.* London: Kegan Paul.

Picou, Steven, and Arata, Catalina. 1997. *Chronic Psychological Impacts of the Exxon Valdez Oil Spill: Resource Loss and Commercial Fishers.* Mobile: University of South Alabama.

Pieper, Josef. 1975. *The Four Cardinal Virtues.* Notre Dame, IN: University of Notre Dame Press.

Piliavin, I., and Chang, H. 1990. Altruism: A Review of Recent Theory and Research. *Annual Review of Sociology* 16: 27–65.

———, Rodin, J., and Piliavin, J. 1969. Good Samaritanism: An Underground Phenomenon? *Journal of Personality and Social Psychology* 13: 289–299.

———, and Piliavin, I.M. 1972. The Effect of Blood on Reactions to a Victim. *Journal of Personality and Social Psychology* 23: 353–361.

Piper, Ernest. 1993. *The Exxon Valdez Oil Spill: Final Report, State of Alaska Response.* Anchorage: Alaska Department of Environmental Conservation.

Plato. *The Republic. Collected Dialogues.* Edited by Edith Hamilton and H. Cairns. Princeton, NJ: Princeton University Press, 1973.

——— *Laches. Collected Dialogues.* Edited by Edith Hamilton and H. Cairns. Princeton, NJ: Princeton University Press, 1973.

——— *The Symposium. Collected Dialogues.* Edited by Edith Hamilton and H. Cairns. Princeton, NJ: Princeton University Press, 1973.

——— *Euthyphro. Collected Dialogues.* Edited by Edith Hamilton and H. Cairns. Princeton, NJ: Princeton University Press, 1973.

——— *Meno. Collected Dialogues.* Edited by Edith Hamilton and H. Cairns. Princeton, NJ: Princeton University Press, 1973.

——— *Protagoras. Collected Dialogues.* Edited by Edith Hamilton and H. Cairns. Princeton, NJ: Princeton University Press, 1973.

——— *The Laws.* Translated by T. Prangle. New York: Basic, 1980.

Plautus, Titus. *Stichus, Plautus. The Comedies.* Edited by P. Bovie, D. Slavitt, and S. Bovie. Baltimore, MD: Johns Hopkins University Press, 1998.

Popper, Karl. 1987. Toleration and Intellectual Responsibility. *On Tolerance.* Edited by S. Mendus and D. Edwards. Oxford, England: Clarendon Press.

Powers, S.I. 1982. *Family Interaction and Parental Moral Development as a Context for Adolescent Moral Development.* Unpublished doctoral dissertation, Harvard University.

Prudentius. *The Fight for Mansoul.* Translated by H.J. Thompson. Cambridge, MA: Harvard University Press, 1949.

Putnam, Robert. 1995. Tuning In, Tuning Out: The Strange Disappearance of Social Capital in America. *PS: Political Science and Politics* 664–682.

———2000. *Bowling Alone. The Collapse and Revival of American Community.* New York: Simon and Schuster.

Rachels, James. 1971. *Egoism and Moral Skepticism. A New Introduction to Philosophy.* New York: Harper and Row.

——— 1986. *The Elements of Moral Philosophy.* New York: Random House.

Rahn, Wendy, and Transue, John. 1998. Social Trust and Value Change: The Decline of Social Capital in American Youth 1976–1995. *Political Psychology* 19: 545–565.

Rand, Ayn. 1964. *The Virtue of Selfishness.* New York: Signet.

Raths, L., et al. 1966. *Values and Teaching.* Columbus, OH: Merrill.

Rawls, John. 1971. *A Theory of Justice.* Cambridge, MA: Harvard University Press.

Reid, Thomas. 1788. *Essays on the Active Powers of the Human Mind.* Cambridge, MA: MIT Press, 1969.

Reis, Harry, Kennon, S., Gable, S., Roscoe, J., and Ryan, R. 2000. Daily Well-Being: The Role of Autonomy, Competence, and Relatedness. *Personality and Social Psychology Bulletin* 26(4): 419–435.

Rest, James. 1979. *Development in Judging Moral Issues.* Minneapolis: University of Minnesota Press.

Ricoeur, Paul. 1984. *Time and Narrative.* 3 Volumes. Translated by K. McLaughlin and D. Pellauer. Chicago: University of Chicago Press.

Ridley, Matt. 1996. *The Origins of Virtue.* New York: Viking.

Robinson, J., and Hawpe, L. 1986. Narrative Thinking as a Heuristic Process. Narrative Psychology: *The Storied Nature of Human Conduct.* Edited by T. Sarbin. New York: Praeger.

Rorty, Richard. 1979. *Philosophy and the Mirror of Nature.* Princeton, NJ: Princeton University Press.

Rosenthal, Robert, et al. 1977. The PONS Test: Measuring Sensitivity to Nonverbal Cues. *Advances in Psychological Assessment.* Edited by P. McReynolds. San Francisco: Jossey-Bass.

Rosner, F., and Bleich, D. 1979. *Jewish Bioethics.* New York: Sanhedrin Press.

Ross, W.D. 1930. *The Right and the Good.* Oxford, England: Oxford University Press.

———— 1939. *The Foundations of Ethics.* Oxford, England: Clarendon Press.

Rothman, G. 1976. The Influence of Moral Reasoning on Behavioral Choices. *Child Development* 47: 397–406.

Rousseau, Jean-Jacques. 1755. *On the Origin of Inequality. First and Second Discourses.* Edited by R. Masters. Translated by R. Masters and J. Masters. New York: St. Martin's Press, 1964.

Ruddick, Sarah. 1989. *Maternal Thinking: Towards a Politics of Peace.* Boston: Beacon Press.

Ruff, G., and Korchin, S. 1964. Psychological Responses of the Mercury Astronauts to Stress. *The Threat of Impending Disaster.* Edited by G. Grosser et al. Cambridge, MA: MIT Press.

Rushton, J. 1976. Socialization and the Altruistic Behavior of Children. *Psychological Bulletin* 83: 898–913.

Ruskin, Liz. 1996. Memory of Killing Gone. *Anchorage Daily News,* March 13.

Russell, L.J. 1942. Ideals and Practice. *Philosophy* 17.

Sacks, Oliver. 1995. *An Anthropologist on Mars.* New York: Alfred Knopf.

Sandel, Michael. 1982. *Liberalism and the Limits of Justice.* Cambridge, England: Cambridge University Press.

Sarbin, T. 1986. The Narrative as a Root Metaphor for Psychology. *Narrative Psychology: The Storied Nature of Human Conduct.* Edited by T. Sarbin. New York: Praeger.

Scanlon, T.M. 1992. Rights, Goals, and Fairness. *Theories of Rights.* Edited by Jeremy Waldron. Oxford, England: Oxford University Press, 137–152.

Schank, R., and Abelson, R. 1977. *Scripts, Plans, Goals, and Understanding: An Inquiry into Human Knowledge Structures.* Mahwah, NJ: Erlbaum.

Scheibe, K. 1986. Self-Narratives and Adventures. *Narrative Psychology: The Storied Nature of Human Conduct.* Edited by T. Sarbin. New York: Praeger.

Scheven, Albert. 1981. *Swahili Proverbs.* Washington, DC: University Press of America.

Schiffhorst, Gerald. 1978. Some Prolegomena to the Study of Patience. *The Triumph of Patience.* Edited by G. Schiffhorst. Orlando: University of Florida Press.

Schiller, Friedrich. 1795. *On the Aesthetic Education of Man.* Translated by R. Snell. New York: Ungar, 1965.

Schmidt, G., and Weiner, B. 1988. An Attribution-Affect-Action Theory of Behavior: Replications of Judgments of Help-giving. *Personality and Social Psychology Bulletin* 14: 610–621.

Schopenhauer, Arthur. 1818. *The World as Will and Representation.* Translated by E. Payne. New York: Dover, 1969.

———— 1841. *On the Basis of Morality.* Translated by E. Payne. New York: Bobbs-Merrill, 1965.

Schulman, M., and Mekler, E. 1985. *Bringing Up a Moral Child: A New Approach for Teaching Your Child to be Kind, Just, and Responsible.* Reading, MA: Addison-Wesley.

Seligman, Martin. 1991. *Learned Optimism.* New York: Knopf.

Seneca. c. 49. *On Tranquility. Essential Words of Stoicism.* Edited by Moses Hadas. New York: Bantam, 1961.

Shafer-Landau, Russ. 1997. Moral Rules. *Ethics* 107: 584–611.

Shaffer, L.F. 1947. Fear and Courage in Aerial Combat. *Journal of Consulting Psychology* 11: 137–143.

Shaftesbury, Earl of. 1711. *Characteristics of Men, Manners, Opinions, Times.* 3 vols. Edited by J. Robertson. New York: Bobbs-Merrill, 1964.

Shanab, M.E., and Yahya, K.A. 1977. A Behavioral Study of Obedience in Children. *Journal of Personality and Social Psychology* 35: 530–536.

Shapiro, David. 1981. *Autonomy and Rigid Character.* New York: Basic.

Sharp, F.C. 1928. *Ethics.* New York: Appleton-Croft.

Shepher, J. 1980. *Incest: A Sociobiological Approach.* New York: Academic Press.

Siebers, Tobin. 1992. *Morals and Stories.* New York: Columbia University Press.

Sidgwick, Henry. 1981. *The Methods of Ethics.* 7th edition. Chicago: Hackett.

Sigmund, K. 1993. *Games of Life.* Oxford, England: Oxford University Press.

Simmel, Georg. 1990. *The Philosophy of Money.* London: Routledge.

Simner, M. 1971. Newborn's Response to the Cry of Another Infant. *Developmental Psychology* 5: 136–150.

Singer, Marcus. 1963. The Golden Rule. *Philosophy* 38(146): 293–314.

Smart, J.J.C. 1973. An Outline of a System of Utilitarian Ethics. *Utilitarianism: For and Against.* Edited by J. Smart and B. Williams. Cambridge, England: Cambridge University Press.

Smith, Adam. 1759. *The Theory of Moral Sentiments.* Edited by D. Raphael and A. Macfie. Oxford, England: Clarendon Press, 1976.

Smith, J., et al. 1989. Expertise in Life Planning: A New Research Approach to Investigating Aspects of Wisdom. *Beyond Formal Operations II: Comparisons and Applications of Adolescent and Adult Developmental Models.* Edited by M. Commons, J. Sinnott, F. Richards, and C. Armon. New York: Praeger, 1989.

Smith, John Maynard, and Price, G.R. 1973. The Logic of Animal Conflict. *Nature* 246: 15–18.

Snarcy, J.R. 1987. A Question of Morality. *Psychology Today,* June: 6–8.

Snyder, C.R., et al. 1991. The Will and the Ways: Development and Validation of Individual Differences in the Measure of Hope. *Journal of Personality and Social Psychology* 60(4).

Soble, Alan. 1990. *The Structure of Love.* New Haven, CT: Yale University Press.

Solomon, Robert. 1980. Emotions and Choice. *Explaining Emotions.* Edited by A. Rorty. Berkeley: University of California Press, pp. 251–281.

———— 1992. *Ethics and Excellence.* New York: Oxford University Press.

Sommers, Christina. 1993. Teaching the Virtues. *The Public Interest* Spring, 3–11.

Sorabji, Richard. 1980. Aristotle on the Role of Intellect in Virtue. *Essays on Aristotle's Ethics.* Edited by A. Rorty. Berkeley: University of California Press.

Sowarka, D. 1987. *Wisdom in the Context of Persons, Situations, and Actions: Common-sense Views of Elderly Women and Men.* Unpublished manuscript. Federal Republic of Germany: Max Planck Institute for Human Development and Education.

Sowell, Thomas. 1987. *The Conflict of Visions.* New York: Quill.

Sparks, G. 1984. The Development of a Scale to Assess Cognitive Responses to Frightening Mass Media. Paper presented at the annual conference of the International Communication Association, San Francisco, CA.

———— 1986. Developmental Differences in Children's Reports of Fear Induced by the Mass Media. *Child Study Journal* 16: 55–66.

Spence, Jonathan. 1984. *The Memory Palace of Matteo Ricci.* New York: Viking.

Staub, E. 1975. *The Development of Prosocial Behavior in Children.* New York: General Learning Press.

Steinberg, L., et al. 1992. Impact of Parenting Practices on Adolescent Achievement: Authoritative Parenting, School Achievement and Encouragement to Succeed. *Child Development* 63: 1266–1281.

Sternberg, R. 1985. *Beyond IQ.* New York: Cambridge University Press.

———— 1985a. Implicit Theories of Intelligence, Creativity and Wisdom. *Journal of Personality and Social Psychology* 49(3): 607–627.

———— 1991. Understanding Wisdom. *Wisdom: Its Nature, Origins, and Development.* Edited by R. Sternberg. Cambridge, England: Cambridge University Press.

Stevenson, C.L. 1937. The Emotive Meaning of Ethical Terms. *Mind* 46(181).

———— 1946. *Ethics and Language.* New Haven, CT: Yale University Press.

Stimmer, M.L. 1971. Newborn's Response to the Cry of Another Infant. *Developmental Psychology* 5: 136–150.

Stimson, Henry. 1947. The Decision to Use the Atomic Bomb. *Harper's Magazine,* February.

Stirner, Max. 1845. *The Ego and Its Own..* Translated by David Leopold. Cambridge, England: Cambridge University Press, 1995.

Stockdale, James. 1984. *A Vietnam Experience.* Stanford, CA: Hoover Institution.

Stocker, Michael. 1976. The Schizophrenia of Modern Ethical Theories. *The Journal of Philosophy* 73: 59–69.

Story, Paula. 1997. Zen and the Art of Survival on the Freeways. Associated Press, April 29.

Strauss, H.L. 1944. The Literature on Empathy. *Journal of Abnormal and Social Psychology* 39(3): 319–328.

Stroufe, Alan. 1983. Infant Care-giver Attachment and Patterns of Adaptation in Preschool. *Minnesota Symposium in Child Psychology* 16: 41–83.

Sun Tzu. *The Art of War.* Translated by Samuel Griffith. Oxford, England: Oxford University Press, 1984.

Tacitus, Cornelius. *Agricola and Germany.* Translated by A. Birley. Oxford, England: Oxford University Press, 1999.

Takaki, Ronald. 1996. *Hiroshima: Why America Dropped the Atom Bomb.* New York: Little, Brown.

Tamborini, R., Stiff, J., and Zillmann, D. 1987. Preference for Graphic Horror Featuring Male Versus Female Victimization: Individual Differences Associated with Personality Characteristics and Past Film Viewing Experiences. *Human Communication Research* 13: 529–552.

———, Stiff, J., and Heidel, C. 1990. Reacting to Graphic Horror: A Model of Empathy and Emotional Behavior. *Communication Research* 17: 616–637.

Tavris, Carol. 1989. *Anger: The Misunderstood Emotion.* New York: Touchstone.

Taylor, A.E. 1956. *Plato.* New York: Meridian Books.

Taylor, Paul. 1975. *Principles of Ethics.* Encino, CA: Dickinson.

Taylor, Richard. 1970. *Good and Evil.* Buffalo, NY: Prometheus.

——— 1992. *Metaphysics.* Upper Saddle River, NJ: Prentice Hall.

Taylor, Shelley, and Brown, Jonathan. 1988. Illusion and Well-Being. *Psychological Bulletin* 103: 193–210.

Theroux, Alexander. 1982. Revenge. *Harper's,* October.

Thomson, Judith Jarvis. 1984. Remarks on Causation and Liability. *Philosophy and Public Affairs* 13(2).

Thoreau, Henry David. 1854. *Walden.* Cambridge, MA: Riverside Edition, 1960.

Tice, D., and Baumeister, R. 1993. Controlling Anger: Self-induced Emotional Change. *Handbook of Mental Control.* Edited by D. Wegner and K. Pennebaker. New York: Prentice Hall.

Traub, James. 1997. The Next University. *The New Yorker,* October 20.

Trivers, R.L. 1971. The Evolution of Reciprocal Altruism. *Quarterly Review of Biology* 46: 35–37.

Trotsky, Leon. 1969. *Their Morals or Ours.* New York: Pathfinder Press.

Truffaut, François. 1967. *Hitchcock.* New York: Simon and Schuster.

Truman, Harry. 1955. *Memoirs. Years of Decision.* Vol. 1. New York: Da Capo.

Trump, Donald. 1987. *The Art of the Deal.* New York: Random House.

Turiel, E. 1983. *The Development of Social Knowledge Morality and Conventions.* Cambridge, England: Cambridge University Press.

Turner, R. 1945. *The Modern Approach to Criminal Law.* Cambridge, England: Cambridge University Press.

Twain, Mark. 1995. *Books for Bad Boys and Girls.* New York: Contemporary Books.

Unger, Lynette, and Lakshmi, T. 1997. Trait Empathy and Continuous Helping. *Journal of Social Behavior and Personality* 12: 785–801.

Unknown. 1918. *Patience.* Edited by H. Bateson. Manchester: Manchester State University.

Vaillant, G. 1977. *Adaptation to Life.* Boston: Little Brown.

Valiant, Gayle, 1993. Life Events, Happiness and Depression. *Personality and Individual Differences* 15(4): 447–453.

Van Inwagen, Peter. 1983. *An Essay on Free Will.* Oxford, England: Clarendon Press.

Veatch, Robert. 1995. Resolving Conflicts Among Principles. *Kennedy Institute of Ethics Journal* 5(3): 199–218.

Veenhoven, Ruut. 1994. Is Happiness a Trait? *Social Indicators Research* 32(2): 101–160.

Verducci, Susan 2000. A Conceptual History of Empathy and a Question It Raises for Moral Education. *Education* 50(1): 63–81.

Vitz, Paul. 1990. The Uses of Stories in Moral Development. *American Psychologist* 45(6): 709–720.

Vlastos, Gregory. 1992. Justice and Equality. *Theories of Rights.* Edited by Jeremy Waldron. Oxford, England: Oxford University Press.

Von Wright, Georg. 1963. *The Varieties of Goodness.* London: Routledge and Kegan Paul.

———— 1979. *Practical Reason.* Ithaca, NY: Cornell University Press.

Walker, L., et al. 1984. Sex Differences in the Development of Moral Reasoning: A Critical Review. *Child Development* 55: 677–691.

———— 1987. Moral Stages and Moral Orientations in Real Life and Hypothetical Dilemmas. *Child Development* 58: 842–858.

Wallace, James. 1978. *Virtues and Vices.* Ithaca, NY: Cornell University Press.

Wallace, R. Jay. 1994. *Responsibility and the Moral Sentiments.* Cambridge, MA: Harvard University Press.

Walters, R., and Bandura, A. 1963. *Social Learning and Personality Development.* New York: Holt, Rinehart and Winston.

———— Parke, R., and Cane, V. 1977. Timing of Punishment and the Observation of Consequences to Others as Determinants of Response Inhibition. *Journal of Experimental Child Psychology* 2: 10–30.

Walton, Douglas. 1986. *Courage.* Berkeley: University of California Press.

Walzer, Michael. 1981. Philosophy and Democracy. *Political Theory* 9: 379–399.

———— 1983. *Spheres of Justice.* Oxford, England: Basil Blackwell.

Warnock, Mary. 1987. The Limits of Toleration. *On Toleration.* Edited by S. Mendus and D. Edwards. Oxford, England: Clarendon Press.

Warr, P. 1990. The Measurement of Well-being and Other Aspects of Mental Health. *Journal of Occupational Psychology* 63: 193–210.

Warren, H. Ed. 1947. *Buddhism in Translations.* Cambridge, MA: Harvard University Press.

Wasserstrom, Richard. 1991. Rights, Human Rights, and Racial Discrimination. *Introduction to Ethical Theory.* Edited by K. Rogerson. Chicago: Holt, Rinehart and Winston.

Weed, Steven. 1976. *My Search for Patty Hearst.* New York: Crown.

Weintraub, Stanley. 1995. *The Last Great Victory.* New York: Dutton.

Whately, Richard. 1828. *Elements of Rhetoric.* Edited by D. Ehninger. Carbondale: Southern Illinois University Press, 1963.

———— 1857. *Lessons on Morals.* Cambridge, England: John Bartlett.

Whiting, J. 1967. *Sorcery, Sin and the Superego: A Cross-cultural Study of Some Mechanisms of Social Control. Cross-Cultural Approaches.* Edited by C.S. Ford. New Haven, CT: Human Relations Area Files Press.

Wilkinson, Alec. 1994. Conversations with a Killer. *The New Yorker,* April 18.

Wilkinson, G.S. 1984. Reciprocal Food Sharing in the Vampire Bat. *Nature* 308: 181–184.

Williams, Bernard. 1973. A Critique of Utilitarianism. *Utilitarianism: For and Against.* Edited by J.J.C. Smart and B. Williams. Cambridge, England: Cambridge University Press.

———— 1978. Politics and Moral Character. *Public and Private Morality.* Edited by Stuart Hampshire. New York: Cambridge University Press, pp. 55–71.

———— 1985. *Ethics and the Limits of Philosophy.* Cambridge, MA: Harvard University Press.

———— 1993. *Shame and Necessity.* Berkeley: University of California Press.

Williams, William. 1995. *Future Perfect.* Cincinnati, OH: Patriot Publishing Co.

Wilson, B. J., Hoffner, C., and Cantor, J. 1987. Children's Perceptions of the Effectiveness of Techniques to Reduce Fear from Mass Media. *Journal of Applied Developmental Psychology* 8: 39–52.

————, et al. 1997. Television Violence and Its Content: A Content Analysis 1994–1995. *National Television Study.* Vol. 1. Thousand Oaks, CA: Sage.

Wilson, E.O. 1998. The Biological Basis of Morality. *The Atlantic Monthly,* April.

Wilson, James. 1993. *The Moral Sense.* New York: Free Press.

Wilson, J.R., and Petruska, R. 1984. Motivation, Model Attributes and Prosocial Behavior. *Journal of Personality and Social Psychology* 46: 458–468.

Windmiller, M., Lambert, N., and Turiel, E., Editors. 1980. *Moral Development and Socialization.* Boston: Allyn and Bacon.

Woodforde, John. 1992. *The History of Vanity.* New York: St. Martin's Press.

Wright, Robin. 1994. *The Moral Animal.* New York: Vintage.

Yass, Marion. 1972. *Hiroshima.* New York: Putnam and Sons.

Zahn-Waxler, Carolyn, et al. 1979. Child Rearing and Children's Prosocial Initiations Toward Victims of Distress. *Child Development* 50: 319–330.

Zheng, Yujian. 1998. *Weakness of Will and a Picoeconomic Model of Mind.* Presentation to the Pacific American Philosophy Association, March, 1999. Unpublished manuscript.

Zillmann, D. 1980. Anatomy of Suspense. *The Entertainment Functions of Television.* Edited by P.H. Tannenbaum. Hillsdale, NJ: Erlbaum, pp. 133–163.

———— 1993. Mental Control of Angry Aggression. *Handbook of Mental Control.* Edited by D. Wegner and J. Pennebaker. New York: Prentice Hall.

————, and Bryant, J. 1984. Effects of Massive Exposure to Pornography. *Pornography and Sexual Aggression.* Edited by N. Malamuth and E. Donnerstein. New York: Academic Press, pp. 124–155.

————, and Cantor, J. R. 1977. Affective Responses to the Emotions of a Protagonist. *Journal of Experimental Social Psychology* 13: 155–165.

Zubieta, J.K., et al. 1996. Increased Mu opiod Receptor Binding Detected by PET in Cocaine-Dependent Men is Associated with Cocaine Craving. *Nature Medicine* 11: 1225–1229.

Index

A

Absence of Malice, 207
Accountability, 99, 101-102
Achebe, Chenua, 265, 267-269
Achilles, 31
Acting
  from duty, 42, 152, 254
  in ignorance, 93 ,96, 103, 105-109
  out of duty, 41,152, 254
  out of ignorance, 93, 103, 105
  under duress, 103, 109-111
Action
  deliberate, 102-104
  impulsive, 102-104
  intentional, 97, 98, 217
  involuntary, 103
  negligent, 98, 105
  nonvoluntary,104
  reckless, 98, 105
  unintentional, 97, 98
  voluntary,102-104
Actus reus, 98
Adam and Eve, 223-224, 231
Addiction, 96-97, 107-108
Admiration, 24. *See also* Disgust
Adorno, T., 143, 144
Adventures of Huckleberry Finn, 67
Aesop, 266-267, 269, 324
Aesthetic education, 62
Affluenza, 246
Affluenza, 246-247
Aguirre, The Wrath of God, 206-207
Ainslie, George, 55, 95
Air Force One, 109-110
Akolasia (self-indulgence), 96
Akrasia (moral weakness), 96
Alamo, The, 203
Alexithymia, 28
All My Sons, 208
All the King's Men, 206
Allegory of the Cave, 157
Allegory of the Convention, 357-358
Allegory of Prudence, 265
Allotrioepiscopia, 159
Allinsmith, G. 35
Allport, G, 143
Alternative possibilities, principle of.
    See Principle(s)
Altruism, 28-29, 376

Amato, P. R., 32
Ambition, 155-157, 206-207. *See also*
  Ruthlessness
American dream, the, 244-247. *See*
  Good life
American Psycho, 61
Andacht, F., 288
Anger. *See* Good-temper
Anhedonia, 146, 147
Ankshesbonq, 142
Annas, George, 282, 283
Anscombe, Elizabeth, 272
Antigone, 207-208
Apathy, 155. *See also* Good-temper
Aquinas, Thomas, 138-139, 158, 165,
  198-201, 216, 219, 375-376,
  biography, 376
  on natural law, 375-376, 378
Arendt, Hannah, 37, 252, 285, 348
Aristotle, xi, 7, 9, 14, 44, 48, 58, 82, 93,
  94, 95, 96,97, 102-112, 140-141,
  145- 146, 147, 148-154, 155,
  158, 165, 166, 167, 168, 171,
  177, 178, 179, 188, 189, 192,
  194, 198-201, 213, 214, 215,
  216, 217, 218, 219, 220, 234-
  241, 242, 244, 251, 252-255,
  272, 273, 274, 275, 375
  and Kant, 301-302
  and Plato, 93, 297-301
  biography, 9
  on decision, 283
  on deliberation, 259-261
  on flourishing, 234-241
  on happiness, 234-241
  on judgment, 283
  on justice, 177-179
  on moral weakness, 92-96
  on natural law, 375
  on practical reason, 297-302
  on practical reasoning, 214-218,
    259-261, 297-302
  on practical wisdom, 212-218
  on responsibility, 97, 102-112
  on the golden mean, 140-141
  on the good life, 234-241, 252-255
  on the life of virtue, 252-255
  on tragedy, 58
  on virtue, 137-142, 145-146, 147,
    148-154, 155, 158, 165,

    166, 167, 168, 171, 177-
    178, 179, 188, 189, 192,
    194, 198-201
  on virtue and pleasure, 148-154
  on voluntariness, 102-112
Arētē (virtue), 238
Armageddon, 224
Aronfeed, J. 55, 56
Arras, J., 278, 282
Arrogance, 189. *See* Pride
Asceticism, 153-154. *See* Stoicism
Ataraxia, 148, 149. *See also* Epicureanism
Atomic bomb, decision to drop, 293-
  296
Attachment, 55
Augustine, 94, 158, 168, 225
  biography, 158
Autism, 27-28. *See also* Empathy;
  Grandin, Temple
Autonomy, 80-81, 120-130, 139, 340,
  341, 343, 345-346, 350
  and self-control, 87, 121, 122, 123,
    127-130
  and self-direction, 121-122, 123
  and self-efficacy, 121, 122, 123
  and self-mastery, 121, 122, 123
  as basis for deontological princi-
    ples, 341, 343, 345-346, 350
  as self-determination, 89, 121
  as self-legislation, 89, 350
  contrasted with heteronomy, 123
  developing, 127-130
Axelrod, Robert, 361-362
Ayer, A.J., 69-71, 369
  biography, 69

B

Babette's Feast, 208-209
Bacon, Francis, 158, 169, 170, 193,
  194, 196, 197, 198
Bad-temper, 154-155
  types of, 155
  See also Apathy; Good-temper
Bahadur, M., 173
Baier, Annette, 46, 47, 52-55, 63-65
  biography, 53
  on trust, 52-55
Bain, Alexander, 128

Baltes, P., 213, 214, 215, 216, 220, 265, 268
Bandura, Albert, 24, 61, 130
Baron-Cohn, S., 27
Barrow, Isaac, 169
Bataan, 204
Batman, 60
Batson, D., 29, 30, 32
Baumrind, D., 55, 56, 57
Beau Geste, 208
Beckett, Samuel, 226
Bell, Daniel, 242
Bellah, Robert, 233-234, 245-247
Benedict (St.), 94-95
Benedict, Ruth, 21-22, 328-329
Benevolence, principle of. *See* Principle(s)
Benn, S., 34, 38, 383
Bennett, Jonathan, 28, 68
Bennett, William, 58
Bentham, Jeremy, 241, 365-368, 382
  biography
  on utilitarianism, 365-368
Berger, P., 268
Berkowitz, M., 56, 57, 61
Berry, M., 61
Berlin, Isaiah, 80
Bettelheim, Bruno, 57, 221
Billy Budd, 38, 75
Bing, Leon, 37
Binmore, K., 363
Birn, Ruth, 47
Black, Henry, 100, 101
Blair, R, 35, 36
Blame. *See* Responsibility
Block, J., 312
Bloom, Alan, 58
Bloomfield, H., 147
Blue Velvet, 76
Blum, L., 29, 30, 36, 68
Bluntness, 184, 187. *See also* Lying; Truthfulness,
Boastfulness, 191. *See also* Exaggeration
Boe, Vivia, 246
Bok, Sissela, 183, 184, 186
Boorda, J., 44
Boorishness, 192
Boorstein, Daniel, 251
Booth, Wayne, 60, 225
Boren, H., 173
Bourget, Paul, 320
Bouvla, Elizabeth, 280-283
Bowlby, J., 55
Bowers, L.B., 56
Brandt, R.B., 235, 369, 370
Braudy, Leo, 250, 251
Braungart, R., 55
Braveheart, 204
Bravery, 164-168, 202-204
  types of, 167
  See also Courage
Brehm, J., 53
Breugel, Pieter, 30
Britton, J., 21
Brown, Jonathan, 236
Brown, R., 144

Buber, Martin, 338
Buddha, 7, 10, 215
  biography, 10
Buffoonery, 192
Burrell, David, 280, 282
Burton, R., 56
Buschke, A., 129
Bush, Jeb, 200
Bushido, 45
Butler, Joseph, 312, 333
Butterworth, G., 26
Buzzuto, J.C., 61

C

Calculation, 255-257, 260. *See also* Cunning; Deliberation
  irrational, 255
  principle of effective means, 255
  principle of inclusiveness, 256
  rational, 255
  principle of greater likelihood, 256-257
Calumny, 207
Calvin, John, 226, 378
Campbell, A., 247
Canterbury Tales, 169
Cantor, J., 61
Capote, Truman, 34
Cardinal virtues. *See* Virtue(s)
Care, 39, 40, 46-47, 51, 63, 64, 65, 336-340
  and feminism, 336-340
  as moral sentiment, 46-48
Carlson, Richard, 169
Carneades, 261
Carnegie, Andrew, 233-234
Carter, Jimmy, 137-138
Carter, Stephen, 320
Carver, C., 32
Casablanca, 48, 73
Cask of Amontillado, The, 209
Castiglione, B., 190
Casuistry, 269, 277-279
  and memory, 269
  and memory palace, 277-279
Catcher in the Rye, The, 60
Categorical imperative. *See* Principle(s)
Cattell, R., 143
Causation, 84, 85, 86, 87, 88, 99-101
Cause,
  concurrent, 100
  contributing, 100
  in fact, 99-100
  proximate, 100, 102
  relevant, 100
  salient, 100
  See also Causation; Responsibility
Censorship, 59
Character, 142-145
  and virtue. *See* Virtue(s)
  and wisdom. *See* Wisdom
Charm, 191-192
Chaucer, 169
Cheating, 185-187. *See also* Honesty
Chekhov, Anton, 226

Cherry Orchard, The, 226
Chisholm, Roderick, 87
Christmas Carol, A, 227
Cialdini, R.B., 28-29
Cicero, 7, 14, 40, 41, 44, 48, 152, 213, 216, 261-265, 296, 387-388
  biography, 262
  on advantage, 262-265
  on affection, 263
  on casuistry, 237
  on deliberation, 261-265
  on discernment, 263-264
  on foresight, 263-264
  on memory, 264
  on natural law, 375
  on necessity, 262
Citizen Kane, 207
Civil Law. *See* Law.
Civility, 188. *See also* Virtues, of respect
Clarification, stage of. *See* Moral knowledge.
Clark, D., 147
Clark, Kenneth, 84
Clark, R.D., 32
Clarke, Randolph, 87
Clayton, V., 216
Cleanliness, 193
Cleckley, Hervey, 33
Clockwork Orange, A, 76
Codes. *See* Moral codes
Cognitive dissonance, 94
Coleman, Jules, 121
Coles, Robert, 31, 143
Comedy. *See* Stories; Vision, Thalian
Commendation, 192
Common good, 229-234
  administered society vs. economic democracy, 233-234
  ironic vision of, 229-233
  Jefferson-Madison dispute about, 232-235
  neocapitalism vs. welfare state, 233-234
  populism vs. elitism, 233-234
  Thalian vision of, 229-233
Communitarianism, 14, 304-305, 352
Compassion, 30-31. *See also* Sympathy
Compatibilism, 86, 88-90. *See also* Determinism
Competitiveness, 193
Comstock, G., 62
Confucius, 7, 8, 14, 48-50, 140, 199, 215, 267, 270, 311, 363
Conscience, 20, 22, 39, 68
Consequentialist principles. *See* Principle(s)
Contempt, 188
Contentment, 161-162. *See also* Covetousness
Contract ethics, 350-353. *See also* Rawls, John.
Corey, Gerald, 122
Corey, Marianne, 122
Counsels. *See* Proverbs.
Count of Monte Cristo, The, 209
Courage, 139, 140, 164-168, 202-204, 218

Coverdale, Miles, 168
Covetousness, 161, 207. *See also* Contentment
Cowardliness, 168. *See also* Courage, 168
Crime and Punishment, 73
Criminal Law. *See* Law.
Crossing Guard, The, 209
Cruelty, 194. *See also* Kindness
Csikszentmihalyi, Mihali, 146, 213, 215, 219, 237-238, 240-241, 248
Cunning, 257-259, 260. *See also* Deliberation
Curiosity, 157-160, 205. *See also* Docility
Cyprian of Antioch, 168

D

Dacyczyn, A., 160
Damasio, Antonio, 17, 68
Daniels, Norman, 317
Dante, 183
Darley, J., 33
Davidson, Art, 114, 115
Davidson, Donald, 95
Davies, Paul, 85
Davis, M., 129
Davis, M.H., 29, 32
Dawkins, Richard, 362
Dean, John, 156
Death of a Salesman, The, 226
Deception, 186
Decision, 289. *See also* Judgment
Definitions, 11
De Graaf, John, 246
Deigh, J., 33, 34, 35
Deliberation, 255-283
    and bad judgment, 288-289
    and casuistry, 269, 277-279, 283
    and decision, 289
    and discernment, 264-265, 272-275
    and foresight, 264-265, 275-277
    and judgment, 283-297
    and memory, 264-272
    and narrative ethics, 277, 280-283
    Aristotle's model of, 259-261
    Cicero's model of, 261-265
    contrasted with calculation, 255-257
    contrasted with cunning, 255, 257-259
    See also Aristotle; Cicero
D'Entreves, A.P., 378
Deontological principles. *See* Principle(s)
Derstine, C.F., 129
Descartes, René, 219
De Sousa, Ronald, 18
Determinism, 82-86, 87, 88, 89, 90
    and chaos theory, 85
    and genetics, 85
    and quantum theory, 85
    See also Compatibilism; Libertarianism
Devlin, Patrick, 181

De Vos, G., 46
Dewey, John, 271-272, 273, 283, 285
Dharmapada, 215
Dialogic principle, the. *See* Principle(s)
Diana (Princess), 106
Dichotomous thinking, 327-328
Didion, Joan, 188, 190
Diener, Carol, 235
Diener, Edward, 235, 248
Diogenes, 7, 9
Directionlessness, 156. *See also* Ambition
Discernment, 272-275
Discourse ethics, 353-358. *See also* Dialogic principle
Disgust, 24-25. *See also* Admiration
Dishonesty,183-186. *See also* Self-deception; Stealing
Disneyland, 243
Dispositions. *See* Virtue(s).
Disrespect, 188
Dobu, the, 6
Docilitas, 158
Docility, See also Curiosity, 158
Doctors Without Borders, 47
Doggedness, 170. *See also* Perseverance
Doi, Takeo, 20-21, 45
Dominguez, J., 161
Donnerstein, E., 62
Doors, The, 209
Douglas, Frederick, 80
Douglas, Kirk,, 129-130
Dr. Jekyl and Mr. Hyde, 158, 205
Duan, C., 25
Dunn, J., 26
Dupery, 186
Duplicity, 186
Durbin, D.L., 57
Duress, acting under. *See* Acting
Duty, 40-43, 51, 66-69, 101, 124-125, 152, 153, 261, 262
    acting out of, 41
    acting from, 41
    of the corporation, 42
    prima facie, 42
    See also Obligation; Kant, Immanuel
Dworkin, Andrea, 59
Dworkin, Ronald, 381-385

E

East of Eden, 76
Eckhardt, Eric, 22
Edwards, Carolyn, 313
Edwards, E., 61
Edwards, Jonathan, 29, 226
Effective means, principle of. *See* Principle(s)
Egoism, the principle of. *See* Principle(s)
Ego-strength, 92
Eichmann, Adolf, 348
Eisenberg, N., 30, 32
Ekman, Paul, 18
El Norte, 204

Eliot, George, 275-277, 337
Emotional contagion, 26
Emotional hijacking, 94, 96
Emotions, general characteristics, 18-19, 58, 139
Emotivism, 69-71
Empathy, 25-28
    and autism, 27-28
    contrasted with sympathy, 25-28
Empirical claims, contrasted with normative ones, 11
Enjoyment. *See* Pleasure
Entertainment. *See* Good life, the
Entitlements, 381
Envy, 158
Epictetus, xi, 7, 9, 19, 148, 152-154, 159, 253. *See also* Stoicism
    biography, 9
Epicureanism, 148-154
Epicurus, 7, 9, 148-154, 163, 333
    biography, 9
Epimarchus, 145, 215, 275
Epistēmē, 213
Erikson, Eric, 52
Ethical principles. *See* Principle(s)
Ethics,
    classic tradition, 7-15
    modern tradition, 7-15
    study of, 7-15
Eubolia, 259
Eudaimonia, 150
Eudaimonism, 148-154, 163
Euthanasia, 390-393
Euthymia, 153. *See also* Stoics
Evans, C., 326
Evolutionary ethics, 360-363. *See also* Tit-for-tat
Exaggeration,187. *See also* Boastfulness
Extravagance, 160
Exxon Valdez, the, 113-117
Eyesenck, H., 143

F

Fairmindedness, 139, 140, 170-180
    and its relation with temperance and courage, 139, 140, 170
    as a cardinal virtue, 139, 140
    characteristics of, 171-173
    contrasted with fairness, 171
    contrasted with justice, 171
Fairness, 171-180
    conditions for, 173-174
    contrasted with fairmindedness, 171
    contrasted with justice, 171
Fame, life of. *See* Good life, the
Fastidiousness, 193-194
Fatalism, 82-84
Fearlessness, 167. *See also* Bravery
Federman, J., 61
Feinberg, Joel, 382, 385
Feldman, R., 32
Felsman, J.K., 312
Feminist ethics, 46-47, 52-55, 63-65, 70, 71, 336-340

Feminist ethics, *continued*
   and caring, 46-47, 336-340
   and Carol Gilligan, 46, 336-340
   and David Hume, 46, 63, 65
   and Immanuel Kant, 47, 63, 65
   and John Rawls, 65, 352
   and moral sentiment, 63-65
   and the principle-and-rules
      approach, 336-340
   and trust, 52-55
Festinger, Leon, 94, 127
Finkelstein, Norman, 47
Fitzcarraldo, 204
Flack, R., 55
Flanagan, Owen, 7, 142-145, 236, 253
Flattery, 193. *See* Vanity
Flinn, Kelly, 274
Flourishing, 148, 150-152, 234-241,
    252-255
   and eudaimonism, 148, 150-152
   and flow, 240-241
   and pleasure, 238-239
   and the life of virtue, 252-255
   Aristotle's account of, 234-241,
    252-255
   as living-well, 234-241
   contrasted with happiness, 236-
    241
   contrasted with prosperity, 236-
    238
   contrasted with success, 236-238
   See also Happiness
Flow, 240-241, 254. *See also* Flourishing
Foolhardiness, 167-168
Foot, Phillipa, 165, 199, 253
Foresight, 275-277. *See also* Delibera-
   tion
Forgiveness, 195-198
Fortune, Reo, 6
Four Feathers, The, 204
Frankena, William, 376-377
Frankenstein, 158, 205
Frankfurt, Harry, 84, 88-89
Frankl, Victor, 239
Franklin, Benjamin, 128, 331
Free will. *See* Compatibilism; Deter-
   minism; Libertarianism
Friedman, Marilyn, 64
Friendliness, 192
Friesen, W., 18
Frost, David, 248, 249
Frugality, 160-161. *See also* Work ethic,
   the
Fujita, F., 235
Fukuyama, Francis, 2-5, 53
Fulghum, Robert, 312

G

Gable, Clark, 251
Gacy, John Wayne, 35
Gadamer, Hans-Georg, 219, 335
Gailbraith, John, 246
Gallipoli, 207
Game theory, 361-363. *See also* Tit-for-
   tat principle
Gandhi, 156, 227-228, 230, 231

Gardner, Howard, 144, 145, 312
Gates, Henry Louis Jr., 159
Gauthier, David, 255-256, 303-304,
   344, 353
Geach, Peter, 198-199
Gearan, A., 195-196
Generosity, 194-195
Genovese, Kitty, 33
Gert, Bernard, 318, 386
Gettysburg, 203
Gill, M., 119
Gilligan, Carol, 46, 47, 64, 65, 322, 324-
   326, 337. *See also* Feminist
   ethics; Kohlberg, Lawrence
Glory, 204
Godwin, William, 314-315
Golden mean, the, 140-141
Golden rule, the. *See* Principle(s)
Goldhagen, David, 47
Goldstein, Kurt, 121
Goldman, A. 26, 48
Goleman, Daniel, 17, 22, 28, 37, 55,
   56, 90, 94, 96, 122, 139, 145,
   154, 191, 215-216, 238, 240
Golzius, Hendrik, 169
Goodfellows, 57
Good life, the, 211, 219, 234-255
   and vision, 218-221
   as fame, 250-252
   as living-well, 234-241
   as pleasure, adventure, and enter-
    tainment, 241-244
   as power, 250-252
   as security and comfort, 244-247
   as the American dream, 244-247
   as the life of virtue, 252-255
   as wealth, 247-250
Good will, the, 123-125. *See also* Kant,
   Immanuel
Goodwill, 52-55
Good-temper,154-155
Gordon, R., 25, 27
Gracian, Balthasar, 137, 183
   biography, 183
Grandin, Temple, 27-28
Gray, Glenn, 167-168, 273
Greater likelihood, the principle of.
   See Principle(s); Calculation
Greatest liberty principle, the. *See*
   Principle(s)
Greed, 195, 207
Greenberg, B. S., 61
Greene, Robert, 257, 259
Gregory the Great, 94, 214
Grim, P.F., 92
Grotius, Hugo, 378-379
Groves, Leslie, 293-296
Guilt, 19-22, 40
Guiness Book of Records, 251
Gulliver's Travels, 228
Gunter, B., 61, 62
Gyges, ring of, 39. *See also* Plato

H

Haan, N., 325
Habermas, Jürgen, 303, 353-358
   biography, 353

Habits, 128-129. *See also* Virtue(s)
Hackworth, D., 44
Hallie, Philip, 22, 43
Hamilton, Alexander, 233
Hamilton, W., 32, 363
Hamlet, 209, 227
Hammurabi, 174
Happiness, 234-255
   and self-actualization, 238
   and utilitarianism, 234
   as contentment, 234
   as well-being, 234-235
   contrasted with flourishing, 234-
    241
   contrasted with living-well, 234-
    241
   contrasted with prosperity, 236-
    238
   contrasted with success, 236-238
   See also Flourishing
Harding, Sonja, 22
Hare, R.M., 318
Hare, Robert, 34, 35, 36
Harsanyi, J.C., 351
Hart, H.L.A., 98, 105, 181
Hartshorne, H., 142, 144
Hauerwas, S., 280, 282
Hawking, Stephen, 85-86
Hayek, F.A., 314-315
Hazelwood, Joseph, 113-117
Hearst, Patty, 111
Hedonism, 148-154, 241-244
   and eudaimonism, 148-154
   and stoicism, 148-154
   epicurean, 148-154
   sybaritic, 148
Hefner, Hugh, 242-243, 253
Hegel, Georg, 37, 219, 227
Heidegger, Martin, 219, 220
Heil, John, 95
Heisler, G.H., 61
Held, Virginia, 63, 64, 65, 352
Heraclitus, 137, 142
Heteronomy, 123. *See also* Autonomy
High Noon, 72-73
Hill, Paul, 21,
Hillsdale College, 200
Hiroshima, the decision to drop the
   atomic bomb on, 293-296
Hitchcock, Alfred, 60
Hitler, Adolf, 126, 156, 231, 359
Hobbes, Thomas, 230, 231, 232, 341,
   342, 378, 380, 381
   biography, 342
Hoffman, M.L., 26, 33, 56, 57
Holliday, S., 214, 215
Holloway, W.,
Holmes, Margaret, 196-197
Holmes, Oliver Wendell, 314
Holmgren, Margaret, 196-197
Homicide, 100, 101, 103-104
Homosexuality, 180-181
Honesty, 182-187, 208. *See also* Truth-
   fulness; Lying
Honor, 40, 44-46, 51
   code, 45
   killing, 45

Hope, 170
Horace, 140, 141
Hornstein, H., 32
Horowitz, D. 242
House of Games, 208
Hubris, 189
Hugh Hefner: Once Upon A Time, 242-243, 253
Hume, David, 11-12, 13, 16, 17, 18, 25, 29, 31, 46, 52, 63-65, 69, 70, 71, 232, 253, 365
  and feminism, 63-65
  and emotivism, 69
  and Kant, 63, 64, 65
  and moral emotions, 16, 17, 18, 25, 29, 31
  and sympathy, 25, 29, 31
  biography, 17
Humility, 188
Hutcheson, Francis, 13, 212, 312, 333, 365
Hypocrisy, 186

I

Iago, 54-55
Ibsen, Henrik, 226
Iliad, The, 31, 57, 83, 206
Ill-temper. *See* Bad-temper; Good-temper
Impatience, 169. See also Perseverance
In Cold Blood, 34, 76
Incest, 328-329
Inclusive fitness, theory of, 32
Incompatibilism, 86
Incompetence, 106
Independence Day, 224
Indeterminancy, 86, 87
Industry, 161. *See also* Work ethic, the
Insensitivity,147
Insincerity, 186
Instrumental theory of virtue, the. *See* Virtue(s)
Integral theory of virtue, the. *See* Virtue(s)
Integrated approach to the study of ethics, xii
Integrity, 320-321
  and moral codes, 320-321
  and stage of systematization, 320-321
  conditions of, 320
Intentional. *See* Action
Intentionality, 18-19, 87-88
Internalization, 13, 39
Intoxication, 106-109. *See also* Incompetence
Irony. *See* Stories

J

Jacobsen, L., 34
James, William, 94, 97, 128, 129, 219
  biography, 129
Jealousy, 161, 205-206
Jean de Florette, 207

Jefferson, Thomas, 200, 232-234, 379, 380
Jesus, 7, 10, 82, 92, 215, 267
  biography, 10
Job, 169
Johnson, B.R., 61
Johnson, Mark, 221, 228, 275
Johnson, Samuel, xi, 189, 321
Jonson, Albert, 261, 277-279
Jouvenal, Bertrand de, 252
Judgment, 215, 284-288
  as a moral dilemma, 284, 286-288
  as a moral temptation, 284, 285-286
  as a tragic choice, 284-285
  bad, 215, 288-289
Julius Caesar, 155-156
Junzi (noble person), 48-50
Justice, 170, 171, 174-180
  contrasted with fairmindedness, 171
  contrasted with fairness, 171
  corrective, 177-180
  distributive, 177-180
  precepts of, 175-177
  retributive, 177-180
  versus mercy, 287-288
Justification, stage of. *See* Moral knowledge

K

Kafka, Franz, 226
Kagan, Jerome, 143, 313
Kagan, Shelley, 320
Kant, Immanuel, 7, 13, 29, 41, 47, 54, 63, 64, 65-69, 70, 81, 145, 146, 152, 159, 184, 188, 189, 190, 193, 196, 197, 199, 219, 220, 254, 321, 334-335, 341, 343, 345-350, 383-385
  and Aristotle, 301-305
  biography, 66, 346
  on autonomy, 345-350
  on duty, 41, 65-69, 123-125, 345-350, 383-385
  on moral sentiment, 65-69, 124-125
  on obligation, 65-69, 345-350, 383-385
  on practical reason, 301-305
  on the categorical imperative, 345-350
  on the good will, 123-125, 254
Kaufman, J., 56
Kawachi, I., 53
Kekes, John, 122-123
Kenny, A., 18
Kerrigan, Nancy, 22
Keyes, Dick, 57, 166, 251
Kidder, Rushworth, 1,5,185, 284-288, 362
Kilpatrick, William, 58, 59, 60, 221, 316
Kim, Peter, 2, 3
Kindness, 194
  virtues of. *See* virtue(s)

King, Martin Luther, 48, 49, 92, 156, 219, 230, 231
King, Larry, 248-249
King Lear, 227
Kirk, K., 278, 279
Kirkpatrick, Jeane, 379
Kitchener, K., 217, 325
Klausner, Samuel, 127-130
Klein, Donald, 146
Klimes-Dougan, B., 56
Klineberg, O., 55
Knack, S., 53
Kohlberg, Lawrence, 57, 321-326, 333, 334, 337
  and Carol Gilligan, 324-326, 337
  stages of moral reasoning, 321-326
Kornet, A., 186
Krakauer, Jon, 290-293
Kramer, Peter, 146, 147
Ku Klux Klan, 180, 182

L

Labouvie-Vief, G., 215, 216
Lactantius, 168
Lake, Daniel, 164
Landscape with Fall of Icarus, 30
Lane, Robert, 247-248
Laplace, Pierre, 85
La Porta, R., 53
Last Temptation of Christ, The, 61
Latane, B., 33
Lauritzen, Paul, 282-283
Law
  civil, 98
  criminal, 98
  natural, 224, 261, 262, 332-333
  tort, 98, 112-119
LeDoux, Joseph, 17, 18, 96
Lee, B., 296
Levenson, R., 18
Lewis, C.S., 158
Lews, Linda, 193
Lex talionis, 179
Lexical ordering. *See* Principle(s)
Liability, 101, 112-113, 118-120
  and restatement of agency, 112
  fault standard of, 112
  strict, 112
Libel, 186
Libertarianism, 86-88
  and chaos, 86-87
  and free will, 86-87
  as a moral principle. *See* Principle(s)
  See also Compatibilism; Determinism
  See also Compatibilism; Determinism
Lickona, Thomas, 58, 316
Life of pleasure and entertainment. *See* Good life, the
Life of virtue. *See* Good life, the
Life of wealth. *See* Good life, the
Lifton, Jay, 293-296
Lincoln, Abraham, 142, 359
Linde, Charlotte, 270-271

Lippman, Walter, 220, 311, 364
Little Red Riding Hood, 60
Living-well. *See* Happiness
Lloyd, G., 63
Locke, John, 231, 232, 332, 343-344, 380
  biography, 344
Lockean proviso, 344
Logical inferences in ethics, 11
Lomax, Eric, 196
Lord Jim, 203
Lord of the Flies, The, 75-76
Lorenz, Konrad, 150
Love, 31
  as contrasted with sympathy, 31. *See also* Sympathy
Lowliness, 192
Loyalty, 207-208
Lucretius, 149
Luks, Allan, 377
Lust, 162. *See also* Sexual continence
Luther, Martin, 226, 378
Lying, 182-187, 348-349. *See also* Truthfulness
  types of, 186-187
Lykken, David, 36, 235-236
Lynd, H., 21

M

Mabbott, J.B., 380
Macbeth, 156, 227
Machiavelli, N., 252, 257-259
Mackie, J.L., 381-385
MacKinnon, Catherine, 59
MacIntyre, Alasdair, 14, 15, 198-201, 237, 254, 280
  biography, 198
Macrobius, 265
Madison, James, 232-234
Magid, Ken, 35
Magnificent Seven, The, 81
Mandela, Nelson, 48
Mann, L., 28
Mannered, 192
Manning, Rita, 46, 324-325, 338-339
Martens, W., 35
Martin, M., 324
Martinez-Coll, J., 363
Maslow, Abraham, 238, 240
  hierarchy of needs, 240
Mass killings of the twentieth century, 38
Master morality, 125-127. *See also* Nietzsche, Friedrich
Matching law, the, 95
Mathai, J., 61
Matrix, The, 152
May, Larry, 113
McCabe, Donald, 185
McCloy, John, 293-296
McCord, W., 35
McFeeley-Wackerle-Jett survey, 1, 5
McKelvey, C., 35
McNamara, Robert, 276-277
McPherson, James, 51, 198
McVeigh, Timothy, 23

McWilliam, C., 189, 190
Meacham, J., 216
Meddling, 158. *See also* Allotrioepis- copia
Medlin, Brian, 359
Medred, C., 164
Meilaender, G., 158
Melden, A.I., 87
Mele, A., 95
Melville, Herman, 38
Meltzhoff, A., 26
Memory, 264-272
  and casuistry, 269-270
  and deliberation, 264-265
  and personal identity, 270-272
  and proverbial wisdom, 267-269, 270, 271
  and stories, 265-267, 270-272
  palace, 277-278
  working, 215-216
Memory palace. *See* Memory
Mencius, 7, 14, 48-50
Mental illness. *See* Incompetence; Acting in ignorance
Mens rea, 98
Mercy, 196
Meticulousness, 194
Meyerowitz, R., 167
Midsummer Night's Dream, A, 227
Milgram, Stanley, 143, 144
Milken, Michael, 362
Mill on the Floss, The, 275-277, 289, 337-338
Mill, John Stuart, 7, 12, 180, 234, 344, 349-350, 367-374, 382-383
  and Bentham, 367-368
  and Kant, 349-350
  and libertarianism, 344
  and utilitarianism, 7, 367-374
  on rights, 382-383
  on tolerance, 180
Miller, Arthur, 226
Miller, C., 218
Miller, William, 24-25
Mills, C. Wright, 248, 250, 251, 252
Milton, John, 95-96
Minimal psychological realism, principle of. *See* Principle(s)
Mischel, Walter, 145
Miserliness, 160
Mitchell, D., 35
Moby Dick, 209
Modesty, 188, 190
Mohammad, 7, 10, 215
  biography, 10
Montaigne, Michel, 157, 183, 189, 197, 328
Montesquieu, Charles-Louis de, 231-232, 233
Moore, G.E., 12, 370
  biography, 370
Moral character, 142-145, 402-405
  and virtue, 142-145
Moral codes, 320-321. *See also* Integrity
Moral competence, xii, 15, 80, 137, 212, 311, 400-402
Moral decline, 2-5

Moral dilemma, 284, 286-288
  individual vs. community, 286
  justice vs. mercy, 287-288
  short-term vs. long-term, 286-287
  truth vs. loyalty, 286
Moral education, 57-63
  and art, 57-63
  and music, 57-63
  and parenting styles, 55-57
  and stories, 57-63
  and values clarification, 316-317
  Plato on, 57-58, 62-63
Moral emotions, 13, 17-39, 58, 80. *See also*, Admiration; Disgust; Guilt; Outrage; Regret; Remorse; Shame;
  and stories, 18-19, 221-222
Moral intuition, 312-315
  acquisition of, 313
  and justification of principles, 312-313
  and stage of clarification, 316-317
  and stage of systematization, 317-320
  Enlightenment view of, 313-315
  Evolutionary view of, 313-315
  Hayek's view of, 313-315
  versus moral knowledge, 313-315
Moral knowledge, xii, xiii, 207-305, 311-393, 400-402
  and intuition, 313-315
  and wisdom, 311-312
  Aristotle's account of, 297-302
  justification of, 315, 321-340
  Kant's account of, 301-305
  Plato's account of, 297-301
  stage of clarification in, 315-317
  stage of justification in, 321
  stage of systematization in, 317-321
Moral luck, 90-92, 97
Moral outrage, 23-24
Moral principle. *See* Principle(s)
Moral psychology, laws of, 52
Moral reasoning,
  stages of, 217-218. *See* Kohlberg, Lawrence
Moral rule(s), 318-320
  and generality, 318-320
  and scope, 318-320
  and universality, 318-320
  contrasted with principles, 318-320
Moral sentiment, xii, 38-71, 80, 124-125, 212, 311, 400-402
  and feminism, 52-55, 63-65
  and Hume, 63-65
  and Kant, 63-65
  and moral competence, xii, 400-402
  as basis of morality, 63-65
  as caring, 46-48
  as duty, 40-43
  as honor, 44-46
  as nobility, 48-52
  cultivation in children of, 55-62
  development in children of, 52-57

Moral strength, xii, xiii, 92-97, 212, 311, 400-402. *See also* Moral weakness
Moral vision. *See* vision
Moral weakness, 92-97
    explanation of, 93-95
    See also Moral strength
Moral wisdom. *See* Wisdom
Moreira, I., 218
Morgan, K., 64
Moses, 7, 10
    biography, 10
Mother Teresa, 46, 144, 359
Mt. Everest, tragedy on, 290-293
Mrozek, Slawomir, 81-82
Much Ado About Nothing, 227
Mundorf, N., 61
Murphey, J., 34
Murphy, Jeffrie, 196
Murphy, Thomas, 80
My Lai massacre, 110
My Left Foot, 204
Myers, David, 248

N

Nagel, Thomas, 84, 85, 89, 90-92
Napoleon, 257
Narrative. *See* Stories
Narrative ethics, 279-283
Natural law, 374-385
    and Aquinas, 375-376
    and Aristotle, 374-375
    and Cicero, 375
    and Sophists, 374
    and Stoics, 375
    as principle of benevolence, 376-378
    history of, 374-376
    See also Law
Natural law theory, 374-378
Natural rights. *See* Rights
Naturalistic fallacy, 12, 150, 370
Needleman, Jacob, 246-250, 267, 285-286
Negligence. *See also* Acting, out of ignorance; Recklessness
Newton, Adam Zachary, 280
Nicholson, Peter, 180
Nielsen, Kai, 317, 335
Nietzsche, Friedrich, 1, 50-51, 125-127, 196, 219, 342-343
    and master morality, 125-127
    and the strong will, 125-127
    biography, 125
1984, 226
Niven, David, 251
Nobility, 40, 48-50, 51
Noddings, Nel, 46, 47, 336-337, 338, 339
Nomos, 374
Nondisclosure, 183. *See also* Lying
Nonmaleficence, the principle of. *See* Principle(s)
Norma Rae, 204
Normative claims, 11, 69, 70
Normativity, 11-14, 330-336

Nous, 213
Nozick, Robert, 151, 343, 369
Nussbaum, Martha, 221, 273-275, 300, 301, 318

O

O'Connor, T., 87
Oakley, J., 24
Obedience, 207
Obligation, 12, 39, 40-42, 101, 102, 124, 125, 152, 153, 330-336, 340, 381-385. *See also* Duty
Odyssey, The, 57, 204
Oedipus Rex, 82-83, 227
Ohlendorff, Otto, 43
Ohlms, David, 97
Oliner, Samuel and Pearl, 23-24, 32, 55
Oppenheimer, Robert, 293-296
Optimism, 170
Original position, the,. 351. *See also* Rawls, John
Orwoll, L., 216
Othello,
O'Toole, John, 183
Ought-is distinction, 11-12
Ovid, 328

P

Paine, Thomas, 320
Palmer, E.L., 61
Pandora, 157
Papworth, J., 186
Parenting, 55-57
    authoritative, 55, 56
    authoritarian, 55-56
    permissive, 55-56
Panaetius, 261
Parfit, Derek, 370
Park, K.A., 55
Passivity, 169
Pathological weakness, 96-97
Patience, 168-170, 204-205
Patterson, James, 2, 3
Paul (the Apostle), 92, 225
Payne, M.A., 61
Peak experience, 240. *See* Flow
Peirce, Charles, 12, 288
Pence, G., 281
Pentimento, 203
Perkins, K., 235
Perry, Bruce, 36
Perry, W. I., 215
Perseverance, 170, 204-205
Persistence, 170
Pessimism, 170
Peter (the Apostle), 82
Peters, R.S., 383
Petrarch, 265
Philips, N., 115
Phronesis, 213
Physician-assisted suicide, 280-282
Physis, 374
Piaget, Jean, 123
Picasso, Pablo, 237
Pieper, Josef, 139, 140, 213

Piliavin, I., 28, 32
Piper, E., 116
Pity, 30. *See also* Sympathy
Plato, 7,8,39,57-63,93,95, 127, 157, 164-165, 213, 219, 220, 222-223, 341
    and Aristotle, 297-301
    and stories, 57-63, 222-223
    and practical reason, 297-301
    and the allegory of the cave, 157
    and the myth of Er, 222-223
    and the ring of Gyges, 39
    biography, 8
    on courage, 164-165
    on moral education, 57-63
    on moral knowledge, 297-301, 302
    on moral weakness, 93, 95
Plautus, 158
Pleasure, 139, 140, 141, 145-154
    and anhedonia, 146
    and eudaimonism, 148-154, 163
    and epicureanism, 148-154
    and insensitivity, 147
    and self-indulgence, 146, 147
    and sexual continence, 163
    and stoicism, 148-154, 163
    and sybaritism, 148
    and temperance, 145-148
    and utilitarianism, 365-374
    and virtue, 148-154
    appetitive, 146
    catastematic, 148, 149
    consummatory, 146
    contrasted with enjoyment, 146
    kinetic, 146
    life of, 241-244
Plautus, 227
Pliny, 192
Plummer, J., 195-196
Polite virtues. *See* Virtue(s)
Politeness, 191
Popper, Karl, 181
    biography, 181
Positivism, 69
Powers, S.I., 57
Practical reason, 297-305
    different senses of, 301-305
    See also, Aristotle; Kant, Immanuel; Plato
Practical reasoning, 14-15, 217-218, 255-283, 297-301
Practical syllogism, 260-261
Praktikē, 213
Precepts. *See* Justice
Pretense, 187
Pretentiousness, 192
Priam, 31
Pride, 188-191. *See also* Arrogance
Priebke, Karl, 43
Princess Diana, 144
Principle(s), 318-393
    and appeal to authority, 331-332
    and circularity, 333-334
    and generality, 318-320
    and reflective equilibrium, 317-318
    and rules approach, 336-340

Principle(s), *continued*
  and scope, 318-320
  and universality, 318-320
  average, the, 368
  balancing, 386-390
  categorical imperative as, 334-335,
    340, 345-350
  characteristics of, 318-320
  consequentialist. *See* teleological
  contrasted with rules, 318-320
  deontological, 302, 334-335, 340-
    358, 381-393
  dialogic, 340, 353-358, 386-393
  difference, the, 351-352
  divisions of, 340
  feminist criticisms of, 336-340
  golden rule, the, as, 319-320, 340,
    363-365, 386-393
  greatest happiness. *See* utilitarian-
    ism
  greatest liberty, the, 350-353
  justification of, 330-340
  lexical ordering of, 386-390
  libertarian, 340, 343-345, 386-393
  mixed approach to using, 386-393
  natural law, 340, 374-378
  natural rights, 385
  of alternative possibilities, 86, 87
  of benevolence, 340, 376-378
  of effective means, 255-256
  of egoism, 340, 341-343, 358-360,
    386-393
  of greater likelihood, 256-257
  of minimal psychological realism,
    7
  of nonmaleficence. *See Libertarian*
  rights-based, 381-390
  role of, 340, 400-402
  teleological, 302, 333, 340, 358-
    374, 385-393
  tit-for-tat, 340, 360-363, 386-390
  total, the, 367, 368
  types of, 340
  using for moral decision-making,
    385-393
  utilitarian, 340, 365-374, 386-393
Prisoner's dilemma, 361-362
Prodigality, 195
Professional ethics, 319
Promise-making, 186
Prosperity, 235, 236-238. *See also* Flour-
  ishing; Happiness; Success
Proverbs, 267-269, 270, 271
  Achebe on, 267-269
  Aesop's, 269
  Confucius's, 270
  Swahili, 271
  use in memory and deliberation,
    267-269
  Whately on, 268
Prudence. *See* Wisdom
Prudentius, 168
Prudishness, 162. *See also* Sexual conti-
  nence
Psychopathy, 33-36
Punctuality, 194
Putnam, Robert, 2-4, 6, 52-55

Q

Quiz Show, 208

R

Rachels, James, 329, 359
Rahn, W., 53
Raiders of the Lost Ark, 158
Rand, Ayn, 342
  biography, 342
Rapoport, Anatol, 362
Raths, L., 316
Rationalists, 13
Raven (Tlingit), 223
Rawls, John, 19, 20, 21, 23, 37, 39, 52,
    65, 171, 172, 173, 174, 255-256,
    305, 317-318, 350-353, 371-
    372, 374, 386
  and communitarianism, 305, 352
  and contract ethics, 350-353
  and fairness, 171-174
  and feminism, 52, 65, 339, 352
  and reflective equilibrium, 317-
    318, 335-336
  and the greatest liberty principle,
    351-352
  and the original position, 351
  and the three laws of moral psy-
    chology, 52
  and the veil of ignorance, 350-351
  on calculation, 255-256
  on moral emotions, 19, 20, 21, 23,
    37
  on moral sentiment, 39
  on utilitarianism, 371-372, 374
Recklessness, 98, 105. *See* Acting, in
  ignorance; Negligence
Red Badge of Courage, The, 202-203
Reflective equilibrium, 317-318, 335-
  336. *See also* Rawls, John
Regret, 22-23. *See also* Remorse
Reid, Thomas, 312, 333
Reis, H., 235
Relativism, 6, 328-330
  empirical, 328-329
  normative, 330
  cultural, 329-330
Remorse, 22-23. *See also* Regret
Resignation, 170. *See also* Perseverance
Respect, virtues of. *See* Virtue(s)
Responsibility, 97-120
  and addiction, 107-108
  and causation, 99-101
  and children, 106-107
  and intoxication, 107-18
  and mental illness, 108-109
  diminished, 106-107
  factors in, 99
  in criminal law, 98-99
  in tort law, 112-113
  various senses of, 98
  vicarious, 112-113, 118-120
Rest, James, 92, 312
Revenge, 209
Ricci, Matteo, 277-278
Richard III, 227

Ridley, Matt, 360, 361, 362, 363
Rights, 177, 332-333
  as entitlements, 381
  Bill of, 232-234, 332
  natural, 332-333, 378-381
  United Nations Declaration of
    Universal, 379, 380, 384
Rights-based ethics, 381-385
  contrasted with deontology, 382-
    385
  contrasted with utilitarianism,
    382-385
Ring of Gyges, 39
Ripa, Caesare, 213
Robin, Vicki, 161
Robinson, J., 58, 221
Robinson, Jackie, 166
Romance. *See* Stories
Romantic vision. *See* Vision
Rorty, Richard, 335-336
Rosenthal, R., 55
Ross, W.D., 42, 386
  biography, 42
Rothman, G., 92
Rousseau, Jean-Jacques, 16, 31, 46,
    230, 343
  biography, 343
Rowling, J.K., 60
Ruddick, Sarah, 64
Ruff, G., 165
Rules. *See* Moral Rules
Run Lola Run, 90
Rushton, J., 32
Russell, L.J., 364
Ruthlessness, 156

S

Sacks, Oliver, 27-28
Sagacious tradition in ethics, 7-15
Saintliness, 144
Samurai, way of the, 45
Sandel, Michael, 14, 304-305, 352, 353
Sarbin, T., 58, 221
Sartre, Jean-Paul, 349
Satire. *See* Stories
Satiric vision. *See* Vision
Satyagraha, doctrine of, 227-228
Scanlon, Thomas, 382
Scarlet Letter, The, 74
Schab, Fred, 1
Schadenfreude, 29. *See also* Sympathy
Schalling, D., 34
Schank, R., 266
Scheven, A., 155, 168
Schiffhorst, G., 168, 169
Schiller, Friedrich, 62, 69
Schindler, Oskar, 24, 74-75
Schindler's List, 24, 74-75
Schmidt, G., 33
Schopenhauer, Arthur, 31, 37, 38, 41,
    46, 68, 194
  biography, 38
Schulman, M., 57

Schwarzenegger, Arnold, 60
Scott, Dred, 180
Searchers, The, 209
Security, 161, 244-247
    and jealousy, 161
    and the American dream, 244-247
Seligman, M., 170
Self-actualization, 238. *See also* Happiness
Self-construction of moral intuitions, 313
Self-control, 87, 92, 127-130, 139, 170, 212-213
    and autonomy, 87, 121, 122, 123, 127-130
    virtues of, 139, 140, 145-163
    See also Autonomy
Self-controlled person, 92, 94
Self-correction, 80-81, 91
Self-debasement, 190. *See also* Pride
Self-deception, 187, 189. *See also* Lying
Self-determination, 89-90. *See also* Autonomy
Self-direction, 121-122, 123. *See also* Autonomy
Self-efficacy, 139, 163-170, 212-213
    and autonomy, 121, 122, 123
    virtues of, 139, 163-170
    See also Autonomy
Self-evidence, 379-380
Self-indulgence, 96, 146, 147
Self-interest, 256, 257
Self-knowledge, 216
Self-legislation, 350. *See also* Autonomy
Self-mastery, 121-123. *See also* Autonomy
Self-reflexivity, 85-86
Self-respect, 188, 189, 190
Seneca, 153
Sentimentalism, 13
Seven deadly sins, the, 145
Seven Samurai, The, 73
Sexual continence, 162-163, 316-317
Sexual harassment, 118-119
Sexual offense policy, Antioch's, 317
Shaffer, L.F., 129
Shaftesbury, Anthony, 312, 333
Shame, 20-22
Shamelessness, 191. *See also* Modesty
Shapiro, David, 90, 96-97, 121-122
Sharp, F.C., 359
Shaw, George Bernard, 364, 365
Shearson-Lehman Brothers survey, 1
Shepher, J., 85, 328
Shelley, Mary, 158
Shiloh, 182
Sidgwick, Henry, 69
Siebers, Tobin, 43, 265, 268
Sigmund, K., 363
Simmel, Georg, 247
Simon, Herbert, 376
Simple Plan, A, 226
Simpson, O.J., 32, 179, 269
Singer, Marcus, 364-365
Slander, 193
Sloth, 161. *see also* Industry
Smart, J.J.C., 350, 369-370

Smith, Adam, 13, 28, 29, 30, 41, 46, 230, 231, 365
    biography, 28
Smith, Jacqui, 214, 268
Smith, Susan, 16-17, 18, 23
Snyder, C.R., 170
Sociopathy, 36-38
Socrates, 7, 8, 157, 164, 212, 216, 267, 297-301
    biography, 8
Soft-hearted, 196
Softness, 194
Solomon, 267
    biography, 8
Solomon, Robert, 18, 320
Solon, 137
Sommers, Christine Hoff, 58
Sophie's Choice, 75, 284-285
Sōphōn (self-control), 92
Sorabji, Richard, 215
Sowarka, D., 215
Sowell, Thomas, 220, 314
Sparks, G., 61
Sportsmanship, 193
Stage of clarification. *See* Moral knowledge
Stage of justification. *See* Moral knowledge
Stage of systematization. *See* Moral knowledge
Stages of moral reasoning, 321-326
    Gilligan's, 324-326
    Kitchener's, et al., 325-326
    Kohlberg's, 321-326
Stalin, Josef, 156, 296
Star Wars, 224
Staub, E., 57
Stealing, 185-187
Steinberg, L., 57
Sternberg, R., 213, 214, 215, 218, 312
Stevenson, Charles, 69-71
Stevenson, Robert Lewis, 158
Stimmer, M., 26
Stimson, Henry, 293-296
Stirner, Max, 341-342
    biography, 341
Stockdale, James, 45
Stocker, Michael, 69
Stoicism, 148-154, 163, 169-170, 261, 375
    and duty, 148-154
    and *euthymia,* 153
    and natural law, 375
    and patience, 169-170
    and pleasure, 148-154
Stories, 18-19, 57-63, 218-229, 230-232, 270-272, 275-277
    and emotions, 18-19, 221-222
    and moral education, 57-63
    and moral vision, 218-234
    and personal identity, 270-272
    and role types, 229
    comedy, 224, 227-228
    irony, 224, 226-227, 228, 229
    life, 270-272
    melodrama, 224-225, 226, 227, 228, 229

romance, 224-229
    satire, 224, 228-229
    tragedy, 224, 226-227, 228, 229
    use in deliberation of, 265-267, 270-272
    use in foresight of, 275-277
    use in memory of, 265-267
    See also Vision
Strange Days, 151
Strauss, H., 129
Striptease, 81-82, 83
Studiositas, 158
Styron, William, 284
Subjectivism, 326-327
Success, 236-238. *See also* Flourishing; Prosperity
Sun Tzu, 257-259
Swahili, the, 161, 168, 169
Swift, Jonathan, 228
Sybaritism, 148-149. *See also* Hedonism
Sympathy, 17, 25-34, 35, 66, 67
    and psychopathy, 33, 35
    characteristics of, 25-26, 28-30
    contrasted with compassion, 30-31
    contrasted, with empathy, 26-28
    contrasted with love, 31
    contrasted with pity, 30
    contrasted with Schadenfreude, 31
    deterrents to, 32-33
    motivation for, 32-33
Synesis, 216
Systematization, stage of. *See* Moral knowledge

T

Tae Kwon Do, 130
Takaki, R., 296
Talmudic ethics, 386
Tamborini, R., 61
Taste, 62
Taylor, A.E., 300
Taylor, Paul, 328
Taylor, Richard, 46, 87, 194
Taylor, Shelley, 236
Tellegen, Auke, 235-236
Tell-Tale Heart, The, 75
Teleological principles. *See* Principle(s)
Temperance, 139, 140, 141, 145-154, 170, 208-209, 215-216. *See also* Epicureanism; Eudaimonism; Hedonism; Insensitivity; Self-indulgence; Stoicism,
Tender Mercies, 147
Theroux, A., 197
Thoreau, Henry David, 228
Thornton, Robert, 184
Thrasymachus, 341
Tice, D., 155
Titian, 265
Tit-for-tat principle. *See* Principle(s)
Tlingit, the, 223-224, 328, 329
Tolerance, 180-182
Tolstoy, Leo, 219
Tort law. *See* Liability
Tosca, 360

Total principle, the. *See* Principle(s)
Toulmin, Stephen, 261, 277-279
Tragedy. *See* stories
Tragic vision. *See* Vision
Traub, J., 237
Treasure of the Sierra Madre, The, 207
Trial, The, 226
Trivers, R., 363
Tricipitum, 213
Trollope, Anthony, 225
Trotsky, Leon, 156
Truman, Harry, 293-296
Trump, Donald, 247
Trust, 3, 6, 52-55
    thick, 53
    thin, 53
    See also Feminist ethics
Truthfulness, 182-187. *See also* Honesty; Lying
Turiel, E., 313
Turner, Fred, 1, 6
Turner, Ted, 248
Tzaddik, 144

U

Uncle Vanya, 226
Unforgiven, The, 226
Unfriendliness, 192
Unger, L., 29
Unpretentiousness, 192
Usual Suspects, The, 92
Ut, Nick, 195
Utilitarianism, 7, 150, 333, 365, 374, 382-383
    act, 369-370
    and pleasure, 365-368
    and rights-based ethics, 382-383
    average principle of, the, 368-369
    Bentham's account of, 365-367
    happiness account of, 369
    Mill's account of, 367-368, 370-371
    preference version of, 369
    principle of, 365, 367
    rule, 369-370
    total principle of, the, 368

V

Vaillant, G., 312
Valiant, G., 236
Values clarification, 316-317
Van Inwagen, Peter, 87
Vanity, 189-190
Veatch, Robert, 386-390
Veenhoven, R., 236
Veil of ignorance, 350-351. *See also* Rawls, John
Vengefulness, 197-198. *See also* Forgiveness
Verducci, S., 25
Vice. *See* Virtue(s); Seven Deadly Sins
Virgin Spring, The, 209

Virtue(s), xii, xiii, 137-201, 212-214, 252-255, 400-402
    and character, 142-145
    and flourishing, 237-240, 252-255
    and pleasure, 145-154
    and wisdom, 212-214
    as a habit, 142-145
    as a disposition, 142-145
    as a trait, 142-145
    as the golden mean, 140-141
    cardinal, 139, 140
    classification of, 141, 142
    integral theory of, the, 198-201
    instrumental theory of, the, 198-201
    life of, 252-255
    natural, 214
    of kindness, 194-198
    of regard, 170-187
    of respect, 187-194
    of self-control, 145-163
    of self-efficacy, 163-170
    polite, 191-194
Virtue ethics, 14
Vision, 218-255
    and stories, 221-229
    and the common good, 229-234
    and the good life, 234-255
    characteristics of, 218-221
    Christian, 222, 223, 224, 225, 226, 227, 228, 229
    comedic. *See* Thalian
    cosmic, 221-229
    ironic, 229, 230-232, 233, 257-259
    moral, 218-255
        aspects of, 219
        as horizon, 219
    romantic, 224-229
    satiric, 224, 228-229
    Thalian, 227-228, 229, 230-232
    tragic, 224, 226-227, 228, 229
Vitz, Paul, 33, 58, 59, 221
Vlastos, Gregory, 382
Volitions, 89, 90, 91, 96
    first-order, 89, 90, 91, 96
    second-order, 89, 90, 91, 96
Voluntariness, 99, 102-113
Voluntary action. *See* Action
Von Wright, Georg, 165, 217
Vulgarity, 191-192

W

Waiting for Godot, 221
Walker, L., 325
Wallace, James, 194, 195
Wallace, R. J., 89, 165
Wallenberg, Raoul, 46
Walters, R., 19
Walton, Douglas, 164-165, 170
Walzer, Michael, 304-305
War and Peace, 219
Warhol, Andy, 250
Warr, P., 234

Warren, Robert Penn, 60
Wasserstrom, Richard, 381-385
Wealth, life of. *See* Good life, the
Weintraub, S., 296
Well-being. *See* Happiness.
Whately, Richard (Bishop), 268-269, 364, 365
Whiting, J., 313
Whitsett, Gavin, 377
Wickedness, 36-38. *See* Sociopathy
Wild Duck, The, 226
Wilde, Oscar, 145
Wilkinson, Alec, 35
Will, 80-90, 92-97, 123-127
    free, 81-90, 97
    good, 123-125
    holy, 124
    strong, 92-97
    weak, 92-97
Will-to-power, 125-127. See also Nietzsche, Friedrich
Williams, Bernard, 14, 15, 20, 21, 41, 253-255, 259, 335-336, 374
    biography, 253
Williams, William, 120-121
Wilson, B. J., 61
Wilson, James, 32, 40, 44, 45, 46, 55
Windmiller, M., 56
Wisdom, xii, xiii, 212-310, 311, 400-402
    acquisition of, 215-216
    and character, 215-216
    and deliberation, 255-283
    and experience, 216
    and judgment, 215-216, 283-297
    and moral knowledge, 297-305
    and moral vision, 218-255
    and perspicacity, 215
    and reasoning, 215, 217-218
    and sagacity, 215, 216
    and the good life, 234-255
    and virtue, 213-217, 252-255
    features of, 214-215
    role in moral competence, 218, 400-402
Wise counsel, 213
Wittiness, 192
Woodforde, John, 189, 190
Work ethic, the, 160-162. *See also* Contentment; Frugality; Industry
Workaholism, 161

Y

Yahweh, 223-224
Yass, M., 296
Yeager, Chuck, 40

Z

Zahn-Waxler, C., 55
Zheng, Yujian, 95
Zillman, D., 61, 154, 155